RESURRECTION *AND* ESCHATOLOGY

THEOLOGY *in* SERVICE *of the* CHURCH

ESSAYS IN HONOR OF

RICHARD B. GAFFIN JR.

EDITED BY

LANE G. TIPTON AND JEFFREY C. WADDINGTON

PUBLISHING
P.O. BOX 817 • PHILLIPSBURG • NEW JERSEY 08865-0817

Scripture quotations in chapters 1, 3, 6, 11, 15, and 20–22 are from The Holy Bible, English Standard Version, copyright © 2001 by Crossway Bibles, a division of Good News Publishers. Used by permission. All rights reserved.

Scripture quotations in chapters 2 and 4 are from the HOLY BIBLE, NEW INTERNATIONAL VERSION®. NIV®. Copyright © 1973, 1978, 1984 by International Bible Society. Used by permission of Zondervan Publishing House. All rights reserved.

Scripture quotations in chapters 5, 7, 8, and 14 are from the NEW AMERICAN STANDARD BIBLE®. Copyright © 1960, 1962, 1963, 1968, 1971, 1972, 1973, 1975, 1977, 1995 by The Lockman Foundation. Used by permission.

All other Scripture quotations, unless otherwise noted, are the author's own translation.

Italics within Scripture quotations indicate emphasis added.

Printed in the United States of America

Library of Congress Cataloging-in-Publication Data

Resurrection and eschatology : theology in service of the church : essays in honor of Richard B. Gaffin, Jr. / edited by Lane G. Tipton and Jeffrey C. Waddington.
   p. cm.
Includes bibliographical references.
ISBN 978–1–59638–126–1 (cloth)
1. Reformed Church—Doctrines. 2. Orthodox Presbyterian Church—Doctrines. 3. Theology. 4. Gaffin, Richard B. I. Gaffin, Richard B. II. Tipton, Lane G. III. Waddington, Jeffrey C., 1964–
BX9422.5.R47 2008
230'.51—dc22
                2008007805

Contents

Foreword: Little Exercises by Theologians Young and Old

THEOLOGY IS, as the word suggests, talk about God; it therefore arises out of God's own revelatory speech to human beings; and God is thus always the subject, not the object, of theology. In addition, the context for theology is the church, the community of the faithful who hears God's words in faith and respond to him in a manner regulated and informed by the priority of divine speech. This was the intentional approach of all the great pre-Enlightenment church theologians, who sought to move in faith from scriptural text through exegesis to doctrinal synthesis and application, and to do it all within the context of the church herself.

Today, of course, much that passes for "theology" does not actually correspond to what I have just described. University theology departments pursue a discipline which, by and large, they regard as incoherent in terms of its classical conception. Indeed, the unity of the university discipline is found more in the administrative structures within which theological teaching takes place—in other words, in an external rationale rather than in any internal principle. Once the uniqueness of Scripture had been denied, whether theoretically or practically—it makes no difference—the whole reason for Christian theology to be seen as a unified, coherent discipline simply disappeared. And once theology had been removed from the church, its whole purpose—that of guarding and explicating the faith once delivered, and of thus edifying the saints—was radically subverted and transformed into something more abstract and, inevitably, more nebulous.

Richard B. Gaffin Jr.'s academic life has, of course, been profoundly counter-cultural in this regard: for him, theology is rooted in, and regulated by, God's uniquely authoritative revelation. In Scripture, the Father has spoken; it is not for the children to question what he says but rather to explicate it, apply it, and, when necessary, to defend it. Dr. Gaffin has also lived out his professional life in the context of the church: the terminus of his work has not been profundity or originality for their own sakes, though he has made contributions which are both profound and original. Rather, his work has been consistently aimed at the upbuilding of the church, an upbuilding which uses scholarly excellence as a means to an end and which takes with the utmost seriousness the statements and methods that the church herself has sanctioned over the years as reflecting sound patterns of words and God-honoring procedures. It is thus fitting that the collection of essays which have been commissioned in his honor should reflect the same set of priorities. Coming variously from the pens of biblical scholars, systematicians, church historians, and perhaps most importantly of all, churchmen and preachers, these contributions demonstrate that the tradition of theologizing in and for the church, that of real faith seeking true understanding, is not dead.

We live in an age where taste, not truth, holds sway; or, perhaps better, we live in an age where taste is truth. Thus, to claim truth relative to God is distasteful because it automatically implies that some other position is wrong or inferior. This has had a baneful effect on modern theology, systematic and biblical. Some today delight in the quintessential postmodern aesthetics of tension, uncertainty, and systematic agnosticism; others seem positively delighted to surrender their virtue to the disciplinary fragmentation of the modern scholarly cults of specialization, with their elitism and quasi-Gnostic attitude to criticism which comes from outside their specific guilds. Still others might posit a radical separation of biblical and systematic theology which functions in practice as a virtual theory of double truth rooted in what one friend calls "the genre trick"—that academic *deus ex machina* which can be wheeled in at any point to avoid a particularly pressing question about truth or coherence; and yet others see novelty and innovation as the essence of true theology, buying into cultural paradigms which are lethal to the preservation, proclamation, and propagation of the gospel. *Church* theologians, however, are cut from a different cloth: they rejoice in the cross-fertilization of their work by others and are happy to lay their work open not only to the scrutiny of their chosen guild but of the church in general, and to see their individual contributions as combining together with those of others to clarify and strengthen the church's ongoing, historic, certain, and firm declaration of the gospel.

It is in this spirit that the following essays are offered. They are each contributions designed for the upbuilding of Christ's church, whether by way of original biblical scholarship or pungent application of Scripture in preaching. As such, they serve not simply the material function of adding to the great tradition of Christian literature which the church has at her disposal for the encouragement and strengthening of God's people; they also offer patterns of how thoughtful theologizing can and should be done in the present age.

Those looking for the thrill of the new, the doubtful, or the iconoclastic should look elsewhere. These essays are offered in a different spirit, that of humility and a desire to be faithful to those little, simple things of the faith once for all delivered to the church, things which can be grasped by a child and yet which take more than a lifetime to master. Indeed, perhaps that spirit of submission to the life and mission of the church, and its contrast to those for whom cleverness is an end in itself, is captured nowhere better than by the great Martin Luther in his introduction to his Large Catechism:

> As for myself, let me say that I, too, am a doctor and a preacher—yes, and as learned and experienced as any of those who act so high and mighty. Yet I do as a child who is being taught the Catechism. Every morning, and whenever else I have time, I read and recite word for word the Lord's Prayer, the Ten Commandments, the Creed, the Psalms, etc. I must still read and study the Catechism daily, yet I cannot master it as I wish, but must remain a child and pupil of the Catechism, and I do it gladly. These dainty, fastidious fellows would like quickly, with one reading, to become doctors above all doctors, to know all there is to be known. Well, this, too, is a sure sign that they despise both their office and the people's souls, yes, even God and his Word. They need not fear a fall, for they have already fallen all too horribly. What they need is to become children and begin learning their ABC's, which they think they have outgrown long ago. Therefore, I beg these lazy-bellies and presumptuous saints, for God's sake, to get it into their heads that they are not really and truly such learned and great doctors as they think. I implore them not to imagine that they have learned these parts of the Catechism perfectly, or at least sufficiently, even

though they think they know them ever so well. Even if their knowledge of Catechism were perfect (though that is impossible in this life), yet it is highly profitable and fruitful daily to read it and make it the subject of meditation and conversation. In such reading, conversation, and meditation the Holy Spirit is present and bestows ever new and greater light and fervor, so that day by day we relish and appreciate the Catechism more greatly. This is according to Christ's promise in Matt. 18:20, "Where two or three are gathered in my name, there am I in the midst of them."[1]

Amen. So let it be.

Carl R. Trueman

1. Tappert, Theodore G.: *The Book of Concord: The Confessions of the Evangelical Lutheran Church* (Philadelphia: Fortress Press, 2000), 359.

Introduction: A Tribute to
Richard B. Gaffin Jr.

AS HERMAN RIDDERBOS indicates in his personal word at the beginning of this volume, Dr. Richard B. Gaffin Jr. has reached a milestone in his distinguished career. On this occasion, the contributors to this volume are delighted to present this festschrift, honoring Dr. Gaffin for his tireless service to Jesus Christ in the Orthodox Presbyterian Church and at Westminster Theological Seminary.

Dr. Gaffin was born in Peiping (now Beijing), China, on July 7, 1936, to missionaries in the Orthodox Presbyterian Church. He received a BA from Calvin College, and pursued graduate theological studies at Westminster Theological Seminary, where he received a BD in 1961, a ThM in 1962, and a ThD in 1969. He also studied for one year at Georg-August Universität, Göttingen (1962–63) and joined Westminster's faculty in 1965, where he has taught with distinction for over forty years.

Dr. Gaffin is, first and foremost, a churchman. His service to the Orthodox Presbyterian Church is astounding, especially in light of his numerous seminary responsibilities. He has the longest continuous presidency of a standing committee in OPC history (Committee on Foreign Missions, 1969–present; president 1972–76) and has also served on the Committee on Ecumenicity and Interchurch Relations (1989–2004). He has served on the following special committees: Committee on Sabbath Matters (1969–72); Committee on Scripture and Inspiration (1969–72; chairman); Committee on Proof Texts for the Shorter Catechism (1971–78); Committee on Baptism of the Holy Spirit (1975–76); Committee on Baptism and the

Gifts of the Holy Spirit (1977); Committee on Reformed Ecumenical Synod Matters (1973–87; chairman, 1986); Committee on Principles of Diaconal Ministry (1980); Committee to Study the History and Development of the OPC (1982); Committee on Hermeneutics (1984); Committee on the Hermeneutics of Women in Office (1985–87); Committee to Study the Involvement of Men and Women in Places of Leadership in Worship Services (1988–89); Committee on the Involvement of Unordained Persons in the Regular Worship Services of the Church (1990–91); Committee to Study the Method of Admission to the Lord's Supper (1991–93); Committee on the Doctrine of Justification (2004–06). He also moderated the 51st General Assembly of the OPC in 1984 and served as a commissioner to the General Assembly twenty-four times.

But Dr. Gaffin is not only a churchman; he is also a theologian of the highest order. Among Reformed interpreters of Scripture in the twentieth and twenty-first centuries, Dr. Gaffin stands out as a giant. Finding peers only in theologians such as B. B. Warfield, Geerhardus Vos, Herman Ridderbos, John Murray, and M. G. Kline, Gaffin has introduced generations of students to the riches of Reformed biblical and systematic theology.

From the earliest stages of his career, Gaffin demonstrated a mastery of the biblical material that would distinguish him as a uniquely gifted exegete and theologian. His doctoral dissertation, entitled *The Centrality of the Resurrection: A Study in Paul's Soteriology*, which was later published under the title *Resurrection and Redemption: A Study in Paul's Soteriology*,[1] significantly advances Reformed scholarship in the area of biblical soteriology. In that volume he corrects a longstanding lack of attention in Reformed theology with regard to the resurrection of Jesus Christ, particularly its bearing on the structure and nature of the once-for-all accomplishment of redemption *by* Christ and its application to believers *in* Christ. His *Perspectives on Pentecost: New Testament Teaching on the Gifts of the Holy Spirit* constitutes another seminal work that both develops and defends the cessationist view of tongues and prophecy in the apostolic age. Gaffin's sensitivity to the bearing of biblical theology on various *loci* in systematic theology is evident in both of these landmark works.

But Gaffin is not merely a constructive theologian who has advanced the Reformed tradition in stimulating and orthodox ways. He is also a

---

1. Full bibliographic information for this and all of Gaffin's publications may be found in the appendix.

polemicist for the orthodox doctrine of Scripture he learned from the founding faculty of Westminster Theological Seminary, particularly from the contributions of John Murray, E. J. Young (his father-in-law), and Cornelius Van Til in the original faculty symposium on Scripture, titled *The Infallible Word*. He has fought vigorously and consistently throughout his career against the inroads of doctrinal error in the forms of liberalism and neoorthodoxy. Gaffin's reviews of Deewey Beegle and Helmut Thielicke's works on Scripture (1964, 1965), along with his response to John Franke's Post-Conservative Evangelical paradigm (2003) supply bookends of sorts to a career of passionate defense of a Reformed doctrine of Scripture. His "Old Amsterdam and Inerrancy," now republished under the new title *God's Word in Servant Form: Abraham Kuyper and Herman Bavinck and the Doctrine of Scripture*, masterfully maps out a properly Chalcedonian and Reformed use of the incarnational analogy in the development of the doctrine of Scripture. In the past year he wrote the introduction to E. J. Young's republished collection of essays titled *The God-Breathed Scripture*, published by the Committee for the Historian of the Orthodox Presbyterian Church.

Additionally, Gaffin reviewed E. P. Sanders and James Dunn's versions of the so-called New Perspective on Paul (2000), demonstrating a keenly analytical mind that is uniquely capable of leveling penetrating criticisms of theological positions that depart in significant ways from biblical teaching. His recent volume, *By Faith Not by Sight: Paul and the Order of Salvation*, extends his critique of recent misinterpretations of Pauline theology and offers a constructive alternative based on careful biblical exegesis.

Representing Westminster's tradition in a unique way in the twenty-first century, Dr. Gaffin bridges the present Westminster back to its founding faculty. Gaffin, as indicated earlier, studied under many of Westminster's original faculty members, and it is particularly through Murray and Van Til that he has developed, and continues to develop, theological distinctives found in the works of Geerhardus Vos and Herman Bavinck. Gaffin has given to students, both in written and oral form, a thoroughly non-speculative theology that is regulated by redemptive-historically conditioned exegesis. It is especially through the influence of Murray that Gaffin offers to the church an essentially *biblical* systematic theology.

Through his forty-three years of teaching at Westminster Theological Seminary, Dr. Gaffin has left an enduring legacy for the church of Jesus Christ. He has influenced thousands of students through his classroom lectures. Those who have sat under Dr. Gaffin's teaching are impressed by its crystal clarity and close fidelity to the biblical text. And students frequently express their desire to emulate Dr. Gaffin's faithfulness to Scripture in their own preaching and teaching ministries.

For these reasons, and many more, it is fitting to offer Dr. Gaffin this festschrift in profound appreciation for his service to the church and the academy. His work has both upheld and advanced the very best of the Westminster tradition in biblical and systematic theology. Perhaps the best way to describe his labors among us can be summed up in a simple phrase: *faithfulness to the self-attesting Christ of Scripture.* May the Lord continue to bless the labors of his humble and faithful servant, Dr. Richard B. Gaffin Jr.

Lane G. Tipton

Abbreviations

AB	Anchor Bible
ANET	*Ancient Near Eastern Texts Relating to the Old Testament*, 3rd ed., ed. J. B. Pritchard (Princeton: Princeton University Press, 1969)
ANEP	*The Ancient Near East in Pictures Relating to the Old Testament*, ed. J. B. Pritchard (Princeton: Princeton University Press, 1954)
AOAT	Alter Orient und Alest Testament
BDB	F. Brown, S. R. Driver, and C. A. Briggs, *A Hebrew and English Lexicon of the Old Testament* (Oxford: Clarendon, 1907)
BECNT	Baker Exegetical Commentary on the New Testament
BETL	Bibliotheca ephemeridum theologicarum lovaniensium
BNTC	Black's New Testament Commentary Series
BST	Bible Speaks Today Series
CH	*Church History*
CTJ	*Calvin Theological Journal*
DSD	*Dead Sea Discoveries*
FOTL	Forms of the Old Testament Literature
GKC	*Gesenius' Hebrew Grammar*, 2nd ed., ed. E. Kautzsch, trans. A. E. Cowley (Oxford: Clarendon, 1910)
HALOT	L. Kohler, W. Baumgartner, and J. J. Stamm, *The Hebrew and Aramaic Lexicon of the Old Testament*,

	4 vols., trans. and ed. under supervision of M. E. J. Richardson (Leiden: Brill, 1994–99)
HTR	*Harvard Theological Review*
IBHS	*An Introduction to Biblical Hebrew Syntax*, B. K. Waltke and M. O'Connor (Winona Lake, IN: Eisenbrauns, 1990)
ICC	International Critical Commentary
JETS	*Journal of the Evangelical Theological Society*
JNES	*Journal of Near Eastern Studies*
JPS	Jewish Publication Society Bible
JSOT	*Journal for the Study of the Old Testament*
JSOTSup	Journal for the Study of the Old Testament: Supplement Series
JTS	*Journal of Theological Studies*
LCL	Loeb Classical Library
LXX	Septuagint
MR	*Modern Reformation*
MT	Masoretic Text
NAB	New American Bible
NASB	New American Standard Bible
NBD	*New Bible Dictionary*, 2nd ed., ed. J. D. Douglass and N. Hillyer (Downers Grove, IL: InterVarsity, 1982)
NCB	New Century Bible
NEB	New English Bible
NH	*New Horizons*
NIB	*The New Interpreter's Bible*
NICNT	New International Commentary on the New Testament
NICOT	New International Commentary on the Old Testament
NIV	New International Version
NJB	New Jerusalem Bible
NLT	New Living Translation
NovT	*Novum Testamentum*
NovTSup	Novum Testamentum Supplements
NT	New Testament

NTOA	Novum Testamentum et Orbis Antiquus
OPC	Orthodox Presbyterian Church
OT	Old Testament
PCA	Presbyterian Church in America
PSB	*Princeton Seminary Bulletin*
PTR	*Princeton Theological Review*
TDOT	*Theological Dictionary of the Old Testament*, 8 vols., ed. G. J. Botterweck and G. Ringgren, trans. J. T. Willis, G. W. Bromiley, and D. E. Green (Grand Rapids: Eerdmans, 1974–)
TJ	*Trinity Journal*
TNIV	Today's New International Version
TNTC	Tyndale New Testament Commentaries
TOTC	Tyndale Old Testament Commentaries
TWOT	*Theological Wordbook of the Old Testament*, 2 vols., ed. R. L. Harris, G. L. Archer, and B. K. Waltke (Chicago: Moody, 1980)
TynBul	*Tyndale Bulletin*
TZ	*Theologische Zeitschrift*
UT	Ugaratic Text
VE	*Vox evangelica*
WBC	Word Biblical Commentary
WCF	Westminster Confession of Faith
WSC	Westminster Shorter Catechism
WTJ	*Westminster Theological Journal*
ZAW	*Zeitschrift für die alttestamentliche Wissenschaft*

A Personal Word from Herman Ridderbos[1]

I FEEL HONORED to open this "Festschrift" for Professor Dr. Richard B. Gaffin Jr. with a personal word.

All of us are aware of the important contribution of Dr. Gaffin, especially in the field of the New Testament Studies, during the long time of twenty-five years. The line of his investigations remember to those of Geerhardus Vos, in the sense of what we may call the "heilshistorische" way of exposition of the New Testament: an indication on the one side of a real difference of the *dogmatic* method of exposition, on the other side of the far more biblical approach than that of the consequent historic-critical school.

Here we may congratulate our esteemed colleague for reaching this "milestone" of his life, together with our best wishes for the continuation, not only of his way of scholarship, but no less that we may continue to take part in the gift of his cordial friendship, of which he knows the secret.

Herman Ridderbos
Kampen, the Netherlands
March 22, 2004

---

1. This letter has been left largely unedited.

PART 1

Studies in Biblical and Systematic Theology

I

The Function of Romans 7:13–25 in Paul's Argument for the Law's Impotence and the Spirit's Power, and Its Bearing on the Identity of the Schizophrenic "I"

DENNIS E. JOHNSON

IT IS A PRIVILEGE to have the opportunity to honor Dr. Richard B. Gaffin Jr., the professor who introduced me to the illuminating insights of Reformed biblical theology for the interpretation of the New Testament Scriptures and who has continued to model for me what careful exegesis, informed by wider and deeper theological perspectives, entails. We who have been privileged to sit under Professor Gaffin's instruction have benefited in ways too numerous to count from his lectures, with their attentive observation of the features of the text, their carefully constructed arguments that expose each passage's contribution to the broader system of revealed truth and redemptive history, and their concern to address the theological issues and needs confronting Christ's church.

One of Dr. Gaffin's early and lasting contributions to New Testament theology has been the focus of his doctoral dissertation, *Resurrection and*

Redemption, completed under the supervision of Professor John Murray and subsequently published under the title *The Centrality of the Resurrection*. [1] This study argued that Christ's resurrection is more central to Paul's Christology, soteriology, and (of course) eschatology than has often been recognized, and therefore that the resurrection of the Messiah deserves greater theological attention and reflection (alongside the atoning death of Jesus, which has often overshadowed the resurrection in Protestants' proclamation of Pauline soteriology). Extending the groundbreaking work of Geerhardus Vos, [2] Herman Ridderbos, [3] and others, *Resurrection and Redemption* argues that Jesus' death and resurrection together constitute the redemptive-historical/eschatological watershed between "the present age" and the inbreaking of the "age to come."

Among the themes highlighted in *Resurrection and Redemption* was that 1 Corinthians 15:45 links the resurrection of Jesus, as the Last Adam, to the life-giving dynamic of the Holy Spirit, now operative in the lives of believers and of the church under the new covenant. [4] One significant implication of this is that Paul's frequent contrast between "flesh" and "Spirit" is not primarily ontological (material v. immaterial) or anthropological-psychological (bodily existence v. consciousness). Rather, it is redemptive-historical or eschatological, distinguishing the natural frailty (and now fallenness) and sub-eschatological character of the original creation and "the present age" from the supernatural and eschatological life of the age to come, now operating proleptically but genuinely in those who are united to the risen Lord Jesus through Holy Spirit-wrought faith.

This redemptive-historical perspective on Paul's flesh/Spirit antithesis has, I believe, an important contribution to make to our understanding of the long-controverted issue of the "identity"—better yet, the spiritual condition—of the frustrated and defeated "I" who speaks

---

1. Richard B. Gaffin Jr., *The Centrality of the Resurrection: A Study in Paul's Soteriology* (Grand Rapids: Baker, 1978). The ThD dissertation submitted to Westminster Theological Seminary was originally titled *Resurrection and Redemption: A Study in Pauline Soteriology* (1969). The second published edition now returns (almost) to the dissertation's title, *Resurrection and Redemption: A Study in Paul's Soteriology* (Phillipsburg, NJ: P&R, 1987).

2. Geerhardus Vos, *The Pauline Eschatology* (Princeton: by the author [printed by Princeton University Press], 1930; repr. Grand Rapids: Eerdmans, 1952; Phillipsburg, NJ: P&R, 1979).

3. Herman N. Ridderbos, *Paul: An Outline of His Theology* (Grand Rapids: Eerdmans, 1975), 44–68.

4. Gaffin, *Resurrection and Redemption* (1987), 78–92.

in Romans 7:13–25.[5] Until the twentieth century, the Augustinian and Reformational traditions (both Lutheran and Calvinist) have consistently understood Romans 7:14–25 as reflective of Christian believers' ongoing struggle with sin and our frustration over the contradiction between our conscious concurrence with the standards of God's law (an implicit evidence of the Spirit's renewing work), on the one hand, and the violation of the law that we observe in our own actions, on the other. The personal and present intensity of the speaker's distress over the contradiction of his law-affirming conviction by his flesh-driven members convinces these interpreters that here Paul speaks autobiographically of his own struggle as a believer in Christ (as representative of normal Christian experience in this period of the "overlap of the ages").[6] Recent proponents of this view—for example, James D. G. Dunn and Donald B. Garlington—have based their argument for a Christian "I" in Romans 7:13–25, specifically on the Pauline motif of the semi-eschatological overlap of the present and coming ages, in which believers now live in the interim between Christ's inauguration

5. Resources addressing the puzzling question of the spiritual condition articulated by the "I" who speaks in Romans 7 are so abundant that it is pointless to try to list them all. A representative bibliography of scholars representing various viewpoints through the late 1980s can be found in D. B. Garlington, "Romans 7:14–25 and the Creation Theology of Paul," *TJ* 11 NS (1990): 198–99, nn5–12. See also the bibliographical resources cited by Douglas Moo, *The Epistle to the Romans*, NICNT (Grand Rapids: Eerdmans, 1996), 410–67.

6. Those who understand Romans 7:13–25 as descriptive of the experience applying to the Christian: the later Augustine and the Augustinian tradition generally, including commentaries by M. Luther, J. Calvin, C. Hodge, A. Nygren, J. Murray (NICNT), C. K. Barrett (BNTC), C. E. B. Cranfield (ICC), L. Morris, F. F. Bruce (TNTC), J. R. W. Stott, and J. D. G. Dunn (WBC); and essays such as J. D. G. Dunn, "Rom 7,14–25 in the Theology of Paul," *TZ* 31 (1975): 257–73; R. Y. K. Fung, "Impotence of the Law," in *Scripture, Tradition and Interpretation* (E. F. Harrison festschrift), ed. W. W. Gasque and W. S. La Sor (Grand Rapids: Eerdmans, 1978), 34–48; D. B. Garlington, "Romans 7:14–25 and Creation Theology"; J. I. Packer, *Keep in Step with the Spirit* (Tappan: Revell, 1984), 263–70; J. R. W. Stott, *Men Made New* (Chicago: InterVarsity Press, 1967), 70–79; and D. Wenham, "The Christian Life: A Life of Tension?—A Consideration of the Nature of Christian Experience in Paul," in *Pauline Studies* (F. F. Bruce festschrift), ed. D. A. Hagner and M. J. Harris (Grand Rapids: Eerdmans, 1980), 80–94. Those advocating this general reading of Romans 7 exhibit variations of perspective. Fung and Wenham, for example, view the "speaker" of Rom. 7:13ff. as reflective of the *subnormal* Christian experience of a believer who attempts to keep the law without dependence on the Spirit. Others insist that the intense frustration that the "speaker" expresses over the contradiction between his inward agreement with God's law and his actual behavior is simply normal Christian experience for believers living in the overlap of the ages, between the "already" of Christ's death and resurrection and the "not yet" of his parousia.

of the kingdom of God in his incarnation, death, resurrection, and ascension, on the one hand, and his consummation of the kingdom in his future parousia, on the other.[7]

From the Patristic period the Greek Fathers understood the "I" of Romans 7:7–25 to represent the spiritual enslavement of those who stand outside the sphere of Christ's redemptive and renewing grace. Since the early twentieth century, a growing circle of interpreters in the West has embraced this perspective with various refinements, challenging the Augustinian-Reformation understanding of Romans 7:13–25 and arguing that the "I" who speaks in this passage represents Paul's pre-Christian frustration as a conscientious and would-be law-observant Jew still mired in the impotence of "the flesh," or (more corporately) dramatizes the inability of Israel as a whole to keep the law acceptably under the old covenant, or (even more comprehensively) portrays the impotence of fallen humanity in general, as descendants of the first Adam, to comply with the divine will, despite a recognition of its holiness.[8] Those advocating a reading of Romans 7:13–25 as reflective of pre- or non-Christian experience include exegetes and theologians who stand solidly in the Augustinian

---

7. J. D. G. Dunn, "Rom 7,14–25 in the Theology of Paul"; Dunn, *Romans 1–8*, WBC 38A (Waco, TX: Word, 1988), 374–412; Garlington, "Romans 7:14–25 and Creation Theology."

8. Those who understand Romans 7:13–25 as descriptive of a person or group (variously identified) not in union with Christ include such commentators as the Greek Fathers, the earlier Augustine, F. Godet, W. Sanday and A. C. Headlam (ICC), E. F. Harrison, Herman Ridderbos (*Aan de Romeinen* [Kampen: J. H. Kok, 1959]), E. Käsemann, Douglas Moo (NICNT, succeeding Murray), N. T. Wright (NIB), and R. Jewett (Hermeneia). This view is also articulated and defended, with variations, in A. J. Bandstra, *The Law and the Elements of the World* (Kampen: Kok, 1964), 134–49; R. H. Gundry, "The Moral Frustration of Paul before His Conversion: Sexual Lust in Romans 7:7–25," in *Pauline Studies*, 228–45; A. A. Hoekema, *The Christian Looks at Himself* (Grand Rapids: Eerdmans, 1977), 61–67; W. G. Kümmel, *Römer 7 und das Bild des Menschen im Neuen Testament* (Munich: Kaiser, 1929, repr.1974); D. M. Lloyd-Jones, *Romans: An Exposition of Chapters 7:1–8:4* (Grand Rapids: Zondervan, 1974), 229–57; H. N. Ridderbos, *Paul*, 126–35; J. A. T. Robinson, *Wrestling with Romans* (Philadelphia: Westminster, 1979); K. Stendahl, "The Apostle Paul and the Introspective Conscience of the West," *HTR* 56 (1963), 199–215; S. Westerholm, *Israel's Law and the Church's Faith* (Grand Rapids: Eerdmans, 1988), 181–86. Harrison, Robinson, and Westerholm view the "speaker" of Rom. 7:13ff. as representative of human experience of the law of God in general, "mere human nature left to itself . . . in its own strength" (Robinson), whereas others associate the experience described by the "speaker" as a personalized and dramatized summation of the experience of ancient Israel under the law, prior to the coming of the Messiah. Another variation worth noting in this "camp" is the view of Lloyd-Jones that the "I" of Rom. 7:13–25 articulates the experience of a person under conviction of sin through the preaching of the law, but not yet converted to faith in Christ—in transition from confident unbelief toward repentance and saving faith.

and Reformed traditions and have no sympathy for the Pelagian, semi-Pelagian, Arminian, and perfectionistic tendencies previously associated with this exegesis of the passage.[9] Therefore, although it may have been plausible in previous generations to answer the question of the spiritual status being portrayed by the "I" of Romans 7:13–25 largely on the basis of one's overall understanding of Christian soteriology, the boundaries between contrasting understandings of this passage are no longer so sharply defined by exegetes' commitments to a specific theological school or tradition. If a particular understanding of Romans 7:13–25 can no longer be assumed to come "bundled and pre-installed" with one's general system of soteriology, a fresh examination of the passage itself within the context of Paul's argument in Romans (and within the wider framework of the Pauline eschatology) seems both appropriate and necessary.

This essay argues that Paul's purpose in Romans 7 is fourfold: (1) to *defend God's "holy and righteous and good" law* from any charge of causation or complicity in the human disobedience and death that sin provokes through the law's prohibition of evil; but also (2) to *dramatize the law's impotence* to effect, in those still enslaved to the spiritual death of the present age, the upright behavior that it enjoins; and, in the course of achieving the first two purposes, (3) to *demonstrate the depth of sin's enslaving grip* on those who are "in the flesh," a tyranny that cannot be broken merely by a conscious and conscientious affirmation of the law's goodness; leading finally to his objective (4) to *extol the power of God's Spirit*, who now achieves in those who trust Christ what the law itself could not, namely, the fulfillment of its righteous requirements (Rom. 8:4). Integral to this argument is the flesh/Spirit antithesis that Paul articulates in Romans 7:5–6, a contrast that the apostle identifies as *temporal*—I will argue, *redemptive-historical*—in character: "when we were . . . but now. . . ." Equally integral is the contention that Romans 7:5–6 and the questions that these verses raise (7:7, 13) set the agenda for the development of Paul's argument throughout Romans 7:14—8:17 (and perhaps as far as 8:39). I conclude, finally, that Paul's theological purpose and rhetorical strategy at this point in the epistle demonstrate that the "I" who speaks *throughout* Romans 7:7–25 portrays the inability of humanity "in the flesh"—that is, apart from vital union with the risen Christ and therefore devoid of the re-creating power of the

---

9. For example, Bandstra, Hoekema, Lloyd-Jones (see comment in previous note), Moo, and Ridderbos.

Spirit—to comply with the divine law, despite the conscience's affirmation that the law is "holy and righteous and good."[10]

Before setting out this argument, however, I will briefly survey the apparently conflicting evidence regarding the identity (spiritual condition) of the "I" who speaks in Romans 7:13–25, to illustrate why exegetes and theologians for centuries seem to have encountered an irresolvable impasse, when approaching this text primarily from the standpoint of the question, "Who is this 'I' who approves God's law but cannot fulfill it?"

THE "I" IDENTITY IMPASSE THAT RESULTS FROM ASKING "OUR QUESTIONS" FIRST

My observation above—that in past generations one or another understanding of the spiritual status being portrayed in Romans 7:13–25 tended to be associated with one or another perspective on soteriology generally, whether the Augustinian-Reformational tradition that stresses divine sovereignty in grace and remains pessimistic regarding the capacities of fallen human nature, or the Pelagian/semi-Pelagian/perfectionist tradition that cultivates more cheerful expectations regarding human capacities and consequently sees God and his grace in a more responsive role—is not intended to minimize the difficulties within the passage itself that have contributed to the controversies that have swirled around it. The speaker of Romans 7:14–25 certainly seems in one breath to articulate convictions and aspirations that could only characterize the Christian believer as described elsewhere by Paul, and then in the next breath to lament his spiritual impotence in terms so strong that nothing but the experience of an unbeliever still "dead in trespasses and sins" (Eph. 2:1) would appear to fit his plight. With good reason Thomas Schreiner begins a lengthy discussion of the identity of the "I" with the assessment that "neither view [i.e., that Romans 7:13–25 describes Christian or pre-Christian experience] is precisely on the mark," but that "there is truth in both views."[11]

10. These conclusions and the arguments supporting them took shape during the years in which I taught Westminster Seminary California's course on the Pauline epistles (1982–91). As I have updated bibliographical references and engaged recent scholarship in the preparation of this essay, I note that the factors I found persuasive have led Douglas Moo to similar conclusions in his *Epistle to the Romans* (NICNT).

11. Thomas Schreiner, *Romans*, BECNT (Grand Rapids: Baker, 1998), 379. His discussion covers 379–92.

Among the strongest and most frequently cited arguments[12] in favor of the Augustinian-Reformational reading of Romans 7:13–25 as demonstrating that *normal Christian experience* is characterized by painful frustration and frequent failure in the attempt to obey God's law are these:

(1) The "I" of our text professes agreement with and delight in the law of God in his mind, his "inner man" (vv.15–18, 20–23), an inward and spiritual allegiance to God's holy standards that is beyond the experience of unbelievers. Paul will go on to affirm in 8:7 that the mind controlled by "flesh," the mind of the person untouched by the resurrection power of God's Spirit, does not and cannot submit to God's law. After all, Paul is speaking not of a merely outward conformity of actions, but of the delight of the "inner man" in the law of God. He would not speak of a non-Christian's relationship to the law in this way.

(2) The intensity of the struggle and frustration portrayed here goes beyond anything that we would expect Paul to attribute to a non-Christian's experience. Although pagan philosophers and Jewish rabbis alike[13] noted the inconsistency between people's convictions concerning right and wrong, on the one hand, and their actual behavior, on the other, none of these statements reaches the level of anguish expressed by the speaker of Romans 7:14–25. This can only be an aspect of the "groaning" and longing for the final deliverance that the Spirit's presence evokes within believers, who live in the overlap between the old, Adamic age and the age to come (8:23).

(3) Paul's self-righteous confidence as a Pharisee, as he expresses it in Philippians 3:6 and as we see it implied in the narrative of Acts (e.g., 8:1; 9:1–2; 26:4–11; see also Gal. 1:14), gives no evidence that prior to his conversion Paul experienced a painful struggle of conscience over his inability to keep the law. The NT offers no evidence that Paul's pathway to faith was parallel to Luther's struggles with an "introspective conscience."[14] Again, if

---

12. These arguments will be referred to throughout this essay in the shorthand form, "Augustinian argument 1," "Augustinian argument 2," etc., not because Augustine employed them all but because they represent the classic arguments that various advocates have cited over the centuries in support of the view that Rom. 7:14–25 describes Christians' struggles in the process of sanctification.

13. See below, notes 68–71.

14. Krister Stendahl, "The Apostle Paul and the Introspective Conscience of the West," *HTR* 56 (1963): 199–215. Stendahl, however, sees the absence of evidence that Paul experienced distress of conscience prior to coming to faith in Jesus, not as demonstrating that Paul intends Rom. 7:13–25 as a portrait of Christian experience, but rather as showing that Paul is not speaking autobiographically at all.

Romans 7:14–25 is autobiographical (an important qualification!), it can only refer to Paul's experience as a Christian, for prior to being captured by Christ Jesus on the Damascus road, Saul of Tarsus seemed quite satisfied with his performance as a keeper of the law.

(4) The transition from past tense verbs to present tense verbs at 7:14 signals that Paul is moving the discussion from his pre-Christian experience of death under sin through the law (7:7–13) to his present experience of "death" (as moral frustration) as a result of sin's continuing presence and power, despite Paul's joyful concurrence with the law of God, insofar as his "inner man" is concerned.

(5) The parallel with Galatians 5:17 suggests that the speaker of Romans 7:14–25 is a Christian, for all parties agree that Paul is speaking of the frustration of Christians when he writes to the believers of Galatia, "The flesh desires against the Spirit, and the Spirit against the flesh; these oppose each other, so that you do not do the things that you want."[15]

(6) The speaker of Romans 7:14–25 is caught in the overlap of ages—between the "already" and the "not yet" of eschatological salvation—and this is the source of his intense frustration.[16] In 7:14–25 the Christian is viewed from the perspective of his or her continuing involvement in the Adamic order, weakened and thwarted by sin, its influence over "the flesh" (which includes, though it is not limited to, the body and its members), and its use of the law as an opportunity or bridgehead (*aphormēn*, vv. 8, 11) to launch its attack on the new, godly desires of the mind. The lament and appeal of verse 24 express desperate longing for nothing less than final resurrection-deliverance from "the body of this death." There is, nevertheless, a hint of the speaker's participation in the Spirit's power not only in the confident exclamation of verse 25a but also in his references to joyful concurrence with God's law and service to God's law in the "inner man," the mind (vv. 16, 22, 25b). Both the law and the "I" are divided, since both the law and "I" are simultaneously related to both the old age and the coming age.[17] The law is sin's instrument, but it is also "spiritual," related to the Holy Spirit, who, as the power of the age to come, has already invaded the present age bringing a real, albeit limited, foretaste of resurrection life into the experience of those who believe in Jesus. The "I" is imprisoned by the law of sin, but

15. Unless otherwise identified, Scripture citations are the author's translation or paraphrase.
16. Dunn, "Rom. 7,14–25," 264–71; Dunn, *Romans*, 387–88, 403–12.
17. Dunn, *Romans*, 397–99, 405–7.

it is also in joyful inner agreement with God's law. A whole and balanced picture of the Christian life can be maintained only if we read Romans 7 and 8 together, for chapter 8 places emphasis on the believer viewed from the standpoint of our participation in the new order of the Spirit, inaugurated by Christ the last Adam.

(7) The speaker of 7:25 confesses Christ, but serves sin. The summary statement of verse 25b, "Consequently, therefore, I myself with respect to the mind am slave to God's law, but with respect to the flesh I am slave to sin's law," encapsulates the situation described in verses 14–24. But it also *follows* the exclamation of faith and hope in verse 25a ("Thanks be to God through Jesus Christ our Lord!"). This argues against the idea that verses 14–24 portray non-Christian or pre-Christian experience, in contrast with the Christian experience described in chapter 8.

(8) Some scholars have argued that the order of topics in the epistle as a whole moves from a discussion of non-Christian experience in 1:18–3:20 to a discussion of Christian experience in 3:21–8:39 (justification in chap. 3–5; sanctification leading to resurrection/glorification in chap. 6–8). In this understanding of the flow of topics and the development of Paul's discussion, to interpret Romans 7:13–25 as descriptive of non-Christians' experience of spiritual inability to obey God's law would entail a topical dislocation that interrupts the epistle's thematic flow.

(9) The frustration and failure confessed by the "I" of Romans 7:14–25 ring true to the struggles in sanctification that genuine Christians regularly experience. Many find it inconceivable that the speaker of 7:14–25 could *not* be a Christian because of the way Paul's words so aptly summarize our own experience. Perhaps we remember no struggle of conscience such as Paul describes *prior* to our conversion (although Lloyd-Jones observes that being "under conviction" through the law is, for some at least, a painful prelude to joyful trust in Christ). Since divine grace awakened us to God's holiness and imparted a grateful longing to show our love by keeping the Father's commands, however, we often grieve to see our behavior contradict our conscious, inward commitment to obedience. Some find the view that Paul would *not* describe Christian experience in the words of 7:14–25 threatening to their assurance, since it is so natural to describe their own struggle with sin, as Christians, in these terms. Does such struggle and defeat mean that we have deluded ourselves in thinking that we are trusting in Jesus, that his Spirit is at work, however imperceptibly at times, conforming us to his

image? Consequently, we may feel that to place the words of 7:14–25 in a non-Christian's mouth is to call into question the reality of our faith, or unrealistically to portray the Christian life as one of sinless perfection.

Taken together, these arguments certainly seem to constitute a strong case for identifying the "I" who speaks in our text as a believer who is caught in the overlap of the present age, still living "in the flesh" (by faith in the Son of God, as Paul says in Gal. 2:20), but also inhabiting the age to come, giving evidence of the Holy Spirit's work in his inner desire to adhere to God's law (which is "spiritual," 7:14) and expressing intense longing for future liberation from "the body of this death" and our present divided existence at the final resurrection.

Other elements in Romans 7:13–25,[18] however, seem to point to a very different conclusion regarding the spiritual condition that evokes the anguish and lament of the "I" who speaks here. In view of striking discontinuity between the frustrated impotence of the "I" who speaks in Romans 7:13–25 and Paul's description of the new liberty to keep God's law that characterizes life in union with Christ in the preceding and the following contexts, the conclusion seems almost inescapable that the speaker in our text articulates the experience of a person (or group) who stands *outside the sphere of the renewing work of the Spirit of God* through faith in Jesus the Messiah. Several of the strongest items of evidence supporting this understanding of the "I" in this text are:

(1) The speaker describes himself as "fleshly [*sarkinos*], sold [*pepramenos*[19]] under sin" (7:14), "taken captive by sin [*aichmalōtizonta me*]" (7:23), and "sin's slave [*douleuō . . . nomō hamartias*]" (7:25). These descriptions are applied by Paul in the preceding (6:16–22; 7:5) and the following (8:2–9) contexts to non-Christian experience, in contrast with the identity of believers, who are in union with Christ and therefore participate in his death to sin and resurrection life in the power of the Holy Spirit. Paul's Christian

18. The larger pericope, Rom. 7:7–25, is often divided into two sections, 7:7–13 and 7:14–25, on the basis of the transition from past-tense verbs in 7:7–13 to present-tense verbs in 7:14–25, and Augustinian interpreters often (but not uniformly) see this *syntactic* shift as signaling a *thematic* transition in Paul's discourse (Augustinian argument 4). I will argue below that Paul's rhetorical strategy throughout Romans indicates that the "break" in his argument (which is relatively minor conceptually) falls between vv. 12 and 13, with a new phase of the discussion opening with the rhetorical question of v. 13a, which finds its answer in vv. 13b–25.

19. Perfect passive participle of *pipraskō*. See Matt. 18:25 and Lev. 25:39, 42, 47–48 LXX for the sale of a person into slavery. Cf. the metaphor "sell oneself to do evil" in 3 Kgdms 20:25 [1 Kings 21:25]; 4 Kgdms [2 Kings] 17:17.

readers were formerly "in the flesh" (7:5), but they are "in the flesh" no longer (8:9)—at least in the sense in which Paul is using the expression "in the flesh" in this stage of his argument. In a similar vein, the metaphors of military capture and being "sold" are acknowledged by interpreters espousing both views as signifying enslavement, even before the use of the verb *douleuō*, "I serve as slave . . . to sin's law," in the summary statement of 7:25.[20] Having grounded his exhortation to a life of righteousness in the unequivocal announcement that his Christian readers, who were once slaves to sin, have been *set free from that slavery* in order to serve righteousness (6:16–23), is it plausible that he would now undermine his earlier argument by portraying them as sin's helpless captives, bound to perform sin's bidding, as slaves to a tyrannical master?

(2) Romans 7:5–25 flows out of a marriage analogy employed by Paul to express the change in our relationship to the law brought about by our death in union with Christ: prior to this death, we were bound to the law as a wife is bound for life to her husband, but now that death has occurred (not the law-husband's death, but our own), the marital bond has been severed and we are free to marry another "husband," "the one who was raised from the dead"—namely, Jesus the Christ (7:1–4). Verses 5 and 6, then, apply the marital metaphor to the experience of Paul's readers, reminding them *first* of their experience prior to believing in Christ, when they were "in the flesh," bound to the law (through which sin's passions operated), and on a trajectory toward death (v. 5), and *then* noting the sharp contrast to their present condition ("but now," *nuni de*), in which their marital commitment to the law has been dissolved (*katērgēthēmen* echoes the application of the same verb to the dissolution of marital obligation in 7:2) by death, and their service to God has been placed on a new footing, "the newness of the Spirit, not the oldness of the letter."

The "before-and-after" contrast drawn in Romans 7:5–6 sets the agenda for Paul's discussion in the rest of chapter 7 and well into chapter 8. In non-Christian experience under the influence of "the flesh," sinful passions

---

20. E.g., Dunn, *Romans*, 388: "With [*pepramenos*], from [*pipraskō*], the metaphor of slavery so prominent in 6:16–23 is recalled; though since defeated captives in war were usually sold as slaves, the imagery of successful surprise attack (vv 8, 11) also naturally leads into that of slavery." And on 7:23: "The metaphor [of warfare] is expressed in its most extreme form here since it speaks not only of warfare but of defeat [*aichmalōtizesthai*]. This is consistent with the other most prominent metaphor in preceding sections, slavery, since defeat in battle usually resulted in the prisoners of war being sold as slaves" (395).

evoked through the law operated in the members of the body, producing death (7:5). Romans 7:7–25 explains this claim of Paul, particularly with a view toward defending the law from any culpability in human sin, while also demonstrating its inability to deliver from sin's devious dominion. On the other hand, Christian experience "in the newness of the Spirit" entails a decisive break with the law through the death of Christ, but also a freedom and power to serve God (7:6). Romans 8:1–39 explains this claim of Paul, demonstrating that God's work in Christ has done what the law was not intended to do and could not do, condemning sin in the flesh and—a grace-effected serendipity—actually producing *the fulfillment of the law's righteous requirement* in those who walk by the Spirit (8:3–4).

(3) Consistent with the interpretation that 7:7–25 elucidates Paul's description of life "in the flesh" apart from Christ, and 8:1ff. unfolds the implications of life lived "in the newness of the Spirit" in union with Christ, is the noticeable *absence of any mention of the Holy Spirit* in the experience of the "I" who speaks in Romans 7:7–25. In fact, the only lexical allusion to the Spirit is (possibly) the comment in verse 14 that "the law is spiritual" (*pneumatikos*), but there the "I" is specifically *set over against the law's spirituality* as "fleshly" (*sarkinos*) and enslaved.

These three strands of evidence, among others (to be discussed below), suffice to show that the numerous arguments and honorable array of theologians who have held that Paul here portrays normal Christian struggles in sanctification must deal with some weighty pieces of exegetical counterevidence. Schreiner's survey of the debate, in fact, leads him to the conclusion that the competition is too close to call:

> The arguments on both sides are remarkably strong. . . . I would suggest that the arguments are so finely balanced because Paul does not intend to distinguish believers from unbelievers in this text. . . . Paul reflects on whether the law has the ability to transform human beings, concluding that it does not. The law puts to death unbelievers who desire to keep it, since they lack the power to keep it. . . . On the other hand, believers are not absolutely excluded from this text either. . . . Since believers have not yet experienced the consummation of their redemption, they are keenly aware of their inherent inability to keep God's law. When believers contemplate their own capacities, it is clear that they do not have the resources to do what God demands. . . . [21]

21. Schreiner, *Romans*, 390.

Although I would by no means minimize the challenge posed by the apparently conflicting lines of evidence in the passage itself, I nevertheless believe that a fresh examination of the text, in the context of Paul's argument at this point in the epistle and in the perspective of his two-age, semi-realized eschatology, will open a path through the "I" identity impasse.

The way forward, I believe, is to pay close attention to the textual indicators that Paul gives for his purpose in taking his discussion in the directions that he does, before we try to address (1) the place of this text in the whole system of Pauline anthropology and soteriology, and then, at last, (2) the connection of the "I" of Romans 7 to our own religious experience. In other words, we must attend to *Paul's* questions and the answers he offers to them before we query his text for answers to *our* questions.

ASKING (AND ANSWERING) PAUL'S QUESTIONS FIRST

Significant progress in breaking through the "identity impasse" can be made through a deliberate effort to focus our attention not, first of all, on the sorts of questions and concerns that the text evokes *in us* as we encounter it in the context of our own spiritual experience (whether before or after coming to faith in Christ), but rather on the precise question (actually a twofold question) that Paul specifically tells us that he is answering.

Admittedly, a host of urgent, theologically and pastorally significant questions could be asked of this text: Does Paul teach that Christians live in the overlap of the ages, between the "already" and the "not yet"? (He certainly does, as other Pauline texts show.) Does Paul teach that sinless perfection is possible for Christians in this life? (He does not, as other Pauline texts show [Gal. 5:17; Phil. 3:12–15].) Does Paul himself still struggle with sin? (He acknowledges as much, admitting that he has not yet reached perfection [Phil. 3:12–14].) Does my own struggle with sin mean that I am not united to Christ, have not received the Spirit? (It does not, for it is specifically those who are united to Christ in his death to sin and resurrection to new life whom Paul calls to resist the efforts of sin to reassert its lordship [Rom. 6:12].) Of course, it is also legitimate to ask the question that has generated such controversy for so many centuries: "What is the spiritual condition of the person whom Paul presents as speaking in the first person, whose experience so traumatically demonstrates the power of sin to capture and kill through God's good law?"

15

None of these, however, is the question that the apostle himself raises, the question that he most explicitly intends to answer *here*, as he develops his case for the gospel as the power of God for salvation (Rom. 1:16–17). Our first objective in interpreting Romans 7:14–25 should be to answer the question of this text's place in and contribution to the development of Paul's argument: why does it follow 7:13 and precede 8:1? In order to answer that question, we need to explore how it answers the questions that Paul overtly raises, as he anticipates objections and misunderstandings that he had, no doubt, often encountered when presenting the gospel in person: "Is the law sin?" (7:7) and "Did that which is good [the law], then, bring death to me?" (7:13). In other words, "How, Paul, can you assert that the law is *sin's* tool of *death*, unless you are indicting the law itself as *sinful* and *death*-inflicting?"

When we have seen how Paul answers his own questions (actually, the predictable questions of his religious opponents), we will be in a better position to discern how and to what extent Romans 7 addresses the questions that we bring to it from the church's theological controversies and our own spiritual struggles.

PAUL'S POLEMICAL STRATEGY IN ROMANS

To understand the flow of thought in the Epistle to the Romans, it is imperative to recognize that this majestic exposition of the gospel is not an abstract or dispassionately articulated discourse on soteriology. Paul is, rather, *arguing his case* for the message of Jesus the Christ, presupposing a context in which this amazingly good news will meet objection, caricature, and misunderstanding from those who both resist and desperately need the sweet grace offered in it. Paul knows from ample experience, in countless encounters with his unbelieving Jewish kinsfolk, with pagan Gentiles, and with confused fellow believers, the resourcefulness of the human heart in its self-defense against divine mercy. He knows how counterintuitive the gospel is, beyond invention by human reason or imagination and beyond human comprehension and trust apart from the Spirit's regenerating power. So in this epistle, written to introduce his gospel to the church at Rome as preparation for his anticipated future visit (Rom. 1:1–17; 15:22–29), the apostle provides an epistolary "transcript" of his persuasive oral defense of the gospel to its detractors, whether in dispersion synagogues or in pagan philosophical schools or even in Christian congregations of intermingled Jewish and Gentile backgrounds.

The apostle's rhetorical style of argumentation in Romans, as well as occasionally elsewhere in his correspondence,[22] is a literary "diatribe,"[23] reflecting the spoken "thrust and parry" of his face-to-face presentation of the gospel and efforts to persuade its opponents. Not only does he address debating opponents whom he does not necessarily expect to be in the Roman Christian congregations to whom his epistle is addressed (e.g., 2:1–5, 17–24). He also anticipates, articulates, and answers the objections and false conclusions that have often been evoked by his gospel of grace (3:3–4, 5–6, 30–31; 6:1–2, 14–15; 7:5–7, 11–13; 9:11–14; 10:19–11:1, 9–11). Throughout Romans 5:20—8:39 in particular, Paul's presentation and defense of the good news of God's righteousness through faith follows a four-step "diatribe" pattern, in which Paul's "dialogue" with a fictional objector or "imaginary interlocutor" allows him to further explain and support the astonishing message that God has given him to preach. The four steps are:

a. *Provocative statement* of Paul's gospel, or some corollary of the gospel. The vividness of these statements and the fact that they contradict conventional wisdom—and particularly Jewish expectations regarding the role of the Torah in God's relationship to his people—virtually invite offense and misunderstanding. For example, " . . . the law came in to increase the trespass, but where sin increased, grace abounded (*pleonazō*) all the more. . . ." (5:20).

b. *Misunderstanding expressed in questions that draw an erroneous inference from Paul's statement*: "What then?" (*ti oun*) is followed by a further question that expresses a misunderstanding of Paul's provocative statement, suggesting a false conclusion that could mistakenly be drawn from the apostle's striking, even shocking claim. The question typically implies that Paul's gospel logically entails a conclusion that sanctions disobedience and dishonors God. For example, "What shall we say then? Are we to continue in sin that grace may abound (*pleonazō*)?" (6:1).

c. *Strong denial*: "May it never be!" or "God forbid!" (*mē genoito*). In the strongest possible terms Paul distances himself from the "logical"

22. E.g., Gal. 2:17; 3:21.
23. Abraham J. Malherbe, "*MH GENOITO* in the Diatribe and Paul," *HTR*, 73.1/2 (Jan.–Apr., 1980): 231–40.

conclusion expressed in his opponent's question. For example, "By no means!" (6:2a).

d. *Clarification and expansion.* Paul follows up his strong denial with an explanation of his original statement that shows *why* it does not lead to the evil conclusion suggested by the opponent, but rather why the gospel of God's grace in Christ is the *only* viable means to righteous and God-glorifying living. For example, "How can we who died to sin still live in it? Do you not know that all of us who have been baptized into Christ Jesus were baptized into his death?" (6:2b–3).

Paul's use of this fourfold diatribe/dialogue style pervades this section of the epistle:

Provocative Statement	Misunderstanding	Denial	Clarification
5:20	6:1a–b	6:2a	6:2b–14
6:14	6:15a–b	6:15c	6:16–7:6
7:5	7:7a–b	7:7c	7:7d–12
7:(5), 10–11	7:13a	7:13b	7:13c–8:11

Of special interest for our purposes are the last two of these cycles:

a. Paul speaks provocatively of "the passions of *sins* which are *through the law*" and which "bear fruit in *death*" (7:5). Paul infers from his marriage analogy (7:1–4) that a believer's death in union with Christ has severed his or her "marital obligation" to the law and set the believer free for a new marital union with the risen Christ, and that this new marriage holds the promise of Spirit-empowered obedience to God *as the old marriage to the law never could achieve.* He draws this conclusion in wording that shockingly associates God's good law with both the power of sin and the outcome of death.

b. "What then shall we say? Is the law sin?" (7:7). In other words, does the fact that "the passions of the sins" (7:5) were operative through the law make the law itself sinful, and the direct and culpable cause of my disobedience?

c. "Never!" (7:7).

d. Paul clarifies his disturbingly concise "passions of sins which are through the law" (7:5) by personifying sin itself, now mentioned in the singular (which cannot be reduced, as the plural "sins" in v. 5 might be, only to distinct evil actions), as a hostile force capable of co-opting the law's holy prohibition of inappropriate desire (*epithumeō*, "coveting," as our English versions typically render the tenth commandment, cited here), turning the law's summons to contentment and purity into an occasion to stimulate the very desire that the law forbids (7:7–12).

In the course of clarifying the relationship between God's good law and the malicious sin that exploits it in fallen humanity, Paul makes another shocking claim:

a. "For sin, seizing opportunity through the commandment, deceived me and through it *killed* me" (7:11). Thus the commandment that was directed toward life, which Paul also extols as "holy and righteous and good," proved in practice to be an instrument of death (7:10–12). This motif was also present in Romans 7:5, where Paul spoke of sin's abuse of the law to "bear fruit for death."

b. "Did that which is good, then, bring death to me?" (7:13). In other words, Am I now claiming that God's good law was the direct and culpable cause of my death under its curse-sanctions? Whereas Paul's first response and clarification concentrated on the relation of the law to *sin* (while defending the law's intrinsic sinlessness), his next response will clarify the relation of the law to *death* (while defending the law's intrinsic link to life).

c. "Never!" (7:13). Again the apostle rejects the inference in the strongest of terms.

d. Paul clarifies the relationship of the law to his death by emphasizing that it is sin's diabolical effectiveness in producing death through the good, God-given law that shows *how utterly sinful sin really is* (7:13–25). Against so formidable an opponent, the "I" has no hope of survival, much less victory, unless a divine, eschatological Ally intervenes on his behalf. The "death" produced by sin through the commandment has been executed long before the cessation of physical life and is dramatically portrayed in the utter incapacity of "I" to perform the good that the law commands, despite his concurrence with the law's standard and desire to achieve it.

Thus the purpose of Romans 7:7–12 is to explain how *sin* could "come to life" in flagrant violations when the law was introduced with its commands and prohibitions, while *the law itself* nevertheless retains its holy character as a good gift from God. Likewise, the purpose of 7:13–25 is to explain how *death* can have resulted from the arrival of the law (7:11), yet the law be good (7:12) and even "unto life" (7:10), rather than the law's being the direct cause of that death (7:13). That the extended discussion (vv. 15–25) of the conflict—between the speaker's approval of the law's requirement and his inability to obey it—is intended *in its entirety* to dramatize sin's death-dealing power operating through the law is confirmed when the apostle draws the discussion to a climax with a repetition of the term "death" (*thanatos*) (closing the *inclusio* introduced in 7:13) in the anguished cry, "Who will deliver me from the body of this *death*?" (7:24).[24] Moreover, the conclusion that this is the controlling issue for the entirety of Romans 7:13–25 is demonstrated not only by this appeal for rescue, but also by the contrasting language of *life* in 8:2 (cf. 8:6, 10–11). These two questions and their respective answers are the apostle's elaboration on the linkage among death, sin, and the law that he had earlier drawn in 1 Corinthians 15:56: "The sting of death is sin, and the power of sin is the law." Writing to Corinth, he did not pause, as he does now for the Roman Christians, to explain how he could dare to attach God's good law to sin and its lethal outcome; but the same problematic relation of the law to sin and death was in view in that earlier epistle as he now explores fully in our text. Yet in both texts Paul is compelled to answer the law-sin-death dilemma with a cry of triumph: "Thanks be to God who gives us the victory through our Lord Jesus Christ!" (1 Cor. 15:57; cf. Rom. 7:25a).

So Paul uses the rhetorical device of raising and answering the misunderstandings of an "imaginary interlocutor" to advance his argument for the gospel as the power of God for salvation to Jew and Gentile alike (Rom. 1:16–17) throughout the epistle, and specifically in Romans 6–8. His burden in Romans 1:18–5:21 had been to demonstrate the universal human need, shared by Jews who treasured Israel's law and Gentiles who lacked it, for a justifying verdict from God not grounded in or mediated by the human defendant's performance, but rather pronounced on the basis of "the righteousness of God" (1:17), and specifically the "one act of righteousness" and "one man's obedience" by which Jesus reversed the damage done by Adam (5:15–21), and to demonstrate that this righteousness is imputed through faith in the God of promise (4:2–8).

---

24. The ESV apparently associates the demonstrative pronoun "this" more closely with "body" than with "death." Either is grammatically possible, although the word order seems to favor associating "this" with "death" (*ek tou sōmatos tou thanatou toutou*), in which case the demonstrative pronoun emphasizes the sort of "death" from which release is sought rather than expressing longing for deliverance from *the body* in which "this death" has been experienced (contra Moo, *Romans*, 466n83).

As Paul draws the discussion of justification to a conclusion, his surprising dual claim in 5:20, that (a) a purpose of the law was to evoke the proliferation of its violation and that (b) where such trespasses multiplied, grace "abounded all the more," provides a segue into his defense of the gospel's "power for salvation," in contrast with the law's impotence, not only with respect to forensic issues of justification or condemnation but also with respect to the subjective captivity of the fallen human heart to the tyrannical hegemony of sin. Therefore the overarching theme of Romans 6–8 is that justification through faith in Christ apart from the works of the law, far from producing or promoting a sinful pattern of life, is the *only* means to a *pattern of obedient living* that is pleasing to God.

Above we noted that some defenders of the Augustinian-Reformational interpretation offer a plausible generalization concerning the order of topics addressed by Paul in Romans (Augustinian argument 8). They contend that Paul's discussion moves from the need of fallen humanity, Gentile and Jew (1:18–3:20), through God's provision for believers' justification through faith alone (3:21–4:25), and then into God's provision for believers' sanctification and ultimate glorification through the indwelling Holy Spirit (5:1–8:39). This generalization needs to be nuanced by an appreciation of the polemical-rhetorical strategy that Paul employs throughout this epistle, a strategy that requires him repeatedly to set the beauties and benefits of the gospel—both forensic and transformative—in sharp contrast with every rival soteriology that offers an alternative to the crucified and risen Christ, and especially in contrast with Judaism's devotion to Torah. The structure of Paul's argument throughout Romans 6–8 demonstrates that he was as concerned to answer assaults on the gospel's sufficiency in the sphere of sanctification as he was to defend the gospel in the matter of justification. To put it another way, Paul is as prepared to expose the inadequacy of a vigorous commitment to law observance as the route to freedom from sin's controlling power (sanctification) as he is to demonstrate the failure of rigorous law observance to warrant vindication from sin's condemning verdict and sentence (justification). At the same time Paul demonstrates that the gospel of grace that he preaches, far from undermining the law's divinely designed purpose, reinforces its authority (Rom. 3:31) and fulfills its righteous norms (8:4).

In Romans 6–7 Paul's argument advances in three stages, using three controlling paradigms, each in response to a misunderstanding expressed in question form, as we have noted:

a. The analogy of *death and resurrection*: Christians cannot remain in sin because they have *died to sin* in Christ's death *and been raised* to newness of life in Christ's resurrection (6:1–14).

b. The analogy of *slavery, liberation, and enslavement to a new master*: Christians cannot remain in sin because they have been *liberated from sin* through the gospel in order that they might be *enslaved to righteousness* (6:15–23).

c. The analogy of *marriage, the marital bond severed by death, and remarriage*: Christians cannot remain in sin because *their "marriage" to the law*, involuntarily co-opted as a provocateur of sin's passions, *has been dissolved* through their death with Christ, so that they might be *united to the Risen One* (7:1–8:17). Because Romans 7:13–25 is part of the clarification arising out of Paul's use of this marriage analogy, we now need to examine this analogy more closely.

THE MARRIAGE METAPHOR OF 7:1–4 AND THE FLESH/SPIRIT CONTRAST OF 7:5–6

Earlier statements on the law's link to sin, leading to 7:5. At several points earlier in the epistle Paul has made statements suggesting that the law of God given to Israel, despite its divine origin, cannot solve the problem of sin but instead exacerbates it: "Through the law comes knowledge of sin" (Rom. 3:20). "The law brings wrath, but where there is no law there is no transgression" (4:15). "Sin indeed was in the world before the law was given, but sin is not counted where there is no law" (5:13). "The law came in to increase the trespass" (5:20). "Sin will have no dominion over you, since you are not under law but under grace" (6:14). The order of these statements linking the law and sin is intentional and strategic. First the law's role is described as revelatory, exposing and identifying as sinful those attitudes and actions that contradict God's holy character and humanity's covenantal obligation. Then the law is shown to hold sin accountable, not only defining boundaries that are not to be trespassed but also holding trespassers liable to divine wrath. Then the apostle broaches the delicate topic of the law's inadvertent role in stimulating in sinful humanity a reaction that proliferates its own violation and keeps sinful people captive to the very sin that it proscribes. Therefore, far from shielding Israel from God's wrath against human unrighteousness, possession of the Torah, the written Law, has exposed Israel to God's judgment and wrath (4:15) not only by revealing sin (3:20) but also by provoking transgression (4:15; 5:20). Although Adam's sin (obviously) predated the giving of the Torah to Israel through Moses, Adam nevertheless violated an explicit, spoken divine command (like the words of the covenant spoken at Sinai) (Rom. 5:14). Thus he brought the guilt of sin and the penalty of death on all those whom he represented, whether Gentiles who lack the Torah or Israelites to whom it was given. Since "sin is not reckoned where there is no law," the death of those who lived between Adam and Moses—even those who did not imitate Adam's transgression of a specific command—demonstrates that, even prior to the giving of the written Torah, human history was being poisoned by the violation of some concrete command that had been delivered by God prior to the covenant at Sinai. That command was specifically the prohibition of eating from the Tree of the Knowledge of Good and Evil, spoken by God to Adam himself (5:13–14). Hence even between the law-covenant of Eden and the law-covenant of Sinai, in the period dominated by the gracious promise of God to Abraham, death was a pervasive element of human experience.[25] When the written law was added, its purpose was to compound that Adamic transgression, fanning into flame the sometimes tacit but always present rebellion of the human heart in overt violations of God's commands. But this is only the proximate purpose of the law's introduction into the history of Israel. The multiplication of transgression serves the ultimate end of providing the context in which grace increases in overwhelming measure.

In Romans 6:14 Paul draws the connection between sin and law even more closely. Contrary to Jewish expectation, in which submission to the Torah is the means to the avoidance of sin, Paul asserts that Christians are free from sin's domination because they are *not* under the law! The implication is clear: to be under the law is to remain under sin's lordship. Paul's gospel has been slanderously accused of promoting sin (3:8; 6:15), since Paul steadfastly resists the imposition of the law on the Gentiles as a

25. See M. G. Kline, "Gospel Until the Law: Rom 5:13–14 and the Old Covenant," *JETS* 34 (1991): 433–46.

requirement for inclusion among those who experience God's salvation.[26] In fact, though, the opposite is true: those who are under the law are the ones who remain enslaved to sin!

Romans 6:15–23 employs the metaphor of *slavery/emancipation* to underscore that the recipients of God's grace in Christ are no longer under sin's enslaving domination, and therefore must no longer act as though they were sin's slaves. This paragraph is pervaded by the contrast between believers' previous condition as sin's slaves and their present condition as those now liberated from sin to become slaves of righteousness and of God:

> 6:16: Obedient slaves of "sin, which leads to death," or of "obedience, which leads to righteousness."

> 6:17: "You who were once slaves of sin" are now heartily "obedient to the standard of teaching [i.e., the gospel]."

> 6:18: "Having been set free from sin" you "have become slaves of righteousness."

> 6:19: You formerly "presented your members as slaves to impurity . . . leading to more lawlessness," but "*now* present your members as slaves to righteousness leading to sanctification" (emphasis added).

> 6:20–22: In the past "you were slaves of sin," and the fruit of that relationship was both shame and death. "But *now* that you have been set free from sin and have become slaves of God," this new relationship bears fruit in sanctification and leads to eternal life (emphasis added).

> 6:23: The wages that sin paid its slaves spelled death, but the gift that God gives to his slaves is "eternal life through Jesus Christ our Lord."

When Paul's subsequent discussion of the relationship of the law to sin and death in Romans 7 is read in the light of these almost excessively repetitive declarations that *believers united to Christ are no longer sin's slaves*, the conclusion seems inescapable that Paul sees slavery to sin

---

26. In Rom. 3:8 it seems that the slanderers are Jewish opponents to the gospel. In 6:15ff., the interlocutors seem to need Paul's warning against pressing their freedom from the law in an antinomian direction. Ironically, legalists and antinomians alike hear the gospel of grace as license to sin.

(and accompanying it, the bond of obligation that he tersely describes as being "under law" in contrast with being "under grace" [6:14]) as characteristic of those outside Christ, whether they be law-admiring Jews or law-defying pagans.

The Marriage Metaphor of Romans 7:1–4. In Romans 7:1–4 Paul rehearses the same redemptive transition effected by the work of Christ and our union with him by faith that he traced in chapter 6, but with two changes in perspective: (1) the metaphor is not the slavery bond between master and slave, but the marriage bond between husband and wife; and (2) the dominant "partner" is not sin (a slave master), but the law (a husband).

Nevertheless, terminology in this paragraph echoes that used in the preceding discussion. The law rules (*kyrieuei*), as sin has ruled (7:1; 6:14). Death "liberates" a wife from the law (*eleuthera apo tou nomou*, 7:3) as Christians have been liberated from sin (*eleutherōthentes apo tēs hamartias*) (6:18). By implication, "marriage to the law" bore fruit for death (*karpophorēsai tō thanatō*, 7:5), just as slavery to sin produced the fruit (*karpon*) of shame and the end of death (6:21). The clear implication of the marriage analogy is that to be "under the law" (6:14) is to be under sin's dominion. This point is reinforced by Paul's choice of *hupandros* (etymologically, "under a husband"[27]) to describe a married woman (7:2). A wife is a woman "under her husband's authority," reflecting the non-Christian Jews' status *hupo nomon*, "under the law." Only a death that severs our marital obligation to the law, leaving us free to become the bride of the One who has been raised from the dead (7:4), can set us free from sin to serve God.

The marriage analogy, admittedly, has its limitations. When a spouse in human marriage has died, obviously only the surviving spouse is alive to remarry. Hence Paul portrays the situation in which the husband dies, leaving the wife free to marry another. In the spiritual realities that Paul is illustrating, however, Christians (who were the law's "wife") have been put to death through union with Christ (7:4), yet they live to be united in marriage to their new bridegroom, the Risen One.[28] The point, however is clear: our

---

27. See Moo, *Romans*, 412n17.

28. John Murray, *The Epistle to the Romans*, NICNT (Grand Rapids: Eerdmans, 1959), 1:241–44, rightly observes Paul's readiness to exercise "some inversion, if not dislocation, in the application" (241) of the marriage analogy to the believer's relationship to the law as

death in union with Christ has not only broken the dominating power of sin (6:6, 10–11); it has also dissolved our marriage to the law (7:2, 4, 6).

The temporal contrast of 7:5–6. Following his practice in Romans 6:16–23 and applying his marital analogy in 7:1–4, Paul now continues, in two compact yet comprehensive statements, to draw a contrast between the situation of the person who is under the law and that of the person who has died to the law through Christ's body and has been united to Christ in his resurrection life (7:5–6). The contrast is temporal: "when we were . . . " (*hote gar hēmen*, v. 5) is set over against "but now . . . " (*nuni de*, v. 6). Does this temporal "past-to-present" contrast refer specifically to the individual experience of Paul's readers as they make the transition out of paganism or Judaism and into faith in Christ and identification with his church, or is it also reflective of a more overarching redemptive-historical transition from the age of promise to the age of fulfillment? Without excluding reference to the readers' own conversion, I am inclined to interpret Paul's "but now" (*nuni de*) here, as earlier in the epistle (especially 3:21), as marking the transition of redemptive-historical epochs. This redemptive-historical (and not merely personal-experiential) understanding of the temporal contrast between 7:5 and 7:6 is also supported by the "oldness of the letter"/"newness of the Spirit" contrast in verse 6, since in previous correspondence Paul has applied these terms to the contrast between the old covenant mediated by Moses and the new covenant initiated by Jesus and proclaimed by his apostles (2 Cor. 3:6, in a context that alludes to the new covenant prophecy of Jer. 31:31–34).

In Romans 7:5 Paul identifies four elements as characteristic of life under the law, life in the old, pre-eschatological era: (1) being "in the flesh" (cf. 8:9); (2) having sinful passions, which function through the law, operating in one's members (*en tois melesin hēmōn*); (3) serving "in the oldness of the letter" (indicated in the contrast in v. 6); and (4) conducting a pattern of life that bears fruit in death. By contrast, then, Paul describes Christians' new life in union with Christ as characterized by the following: (1) not being "in the flesh" (further clarified in 7:14; 8:3, 9); (2) having

---

motivated by the apostle's deliberate decision to avoid implying the death of the law (parallel to the husband in the analogy) per se, as well as by his insight that it is *our* (i.e., the "wife's") union with Christ in his death that has severed our previous "marital" bond with the law, freeing us to be united as the Messiah's bride.

been released from "marital" obligation to the law (an obligation to be articulated in 9:30–10:4 in terms of reliance on one's law-observance to establish and maintain one's righteousness); (3) serving "in the newness of the Spirit"; and, by implication, (4) conducting a pattern of life that bears fruit for God, leading to eternal life.

In verses 5–6, then, Paul makes explicit this intimate connection between the law and sin in his most daring statement yet regarding the law: "the passions of the sins, [passions] which were *through the law* [*dia tou nomou*], were working in our members so as to produce fruit for death" (7:5). How dare Paul suggest that sinful passions somehow came about (or "came to expression") through the holy law of God? The very ambiguity of Paul's phrase *ta dia tou nomou* would be troubling to a Jewish reader. This is the provocative conclusion that seems inevitably to invite the question, "Is the law sin?" And this question gives Paul the opportunity to explore more deeply the complex relationship through which the law can function as sin's instrument of domination while remaining itself "holy and righteous and good."

The structural significance of 7:5–6 for 7:7–8:39. The movement in thought from the life "in the flesh" under the law, in which sinful passions in one's members lead to death (7:5), to the life "in the newness of the Spirit" apart from the law, in which service is rendered which pleases God and leads to life (v. 6), previews in compact miniature the movement that we observe between 7:7–25 and 8:1–39. Even James Dunn, who in the course of his Romans commentary argues that 7:14–25 "includes" Paul as a believer[29] and finally that it can *only* refer to believers,[30] begins his discussion of this section with a cogent statement of the relation of 7:5–6 to the ensuing argument: "7:5 in effect traces the course of the discussion in 7:7–25: 7:5a (vv. 14–25), 7:5b (vv. 7–13), 7:5c (vv. 10–11, 13, 24). Likewise 7:6 foreshadows the course of chap. 8: 7:6a (8:1–3); 7:6b (8:4 ff.)."[31] Dunn also recognizes that 7:5a ("for when we were in the flesh") "is clearly a description of their *pre-Christian* position and experience."[32] One wonders, therefore, whether Dunn's (correct, in my view) identification of 7:5a

---

29. Dunn, *Romans*, 388.
30. Ibid., 394.
31. Ibid., 358.
32. Ibid., 363 (emphasis added).

as referring to the Roman believers' "*pre-Christian* position and experience," and of 7:14–25 as an expansion of verse 5a, can be reconciled with his later argument that 7:14–25 portrays the plight of the *Christian* caught in the tension of the overlapping ages of redemption.

The repetition of terms and concepts from 7:5 in 7:7–25 *and the absence of terms and concepts from 7:6* in 7:7–25 further support the view that 7:7–25 *as a whole* is a clarification and exposition of 7:5—which is to say, an explanation of the way in which the law provides an occasion for sinful passions in people who are "in the flesh" and attempting to serve God "in the oldness of the letter" rather than "in the newness of the Spirit."[33] As we have seen, the speaker of 7:13–25 is painfully aware that he is "fleshly" (7:14). He finds that nothing good dwells in him, that is, "in my flesh" (7:18). The speaker of 7:13–25 watches in horror as "the law of sin which is in my members" *wages war* against the law (of God) with which his mind agrees, and as that evil aggressor *takes him captive* as a prisoner of war (7:23). The speaker of 7:13–25 pleads for deliverance from "the body of this death" (v. 24). He is *sold* (into slavery) under sin (v. 14; cf. 6:16–17, 19–20).[34] Meanwhile, this speaker *never speaks of the power of the Spirit*, even though Paul has just spoken for Christian believers in verse 6, affirming that we serve God "in the newness of the Spirit." In fact, the "I" of 7:13–25 cannot mention any obedience to God's law that he has actually carried out in practice, through the members of the body, unlike Paul's description of believers, who now can and must present their members to God as weapons of righteousness, 6:13. Only when we reach Romans 8 do we hear of the Spirit, by whose power the law's righteous requirement is fulfilled in practice by those who "walk according to the Spirit" (8:4ff.).

These structural observations lead to the following conclusions:

(1) Romans 7:5 provides a general description of the experience of human beings "in the flesh"—outside the sphere of the Spirit's new creation power to impart spiritual life. In such a situation the exposure of fallen humanity to God's law reveals sin in concrete violations of specific commandments, but it also multiplies those transgressions and compounds the culpability of fallen, "fleshly" humanity, issuing in death. As we will see, this function of the law in diagnosing and inflaming sin

---

33. See Herman N. Ridderbos, *Romeinen*, 162.

34. On the condition of enslavement implied in "sold," see Dunn, *Romans*, 388, cited in note 20 above.

even on the part of those who consciously affirm the law's divine origin and authority can be seen in Israel's national/covenantal experience under the law in the redemptive-historical epoch between Sinai and the redemptive work of Christ and (even more widely) in the experience of the human race from the standpoint of its solidarity in Adam, its covenant head.

(2) Romans 7:7–25 is an exposition of the situation of those "in the flesh" introduced in 7:5, just as 8:1–39 is an exposition of the experience of those "in the Spirit," introduced in 7:6.

(3) Therefore Romans 7:7–25 as a whole demonstrates the inability of the law to liberate the human heart from sin's tyrannical and lethal control. As will be argued below, Romans 7:7–12 personalizes, as if it were Paul's individual "in the flesh" (= pre-Spirit) experience, Israel's national/covenantal experience under the law before Messiah's coming, portraying the inauguration and violation of the covenant at Sinai in terms that suggest a reflection of the wider horizon of fallen humanity's moral impotence as a result of our fall in Adam. The law remains good, yet sin seizes this good law as a weapon to provoke corrupt humanity to violate its holy commands, thereby inflicting the law's sanction of death. Then, in response to the possible misperception that he blames the law itself for the death that ensued from Israel's (and Adam's) breach of the Lord's covenant law, in Romans 7:13–25 Paul dramatizes in vivid terms the agonizing death that sin inflicts through the law. This death consists in the stark fact that *the very best* that humanity without the Spirit can generate—admiration for the goodness of the law's demands, and desire to achieve the standard it sets—is utterly powerless to conform actual behavior to the norm it acclaims, thirsting like Tantalus for a righteousness that remains perpetually out of reach.

These conclusions seem to fit the flow of Paul's thought and his polemical strategy in demonstrating that the law, though given by God and holy in the norms it imposes, lacks the intrinsic power to produce, even in those who extol it as God's good gift to his covenant people, the obedience that it demands. Yet these structural considerations must be put to the test in the crucible of the specific features of the failure and confusion that so frustrate the "I" who speaks in Romans 7:13–25. The case that this "I" speaks from and for the condition of corporate Israel (as reflective of humanity fallen in Adam) apart from the renewing power of the Spirit—prior to the outpouring of the life-giving Spirit by the exalted Christ[35]—must answer the evidence and arguments surveyed above, which have persuaded so many accomplished and sober exegetes and theologians of the Augustinian-Reformational perspective that understands Romans 7:14–25, at least, as expressing Christian believers' lifelong frustration in our pursuit of holiness.

Question 1: Is the Law Sin? How Sin Used God's Good Law to Deceive and Kill Paul—In Israel and Adam (7:7–12)

Interpreters holding various views of the spiritual condition portrayed in Romans 7:14 and following generally agree that 7:7–12 reflects the effect of the law *outside the sphere of Christian faith and the work of the Spirit.* There is no consensus, however, regarding the situation portrayed in this description of the "I" who was first alive, then experienced illicit desire (or coveting) through the commandment's prohibition, whereupon sin sprang to life, deceived, and killed this hitherto-living "I." Is this an autobiographical reference to Saul's own experience of "coming of age," reaching a stage of physical puberty and moral sensitivity at the very time in which his accountability to the Torah became an issue in his religious community?[36] Or does the period when "I was living apart from the law" refer to a condition of spiritually naïve, self-satisfied complacency, before the true gravity of one's violation of God's commands is borne home to the heart?[37] Or are the echoes of Adam's original "life" (*ezōn*) in Eden, the

---

35. This is not to imply that the Spirit of God was in no sense active and present among the people of God under the old covenant. Not only did he anoint prophets, judges, kings, artisans, and others for various positions of leadership and service to the covenant community; but also we may infer from the New Testament's diagnosis of the innate spiritual morbidity of humanity "in the flesh" that no patriarch or later Israelite could or would have embraced God's promises of the coming Savior apart from a regenerating work of the Spirit. Nevertheless, the OT offers us only scattered glimpses and subtle hints of the Spirit's work prior to the accomplishment of Christ's redemptive mission, and the latter prophets direct the hearts and hopes of Israel *as a covenant community* forward in time to a future, eschatological outpouring of the Spirit in such fullness that ancient Israelites' tastes of the Spirit's life-refreshing water would seem like raindrops before a deluge. See B. B. Warfield, "The Spirit of God in the Old Testament," in Warfield, *Biblical and Theological Studies*, ed. S. G. Craig (Philadelphia: Presbyterian & Reformed, 1952), 127–56; and Richard B. Gaffin Jr., *Perspectives on Pentecost: Studies in New Testament Teaching on the Gifts of the Holy Spirit* (Phillipsburg, NJ: Presbyterian & Reformed, 1979), 35–39.

36. So Gundry, "Moral Frustration," 228–45.

37. So Murray, *Romans*, 1:251.

deception (*exēpatēsen*) and desire (*epithumian*) that precipitated his fall, and the death (*apethanon, thanaton*) that ensued intended to universalize the "I" by identifying him with the father of the human race whose one trespass brought condemnation on all (Rom. 5:12–21)?[38] Or are we to think primarily of the initiation of the "old covenant" with Israel at Sinai as a recapitulation of the original temptation and fall?[39]

There is good reason to conclude that Romans 7:7–12 is Paul's portrayal of the inauguration of the Mosaic covenant at Sinai, but in terms calculated, on the one hand, to emphasize (1) the parallels between that covenant-making which "created" Israel as God's covenant people and the period of Adamic innocence at the dawn of creation and, on the other, to emphasize (2) Paul's *representative, but personally significant, participation* in those events by which sin and death entered, first, human experience and, second, Israel's corporate experience as a covenant community by the shocking avenue of God's own commandment.

The Adamic overtones of Paul's portrayal of sin's seizing the law as its weapon of death against the "I" are noteworthy especially in three themes: (1) *Life before the law*: The prelapsarian, Edenic period was not a time "without law" in an absolute sense, of course, since the prohibition of eating from the Tree of the Knowledge of Good and Evil (as well as the cultural mandate) was built into the covenant relationship between God and his human image bearers from the start. Humanity was created for the purpose of being summoned into covenant with the Creator whose image we bear, and the terms of continuing in covenantal communion and blessing are articulated in God's first words to his human image bearers in Genesis 1 and 2 (see Hos. 6:7). In another sense, though, Adam endured the bitter transition from "I was once alive" to "I died" (Rom. 7:9) in a way that none of his descendants have faced it, as sin sprang to life through the commandment, lured Eve and Adam into disobedience, and thus inflicted death. (2) *Deception of sin*: This word/concept suggests that Paul is alluding to the temptation narrative in Genesis 3. Paul's use of *exapateō* here is to be compared with the LXX of Gen. 3:13 (*apateō*), as well as with Paul's

---

38. So, for example, Dunn, *Romans*, 381–83.

39. N. T. Wright, "Romans," in *NIB*, 10:563, sees a reference to Israel's reception of the law at Sinai and subsequent apostasy as a recapitulation of Adam's fall in Eden. Moo, *Romans*, after a lengthy discussion (423–31), concludes, " . . . we argue for a combination of the autobiographical view with the view that identifies *egō* with Israel. *Egō* is not Israel, but *egō* is Paul in solidarity with Israel" (431).

terminology in his other descriptions of the temptation in Eden (2 Cor. 11:3 [*exapateō*] and 1 Tim. 2:14 [*apateō, exapateo*]). (3) *Death through sin*: On this theme we recall Romans 5:12–21, in which Paul had already laid the foundation for this discussion in Romans 7:7–12. It was in the transgression of the one man Adam that all sinned, all were condemned, and all died.

Yet the connection with the Mosaic-Sinaitic covenant is unmistakable as well. The commandment that provokes the speaker's transgression and, thereby, his death, is the last of the Ten Words, "You shall not covet" (Ex. 20:17). With respect to the puzzling "I was once alive apart from the law," we should note that, although individual Israelites of every generation, like all of Adam's descendants, lived under the shadow of death (as Paul noted death's reign in the era between Adam and Moses, Rom. 5:14[40]), in one sense biblical authors could regard the covenant people, newly liberated in the exodus, as "alive" prior to the covenant ratification ritual narrated in Exodus 24:1–8. In that ritual, in which the blood of slain animals was sprinkled both on the Lord's altar and on the people who professed their readiness to keep his commands, Israel bound themselves to obey by the sanction of death, symbolized in that sprinkled blood and the victims from which it had been drawn (Ex. 24:6–8; see Heb. 9:15ff.).[41] Commenting on this bloody ritual of covenant ratification, the author to the Hebrews notes that covenants are confirmed "over corpses" (*epi nekrois*), the bodies of slain animal sacrifices, and draws the conclusion from this symbolism that the covenant "is not in force" (*ischuei*) as long as the one contracting the covenant remains "alive" (*hote zē*)—that is, until he has sealed his loyalty in the blood that signifies the curse sanction that would fall if the obligations of loyalty are violated (Heb. 9:16–20). In this sense, then, Israel "was alive" as they approached Horeb, the mount of God, and gladly entered into a bond of loyalty (or death!) through the blood-sprinkling ceremony of Exodus 24:1–8. Then, tragically and culpably, Israel soon followed that eager pledge of allegiance to the Lord and his law with spiritual harlotry with the golden calf, and death quickly ensued for the idolaters (Ex. 32).[42]

40. See note 25 above.

41. John J. Hughes, "Hebrews ix 15ff. and Galatians iii 15ff. A Study in Covenant Practice and Procedure," *NovT* 21 (1979): 27–96.

42. Similar patterns of verbal (not necessarily hypocritical, but at least superficial and unreflective) agreement with the law and commitment to its observance, followed by griev-ous violation of the law, recur later in Israel's history. At the end of Joshua's life the captain

The way that Paul personalizes the covenantal history of Israel (and Adam) through his first person references—"*I* was alive ... sin killed *me*"—can be explained by two factors. The first is a rhetorical feature observable elsewhere in Paul's correspondence, particularly in polemical contexts, where we hear the apostle using first person references even though the context makes it clear that he is not personally the agent under discussion. For example, in Galatians 2:18 Paul writes, "For if *I* rebuild what *I* tore down, *I* prove myself to be a transgressor." The preceding context, however, demonstrates that Paul is certainly *not* the one who may be tempted to rebuild the barriers between Jews and Gentiles, which the law had maintained but which had now been dismantled through the sacrifice of Christ (2:19–21). If Paul had a single person in mind in verse 18, it would be Cephas, whose action in withdrawing from table fellowship with Gentile believers for fear of Jewish Christian criticism Paul indicted as a failure to "walk straight toward the truth of the gospel" (2:14). Paul's "I" in Gal. 2:18 may also include the Galatian Gentile believers themselves, since they stand in danger of being persuaded to "Judaize," submitting to circumcision and all the legal obligations incumbent on proselytes to Judaism, rather than resting in the redemption accomplished by Christ crucified and received by faith in the message they had heard (Gal. 3:1–5). Paul was the one person mentioned in Galatians who would *not* be inclined to rebuild the law's barrier, excluding believing Gentiles. Yet for the sake of the argument, he rhetorically injects himself into the intolerable hypothetical situation: "If I rebuild what I tore down . . . " (see also Gal. 1:8).

---

of the conquest challenged the Israelites to whom the Lord had given his land, "Choose this day whom you will serve," whether the gods their fathers served beyond the River or the gods of the Amorites whose land they had come to occupy. "But as for me and my house, we will serve the Lord" (Josh. 24:14–15). The people immediately swore exclusive allegiance to the Lord, but Joshua responded with sobering realism, "You are not able to serve the Lord. . . . If you forsake the Lord and serve foreign gods, then he will turn and do you harm and consume you." When they persisted in their protestations of loyalty, Joshua erected a stone monument to stand in testimony to the people's oath when (not if) they would abandon the Lord in future generations (vv. 19–27). In fact, the comment that "Israel served the Lord all the days of Joshua, and all the days of the elders who outlived Joshua" (v. 31) ominously foreshadows the repeated apostasies soon to follow, as recorded in Judges. Likewise, after the Lord's defeat of the prophets of Baal at Mount Carmel, the Israelites confess in terror and wonder, "The Lord, he is God; the Lord, he is God," and they aided God's prophet Elijah as he executed the purveyors of paganism among God's people (1 Kings 18:39–40). That same prophet, however, saw through their spontaneous and superficial response. Soon thereafter his indictment of Israel (perhaps jaundiced by his own pessimism and self-pity, but too true nonetheless) was, "The people of Israel have forsaken your covenant, thrown down your altars, and killed your prophets with the sword" (1 Kings 19:10, 14).

Here, however, Paul is involved in some way in the drama of death inflicted through the law, yet this involvement need not refer to his individual autobiography. Paul has a livelier sense of his covenantal identification with Israel (and with Adam) than do we who have absorbed the individualistic mindset of modern Western cultures. Paul can say about Israel at Sinai, "The law came, and *I* died," because Paul is profoundly aware that he is "in" Israel (and "in" Adam as well). Israel's history is Paul's history, whether or not his subjective experience as an individual has precisely mirrored Israel's trajectory of exodus-liberation from Egypt, marriage-covenant to the Lord at Sinai, almost-immediate spiritual adultery (the golden calf) and death, followed by a recurrent pattern of adultery with other gods, exile, and return to God's land, as recorded in the Hebrew Scriptures. The question is not whether Paul personally recalls an experience such as he describes in Romans 7:7–12, of passing from pre-law "life" into post-law "death," of being killed by the law's arrival. Paul can speak so personally and concretely of his death at the hands of sin, as it wielded the law as its lethal weapon, because he has a lively sense of his identification with his people as the nation called into covenant with God, yet squandering its privilege in spiritual adultery. The same profound and emotionally charged sense of identification with his wayward people is expressed in the prayer of Daniel, whose personal piety, demonstrated consistently in the preceding narrative, drops wholly out of view as he appeals for God's mercy: "To us, O LORD, belongs open shame, to our kings, to our princes, and to our fathers, because we have sinned against you. . . . [We] have not obeyed the voice of the LORD our God by walking in his laws. . . . We have sinned, we have done wickedly" (Dan. 9:8, 10, 15). Admittedly, Daniel employs the first person plural (rather than Paul's *singular* "I") throughout his confession of sin; but his sense of identification with his sinful people—despite the evidence that Daniel himself is a striking exception to Israel's infidelity—is demonstrated in the depth of his distress over the corporate evils that he is confessing.[43]

43. Moo, *Romans*, 431, mentions Mishnah Pesahim 10 as evidence of an ancient Jewish expression of personal involvement through covenantal representation (which he calls "a lively sense of 'corporate' identity") in the events of Israel's history: "Most famous in this regard, of course, is the Passover ritual, in which each Jew confesses that he or she was a slave in Egypt and was redeemed through the events of the Passover." Mishnah Pesahim 10.5 reads in translation: "In every generation a person is duty-bound to regard himself as if he personally has gone forth from Egypt, since it is said, *And you shall tell your son in that day saying, It is because of that which the Lord did for me when I came forth out of Egypt* (Ex.

Recognizing that Paul is speaking, not only in 7:7–12 but also in 7:13–25, not of his personal, individual experience but of the inability of Israel throughout redemptive history to keep the law that the people of God had welcomed at the foot of Mount Sinai helps us to understand how this text's dire portrait of defeat, slavery, and death "under the law" can be reconciled with the apostle's reports elsewhere concerning his previous achievements in Judaism (Phil. 3:6; cf. Gal. 1:13–14) (Augustinian argument 3). Paul is not intending us to understand his description of sin's wielding of the law to inflict death (Rom. 7:7–12) or of sin's enslavement that thwarts every desire of the fleshly "I" to obey the law's commands (7:13–25) as personally autobiographical. If the "I" who once lived when the law had not come is Paul *in Adam and in Israel*, then the defeat of this "I" when confronting sin's aggressive and enslaving power dramatizes the helpless plight in which the law, through the weakness of the flesh, leaves anyone. Garlington may well be right when he admits:

> Therefore Paul demonstrates from his pre-Christian life that the law does indeed reveal sin and increase the trespass. . . . This in itself argues that, notwithstanding Gal 1:14 and Phil 3:4–6, at some point in his Pharisaic career Paul was confronted with the condemning letter of the law, perhaps—though by no means for certain—just prior to his conversion and contributory to it.[44]

Paul's primary focus in Romans 7, however, despite his intensely personal mode of expression, is not the psychological trajectory of his individual narrative of conversion. Throughout his correspondence he exhibits little interest in probing or exposing the psychological dynamics of his transformation from persecutor to propagator of faith in Jesus as the Christ. More central to his theological substructure is the historical shift effected by Christ's accomplishment of redemption and bestowal of the Spirit as the inaugurator of the age to come and the firstfruits of believers' eschatological inheritance—the redemptive-historical movement signaled in the contrast between "flesh/sin/law/oldness of the letter" and "now/newness of the Spirit" in 7:5–6.

13:8)." Jacob Neusner, *The Mishnah: A New Translation* (New Haven, CT: Yale University Press, 1988), 250 (emphasis original to the translator).

44. Garlington, "Romans 7:14–25 and Creation Theology," 207.

QUESTION 2: DID GOD'S GOOD LAW BECOME MY DEATH? SOUNDING THE DEPTH OF THE DEATH THAT SIN INFLICTED THROUGH THE LAW (7:13–25)

If it is correct to view Romans 7:7–12 as referring to the giving of the law covenant to Israel at Sinai, their eager and voluntary submission to the covenant's sanctions, and virtually immediate violation of the covenant, incurring the curse of death (a recapitulation of Adam's failure in the original Edenic law-covenant with its adverse effects for all humankind), this interpretation clarifies the relationship between the experience of the "I" in 7:7–12 and the "I" in 7:13–25.[45]

As we have seen, many interpreters who attribute the anguish of the "I" who speaks in Romans 7:14–25 to Christian experience draw attention to the transition from past (mainly aorist) tense verbs in 7:7–12 to present tense verbs in 7:14–25,[46] inferring that by this grammatical shift Paul intends to signal a *temporal* transition from his (or others') pre-Christian experience of the law's seductive and lethal power to the believer's present, ongoing experience of inability to keep the law's commands (Augustinian argument 4). Sometimes this argument is combined with Augustinian argument 2 and articulated as follows: Paul's primary purpose is to exalt the gospel by demonstrating that God's law, although not intrinsically sinful, cannot enable human beings affected by the fall into sin to comply with its commands. This is true for those outside Christ, whether Jews or Gentiles, as Paul's past experience as a Pharisee and a persecutor of the church (now interpreted retrospectively by the apostle from the vantage point of his faith-informed appreciation of the law's spiritual depth) demonstrated (7:7–13). Yet it is equally true for believers united to Christ and sensitized to the law's true holiness, righteousness, and goodness—the law's spirituality (as originating from the Spirit of God)—that the law *in itself* can only reveal God's standard of holiness, a standard that remains out of reach for believers who have received the firstfruits of the Spirit (and with him an inner delight in God's law not previously experienced) and yet who continue to live their lives in "the present age" in which the continuing influence of sin is

45. See Ridderbos, *Romeinen*, 162–63.

46. The lack of an indicative verb in v. 13bc leaves the timing of sin's production (*katergazomenē*, present/progressive participle) of death through the law indeterminate, but the aorist *egeneto* in the question of v. 13a, "The good thing, then—*did it become* death to me?" implies that Paul's answer in v. 13bc refers to the pre-Christian past described in vv. 7–12.

all too evident in the actions of their "members," the cravings of their physical bodies that persistently resist control by the conscious mind that now concurs and rejoices with God's law (7:14–25). Whereas the nonbeliever's experience of sin's power working through the law was one of *passive non-resistance* ("sin came alive and I died," 7:9), the believer's experience is one of *struggle against the power of sin* and distress over his inability to perform the good he wishes to do. Garlington expresses this contrast:

> . . . the conspicuous feature of these verses [7:14–25] is Paul's struggle. Yet, I would submit, it is the very presence of the struggle that argues forcefully that this segment of Romans is the product of Paul's Christian consciousness. Whereas in vv. 7–13 Paul is simply dead because of the sin-revealing law, in vv. 14–20 (21–25) he is actively resistant to the impulses of indwelling sin because he wills to do what is right—in itself a sign of life. Paul's awareness of covetousness (= idolatry, Col 3:5) was a death experience: all he could do was acquiesce, as it were: lie down and die before the law's accusations. But now, because Paul delights in the law of God in the inner person, he strives to do what he knows is acceptable according to the law's prescriptions.[47]

It must be asked, however, with respect to Augustinian argument 4, whether at 7:14 Paul so obviously calls attention to his shift of verb tense from past (aorist, pluperfect, imperfect) to present as to warrant the conclusion that Paul intends readers to infer that his narrative of sin's exploitation of the law to inflict death is moving from a pre-Christian past to present Christian experience. Dunn, in fact, admits that "Paul does not make much of the transition, that his thought moves from past to present [as Dunn understands it] almost unconsciously."[48] Calvin, recognizing that the descriptions "fleshly" and "sold under sin" in verse 14 most appropriately characterize the *non-Christian's* spiritual status, finds the transition to a description of Christian experience not at verse 14 but at verse 15— implying, in other words, that Paul uses the present "I am" (*eimi*) in verse 14 to describe his and others' condition *outside* Christ. On verse 14 Calvin comments, " . . . By nature

---

47. Garlington, "Romans 7:14–25 and Creation Theology," 211–12.
48. Dunn, "Rom. 7,14–25," 261–62. Dunn, *Romans*, 405, admits: "[Paul] makes the transition [from past to present] without fanfare, though no less deliberately (using both 'I' and 'am'), and perhaps the first listeners would not notice it straightaway." One wonders, is a transition so subtle that the first listeners might miss it *really there* at all?

man is no less a slave to sin, than the bondmen whom their masters buy and ill-treat at will, as if they were oxen or asses. . . . "[49] Turning to verse 15 Calvin notes, "[Paul] *now* comes to a more particular example of a man who has already been regenerated."[50] Thus Calvin implicitly discounts (rightly, I believe) the present tense of the verbs *estin* and *eimi* in verse 14, interpreting these "present" statements as actually elaborating on the pre-Christian *past* experience described in verses 7–12. If Paul's shift of tenses is so subtle and the descriptive terms (fleshly, sold under sin) that he applies to the "I" in verse 14 (where verbs in the present tense first appear) most aptly apply (as Calvin indicates) to fallen humanity apart from Christ, there is little reason to point to verb tenses *per se* as indicative of a change in the spiritual status of the "I" as Paul moves from verses 7–13 to verses 14–25. The way that Paul draws together *as one argument* the description of sin's death-wielding power articulated in past tenses (7:7–13) and the description of sin's death-wielding power (7:14–25) dramatized in a "present tense" narrative suggests that the temporal shift in Paul's verb forms is not as significant as Dunn and Garlington and others before them have believed.

This observation also calls into question Augustinian argument 2, particularly in the form that contrasts an "acquiescent" passivity in death (7:7–12) to an active resistance to sin's power (7:14–25)—supposedly a tacit indication that the "I" whose experience is described in the latter text has experienced the regenerating power of the Spirit. To infer that Paul would characterize the struggle, defeat, and enslaved captivity described in verses 14–25 as evidence of "life" as opposed to "death" is to misperceive what Paul considers to be "death" in this chapter. The "death" that sin has produced through the law (7:13b) is precisely the anguish that we observe in 7:13–25, leading to the cry for deliverance from "the body of this death." This death is not a cessation of struggle against sin, but rather the constant but unremittingly frustrated agony of a prisoner of war, a slave who recognizes sin as evil, yet finds himself powerless to overthrow its mastery.

The view that Paul's intention *throughout 7:13–25* is to demonstrate how sin could have turned God's good law into an implement of death for Israel, and (in a wider horizon) for all who are "in" the first Adam but

---

49. John Calvin, *The Epistles of Paul the Apostle to the Romans and to the Thessalonians*, trans. Ross Mackenzie, ed. David W. Torrance and Thomas F. Torrance (Grand Rapids: Eerdmans, 1961), 147.

50. Calvin, *Romans*, 148 (emphasis added).

not "in" Christ, finds support in the *tightly interlocking logic and series of inferences* by which the apostle links verses 14–25 to his initial answer to the incorrect inference expressed in the question of verse 13a. Paul's answer to this question, "Did that which is good, then, bring death to me?" is not confined to the remainder of the verse (which recapitulates the "past history" summarized in 7:7–11): "It was sin, producing death in me through what is good, in order that sin might be shown to be sin, and through the commandment might become sinful beyond measure." Rather, Paul's elaboration of the utterly evil power of sin to wield the law as a lethal weapon continues throughout 7:14–25. The first syntactic signal that the apostle is presenting verses 14–25 as further elaboration of his answer in 7:13b is the conjunction "for" (*gar*) that binds 7:14 to 7:13. "I am fleshly, sold under sin" (v. 14) provides *a supportive rationale* for the assertion that sin's utter sinfulness is demonstrated in its exploitation of God's law as an instrument of death (v. 13bc). Paul reasons: "Sin could produce death in me through God's good law . . . *because* (as we know), although the law is spiritual, I am fleshly, sold to serve sin."

Moreover, another *gar* links verse 15 to verse 14, invoking the conflict between the law-approving will of the "I" and his law-violating behavior (v. 15) as *illustrating and supporting* the distance between the weakness of the fleshly "I" and the demand of the spiritual law (v. 14). Paul reasons, "It is evident that I am fleshly, sold into slavery to sin, *because* the good that I wish to do I cannot, and the evil I hate I find myself doing." If, therefore, Calvin is right (as I think he is) to conclude that "fleshly, sold under sin" describes natural man apart from the renewing life of the Spirit (v. 14), then the confusion and frustration of the "I" in verse 15 shows what that spiritual slavery entails in experience, namely, inability to do the good that one desires and performing instead the evil that one abhors. The inferential links in Paul's chain of reasoning draw us to the conclusion (contra Calvin) that verse 15, no less than verse 14, describes the condition of humankind "in the flesh," not of those who are experiencing the work of the Spirit, whose transforming action Calvin rightly describes (in his comment on v. 14) as "the renewing of our corrupt nature, while God reforms us after His own image."[51]

If, then, the disjunction between the fleshly "I" and the spiritual law in Romans 7:14 explicates Paul's narrative of the way that sin has inflicted

51. Calvin, *Romans*, 147.

death through the law on those who were "in the flesh" (v. 13bc) and if, in turn, the disjunction between good intention and actual behavior in verse 15 explicates the fleshly weakness and slavery to sin spoken of in v. 14, how should we go on to understand verses 16–21? Interwoven throughout these verses is the pervasive theme of the conflict between what the "I" wills (*thelō* in vv. 15, 16, 18, 19, 20, 21) and what he actually does (*katergazomai*, *prassō* and/or *poieō* in vv. 15, 16, 17, 18, 19, 20, 21). This motif shows this entire section to be an extended dramatization and clarification of verse 15: "What I am producing [*katergazomai*] I do not know [either 'understand' or 'approve']. For I do not do [*prassō*] what I want [*thelō*], but what I hate, this I do [*poiō*]."

The unremitting failure—and Paul does here present it as *unremitting*—to perform the good that the law requires and the "I" approves is traced to the sobering truth that "nothing good dwells in me, that is, in my flesh" (v. 18). If we interpret the clarification, "that is, in my flesh," in the context of Paul's discussion in Romans 6–8, we will recognize that the distinction that the apostle has in view is neither generically anthropological ("flesh" as body in contrast with soul or spirit[52]) nor psychological ("flesh" as a sinful nature coexisting alongside and in conflict with a new "spiritual" nature). Rather, it is redemptive-historical: "in my flesh" is Paul's deliberate signal that, though he is now employing "present tense" verbs for dramatic effect, he is not portraying his present experience as one set free to serve God in the newness of the Spirit (7:6) but rather the condition of Israel, his Roman readers, and himself when "we were in the flesh" (v. 5), when we were "fleshly" (v. 14). Then, indeed, "nothing good" dwelt (*oikei*) in those whose lives were defined by the frailty and fallenness that was Adam's legacy, but now the Spirit of God dwells (*oikei*) in those who belong to Christ, securing their hope of future bodily resurrection through the life-giving power of the indwelling Spirit (8:9–11).

Consequently, verse 14 (linked to v. 13 by *gar*) opens an exploration of how sin could have exploited God's good law to inflict death (v. 13bc is both an answer to the misperception expressed in verse 13a and a retrospective summary of vv. 7–11); and verses 15–21 (linked to v. 14 by another *gar*) continue the exploration of that death in the impotence of the will to overcome the malevolent power of sin operating at some depth beyond the

---

52. Contra Moo, *Romans*, 459.

reach of the conscious will. The relentless consistency of Paul's argument, with each link in the chain tightly interlocking with those that precede it syntactically (the inferential conjunction *gar*) and/or lexically (repeated vocabulary), shows that throughout verses 13b–21 he develops his response to the allegation that his message blames the law itself for the death that sin effected through the law.

The climax of this exploration of sin's utterly sinful power and the fleshly self's (and the law's) impotence to combat sin's subtle strength comes in verses 22–23, and again *gar* binds this conclusion tightly to the preceding argument: the shocking reality that Paul has "found" (*heuriskō*), namely, that though he wants to do the good, "evil lies close at hand" (*parekeitai*) (v. 21) finds perhaps its most poignant and stark expression in the paradox that, though his delight (*sunēdomai*) is in God's law (v. 22), he sees operating in his members a hostile alien force, which assaults the (God-given) law that his mind wants to serve and takes him captive, making him sin's prisoner of war (*aichmalōtizonta me*) (v. 23). This is the death—a death that consists in agreeing with God's law and delighting in it (vv. 16, 22), on the one hand, yet finding oneself incapable of translating conscious assent into obedient action, on the other—from which the miserable captive cries out for rescue (v. 24). Paul's syntactic and lexical signals show that he intends the entire discussion (7:7–24) to hang together as an indictment of sin's devious, enslaving, and lethal power and a dramatic illustration of the law's impotence to deliver those "under the law," wed to the law, from sin's death-grip. Another, stronger Rescuer was needed, and has now come, as Paul well knows and now, unable to contain his joy any longer, gladly exclaims, "Thanks be to God through our Lord Jesus Christ!" (v. 25a).

My conclusion, then, is that Paul's tightly-linked logic directs us to read this entire section (7:7–24) as explaining how the law was made weak by the flesh and turned into an implement of slavery and death until the coming of the Messiah and the life-giving power of his resurrection, applied in the Spirit, burst into the history of redemption. When we read the "I" of Romans 7 in this light, we can give full weight to the negative force of the terms that Paul uses to articulate the utter helplessness of those who are "married" to the law, under the law, "in the flesh," and enslaved to sin. This interpretation can also account credibly and even helpfully for the self-descriptive statements in Romans 7:14–25 that lead Augustinian interpreters to conclude that this text must describe the Christian believer's struggles in sanctification, while other exegetes conclude that the "I" who speaks here is so schizophrenic as to make determining his spiritual identity an exercise in exegetical frustration.

ANOTHER LOOK AT THE SCHIZOPHRENIC "I" OF ROMANS 7:13–25

The agenda-setting function of the rhetorical questions in Romans 7:7 and 13 as signaling the interlocking problem that Paul intends to address, together with the syntactic and lexical links that unify his tightly reasoned response to the problem, provide strong evidence that Paul intends the entire discussion, from 7:7 through 7:25, not only to defend the law from the charge of complicity in human sin and death, but also to demonstrate that the law, although given by God as the holy norm for his human servants, lacks the power to produce the obedience that it demands. Especially in his portrayal of the conflicted "I" in verses 13–24, Paul has dramatized in the most vivid way imaginable the point that he makes more succinctly in Galatians 3:21: "If a law had been given that could give life [*zōopoieō*], then righteousness would indeed be by the law." Paul's point, both in Galatians 3 and in Romans 7, is that no such life-giving law has been given by God. The law is holy, righteous, and good *as a standard* defining the conduct that God approves. But *as commandment* its role in the divine economy of salvation was never to give life, never to impart to fallen human beings the capacity to fulfill its standard. This is its weakness as letter (*gramma*) in contrast with the Spirit, who can and does "give life" (*zōopoieō*) (2 Cor. 3:6; Rom. 8:11; cf. 1 Cor. 15:45; John 6:63; 1 Pet. 3:18). Hence Paul's mention of the "oldness of the letter" in 7:6 anticipates 8:3, where he will encapsulate the struggle, defeat, and death experienced by the "I" of 7:7–25 in the terse expression, "what the law, weakened by the flesh, could not do." Then, in 8:4, the apostle will declare that the goal that lay beyond law's power (*to adunaton tou nomou*) has been achieved by God through Christ's sacrifice: "that the righteous requirement of the law might be fulfilled in us, who [unlike the 'I' of 7:7–25] walk not according to the flesh but according to the Spirit." This interpretation enables us to take the dire self-description of the "I" who speaks in 7:13–25 "full strength," without watering down the starkness of his plight, doing justice to at least five facets of the desperation, defeat, and death portrayed in our text.

1. *"Fleshly, in flesh" (vv. 14, 18, 25).* The speaker's self-description in verse 14, "I [in contrast to the law, which is spiritual] am *fleshly* [*sarkinos*]," is to be understood in the light of Paul's use of the phrase "in the flesh" both in 7:5 and again in 8:8 to describe the pre-Christian condition of those who had not yet entered into "the newness of the Spirit" through union with Christ by faith, and were thus devoid of the Spirit's life-giving power. To be "in the flesh" or "fleshly" is, at best, to be shut up to the resources of the first creation and "the present age," but the reality of "the flesh" is far worse than this may at first appear. The bitter legacy of Adam's sin has made "the flesh" not merely a sphere of creaturely weakness but also a center of creaturely defiance, unwillingness and inability to submit to God's law. From this sphere Christ has liberated those who trust in him by his indwelling Spirit (8:9), delivering them from "the present evil age" (Gal. 1:4).

Yet Dunn, followed by Garlington, asserts that it is characteristic for Paul in Romans 6–8 to state the contrast between the two ages in absolute terms ("we were living in the flesh . . . but now . . . we serve . . . in the new life of the Spirit," 7:5–6), and then to qualify the absoluteness of the contrast by taking account of the fact that Christians, who in Christ belong to the age to come, nevertheless also belong to the old order characterized by Adam's disobedience and the resultant miseries.[53] Consequently they cite such passages as 2 Corinthians 10:3, Galatians 2:20, Philippians 1:22, and Philemon 16 as evidence that Paul can speak of Christians as still living "in the flesh."[54] In such texts, however, Christians are said to live "in the flesh" not in the sense of lying under the domination of the old order (as, Dunn acknowledges, is the significance of "in the flesh" in Romans 7:5), but in the sense of their continuing to inhabit a world characterized by injustice, suffering, and danger, inasmuch as they have not yet received the consummative eschatological gift, the resurrection of the body. Garlington writes with respect to Romans 7:14, 18, and 25:

> Therefore during the period of concurrent ages "flesh" characterizes Paul and all like him. Rather than being a sign of his pre-Christian state, "flesh" within the present setting is indicative of Paul's continued

---

53. Dunn, *Romans*, 388; Garlington, "Romans 7:14–25 and Creation Theology," 216.
54. Dunn, "Rom 7,14–25," 266.

belongingness—as a whole person—to the present evil age, which has not yet been superceded by the age to come in its fullness.[55]

Dunn and Garlington (with Murray[56] and others) therefore read "fleshly" and "in my flesh" as Paul's nuancing of his earlier (and later) announcements that believers are no longer "in the flesh," controlled by the fallen human nature inherited from Adam. Although believers have tasted the powers of the coming age in the mighty presence of the Spirit, they still encounter both temptation and suffering and are in this sense "fleshly," despite the fact that they belong to the new creation.

This softened reading of "fleshly" is possible, but its plausibility is damaged by several factors. First, the closest and most relevant usage of "flesh" (sarx) to 7:14 is in the phrase "in the flesh" in verse 5, which Dunn himself acknowledges to describe a situation "prior to and exclusive of being 'in Christ,' 'in flesh' as a kind of living dominated or characterized by the weakness and appetites of this life. . . ."[57] Second, the succeeding context likewise indicates that Paul continues to think of "fleshliness" as the opposite of being in Christ. Most pointedly, as noted above, there is the absolute statement of 8:9, "But you are not in flesh but in Spirit, since in fact the Spirit of God dwells in you." The earlier verses of Romans 8 likewise speak of "those who are according to the flesh" (8:5), "the mind of the flesh" (vv. 6–7), and "those who are in flesh" (v. 8), and all of these refer to those who are outside Christ and his Spirit's power.[58] Third, within the very structure of verse 14 the "I" who is fleshly is placed in contrast with the law which

---

55. Garlington, "Romans 7:14–25 and Creation Theology," 224.

56. Murray, *Romans*, 1:260.

57. Dunn, *Romans*, 370.

58. Murray, *Romans*, 1:260, distinguishes being "fleshly" from being "in the flesh" (7:5; 8:5, 8) on the grounds that Paul rebukes the Corinthian believers as "fleshly" (1 Cor. 3:1, 3) and that "Paul recognizes that the flesh still resides in him (vv. 18, 25), although he is regenerate by the Spirit." Dunn, *Romans*, 406, paraphrases 7:14, "'I' am still within sin's power, my slavery to sin unbroken; as such 'I' am still sin's chattel, sin can have its way with me," on which he comments, "The answer is so astounding that many would probably jump to the conclusion that Paul must after all be speaking of his previous condition (as many have since). How can he who has died to sin (6:2), who has been liberated from sin (6:18), still be sin's bondslave?" Dunn tries to resolve the contradiction that he so frankly acknowledges by contending that in 7:14 Paul is balancing his emphasis in 7:1–6 on the *dis*continuity of the present and coming epochs by now stressing that believers still "belong to this world, to the old epoch which is to pass." Garlington, "Romans 7:14–25 and Creation Theology," 224, does not refer to 7:5 or 8:9 in his interpretation of "fleshly" in 7:14.

is "spiritual" (*pneumatikos*). Garlington correctly notes that this adjective implies the law's origin in the Holy Spirit and consequently the law's connection (in some sense) with the age to come, which is characterized by the Spirit's power.[59] He is on shakier ground exegetically when he claims (Augustinian argument 6) that the "I" who speaks in 7:13–25 is a person "in the Spirit."

> It is true that Paul does not say in so many words that he is "Spirit." However, his self-assessment throughout Rom 7:14–25 is to the effect that he is squarely within the era of the Spirit; he has been enrolled in the new covenant, proof of which is his delight in the law of God, his desire to do God's will, and his hatred of sin.[60]

I will deal below with Garlington's contention that the speaker's delight in the law can be explained only as evidence of the Spirit's life-imparting power at work in his life. At this point, I would simply observe that the *contrast* between the "*Spirit*-ual" law and the *flesh*-ly "I" would seem to support our understanding of the speaker's condition as "fleshly" in the sense of 7:5 and 8:5–9—namely, as belonging to the sphere *outside* the power of the Spirit, prior to and exclusive of being "in Christ."[61]

In fact, two significant differences distinguish the situation portrayed in Romans 7:7–25 from that which Paul attributes to the Christian experience of frustration in the crossfire between the flesh and the Spirit in Galatians 5:17 (contra Augustinian argument 5). First, of course, is that the "protagonists" in the conflict of Galatians 5 are the flesh and the Spirit, whereas in Romans 7 it is the "I"—with no mention of the Spirit—who finds himself under assault and enslaved by the law of sin at work in the flesh. The second, and related, difference is that, although the wording of Galatians 5:17, if read in isolation, seems to portray a stalemate between the flesh's desire and the Spirit's desire "so that you do not do the things that you wish," this statement is immediately preceded and followed by assurances of victory through the Spirit's presence and power: "Walk by the Spirit and you will certainly not [*ou mē* = strong negation] accomplish the desire of the flesh"

---

59. Garlington, "Romans 7:14–25 and Creation Theology," 214–15.

60. Ibid., 224. Also see his *Faith, Obedience, and Perseverance: Aspects of Paul's Letter to the Romans* (Tübingen: J. C. B. Mohr, 1994), 132. In this version of the quotation, the word "spirit" in the first sentence remains uncapitalized.

61. So Ridderbos, *Paul*, 126–30; and Ridderbos, *Romeinen*, 153–70.

(v. 16) and "If you are led by the Spirit, you are not under law. . . . Those who belong to Christ Jesus have crucified the flesh with its passions and desires. Since we live by the Spirit, let us also keep pace with the Spirit" (vv. 18, 24–25). In Romans 7:13–25, on the other hand, the "I" can accomplish *nothing but the desire of the flesh*, the law of sin, despite his mind's desire to practice the good commanded in God's law.

The expression "in my flesh" in verses 18 and 25 should be interpreted in the light of Paul's redemptive-historical contrast between flesh and Spirit in 7:5–6 and 8:1–17. Paul is not performing anthropological or psychological dissection, as though he were saying that nothing good dwells in some part of him, the fleshly part as opposed to some other part (v. 18). Nor is he, in verse 25 or earlier in the chapter, blaming his "flesh"—his bodily members—for running amok in rebellion against his law-abiding mind, so as to exonerate his consciousness from responsibility for his sinful behavior. Nor is he engaging in a subtle distinguishing of perspectives at this point: "Viewing myself, the Christian, in terms of Adam and the old age I find nothing good. On the other hand, viewing myself in Christ and the age of the Spirit is another story, which I shall recount presently." Rather, he is making clear that, despite his use of present tense verbs for dramatic effect, he is in fact voicing the plight of the person, and the covenant people, "in the flesh"—a plight in which he himself was once trapped as a member of Israel and of the first Adam. *Hence, "in my flesh" is Paul's shorthand for "when I myself was controlled by the sinful desires of the old order, there was nothing in me strong enough to curb sin's domination over my members, despite my conscious concurrence with the goodness of God's law."*

2. "Sold under sin" (v. 14). We have already noted the frank acknowledgement by Calvin and Dunn that Paul's metaphor entails the imagery of slavery, and portrays sin as a master whose will his slaves cannot resist.[62] Having admitted forthrightly that "sold under sin" is indeed the language of enslavement, however, Dunn goes on to assert that the speaker's "capture and subjection to death at the hands of sin . . . does not exclude Paul the believer."[63] But is this really plausible in the context of Paul's discussion? A description of the Christian life as one of *slavery under sin* would be, to say the least, unprecedented throughout these chapters of Romans

---

62. Calvin, *Romans*, 147; Dunn, *Romans*, 388, cited above in note 20.
63. Dunn, *Romans*, 388.

(in which, as we have seen, Paul so often asserts the contrast between slavery to sin and slavery to God and his righteousness through union with Christ). In fact, to allege that Paul here intends to portray Christians as sold into slavery to sin, unless the metaphor is nuanced and qualified almost beyond recognition, is to bring Paul into conflict with his own declarations that believers have been liberated from sin's mastery in both the preceding and the following portions of the epistle, and thus to undermine his rationale for summoning believers to resist sin's sway (6:16–22; 8:24).

Murray and Garlington do attempt to nuance and qualify the "slavery" into which the "I" of 7:14 has been sold. They resist the parallel that we noted earlier to such OT passages as 1 Kings 21:20, 25 and 2 Kings 17:17, in which individuals are said to have "sold themselves to do evil." Murray insists that *selling oneself* to do evil differs from *being sold by another* into a condition of slavery, "subjected to a power that is alien to his own will," and against which Paul's "sanctified sensibility" and "most characteristic self" protested.[64] Garlington contends that Paul's wording does not imply that the speaker "can never perform the will of God," but he does not indicate why he believes that this expression allows for the possibility that the "I" might, on occasion, escape sin's control and perform the good that the law demands. Such a glimpse of emancipation from sin and actual obedience to God seems utterly foreign to the experience of the "I" throughout Romans 7:13–25.[65]

3. *"Taken captive by the law of sin" (v. 23).* This description, like "sold under sin," evokes the imagery of a hostile capture as a result of defeat in battle, leading to subjugation, slavery, and even death.[66] Despite the speaker's conscious agreement that the law is good, inasmuch as it is God's standard for human life, this speaker finds himself not only warred against but actually conquered by the power of sin, operating at a level deeper than his conscious thoughts to control his behavior.

4. *Deliverance "from the body of this death" (v. 24).* The plaintive question of verse 24, "Who shall deliver me from the body of this death?"

64. Murray, *Romans*, 1:261.
65. Garlington, "Romans 7:14–25 and Creation Theology," 216n86.
66. Dunn, *Romans*, 395, cited above in note 20.

is sometimes interpreted as the Christian's groan of longing for resurrection life, for rescue from the body that exhibits sin's ongoing influence in its members (8:23). In the preceding context, however, the death in view has been neither physical death nor the physical decay that anticipates it. Rather, it is the death that sin brought about through the law (vv. 10, 11, 13), the death that consists in the inability to do what the law demands, and the condemnation resulting from that failure (cf. 5:12–21). A parallel is sometimes drawn to the expression "body of sin" in 6:6. There the crucifixion of our old man with Christ, which has taken place, is said to have two results or purposes (or one expressed in two ways): that the body of sin might be destroyed (*katargeōmai*, also used in 7:6), and that we might no longer serve as sin's slaves. In the context it is clear that the destruction of the "body of sin" does not refer to the physical resurrection-transformation, which is yet future; rather, it refers to the nullification of sin's tyranny over believers and their bodies/members *now*, as a result of our union with Christ in his death. Now that Christ has died to sin and been raised, death can no longer rule over him (6:9); neither can sin rule over us, since we have died (the body of sin destroyed) and been raised with him (6:11–12). Thus it turns out that the parallel between the "body of death" in 7:24 and the "body of sin" in 6:6 reinforces our conclusion that in both texts Paul is referring to the transition from enslavement to sin, on the one hand, to freedom for obedience that occurs upon union with Christ by faith.

5. *"I myself . . . in the flesh serve as slave to sin's law" (v. 25).* The concluding and summative statement of verse 25bc, "So then I myself with respect to my mind am slave to God's law but with respect to the flesh I am slave to sin's law," encapsulates the struggle that has been dramatized in verses 15–23 and has issued in the lament and question of verse 24. This important summary statement, which looks back over 7:7–24 toward the introductory statement in 7:5 and is placed immediately before the summary statement of 8:1—which, in turn, looks back to 7:6 and introduces the life in the Spirit, 8:2ff.—states the speaker's relationship to sin as one of *slavery (douleuō)*. This enslavement to sin of the conflicted and captive "I" stands in direct contradiction to Paul's affirmation to Christian believers in Romans 6:17–18 that through faith in the gospel they are no longer slaves to sin, but have been set free from sin to be slaves to righteousness.

48

On the other hand, those who believe that Paul has articulated his frustrations in sanctification as a believer in Jesus throughout this section find support for their view in two features of this conclusion. First, its placement following the joyful answer to the plea for deliverance, "Thanks be to God through Jesus Christ our Lord" (v. 25a), is thought to affirm that the retrospective in v. 25bc must sum up the experience of one who has found hope in Jesus (Augustinian argument 7). Second, many who take seriously (as I do) the biblical (and specifically Pauline) teaching that apart from the renewing work of Christ's Spirit no fallen human heart does submit or can submit to God's law (8:7–8) conclude that Paul would never describe a non-Christian (of any background) as serving God's law with his mind (7:25) or rejoicing with it in the inner man (7:22) (Augustinian argument 1).

It would seem, then, that in verse 25 we find the schizophrenia of the mysterious "I" displayed "full strength," confronting the interpreter with an irresolvable dilemma: Are Christians still sin's slaves? Can non-Christians internally, mentally, exhibit allegiance to God's law? On further examination, however, I am convinced that both of the elements in verse 25 that have been thought to support a Christian identity for the "I" of Romans 7:14–24 can be credibly accounted for by the view that takes with complete seriousness the utter impotence of the "I" as a slave of sin, and therefore understands 7:25b as summarizing the utter impotence of the law to liberate from sin's tyranny those who remain "under the law"—Israel (and Saul in Israel), apart from and prior to union with Christ in the power of the Spirit.

Consider, first, the textual flow of Romans 7:25, or, better yet, the flow of 7:25–8:4. The placement of the cry of confident faith in Christ at 7:25a is often thought to be an insurmountable difficulty to the view that 7:13–25 describes non-Christian experience, since it is recognized that 7:25bc is a summary of 7:13–24. I would suggest, however, that the cry of victory, "Thanks be to God through Jesus Christ our Lord" is inserted by Paul in his dictation process because he cannot let the mournful question of verse 24 remain unanswered, even for a moment. This is an outburst of joy, relief, and exultant thanksgiving: there is an answer to such helpless and hopeless enslavement! "Thanks be to God through Jesus Christ our Lord!" anticipates in both tone and content Paul's elaboration of the life of those liberated through faith in Christ in Romans 8.

Then, having offered a tantalizing foretaste of freedom in Christ, Paul returns to *a two-sided* conclusion, each introduced by "consequently" (*ara*).

The first concluding statement (7:25bc) encapsulates the radical frustration of the best that "the flesh" has to offer: the person (especially the conscientious Jew) who knows the law and joyfully concurs with its goodness, insofar as his mental attitude is concerned, nevertheless finds himself constantly thwarted by a slavery to sin that lies beyond the control of his mind. Even the law, as commandment, cannot break this slavery nor bring life into this situation of death.

The second conclusion is 8:1–4 (and following). Paul picks up the theme of 7:13–25 when he notes that the law could not condemn sin in the flesh because it was weakened by that same flesh (8:3). As he notes elsewhere, the law was not given to impart life (Gal. 3:21). By contrast, those who are "in Christ" now (*nun*) face no condemnation. Deliverance from the complex of law-sin-transgression-condemnation-death has been accomplished through the death of Christ. The law's goodness (the point at issue in the questions of 7:7, 13) is vindicated *not only* by Paul's showing that it was sin's devious maliciousness that turned the good law into an instrument of death, but also by his affirmation that the Spirit's power so applies the benefits of union with Christ in death and resurrection that the law's righteous demand is fulfilled in those who are "in Christ," who walk by the Spirit (8:4).

It is not unusual for Paul to overlap the stages of his argument, or to recapitulate an earlier conclusion after the next step in the argument has been introduced. Romans 8:3a, "That which was impossible for the law because it was weakened through the flesh," is itself such a recapitulation, a retrospective on the law's incapacity to set sin's slaves free, just dramatized so vividly in 7:7–24. Likewise, in Romans 3:21–24, Paul recapitulates the conclusion of his extended discussion of human depravity, Gentile and Jewish (Rom. 1:18—3:20), in the summary, "For there is no distinction, for all have sinned and 'come up lacking' the glory of God" (3:23), in the midst of his exposition of the revelation of God's righteousness in Christ, the solution to the human catastrophe. The movements of Paul's discourse interlock with each other, both logically and emotionally, so it is not surprising to hear 7:25a, as it strains forward to the joy and freedom of Romans 8, followed by 7:25bc, which consolidate the sobering portrait of slavery to sin for those under the law (7:7–24), making unavoidably clear the need for the rescue that only God through Christ could accomplish.

Perhaps the most formidable *theological* objection to interpreting the "I" of Romans 7:14ff. as reflective of Israel's and observant Jews' experience apart from the regenerating work of Christ's Spirit is the conviction that a non-Christian can neither delight in God's law in the inner person nor feel the pain of a conscience that, approving God's law, is appalled at his own evil actions (Augustinian arguments 1 and 2). As a generalization regarding the pervasiveness of depravity in fallen human beings, this conviction has warrant in Scripture, and specifically in this very epistle (3:9–20; 8:6–8). Yet Paul's theological anthropology and pastoral wisdom add necessary nuances to our understanding of the ways in which unregenerate persons may manifest and experience their resistance to and inability to obey God's law. I argued earlier that the Exodus narrative concerning the giving of the law at Sinai and its aftermath illustrates the sobering truth that a conviction that the Torah is good and God-given did not in itself impart to Israel the power to keep the Torah's demands. Paul has already alluded to this disjunction between his fellow Jews' admiration for the law and their failure to adhere to the law in Romans 2:17–29. In verses 17–20 he acknowledges his fellow Jews' devotion to the law, at least with respect to their conscious convictions: "You call yourself a Jew and rest in the law and boast in God and know 'the will' and approve what is preferable because you are instructed from the law. . . . you have the very image of knowledge and truth in the law." All such "credentials," of course, only compound the culpability of those who teach others while failing to conform their own behavior to the God-given norms they propound, dishonoring God by violating the very law in which they boast (vv. 21–24). Such incongruity between professed admiration for the law and practiced violation of it may, of course, be symptomatic of conscious and willful hypocrisy. It could also be attributed, however, to the troubling phenomena of sinful human inconsistency and unruly desires that seem bent on defying the ethical norms that the conscience acknowledges as right and true. In a similar vein in Romans 10:2–3, Paul bears witness (*marturō*) on behalf of his Jewish kinsmen who are yet outside Christ that "they have a zeal for God, but not according to knowledge. For ignoring God's righteousness and seeking to make their own righteousness stand, they are not submissive to God's righteousness." He does not challenge the sincerity of their zeal for God, although it is mired in ignorance and mingled with resistance to God's righteousness, now revealed in the gospel and bestowed graciously through faith. Throughout Romans, Paul returns to this motif: the conflict between the law-affirming conscious mind and law-violating passions cannot be resolved by a greater exertion of human willpower (reliance on "the flesh") to subdue wayward desires. What is needed is "circumcision of the heart, in the Spirit not the letter" (2:29), "the law of the Spirit of life in Christ Jesus" to liberate us from the law of sin and death (8:2), the imputation of divine righteousness through faith in the heart, confessed by the lips (10:4–11). Ridderbos observes:

> It is in harmony neither with the teaching of Jesus nor with that of Paul to deny zeal for the law or desire for the good to every man outside Christ, or to consider such impossible in him. It is likewise not in harmony with the reality to which Paul, without fear of being wrongly understood, appeals with a certain degree of self-evidentness (Rom. 2:14ff.). This takes away nothing from the necessity of total renewal.[67]

A profound theologian as well as a strategic debater, Paul refuses to caricature the mindset of those outside Christ, whether Jew or Gentile. Acknowledging the best convictions that God's common grace has preserved in the consciousness and the communities of the unregenerate, he insightfully shows that their human "best" falls infinitely short of the divine norm that they acknowledge and in some sense want to achieve. He therefore shows that there is, in fact, no way of escape, even for those bound to God through the patriarchs and the covenants, except through Jesus.

Paul's stark but nuanced assessment of the impotence of fallen human nature apart from Christ's Spirit (and the law's impotence to rescue those who are "in the flesh") finds resonance with other ancient sources, which also evidence the awareness that human behavior too often contradicts the better judgment of human conscience. The rabbis of Paul's day spoke of the internal warfare between the "evil inclination" (*hayetzer hara'*) and the good inclination within human beings. Whatever they were referring to by the "good inclination," they considered that its goodness was defined in terms of its concurrence with the law of God.[68] Their discussions illustrate a recognition that the covenant people's conscious assent to the Torah's righteous standards faced strong opposition from a malevolent force within, the two inclinations locked in a struggle that too often failed to issue in victory over temptation.

---

67. Ridderbos, *Paul*, 128.

68. For bibliographical sources on the rabbinic discussion of the conflict between the "evil impulse" and the "good impulse" in human nature, see Garlington, "Romans 7:14–25 and Creation Theology," 221n105.

Even pagan writers, by God's common grace, noted the frustration and conflict of conscience that arise from failing to do what one recognizes to be good and right. Several centuries before Paul, the Greek playwright Euripides (ca. 480—406 B.C.) placed the following observation in the mouth of the mythical Phaedra, wife of Theseus and lover of his son Hippolytus: "Oft sleepless in the weary-wearing night have I mused how the life of men is wrecked. 'Tis not, meseems, through inborn folly of soul they fare so ill—discretion dwells at least with many,—but we thus must look hereon: *that which is good we learn and recognize, yet practice not* [*ta chrēst' epistametha kai gignōskomen, ouk ekponoumen d'*], some from sloth, and some preferring pleasure in the stead of duty."[69] The Roman poet Ovid (ca. 43 B.C.–A.D. 17), an older contemporary of Paul, gave the Princess Medea these lines to express her inner conflict between filial duty and romantic attraction: "Ah, if I could, I should be more myself. But some strange power draws me against my will. Desire persuades me one way, reason another. *I see the better and approve it, but I follow the worse* [*video meliora proboque, deteriora sequor*]."[70] A generation after Paul's ministry, Epictetus (ca. AD 55—135), a Stoic philosopher, likewise noted the contradiction intrinsic to moral failure in words that closely parallel Romans 7:15: "Every error [or 'sin,' *hamartēma*] involves a contradiction. For since he who is in error [*ho hamartanōn*] does not wish to err [sin] but to be right, it is clear that . . . he is not doing what he wishes and what he does not wish he does [*ho thelei ou poiei kai ho mē thelei poiei*]."[71] Epictetus' full discussion shows, however, that he was far more optimistic than was Paul regarding the potential of reasoned persuasion to expose the contradiction at the root of "sin" (or "error"), disabusing the confused "sinner" of the irrationality of his actions, thereby turning behavior toward the good. Although Scripture has a less irenic view of human rationality and human nature in general, these

---

69. Euripides, *Hippolytus*, 375–83, trans. Arthur S. Way, LCL (Cambridge, MA: Harvard University Press, 1912), 192–95 (emphasis added). Cf. also Euripides, *Medea*, 1078–80, trans. Arthur S. Way, LCL (Cambridge, MA: Harvard University Press, 1912), 366–67: "Now, now, I learn what horrors I intend: but passion overmastereth sober thought, and this is cause of direst ills to men." "Sober thought" might be translated "my better purposes" (*kreissōn tōn emōn bouleumatōn*)—hence, Medea experiences the conflict of her "passion" (*thumos*) against her more rational and nobler desires, and expects passion to gain the upper hand.

70. Ovid, *Metamorphoses*, 7.18–21, trans. Frank J. Miller, LCL (Cambridge, MA: Harvard University Press, 1984), 343 (emphasis added).

71. Epictetus, *Discourses*, 2.26.4, trans. W. A. Oldfather, LCL (Cambridge, MA: Harvard University Press, 1925), 1:430–33. The full discussion is in *Discourses*, 2.26.1–7.

comments from ancient pagan writers at least illustrate that the conflict between one's actions and the ethical standard to which one's conscience bears witness is not an experience unique to regenerate persons. Although the traitor Judas's conscience may have indicted his evil act only in retrospect, his despairing regret provides further biblical confirmation of this insight (Matt. 27:3–5).

WHAT ARE PAUL'S PURPOSES IN ROMANS 7:7–25?

Paul has two purposes for inserting at this point in his discourse this extended dramatization of sin's exploitation of the law to deceive, defeat, captivate, and kill through God's good law. His first purpose is polemical. As signaled in the questions of 7:7 and 7:12, he continues to engage the rhetorical diatribe form to answer misrepresentations of his gospel that the Roman believers may well have encountered, as he has, from Jewish objectors. While penning this epistle from Achaia, before traveling to Jerusalem with the relief offering of the Gentile churches (15:25–28), Paul was no doubt already well aware of the slander that had reached the ears of the church's leaders in Judea: "Jews . . . who have believed . . . are all zealous for the law, and they have been told about you that you teach all the Jews who are among the Gentiles to forsake Moses, telling them not to circumcise their children or walk according to our customs" (Acts 21:20–21). Against such libelous reports, which may well have reached Rome as well, Paul asserts in the strongest terms, "So the law is holy, and the commandment is holy and righteous and good" (Rom. 7:12). It is not the initiating cause of sin or of death (7:7, 13). It is spiritual (7:14). Its flawless observance, if such were possible to fallen humans, would lead to life (7:10). Paul the Christian apostle loves God's law, and his gospel causes the law to stand in its proper, divinely purposed place of honor (3:31)!

Paul also has a second, pastoral purpose, however, and this purpose requires him to display the law's limitations in the starkest possible terms. He states the main point of 7:7–25, as we have seen, most succinctly in 8:3: the law was weak because of the flesh. Although it is to be praised and delighted in as the revelation of God's holy character and righteous norm for his covenant servants, the law in itself lacks the power to liberate those "under law" and "in the flesh" from "another law" that wages war against the divine norm that conscience approves, the law of sin that assaults, overcomes, enslaves, and kills. An observant Jew's shock at seeing violations of the law in his "members," despite the joyful agreement of his conscious mind with the holiness and righteousness of the commandments, points to a fundamental flaw, a weakness of fallen humanity that reaches too deep for any human solution. Israel's glad agreement at Sinai to obey all the Lord's commands (Ex. 24:7), soon followed by their spiritual harlotry with the golden calf (Ex. 32), magnifies from the individual level to that of the ancient covenant community the evidence of the law's impotence to enable compliance to its demands.

If, insofar as I know my mind, I agree with God's law while my members go their own way, I am indeed out of control, in a desperate plight unless there is Someone to rescue me. The question to which Paul is responding is not, "If you have entered the new creation, why are you not perfect according to the law of God?"[72] Paul tells us plainly the question that he is answering, and it is: "Did the good law of God (which was given for life) become death to me?" Can we maintain that the law is still good, even if it is so intimately bound up in the complex of sin and death?

It is a pastoral purpose that leads Paul to portray at such length and in such vivid terms the utter helplessness of Israel "under the law" and apart from the Spirit. He knows, on the basis of his experience with the Galatian Gentile believers and others, how plausible a Judaizing "gospel" (which is not "good news" at all) can sound to those who long to put their pagan past far behind them. He is well aware that those accustomed to serving "the weak and worthless elementary principles (*stoicheia*) of the world" (Gal. 4:8–9) in the form of pagan idolatry can easily be lured back into a different variety of that same slavery to the world's elements (*stoicheia*) by misunderstanding and so misusing God's law (4:3), failing to grasp that the sending of God's Son and God's Spirit in the fullness of time has brought a new era of liberty and sonship (4:4–6) to all who believe.

Writing earlier to the Corinthian church, Paul presented the same contrast between the law's letter and the Spirit's power, calling the former a ministry of death and the latter the ministry of life (2 Cor. 3:6–18). Why does the letter kill, but the Spirit make alive? Is it not because the letter (the Mosaic covenant as a law administration) is a ministry of condemnation (v. 9), able only to pronounce covenant curse on those who have violated

---

72. Contra Garlington, "Romans 7:14–25 and Creation Theology," 210.

its stipulations but lacking the life-giving power to evoke the obedience that would warrant its blessings? The ministry of the Spirit (v. 8), inasmuch as it is contrasted with the ministry of death (v. 7), is the ministry that imparts life (v. 6) and righteousness (v. 9). Writing later to Philippi from a prison cell, Paul again warns believers against those who would tempt them to put confidence in the flesh by pursuing "perfection" through circumcision and the other credentials (including "blameless" righteousness in the law) that Paul has now gladly jettisoned for the infinitely better prize of being found in Christ, "not having a righteousness of my own that comes from the law, but that which comes through faith in Christ, the righteousness from God that depends on faith" (Phil. 3:2–9).

Paul the pastor was vividly conscious of how easy it is for impressionable Christians (perhaps especially those from pagan backgrounds) who began well, relying on the crucified Christ in the power of the Spirit, to be "bewitched" and led astray, returning to reliance on their own performance to reassure their uneasy consciences of their standing before God and their place in his new covenant community (Gal. 3:1–5). It is precisely because Christians now live in the overlap of the present age and the age to come (Augustinian argument 6) that we are tempted by so-called "gospels" that invest God's law with life-giving, behavior-transforming power (Gal. 3:21), turning struggling hearts back on themselves rather than fixing our gaze on Christ, who has become "life-giving Spirit" (1 Cor. 15:45) and whose radiance alone transforms those who behold him by faith into his glorious image (2 Cor. 3:18). Therefore Paul will not let the Roman believers forget that their only hope, not only with reference to God's vindicating verdict but also with respect to the lifelong process of growth in godly affections and behavior, lay in what God alone could do and has done in Christ, condemning sin in the flesh, severing their "marital" obligation to the law through union with Jesus in his death (thereby also liberating them from sin's otherwise-unbreakable tyranny), and setting them free so that the law's righteous requirement is fulfilled in them as they walk "not according to the flesh but according to the Spirit" (Rom. 8:4). To whatever degree his Roman readers may have experienced subjectively sin's paralyzing and death-dealing power operating through God's good law in their individual journeys to Jesus, they all need to hear the desperate lament of Israel under the law—and of Saul of Tarsus, Hebrew of Hebrews and Pharisee of Pharisees—throughout the old covenant era, crying out for the rescue that could be accomplished only by the death and resurrection of Jesus the Messiah and applied by his life-creating Spirit.

ASKING (AND ANSWERING) OUR QUESTIONS AT LAST

Who then is the "speaker" in Romans 7:7–25? I have been arguing that the "speaker" whose experience is described in Romans 7 is the person who is confronted with God's command but not renewed by God's Spirit. Since the "sin" that lurks within, waiting to seize the divine command as an opportunity to express its rebellion, is ultimately our inheritance from our father Adam, Paul's first description of "my" experience of death inflicted by sin through the commandment contains echoes of the account of the fall in Genesis 3 (Rom. 7:7–13). But of course for a biblical theologian of Paul's stature, the history of Israel as a people would be the classic example of the way in which sin used God's commandments to produce death.[73] Therefore the "I" of Romans 7:13–25 is the personified nation of Israel under the old covenant. It is also true that Israel's corporate experience in covenant with God would be reflected in the experience of the conscientious individual Jew who seriously sought to keep the Torah, whether or not Saul of Tarsus personally experienced such inner distress prior to being confronted by the risen Lord Jesus on the Damascus road.[74]

CONCLUSION: EMPLOYING THE THEOLOGY OF ROMANS 7 IN SERVICE OF THE CHURCH

Exegetes and theologians over the centuries who have concluded, following Augustine, that in Romans 7:14–25 Paul is describing an aspect of normal Christian life, have supported their view with weighty exegetical and theological argumentation. I share their basic conviction that Christians

73. Moo, *Romans*, 417: " . . . Paul views the Jewish experience with the Mosaic law as paradigmatic for the experience of all people with 'law.' Israel stands in redemptive history as a kind of 'test case,' and its relationship with *the* law is *ipso facto* applicable to the relationship of all people with that 'law' which God has revealed to them (cf. 2:14–15)."

74. Robert Jewett, *Romans,* Hermeneia (Philadelphia: Fortress, 2007), 461–62, argues that Romans 7 focuses on that confrontation on the Damascus road, when Saul discovered to his shock that his zealous pursuit of righteousness through Torah observance had set him on a collision course with the God who gave the Torah, who had sent his Messiah to suffer under the curse as one hanged on a tree.

should expect a continuing battle against sin until we enter fully into the age to come at Christ's visible, physical return and our physical resurrection. The element of frustration that apparently makes Romans 7:14–25 "ring true" to our experience as believers (Augustinian argument 9) is indeed taught as an aspect of Christian experience in Galatians 5:17 (Augustinian argument 5). The teaching of perfectionism is not only theologically and exegetically erroneous; it is also pastorally harmful, planting doubt and even despair into the hearts of believers who are valiantly waging spiritual warfare as part of the church militant. We do live in the overlap of the ages, when God's eschatological redemption has entered Christian experience by the Spirit "already," and yet the climax of our salvation in resurrection glory is "not yet" (Augustinian argument 6).

But if the exegesis offered in this essay is correct, *even more positive* pastoral implications follow from recognizing that Romans 7:7–25 portrays the inability of the law to empower obedience to its commands apart from the life-giving power of the Spirit of Christ. Christians can be safeguarded from *misapplying* this passage to themselves, portraying themselves to themselves as though they were victims who are powerless to resist sin's control of their members, in contradiction to the force of Paul's argument throughout Romans 6–8. Admittedly, the most responsible proponents of the Augustinian interpretation "water down" Romans 7's terminology of slavery and captivity, so that believers who have been taught to view their present Christian experience in the "mirror" of the frustrated "I" of Romans 7:14–25 will not necessarily fall into the error of perceiving themselves as sin's helpless victims. Yet the pastoral danger remains that some Christians will believe themselves to be diagnosed so accurately in the ethical paralysis portrayed in this text that they will "trust" this diagnosis (false, in my judgment, for those truly united to Christ by faith) *more firmly* than they trust what the apostle so plainly declares about all who are "in Christ": "But thanks be to God, that you who *were once* slaves of sin *have become obedient from the heart* to the standard of teaching to which you were committed, and, *having been set free from sin*, have become slaves of righteousness" (6:17–18).

Even beyond the avoidance of this potential negative outcome of the traditional Augustinian-Reformational view, when we understand rightly the role of this passage in Paul's exposition of his gospel, we can appreciate and communicate even more fully the true glory of God's grace in Christ. Here Paul has shown us the best of all possible situations within the sphere of "the flesh," unaided human nature. Here we see, not the idolatrous and sensual Gentile sinner, bent on pleasing himself and hating God, but rather the situation of the Jew who knows the law, confesses its goodness, and even experiences distress that his behavior falls so far short of the righteousness required in the law. Even for such a person the law as commandment, the law that casts him back on his own willpower, proves to be a blind alley. There is only One who can deliver from the death portrayed in Romans 7:13–25, the death of captivity to sin: "There is therefore now no condemnation for those who are in Christ Jesus. For the law of the Spirit of life has set you free in Christ Jesus from the law of sin and death" (8:1–2). "Likewise, my brothers, you also have died to the law through the body of Christ, so that you may belong to another, to him who has been raised from the dead, in order that we may bear fruit for God" (7:4). Romans 7 presents theology that is both systematic and practical "in service of the church": not a whisper of introspective self-confidence or naïve, over-realized eschatology that ignores our continuing warfare of faith, but rather an "extrospective" assurance that Christ's sovereign Spirit is indeed applying to us, silently but surely, the comprehensive rescue that Jesus achieved once-for-all in his sacrificial death and glorious resurrection.

2

Psalm 110: An Exegetical and Canonical Approach

BRUCE K. WALTKE

LET ME TAKE this opportunity to thank the editors for honoring me with an opportunity to contribute to Professor Richard Gaffin's festschrift. Professor Gaffin is a solid rock of orthodoxy; his writings reflect the best of Reformed theology. Nevertheless, he reflects on that rich heritage with originality and fresh expression. Although he has been a professor of New Testament and of systematic theology, he is also a biblical theologian.

Psalm 110 is a crucial text for all his interests: New Testament studies (it is quoted in the New Testament more than any other Old Testament text); systematic theology (for its importance to Christology and eschatology); biblical theology (an excellent test case of the use of the New Testament in light of contemporary exegesis of Old Testament texts); and the book of Hebrews (one of the three psalms on which Hebrews is built). Therefore, it seems fitting to present in honor of Professor Gaffin a careful exegesis of that psalm in the light of recent research on the book of Psalms and reflection on its contribution to

Christology. The essay has five parts: Translation, Introduction, Exegesis, Identification of "My Lord" (i.e., reflections on the psalm's Christology), and Conclusion.

TRANSLATION[1]

> By David. A psalm.
>
> An oracle of I AM[2] to my[3] lord:
>
> "Sit at[4] my right hand
>
>> until I make your enemies a footstool for your feet."
>
> I AM will extend[5] your mighty scepter[6] from Zion.
>
>> "Rule in the midst of your enemies."
>
> Your troops[7] offer themselves freely[8] on the day of your strength.[9]
>
>> Arrayed in holy splendor,[10] from the womb of[11] the dawn,
>
>> the dew of your youth comes[12] to you.[13]

1. Author's own translation. Throughout the essay, the NIV is used unless otherwise noted. In quotations from the NIV and other translations, the tetragrammaton is displayed as "I AM."

2. Genitive of authorship. See *IBHS*.

3. Genitive of relationship (*IBHS*, 145, P. 9.5.1i).

4. The preposition *lamedh* marks location (*IBHS*, 205, P. 11.2.10b).

5. Construed as a specific future, not as a jussive ("may he send") in spite of the parallel imperative "rule," because the rest of the psalm predicts victory.

6. Construing genitive as attributive, but it could be possessive: "scepter of your strength" (*IBHS*, 149, P. 9.5.3a; 145, P. 9.5.1g).

7. Collective singular (*IBHS*, 113, P. 7.1c).

8. Lit. "are volunteerism," an abstract plural signifying state, condition (*IBHS*, 121, P. 7.4.2a).

9. Instead of "Your people are willingness," the LXX reads *meta sou hē archē*, which retroverted is *'immka nediboth*. MT makes a better parallelism between the first and last words of the verse: "your troops" and "your youths," than "with you . . . your youths."

10. Several medieval Hebrew manuscripts, a Cairo Geniza fragment, Symmachus, and Jerome read *hare* as "mountains of." *Dalet* and *resh* are commonly confounded. With "holy," however, one expects a singular "mountain" (i.e., Zion) as in Psalm 2. Also, this alternative is attractive only with the alternative reading *yelidtika* ("I brought you forth from the womb before the morning").

11. The Greek translations (LXX, Origen, Theodotian) and Syriac read *mishshakhar* ("from the womb, from the dawn"). The Massoretes probably thought that *mishkhar* was a bi-form of *shakhar*. More probably neither understood enclitic *mem*. The text should be normalized as *rkhm mshkhr* (see *IBHS* , 158–60, P. 9.8).

12. See n7.

13. So MT. Others change MT's accents so that "in holy splendor" modifies the preceding clause and refer "from the womb of the dawn you have the dew of your youth" to the king's youth. The emendation questionably separates the foci of v. 3 from Messiah's troops (3A) to his person (v. 3B).

I AM swears[14] and will not change his mind:[15]

"You are a priest forever,

like[16] Melchizedek."

The Lord is at your right hand;

he will crush kings on the day of his anger.

He[17] will judge[18] the nations, he will fill[19] the valley with corpses,[20]

and smash the heads that are[21] over the whole earth.

From the wadi beside the way he will drink;

therefore he lifts up his[22] head.

INTRODUCTION

"This brief but weighty Psalm—*brevis numero verborum, magnus pondere sententiarum,* as it is called by Augustine"[23]—is so because its seven verses lay an Old Testament foundation for Jesus Christ's claim that he is more than the son of David, for the apostolic testimony of his ascension into

14. Construed as an instantaneous or performative perfective (*IBHS*, 488, P. 30.5.1d). I have avoided "has sworn" lest it be construed as a reference to the Davidic covenant, which makes no mention in the biblical texts (2 Sam. 7; 1 Chron. 17; Ps. 89) that Solomon is a priest (*pace, TNIV Study Bible* [Grand Rapids: Zondervan, 2006], 973). I will return to this interpretive *crux* below.

15. Some English versions gloss *nkhm* Ni. by "repent" (KJV, JPS) or an equivalent such as "is not sorry" (C. A. Briggs and Emilie Grace Briggs, *The Book of Psalms*, ICC [Edinburgh: T. & T. Clark, 1907], 2:378). These glosses mislead because they connote "to turn from sin," "to amend one's life," "to feel contrition." Better glosses are "relent," "retract," "waver," or "break one's vow."

16. The final *yod* of the construct *dibrathi*, an unexplained connecting suffix (*IBHS*, 127f., P. 8.2.e), may have been chosen for its assonance with the same suffix in its absolute counterpart, *malkitsedeq*, also composed of the construct *malki* and its absolute *tsedeq*.

17. I.e., the Messiah.

18. Construing the non-perfective as a specific future (*IBHS*, 512, P. 31.6.2b).

19. Construing the suffix conjugation as an accidental (traditionally prophetic perfective) (*IBHS*, 490, P. 30.5.1e).

20. On the basis of *pharanges* in Aquila and Symmachus and of *valles* in Jerome, Bardtke rightly emends MT's *male' gewiyoth* to read [with slight modification on my part] *mille'* (Piel) *ge'ayoth gewiyoth*. The consonance (i.e., similar consonants) and assonance (i.e., similar sound) of *ge'ayoth* and *gewiyoth* are fertile soil for haplography (*IBHS*, 23, P. 1.6.2c). If the skipped word was *ga'* (valley [singular]), it would be a simple case of homoiarchton. Furthermore, textual corruption in MT may prompt the accompanying oral tradition to adjust to the new reading (*IBHS*, 25, P. 1.6.3e). The emended text construes *ge'ayoth gewiyoth* as a double accusative (*IBHS*, 176, P. 10.2.3e).

21. Added to show that prepositional phrase modifies "heads," not "smash."

22. Added *ad sensum*. The absolute form serves best as a catchword with v. 6.

23. A. F. Kirkpatrick, *The Book of Psalms*, The Cambridge Bible for Schools and College (Cambridge: Cambridge University Press, 1916), 660.

heaven, and for the teaching of the book of Hebrews about Christ's royal priesthood in heaven. The New Testament cites this psalm more frequently than any other single passage of Scripture.[24] In addition to its profound Christology, the psalm speaks of I AM's awful power on the day of his anger (v. 5) in connection with Jesus Christ on the day of his strength (v. 3) and their consummate victory over evil. The psalm, like Psalm 2, probably was sung as part of Israel's royal enthronement ritual, and, as a God-inspired oracle, functions as an investiture of priesthood on the Messiah. The New Testament gives primacy to this predictive dimension of the psalm, and does seem to be aware of an inferred historical use in Israel's coronation ritual.

Modern scholarship, however, does not give primacy—if any importance—to its predictions as understood in the New Testament. Rather, these scholars give primacy to its inferential historical use as part of the coronation ritual for David's non-supernatural sons or for a post-exilic royal priest. For most scholars—at best—the New Testament re-interprets the original intention of the psalm. According to them, an exclusively human son of David during Israel's pre-exilic monarchy is the lord and priest-king celebrated in the psalm, and it uses courtly hyperbole, not necessarily substantial prophecy. Most deny Davidic authorship, and some deny the psalm's unity.

According to the commentary that follows, the psalm (or better, oracle) was used in Israel's enthronement festival, but its primary focus is on the psalm's predictive element about the Messiah, or better, as Jesus preferred to refer to himself, the Son of Man. To establish this is its original intention according to the accredited grammatico-historical method of interpretation, we begin with its form as a unified royal prophecy from the time of the monarchy. We then argue that Jesus Christ uniquely fulfills the predications about the "lord," the subject of the psalm. Modern scholarship, we argue, reinterprets the psalm from its plain sense in order to fulfill the dogma of historical criticism, *vaticinium ex eventu* ("proclamation from the event").

Form

The similarity between Psalm 110 and Assyrian royal prophecies identifies beyond reasonable doubt that the psalm is a royal prophecy. This

---

24. Matt. 22:41–45; Mark 12:35–37; Luke 20:41–44; Acts 2:34–35; 1 Cor. 15:25; Heb. 1:13; 5:6; 7:17, 21; 10:13.

also supports the notion that Psalms 2 and 110 are sung as part of Israel's royal coronation ritual. John Hilber in his 2005 Cambridge doctoral dissertation documents the correspondences between the two:

1. An introduction formula in both: 110:1
2. Subdivision of oracle with a second introduction formula: 110:4
3. Change in person, both of the addressee and the divine speaker: 110:4–5, 6–7
4. Legitimization of relationship between deity and king ("at the right hand"): 110:1
5. Enemies at the king's feet: 110:1
6. Promise of the destruction of enemies: 110:2, 5–6
7. Promise of universal dominion: 110:1, 6
8. Presence of loyal support: 110:3
9. Divine promise accompanied by denial of lying: 110:4
10. Affirmation of priestly responsibility: 110:4
11. Eternality of royal prerogatives: 110:4[25]

Implicitly, the author is a prophet. Wieppert, from his broad study of ancient Near Eastern literature, defines a prophet(ess) as one who has a cognitive experience by vision, audition, or dream that shares in a revelation from deity, and who has an awareness of a commission from the deity to transmit the revelation.[26] The introduction to Psalm 110 shows the author speaks, as Jesus says, "in the Spirit" (Matt. 22:43 ESV): "An oracle [inspired utterance] of I AM" (see commentary). The Assyrian parallels show that the entire psalm is conceived of as an oracle—that is to say, no distinction as to the poem's inspiration is made between divine citations (vv. 1B, 4B) and the prophet's reflections (vv. 2–3, 5–7). The prophet mediates both. Switching of pronouns from first person to third person to view a subject from the divine and human perspectives, respectively, is common to the Old Testament and Assyrian prophetic literature (cf. Isa. 3:1–4; Hos. 5:1–7;

25. J. W. Hilber, *Cultic Prophecy in the Psalms*, ZAW (Berlin: Walter de Gruyter, 2005), 76–88, esp. 76–80. His work has been of considerable help to me in writing a commentary on this psalm.

26. M. Weippert, "Aspekte israeliticher Prophetie im Lichte verwandter Ersheinungen des Alten Orients," *Ad bene et fideliter seminandum: Festgabe für Karlheinz Deller zum 21. February 1987*, ed. Gerline Mauer und Ursula Magen, AOAT 220 (Neukirchen-Vluyn: Kevelaer, 1988), 287–319, esp. 289f.

Amos 3:1–7; Mic. 1:3–7). Hilber comments: "The Assyrian oracles . . . display a rapid shift between persons within the same relatively short oracle."[27]

The prophet *probably* participates in Israel's cultus. Scholars have debated Sigmund Mowinckel's thesis in 1922 that certain psalms come from permanent cultic servants with recognized prophetic gifts.[28] He argues: 1) these psalms look in form and style like known prophetic literature (e.g., Psalm 81, 86); 2) the prophets Moses, Deborah, Joel, and Habakkuk combine oracles and hymns into a unified corpus; and 3) priest and prophet mediate the deity's mind (Jer. 23:33–40). Furthermore, we first encounter a band of prophets coming from a high place (1 Sam. 10:5); prophets locate at cultic centers (Num. 11:24–30; 1 Sam. 3:21; 19:19–20; 2 Kings 2:3; 2 Kings 4:22–23; Jer. 26:7); and prophets serve at the temple under the oversight of priests (Jer. 29:26), and some live there (Jer. 35:4; cf. Jer. 23:11). Finally, prophetic ecstasy is linked with music (2 Kings 3:15; Ps. 49:4 [5]; 2 Chron. 20).[29]

The Assyrian prophetic texts suggest the prophet(ess) is closely linked with the deity's cult; some prophecies are delivered at the temple. One Assyrian text represents a prophetess as a votaress of the temple, and other Assyrian data suggest that prophets were supported by the temple. Hilber concludes: "On the whole it seems reasonable to conclude that the temple was significant for prophetic activity and that the primary identification of prophets was with the cultic community."[30]

The combined evidence suggests that Psalm 110 was delivered at the temple by a prophet, possibly a temple functionary, as a part of Israel's cultus, and pertains to the newly minted king. The king extends his scepter from Zion. The divine command, "Sit at my right hand," can be fitted into an enthronement ritual. One collection of Assyrian prophetic texts is linked to enthronement. Antti Laato (1996) associates the Assyrian corpus with Psalm 110 as follows: 1) legitimating of kingship; 2) destruction of enemies; 3) presence of loyal supporters; and 4) priesthood of the king.

---

27. Hilber, *Cultic Prophecy*, 81.

28. For a helpful survey of the debate, see Hilber, *Cultic Prophecy*, 1–39.

29. These data show a close connection between the sanctuary and prophets but do not prove that professional prophets are members of Israel's cultus. Priests and others within the cultus, besides professional prophets, can have prophetic experiences. During the second temple epoch Josephus reports two incidents of divine revelation to the high priest, John Hyrcanus, and there are reports of special revelation to the high priests Jaddua (Neh. 12:11) and Onias III (early second century B.C.). Zechariah, father of John the Baptist, received a revelation while serving as a priest at the altar of incense within the temple (Luke 1:5–25).

30. Hilber, *Cultic Prophecy*, 61.

Hilber draws the conclusion: "It is likely that Psalm 110 was a prophetic oracle originating and subsequently used in conjunction with cultic celebration of the king's enthronement."[31]

Structure, Rhetoric, Message

Psalm 110 has two parts (vv. 1–3, 4–7), and like Assyrian royal prophecies, a second introduction formula introduces the second part (v. 4). In one Assyrian single oracle a scribe bracketed the two parts by scribal divisions and colophons.[32] The psalm's two parts have similar structures: 1) introduction naming I AM as the speaker and addressee (1A; 4A); 2) a divine citation (1B; 4B); and 3) the prophet's reflections (2–3; 5–7). The first introduction formula also introduces the whole psalm as an oracle. Note the couplets: verses 1–2, 4–5 pertain to I AM and king; verses 6–7 are addressed to the congregation about "heads" (v. 6) and "his head" (v. 7). Isolated verse 3 pertains uniquely to the army. Nevertheless, verses 3 and 4 are uniquely tristichs of 1:2 and 2:1 stichs. In other words, v. 3 to some extent is also a janus.

The form profiles the similarity and dissimilarity of the two parts. The first part designates "my lord" as king; the second, as priest. In the first, the lord is at I AM's right hand; in the second, the Lord is at the lord's right hand. The psalm moves from the priest-king's exaltation in the register of heaven to his exaltation in the register of earth. Other wordplays closely link I AM and his priest-king: "my lord" [i.e., the priest-king] (*'dhoni*, v. 1) and Lord [i.e., I AM] (*'adhonay*, v. 5);[33] the day of the king's power (v. 3) and the day of I AM's anger (v. 5). Both parts prophesy that I AM and his king establish from Zion a universal and eternal kingdom by vanquishing their enemies. This is the message of the psalm.

Here is a sketch of the Psalm's structure:

I. Superscription: author (David), genre (psalm) (v. 1Aa)

II. Introduction: genre (prophecy), author (I AM), addressee (lord) (v. 1Ab)

III. First Part: Lord as King (vv. 1B–3)

---

31. Ibid., 85.
32. Ibid., 78.
33. Other wordplays, noted in the commentary, connect the stanzas and their strophes.

A. Divine citation: "Sit at my right hand" (v. 1B)

B. Prophetic reflection: address to Lord (vv. 2–3)

    1. I AM initiates holy war (v. 2)

    2. Lord's troops willing to fight (v. 3)

IV. Second Part: Lord as Priest (vv. 4–7)

  A. Divine Citation (v. 4)

    1. Introduction: genre (an irrevocable oath) (v. 4A)

    2. Citation: an eternal priest like Melchizedek (v. 4B)

  B. Prophetic reflections (vv. 5–7)

    1. Address to Lord: he will smash kings (v. 5)

    2. Address to congregation

      a. Lord judges whole earth (v. 6)

      b. Lord consummates victory (v. 7)

The two parts consist of seven verses: 3 + 4, the number of perfection. Moreover, there are ten lines of poetry, 5 + 5 (see translation), the number of fullness.[34] Both numbers figure prominently in the Davidic covenant, which this oracle supplements.[35] D. N. Freedman strikingly observed that each stanza contains 74 syllables.[36] In sum, thematically and structurally the psalm has two equal parts. The prophet may have been in ecstasy, but he is in full control of his thoughts and emotions.

EXEGESIS

Superscript (v. 1Aa)

By David a psalm (*ledhawidh mizmor*, see Ps. 3:1). Authorship is important for Jesus' argument that he is more than a son of David (see conclusion).[37] Academics who deny that *ledhawidh* refers to David as the historical author reach no consensus about the date of Psalm 110. Dahood locates the psalm in the tenth century because of its similarity to Psalm 2, but Gerstenberger locates it in the post-exilic period because of its messianic

---

34. Verse 1 is a tetrastich; vv. 2, 5, 6, 7 are bistichs, and vv. 3, 4 tristichs.

35. So *BSH* and NIV/TNIV. See B. Waltke with C. Yu, *An Old Testament Theology* (Grand Rapids: Zondervan, 2007), 661.

36. M. Dahood, *Psalms III 101–150*, AB 17A (Garden City, NY: Doubleday, 1970), 113.

37. His argument, however, does not prove authorship; it assumes, not teaches, the Jewish tradition.

expectation.[38] Assyrian prophetic oracles (seventh century B.C.) support an oracle from the monarchy, not a post-exilic date. The expectation of a universal dominion finds a parallel as early as the Egyptian Execration Texts (20th–18th centuries B.C.). If the psalm is pre-exilic, as most scholars think, there is no reason to deny David's authorship. He is the only king in Israel's memory through whom divine communication occurs (2 Sam. 23:1–2). *Ne'um* ("inspired utterance") uniquely occurs in another hymn by David (2 Sam. 23:1). *Mizmor* indicates that plucking of stringed instrument(s) accompanied the prophecy, a natural connection.

Introduction (v. 1Ab)

"The oracle of I AM" (*ne'um yhwh*) is preferable to the traditional rendering, "The LORD says." That tradition masks that *ne'um* in its other 375 occurrences is used exclusively of divine speech.[39] God's name I AM (*yhwh*) is his covenant name with Israel. This name is expressed by the author of the Mosaic covenant, whose key catechetical teachings demand love for the God of justice and salvation and for one's neighbor as oneself. The Davidic covenant also commissions the house of David to spread that catechetical teaching universally according to Psalm 2. Those covenants are fully realized in Jesus Christ.

David addresses his oracle to *my lord* (*'dhoni*, not *'adhonay*, I AM), his master, to whom he is a slave.[40] *'Adhon* occurs almost exclusively with a genitive of relationship (see n3) to signify the authority of one over another. The epithet, however, veils the identification of "my lord." We will return to his identification in the conclusion. Suffice it to assume here that he is the Messiah, or better, the Son of Man, and that the absence of the appellative "king" or its equivalents, such as "anointed," does not prove the psalm is

---

38. Dahood, *Psalms III*, 112. E. S. Gerstenberger, *Psalms Part 2 and Lamentations*, FOTL 15 (Grand Rapids: Eerdmans, 2001), 266f. Dahood interprets the psalm by the use of words in Northwest Semitic, not by biblical usage, and no scholars follow his lead.

39. Bruce K. Waltke, *The Book of Proverbs: Chapters 15–31* (Grand Rapids: Eerdmans, 2005), 454n6. Gerstenberger thinks Prov. 30:1, 2 Sam. 23:1, and Ps. 36:2 are exceptions; they are not. In Prov. 30:1 *ne'um* parallels *massa'* ("prophetic burden") and is used with *haggever* ("the powerful man says") as in Num. 24:3 (of Balaam's oracle). Second Sam. 23:2 names I AM as speaking through David. TNIV glosses the term in Psalm 36:2: "I have a message from God in my heart." For a detailed discussion, see R. Rendtorff, "Zum Gebrauch der Formel n'um Jawe im jeremiah-buch," *ZAW* 66 (1954), 27ff.

40. Only once does *'adhon* appear in the sense of authority over impersonal spheres (1 Kings 16:24).

post-exilic. Hilber notes one Assyrian royal prophecy from the seventh century B.C. that also does not use the word "king" or its equivalents.[41]

Part 1: Lord as King (vv. 1B–3)

After the introduction, the first part consists of a divine citation and a prophet's reflection.

Divine Citation to Lord: "Sit at my right hand"

The divine invitation *sit* (*shev*, "enthrone" in Ps. 2:4) *at my right hand* (*limini*, note the alliteration and assonance with *'adhoni*), gives David's lord the highest place of honor (cf. 1 Kings 2:19), assures him of divine protection (see Ps. 16:8; cf. 74:11). To sit symbolizes the king's authority in contrast with his attendants who stand to wait on him. To sit at the right hand signifies serving I AM as his viceroy.[42] Some argue the language is metaphorical to represent the king's favored position and his inviolable protection (Ps. 16:8; 74:11). This is possible because its counterpart, "I AM is at your right hand," is metaphor. Others guess that there is an allusion to a special ceremonial place in the temple (cf. 2 Kings 11:14; 23:3).[43] More probably God's right hand refers to the throne hall, the Hall of Judgment, where the king sits to judge (1 Kings. 7:7).[44] The temple housing I AM's earthly throne, the ark (1 Sam. 4:4; Isa. 66:1; cf. Matt. 5:34), faces eastward in the great courtyard.[45] The Hall of Judgment housing the king's throne seems to be on the south side, to the right of God's throne, facing northward in the great courtyard. Recall that the Egyptian coronation ceremony had two parts: first the king was crowned in the temple, and thus crowned "he was conducted to his palace where he ascended his throne where in a more or less threatening way he announced *urbi et orbi* the start of his rule" (see Ps. 2).[46] David, limited by his sociological knowledge, envisions the ascent of his lord to the throne

---

41. Hilber, *Cultic Prophecy*, 86n26.

42. J. J. Stewart Perowne, *The Book of Psalms* (1878; repr. Grand Rapids: Zondervan, 1976), 304.

43. A. Weiser, *The Psalms*, Old Testament Library (Philadelphia: The Westminster Press, 1962), 694.

44. Surprisingly, to my knowledge, no one has proposed this *Sitz im Leben*.

45. D. Ussishkin, "King Solomon's Palaces," *Biblical Archaeologist* 36 (1973): 78–105.

46. G. Van Rad, *Old Testament Theology*, 2 vols., trans. D. M. Stalker (New York: Harper & Row, 1965), 1:319. See now Lanny Bell, "Luxor Temple and the Cult of the Royal Ka," *JNES* 44 (1985): 251–94.

in the Hall of Judgment as the site of the coming universal kingdom.[47] Its fulfillment in the ascension of Christ shows the temple-palace complex is a type of the heavenly reality that broke into history (see Ex. 25:40; Heb. 8:5; 9:24).[48] What is certain is that "sit at my right hand" is fulfilled in the resurrected-bodily ascension of the Lord Jesus Christ into heaven where today the Son of Man sits at God's right hand and is given a kingdom (Dan. 7:13f.; Acts 2:34–36).

The lord's final triumph is depicted by until I make ('ashith, Ps. 3:7) your enemies ('oyeveyka, Pss. 3:8; 8:2 [3]) the footstool of your feet (leragleyka, Ps. 8:7 [8]). Until ('adh) here "expresses a limit which is not absolute (terminating the preceding action), but only relative, beyond which the action or state described in the principal clause still continues."[49] The six uses of the term footstool (hadhom) always occur with "feet." The royal footstool, a part of the throne (2 Chron. 9:18), symbolizes power and authority (Isa. 66:1); a victor making his enemies his footstool depicts the victor's complete power and authority over them (cf. Josh. 10:24; 1 Kings 5:3). On the young Tutankhamen's footstool are representations of foreign captives, prostrate, with their hands behind their backs, to depict symbolically his enemies as already bound and under his feet.[50] From the victor's perspective it connotes his disdain and judgment; from the victim's perspective it connotes his shame and humiliation. The New Testament stresses the authority of Christ over all things by imaging it as under his feet (1 Cor. 15:25; Eph. 1:22).

Reflection: Prophetic Address to Lord (vv. 2–3)

"Your enemies" links the divine citation and the inspired reflection.

I AM Initiates Holy War (v. 2)

The divine command prompts the prophet to commission his king to rule the earth, using the symbol of his scepter. The command and commission fulfill Israel's covenant mandate to subdue her enemies and to bless

---

47. See suggested arrangement of the buildings of Solomon's palace in NBD, 1129.

48. Waltke with Yu, Old Testament Theology, 818f.

49. IBHS, 215, 11.2.12b, n102. GKC, 164f. An Ugaritic text also rebuts this claim: "A throne is placed and he's [Kothar] seated at the right hand of Puissant Baal" (UT, 51:108–10; ANET, 134).

50. F. Gössmann, "Scabellum pedum tuorum," Divinitas 11 (1967): 30–53; cf. Biblical Imagery of the Bible, 906. Turning from Egypt to Mesopotamia, a relief shows Sennacherib, king of Assyria, sitting on his throne held up by twelve Israeli captives (ANEP, 129, No. 371).

respectful nations: originally to Abraham (Gen. 12:3; 22:18); then to Israel through Moses (Deut. 20:10–15; 28:10–15); and climactically to David (2 Sam. 7). *Scepter (matteh)* means stick or staff, but in royal context becomes the king's badge of authority and of power to punish his enemies (Isa. 10:5). *Your strong* (*'uzzeka*, n4) connotes he will wield his coercive mace forcefully without breaking it and so symbolically losing his kingship (cf. Jer. 48:12). The scepter is usually made of gold or iron; the latter probably is in view (cf. Ps. 2:9). *I AM will stretch out* (*yishlakh yhwh*, n4) has this specialized sense of "to send" with reference to something attached to something else (1 Chron. 13:10; Isa. 18:9; Ezek. 17:6). The depiction connotes ever-widening circles of dominion *from Zion* (i.e., Jerusalem; see Ps. 1:6), conceptualized as the center of the world (2 Sam. 5:7, 9; 9:11; Ps. 4; 48; 132:13–18).[51] Elsewhere, the king's scepter establishes justice (Ps. 45:6; Heb. 1:8).

The command: *rule in the midst of your enemies* (*redheh beqerev* [Ps. 51:10 (12)], *'oyeveyka* (see v. 2)]) initiates the holy war. The imperative also connotes assurance.[52] One time *radhah* means "to tread [the wine press]" (Joel 4:13), and many other times *to rule* with the associated meaning to compel obedience by punishing disobedience and so commanding respect (cf. Lev. 25:43; 26:17; Ezek. 34:4).[53]

Lord's Troops Willing to Fight (v. 3)

As in Assyrian royal prophecy, mention is made of the king's army. To fortify the king to initiate holy war, the prophet assures him of the competence of *your troops* (*'am*, a specialized sense of "people" in this holy war context). His army *freely offers itself* (*nedhavoth*) glosses a more literal, "is volunteerism," an idiom meaning, "wholly/freely volunteers."[54] Holy war is conducted only with dedicated, fearless warriors to support their leader on the battlefield (Deut. 20:1–9; Judg. 5:5:2; 1 Sam. 25:28; 2 Chron. 13:8, 12; 20:13–21; Isa. 13:3f.), not with mercenaries and/or draftees. The stout-hearted freely volunteer themselves because they love and trust their king, and know God is with them for their cause is justice. Jesus calls this army to follow him in his church militant (cf. Matt. 10:34; Luke 9:57–62; 2 Cor.

---

51. See Waltke, *Old Testament Theology*, 554.
52. GKC, 324, P. 110c.
53. *HALOT*, 4:1190, s.v. *rdhh*.
54. "I am prayer" means "I am wholly given to prayer" (Ps. 109:4); "I am peace" means "wholly given to peace" (Ps. 120:7); and "I am delights" means "I was wholly delighting" (Prov. 8:30).

4:7–12; 2 Tim. 2:3). Paul offered himself to God as a "drink offering" (Phil. 2:17). Concerning the church's faith in the resurrection of their Lord, Chesterton wrote: "A real Christian who believes should do two things: dance, out of the sense of sheer joy; and fight, out of the sense of victory."[55]

On the day of glosses *beyom*, a collocation normally equivalent to the semi-prepositional phrase meaning "when," but when *yom* is further defined, as by "of your strength," it specifies a period of time. *Of your strength* (*kheleka*, cf. Eccl. 12:3; Ps. 33:17; Job 20:18) is a metonymy for the time of holy war. Christ's worldwide conquest to his law of liberty begins when he ascends into heaven and pours out his spirit. After Pentecost his disciples surrender their lives in service to him, even to martyrdom (Acts 7:57–59).

Verse 3Ba adds two images of these troops. First, *arrayed in holy splendor* (*behadhre* [see n9; Ps. 8:7 (6)]) *qodhesh* [see Ps. 2:6], literally, "holy splendors," is a metonymy for their regalia (cf. Ps. 45:3 [4]). "Holy" signifies that their garments mark them as set apart to God and so as a pure army (1 Sam. 21:4f.). Perhaps the army wears the garments of priests, in accordance with the conception of the nation as a kingdom of priests (Ex. 19:6). The second image, *from the womb* (*merekhem*), pictures the dawn of the final king's rule as giving birth to this dedicated army. *Of the dawn* (*shakhar*, see n9) signals dispelling the night in which people weep, and presages the beginning of hope and joy in human experience (Ps. 30:5). This army, as copious as morning dew, mysteriously appearing and glittering on every blade and leaf, refreshes a languishing earth. *Dew* or "light rain" (*tal*) evokes the heavenly origin of the troops, for in the Old Testament dew is thought of as coming from the sky and descending on the earth (cf. Gen. 27:28, 39; Deut. 33:28; Hag. 1:10; Zech. 8:12; Prov. 3:20). Because its descent is imperceptible, it may evoke the invisible working of God. Also, in Israel's agrarian economy, dew is associated with life. In sum, God mysteriously raises this holy army to refresh the earth with justice and love, after the long night of satanic tyranny (cf. Zeph. 3:5). *Of your youth* (*yaldhutheyka*, see n12), according to the Masoretic text, completes the metaphor about the army, not the king. *Come to you* (*leka*, see n9) shows "youth," the last word of the verse, is a parallel metonymy of the army, the first word of the verse. "Youth" connotes freshness, prime strength, prowess, promise and endur-

---

55. Cited by Samuel Young, *God Makes a Difference* (Holiness Data Ministry, Digital Reproduction, copyright 1993–2006).

ance (cf. Lam. 4:7). Holy war is a time when God and humans in their true strength join forces against impious and immoral despots.

Part 2: Lord as Priest (vv. 4–7)

As noted above, Assyrian royal oracles can display two parts, and the second also stands under the umbrella of the first: "An oracle of I AM" (v. 1Aa).

Divine Citation to Lord (vv. 4–5)

Introduction to Genre of Divine Citation: An Irrevocable Oath (v. 4A)

I AM's oath and his denial that he changes his mind underscore the importance and truth of what he is about to say. The investiture of priesthood on the ruler reverses the old Mosaic dispensation that radically separated the two theocratic offices, symbolized by throne and altar. I AM *swears* (*nishba' yhwh*, see Ps. 15:4) to assure his newly minted king that he is also a priest. Also, perhaps I AM uses the oath formula to supplement his original oath to David deeding him an eternal house, throne, and kingdom (2 Sam. 7; Ps. 89:3–4). God changes his prophecies when circumstances change (see Jer. 18:5–10), but never changes his oaths (Heb. 6:13–17).[56] A tautology certifies the oath's inviolability: "and will not change his mind" (*welo' yinnakhem*, see n16).

Citation: An Eternal Priest like Melchizedek (v. 4B)

I AM's proclamation about the lord's identity, *you are a priest* (*'attah kohen*), asserts that this ideal, hoped-for king will sit on a throne and serve at an altar. In these combined roles he is uniquely qualified to fight holy war: purifying his troops to fight as victors. Unlike the Egyptian and Mesopotamian religions, in the old dispensation the king could not intrude on the altar as proud Uzziah/Hezekiah learned the hard way (2 Chron. 26:16–21).

Presumably, the nature and duties of this royal priesthood can be inferred by comparing and contrasting the priesthoods of the Old Testament and of the New Testament. In the former, only the tribe of Levi,

---

56. R. L. Pratt Jr. "Historical Contingencies and Biblical Predictions," in *The Way of Wisdom: Essays in Honor of Bruce K. Waltke*, ed. J. I. Packer and Sven K. Soderlund (Grand Rapids: Zondervan, 2000), 180–203.

not the tribe of Judah, could enter the sanctuary and offer sacrifices, and only the primogeniture descendant of Aaron could serve as the temple's highest official, called *hakkohen*, "the priest" (i.e., the high/chief priest, 2 Chron. 26:18).[57] In sum, the high priest protects the sanctity of the temple and performs what properly goes on there: offering sacrifices, singing, and other worship activities (Leviticus; Num. 1:53; 3:28, 32).[58] The high priest also dispenses oracles (1 Sam. 14:36f.; 23:2; 30:7f.; cf. Judg. 18:5), and with all the Levites is involved in teaching *Torah* (Deut. 31:9f.; 2 Chron. 17:8f.; Ezek. 44:23; Hag. 2:11ff.; Mal.2:7). Closely related to the priest's teaching functions is his role in jurisprudence. In disputed cases (lawsuits) they joined other judges to arrive a ruling together (Deut. 17:8–13; 21:5). For these sacred responsibilities the priest is holy and must be free from physical and moral defects and have no association with death such as a corpse (Lev. 21:10–15). He is rewarded with the best of the land and of the animals. Dommershausen draws the conclusion:

> It would be difficult to overstress the importance of the priesthood for OT religion. The priests represent Israel's relationship with God; in a sense, they are mediators of the covenant. The high priest, bearing the names of the twelve tribes on his breastplate, represents as it were the entire nation. The priests actualize Yahweh's presence in the words of their many liturgical functions. The holiness that worship demands is symbolized in the priesthood, which makes a visible statement that Yahweh is the lord and master of the nation.[59]

If this is true of the priesthood of Levi, how much more is it true of the higher priesthood of Melchizedek, an authority figure in both the political and religious spheres, and so in a position to bless (3x, Heb. 7:4–10). Melchizedek's priesthood is founded on his righteous character—his name means "King of Righteousness," his sound theology that I AM is *El Elyon*, the Only High God, and his being God's agent of peace. In the Abraham narrative his appointment as a king-priest functions as a foil to the king of Sodom, a Satanic pretender to rule the earth. Christ's priesthood is grounded

---

57. From the time of David (1000 B.C.) to the destruction of the temple (70 A.D.), the high priests were Abiathar, succeeded by the Zadokites until 171 B.C., when Antiochus IV transferred it to Menelaus and the Hasmoneans.

58. Presumably kings offered sacrifices through the priests.

59. Werner Dommershausen, *TDOT*, 7:72, s.v. *kohen*.

in his sinless perfections, his orthodoxy, and his bringing true peace, and in God's appointment in contrast to Satan's usurpers of his rightful rule. Both type and antitype bring bread and wine to the faithful. The priesthood of Melchizedek is superior to that of Aaron for, unlike Aaron, his is eternal: "You are a priest *forever* (*'olam*, see Ps. 15:5) *like* (*'al divrathi*) *Melchizedek.*" As for *'al divrathi, divrah*, in its one absolute usage it means "cause" (Job 5:8) and in its five other uses as a collocation with *'al* means "for the cause/reason that" (Job 5:8; Eccl. 3:18; 7:14; 8:2; Dan. 2:30; 4:17).[60] In that light the lord, whom David envisions, wears a crown as a cache of his kingship and priesthood on account of Melchizedek, albeit *'al divrathi* is normally glossed in most English versions—probably following *taxin* of LXX—by "in the order of," "in the succession of" (NEB), "in the line of" (NLT). But that use is otherwise unattested and unnecessary, and so improbable. More probably, David intends, as the writer of Hebrew perceives, that because Melchizedek, priest of I AM, *El Elyon* ("The Most High God"), is represented as an eternal king-priest before the Mosaic covenant, I AM similarly (cf. Heb. 7:3) ordains David's lord to be his priest-king forever when the final kingdom comes. The NAB glosses the syntagm by "like," my proposal before consulting the translations. In sum, Christ's priesthood under the new covenant is similar to that of Melchizedek's priesthood before the old covenant.

The Teacher of Righteous and his sect at Qumran separated themselves from the Jerusalem priesthood and its temple, and in that context spiritualized the notion of sacrifice.[61] Since atonement could not be effected by sacrifice, prayer and moral conduct served as its substitute (1QS 9:3–6). The same thing occurred in Judaism with the destruction of the temple. In the New Testament, the reality of the symbolic temple, with its priesthood, appeared in the person of Jesus Christ and rendered the old religion obsolete. The impeccable Christ is the perfect sacrifice, and his church offers spiritual sacrifices of prayer and praise (Heb.13:15), and her members, a royal priesthood (1 Peter 2:9), offer themselves as living sacrifices in the service of Jesus Christ, including doing good to and sharing with others (Rom. 12:1–2; Heb. 13:16).

---

60. *BDB*, 184, s.v. *divrah*, gives the meanings "cause, reason, manner," but for this text curiously opts for "in the order of." *HALOT* (1:212, s.v. *divrah*) gives "manner" as the only option for this text.

61. There is questionably an altar of incense, not of sacrifice, at Qumran, Torleif Elgvin and Stephen J. Pfann, "An Incense Altar at Qumran?" *DSD* 9 (Leiden: Brill, 2002): 20–33.

Prophetic Reflections (vv. 5–7)

David first addresses his reflections to the Messiah and then to the congregation. Ancient Near Eastern literature, as in the Tell Fekherye Inscription, shifts pronouns between first, second, and third persons without formally signaling the change of perspectives.[62] This occurs especially in prophecy (see above). The shift of pronouns from "you" (v. 5) to "he" (vv. 6–7) signals the rhetorical change of perspective from addressing the lord to addressing the congregation within the unified oracle. Although the nearest antecedent of "he" is "Lord [I AM]" (v. 5), semantic pertinence demands an earthly antecedent—that is to say David's lord. The two parts of David's reflections are held together by the same subject, Messiah, the predicate catchword "smash" (*makhats*), and its common object, "kings" and "nations" (vv. 5, 6; see Psalm 2:1–2). A second catchword, "head" (*ro'sh*), also links the two halves: the head of the enemy is smashed; the head of the lord rises up in triumph. The first half of this address represents the lord as smashing the tyrannical kings, and the second half draws his conquest to a climactic conclusion: an enduring victory.

Address to Messiah: Lord of All Will Smash Pagan Kings (v. 5)

The epithet Lord (*'adhonay*) refers to I AM as Lord of lords, the Lord of all,[63] and signifies that I AM is Messiah's master and that Messiah is his slave-king (see v. 1). This Lord of all, David says, is at *your right hand* (*'al yeminka*), thereby assuring him of divine protection and power (see v. 2). Unlike I AM's plunder of Egypt, when Israel did almost nothing, True Strength *smashes* (*makhats*) *kings* (*melakim*), who represent sinful gods and are empowered by demonic forces (cf. Ps. 2:1–2, 10; cf. Eph. 6:10–20). Their defeat is certain because their king has been dethroned from heaven (Luke 10:18) and been bound in the sense that today Jesus Christ takes captives from nations formerly under his rule and frees them from sin and death to join him in his battle for truth and justice (Eph. 4:1–13). *Makhats* ("smash") occurs fourteen times, always in poetry, to signify the victor's

---

62. A. Abou-Assaf, P. Bordreuil, and Alan Millard, *La Statue del Tell Fekherye et Son Inscription Bilingue Assyro-Arméenne*, Recherche sur les Civilisation, Cahier 7 (Paris: ADPF, 1982). In this inscription an index of the stylistic freedom is the fact that the first change of persons does *not* take place at exactly the same point in the Akkadian and Aramaic versions.

63. *IBHS*, 123f., P. 4.4.3e,f.

absolute power. Its subjects are I AM (Deut. 32:39; 33:11; Ps. 68:21, 23 [22, 24]; 110:5, 6; Job 5:18; 26:12; Hab. 3:13), or his "star" from Jacob (Num. 24:17), or Israel (Num. 24:17), or an Israelite warrior such as Jael, who crushed the head of Sisera with a tent peg (Judg. 5:26), and David (2 Sam. 22:39 (= Ps. 18:29).

Address to Congregation (vv. 6–7)

To better interpret David's second reflection, it is important to bear in mind that the representation of Old Testament prophecies about the spiritual realities of the New Testament dispensation are contingent on the Old Testament culture. As prophets must foretell the future in their own language to think intelligently and to speak lucidly, so their language also represents their world. An Old Testament prophet *cannot* speak in the terms of present-day culture because prophecy is God's Word incarnate, adapted to the intellectual capacity of the speaker and his audience.[64] In other words, their imagination is restricted by what sociologists call the sociology of knowledge. For this reason the language of Psalm 110 must be interpreted spiritually after Pentecost when the Spirit broke spiritual realities into salvation history. Christ introduces this method of interpretation: the temple, Jacob's well, and manna all become symbols of his life and body (John, 2, 3, 4, 5, *passim*). His apostles follow suit: military armor becomes spiritual armor; temple becomes heavenly sanctuary; and so forth. This address represents holy war in the political terms of the old dispensation; these terms must be reinterpreted to refer to the spiritual realities of the new dispensation.

Lord Will Judge Whole Earth (v. 6)

He will judge (*yadhin*) means he "gives right and just verdicts," in contrast with "judge" *shaphat*, "to right wrongs." The lord rewards the good with good and the evil with evil. *Among the nations* (*baggoyim*) replaces the synecdoche "kings" (v. 5). At his first advent Jesus Christ commands his disciples to baptize nations and to teach them, and he foretells that at his second advent he will judge among the nations: rewarding those who showed compassion to the poor and punishing those who oppressed them (Matt. 25:31–46).

---

64. Waltke, *Old Testament Theology*, 818.

His punishing the wicked is instantiated first by *he will fill the valleys with corpses* (*mille' Piel ge'ayoth gewiyoth*, see n16; cf. Isa. 66:24; Rev. 19:17).[65] Prior to that, presumably with his mighty mace, *he will smash* (*makhats*, see v. 5 with his mace) *the heads* (*ro'sh*). *Ro'sh* is ambiguous, for it could be either a countable singular for the head over the nations (cf. Ex. 18:25; Num. 1:16; so LXX [*kephalas*, also ambiguous], JPS), or a collective singular for all the leaders of the nations (i.e., "heads," Ps. 68:22; so Targ. ["heads of kings"] and most English versions). The latter option is preferable; the collective singular was probably chosen for its play with the countable singular "head" in verse 7. If a countable singular is intended, there could be an intertextual allusion to Genesis 3:15, which foretells a battle of champions in which the Seed of the woman will crush the head of the Serpent, who is unmasked in later revelation to expose Satan/the Devil (Rev. 19:20; 20:2); the singulars in verses 6–7 would then signal the final showdown battle of the two seeds. *Who are over the broad earth* or "a wide land" (*'erets rabbah*, "much land"; see n22) is a metonymy for all nations.[66]

Lord Will Consummate His Victory (v. 7)

The second concrete image, *from the wadi* (*minnakhal*), refers to a sharply defined depression of a valley or streambed, usually in desert areas, that is bone dry in summer and becomes a gulley washer in the rainy season, forming its sharp contours.[67] The image connotes that even in desert areas of the broad earth God will supply the Messiah with an abundant amount of water to quench his thirst and refresh him (cf. Deut. 8:7; Ps. 36:8 [9]).[68] *Along the way* (*badderek*) adds to this image the Messiah's marching triumphantly in his conquest of the whole earth. *He will drink* completes the image. In his

---

65. Such a valley is Jerusalem's Valley of Hinnom, whose exact location is uncertain, but whichever of three possible valleys is intended, all three include Jerusalem's southeast extremity. This valley was used for burning the corpses of criminals and animals, and indeed refuse of any sort. Although references to this valley occur after the time of David, ancient Jebus and other cities must have had such incinerators. I spent several days excavating a garbage dump at Gezer!

66. Cf. *HALOT*, p. 1171, s.v. *rav*, entry 1.

67. Wadis are common in North Africa and southwestern Asia, including Israel, especially along the Jordanian rift (Deut. 8:40; Isa. 35:6).

68. Some scholars speculate with no evidence that during the royal ritual, the king drinks from a brook (the spring of Gihon?) to refresh himself for battle (see A. A. Anderson, *Psalms*, vol. 2, *Psalm 73–150*, New Century Bible [Greenwood, SC: The Attic Press, 1977], 772).

hurry, he takes a momentary break to refresh himself but does not linger. Neither desert nor fatigue will stop him in his zeal to end tyranny. *Therefore* (*'al ken*) introduces a state of later effects:[69] the priest-king's distinguished and exalted authority and joy. As a result of refreshing himself, he pursues his foes until *he will lift up his head* (*yarim*, Ps. 3:3 [4]), a signal that he has distinguished himself, is worthy of honor and dominion (cf. Gen. 40:13; Judg. 8:28; 1 Sam. 2:10; Ps. 3:3 [4]; 27:6), and is full of joy (Ps. 24:7, 9).[70] In contrast with the abased kings whom he makes his footstool (v. 1), I AM's king holds his head high.

IDENTIFICATION OF "MY LORD"

Returning to the introduction, we again address the identity of the psalm's lord. Modern scholarship has supported four candidates and *usually* accepts the dictum of historical criticism: *vaticinium ex eventu* ("proclamation at the time of the event"). Form critics *infer* this royal psalm was used in a coronation ceremony. If one accepts this hypothesis, as I am inclined to do, the issue is whether the king, when he ascended his throne, was hailed with messianic enthusiasm,[71] and, more than that, whether the oracle contains predictions that this Messiah is superhuman, combines throne and altar under his crown, and achieves a consummate, universal victory over his enemies.

A Cultic Servant of a Maccabean or of Joshua

Many historical critics at the turn of the twentieth century thought "lord" refers to a Maccabean prince, particularly to Jonathan (1 Macc. 9:30f.; 10:20) or Simon (1 Macc. 14:35, 38, 41). This theory faces insuperable difficulties. 1) The Maccabees are not of David's posterity; 2) They are priests, but the psalm crowns a prince; 3) Psalms of Solomon 17:23f. (first century B.C.) [and the Talmud and Midrash] look for a son of David as Messiah, not for a son of Aaron;[72] 4) the priesthood of the sons of Aaron did not

---

69. '*Al ken*, also glossed "therefore," introduces a proposed or anticipated response after a statement of certain conditions.

70. A. Bowling, in *TDOT*, 2:838.

71. G. A. F. Knight, *A Christian Theology of the Old Testament* (Richmond: John Knox Press, 1959), 300.

72. Briggs and Briggs, *Book of Psalms*, 2:374.

last forever;[73] 5) the psalm is a prophecy, but the Maccabean age is sadly conscious that the voice of prophecy was silent (1 Macc. 4:46; 9:27);[74] and 6) the language of the Qumran hymnic literature, roughly contemporary with the Maccabean age, "is neo-classical, not classical."[75]

Some contend the psalm was composed for the crowning of the high priest Joshua, because Zechariah (520 B.C.) prophesied at the crowning of the high priest Joshua (Zech. 6:11) that the high priest's royal crown would become a memorial of the uniting of the two offices and so foreshadows the crowning of a Messianic King-Priest (Zech. 6:12–13). This view obviates the last two objections against a Maccabean referent but not the first four, which pertain to any post-exilic Jewish ruler.

A Cultic Servant of Zadok

Some think that during the coronation liturgy the speaker(s) turn(s) and address(es) the high priest Zadok.[76] They argue that Zadok derives from Melchizedek.[77] Others think that Zadok addresses David in vv. 1–3, 5–7 and that David addresses Zadok in v. 4. But the prophet addresses his whole oracle to "my lord" whom he consistently addresses as "you" in both parts of the psalm (vv. 2–3, 4–5). The interpretation that the antecedent of "you" changes back and forth between king and priest is arbitrary. Moreover, the poet's lord is a champion warrior who rules universally in time and space. No historian makes such a claim for Zadok.

David of Solomon

Several academics accept David as the antecedent of "my" in the term "my lord," but nevertheless historicize the "prophecy" and preempt it of true predictions. They argue the aged David calls Solomon his lord in view

---

73. First Maccabees speaks of Simon as "high priest for ever," but immediately qualifies it: "until there should arise a faithful prophet."

74. Did the writer of Maccabees evidently discount Josephus's reports of high priests' giving prophecies (see n30)?

75. F. M. Cross, *Ancient Library of Qumran* (Garden City, NY: Doubleday, 1958), 166.

76. H. H. Rowley ("Melchizedek and Zadok," Festschrift, Alfred Bertholet zum 80. Geburtstag / gewidmet von Kollegen und Freunden; herausgegeben durch Walter Baumgartner . . . [et al.] [Tubingen: J. C. B. Mohr, 1950]), 467f., thinks Zadok is the speaker in verses 1–3, 5–7, and that the king addresses Zadok in v. 4.

77. C. Broyles, *Psalms*, New International Biblical Commentary (Peabody, MA: Hendrickson, 1999), 415.

of Solomon's new status as king. In so doing, they further argue, David spoke a word far greater than he knew. This interpretation is not tenable. First, the entire prophecy represents David's "lord" as a warrior-king who harshly subdues the whole earth in holy war, but David expected Solomon (i.e., "Peace") to concentrate that nation's strength and resources to building I AM's temple, not to engage in holy war (2 Sam. 7:10; 1 Kings 5:1–6). Second, the subject of our psalm is a priest; Solomon was not. To rebut this anticipated objection it is argued:

> David and his royal sons, as chief representatives of the rule of God, performed many worship-focused activities, such as overseeing the ark of the covenant (see 2 Sam. 6:1–15, especially v. 14; 1 Kings 8:1), building and overseeing the temple (see 1 Kings 5–7; 2 Kings 12:4–7; 22:3–7; 23:4–7; 2 Chron. 15:8; 24:4–12; 29:3–11; 34:8) and overseeing the work of the priests and Levites and the temple liturgy (1 Chron. 6:31; 15:11–16; 16:4–42; 23:3–31; 25:1; 2 Chron. 17:7–9; 19:8–11; 29:25, 30; 35:15–16; Ezra 3:10; 8:20; Neh. 12:24, 36, 45).[78]

These texts, however, cannot bear the weight of the argument. In the ancient Near East, temple building is a royal responsibility; magistrates oversee it, and to some extent the priest's activity. Moses, not Aaron, oversees the building of the tabernacle and legislates the Levitical cultus; David has the inspiration for building the first temple, provides for it, and supplements the Mosaic cultus with musical directions (1 Chron. 22:2–5; 28:2; Ps. 30 title). In post-exilic times Zerubbabel, Ezra, and Nehemiah performed similar duties. Herod the Great greatly expanded the temple. But Moses, the house of David, and the post-exilic Reformers are never called priests.[79] Moreover, in contrast with other ancient Near Eastern cultures and Melchizedek's El Elyon cult (see below), in the old dispensation (from Aaron until the Maccabees), Israel kept separate the roles of kings and priests. Similarly, the president and Congress of the United States

---

78. *TNIV Study Bible*, 973. Surprisingly, this note does not mention specifically that David was wearing a linen ephod, the garment of a priest, when he accompanied the bringing up of the ark to Jerusalem. Nevertheless, the garment does not qualify him to assume the appellation or duties of a priest; the narrative makes no mention of Melchizedek; and the oracle is about his royal sons, not himself.

79. Second Sam. 8:17 may be the sole possible exception. In the lists of David's officials, David's sons are labeled *kohanim*, which probably means "chief/court officials" (2 Sam. 8:17) as understood in the LXX [*aularchai*], Targ. [*ravrevin*], and 1 Chron. 18:17 [*hari'shonim*].

commission the construction of the Supreme Court building, appoint its chief justice and associate justices, and oversee the federal judicial system, but they are neither called judges nor allowed to function as judges. Then, too, why is a solemn oath needful to permit Solomon to perform what are commonly royal functions with regard to the temple? Finally, taxes, not tithes, are paid to Israel's kings. In sum, the psalm's predicates defining David's lord are not fulfilled in Solomon nor are they expected to be.

A Cultic Servant of the House of David

Most deny Davidic authorship and argue that a cultic servant is addressing an exclusively human son of David as his lord. To explain his priesthood, they use the same flawed arguments as in the preceding interpretation: David of Solomon. Others argue that the oracle grants or assumes the house of David inherits an El Elyon cultus at Jerusalem of which Melchizedek was the priest in the time of Abraham; this supposedly occurs when David conquers Jerusalem and makes it his royal city, "the city of David" (Gen. 14:18–20; 2 Sam. 5:6–8).[80] This interpretation is unlikely.

First, at the time of Joshua a true El Elyon cultus—the one Abraham respects—does not exist in Jerusalem, for I AM commands Joshua to exterminate the city, leaving no survivors including its king (Gen. 15:17–21; Deut. 7:1–2; Josh. 10:1–27; Judg. 1:4–8). It is unlikely the house of David desires to resurrect and reckon itself as heir of a failed and shamed Canaanite cultus and synthesize it with the cult of I AM. Second, this alleged priesthood would have a higher rank than Aaron's. Melchizedek's superiority to Abraham and so to his descendants Levi and Aaron is implied by Abraham's paying tribute to Melchizedek and by Melchizedek's blessing Abraham. If this theory has historical substance, the king would trump the high priest and have no need to submit to his rule in the sanctuary. Is this possible in the old dispensation? Yes. Evidence? None.

Third, the theory lacks any external validation. To use this psalm to prove the interpretation commits the logical errors of begging the issue and/or circular reasoning; it substantiates the theory from the psalm itself. The Melchizedek in the Abraham narrative appears out of the blue and just as mysteriously disappears. This is more than an argument from silence.

80. A. Weiser, *The Psalms: A Commentary* (Philadelphia: The Westminster Press, 1962), 695; A. A. Anderson, *Psalm 73–150*, New Century Bible (Greenwood, SC: Attic Press, 1977), 2:771.

The Bible is all about true religion. Its failure to preserve a tradition that David and his sons inherit Melchizedek's priesthood is too glaring to be an oversight or an accident.

Fourth, unlike Psalms 89 and 132, this royal prophecy makes no reference to David's sons. In sum, the interpretation is made up whole cloth with no external validation.

Fifth, if one argues that the prophet has in mind only Israel's kings during the monarchy, his prophecy is either false, or, if his audience understands he is using *Hofstil*, courtly hyperbole, has no real substance. No son of David during the first temple period fulfills it. In contradistinction to this prophetic vision of the universal rule of this "lord," no son of David before Jesus Christ rules beyond those of David's empire. Rather than establishing a universal kingdom, the house of David loses its kingdom until Jesus Christ restores it (Acts 15:12–18).

Sixth and correlatively, the preservation of the psalms argues against this interpretation. If the historical circumstances are thought to falsify a prophecy, the prophecy is not preserved. The notion that post-exilic Judaism re-interpreted royal psalms to refer to the Messiah morally tarnishes the tradition that saved it and diminishes the psalm's credibility.

David of the Son of Man

The New Testament does not accept the historical critics' dictum of *vaticinium ex eventu*, but interprets David's lord as a true prediction of Jesus Christ. This conviction uniquely satisfies the accredited grammatico-historical method of interpretation, provided one accepts the canon that prophecy represents the spiritual realities of the new dispensation in terms of its historical conditioning. Delitzsch rightly labels it a unique prophetico-Messianic psalm: "In dying he [David] seizes the pillars of the divine promise, he lets go the ground of his own present, and looks as a prophet into the future of his seed." Delitzsch's arguments, however, are not equally cogent.[81] We argue:

First, the introduction formula identifies the coming Messiah as superhuman:

81. F. Delitzsch, *Commentary on the Old Testament*, vol. 5, trans. Francis Bolton (Peabody, MA: Hendrickson, 1996; reprinted from the English edition originally published by T. & T. Clark, Edinburgh, 1866–1891), 691–99, esp. 693.

> While the Pharisees were gathered together, Jesus asked them, "What do you think about the Messiah? Whose son is he?"
>
> "The son of David," they replied.
>
> He said to them, "How is it then that David, speaking by the Spirit, calls him 'Lord'? For he says,
>
> 'The Lord said to my Lord:
> "Sit at my right hand . . . ."'
>
> If then David calls him 'Lord,' how can he be his son?" No one could say a word in reply, and from that day on no one dared to ask him any more questions. (Matt. 22:41–46)

Jesus' argument assumes the disputants agree that: the psalm is inspired; David is the author; a father is superior to the son, who owes his life to his father; and a lord, by definition, has authority over his slave. Accordingly, David's lord must be superhuman in his nature. Jesus Christ uniquely validates these assumptions by his being born Son of David and Son of God; his sinless life; his bodily resurrection from the dead; and his ascent into heaven (cf. Matt. 22:44f.; Mark 12:36f.; Luke 1:32; 20:42–44).

Some contend, however, that Jesus merely uses these wrong assumptions of Judaism, without endorsing them, for the sake of his argument.[82] But if Christ is using false, Jewish assumptions, his argument for his superhuman nature based on this prediction is no longer cogent for Christian apologetics and doctrine.[83] In short, the theory of false assumptions undermines sound doctrine. Finally, the next two arguments, based on the divine citations (vv. 1B, 4) and the prophet's reflection (vv. 2–3, 5–7), validate that the psalm contains true predictions, and if this is so in vv. 1B–7, why not allow that David gives a real prediction in v. 1A?

Turning from the psalm's introduction, its two divine citations (vv. 1B, 4) assert that David's lord sits at God's right hand, and by divine appointment serves as his eternal priest-king, resembling the venerable, pre-Aaronic priesthood of Melchizedek, not a hereditary priest of the line of Aaron. Christ's apostles lay down their lives to bear witness that they saw Jesus Christ ascend into heaven where, the writer of Hebrew teaches, he serves God as his priest-king in the heavenly sanctuary (Acts 2:30–36; 5:31; 7:55–56;

---

82. Kirkpatrick, *Psalms*, 662f.
83. Perowne, *Psalms*, 297f.

Rom. 8:34; Eph. 1:20; 4:7–9; Col. 3:1; Heb. 1:3; 5:6–10; 7:11–28; 8:1; 10:12; 12:2). The apostles frequently mention his ascension in connection with his sitting "at the right hand of God," a term molded and minted by Psalm 110. In other words, the historical temple-palace arrangement discussed above is a type of the heavenly reality.

Turning to the prophet's two reflections (vv. 3, 5–7), the scene shifts from the royal throne to the battlefield. He extends his reign in ever-widening circles throughout the world in a holy war through his dedicated troops. So also in ever-widening circles the ascended Christ and his church militant raise his flag of the new covenant on every continent and win disciples to Jesus Christ in almost every nation by the sword of the Word and the power of the Holy Spirit (Matt. 16; Acts 1:8).

Conclusion

Those who support a different candidate from Jesus Christ contend that the New Testament and/or the superscripts in the book of Psalms reinterpret the oracle's original intention. In truth, no other candidate than Jesus satisfies the plain sense of the predications of this unified oracle addressed to David's lord. Historical critics, not the New Testament, reinterpret the psalm from its plain meaning to fit their dogma. David's lord is Daniel's Son of Man, a term Jesus preferred to the political title Messiah. This is so because he, like Daniel's Son of Man, rides the clouds to the Ancient of Days and brings all nations under his dominion (Dan. 7:13f.; Matt. 24:36; 1 Cor. 15:24).[84]

David probably composed his royal prophecy to be sung by cultic functionaries at the coronation ceremony of his heirs, hoping that in the end of salvation history a final successor of his would fulfill and consummate his prophecy. He is probably unaware, however, that his language is a type of the spiritual reality that his eternal son introduced into salvation history. David's royal prophecy of Psalm 16:11 envisions his uncorrupted body at God's right hand forevermore. Psalm 110 adds to that vision the prophecy that his transcendent son, a David *redivivus*, in a type ascends to his throne of judgment and eliminates his self-serving enemies (Matt. 25:31ff.). His hope is not put to shame in the resurrection, ascension, and present reign of Jesus Christ.

84. Waltke, *Old Testament Theology*, 568.

3

The Quest for Wisdom[1]

VERN SHERIDAN POYTHRESS

The LORD by wisdom founded the earth;
> by understanding he established the heavens. (Prov. 3:19)

For the LORD gives wisdom;
> from his mouth come knowledge and understanding. (Prov. 2:6)

At the mall, a child begins to cry and scream when his mother does not buy him a cookie. The mother, embarrassed by the public display, tries desperately to quiet the child. The noise from the child subsides while the mother speaks a sentence or two. Then the child breaks out louder than ever. The mother, exasperated, finally buys the cookie, and all is calm again.

As I look on, I can see a history in which the mother, by giving in to screaming, is actually training her child to scream in order to get his way. By rewarding him for bad behavior, she is encouraging him to do it again. Unfortunately, the mother does not see what she is doing. She is too

---

1. Materials from this essay are to appear in another form in Vern S. Poythress, *Language: A God-Centered Approach* (Wheaton, IL: Crossway, forthcoming).

immersed in the situation and does not step back to think, to consider the larger pattern. The mother needs wisdom and does not have it. I wish I could give it to her.

The writer of Proverbs had a similar experience when he observed folly of another kind:

> For at the window of my house
>   I have looked out through my lattice,
> and I have seen among the simple,
>   I have perceived among the youths,
>   a young man lacking sense,
> passing along the street near her corner,
>   taking the road to her house
> in the twilight, in the evening,
>   at the time of night and darkness.
>
> And behold, the woman meets him,
>   dressed as a prostitute, wily of heart. . . .
>
> All at once he follows her,
>   as an ox goes to the slaughter,
> or as a stag is caught fast
>   till an arrow pierces its liver;
> as a bird rushes into a snare;
>   he does not know that it will cost him his life. (Prov. 7:6–10, 22–23)

The observer at the mall and the observer at the window in Proverbs are able to step back and see long-range consequences. In their ability to step back, they transcend the pressing demands of the situation. They have a deeper understanding, in comparison with the animal-like instincts of the mother who thinks only of immediate relief and of the young man who thinks only of immediate pleasure.

WISDOM

We may be able to acquire bits of wisdom by watching mothers in malls. But how can we look down on human life as a whole "from above," when we are immersed in it? We can never surmount it by focusing analytically on everything simultaneously, and being perfectly conscious of everything. We are always focused and conscious *from a particular point of view*, and of that point of view we are never exhaustively conscious.

A view of human life as a whole requires transcendence. We must somehow transcend the limits of our lives, and be able to view life as an object rather than merely have it as a subliminal environment. Or, to put it another way, a sound view of life requires wisdom. We must be able to position our lives in a measured way that gives us guidance and appreciation for both the powers and limitations of our lives. We must have something like a God's-eye view.

Access to Wisdom

The Bible says that wisdom comes from God (Prov. 2:6; 1 Cor. 1:30). God knows everything, and knows each of our lives exhaustively. God is aware of every aspect of a child's screaming and a young man's lust and the history of both. He has the wisdom we need.

Receiving wisdom from God involves communion with God. And how do we have communion? Since the fall, as sinners we are alienated from God. After the fall, Adam and Eve were expelled from the Garden of Eden, the place of communion with God (Gen. 3:23–24). Cherubim barred the way back. We have a three-sided problem. First, as human beings we have the need and the longing to return to God. Second, our own sin and rebellion make us want to avoid God and to flee from him (Gen. 3:8). Third, God prevents return, because sinners cannot stand in the presence of the holiness of God (Isa. 6:3–5).

The barriers to returning to Eden are analogous to the barriers in the tabernacle, in the form of curtains barring the way to the presence of God. In still other passages of Scripture, the barriers are re-expressed as barriers to receiving wisdom, or as barriers to ascending to heaven. Since the tabernacle of Moses is an image of heaven, its barriers correspond by analogy to the seeming impossibility of ascending to heaven. Consider the language in Proverbs 30:1–4:

> The words of Agur son of Jakeh.
> The oracle.
>
> The man declares, I am weary, O God;
>   I am weary, O God, and worn out.

Surely I am too stupid to be a man.
    I have not the understanding of a man.
I have not learned wisdom,
    nor have I knowledge of the Holy One.
Who has ascended to heaven and come down?
    Who has gathered the wind in his fists?
Who has wrapped up the waters in a garment?
    Who has established all the ends of the earth?
What is his name, and what is his son's name?
    Surely you know!

Agur's confession in Proverbs begins with weariness. It appears that Agur is worn out from seeking wisdom and not achieving it. And wisdom is linked with "knowledge of the Holy One." That observation in turn leads him to reflect on the wisdom of God's governance ("gathered the wind in his fists"). Agur perceives the need to ascend to heaven to receive wisdom, and then to come down. One would think that such an ascent is impossible, and so come to despair. But that is not where the passage ends. The very next verse shows a way forward: "Every word of God proves true; he is a shield to those who take refuge in him" (Prov. 30:5). In other words, God provides wisdom for those who receive his word. This thought is confirmed at the beginning of Proverbs: "The fear of the LORD is the beginning of knowledge; fools despise wisdom and instruction" (Prov. 1:7).

Similar language can be seen in Deuteronomy.

> For this commandment that I command you today is not too hard for you, neither is it far off. It is not in heaven, that you should say, "Who will ascend to heaven for us and bring it to us, that we may hear it and do it?" Neither is it beyond the sea, that you should say, "Who will go over the sea for us and bring it to us, that we may hear it and do it?" But the word is very near you. It is in your mouth and in your heart, so that you can do it. (Deut. 30:11–14)

In context, Moses is exhorting the Israelites before they enter the promised land. He envisions both their future disobedience (Deut. 30:1) and restoration (Deut. 30:2–10). So it is debated whether the nearness of God's word in Deuteronomy 30:14 has already been brought about by

God's speaking through Moses, or whether it is to be accomplished only in connection with the restoration that Moses prophesies.[2] From a theological point of view, God did come near to Israel at Mount Sinai, when he gave the nation the Ten Commandments. The Ten Commandments are a linguistically accessible expression of God's wisdom. Yet the giving of the Ten Commandments did not succeed in penetrating to the heart of each Israelite and giving him a new heart that loved God and obeyed him. So Deuteronomy 30 does look forward beyond what was accomplished at Mount Sinai. It looks forward to Christ, as is clear in Romans 10:5–10:

> For Moses writes about the righteousness that is based on the law, that the person who does the commandments shall live by them. But the righteousness based on faith says, "Do not say in your heart, 'Who will ascend into heaven?'" (that is, to bring Christ down) or "'Who will descend into the abyss?'" (that is, to bring Christ up from the dead). But what does it say? "The word is near you, in your mouth and in your heart" (that is, the word of faith that we proclaim); because, if you confess with your mouth that Jesus is Lord and believe in your heart that God raised him from the dead, you will be saved. For with the heart one believes and is justified, and with the mouth one confesses and is saved.

The revelation of the word of God at Mount Sinai took place in connection with Moses ascending Mount Sinai, and then descending with a copy of the law in his hands. His ascending symbolized ascent to heaven and to the presence of God. His descent symbolized descent from heaven, bringing the word of God to man. In this way, Moses mediated between God and the sinfulness of the people. He foreshadowed and typified Christ's mediation (1 Tim. 2:5–6).

Christ's Fulfillment of the Quest

Christ's ascent and descent fulfill the picture in Exodus 19–20 and in Deuteronomy 30. Ephesians 4 uses similar language with respect to Christ:

2. See Steven R. Coxhead, "Deuteronomy 30:11–14 as a Prophecy of the New Covenant in Christ," *WTJ* 68/2 (2006): 305–20.

Therefore it says,

> "When he ascended on high he led a host of captives,
>   and he gave gifts to men."

(In saying, "He ascended," what does it mean but that he had also descended into the lowest parts of the earth? He who descended is the one who also ascended far above all the heaven, that he might fill all things.) (Eph. 4:8–10)

There are still some notable complexities. Christ descended from heaven in his incarnation. "The lowest parts of the earth" (Eph. 4:9) might refer either to the incarnation or to Christ's descent into the realm of death at the time of his death. Both are aspects of Christ's identification with humanity. He underwent death as the penalty for the sins of others, which he bore (1 Peter 2:24). His incarnation and his death, as acts of identification with us, belong together theologically. Both of these *precede* his ascension, to which Eph. 4:8 and 10 refer. By contrast, in Proverbs 30:4 the ascent comes *first*, before descent. Ascent also precedes descent in Moses's movements in Exodus 19 and in Deuteronomy 30:12.

Actually, the Old Testament examples are fully compatible with Ephesians 4, once we see a fuller picture. According to Ephesians 4:8–10, Christ ascended and then "gave gifts to men" (v. 8). The gifts are further explained in verse 11 and what follows. "And he gave the apostles, the prophets, the evangelists, the pastors and teachers, to equip the saints . . . ." Christ did not descend bodily after his ascension, but he gave the church his representatives and those who would teach his word. He speaks to the people on earth through these representatives. So, theologically speaking, he *has* descended. To put it another way, he has poured out the Holy Spirit, who empowers his representatives (Acts 2:33). The giving of the Holy Spirit at Pentecost is parallel to the giving of the law at Mount Sinai. Moreover, the Spirit of Christ brings Christ's presence to his people: spiritually speaking, Christ descends in the descent of the Holy Spirit (John 14:16–18, 23).

Then what about the incarnation? It too is a descent of God from heaven. Jesus more than once speaks of having "come down from heaven" (John 6:33, 38, 51). In the incarnation, "the Word became flesh and dwelt among us" (John 1:14). His "dwelling" or "tabernacling" among us is parallel to the symbolic picture of God dwelling in the midst of Israel through the tabernacle of Moses.

The incarnation, as a fulfillment of the tabernacle dwelling, is an act of God's coming near to man to bless him, to dwell with him, and to establish communion with him. As such, it already anticipates the further work that Jesus will accomplish in his crucifixion, death, resurrection, and ascension. In fact, as a blessing of God's communion, it anticipates the communion with God in Christ through the Holy Spirit, who is poured out to make us into a temple of God, both corporately (the church: 1 Cor. 3:16) and individually (1 Cor. 6:19).

Let us put it another way. The "descent" of God to man in Christ's incarnation is one historical stage in a progression of works of God that redeem man, establish communion between man and God, bring God's wisdom down to man and make it accessible to man in Christ's teaching, and transform the heart of man by remaking him a dwelling of God and transforming him into the image of Christ (2 Cor. 3:18). The appearance of God in the flesh is the appearance of the redeeming God, and so already implies in a nutshell all the works to come.

The descent of the Holy Spirit is the descent of the presence of the resurrected and ascended Christ. Christ comes through the Spirit who represents him. The Spirit is "another Helper" (John 14:16). The coming of the Spirit is thus integrally related to the incarnation, even though it is a distinct event. The same holds for the "descent" of gifts to the church. Through the apostles and prophets and evangelists and pastors and teachers (Eph. 4:11), the church hears the voice of Christ proclaiming the good news of his resurrection and ascension and their implications (Eph. 2:17). "For through him [Christ] we both [Jews and Gentiles] have access in one Spirit to the Father" (Eph. 2:18). "Access" is access to heaven. Each of us who is "in one Spirit" may now ascend:

> Therefore, brothers, since we have confidence to *enter* the holy places [in heaven] by the blood of Jesus, by the new and living way that he opened for us through the curtain, that is, through his flesh, and since we have a great priest over the house of God, let us *draw near* with a true heart in full assurance of faith, with our hearts sprinkled clean from an evil conscience and our bodies washed with pure water. (Heb. 10:19–22)

We are to "draw near," that is, draw near to the presence of God in heaven. We are able to do so because of the completed work of Christ, which is referred to by mention of "the blood of Jesus" and the sprinkling and washing accomplished by his priesthood and self-sacrifice. Jesus the great high priest is the mediator between God and man, just as 1 Timothy 2:5 indicates. Through him we have permanent, unimpeded access to God. Through him the barrier of the cherubim in Genesis 3:24 has been removed. Through him we have access to wisdom, because Jesus is the wisdom of God (1 Cor. 1:30; see Col. 2:3).

So Jesus Christ turns out to be the answer to Agur's unanswered longings for access to the wisdom of God. Agur asks, "What is his name [the name of God], and what is his son's name?" (Prov. 30:4). The name of God is not just a meaningless sound, but in a biblical context it indicates the revelation of his character. Through the name of the Son, the character of the Father is revealed. And with that climactic revelation, we receive the wisdom of God:

> Long ago, at many times and in many ways, God spoke to our fathers by the prophets, but in these last days he has spoken to us by his Son, whom he appointed the heir of all things, through whom also he created the world. He is the radiance of the glory of God and the exact imprint of his nature, and he upholds the universe by the word of his power. (Heb. 1:1–3a)

Agur, without knowing in detail what he was longing for, was inspired by the Spirit to speak beyond himself, and prophetically to anticipate the satisfaction of his longing, when one comes to know the name, that is, the character, of the Son of God.

Elsewhere in the Old Testament one may see similar longings. Job longs for wisdom, because what is happening to him does not make sense:

> But where shall wisdom be found?
> 　And where is the place of understanding?
> Man does not know its worth,
> 　and it is not found in the land of the living.
> The deep says, "It is not in me,"
> 　and the sea says, "It is not with me."
> It cannot be bought for gold,
> 　and silver cannot be weighed as its price. . . .

From where, then, does wisdom come?
    And where is the place of understanding?
It is hidden from the eyes of all living
    and concealed from the birds of the air.
Abaddon and Death say,
    "We have heard a rumor of it with our ears."

God understands the way to it,
    and he knows its place.
For he looks to the ends of the earth
    and sees everything under the heavens.
When he gave to the wind its weight
    and apportioned the waters by measure,
when he made a decree for the rain
    and a way for the lightning of the thunder,
then he saw it and declared it;
    he established it, and searched it out.
And he said to man,
"Behold, the fear of the Lord, that is wisdom,
    and to turn away from evil is understanding." (Job 28:12–15, 20–28)

The fear of the Lord is wisdom, because it sets a person in communion with God and sets him on the path to the fullness of knowledge that will dawn in Christ. Indeed, the fear of the Lord is granted to a sinful person only for the sake of Christ. God acts in mercy toward people in Old Testament times by reckoning for their benefit beforehand the grace that will be accomplished in Christ (Rom. 3:25). Even in the Old Testament, godly people experienced some foretaste of the wisdom of God and the communion with God. The full realization of that communion awaited the coming of Christ. And of course we still await a yet-fuller communion with God in the new heaven and the new earth (Rev. 21:1–4; 1 Cor. 13:12).

Multiple Quests for Wisdom

The Bible claims to be the Word of God (2 Tim. 3:16–17; 2 Pet. 1:21). As the Word of God, it offers us wisdom from God. At the heart of that wisdom is personal knowledge of God through Jesus Christ. Christ is the wisdom of God, and we may know him because he speaks to us in the Bible.

The Bible is not only the Word of God, but the word of the Son of God who is God (John 1:1). And Christ promises the Holy Spirit, to open our minds to understand him (John 16:13–15).

But not everyone accepts this. Many people remain in rebellion against God; and yet, because they are human beings, they are still made in the image of God. They still rely on God. And, more painfully, they have an unquenchable longing for God, because they were originally created not only to be like God but to have communion with God, to enjoy the presence of God forever (Ps. 16:11).

In particular, they long for wisdom. They have an intellectual thirst to understand. And God is the all-wise One. He is the obvious source of transcendent wisdom. At some level, human beings know this instinctively. God manifests his wisdom in the created world (Rom. 1:18–23). He manifests his wisdom in the very constitution of the mind, which knows the need for rationality, a rationality that reflects the rationality of the mind of God. And so in longing for wisdom they long for God.

But simultaneously they rebel. They would have an autonomous wisdom, a wisdom coming from virtually being a god. Each person would like to see and understand everything by himself and for himself, locked up in the narcissism and wilderness of loving only oneself—and simultaneously hating oneself, because a self turned on itself is no longer beautiful.

Of course no one is really by himself. He needs to rely on God, but in rebellion he falls victim to Satanic deceit. He is enslaved in his mind as well as his body:

> Now this I say and testify in the Lord, that you must no longer walk as the Gentiles do, in the futility of their minds. They are darkened in their understanding, alienated from the life of God because of the ignorance that is in them, due to their hardness of heart. They have become callous and have given themselves up to sensuality, greedy to practice every kind of impurity. But that is not the way you learned Christ! (Eph. 4:17–20)

Because people are alienated from God, their quest for wisdom takes strange, distorted forms. It takes counterfeit forms, and leads to counterfeit wisdom. Satan is the great deceiver (Rev. 12:9), the great counterfeiter who tries to make his deceit close enough to the truth to entrap people.[3] He tries to appear like an angel of light (2 Cor. 11:14).

The counterfeit has to be close to the truth in order to be effective. The counterfeit of true religion is still in essence religion. If you will not worship and serve God, you will serve a substitute god. Ultimately you will worship yourself: "You will be like God, knowing good and evil" (Gen. 3:5). But you are finite, and can never succeed in being an adequate substitute for the true God. And so the gods multiply. Not only the self, but Satan, and Satanic ideas, and physical idols, and money, and pleasure, and sex, and the health of one's body, and fame, and so on and on.

In the intellectual arena, we have a continuing quest for wisdom. This quest is in essence a *religious* quest, even if it is undertaken by an atheist. It is a quest to ascend to heaven, to be like God. Because each of us is finite, the quest for the infinite needs mediation. Moses mediated in his limited way between God at the top of Mount Sinai, and the people of Israel at the bottom (Ex. 19). The priests in the tabernacle mediated between God's presence in the innermost room, and the people who stood outside. Animal sacrifices, through substitutionary sin bearing, expressed the principle of mediation that deals with the sins of man, and more broadly with his failures, including his intellectual failures. All of these Old Testament symbolic institutions pointed forward to Christ, who is the final mediator (1 Tim. 2:5). If, now, we do not come to Christ, we will embark on some other religious quest for mediation, and through mediation, a quest for the infinite wisdom of God.

So what forms does man-made wisdom take? Let us consider some examples. In order to see the main point, we consider them only in a highly simplified, "skeletal" form.

PLATONISM

In Plato's allegory of the cave, people are chained to one place in a subterranean cave and see only shadows on the wall.[4] In the allegory, the cave dwellers represent ordinary people, who live in a shadow world, with confused

3. On counterfeiting, see Vern S. Poythress, *The Returning King: A Guide to the Book of Revelation* (Phillipsburg, NJ: P&R, 2000), 16–25.
4. Plato, *Republic*, Book 7, 514a–520a.

and muddled thoughts. Outside the cave, where the sun shines, one is able to see the world as it is, and to see the realities that produced the shadows on the cave wall. The person who is outside the cave corresponds to the enlightened philosopher. He has wisdom because he has ascended from the subterranean cave to enjoy the light of the sun. The physical ascent pictured in the allegory represents spiritually an ascent "to the intelligible region,"[5] a kind of ascent to heaven. Plato conceives of this philosophical wisdom mainly as a recovery of the eternal knowledge of eternal forms or ideas. The idea of the good is supreme, but one may also seek to grasp the idea of justice, the idea of piety, the idea of temperance, the idea of love, and so on.

Who has such knowledge? According to Plato, the individual soul is eternal, indestructible, and preexistent. In its preexistence it had immediate access to and grasp of the eternal ideas. It had virtually divine knowledge. The claim for preexistence is interesting. In biblical terms, we would say it is a claim to be "like God" in the non-Christian sense. Christ existed even before his incarnation, and that is one evidence for his transcendent wisdom (John 1:1–3). In Platonic thought, the individual soul counterfeits the role of Christ.

According to Platonic thought, when the soul becomes embodied, it forgets its former knowledge. The task of the philosophical quest is recovery of what the soul has "forgotten."

So what plays a mediating role, offering access to a divine vision of the ideas? The soul itself does. Man, conceived of as capable of virtually divine vision and knowledge, has made himself the mediator. In practice, Plato uses "dialectic," a process of dialog involving interchange and critical analysis of imperfectly grasped ideas. Using dialectic, one may cast off the imperfections and see more and more clearly the "essence" of the idea, through the vision of the soul. In this respect, dialectic, and the mind that plays through the process of the dialectic, is itself the mediator. Plato must know that even he has not yet *actually* come to a perfect grasp of the ideas. The full vision (that is, something akin to divinity) awaits the time when, through death, the soul breaks free from the body. Socrates does not fear death, but rather welcomes it, because it is the gateway and final mediator[6] leading to the heavenly deification of his knowledge.

5. Ibid., 517b.
6. That is, a person's own literal death, rather than the death of Christ, becomes the mediator for achieving wisdom.

In the meantime, grasp of the ideas is partial. But the dialectic, faithfully used, will lead onward toward the goal. The dialectic itself, the process, I would guess is a deeper religious certainty than even the state of knowledge that a Platonist has already attained. And how does one know for sure that the dialectic itself is pure and not misleading? It is the operation of eternal reason. It is self-correcting, because reason can always catch out an earlier lapse in the operation of a human dialog. And one knows its power, one knows its promise, by the vision already afforded by previous experience. One has experienced the destruction of the illusions and the half-baked opinions of ordinary people through its operation.

Socrates admits that, for the most part, he does not know. But at least he knows that he does not know. That is, through the dialectical critical analysis of others' opinions, he sees flaws and contradictions in those opinions, and he then knows that they do *not* represent truth. Through an accumulation of these experiences, each of which is a *revelation*, a moment of insight, he gains experientially a confidence in the dialectic. Reason is virtually divine, and he has achieved it as a process even if he has not yet arrived at the heavenly vision where the soul sees the eternal ideas in an unimpeded way.

This quest for wisdom is a counterfeit. Yet there are still some positive insights in Plato. From a Christian point of view, how can this be? It is a product of common grace.

God's mind is the original for which the human mind is an analogue. Man's reason images God's reason. So Plato is partly right about his rational powers. God is rational, because he is faithful to his own character. He is consistent with himself. Or, to put it another way, the Son of God, the Second Person of the Trinity, is the Word (John 1:1). He is not only "with God from the beginning," but he *is* God. He is in harmony with the Father. That harmony includes the harmony of word, of discourse. The Greek word used in John 1:1 is *logos*. This word can mean "discourse," but it is also closely associated with reason. He is the mediator for those who would grow in human wisdom.

Now Plato thinks of wisdom as the fruit of communion with reason. But for him it is still the self-achieved wisdom of the insight of the autonomous soul. His own would-be autonomous soul, and especially its reason, is the religious substitute for Christ. It is man listening to the voice of Satan, "You will be like God." According to Platonic thinking, man, when properly reasoning, is the ultimate standard for truth, because in such a mode his mind is virtually identical with the divine mind. This is non-Christian rationalism. At the same time, the soul's captivity within the body drags the soul down into the world of shadows, where there is virtually no access to truth. How then can Plato know, as long as he is in the body, whether his whole experience of enlightenment is not a gigantic deception? The lack of foundation for knowledge is non-Christian irrationalism.[7]

If one has given oneself to Platonism, as a religious commitment, one might still ask how many people are directly capable of achieving the exalted insights that Plato achieved. Is every soul as pure in its grasp of reason? It does not seem so. And thus there comes the need for more mediation. We must have earthly priests who help the unenlightened toward enlightenment. Socrates and Plato offer themselves as mediatory priests who claim to have access to the light, and to stand in heaven, in order to come down and speak to ordinary people. They give them insights, adapted to their level of enlightenment, and lead them higher. We have here substitutes for the exclusive mediation of Christ, who as man is one with us, and who as God has the eternal wisdom of the divine vision.

Plato frames his discussion primarily in terms of ideas, rather than in terms of language. But the two correlate closely. One could easily transcribe Plato's reasoning into the realm of language. The ideas, instead of being primarily located in thought, are concepts in an eternal, heavenly language. The challenge of Plato and his friends would then be to grasp that heavenly language in its essence. Human language points to the heavenly original, but is distorted through the presence of the body. Purification takes place through discourse, discussion, and dialog. That is, we use language, in accordance with the rules of language, in service of language purification. Rules of language include logical rules. Rules of language, and particular rules concerning dialectic, offer the mediatorial substitute for Christ.[8] Those who have already managed to purify their language serve as priests for those who are beginning.

Is Plato really this bad? Yes and no. Underneath the surface, Plato represents a counterfeit offer of wisdom, and therefore a counterfeit religious direction. But like all counterfeits, Platonic thought also includes many

---

7. On non-Christian rationalism and irrationalism, see John M. Frame, *The Doctrine of the Knowledge of God* (Phillipsburg, NJ: Presbyterian and Reformed, 1987), 13–15.

8. One might ask whether something very similar to this program for language was in process in the work of Ludwig Wittgenstein.

attractive and helpful insights. There is common grace. Elements of truth make the whole more attractive. Sorting of good and bad is required.[9]

Similar things could be said about other thinkers who endeavor to bring us wisdom. For the ones below, I will indicate what I see as counterfeit features. But I will not delay very much to make the legitimate point that each is a subtle combination of truth and distortion of truth.

IMMANUEL KANT

Next consider Immanuel Kant. At the heart of Kant's philosophical reflections lies his reasoning about the nature and limits of human reason. According to Kant, people analyze the *phenomena* of human sense experience, but never succeed in directly grasping things as they really are. Why not? The phenomena are what they are because they have already been conformed to the nature of man's sensory apparatus and the character of his mind. The mind necessarily thinks in terms of the categories of space, time, and causality. So these categories are imposed on the phenomena in the process of their becoming phenomena accessible to human consciousness.

Human reason can operate confidently in analyzing the phenomena, since these are always automatically conformed to the natural categories of human reason. But reason produces antinomies if it is inappropriately applied to the noumenal realm, which includes God, morality, and human freedom.

The interesting aspect of the picture that Kant paints is its transcendent vision. Kant speaks confidently about the noumenal realm, about things in themselves, about human reason and its limits, about the human capacities of understanding and imagination, about the innate categories of the human mind, and about the impossibility of a direct appearance of God (revelation). It would seem that he must himself first exceed the limits that he has postulated for reason, in order to write his account of those limits and their relation to what lies beyond them. His own books confidently use reasoning, and apply it *beyond* the realm of the phenomena, in order to show what goes wrong when ordinary people use reason without noticing its limits. But in using reasoning in this way, Kant has gone beyond the

---

9. For further discussion of Plato and the larger field of Greek philosophy, see John M. Frame, "Greeks Bearing Gifts," in *Revolutions in Worldview: Understanding the Flow of Western Thought*, ed. W. Andrew Hoffecker (Phillipsburg, NJ: P&R, 2007), 1–36.

limits for reason that he has prescribed for everyone else.[10] In an intellectual sense, he has ascended to heaven, and achieved a divine vision.

At the same time, Kant's philosophy forbids human beings in general from transgressing the limits of reason. Through his philosophy, then, he attempts to forbid any *other* ascent to heaven. Kant assures us that, in the nature of the case, the ascent is impossible for human reason. So his philosophy claims for itself an exclusive, monopolistic role in the quest for wisdom.

Additional questions arise. How shall we know whether Kant's reasoning gives us illusions rather than the truth? Actually there are hidden assumptions in his reasoning. But even if his reasoning appeared completely sound, how do we know—given his concerns about the possible limits of reason—whether his arguments describe reality, as opposed to merely being postulated in conformity with the natural categories of our finite minds? We could know this if we could achieve a second ascent to heaven, to a heaven above the heavens. From there, we might discern whether our minds are constituted in such a way that they can achieve an accurate vision from the first heaven.

From a third heaven, higher than the second, we could then check as to whether our vision achieved from the second heaven is really authentic. And from the vantage point of a fourth heaven, we could check the authenticity of the third heaven. An infinite regress threatens. Why? Man is attempting to make himself God. He never achieves exhaustive consciousness of the relation of his consciousness to an outside reality, because he does not have direct divine knowledge of that outside reality nor of his own consciousness. He never achieves deity.

At the same time, a human being does have the ability to stand back, to look at his limitations. He thinks about what it might be like to see things from an all-knowing point of view, that is, from God's standpoint. Though he is a finite creature, he has the ability to think like God, to imagine things from God's standpoint, to think God's thoughts after him. That ability is one aspect of his being made in the image of God. Since he is made in the

---

10. Richard Rorty comments:

" . . . Kant seems never to have asked himself how, given the restrictions on human cognition the *Critique of Pure Reason* had discerned, it was possible to assume the 'transcendental standpoint' from which that book was purportedly written. . . ." (Rorty, *Contingency, Irony, and Solidarity* [Cambridge: Cambridge University Press, 1989], 110).

image of God, he can project images of himself looking at himself, or God looking at him, or a whole indefinite series of images of higher heavens from which he looks down on the limitations of the lower heavens.

If a questing person does not find rest by trusting in the all-knowing God, he ascends and ascends through these mental images, in an endless quest. His thirst does not come to an end. Like Kant, he may perhaps assure himself that the thirst for scientific knowledge of the phenomena can be satisfied, but that thirst for knowledge of the noumena is vain. But then he finds that he still thirsts for a third knowledge, a knowledge of whether he is right in thinking that this second thirst is vain.

As in the case of Platonism, so also here we can transform Kant's reflections into reflections about language and its rules, instead of reflections about thought and reason. According to this kind of thinking, man cannot escape the bounds of his language and its rules. He sees the world, not as it is in itself, but in the form to which it has been conformed by being seen through the windows of the categories of language with which man is supplied. In this situation, Kant's attempt to ascend to discover the limitations of thought is transformed by analogy into an attempt to ascend to see the limitations of language. The ascent takes place, not through reason that inspects reasoning, but through language that inspects language use. That is, we look at linguistics, discourse that uses language to take language as its subject matter. And to see the limitations of linguistics itself, one would use metalinguistic discourse that talks about the philosophy of linguistics. To guarantee the authenticity of metalinguistic discourse, one would need to ascend further, to meta-metalinguistic discourse that has metalinguistic discourse as its object. Again, one must ascend forever.

Evolutionary Naturalism

In the late twentieth century and the early twenty-first century, the overt cultural influence of Kant and other philosophical system-builders has perhaps waned. In the West, two dominant worldviews remain, evolutionary naturalism or materialism, and postmodern contextualism. Let us consider how they build a worldview.

First, what is the typical approach of evolutionary naturalism? Evolutionary naturalism uses the neo-Darwinian theory of evolution as a platform to propound a materialistic worldview.[11] This materialistic worldview contrasts not only with views in which God works miraculously to create some forms of life, but with the view, often called theistic evolution, that God has worked out his purposes for various forms of life using the secondary means of evolutionary gradualism, a means that he sovereignly controls. The contrast is between the work of a purposeful God on the one hand, and on the other hand the purposeless development of life in a situation in which God is absent or nonexistent. This contrast shows that evolutionary naturalism is not just a narrow scientific theory for explaining specific material phenomena, but a worldview with close ties with philosophy.[12] According to this worldview, the world consists primarily in matter and energy in interaction. There is no God or gods, and mind and consciousness have arisen without the influence or guidance of God or gods. All of life has arisen by gradualistic, chance processes that take place without any purpose to direct them.

Evolutionary naturalism, as a worldview, offers us answers to "big" questions. Who are we? Where did we come from? Who or what made us? Where are we going? What is our purpose? Which kinds of questions have answers? Naturalism, by offering answers to such questions, offers wisdom. But its answers differ from the answers in the Bible, and so it is a counterfeit wisdom.

How did naturalism achieve its wisdom? From science. It has begun with scientific analysis that enters into a minute causal, physical, material explanation of physical things and of life processes. It has ended up by concluding that the material aspect is all that there is. That itself involves a leap. How could a scientist confidently make that leap? How could he logically go from the success of science in explaining some things to the conclusion that what it does not explain does not exist? The leap is all the more problematic because in its beginnings, the procedures for science focus on the physical and the material. It follows almost by necessity that such procedures will end with only physical and material conclusions. The general nature of the conclusions follows not from the details of the investigation in the middle, but from the assumptions and commitments

11. See Vern S. Poythress, *Redeeming Science: A God-Centered Approach* (Wheaton, IL: Crossway, 2006), 79–80.
12. See ibid., 79–81, 259–83.

made at the beginning. The leap to a materialistic worldview seems to have been the result of a sleight of hand by which the materialist simply overlooks the starting assumptions.

The leap is nevertheless very appealing to many. By calling it a "leap," I have already hinted at one possible reason. This "leap" is another form of an ascent to heaven. We have a quest for wisdom. For a human quest, the most valuable wisdom would not be the minute wisdom that understands the mechanisms of chromosomal duplication in a cell, but the wisdom that understands the world as a whole—a worldview. We want transcendence. Evolutionary naturalism gives it to us, by means of the leap, the extrapolation from a narrow materialistic *procedural* focus within scientific practice to *philosophical* materialism.

The leap also needs for its success a conception of scientific law. Elsewhere I have discussed the topic of law at some length.[13] Within the worldview set forth in the Bible, "scientific law" is one aspect of God's word of providence governing the universe. God governs as a person. His faithfulness produces the regularities that scientists observe. But generally speaking, secular science today, by its training, pushes people in the direction of conceiving of scientific law as impersonal and therefore able to be perfectly mastered. As a result, there must be no exceptions to the ordinary patterns of cause and effect that we observe. The principle of no exceptions effectively allows man to master the law. He conceives of the law not as God exercising his rule through speaking (God's word of providence), but as an impersonal rule that in principle his human mind must be able to fully grasp. At the moment of full grasping, his mind has ascended to heaven, and he sees the world as it really is.

Through conceiving of the law as impersonal, the evolutionary naturalist can achieve certainty that there is no God and that everything is reducible to matter and energy. This certainty is fundamentally a mystical *religious* vision. It is religious because it involves an ascent to heaven in order mentally to grasp the law as impersonal. It is mystical because the ascent actually exceeds the bounds of scientific evidence and human consciousness. Materialist reasoning has smuggled in, from the beginning, its commitment to reducing phenomena to the material level, and only so can it achieve its goal.

13. Poythress, *Redeeming Science*, 13–31, 259–83.

Finally, this religious vision is *satisfying*, because it terminates the quest for wisdom. Wisdom has been achieved by accessing a worldview. The soundness of this wisdom is allegedly guaranteed by science. And this worldview assures those who adhere to it that they have essential guidance concerning wisdom in other spheres of life. What about wisdom in knowing moral right and wrong, wisdom in knowing God, wisdom in knowing oneself, wisdom in knowing the purpose of one's life? Such questions about wisdom either ask fruitlessly about what is illusory or have already received the essence of their answer within the worldview already in one's possession.

Unfortunately, as John Byl points out in his extended critique of naturalism, the cost to the richness of human life is very high. Byl indicates in brief how naturalism threatens to evaporate reason, mind, consciousness, mathematics, and scientific law itself into an illusion—because none of them is material.[14] Idolatrous religions devour their adherents, because ultimately counterfeits are not the same as the original, and therefore do not succeed.

VARIANT VIEWS OF RELIGIOUS "REVELATION"

Let us go on to consider some other routes in the quest for wisdom. Liberal and neorthodox theologies have often said that revelation from God takes the form of religious feeling or personal encounter. They claim that revelation cannot contain propositional content; that is, it cannot contain assertions that are true. The Bible contains many kinds of language: histories, songs, prayers, sermons, commandments, proverbs, letters. Among this variety, even a casual reading turns up many discourses that contain assertive claims, both about ordinary matters ("Crescens has gone to Galatia," 2 Tim. 4:10) and about matters of God and "religion":

But in fact Christ has been raised from the dead. (1 Cor. 15:20)

He [God] has fixed a day on which he will judge the world in righteousness by a man whom he has appointed. (Acts 17:31)

The LORD is merciful and gracious,
    slow to anger and abounding in steadfast love. (Ps. 103:8)

14. John Byl, *The Divine Challenge: On Matter, Mind, Math, and Meaning* (Edinburgh: Banner of Truth, 2004).

Liberalism and neoorthodoxy have tried to evade the obvious by claiming that the Bible is not itself revelation, but the product of the "real" revelation in religious feeling or in personal encounter. This move conveniently allows modern people to escape claims from the Bible that they do not like or do not agree with. Some people have even admitted that their view is a modern innovation, not found in the Bible. But it is alleged to be necessary to make this adjustment in the face of modern knowledge.

Modern knowledge allegedly shows that the Bible is mistaken in many of its claims. This kind of allegation deserves a detailed response, such as is found in many apologetics books written by modern evangelicals, who are familiar with the modern world and still do believe that the Bible is the Word of God.[15] We cannot pursue this line of argument here, because it would take a book in itself, and because many books have already been written on the subject.

But we can say something about another aspect of liberalism and neoorthodoxy, namely, their positive claims about the nature of revelation. Where do these claims come from? To know the nature of revelation is tied closely together with knowing about the God or gods who can give such revelation. It is a claim to transcendent wisdom or insight. Liberalism and neoorthodoxy thus have their own transcendent claims, and these claims presuppose that the claimant has been able to "ascend to heaven." But if, as liberalism asserts, religion is the product of human religious feelings, it never really rises to heaven.

Religious feelings have been variously interpreted. Indeed, evangelicals who believe the Bible have interpreted their own feelings in a manner consistent with *their* beliefs that the Bible is actually the Word of God. So liberals have no firm ground for a transcendent claim to the contrary.

The situation is a little different for the neoorthodox. They say that we can have a nonpropositional "personal encounter" with God. Could neoorthodox theology, and in particular its theology of revelation, be built on such a personal encounter? But unfortunately the encounter is nonpropositional. So who is to say that neoorthodox interpretation of it is any

---

15. See, in particular, Kenneth D. Boa and Robert M. Bowman Jr., *Faith Has Its Reasons: Integrative Approaches to Defending the Christian Faith*, 2nd ed. (Waynesboro, GA: Paternoster, 2005), which refers to a large number of apologetic works in a variety of traditions. I belong to the tradition of Cornelius Van Til (see *Defense of the Faith*), which acknowledges value in other traditions but also claims that at times they have been inconsistent and have conceded too much to the power of man's would-be autonomous reason.

better than any other? Neoorthodox theology has often attempted to derive its view of revelation from the Bible itself. But in actuality the Bible fights against such an interpretation, as John Frame's articles on neoorthodoxy have shown.[16]

If neoorthodoxy succeeded by using the Bible itself, it *would* be using a legitimate transcendent source of wisdom. It would have "ascended to heaven," not by human power but by being taught by God. The result would, however, still be paradoxical, because neoorthodoxy would have been taught by God the propositional truth that it is impossible to be taught by God in propositional truths.

In fact, an inspection of affinities in the history of ideas shows relationships between both classical liberalism and neoorthodoxy on the one hand, and Kantian philosophy on the other. Kant allegedly has shown that a direct revelation from God into the time and space world of phenomena is impossible. A revelation such as God speaking from the top of Mount Sinai as recorded in Exodus 19 is supposed to be impossible.[17] Kant says that revelation cannot be of the character that simple Bible readers of previous centuries thought it to be. So, in the light of Kant's alleged transcendent wisdom, the reformulations undertaken by liberalism and neoorthodoxy were to be expected. They are just as much counterfeits as was Kant's original vision.

LOGICAL POSITIVISM

Next, consider logical positivism (also called logical empiricism). Logical positivism saw the rigor of symbolic logic, along with the rigor of mathematics and the lesser rigor in hard sciences, as the model for all truth. It said that only two kinds of propositions had cognitive meaning and truth

---

16. John M. Frame, "God and Biblical Language: Transcendence and Immanence," in *God's Inerrant Word*, ed. John Warwick Montgomery (Minneapolis, MN: Bethany Fellowship, 1974), 159–77; Frame, "Scripture Speaks for Itself," ibid., 178–200.

17. A more sophisticated Kantianism might claim not that the Mount Sinai theophany is literally impossible, but rather that it is not direct revelation, because it is a phenomenon, and as such must still be subjected to the critical faculties of human reason as the arbiter of religious claims. Using the word "must" is tantamount to saying that man must insist on being absolute lord of his ideas even when, to do so, he must defy the most overt and overwhelming manifestation of God. In other words, man must seek Satanic autonomy no matter what.

value, namely tautologies and empirically verifiable statements. All other propositions had only "emotive" significance.

Tautologies are statements that can be seen to be true by virtue of an inspection of their meaning: "A is A"; "What is white is white"; and "Bachelors are unmarried." Empirically verifiable statements are statements whose truth can be checked out by empirical means, by inspecting or measuring something within the environment (akin to Kant's phenomenal realm). Thus, "The moon is made of green cheese" is empirically verifiable and false. "An apple seed can be planted and sometimes grows into an apple tree" is empirically verifiable and true. "Being negates itself" (a famous statement from Heidegger) is not empirically verifiable.

Logical positivism blossomed and flourished for a while, especially among people who admired the rigor of science and who felt impatient or skeptical about general philosophical and religious statements ("God is love"). It is a significant movement from the point of view of language, because it was hoping to clean up language and concentrate on the proper and fruitful uses of language for empirical science, while discarding the allegedly fruitless and meaningless uses having to do with philosophy, metaphysics, and religion.

Yet the logical positivism movement died because of its internal problems. Consider its fundamental thesis:

> A statement is cognitively meaningful only if it is either tautologous or empirically verifiable.

Is this thesis a tautology? It can only be so if the expression "cognitively meaningful" has already been secretly redefined to *mean* "tautologous or empirically verifiable," in which case it is trivially true. But then it is useless for the practical task of assigning *genuine* meaning (as opposed to its own hothouse definition of meaning). Or is the thesis empirically verifiable? No, because it is a claim about cognitive meaning, not about the phenomenal world. One cannot specify a series of scientific procedures that would lead to a definitive test of its truthfulness.

So now apply the thesis to itself:

> The thesis of logical positivism is cognitively meaningful only if it is either tautologous or empirically verifiable.

Since the thesis is neither tautologous nor empirically verifiable, it is not cognitively meaningful. Hence the thesis has destroyed its own meaning, and the movement of logical positivism cannot be sustained.

In looking back over the collapse of logical positivism, one can see the theme of ascent to heaven. The central thesis, the thesis about tautology and verifiability, offered a seemingly universal vision about the nature of meaning. But it had to exceed its own bounds—it had to ascend to heaven—in order to obtain this vision. It was in fact a kind of substitute religion. It declared, on the basis of transcendent insight into the nature of truth and verifiability, that all conventional religions and philosophies were meaningless. With that declaration it offered to its adherents transcendent wisdom, and freed them from the alleged deceits of conventional religion. But in the long run it undermined itself, since it could give no coherent account of its access to this heavenly vision.

Postmodern Contextualism

We may also use the analogy of ascent to heaven to understand one aspect of postmodern contextualism. By postmodernist contextualism I mean the skeptical and pragmatic views that think the language and culture in which we are immersed prevent us from accessing reality, or at least prevent us from being certain about truth. The skepticism and uncertainty in contextualism typically build on insights about the influence of language and culture. The influence of culture is expounded particularly in the tradition of the sociology of knowledge.[18] The influence of language is discussed in many contexts. One main line of influence comes from linguistics through French structuralism into deconstruction.[19]

Postmodern contextualism uses the analysis from linguistics and structuralism in order to become aware of the limits of language and the instabilities of meaning. The instabilities are related to the fact that meaning

18. See, e.g., Peter L. Berger and Thomas Luckmann, *The Social Construction of Reality: A Treatise in the Sociology of Knowledge* (Garden City, NY: Doubleday, 1967).

19. For an introduction to postmodernism, see Heath White, *Postmodernism 101: A First Course for the Curious Christian* (Grand Rapids: Brazos, 2006).

is largely constituted by a system of relations within the language system, relations with other elements of meaning, whose meaning is in turn determined by a system of relations, and so on indefinitely.

Contextualism uses "scientific" approaches to language and culture in order to rise to a general view of the function of language and culture. This general view offers a transcendent insight into the limitations of meaning. One climbs up to this insight through scientific analysis of meaning. Once one has completed the climb, one realizes that all language, even the language used in scientific analysis, has instabilities.

Something akin to this situation is described by Ludwig Wittgenstein in his work *Tractatus Logico-Philosophicus*:

> My propositions are elucidatory in this way: he who understands me finally recognizes them as senseless, when he has climbed out through them, on them, over them. (He must so to speak throw away the ladder, after he has climbed up on it.)
>
> He must surmount these propositions; then he sees the world rightly.
>
> Whereof one cannot speak, thereof one must be silent.[20]

In the present case, the "ladder" consists in the social sciences. One climbs on their conclusions. When one has attained the postmodern insight, one "sees the world rightly." Then he also sees that the social sciences are culturally conditioned human opinion. He "throws away the ladder." This achievement is akin to a *religious* vision, not only in its move to transcendence, but in its essential inexpressibility. The limitations of language meanings imply that the vision cannot be made transparent.

Shortly before the analogy concerning the ladder that one throws away after climbing it, Wittgenstein has some telling remarks:

> 6.432 *How* the world is [the facts open to empirical observation], is completely indifferent for what is higher. God does not reveal himself *in* the world. . . .

20. Ludwig Wittgenstein, *Tractatus Logico-Philosophicus* (London: Routledge & Kegan Paul, 1922), 189, propositions 6.54 and 7. I am, of course, using Wittgenstein's picture, but not the specific application that he gave to it.

6.45 The contemplation of the world sub specie aeterni is its contemplation as a limited whole.

The feeling of the world as a limited whole is the mystical feeling. . . .

6.522 There is indeed the inexpressible. This *shows* itself; it is the mystical.[21]

The vision of the whole, which shows the limits of language, is not only inexpressible but "mystical," and is akin to a vision from God's point of view. In the *Tractatus Logico-Philosophicus*, Wittgenstein thought that he had achieved such a vision through indirect expression about the nature of the ideal, logical language. But he later became dissatisfied with this solution and went on to analyze the nature of ordinary language, which he recognized was richer than the formerly envisioned logical ideal. The earlier Wittgenstein had a position similar to logical positivism, and fell into a similar pattern of claiming a transcendent understanding of the limits of language. The later Wittgenstein abandoned the logical ideal, but he did not give up the idea of analyzing the limits of language (in this case, ordinary language) in the hope of dissolving philosophical problems by showing that they transgressed the bounds.

Both of these moves show similarities to postmodern contextualism, in that they hope to use observations about language in order eventually to understand the limits of access to truth. The lure of transcendence and of "mystical" vision remains in both. The quest is in the end religious, even if it is no longer a quest to know "God" as traditionally conceived. Buddhism, remember, also has a quest: not to know God (Buddhism maintains that there is no personal Absolute) but to know final reality, and in knowing to dissolve the restlessness of the questing mind.[22]

21. Wittgenstein, *Tractatus*, 187.

22. Richard Rorty, for example, proposes to find rest, or at least the best way to live life, in the acceptance of the nonexistence of God and the nonexistence of transcendent truth: "To drop the idea of languages as representations, and to be thoroughly Wittgensteinian in our approach to language, would be to de-divinize the world. Only if we do that can we fully accept the argument I offered earlier—the argument that since truth is a property of sentences, since sentences are dependent for their existence upon vocabularies, and since vocabularies are made by human beings, so are truths" (Rorty, *Contingency, Irony, and Solidarity*, 21). Rorty's rhetoric offers us a proposed answer to ultimate questions, and therefore includes a promise of transcendent wisdom.

HOW TO ANSWER RESTLESSNESS

In the end, there are only two options. First, one may find rest in submitting to God. "You have formed us for Yourself, and our hearts are restless till they find rest in You."[23] Or, second, one may continue in the autonomous quest to which the serpent invited mankind.

In the second option, one tries to ascend to heaven by oneself, autonomously. Many counterfeit gods offer themselves as allegedly satisfying substitutes for the true God. But in the end they fail if one gives oneself over to them.

Underneath them all remains one final "god," namely the self, man himself, who aspires to "be like God." In this final "quest," man's mind will be the limits of his self-constructed world, either the world of the early Wittgenstein's atomic empirical facts, or the world that we form for ourselves through the power of language, or the mystical world of Buddhist insight that has seen through the illusion of both the phenomenal world and the world of ordinary thought. One thinks one has arrived at transcendent wisdom.

In ordinary consciousness, a human person experiences limits in his senses, in his knowledge, and in his ability to hold in mind many meanings simultaneously. He is confronted at every moment with his finiteness. He is not God. If he nevertheless persists in the delusion that he is the ultimate arbiter, he makes himself god. Then he forces himself to believe that his mind is the mind of god, and identical with reality. Thus, above or below or within the level of ordinary consciousness, the observer is identical with reality. This identity can take a more Kantian form, in which one claims that the external world is inaccessible, so that in practice one is living in the mental world that one claims is self-constructed. Or it can take a mystical monist form, in which one thinks that one's mind in essence is one with the All. In their focus on the alleged ultimacy of the human mind, the two are more akin than one might think.

For all its apparent secularism and easy tolerance for religious differences, postmodern contextualism cannot evade the essentially religious quest of the restless mind. What is reality, and what can we know about it? Contextualists offer a fundamental vision of reality that limits and reconfig-

---

23. Updated language, from St. Augustin, *The Confessions of St. Augustin*, 1.1.1, in Philip Schaff, ed., *A Select Library of the Nicene and Post-Nicene Fathers of the Christian Church* (Grand Rapids: Eerdmans, 1979), 1:45.

ures the role of traditional religions. That looks secularist in spirit. What is not so obvious is that this vision has a fundamental affinity with mysticism. While pretending to be secular, it offers a religious answer to a religious longing, the longing for transcendent wisdom.

Contextualists may appear to be breezily tolerant of all sorts of religious views, provided that these views keep themselves in their assigned place. That is, the religious viewpoints are to be viewed as finite cultural viewpoints under the hegemony of multicultural tolerance. Tolerance demotes religions from their leading role in premodern cultures to an ancillary role as merely one colorful aspect of culture.

Traditional religions are thus given their place. And ruling over them all is a secularism that privatizes and tames the potency of religion, which otherwise would stir up dangerous absolutist and intolerant claims. This secularism thinks it knows the proper role for traditional religions. And how does it know? Only because it has first secured itself: it has assured itself that no religion can actually access transcendent truth (because of the limits of languages and cultures). This knowledge is the contextualist's own claim to transcendence.

It is mystical, in that it cannot directly reveal itself in words, which are within the limits of language. But it is absolute (as the contextualist secretly assures himself). It gives "rest" by assuring the mind that there is nothing to know beyond its own self-constructed and language-constructed world. An early Wittgenstein aphorism may express it: "6.521 The solution of the problem of life is seen in the vanishing of this problem."[24] That aphorism is right next to the aphorism 6.522: "There is indeed the inexpressible. This *shows* itself; it is the mystical."

COUNTERFEITS DEPENDING ON TRUTH

Many false routes for ascending to heaven offer themselves. They are counterfeits. But counterfeits are always counterfeits of the truth. Each of the routes discussed above—and others that we might add—is not merely a false route, but a route containing within itself many individual insights, many partial truths. Without dependence on truth, these routes would not offer the least attraction. The challenge, then, is not merely to discern

---

24. Wittgenstein, *Tractatus*, 6.521, 187.

the difference between true and counterfeit, but to discern even within a counterfeit its dependence on truth.

For instance, in the twentieth century not only logical positivists but also Martin Heidegger, post-Wittgensteinian ordinary-language philosophy, and some postmodernists have looked at language as a key to transcendent wisdom. And in one sense they are right. God created and governs the world through speaking. If indeed philosophers could get to the bottom of language, they would understand everything important about the world, because they would understand God's language ruling the world. In fact, they would understand God himself. They would understand the Word, the Second Person of the Trinity.

Unfortunately, that is not the way it has turned out. The philosophers' search after wisdom shows not only a profound insight into the fact that language is a fruitful source of wisdom, but also a profound failure. Which of the philosophers has managed to become aware of the true God, and his profound presence in language? No, God is not found through human wisdom. Rather, God chooses to find out and reverse human rebellion through the "folly" of the cross (1 Cor. 1:18–25):

> Where is the one who is wise? Where is the scribe? Where is the debater of this age? Has not God made foolish the wisdom of the world? For since, in the wisdom of God, the world did not know God *through wisdom*, it pleased God through the folly of what we preach to save those who believe. (1 Cor. 1:20–21)

4

Biblical-Theological
Ruminations on Psalm 1

D. A. CARSON

RECENT DECADES have witnessed an extraordinary amount of work on the way the New Testament quotes the Old. Within confessional scholarship, this work has been wedded to a desire to think through systematically and in detail what we mean when we speak of christological readings of the Old Testament or, otherwise put, how we justify Christ-centered preaching from the entire canon—genuinely grounded in the text of Scripture. In this essay I wish to select one Old Testament passage, Psalm 1, and use it as a springboard to canvass some of the hermeneutical options in order to arrive at a slight tweaking of the options. I shall avoid unnecessary technical discussion, this essay being rather more a rumination than a technical argument. Despite its limitations, I am delighted to offer it in honor of Richard Gaffin, whose scholarly and pastoral interests have encompassed both testaments, substantial questions surrounding the field of hermeneutics, the unity of the canon, and the interplay between responsible exegesis and responsible dogmatics.

Psalm 1

The place to begin is with a brief reminder of what Psalm 1 says, of how it is put together. It offers a contrast between the righteous and the unrighteous. The righteous are described in verses 1–3, the unrighteous in verses 4–5, and a summarizing contrast closes the psalm in verse 6. The first unit, where the righteous are described, depicts them negatively in verse 1, positively in verse 2, and metaphorically in verse 3.

Negatively, then, the righteous do *not* do certain things: "Blessed is the man who does *not* walk in the counsel of the wicked, or stand in the way of sinners, or sit in the seat of mockers." The person who walks (a common metaphor to describe one's behavior, one's ethical life) in the counsel of the wicked is listening to the wrong counselor: the frame of reference is wrong, the values are wrong, the priorities are wrong. Continuing in such counsel can have only one result: the person so influenced will "stand in the way of sinners." That is simultaneously an accurate formal translation of the Hebrew and a thoroughly bad translation (even though it is adopted almost universally; the exception is the NET Bible, "or stand in the pathway with sinners"). In English, "to stand in someone's way" means "to hinder someone," in some sense to block him or her. One thinks of Robin Hood and Little John on the bridge: one of them will end up in the stream. In Hebrew, however, "to stand in someone's way" means to do what he does, to act indistinguishably from him—or, as we might say in North America, to walk in his moccasins. The person who constantly walks in the counsel of the wicked will do wickedness, of course, and sooner or later he will *be* wicked in the same way that the person who is giving the advice is wicked. It is painfully easy to slide into the third line: he now sits "in the seat of mockers." No longer is it sufficient to do your own thing, even if God calls it wicked; now you must sneer condescendingly at those who do not join you in this wickedness. So here in verse 1, then, we find what a righteous person is *not* like. The righteous person is described negatively.

If the antithetic parallelism between verse 1 and verse 2 had been tight, one might have expected the latter, which describes the righteous person *positively*, to offer a straightforward formal antithesis: "Blessed, rather, is the man who walks in the counsel of the righteous, who stands in the way of those who do good, and who sits in the seat of the praising." Instead, it offers a conceptual antithesis, one simple point—for if that point is carefully observed, everything changes, and a sharp conceptual antithesis is established with verse 1: "But his delight is in the law of the LORD, and on his law he meditates day and night" (1:2).

Here is the alternative counsel to the counsel of the wicked. It is not enough simply to become familiar with "the law of the LORD"; rather, it must be our "delight," the content on which a person "meditates day and night." If what the Lord teaches (for *Torah* is better rendered "teaching" or "instruction" than "law") is cherished with delight, and if it becomes the substance of our constant thought, then transparently our behavior will be transformed: we will walk in the way of the Lord. Instead of sliding into sneering condescension, our response will be joyful faith, obedience, and praise.

Passages either commending or exemplifying this positive description of the righteous are many—i.e., passages that make the controlling criterion of the righteous a passionate devotion to the Word of God. Before there is a king in Israel, Moses gives some instruction as to that king's priorities:

> When he takes the throne of his kingdom, he is to write for himself on a scroll a copy of this law, taken from that of the priests, who are Levites. It is to be with him, and he is to read it all the days of his life so that he may learn to revere the LORD his God and follow carefully all the words of this law and these decrees and not consider himself better than his brothers and turn from the law to the right or to the left. Then he and his descendants will reign a long time over his kingdom in Israel. (Deut. 17:18–20)

So the new man comes to the throne: What is his first task? Audit the books of his predecessor? Make sure all the cabinet positions are filled? Review the military? No, his first task is to copy out, longhand, the words of "this law"—apparently referring either to Deuteronomy or, conceivably, to the entire Mosaic code. This is not a matter of downloading text from the Internet to a hard drive without it passing through anyone's brain. The copy is to be so carefully executed that it becomes the king's own copy, which he is then to read every day so as to learn to revere the Lord his God and all his words, and not become puffed up and think himself better than his peers. If only these three verses had been obeyed, all of Old Testament history would have been different. For the steady diet of *this* kind of counsel produces radically different conduct and attitude, compared

117

with what the counsel of the wicked produces. Concretely, when Joshua comes to power, he is told, "Do not let this Book of the Law depart from your mouth; meditate on it day and night, so that you may be careful to do everything written in it. Then you will be prosperous and successful" (Josh. 1:8). One recalls the theme of Psalm 119; one thinks of Jesus' prayer on the night he was betrayed: "Sanctify them by the truth; your word is truth" (John 17:17). A professor long since retired from Trinity Evangelical Divinity School was prone to say, "You are not what you think you are, but what you think, you are": that is what Psalm 1:2 presupposes. Similarly, when Paul wants his Roman readers not to be conformed to the world, he recognizes that the proper antidote to such conformity is transformation by the renewing of the mind (Rom. 12:1–2).

The righteous person described negatively in verse 1 and positively in verse 2 is described *metaphorically* in verse 3: "He is like a tree planted by streams of water, which yields its fruit in season and whose leaf does not wither. Whatever he does prospers." Israel is a semi-arid land. Many streams are intermittent, leaving empty *wadis* in the dry season (akin to *arroyos* in the American Southwest). During the dry season the vegetation either dies or looks dead. But the tree in verse 3 is not a wild specimen that has casually sprung up next to a *wadi* that is usually dry. Far from it: this tree has been carefully "planted" at a confluence of streams, ensuring a steady water supply. The result is that its "leaf does not wither"; equally delightful is the fact that it "yields its fruit in season." The last line summarizes the man who is like such a tree: "Whatever he does prospers." This is not sanction for today's "prosperity gospel." Rather, it is an extension of the watered-tree metaphor: no matter the oppressions of life, understood within the metaphor as dry seasons and drought, the abundance of the fresh water ensures that the tree prospers. And if verses 2 and 3 are conceptually connected, the supply of "water" that the psalmist has in mind for the righteous person is the Word of God, the *Torah*, the law.

Similar uses of the metaphor of the well-watered tree are not uncommon in the Old Testament. For instance (emphasis added):

This is what the LORD says:
"Cursed is the one who trusts in man,
    who depends on flesh for his strength
    and whose heart turns away from the LORD.

He will be like a bush in the wastelands;
    he will not see *prosperity* when it comes.
He will dwell in the parched places of the desert,
    in a salt land where no one lives.

"But blessed is the man who trusts in the LORD,
    whose confidence is in him.
He will be like a tree planted by the water
    that sends out its roots by the stream.
It does not fear when heat comes;
    its leaves are always green.
It has no worries in a year of drought
    and never fails to bear fruit." (Jer. 17:5–8)

So the righteous person is described negatively (v. 1), positively (v. 2), and metaphorically (v. 3). The second part of the psalm (vv. 4–5) begins with a strong negation. One might render the first line, "Not so the wicked, not so!" It is as if anything of significance that can be said of the righteous must be denied with respect to the wicked. Do the righteous avoid walking in the counsel of the wicked? Transparently, "Not so the wicked" themselves. Do the righteous refuse to stand in the way of sinners? Not so the wicked, not so! Do the righteous manage not to sit in the seat of mockers? Not so the wicked, not so! Do the righteous delight in the law of the Lord, and meditate on it day and night? Not so the wicked, not so! Can the righteous be likened to a copiously watered tree that always shows signs of vitality and that brings forth its fruit in season, and that prospers even in a time of drought? Not so the wicked, not so!

Well, what *are* they like, then? "They are like chaff that the wind blows away" (v. 4). The contrast with the watered tree (the righteous) is startling: unlike the tree, chaff is rootless, lifeless, fruitless, worthless, unstable, insignificant, not enduring. In case we do not pick up on the metaphor, the psalmist spells out the results: "Therefore the wicked will not stand in the judgment, nor sinners in the assembly of the righteous" (v. 5). The same point is frequently made in the Scriptures (e.g., Isa. 2:12–21; 1 Cor. 3:12–13; 2 Thess. 1:8–10a).

The psalm ends with a summarizing contrast: "For the LORD watches over the way of the righteous, but the way of the wicked will perish" (v. 6). Strictly speaking, this final contrast is not between the righteous and the wicked, but between the *way* of the righteous and the *way* of the wicked. Not only will the wicked perish, but their *way* will, too. Fifty billion years into eternity (if one may speak of eternity in the categories of time), no one will be celebrating the ways of Pol Pot, Adolf Hitler, Genghis Khan, Joseph Stalin, and a host of others like them. And if there is awareness of the smoke of Babylon's destruction rising "for ever and ever" (Rev. 19:3), it is only because such awareness serves to underscore the utter faithfulness and triumph of God. The way of Babylon is destroyed forever. But every cup of cold water given in the name of the Lord will still be celebrated, for "the LORD watches over the way of the righteous"—he acknowledges it as his and protects it. For this Lord is the God behind his word (v. 2), which has established the "way" of the righteous.

Here, then, is a summary of what Psalm 1 says. It lays out two ways to live, and there is no third.

SOME HERMENEUTICAL OPTIONS

Not all of the options sketched in the following pages are mutually exclusive. Here they are distinguished so as to contribute to clear thinking.

(1) Some read Psalm 1 more or less as I have just outlined it, and apply it directly and in its own moralizing categories to Christians in the twenty-first century. After all, Paul reminds us that all Scripture is profitable for instruction in righteousness (2 Tim. 3:16). Transparently, it is important for Christians to avoid the advice of wicked people, to delight in the Word of God, to pursue the way of the Lord, and so forth. On the eternal scale, the psalmist surely has it right: the unrighteous will not stand in the assembly of the righteous, and God "watches over" or "owns" only the way of the righteous.

Yet how does such a reading ever become integrated with the gospel? Is the final distinction between the righteous and the wicked to be determined by degree of conformity to *Torah*? Moreover, isn't the absolute polarity of the psalm just a tad unrealistic and more than a little frightening—unrealistic because countless millions of Christians fit into neither of the psalm's polarities but somewhere on a spectrum between the two, and frightening because the judgment imposed on the failure to live under the aegis of the psalm's positive pole is unrelenting and catastrophic—damnation by

God? One intrinsically feels that the psalm *ought* to guide our priorities, yet thoughtful and rigorous application of this psalm to our lives may engender despair rather than moral incentive.

(2) It helps to remember considerations of literary genre. Most commentators classify this as a wisdom psalm. The genre of wisdom literature is extraordinarily multi-faceted, but one important characteristic of much of it is its love of absolute polarities. In Proverbs, one is either honoring Lady Wisdom or being seduced by Dame Folly: no place is given for inconsistent behavior that follows now one, now the other, or that seems to follow the one in some domains of life and the other in the remaining domains. Wisdom literature sets out the ideal, principled answer, without footnotes or caveats. "Train a child in the way he should go, and when he is old he will not turn from it" (Prov. 22:6): if we may sidestep for the moment the challenging question about what is meant by "the way" in this passage, most of us eventually recognize that this is deeply principled advice. To treat this proverb as an unqualified promise from the sovereign God finally means that every instance of every child who ever goes astray must be charged directly to the parents. If that is what Scripture teaches, so be it; if that is not quite what Scripture teaches, those who claim that it is are imposing additional pain on some parents who are already facing pain enough. Rapid canvassing of other proverbs quickly discloses that any attempt to read some of them in absolute guise leads to ridiculous conclusions. "Do not answer a fool according to his folly," Proverbs 26:4 tells us, only to be answered by Proverbs 26:5: "Answer a fool according to his folly." Obviously, neither can properly be taken as an absolute injunction. When, then, should one take precedence over the other? One gains some insight by reflecting on the second line of each verse: "Do not answer a fool according to his folly, *or you will be like him yourself*. Answer a fool according to his folly, *or he will be wise in his own eyes*." Still, when does one purpose take precedence over the other? Judgment and discernment are required to make faithful use of these proverbs.

Proverbs (and related forms of wisdom literature) tend to give us the large principles that underlie life in God's universe. The importance of bringing up our children in the nurture and admonition of the Lord must not be gainsaid. But that is a little different from thinking that in one proverb God has given us an exhaustive and exclusive assignment of praise and blame in child-rearing.

Two further pieces of biblical data must enter our reflections at this point.

First, wisdom is not the only genre found in Scripture. Narrative is much more likely to provide a nuanced portrait of a person's strengths and weaknesses, graces and foibles, triumphs and failures. Narrative brings us a David who is a man after God's own heart, but who sins deeply in the matter of Bathsheba and related events (2 Sam. 11–12), in the counting of the people (2 Sam. 24), and in his failure to discipline Amnon (2 Sam. 13:21–22). If one were to read wisdom literature only, such moral complexity and inconsistency would be unthinkable. So the question becomes, How does one properly integrate the somewhat divergent emphases that spring from the Bible's differing literary genres?

Second, one cannot overlook that the canonical Gospels often present Jesus as the New Testament's most illustrious wisdom preacher. He refuses to be reduced to a single literary genre, of course: what is reported of his teaching comes in narratives (parables), extended exchanges, beatitudes, substantial interpretations/expositions of Old Testament texts, enigmatic and symbol-laden explanation, apocalyptic descriptions of the end, and much more. But among these forms is wisdom. Notably, readers come to the end of the Sermon on the Mount to find Jesus confronting them with simple and absolute polarities. Either we enter through the small gate and walk the narrow way that leads to life, or we walk through the wide gate and take the broad path that leads to destruction. Like Psalm 1, there is no third choice. Either we build our houses on solid rock that enables them to withstand the fiercest storms, or we build them on sand, and they are swept away. Hard-pan clay is not an option—something that withstands, say, most storms but perhaps not all. Either the tree brings forth good fruit or it brings forth bad fruit: it never brings forth so-so fruit. In short, Jesus often presents the options in the starkest polarities characteristic of wisdom literature—yet this same Jesus shows himself to be wonderfully compassionate to the broken and the despised. He tells the story of the Pharisee and the tax collector to depict something else again: contrition is more important than the most disciplined human conformity to the law (Luke 18:9–14—a lesson also learned by the apostle Paul: cf. Phil. 3:4–11). This means that the challenge of integrating Psalm 1 with other strands of Scripture is part and parcel of the challenge of integrating the complex and diverse strands within the teaching of the Lord Jesus himself. In the same way, responsible reading of Psalm 1 *on its own terms* must be accompanied by responsible reading of Psalm 1 *within the biblical context.* Consideration of the literary genre of the psalm helps us with the former, but contributes to the latter only by highlighting the diversity found within the canon, rather than by signaling what responsible canonical theology might look like.

(3) This third option is a slightly more sophisticated form of the first. We begin by reminding ourselves that New Testament writers sometimes cite Old Testament narrative texts to extract a moralizing principle. For example, both 1 Corinthians 10:1–13 and Hebrews 3:7–19 refer to the tragic years of the Israelites' wilderness wanderings in order to press the conclusion that good beginnings are not enough: one must display perseverance in faith and obedience to receive the promised inheritance. If someone were to object that this is a moralizing reading of a *narrative* text, it is easy enough to think of similar connections being made across the testaments using other literary genres. James 4:6, for instance, quotes Proverbs 3:34: "But he gives us more grace. That is why Scripture says: 'God opposes the proud but shows favor to the humble and oppressed'" (TNIV). The Letter of James is noted for its wisdom characteristics, and in this passage James cites an Old Testament wisdom book to establish what is a theistic moralizing argument—and of course there are many other examples (e.g., 1 Peter 3:10–12, citing Ps. 34:12–16). By extension, then, why not read Psalm 1 the same way? Are there not numerous instances in which the "laws" of the Old Testament—understood, for the moment, as God's demands on his image-bearers—are reiterated in the New? Adultery is condoned in neither testament; the obligation to honor one's parents is established in both testaments; the demand to love one's neighbor is picked up in the New, citing the Old. So why should today's Christians who read Psalm 1 not apply it to themselves as an ongoing demand, much like other Old Testament demands that continue under the new covenant?

At some level, that is surely right. Nevertheless, at least some of the New Testament passages under review display something a little more complicated than moralizing application. Both 1 Corinthians 10:1–13 and Hebrews 3:7–18, referred to above, presuppose some kind of typology between the people of the old covenant and the people of the new, if their moralizing lesson about perseverance is to have any bite. Moreover, the former includes the extraordinary "rock" typology, and the latter sets the stage for a complex salvation-historical reflection on the trajectory of "rest" within the Old Testament, and the direction in which it points forward to still greater rest (on which more below). Above all, like the first option, this third one does not in itself give us much insight on how to integrate the psalm with the gospel.

(4) Some important suggestions have been made in the past, of course, about how to effect this integration. Historical theology reminds us that the challenges of integrating the disparate strands of Scripture were perceived long before the twentieth and twenty-first centuries. For instance, if one were to ask Puritan divines what is in the Bible, they would most likely answer with the summary, "Law, gospel, and illustrations of both." Lutheran theologians would rejoice at the formulation, of course, though their developed synthesis would not include the "third use of the law" that the Puritans inherited from Calvin. For both groups, the words "law" and "gospel" are "thick" expressions, and the corresponding systematic theologies are not easily summarized in a sentence or two.

Transparently there is something of both demand and promise in the text of Psalm 1. Logically it is easy to factor the psalm's content into such categories. But one must at least ask whether such categories constrained the thinking of the psalmist. At what point do categories derived from theological understanding developed much later in the history of the church begin to sound anachronistic if they are applied too early? Moreover, if one attempts to salvage the argument by appealing rather quickly to God's intentions in the passage (as measured by one's interpretation of God's intentions gleaned from the Bible as a whole, as interpreted by theologians a millennium and a half later!), do we not have to ask exactly how God's intentions in any particular biblical text correspond to the human author's intentions? Is there not at least some danger in appealing to a bottomless chasm between the notion of divine authorial intent and the notion of the authorial intent of the human author? Otherwise put, is there not at least some danger in assigning this much hermeneutical authority to one's systematic theology when it comes to the exegesis of individual biblical texts? This is not to question the legitimacy—indeed, the unavoidability—of allowing one's understanding of the whole to enjoy an important role in the interpretation of the part. At what juncture, however, does such an appeal slide toward the mere domestication of the part?

(5) Some voices, especially popular ones, interested as they are in preaching Christ from the whole Bible, infer that Psalm 1 is really describing Jesus Christ. He alone is the man who does not walk in the counsel of the wicked, who delights in the law of the Lord, and so forth. According to these voices, failure to preach Psalm 1 in this way is indicative of a deep failure to preach Christ from the whole Bible.

I have enormous sympathy with efforts to preach Christ from all the Scriptures. The most responsible of such efforts, however, depend on the legitimacy of complex (and textually authenticated) typologies—I wish I could spend fifteen or twenty pages on an introduction to the use of Psalm 110 in the New Testament—or on about twenty biblical-theological strands that run through the Scriptures (e.g., temple, high priest, sacrificial system, creation, kingship, covenant, and so forth), rather than on a kind of homiletical fiat that simply declares a particular passage is talking explicitly about Jesus. Of course, if one were to argue that, in the light of all of Scripture, the only perfect human being this side of the fall is the Lord Jesus, and therefore Psalm 1 is most perfectly mirrored in him, one would not find strident demurral from most Christians. But that is a little different from saying that when he penned the lines of Psalm 1, the psalmist had the ultimate Messiah in mind, fully intending that his psalm be read eschatologically and christologically. Surely Christian readers are right to look for clear *textual* markers before they affirm such connections in such straightforward claims about the psalm's referents.

(6) There is ample evidence that parts of the New Testament are related to the Old as fulfillment to promise. Paul makes much of these connections, for instance, in his treatment of the Abrahamic covenant (Gal. 3); Hebrews does something similar with its reading of the promise of a new covenant (Heb. 8:7–13; 10:15–18), and so does Matthew with the request to ascertain the birthplace of the coming "shepherd of my people Israel" (Matt. 2:3–6; Mic. 5:2). But there is no textual evidence, whether in the Old Testament or the New, that Psalm 1 should be read as a straightforward promise whose ultimate significance is in the fulfillment to which it points.

(7) Nevertheless the categories of promise and fulfillment easily slide into the subtler streams of typology. Many of the claims by New Testament writers to the effect that Jesus, and many of the events that befall him,

are "fulfillments" of Old Testament texts depend on typological connections—the "Out of Egypt I called my son" fulfillment (Matt. 2:15; cf. Hos. 11:1), for instance, which depends on an Israel/Christ typology (cf. also Matt. 4:1–11), or the many instances of Davidic typology controlling New Testament Christology, or the ease with which categories applied to Israel as the locus of the old covenant people of God are applied to the church as the new covenant people of God (e.g., 1 Peter 2:9).

Debates continue as to whether such typologies should be seen as properly predictive, in the sense that the human authors understood that what they were writing had an anticipatory element that needed to be fulfilled in the future. At the risk of generalization, one can distinguish three positions (though the reality is more like a spectrum):

(a) Some think that these so-called typological trajectories are nothing more than instances of exegetically indefensible proof-texting, the types being "discovered" after the fact with no intrinsic value other than the value of unveiling how the earliest Christians abused and misapplied their sacred texts (e.g., Barnabas Lindars).

(b) Some think that although the human authors of the Old Testament saw no anticipatory element in the typological trajectories they were creating—indeed, they would not have understood them to be what we mean by "typological trajectories"—nevertheless God did so understand them, and disclosed their true meaning to the heirs of the new covenant. This preserves the unity of the canon, but the price is fairly steep: the wider the hiatus between divine authorial intent and human authorial intent, the harder it is to avoid the conclusion that the anticipatory element in Old Testament types is not really there in the text, but only, somehow, in the mind of God. The first Christians "found" the types in the text only *after* they came to Christian convictions about who Jesus is, what he accomplished on the cross, the cruciality of the resurrection, the work of the Spirit, and the true locus of the people of God. This second group of interpreters is distinguished from the first in that it believes this meaning really is of God, and can be seen to be there, even if only after the fact.

(c) Still others argue that there is little evidence in the texts to support the view that the *first* contributors to a typological trajectory would have seen that they were contributing to a typology, but that over the centuries during which the Old Testament documents were written the *later* contributors to at least some typologies would have seen that they were part of a stream, a trajectory that was in some sense pointing forward, even if they still had only very unclear ideas of what it was that was being anticipated. This position implies that the chasm between what God intends by the text (including a predictive element) and what the human authors intend (without a predictive element) is true only at the beginning of a trajectory: as the trajectory unfolds, the chasm narrows. Even so, this must be distinguished from the question of *when* Christians understood the Old Testament Scriptures in this way. The faithful presentation of even apostolic ignorance, preserved in all four canonical Gospels and Acts, demonstrates that the first Christians did not do their exegesis first and then draw correct inferences about Jesus. The process was the reverse: they came to grips with who Jesus was and is, they confronted (for instance) the powerful evidence of the resurrection, and then they came to read their sacred texts in fresh ways. But the remarkable thing is that these Jewish Christians do not then embark on an apologetic to their fellow Jews to say, in effect, "Oh, if only you could examine the evidence of the resurrection of Jesus of Nazareth and become convinced of who he is! Then you would read *Tanakh* the way we do." Rather, they try to convince their fellow Jews *from the Scriptures* that Jesus is the promised Messiah (e.g., Acts 18:28). They have become convinced that their former reading of Scripture was wrong, or at least incomplete, and their current reading is right. The true meaning was there all along, but they simply had not seen it. This is tied, of course, to the "mystery" passages of the New Testament—not only those where the word *mystērion* is used, but those where the theme is invoked (e.g., John 2:19–22). In short, the Christians detected a number of crucial typological trajectories in Scripture, and were convinced that these were not artificially imposed structures but were actually *there*, even while they admitted that they had not always seen them.

Now all of this is important to the next stage of my argument. None of it, however, sheds much light on how to read Psalm 1, not least because typologies are almost universally recognized to be grounded in persons, institutions, or events—and on the face of things, Psalm 1 does not focus on any of these.

(8) In the last few decades, some have understood "law" to have a predictive or prophetic element (cf. Matt. 5:17–20; 11:13). Most of us are already familiar with the notion that some laws—those connected with the sacrificial system, for instance, including the centrality of the priesthood

and tabernacle/temple—are claimed by New Testament writers (especially, but not exclusively, John and Hebrews) to point forward to the ultimate priest, the ultimate sacrifice, the ultimate temple. But now some argue that laws that are normally labeled "moral" also enjoy an anticipatory function, a prophetic/predictive function. In most cases, this works out pretty much the same way, morally speaking, as it does among those who think the Sermon on the Mount establishes an "intensifying" of the law, or those who think that the Sermon on the Mount unpacks the moral overtones of what is really there in the Decalogue's formal statutes—except that the way of arriving at this conclusion is rather different. The older pattern was largely atemporal: one spoke of intensifying the law, or unpacking the layers of intensification already embedded in the law. The more recent pattern of argumentations suggests instead that *along the temporal axis of salvation history*, the stipulation not to commit murder finds its ultimate *fulfillment* not only in the avoidance of murder, but in that to which such a statute points: love, which is the antithesis of hate, which is morally of a piece with murder. The ultimate fulfillment of the prohibition of murder is found in the ethics of the consummated kingdom—and that kingdom, though not yet consummated, has already dawned, and claims our allegiance. I repeat: morally, these two ways of seeing the contemporary significance of the prohibition of murder are equivalent; hermeneutically, they are rather distinctive.

If we grant this way of reading the law some plausibility, may we draw a comparison with the kind of fulfillment one finds in typological trajectories? Certainly there are some fascinating parallels, and if one thinks of the Decalogue as in some sense an institution, then the parallels become closer. Perhaps, however, we are getting caught up in our terminology. Certainly Paul can think of love as "fulfilling" the law in some sense (Rom. 13:10), an insight tied to Jesus' treatment of the first and second most important commandments.

Certainly we are stretching the terminology of typology if we extend the category to Psalm 1. Yet regardless of the terminology we deploy, the deepest moral appeal in Psalm 1—the appeal to delighted, heartfelt obedience to the instruction of God—finds its echo often enough in the New Testament, whether in Jesus' reiteration that "People do not live on bread alone, but on every word that comes from the mouth of God" (Matt. 4:4 TNIV; cf. Deut. 8:3) or on his insistence that his followers are sanctified through the truth, through his Father's word (John 17:17). Inevitably that raises important questions about the relationships between the referent of "law" or "teaching/instruction" in Psalm 1:2 and such terms as "word" and "truth" in New Testament documents.

(9) Finally, a number of New Testament writers deploy what might be called a salvation-historical hermeneutic, an insistent reading of Old Testament documents along a sequential axis, to establish certain nonnegotiable *Christian* readings. In part, Paul's argument in Galatians 3 is that because the Abrahamic promise, to the effect that all the nations of the world would be blessed through Abraham's seed, was established centuries *before* the giving of the Mosaic code, Sinai could not possibly call into question the validity of that promise. The law from Sinai must therefore *not* be understood to have quite the salvific potential that many Jews thought it had. Again, Hebrews 3:7–4:13 argues that a fair exegesis of Psalm 95, which was written *after* the Israelites had entered the land of "rest" in the time of Joshua, and which nevertheless promised rest to its own readers on condition of persevering obedience, establishes that entrance into the promised land could not properly be thought of as the ultimate rest. Pretty soon this is linked to God's rest in creation and to the theme of rest running right through the Old Testament canon (whether or not this then is considered a "type"). Similar arguments are constructed regarding Melchizedek (Heb. 7) and the promise of the new covenant (Heb. 8), all designed to show that what we call the Old Testament Scriptures *themselves* establish the principial obsolescence of the old covenant and point toward something greater. Once that argument is established in the minds of new covenant believers for major turning points in the Bible's story line, of course, then it becomes a contributing grid toward reading a great deal of Old Testament text. Thus even if the arguments found in Galatians 3 and Hebrews 7 have no *direct* bearing on the interpretation of Psalm 1, they become part of the way Christians put their Bibles together, and thus have an *indirect* bearing on how Christians are likely to read Psalm 1.

So Where Do We Go from Here?

The list of hermeneutical options just described is far from exhaustive. Exhaustive or not, they constitute a sufficiently diverse spread to prepare us for this last step in the argument.

Most of these hermeneutical options have *some* kind of usefulness in the interpretation and exposition of Psalm 1. The worst mistakes seem to occur when any one of them becomes the sole key for understanding the psalm in its canonical context. A wiser way forward is to reflect on what kind of bearing any one of them individually, and all of them together, may have.

Option 1 will expound the psalm as it is, so far as the preacher understands that text as it stands and without a lot of explicit recourse to comprehensive biblical and systematic theology. The application will be very direct. One can make a case for this: surely the preacher's first responsibility is to unpack the text at hand. Moreover, if the preacher handles enough biblical texts over time, surely most of the congregation will hear the complementary truths that are necessary to make sense of the Bible as a whole, even though the preacher does not attempt such integration in any one sermon. Yet that argument soon sounds weak. If the preacher were handling, say, one of the Old Testament passages that pronounces death by stoning on the adulterer and homosexual, wouldn't most people think it strange if no attempt were made *within that sermon* to establish how these texts cohere with later streams of revelation, instead of waiting some months or years until complementary texts are expounded? Isn't something more required of the one who expounds Nehemiah than application to a contemporary building program?

Considerations of genre (Option 2) are important, of course, and need to be spelled out from time to time. And of course, it is important to recall that Jesus sometimes chose to address his crowds in the form of wisdom, as also in many other forms. Sooner or later, we must reflect publicly on how genres as disparate as narrative and wisdom complement each other and cohere. Moreover, when we embark on such an exercise we need to be aware of our own cultural biases. We are not living in the Eisenhower years, where the good guys in films were very good and the bad guys in films were very bad. We still produce some films like that, of course, but they are recognized to be cartoonish: a Rambo or a Terminator needs targets that deserve killing, so of course the polarities must be absolute. But the films that win Academy Awards are films such as *Crash*, where all the moral polarities are reversed in the space of two hours. Even a genuinely cartoon character such as Spider-Man has to be morally conflicted. But the difference between this sort of moral ambiguity within narrative and the kind of moral ambiguity one finds in, say, the accounts of David, is stark. The biblical narratives of moral ambiguity, set within the canon, tell the nuanced story of moral ambiguity in a way that preserves the sense of the tragic, the ugliness of evil, the wretchedness and deceptiveness of sin—all of it to be wonderfully overcome in the consummation. Contemporary nuanced stories of moral ambiguity glory in the moral ambiguity as an end in itself, tending to demonize the absolutes while cherishing the mingling of the noble and the corrupt. Our culture thinks this reading is sophisticated; by contrast, scriptural narratives frankly display the seamy contradictions, but scream, "This is not the way it is supposed to be!" If we need narrative to expose our inconsistencies, we need the absolutes to obliterate our self-indulgent excuses.

Psalm 1, then, must be expounded with all the stark directness of Jesus' closing antitheses in the Sermon on the Mount: good fruit or bad fruit, narrow way or broad way, rock foundation or sand. Yet Jesus' antitheses are not all that must be said of Jesus to get the portrait right, and Psalm 1 is not the only psalm, let alone the only passage of Scripture. What shall we make of Psalm 51, or Psalm 102? What shall we make of the fact that the law itself provided a Day of Atonement, and that the hope of the believer is in God's forgiveness, not in achieving perfection as adequate ground for standing in the congregation of the righteous? *Some* sort of integration is surely required.

None of these considerations should weaken the direct thrust of the magnificent antithesis that controls Psalm 1. The New Testament writers *do* read moral principles out of some Old Testament texts (Option 3), and there *are* several long-standing theological traditions that preserve some useful integration by reminding us how often God makes stunning demands that any thoughtful human conscience this side of the fall recognizes we cannot possibly meet (Option 4). Nevertheless an automatic assignment of texts to law, gospel, and illustrations of both is likely to lose sight not only of the richness of literary genre, but how the Bible's entire story line hangs together—and therefore how salvation-historical dimensions must be brought to bear. A simplistic form of law/gospel antithesis (and of course, the best treatments are *not* simplistic) often becomes unbelievable to good readers, simply because it feels like (and is!) a form of reductionism.

What more can be said for Option 5—the one that thinks the blessed "man" is none other than an anticipatory reference to Jesus? If such referentiality is understood in some specific and strictly predictive sense

131

(overlapping with Option 6), this reading is nonsense: there is no evidence to support it. Nor is there the kind of controlled and exegetically grounded typology (tied to person, event, or institution, Option 7) not uncommon in Scripture. One can speak in atemporal generalities, of course: within the Bible, this side of the fall, the only person who perfectly brings to realization the stark antitheses of this psalm is Jesus himself—though in some attenuated sense there is a handful of persons about whom nothing negative is recorded (e.g., Daniel, perhaps Esther).

Yet if one looks at broader streams, perhaps a little more can be said. Perhaps a somewhat analogous parallel will help. Some years ago I was preaching through a substantial part of Ezekiel. On the Sunday of which I am thinking, I tackled Ezekiel 4–5. These two chapters use heavily symbol-laden actions and language to foretell the catastrophic destruction of Jerusalem owing to the multiplied layers of its wretched idolatry. The preacher's first job is to explain the text immediately at hand. But then what? It is possible to offer essentially *atemporal* applications: to talk about idolatry then and now, the inevitability of the wrath of God (perhaps with parallels from other biblical texts, and with contemporary application), and so forth. But if one recalls how these chapters contribute to the prophecy of Ezekiel as a whole, and where this prophecy stands in the stream of biblical redemptive history, then other lines open up. Ezekiel is preaching to the exiles on the banks of the Kebar River, seven hundred miles from home. The message that Jerusalem will be destroyed can scarcely be popular, for if true, the exiles would soon have no home to which to return, and therefore no hope. The thrust of this book is almost unbearably dark until chapter 33, when word reaches Ezekiel that Jerusalem has indeed fallen. From that point on, the messages he conveys from YHWH are full of hope. This, of course, can be fleshed out for homiletical purposes in many ways. Moreover, it is surely worth reflecting on the way that the opposing themes of wrath and mercy, judgment and hope, barrel through the Scriptures until they collide gloriously in the cross and point forward to the consummation.

In other words, in addition to explaining what Ezekiel 4 and 5 actually say, I have a choice of (a) working out how these chapters contribute to Ezekiel as a whole, in order to deepen the exposition and application, (b) working out how its themes cohere with similar or complementary themes (essentially an atemporal/systematic approach), (c) working out how this and related themes are developed along the temporal axis of the Bible's story line, which inevitably takes us toward Christ and the consummation (an essentially salvation-historical, or biblical-theological, approach), or (d) some combination of the first three.

Something similar can be attempted with respect to Psalm 1. Of course, the preacher's first responsibility is to unpack the passage. That surely includes consideration of genre, the moral impact of this wisdom psalm, and the like. But the exposition becomes more telling if the preacher (a) works out how Psalm 1 relates to the Psalms as a whole, esp. Book One (Pss. 1–41), and/or (b) works out how this antithesis between the righteous and the unrighteous is paralleled by other biblical passages, including (say) parts of Deuteronomy and parts of the Sermon on the Mount. This might also be the time to work out how complementary themes are to be handled. We might consider a book such as 1 John. On the one hand, the apostle tells Christians that if they claim they do not sin or have not sinned, they are deluding themselves and calling God a liar, and that the only proper thing to do is to confess our sins, knowing that the only final solution to our guilt before God is Jesus Christ our advocate and the propitiation for our sins (1 John 1:6–2:2). On the other hand, the same John specifies, in sharpest terms, that only those who love the brothers and sisters, obey Christ, and believe the truth, are truly Christ's (see esp. chap. 3): the antitheses are at least as sharp and as absolute as those in Psalm 1. But the preacher may also (c) work out this centrality of the Word of God, this centrality of delighting in the instruction of God, along the axis from creation to consummation, with carefully chosen stops along the way—stops that would show how transient is our obedience, how radical our guilt, how delightful to anticipate the time when our righteousness will be as consistent as Psalm 1 depicts, how necessary forgiveness is, how much Psalm 1 shames, convicts, and threatens the guilty, how powerfully it sets forth that for which the people of God must strive, how eagerly we await that consummation. All such lessons are pretty obvious when Psalm 1 is set along the axis of redemptive history. By the same token, to read Psalm 1 as if it prescribed *how* the people of God, finally, please him enough to know his blessing, will not only appear unnecessarily shallow, but will belong to the same species of error that reads any other text without adequate respect for the larger context. The only difference here is that "the larger context" embraces the entire canon.

In short, I have tried to show some of the wealth of hermeneutical approaches to what it means to preach Christ from all the Scriptures, hermeneutical approaches to the challenging and rich dimensions of the New Testament's use of the Old. This wealth of hermeneutical options, properly integrated, may help to steer the preacher away from, on the one hand, the relative sterility of grammatical exegesis by itself, and, on the other, the relative reductionism of resorting to only one way of seeing how biblical passages are embedded in the fabric of the entire canon.

5

A Specific Problem Confronting the Authority of the Bible: Should the New Testament's Claim That the Prophet "Isaiah" Wrote the Whole Book of Isaiah Be Taken at Face Value?

G. K. BEALE

INTRODUCTION[1]

The authorship of the book of Isaiah is among a variety of issues related to the inerrancy of the Scriptures that are being debated by evangelicals today. A number of contemporary evangelical scholars do not take at face value the repeated affirmations by Jesus and the New Testament writers that the prophet Isaiah wrote the entire Old Testament book known as Isaiah. This debate has significant bearing on the issue of the Bible's authority, since if Isaiah did not write the book attributed to him, the New Testament's assertion that he did

---

1. I am happy to contribute an article for Richard Gaffin's festschrift, since I have benefited greatly from his writings. The following essay is a revised form of a chapter to appear in a forthcoming book: G. K. Beale, *The Erosion of Inerrancy in Evangelicalism: Responding to New Challenges to Biblical Authority* (Wheaton, IL: Crossway, 2008).

write the book is wrong. But, perhaps of greater significance, if the prophet Isaiah was not responsible for the contents of the whole book, then we are left with a christological problem, since Jesus understood that Isaiah wrote the entire book attributed to him.

It is important to recognize that some (including evangelicals) who contend that Isaiah was not the author of the book by that name do not believe such a position is inconsistent with the inspiration of Scripture. Some believe that the New Testament refers only to a collection of writings known as "Isaiah," so that such allusions do not have to be understood as referring to a personal prophet whose handprint is over the whole work. Others believe that Jesus' intention was not to convey that the historical prophet Isaiah was the author, and that Jesus' focus was on communicating only the meaning of the prophecy. Some believe that Jesus knowingly accommodated himself to a false Jewish tradition about Isaiah's authorship. Others think that Jesus did believe, wrongly, in Isaianic authorship, and they attribute this mistake to the mysteries of the incarnation and Jesus' self-emptying. In this way, a high view of his deity is not denigrated nor is the authority of Scripture affected.

The problem with these views that accommodate the multiple authorship of Isaiah is how the Bible can really still be authoritative given the straightforward affirmations of unity of authorship by Jesus, Paul, and other NT writers.

THE SHIFT OF OPINION AMONG NORTH AMERICAN EVANGELICALS CONCERNING AUTHORSHIP CLAIMS BY THE NT ABOUT OT BOOKS

Until the late 1970s, the consensus among evangelical scholars was to accept the Bible's claims about the human authorship of some of its books, whether that be concerning Isaiah,[2] or Mosaic authorship of the Pentateuch, or attribution of many of the Psalms to David. This was, for example, the position taken in the 1978 Chicago Statement on Biblical Inerrancy. It is noteworthy that in as little as thirty years, there has arisen in American evangelical scholarship a willingness to accept what had been considered too-liberal higher critical views of the Bible's claims about authorship of par-

---

2. E.g., see E. J. Young, *The Book of Isaiah*, NICOT (Grand Rapids: Eerdmans, 1972), 538–49; R. K. Harrison, *Introduction to the Old Testament* (Grand Rapids: Eerdmans, 1969), 765–95.

ticular biblical books, including Isaiah.[3] However, some evangelical scholars of the Old Testament still hold to the traditional view about Isaiah.[4]

Among the main conservative arguments for the single authorship of Isaiah are the following, as summarized in the mid-twentieth century by Oswald Allis:

(1) All fifteen of the latter Old Testament prophets begin with a heading of the prophet's name, but Isaiah 40–66 does not begin with such a heading, so it would appear likely that the author of Isaiah 1–39 is the same as that of chapters 40–66.

(2) For twenty-five centuries no one questioned the authorship of Isaiah, except for one little-known Jewish medieval interpreter.

(3) The New Testament writers quote from all parts of the book of Isaiah, and consider that they are all to be attributed to the prophet Isaiah.

(4) The Qumran scroll of Isaiah shows no literary break between chapters 39 and 40, just where the critics locate the most major break in authorship.[5]

RECONSIDERATION OF JESUS' AND THE NEW TESTAMENT'S REFERENCES TO ISAIAH

It is certainly true that cogent arguments are made by Old Testament scholars for multiple authorship of Isaiah, which in fact is the ruling model today for understanding the book's authorship (which we will not rehearse here[6]). Yet viable arguments for the unity of Isaiah's authorship continue to be offered. Interestingly, within the last ten to fifteen years, there has been less study emphasizing evidence for diversity of authorship, and greater strides

---

3. See, e.g., Raymond B. Dillard and Tremper Longman III, *An Introduction to the Old Testament* (Grand Rapids: Zondervan, 1994), 268–74, which is commonly used at many evangelical institutions and is published by a traditionally conservative evangelical publisher.

4. John N. Oswalt, *The Book of Isaiah*, NICOT (Grand Rapids: Eerdmans, 1986), 23–28; J. Alec Motyer, *The Prophecy of Isaiah* (Downers Grove, IL: IVP, 1993), 25–30; see N. H. Ridderbos, "Isaiah: Book of," *NBD*, 513–16, who holds a mediating position, i.e., that it is acceptable to affirm that Isaiah 40–66 contains an Isaianic core, which Isaiah's disciples expanded according to the spirit of Isaiah, but that it is not possible to determine what belongs to the core and what to the later editors.

5. Oswald Allis, *The Unity of Isaiah: A Study in Prophecy* (Philadelphia: Presbyterian and Reformed, 1950), 39–43.

6. For typical critical arguments, see the summary (and responses) in Harrison, *Introduction to the Old Testament*, 765–95.

by those who, while still affirming multiple authorship, nevertheless perceive an overall unity of subject matter from various angles. They propose this as the work of a final editor. The cumulative effect of these arguments has been to highlight the book's unity. The longer these arguments continue to be made, the thinner will be the line between a final redactor who imposed unity on the diverse strands of the book and Isaiah as the original author, responsible for its unity from the beginning.[7]

Though there is much to discuss about the authorship of Isaiah from the perspective of the book itself, the remainder of this excursus will consider primarily the authorship of Isaiah for the most part from the claims of the repeated references to "Isaiah" in the New Testament, in addition to other early Jewish and Christian sources. Most Old Testament scholars holding to multiple authorship consider their arguments for it to be overwhelming, but must explain the New Testament evidence in some way consistent with their conclusion. Such explanations have concluded that Jesus and his followers were wrong like the rest of early Judaism, or that Jesus knowingly accommodated himself to false Jewish tradition or that the New Testament merely refers to a literary collection known as "Isaiah" but not written by the personal prophet himself (a view often preferred by more conservative scholars holding to diversity of Isaiah's authorship).

The intended upshot of the remainder of this essay is that New Testament evidence so strongly supports the personal prophet Isaiah's authorship of the complete book that to hold that there were multiple authors inevitably must lead, if a person is consistent, to only one conclusion: that Jesus and the New Testament writers were wrong in their assessment of the book's authorship. On the other hand, I believe that the New Testament position on this issue vindicates the traditional arguments within Isaiah itself that Isaiah wrote the whole book, and best explains the kinds of unity that scholars have more recently been recognizing yet still attribute to a later redactor or redactors. In arguing this, I am merely trying to develop in more detail and update the traditional argument that the New Testament evidence for Isaianic authorship is significant and cannot be dismissed lightly.

7. See R. Schultz, "How Many 'Isaiahs' Were There and Does It Matter? Prophetic Inspiration in Recent Evangelical Scholarship," in *Evangelicals and Scripture*, ed. V. Bacote, L. Miguelez, and D. Okholm (Downers Grove, IL: InterVarsity, 2004), passim, for a convenient survey of this issue, as well as the current status of evangelical views from an Old Testament perspective on the authorship of Isaiah.

CONSIDERATION OF ACTUAL ATTRIBUTIONS OF QUOTATIONS TO ISAIAH THE PROPHET IN EARLY JUDAISM, THE NEW TESTAMENT, AND EARLY CHRISTIANITY

Probably the best and most precise manner to study this issue of how the ancients viewed Old Testament authorship, especially that of the book of Isaiah, is to survey the evidence about Isaiah in Judaism and early Christianity. Without exception, this literature understands that the prophet Isaiah was the author of the entire book. The following represents all of the references to Isaiah in the Dead Sea Scrolls, Josephus, Philo, Old Testament Apocrypha and Pseudepigrapha, the New Testament, New Testament Apocrypha, and the Apostolic Fathers. This list shows that throughout this Jewish and Christian literature there are references to quotations from all parts of the book of Isaiah (so-called First, Second, and Third Isaiah) that are attributed to the person of Isaiah according to the following expressions (I have highlighted with italics the expressions below that appear to indicate the personal agency of "Isaiah"):

New Testament

For this is the one referred to *by Isaiah the prophet when he said*,

> "The voice of one crying in the wilderness,
> 'Make ready the way of the LORD,
> make His paths straight!'" (Matt. 3:3)

This was to fulfill what *was spoken through Isaiah the prophet.* (Matt. 4:14)

This was to fulfill what *was spoken through Isaiah the prophet*: "He Himself took our infirmities and carried away our diseases." (Matt. 8:17)

This was to fulfill what *was spoken through Isaiah the prophet.* (Matt. 12:17)

In their case the *prophecy of Isaiah* is being fulfilled, which says,

> "You will keep on hearing, but will not understand;
> You will keep on seeing, but will not perceive." (Matt. 13:14)

You hypocrites, *rightly did Isaiah prophesy of you.* (Matt. 15:7)

As it is written *in Isaiah the prophet*:

> "Behold, I send My messenger ahead of you,
> Who will prepare your way." (Mark 1:2)

And He said to them, "*Rightly did Isaiah prophesy of you* hypocrites, as it is written:

> 'This people honors Me with their lips,
> But their heart is far away from Me.'" (Mark 7:6)

As it is written *in the book of the words of Isaiah the prophet,*

> "The voice of one crying in the wilderness,
> 'Make ready the way of the LORD,
> Make his paths straight.'" (Luke 3:4)

And the book *of the prophet Isaiah* was handed to Him. And He opened the book and found the place where it was written . . . . (Luke 4:17)

He said, "I am a voice of one crying in the wilderness, 'make straight the way of the LORD,' *as Isaiah the prophet said.*" (John 1:23)

"This was to fulfill *the word of Isaiah the prophet which he spoke*: 'LORD, who has believed our report? And to whom has the arm of the LORD been revealed?'" (John 12:38)

For this reason they could not believe, for *Isaiah said* again . . . . (John 12:39)

And he was returning and sitting in his chariot, and *was reading the prophet Isaiah.* . . . Philip ran up and *heard him reading Isaiah the prophet,* and said, "Do you understand what you are reading?" And he said, "Well, how could I, unless someone guides me?" And he invited Philip to come up and sit with him. Now the passage of Scripture which he was reading was this:

> "He was led as a sheep to slaughter;
> And as a lamb before its shearer is silent,
> So He does not open His mouth.
> In humiliation His judgment was taken away;

Who will relate His generation?
For His life is removed from the earth."

The eunuch answered Philip and said, "Please tell me, of whom *does the prophet say this? Of himself or of someone else?*" Then Philip opened his mouth, and beginning from this Scripture he preached Jesus to him. (Acts 8:28, 30–35)

And when they did not agree with one another, they *began* leaving after Paul had spoken one parting word, "*The Holy Spirit rightly spoke through Isaiah the prophet to your fathers.*" (Acts 28:25)

Isaiah cries out concerning Israel, "Though the number of the sons of Israel be like the sand of the sea, it is the remnant that will be saved." (Rom. 9:27)

And just *as Isaiah foretold,*

> "Unless the Lord of Sabaoth had left to us a posterity,
> We would have become like Sodom, and would have resembled
> Gomorrah." (Rom. 9:29)

However, they did not all heed the good news; for *Isaiah says,* "Lord, who has believed our report?" (Rom. 10:16)

And *Isaiah is very bold and says,*

> "I was found by those who did not seek Me,
> I became manifest to those who did not ask for Me." (Rom. 10:20)

Again *Isaiah says,*

> "There shall come the root of Jesse,
> And He who arises to rule over the Gentiles,
> In Him shall the Gentiles hope." (Rom. 15:12)

Philo

Change of Names, 169—"But it is not allowed to every wicked man to rejoice, *as it is said in the predictions of the prophet,* 'There is no rejoicing for the wicked, says God' (Isa. 47:22)."

On Dreams Book 2, 172—"They then very fairly compare this vine of which we were only able to take a part, to happiness. *And one of the ancient prophets bears his testimony in favour of my view of the matter, who speaking under divine inspiration has said,* 'The vineyard of the Lord Almighty is the house of Israel' (Isa. 5:7)."

On Rewards, 158—"Then, like an affectionate mother, it shall pity the sons and the daughters whom it has lost, who now that they are dead are, and still more were, when alive, a grief and sorrow to their parents; and becoming young a second time, it will again be fertile as before, and will produce an irreproachable offspring, an improvement on its former progeny; for she that was desolate, *as the prophet says,* (Isa. 54:1) is now become happy in her children and the mother of a large family. Which prophetic saying has also an allegorical meaning, having reference to the soul."

Josephus

Antiq. 9:276 (9.13.3.276)—"But king Hezekiah was not concerned at his threatenings, but depended on his piety towards God, and upon *Isaiah the prophet, by whom he inquired, and accurately knew all future events:*—and thus much shall suffice for the present concerning this king Hezekiah."

Antiq. 10:35 (10.2.2.35)—"Now as to this prophet [clearly Isaiah in context], *he was by the confession of all, a divine and wonderful man in speaking truth; and out of the assurance that he had never written what was false, he wrote down all his prophecies, and left them behind him in books,* that their accomplishment might be judged of from the events by posterity. Nor did this prophet do so alone; but the others, which were twelve in number, did the same. And whatsoever is done among us, whether it be good, or whether it be bad, comes to pass according to their prophecies; but of every one of these we shall speak hereafter."

Antiq. 11:5 (11.1.2.5)—"This was known to Cyrus by his reading the book *which Isaiah left behind him of his prophecies; for this prophet said that God had spoken thus to him in a secret vision:*—'My will is, that Cyrus, whom I have appointed to be king over many and great nations, send back my people to their own land, and build my temple.'"

Antiq. 13:64 (13.3.1.64)—"The chief reason why he was desirous so to do, was, that he relied upon the prophet Isaiah, *who lived about six hundred years before, and foretold* that there certainly was to be a temple built to Almighty God in Egypt by a man that was a Jew. Onias was elevated with this prediction, and wrote the following epistle to Ptolemy and Cleopatra."

Antiq. 13:68 (13.3.1.68)—*"For the prophet Isaiah foretold, that 'there should be an altar in Egypt to the Lord God: and many other such things did he prophesy relating to that place.'"*

Antiq. 13:71 (13.3.2.71)—"But since *thou sayest that Isaiah the prophet foretold this long ago,* we give thee leave to do it, if it may be done according to your law, and so that we may not appear to have at all offended God herein."

War 7:431–432 (7.10.3.431–432)—"Accordingly, he [Onias] thought that by building this temple he should draw away a great number from them to himself. *There had been also a certain ancient prediction made by a [prophet] whose name was Isaiah, about six hundred years before, that this temple should be built by a man that was a Jew in Egypt.* And this is the history of the building of that temple."

The above references to a temple in Egypt are likely to Isaiah 19:18–25, which pertains to the final eschatological restoration of Egyptians and Assyrians at the same time as Israel's end-time restoration.

Qumran[8]

CD 4:13–14—"Belial is unrestrained in Israel, *just as God said by Isaiah the prophet, the son of Amoz,* saying, Fear and pit and snare are upon thee, dweller in the land (Isaiah 24:17[9]). The true meaning of this verse . . . ."

CD 7:10—"to them that is *when the oracle of the prophet Isaiah son of Amoz came true* (in context the reference is to Isa. 7:17)."

4Q174 3:15–16—"as it is written *in the book of Isaiah the prophet* in reference to the Last Days, 'And it came to pass, while His hand was strong upon me, [that He warned me not to walk in the way of] this people'

---

8. The following quotations from Qumran are from *The Dead Sea Scrolls: A New English Translation*, ed. M. O. Wise, M. G. Abegg, and E. M. Cook (New York: HarperCollins, 1996). Brackets indicate lacunae filled in by the editors.
9. This is a text typically viewed as non-Isaianic by many scholars.

(Isaiah 8:11). These are they about whom it is written in the book of Ezekiel the prophet . . . ."

4Q177 1:2—"[as it is written *in the book of Isaiah the prophet,*] 'This year eat what grows [by itself, and next year the aftergrowth' (Isaiah 37:30). The meaning of] 'what grows by itself' is [. . .]."

4Q177 1:5—"[. . . that is written] about them *in the book of [Isaiah the prophet . . . for]* the Law of the [. . .]"

4Q177 1:6—"[. . .] it calls them, [as it is written about them *in the book of Isaiah the prophet,* 'He thinks up plots to [destroy the humble with lying words' (Isaiah 32:7) . . .]"

4Q265 f1:3–5—"[. . . just as] it is written in *the b[ook] of Isaiah the prophet,* [' "Sing, O barren one who did not bear; burst into song and] shout, you who have not been in labor! For the children of the desolate will be more [than the children of her that is married," says the Lord.] Enlarge the site of [your] ten[t and let the curtains . . .' (Isaiah 54:1–2).]"

4Q266 f3i:7—"in Israel, just as God said *by Isaiah the prophet,* the son of Amoz, (CD 4:14) saying . . ."

4Q266 f3ii:1—"[against] them. Al[l of them are kindlers and lighters of brands (Isaiah 50:11); the webs of (CD 5:14) a spider are their webs]."

4Q266 f3ii:2—"[and the eggs of vip]ers are t[heir] eggs (Isaiah 59:5). [Whoever touches them (CD 5:15) shall not be clean. The more he does so, the more he is guilty]."

Old Testament Apocrypha

2 Esdr. 2:18—"I will send you help, my servants Isaiah and Jeremiah. According to their counsel I have consecrated and prepared for you twelve trees loaded with various fruits [this is in a clear context of chapter 2 of God's promise to bring Israel out of captivity into all the blessings of the restoration promises]."

Sir. 48:20—"But they called upon the Lord who is merciful, spreading forth their hands toward him; and the Holy One quickly heard them from heaven, and delivered them by the hand of Isaiah."

Sir. 48:22–23—"For Hezekiah did what was pleasing to the Lord, and he held strongly to the ways of David his father, which *Isaiah the prophet commanded, who was great and faithful in his vision.* In his days the sun went backward, and he lengthened the life of the king."

Sir. 48:24—"*By the spirit of might he [Isaiah] saw the last things, and comforted those who mourned in Zion.*"

Sir. 48:25—"*He revealed what was to occur to the end of time, and the hidden things before they came to pass.*"

4 Mac. 18:14—"He reminded you of the scripture of Isaiah, which says, 'Even though you go through the fire, the flame shall not consume you.' (Isaiah 43:2)."

Old Testament Pseudepigrapha

Mart. Ascen. Isaiah 3:6—"*Isaiah and the prophets who (are) with him prophesy against Jerusalem and against the cities of Judah that they will be laid waste, and also (against) Benjamin that it will go into captivity, and also against you, lord king, that you will go (bound) with hooks and chains of iron.*"

Mart. Ascen. Isaiah 4:8[10]—"*And the rest of the words of the vision [by Isaiah] are written in the vision of Babylon [Isaiah 13]. And the rest of the vision about the Lord, behold it is written in parables in the words of mine [Isaiah] that are written in the book which I prophesied openly. And the descent of the Beloved into Sheol, behold it is written in the section where the Lord says, 'Behold, my son shall understand' [Isa. 52:13, LXX].* [Martyrdom and Ascension of Isaiah is dated variously to the first or second century A.D.]."

New Testament Apocrypha

Pilate 18:1 (2.1)—"O Lord Jesus Christ, the resurrection and the life of the dead, permit us to speak mysteries through the death of your cross, because we have been adjured by you. For you ordered your servants to relate to no one the secrets of your divine majesty which you did in

---

10. In the Charlesworth edition of the pseudepigrapha, this reference is Mart. and Ascen. Isaiah 4:20–21.

Hades. And when we were, along with all our fathers, lying in the deep, in the blackness of darkness, suddenly there appeared a golden heat of the sun, and a purple royal light shining upon us. And immediately the father of all the human race, with all the patriarchs and prophets, exulted, saying: 'That light is the source of eternal light, which has promised to transmit to us co-eternal light.' *And Isaiah cried out, and said: 'This is the light of the Father, the Son of God, as I predicted when I was alive upon earth:* "The land of Zabulon and the land of Nephthalim across Jordan, Galilee of the nations, the people who sat in darkness, have seen a great light; and light was shining among those who are in the region of the shadow of death." And now it has come and shone upon us sitting in death.' "

Pilate 21:2 (5.2)—"And all the multitude of the saints, hearing this, said to Hades, with the voice of reproach: 'Open your gates, that the king of glory may come in.' And David cried out, saying: 'Did I not, when I was alive upon earth, prophesy to you: "Let them confess to the Lord His tender mercies and His wonderful works to the children of men: for He has shattered the brazen gates, and burst the iron bars; He has taken them up out of the way of their iniquity"?' And after this, in like manner, *Isaiah said: 'Did not I, when I was alive upon earth, prophesy to you:* "The dead shall rise up, and those who are in their tombs shall rise again, and those who are upon earth shall exult; because the dew, which is from the Lord, is their health"? (Isaiah 26:19) *And again I said,* "Where, O Death, is your sting? where, O Hades, is your victory?" ' "[11]

Pilate 21:3 (5.3)—"*And when all the saints heard this from Isaiah,* they said to Hades: 'Open your gates. Since you are now conquered, you will be weak and powerless.' "

Apostolic Fathers

2Clem. 3:5—"And in Isaiah he also says, 'This people honors me with their lips, but their heart is far from me.'[6]"

---

11. This last clause is actually a quotation from Hos. 13:14, but the author has taken the verse as an interpretation of the resurrection prophecy of Isa. 25:8 (LXX), probably under the influence of 1 Cor. 15:54–55, where the same Hosea text directly follows the same Isa. 25:8 citation as an interpretation of it. This is quite close to the same phenomenon we observed above in the use of the Old Testament in Mark 1:2–3.

Barn. 12:4—"And *again in another prophet [Isaiah] he says*: 'All day long I have stretched out my hands to a disobedient people who oppose my righteous way' (Isaiah 65:2)."

Barn. 12:11—"And *again, Isaiah says as follows*: 'The Lord said to the Messiah my Lord, whose right hand I held, that the nations would obey him [Isa. 52:15? 60:11–12], and I will shatter the strength of kings.'[114] Observe how David calls him 'Lord,' and does not call him 'son.'"

Conclusion to the Above Isaiah Quotations

References to all parts of the book of Isaiah are found attributed to the personal prophet Isaiah. It is true that some of the general references to "Isaiah" could be taken figuratively to refer merely to a literary collection known as "Isaiah." It is clearer, however, from the majority of the above citations, that they should not be understood to refer only to such a literary collection. That the references are made not merely to a literary collection but to sayings from the personal prophet Isaiah is apparent from the specific language often used, of which the following expressions are a summary.

The allusion is not typically to the "prophecy" or "prophecies" of "Isaiah" but to "Isaiah" as a "prophet" / "Isaiah the son of Amoz" / "what was spoken through Isaiah the prophet" / "referred to by Isaiah the prophet" / "the prophecy of Isaiah" / "rightly did Isaiah prophesy" / "as it is written in the book of the words of Isaiah the prophet" / "the book of the prophet Isaiah" / "the word of Isaiah the prophet which he spoke" / "of whom does the prophet say this" / "the Holy Spirit rightly spoke through Isaiah the prophet to your fathers" / "Isaiah cries out" / "Isaiah foretold" / "Isaiah says" / "the predictions of the prophet" / "one of the ancient prophets bears his testimony" / "as the prophet says" / "Isaiah the prophet . . . and [he] accurately knew all future events" / "reading the book which Isaiah left behind him of his prophecies" / "he relied upon the prophet Isaiah, who lived about six hundred years before, and foretold" / "the prophet Isaiah foretold" / "there had been also a certain ancient prediction made by a [prophet] whose name was Isaiah, about six hundred years before" / "as God said by Isaiah the prophet" / "the oracle of the prophet Isaiah."

When these references are read straightforwardly, they refer to the active personal role of Isaiah in writing and prophesying in all parts of the book. The cumulative effect of these references to quotations of

Isaiah shows no substantial evidence that such references could have been seen to be merely part of a literary work known as "the book of Isaiah." Repeatedly, however, there are a variety of expressions alluding to the personal activity, role, or involvement of a person named "Isaiah." Very interestingly, the quotations come from all parts of the book of Isaiah, whether so-called First, Second, and Third Isaiah, all of which are attributed to the personal prophet Isaiah. The first-century Christian and Jewish view was that the single prophet Isaiah wrote the entire book attributed to him.

In conclusion, any stylistic convention of attributing an Old Testament prophet's name such as "Isaiah" to a quotation not written by that prophet does not appear to be supported from the evidence surveyed above. Therefore, when quotations by Isaiah are mentioned by Jesus or Paul or in Acts, the speaker or writer has in mind Isaiah himself. This is supported by references in early Judaism and other early Christian literature. Either Jesus, Paul, or the writers and speakers in Acts are wrong in so referring to Isaiah, or they are correct. What appears not to be an option is that they were reflecting a stylistic convention that referred only to a literary work known as "Isaiah." At least, the early evidence about Isaianic authorship points away from this option.

Josephus sums up the early Jewish view of Isaiah, which bears repeating from above:

> Antiq. 10:35 (10.2.2.35): Now as to this prophet [clearly Isaiah in context], he was by the confession of all, a divine and wonderful man in speaking truth; and out of the assurance that he had never written what was false, he wrote down all his prophecies, and left them behind him in books, that their accomplishment might be judged of from the events by posterity. Nor did this prophet do so alone; but the others, which were twelve in number, did the same. And whatsoever is done among us, whether it be good, or whether it be bad, comes to pass according to their prophecies; but of every one of these we shall speak hereafter.

Similar to the idea of a stylistic convention is the view that Jesus and the New Testament writers did not intend to speak specifically about actual human authorship when they referred to "Isaiah," but they were concerned only about the divine meaning of the text being quoted. If they did not intend to communicate the identity of the human author, they cannot be charged with inaccuracy, even if a real person known as "Isaiah" did not write the entire book. Thus, according to this view, references to "Isaiah" are like window dressing through which the divine message is conveyed.

But our survey of references to Isaiah shows repeated references to the active personal role of Isaiah in writing and prophesying in all parts of the book. Such references are not merely the pipe through which the water of the real message flows, but are part of the message, because they convey the authority of the prophet who was appointed by God, so his message carries that divine authority. For example, note again some expressions: "*rightly* did Isaiah prophesy of you [hypocrites]" (Matt. 15:7; Mark 7:6); "*to fulfill* what was spoken through Isaiah the prophet" and similar phrases (six times); "the Holy Spirit *rightly* spoke through Isaiah the prophet to your fathers" (Acts 28:25). The word translated "rightly" is *kalōs*, which can be rendered "correctly" or "accurately" (as elsewhere in the NT).[12] The authority of the prophet Isaiah is integral to the message communicated, apparent also from recalling Jesus' comparable appeal to the persons of Moses (Luke 20:37; 24:27, 44; John 1:17, 45) and David. This appeal underscores the authority of the message, so that the authority of these personages is inextricably bound up with the message. Note Jesus' appeal to David in Mark 12:35–37, quoting Ps. 110:1:

> And Jesus began to say, as He taught in the temple, "How is it that the scribes say that the Christ is the son of David? David himself said in the Holy Spirit,
>
> > 'The Lord said to my Lord,
> > "Sit at My right hand,
> > Until I put Your enemies beneath Your feet."'
>
> "David himself calls Him 'Lord'; so in what sense is He his son?" And the large crowd enjoyed listening to Him.

12. See *A Greek–English Lexicon of the New Testament and Other Early Christian Literature*, rev. and ed. F. W. Danker (Chicago: University of Chicago Press, 2000), 505–6, who surveys various ranges of meaning and correctly places the uses in Matt. 15:7, Mark 7:6, and Acts 28:25 in the category of "being in accord with a standard, rightly, correctly."

What is also significant in this regard is that Jesus understands that parts of his ministry are modeled after the prophetic vocation of the actual prophet Isaiah. For example, he views his parabolic ministry as a recapitulation of the ministry of Isaiah, as explained in Matthew 13:13–15, which quotes Isaiah 6:9–10:

> Therefore I speak to them in parables; because while seeing they do not see, and while hearing they do not hear, nor do they understand. In their case the prophecy of Isaiah is being fulfilled, which says,
>
> > "You will keep on hearing, but will not understand;
> > You will keep on seeing, but will not perceive;
> > For the heart of this people has become dull,
> > With their ears they scarcely hear,
> > And they have closed their eyes,
> > Otherwise they would see with their eyes,
> > Hear with their ears,
> > And understand with their heart and return,
> > And I would heal them."

What applied to the historic Isaiah's ministry is now seen by Christ as applying to his own ministry. Isaiah 6:9–10 is a commission that the prophet is to fulfill, and Jesus understands that it "is fulfilled again" (anapleroō) in him. Isaiah's ministry was a historical foreshadowing of the even greater ministry of Jesus. Thus, the authority of this statement by Christ is, at least in part, derived from its origin with the prophet Isaiah. Jesus believed that the prophet Isaiah was a historical figure and that Isaiah's historical ministry was a model for his own. Though most scholars accept the Isaianic authorship of Isaiah 6, what is quite interesting about this is that Jesus' quotation of Isaiah 6:9–10 in John 12:39 is said to be written by the same "Isaiah" whom Jesus has just said in verse 38 prophesied the words of Isaiah 53:1, commonly attributed to an anonymous author living after the time of Isaiah.

> This was to fulfill *the word of Isaiah the prophet which he spoke*: "Lord, who has believed our report? And to whom has the arm of the Lord been revealed?" [quoting Isa. 53:1]. For this reason they could not believe, for *Isaiah said again*, "He has blinded their eyes and He hardened their heart,

so that they would not see with their eyes and perceive with their heart, and be converted and I heal them." (John 12:38–40)

What is further striking about the quotation of Isaiah 6:9–10 in John 12:39 is that Jesus has interlaced the quotation with allusions from other passages later in Isaiah, typically attributed to an author (or authors) subsequent to Isaiah. The phrases "he has blinded their eyes" and "he hardened their heart" is an interpretative paraphrase respectively of "make dim their eyes" and "make the hearts of this people fat," both from Isaiah 6:10. Jesus formulates these two paraphrases on the basis of allusions from elsewhere in Isaiah, which come from parts of the book usually said to have been written by writers other than Isaiah the prophet: [13]

John 12:40	Isaiah
"He has blinded their eyes"	29:9-10—" . . . blind yourselves and be blind . . . He [God] has shut your eyes."
	29:18—" . . . the eyes of the blind . . . ."
	42:18-19—"look, you blind . . . Who is so blind . . . as the servant of the LORD" (cf. Isa. 56:10; 59:10).
"He hardened their heart"	63:17—"Why . . . do You harden our heart . . . ?"*

In fact, Isaiah 29:9–10,18; 42:18–19; and 63:17 are among some of the intertextual developments of Isaiah 6:9–10 found later in Isaiah14. The upshot of this is that Jesus sees Isaiah, not later anonymous writers, to

---

13. These interlaced allusions in John 12:40 have been observed in *Writing and Reading the Scroll of Isaiah*, ed. Craig C. Broyles and Craig A. Evans.

14. For developments of Isa. 6:9–10, see also J. L. McLaughlin, 'Their Hearts *Were* Hardened: The Use of Isaiah 6:9–10 in the Book of Isaiah," *Bib* 75 (1994): 1–25, who sees parts of Isaiah 29 and 44 to be direct developments from Isa. 6:9–10; likewise, see R. E. Clements, "Patterns in the Prophetic Canon: Healing the Blind and the Lame," in *Canon, Theology, and Old Testament Interpretation*, ed. G. M. Tucker, D. L. Petersen, and R. R. Wilson (Philadelphia: Fortress, 1988), 192–94, 198, who sees such passages as Isa. 29:18, 20–21; 32:3; 33:23; 35:5–6; 42:18–21; and 44:18 to have demonstrable links and to develop the themes of blindness and deafness in Isa. 6:9–10; so also see idem., "Beyond Tradition-History," 95–113, which mentions most of the preceding texts in Isaiah 29–55 but adds Isa. 43:8; likewise idem., "The Unity of the Book of Isaiah," *Interp* 36 (1982): 125–26, which discusses the passages from Isa. 42 and 43, as well as Isa. 32 and 35. For Clements, these are some of the best examples of intratextual usage within the book.

be the one executing this development of Isaiah 6:9–10 in later parts of the book.

There is insufficient evidence in these references to Isaiah to conclude that they are merely the insignificant husk that surrounds the message intended. Rather, they are part of the message.

WAS THERE A STYLISTIC CONVENTION IN ANCIENT HELLENISM OR JUDAISM BY WHICH PASSAGES FROM LITERARY WORKS COULD BE ATTRIBUTED TO AUTHORS WHO DID NOT WRITE THEM?

One of the reasons for some to reconsider what it means for Jesus, Acts, and Paul to refer to all parts of Isaiah (so-called First, Second, and Third Isaiah) is the idea that there was a common stylistic convention in the ancient world by which people would refer to passages from literary works by names of persons who had, in fact, not authored those works.

The evidence, however, for such a way of referring *to particular passages from ancient works* is non-existent. More work needs to be done in this area, but we are well-served by Christopher D. Stanley's book on Paul's use of the Old Testament.[15] Stanley's main argument is that it was common for later authors to quote earlier authors, but not verbatim. They would make small or large changes, sometimes without interpretative significance but sometimes representing interpretations by the later author.[16] Stanley surveys early Greco-Roman and Jewish writers contemporary with the New Testament. He argues that Paul appears to follow the same general procedure as the non-biblical writers in his quotation technique.

Stanley does a good job of showing whether or not an author is dependent on earlier textual traditions or whether the changed wording reflects an independent rendering by the author. This is helpful in terms of providing a lot of the manual labor (especially in Paul) of supplying textual comparisons, but Stanley does not discuss much the interpretative significance of these changes when they are seen to be made by the quoting author or even when they represent a textual

15. Christopher D. Stanley, *Paul and the Language of Scripture*, Society for New Testament Studies Monograph 69 (Cambridge: Cambridge University Press, 1992).
16. Ibid., 242–43.

tradition that appears already to be interpreting the earlier text (such as the LXX in relation to the MT). He also makes the point that this style of quoting was not unique to the ancient world but is common even in modern usage.[17] In this respect, Stanley's book does not break much ground.

With regard to the issue at hand, however, he presents no evidence that it was an accepted stylistic convention at the time of Jesus and the New Testament writers to quote from earlier authors and attribute to them quotations that did not come from them. Thus, he gives no support to the idea that it was understandable and acceptable for Jesus to have attributed to "Isaiah" the prophet quotations of so-called Second and Third Isaiah—quotations not actually written by "Isaiah." This is our main purpose in summarizing Stanley's book, though he does not draw this implication. But even if there were evidence of such a stylistic convention in the Greco-Roman world, one would also have to show it operating in early Judaism.[18]

17. See Ibid., 355–56, though on 345 and 350 Stanley contradicts this assessment.

18. It is possible that the Jewish pseudepigrapha could offer a parallel to taking Isaiah 40–66 as written by a different author than Isaiah but in the name of Isaiah, which would have been assumed from chapters 1–39, but we are here more concerned with Jesus and the apostles quoting particular verses from "Isaiah" and attributing these verses to the prophet Isaiah. The pseudepigraphical group of writings, on the other hand, are not taken into consideration here because this body of works, while attributing an ancient heroic biblical name to a later writing composed by someone else, does not primarily quote from or expand on specific passages from a body of writings that were composed by that ancient biblical figure, as is argued for Isaiah 40–66 (though these works do make plenty of allusions to Old Testament passages). Rather, a completely new and later composition is attributed to the earlier biblical character; thus, these pseudepigraphic names are attached to "new" works, not as references to Old Testament works. Furthermore, some of the biblical names attributed to these pseudepigraphical works were people who wrote nothing of which we know (e.g., Enoch, Abraham, Jacob, etc.). In the case of Isaiah, however, the contention is that chapters 40–66 were composed by a school of disciples or editors who expanded on chapters 1–39, which were written by the historical Isaiah. Indeed, one reason the large collection of pseudepigraphical works were not included in the Old Testament canon was likely because they were known not to have been written by the person whose name was attached to them, and thus were seen to lack the same biblical authority as Old Testament writers. Most holding a two-Isaiah or three-Isaiah view believe that chapters 40–66 were written around the sixth century B.C., long before the time when the literary genre of Jewish pseudepigrapha arose and flourished (around the beginning of the second century B.C.). In addition, if Isaiah 40–66 were a pseudepigraph, would not the fake author go to clear and repeated lengths to insert the name of Isaiah at points throughout those chapters, as happens typically in the pseudepigraphical books? The survey of early Jewish and Christian views (including that of Jesus) of Isaianic authorship will clearly reveal that

Stanley does make the point that later writers would "correct" an earlier ancient text to "bring it into line with later sensibilities" (this may involve correcting the ancient author's wrong geographical reference or a statement apparently contrary to the morality of a later age; sometimes such "corrections" are mere additional statements set alongside the original without comment).[19] These kinds of quotations, of course, would not be applicable to, e.g., New Testament writers quoting Old Testament texts and "correcting" them. Stanley concludes this discussion by saying that "modern notions of the inviolability of an author's original text simply cannot be transferred to the ancient world,"[20] yet at other points he asserts that such things are not uncommon in modern quotations,[21] so in this respect, he exhibits some inconsistency.

In another instance, Stanley mentions Heraclitus, who "can quote two or more verses back-to-back with no indication of their diverse origins [i.e., from different parts of Homer]. In every case the materials thus combined deal with similar topics, producing a single 'quotation' that better supports or exemplifies the author's [Heraclitus's] point."[22] After the preceding reference, however, Stanley gives an example:

> One peculiarity worth noting is a single instance in which an introductory formula anticipates a quotation concerning Athena ... is actually followed by a "quotation" that combines one passage on Athena with another that originally referred to Artemis. Though a memory lapse is always possible, it may be that here again one sees a certain willingness on the part of the author to adapt the Homeric text to his own purposes.[23]

If this is not a memory lapse, then it is an interpretative attempt to describe Athena with the attributes of Artemis (similar to a procedure that John uses in Revelation: e.g., the phrase "the one who was and is and is coming" is a name for Zeus, taken and applied to the God of the Bible, though there

---

they did not view the book to be a pseudepigraph. In this connection, neither Jesus nor the apostles ever formally quote from a pseudepigraphical book, presumably because they were held not to have divine canonical authority.

19. Stanley, *Paul and the Language of Scripture*, 274.
20. Ibid.
21. Ibid., 356.
22. Ibid., 283–84.
23. Ibid., 284.

is also Old Testament influence). But both quotations are apparently from Homer, not Homer and a different author.

None of what Stanley has said so far has any parallel with attributing to an author (such as Isaiah) a specific quotation that is not really from that author. Indeed, in surveying the Greco-Roman authors, he focuses on their quotations of Homer, and, as far as I can tell, not one time is there any question of attributing to Homer statements or segments from another author.[24]

Stanley, however, does introduce something that could fit this kind of situation. He cites 1 Esdras 1:58 (55), which I cite here in its immediate context:

> 1 Esd. 1:57–58—"And they were servants to him and to his sons until the Persians began to reign, in fulfilment of the word of the Lord by the mouth of Jeremiah: Until the land has enjoyed its sabbaths, it shall keep sabbath all the time of its desolation until the completion of seventy years."

> 1 Esd. 2:1–2—"In the first year of Cyrus as king of the Persians, that the word of the Lord by the mouth of Jeremiah might be accomplished, the Lord stirred up the spirit of Cyrus king of the Persians, and he made a proclamation throughout all his kingdom and also put it in writing."

Stanley says that 1 Esdras 1:58, "a verse framed as an indirect statement in 2 Chr 36.21 (a midrashic conflation of Jer 25.12 and Lev 26.34), appears as a direct quotation and is attributed in its entirety to the prophet Jeremiah."[25] On the surface, one might say that 1 Esdras is attributing to Jeremiah words from Moses (Leviticus) and the Chronicler. But there is a thin line between what Stanley calls "an indirect statement in 2 Chr 36:21" and "a direct quotation" in 1 Esdras, since both have virtually the same introductory phrasing, "to fulfill the word [or 'for fulfillment of the saying'] of the Lord through the mouth of Jeremiah." Note the comparison of the relevant texts:[26]

---

24. E.g., see Stanley's conclusion in *Paul and the Language of Scripture*, 339.

25. Ibid., 309.

26. Greek script is used here instead of English transliteration in order that the textual comparisons may be observed more readily.

1 Esd. 1:57–58	εἰς ἀναπλήρωσιν του ῥήματος του κυρίου ἐν στόματι Ιερεμιου Ἕως του εὐδοκησαι τὴν γην **τὰ σάββατα αὐτης, πάντα τὸν χρόνον της ἐρημώσεως αὐτης**, σαββατιει εἰς **συμπλήρωσιν ἐτων ἑβδομήκοντα**.	In fulfillment of the word of the Lord by the mouth of Jeremiah; until the land has enjoyed its sabbaths, it shall keep sabbath all the time of its desolation until the completion of the seventy years. [Note: The words in bold are also in the 2 Chronicles text.]
2 Chron. 36:21–22	τοῦ πληρωθῆναι λόγον κυρίου διὰ στόματος Ιερεμιου ἕως τοῦ προσδέξασθαι τὴν γῆν **τὰ σάββατα αὐτῆς σαββατίσαι, πάσας τὰς ἡμέρας τῆς ἐρημώσεως αὐτῆς** ἐσαββάτισεν εἰς **συμπλήρωσιν ἐτῶν ἑβδομήκοντα**. μετὰ τὸ πληρωθῆναι ῥῆμα κυρίου διὰ στόματος Ιερεμιου.	That the word of the Lord by the mouth of Jeremiah might be fulfilled until the land should enjoy its Sabbaths in resting [and] sabbath-keeping all the days of its desolation until the fulfillment of seventy years . . . after the fulfillment of the word of the Lord by the mouth of Jeremiah. [Note: The words in bold are also in the 1 Esdras text.]
Lev. 26:34	τότε εὐδοκήσει ἡ γη **τὰ σάββατα αὐτης** καὶ πάσας τὰς ἡμέρας της ἐρημώσεως αὐτης καὶ ὑμεις ἐσεσθε ἐν τη γη των ἐχθρων ὑμων, τότε σαββατιει ἡ γη καὶ εὐδοκήσει **τὰ σάββατα αὐτης**.	Then the land shall enjoy its sabbaths all the days of its desolation, and you shall be in the land of your enemies; then the land shall also keep its Sabbaths. [Note: The words in bold are also in the 2 Chron. text.]
Jer. 25:12	καὶ ἐν τω **πληρωθῆναι τὰ ἑβδομήκοντα ἔτη** ἐκδικήσω τὸ ἔθνος ἐκεινο, φησὶν **κύριος**, καὶ θήσομαι αὐτοὺς εἰς ἀφανισμὸν αἰώνιον.	And when the seventy years are fulfilled, I will take vengeance on that nation, and will make them a perpetual desolation. [Note: The words in bold are also in the 2 Chron. text.]

First Esdras 1:57–58 is essentially a quotation from 2 Chron. 36:21, as the above chart makes clear (in fact, 1 Esdras 1:1–2:5 is essentially a copying of 2 Chron. 35:1–36:23). Thus, like 2 Chron. 36:21, so 1 Esdras 1:57–58 attributes the saying to Jeremiah. Stanley is likely correct (as can also be seen from the table) that 2 Chronicles itself combines Lev. 26:34 and Jer. 25:12. So the problem is not how 1 Esdras can attribute to Jeremiah a saying that includes what Moses said, but how the Chronicler can do it.[27] The answer seems to be along the following lines: Jeremiah itself could be developing Leviticus (though more conceptually than verbally), or the Chronicler could be interpreting that Jeremiah is developing Leviticus, and so he combines the two. The reason that the Chronicler attributes the entire saying to Jeremiah is likely because the quotation from Jeremiah is the part of the prophecy that he mainly had in mind (Leviticus has become subsumed interpretatively in Jeremiah). This is classic midrash, in which one key biblical text is combined with another to be interpreted by it. The Chronicler is not citing an entire segment of chapters and attributing them to an author who did not write them. The Chronicler is interpreting one verse (in Jeremiah) by another verse (in Leviticus), and the author (Jeremiah) he mentions is the one that he mainly has in mind to interpret, which is interpretatively supplemented by the secondary author (Moses in Leviticus).[28]

This then is not an issue of authorship but one of midrashic interpretation. The same phenomenon occurs with the attribution of Malachi to Isaiah in Mark 1:2–3. Rikki Watts has demonstrated quite plausibly that the reason for this is that Mark is dominated throughout by Isaiah (being concerned with narrating Jesus as inaugurating the end-time second exodus predicted by Isaiah), and that other Old Testament references adduced throughout Mark supplement interpretatively the Isaianic picture.[29] What better way to start off that project than to adduce Malachi to interpret Isaiah 40:3, so that Malachi becomes subsumed interpretatively into Isaiah.[30] This is not, as far

27. First Esdras also appears to supplement two further possible words from Leviticus, following the example of 2 Chronicles: *eudokēsai* and *sabbatiei* (though the latter is merely a minor change in verb form).

28. Stanley concludes his discussion by noting that there is some textual lack of clarity in the 1 Esdras quotation: "The origins of this conflation and adaptation remain obscure [in 1 Esdras 1:57–58] . . ." (*Paul and the Language of Scripture*, 309). So one should be careful of basing too much on this particular example.

29. On which see R. Watts, *Isaiah's New Exodus in Mark* (Grand Rapids: Baker, 1997), 53–90.

30. Indeed, Mal. 3:1 alludes to the leading angel of Ex. 23:20, guiding Israel in the first exodus, which fits admirably with the Isa. 40:3 reference to the messenger preparing for the second exodus.

as I can tell, about a forgetful memory nor a stylistic convention whereby an author is adduced who could be seen to have written a passage that the author, indeed, did not write.[31]

It may be that in some cases only the main text to be interpreted is mentioned, since not only one but more secondary texts brought in to interpret the focus text are present, and it would be too cumbersome to mention all three of the texts or authors.[32] Similarly, would we demand that Paul (or Moses), when intentionally referring to a phrase from an earlier letter in a later letter, say something like, "as I said in Galatians," in order to preserve his historical authorship of that earlier saying? In so doing, does he deny the earlier authorship of the statement? With regard to both questions, I do not think so.

Of course, Isaiah 40–66 may be one big midrashic interpretation of the preceding part of Isaiah; if so, Jesus may have simply attributed parts of this latter section to Isaiah. If such were the case, this anonymous author of Isaiah 40–66 would have been interpretatively expanding the focus text of the first part of the book called and penned by "Isaiah." But this would be an example close to the Jewish pseudepigraphical genre, which we have already determined to be an unlikely category for Isaiah 40–66. This would be quite different from citing specific quotations or combining parts of verses for interpretative purposes, which is the topic of concern here (indeed, we are talking about intertextuality, whereby the main text of concern to be interpreted is mentioned but not the interpreting text).

Why have we included a summary of Stanley's work here? The upshot of the above survey of his work does not support the notion that there was an ancient stylistic convention among Greco-Roman or Jewish writers contemporary with the New Testament period of attributing a quotation to an author when that author did not write that quotation. When scholars assert that there was such a stylistic habit and that this explains New Testa-

---

31. The same thing is going on in Matt. 27:9–10, where Jeremiah and Zechariah are combined but the entirety is attributed to Jeremiah. See D. A. Carson's explanation in *Matthew, Chapters 13 through 28*, Expositor's Bible Commentary (Grand Rapids: Zondervan, 1995), 562–67. This is along the lines that Watts follows.

32. This could be the case in Mark 1:2–3, where Mal. 3:1 and Ex. 23:20 may both be adduced as secondary enhancing texts of the main focus text of Isaiah. Again, see Watts, *Isaiah's New Exodus in Mark*, 53–90, who discusses the influence of Ex. 23:20 in Mal. 3:1, but concludes that only Malachi is present in Mark 1 (though on 89 Watts refers to the Exodus/Malachi conflation in Mark 1); however, both the Exodus and Malachi texts may be in mind, as the margin of NA27 contends.

ment references to particular verses from "Isaiah," such an assertion is not supported by evidence. Until there is further evidence forthcoming to the contrary, scholars should be hesitant to appeal to this kind of argument.[33] I think a number of scholars (I strongly suspect including Stanley himself) who do not hold to Isaianic authorship would accept the above argument, but would affirm simply that Jesus and the apostles thought they really were quoting from the author Isaiah, when in reality, unbeknownst to them, Isaiah actually was not the author. More conservative scholars who hold such a position and would not want to posit an "error" at this point often appeal to some sort of accommodation theory in order still to hold to the infallibility of Scripture, a theory to which we now direct attention.

WAS JESUS' REFERENCE TO "ISAIAH" AN ACCOMMODATION TO AN INCORRECT JEWISH TRADITION?

Many of those who are not convinced that the references to Isaiah were part of an understandable stylistic convention would contend that the belief of Judaism and early Christianity in the authorship of Isaiah was not historically correct, but that such a conviction had become part of their socially constructed tradition. Consequently, it is only natural that Jesus expressed this belief, since he not only had a divine nature but *was* human, speaking Aramaic, and accepting the customs of his Jewish culture, presumably including traditions that were unbiblical or not true to historical reality. This is sometimes understood as part of a "kenosis" theory of Christ's incarnation, whereby "he emptied himself" or "gave up the use" of his divine attributes. Accordingly, he was in part a typical person of his time and culture, naturally and unconsciously accepting some of the untrue traditions of that culture. This may be referred to as an "unconscious accommodation" of Jesus to his culture.

---

33. Though I suspect that it is likely that Stanley would draw the conclusion that Isaiah the prophet was the author of Isaiah 40–66, it would probably be for other reasons than his disagreement with the evidence adduced in this section. Of course, one could hold that Jesus and the apostles thought Isaiah was the original author of sayings from this section, so that from this vantage point their citations still fit with Stanley's study. However, such a conclusion poses other problems dealt with in the remainder of this study, among which are theological problems (e.g., Christology). One could object to my application of Stanley's work to Jesus' quotations, since Jesus never wrote anything but his references to Isaiah were oral, but the same thing could be technically said of Paul's letter to the Romans and Peter's first epistle (on which see below). Anyway, what Stanley has adduced with respect to authors would appear to be just as applicable to speakers.

In further support of this, it is sometimes said that Christ acknowledged that he was ignorant of some things and, therefore, fallible in his knowledge, though the thrust of his message was reliable. A text sometimes adduced for this is Matthew 24:36, where Christ says that the "day and hour" of the end of history "no one knows, not even the angels of heaven, nor the Son, but the Father alone." But ignorance of the future is not the same thing as making an erroneous statement (whereas if Christ had predicted something that did not take place, that would be an error). In support of this, ironically, is the directly preceding verse, Matthew 24:35: "Heaven and earth will pass away, but my words will not pass away." In other words, any assertion about past, present, or future reality that Christ makes has a truthful force that cannot be blunted.[34]

In this respect, some evangelical postmodernists might even conclude that this tradition was not "wrong" for the first-century Jews, even though according to our modern historical standards we would judge it to be erroneous. But, so goes the argument, we should not impose our standards of historical correctness on ancient literature. Thus, God communicated fully inspired truths to them in their own linguistic and cultural language. But, again, Matthew 24:35 says that no matter how many cultures come and go, Christ's truthful word remains the same. Cultures with their own idiosyncratic beliefs will rise and fall until Christ comes a final time; not only will they pass away, but ultimately this "heaven and earth will pass away, but [Christ's] words will not pass away." The truth of Christ's words and teachings is not culturally bound but transcends all cultures and remains unaltered by cultural beliefs. This is said in another way in Isaiah 40:7–8, quoted partly in James 1:10–11 and more fully in 1 Peter 1:24–25: "The grass withers, the flower fades, but the word of our God stands forever" (see also Isaiah 55:10–11; Matthew 5:17–18). As argued elsewhere, ancient cultures had logical categories for observing and assessing the world and distinguishing the true from the false that are in significant ways commensurate to

---

34. I am grateful to J. I. Packer, *"Fundamentalism" and the Word of God* (Grand Rapids: Eerdmans, 1957), 60–61, for this point about the link between Matt. 24:35 and 24:36. In this connection, note also B. B. Warfield's comment on Christology: "in the case of our Lord's person, the human nature remains truly human while yet it can never fall into sin or error because it can never act out of relation with the Divine nature into conjunction with which it has been brought" (*The Inspiration and Authority of the Bible* [Nutley, NJ: Presbyterian & Reformed, 1970], 162f. [cited by Packer, *"Fundamentalism,"* 83, but I have been unable to find this precise quotation in Warfield's book, though he says as much in 158–76]).

our modern categories.[35] In line with this, Jesus' propositional statements about such things as sin, his deity, his saving death, his resurrection, the final resurrection of humanity, and the end of world history are truths that transcend all cultures.

Others contend that Jesus, as the God-man, may have known that Isaiah was not the author of the work that went by his name, but consciously "accommodated" himself to the false Jewish view in order to facilitate his communication of the message from the book. Accordingly, to have exposed the error of the Jewish tradition about Isaiah would have altered the center of attention from the main point of the message of Isaiah to a pedantic point about technical historical authorship. Therefore, Jesus adjusted his message to permit this belief to remain unchallenged.

There is a common problem with both of these perspectives about Christ's "accommodation": it is clear that part of Jesus' mission was to confront and expose the false traditions of Judaism that had gradually grown and come to be held by the first century.[36] J. I. Packer aptly put his finger on this point as far back as the late 1950s, when he concluded that Jesus "did not hesitate to challenge and condemn, on His authority, many accepted Jewish ideas which seemed to him false"[37]; and

> Scripture, indeed, contains emphatic warnings against uncritical deference to traditions and speculations in theology. Christ deals with the question of the authority of tradition in Mk. vii.6–13. The Pharisees claimed their oral law was derived from Moses and should therefore be treated as an authoritative supplement to and exposition of the written law. Christ rejects this idea, contrasting the written word with the oral law as "the commandment *of God*" and "the commandments *of men*" respectively. . . . The fact that they are bowing to man-made tradition rather than God-given Scripture, He says, shows that their

---

35. See Beale, "The Issue of Socially Constructed Cultures, Presuppositions, and Biblical Interpretation," in *The Erosion of Inerrancy in Evangelicalism: Responding to New Challenges to Biblical Authority* (see especially section III.A.).

36. See further, e.g., N. B. Stonehouse, *The Witness of Matthew and Mark to Christ* (Philadelphia: Presbyterian Guardian, 1944; repr. Grand Rapids: Eerdmans, 1958), 195–211; and R. V. G. Tasker, *The Old Testament in the New Testament* (Grand Rapids: Eerdmans, 1954), 32. I am thankful to Packer, "*Fundamentalism*," 56n2, for alerting me to these two sources.

37. Packer, "*Fundamentalism*," 55.

hearts are far from God. To Christ, ecclesiastical tradition was no part of the word of God; it must be tested by Scripture and, if found wanting, dropped.[38]

Significantly, the Jews believed that since a well-known Old Testament figure, Moses, was the author of their oral law,[39] their oral law had equal authority with the written Scripture that had also come from Moses. Jesus says no and that such traditions did not have the authority of Mosaic Scripture. In Mark 7:1–13, Jesus contrasts Isaiah's prophesying (v. 6, citing Isa. 29:13) and Moses's written word (v. 10), which had divine authority, with "the tradition of the elders," which has no divine authority. Therefore, while Jesus opposed the pseudo-authority of untrue Jewish traditions, he always affirmed the definitive authority of the Old Testament (e.g., John 10:35, "the Scripture cannot be broken") and "never qualified the Jewish belief in its absolute authority in the slightest degree."[40] This appears to be a case where Jesus disagrees with a pseudo-oral source (the false attribution of Jewish oral tradition to Moses).

In the light of this, is it possible that Jesus would have gone along with a false Jewish view about the authorship of Isaiah? It is unlikely, especially since the Old Testament was foundational for Jesus' teaching about his vocation and his identity; he made appeal to the Old Testament repeatedly as the primary warrant for the things he did and said. Is it likely, in this light, that he would knowingly or unknowingly be wrong about who was the authoritative author of what some scholars refer to as the "gospel of Isaiah"? If he were wrong here, why should we have confidence that he was not also wrong in other of his important appeals to the Old Testament?[41] As R. V. G. Tasker has concluded, "If He [Christ] could be mistaken on matters which He regarded as of the strictest relevance to His own person and ministry, it is difficult to see exactly how or why He can or should be trusted anywhere else."[42]

38. Ibid., 70–71.
39. See, e.g., J. Neusner, "Rabbinic Literature: Mishnah and Tosefta," in *Dictionary of New Testament Background*, ed. C. A. Evans and S. E. Porter (Downers Grove, IL: IVP, 2000), 895.
40. Ibid., 55.
41. Ibid., 60, though Packer is speaking generally about Christ's view of the authority of the Old Testament and not focusing merely on Jesus' appeals to Isaiah.
42. Tasker, *The Old Testament in the New Testament*, 37.

RECONSIDERATION OF THE MATERIAL IN THE BOOK OF ISAIAH

Superscriptions referring to "Isaiah" in the book of Isaiah are found at 1:1, 2:1, 13:1, and 20:2:

> The *vision of Isaiah* the son of Amoz concerning Judah and Jerusalem, which he saw during the reigns of Uzziah, Jotham, Ahaz and Hezekiah, kings of Judah. (Isa. 1:1)

> *The word which Isaiah the son of Amoz saw* concerning Judah and Jerusalem. (Isa. 2:1)

> *The oracle concerning Babylon which Isaiah the son of Amoz saw.* (Isa. 13:1)

> At that time *the* LORD *spoke through Isaiah the son of Amoz, saying,* "Go and loosen . . . ." (Isa. 20:2)

> Now the rest of the acts of Uzziah, first to last, *the prophet Isaiah, the son of Amoz, has written.* (2 Chron. 26:22)

Judging by the above evidence, I am in agreement with Richard Schultz's recent conclusion about the superscriptions:

> Given 1) the clear assertion in Isa 1:1 that what follows is "the vision of Isaiah son of Amoz, which he saw concerning Judah and Jerusalem in the days of Uzziah, Jotham, Ahaz, and Hezekiah, kings of Judah" and 2) the absence of any additional ascriptions of authorship within the book, the "one Isaiah" position may be the only one that takes the book's own claims seriously.[43]

I still find the traditional view of Isaianic authorship for the whole book preferable (though in the academic guild, I am not considered to be an Old Testament but a New Testament practitioner). The most recent work of which I am aware arguing for this position is Richard Schultz's above-quoted article on the authorship of Isaiah.[44] This article presents a brief but

---

43. Schultz, "How Many 'Isaiahs'?" 153.
44. See also his forthcoming commentary on Isaiah for Baker Book House; note, in addition, Schultz's monograph (based on his Yale PhD dissertation), *The Search for Quotation,*

viable conservative view of the significance of the superscriptions in Isaiah, as well as of the unity of the book.

As evident from reading in the field of Isaiah scholarship, one of the main reasons for reconsidering the authorship of Isaiah 40–66 is that it is so specifically aware of circumstances in Babylon, and it addresses those who were in exile there instead of Isaiah's earlier audience in the land of Israel. In fact, this fits in with a presupposition of the majority of Old Testament scholars, who are convinced of higher critical views of dating, that prophecy had to contain material that was mainly relevant for the contemporary audience of the prophet and not contain predicted events that had no relation to the present audience. Thus, most predictions are viewed as *vaticinium ex eventu* ("prophecy after the event"). In other words, recent events that had happened to a prophet's audience were written down as if they had been prophesied many years, or even centuries, earlier. For myself, I am not convinced of this presupposition about Old Testament books but am convinced generally by the evidence of Schultz's article. Most who hold to a different author of Isaiah believe that it was someone living directly after the prophecies were fulfilled, and writing history to make it look like prophecy. A minority of scholars holding to non-Isaianic authorship still affirm, however, that the anonymous author of Isaiah 40–66 was living in the midst of the Babylonian exile and was genuinely prophesying about events soon to happen (in thirty to forty years or so).

But Isaiah 13 is just as specific in a more extreme manner in discussing the decisive judgment of Babylon at the hand of the Persians. This thirteenth chapter is introduced by the phrase, "the oracle concerning Babylon which Isaiah the son of Amoz saw." Does this not point to a positive answer to the question posed skeptically by some as to whether the only way Isaiah 40–66 could have been written by "Isaiah the prophet" would be if he had a vision of the future (or was transported by vision into the future). Isaiah 13:1 makes just this scenario quite viable. The "oracle" likely continues into Isaiah 14:1–23, where Israel is said repeatedly to have been in bondage to Babylon, that Babylon would be judged, and that Israel would be restored from Babylon. Isaiah 21:1–2 likewise refers to Isaiah's "oracle" and "vision" about the judgment of Babylon ("fallen, fallen is Babylon," 21:9). Of course, I am aware that commentators place Isaiah 13–14 and parts of

---

JSOT 180 (Sheffield, England: Sheffield Academic Press, 1999), which focuses not on authorship issues but on intertextuality in the Old Testament, with a focus on Isaiah.

21:1–10 late as well.[45] And, of course, commentators place Isaiah 24–27 at a late date because of its eschatology (e.g., resurrection, Israel's restoration, etc.). I am not convinced by these arguments, but I cannot elaborate on all my reasons now. Suffice it to say, that wherever Isaiah appears to make specific prophecies, the critics too often assume that such prophecies are *vaticinia ex eventu*. Thus, I think presuppositions drive these late datings of parts of Isaiah.

Interestingly, "I" in 24:16 and 25:1 refers likely to Isaiah in continuation of the fifteen times it occurred previously in Isaiah 6–21 with reference to Isaiah; in addition, "But I say, 'Woe to me! Woe to me! Alas for me'" (Isa. 24:16) appears uniquely similar to Isa. 6:5, "Then I said, 'Woe is me, for I am ruined!'"). In this respect, "oracle" (in Isa. 21:1) is used about ten times in Isaiah (chaps. 13–30) and "vision" (Isa. 21:2) about seven times in the same segment. In addition, the name "Isaiah" occurs about sixteen times in Isaiah 1–39. In particular, the intensive use in Isaiah 37–39 (ten times) may be significant, since there Isaiah is reported to have prophesied the exile to Babylon:

> Then Isaiah the prophet came to King Hezekiah and said to him, "What did these men say, and from where have they come to you?" And Hezekiah said, "They have come to me from a far country, from Babylon." (Isa. 39:3)

> "Behold, the days are coming when all that is in your house and all that your fathers have laid up in store to this day will be carried to Babylon; nothing will be left," says the LORD. "And some of your sons who will issue from you, whom you will beget, will be taken away, and they will become officials in the palace of the king of Babylon." (Isa. 39:6–7)

If one takes this, together with the prophecies of Israel's bondage to Babylon in chapters 13–14 and of her restoration in chapters 24–27, are the prophecies of the very same things in Isaiah 40–66 so alarming and different? The main difference is the extended length of this latter section, but the nature of the material does not appear to be much different, except for the specific reference to the idols of Babylon (intriguingly, "Babylon" appears nine times in Isaiah 13–39 and only four times in chaps. 40–66).

---

45. E.g., with respect to Isaiah 13–14, see S. Erlandsson, *The Burden of Babylon: A Study of Isaiah 13:2–14:23*, Coniectanea biblica 4 (Lund, Sweden: Gleerup, 1970).

But even this theme of idolatry in chapters 40–66 has its clear roots in Isaiah 1–39.[46] Note, in this respect, Isaiah 21:1–10:

> The oracle concerning the wilderness of the sea.
> As windstorms in the Negev sweep on,
> It comes from the wilderness, from a terrifying land.
> A harsh vision has been shown to me;
> The treacherous one still deals treacherously, and the destroyer still destroys.
> Go up, Elam, lay siege, Media;
> I have made an end of all the groaning she has caused.
> For this reason my loins are full of anguish;
> Pains have seized me like the pains of a woman in labor.
> I am so bewildered I cannot hear, so terrified I cannot see.
> My mind reels, horror overwhelms me;
> The twilight I longed for has been turned for me into trembling.
> They set the table, they spread out the cloth, they eat, they drink;
> "Rise up, captains, oil the shields,"
> For thus the Lord says to me,
> "Go, station the lookout, let him report what he sees.
> "When he sees riders, horsemen in pairs,
> A train of donkeys, a train of camels,
> Let him pay close attention, very close attention."
> Then the lookout called,
> "O Lord, I stand continually by day on the watchtower,
> And I am stationed every night at my guard post.
> "Now behold, here comes a troop of riders, horsemen in pairs."
> And one said, "Fallen, fallen is Babylon;
> And all the images of her gods are shattered on the ground."
> O my threshed people, and my afflicted of the threshing floor!
> What I have heard from the LORD of hosts,
> The God of Israel, I make known to you.

Isaiah[47] here sees a vision of the fall of Babylon and hears the message from God about this future fall several generations after his own, includ-

---

46. See G. K. Beale, "Isaiah 6:9–13: A Retributive Taunt Against Idolatry," *VT* 41 (1991): 257–78; see also expanded comments in my *You Become Like What You Worship: A Biblical Theology of Idolatry* (Downers Grove, IL: InterVarsity, forthcoming in 2008).

47. That Isaiah the prophet is in mind is apparent from the repeated first person pronouns (vv. 2–4, 6, 8, 10) in continuation of the repeated first person pronouns referring to "Isaiah" in the preceding chapters.

ing the judgment of her idols, a theme expanded on in Isaiah 40–48. Isaiah 21:2 not only prophesies about the fall of Babylon but explicitly names the nation ("Media") that will defeat Babylon (as also in Isa. 13:17), which is similar to though not as specific as Isaiah 44:28 and 45:1–3, 12–13. Is this not equivalent to Isaiah being transported to the future or seeing a vision of the future or hearing about it in an oracular manner and then prophesying about it?[48]

Likewise, Isaiah 2:1–4 (introduced as "the vision which Isaiah the son of Amoz saw") and its prophecy of the eschatological temple and the coming of Gentiles to Jerusalem is a specific restoration prophecy of distant eschatological events. If all of Isaiah 1–39 is from Isaiah's hand, it would seem that the nature of, especially, chapters 13–14, 21, 24–27, and 39 would assuage one's unease at the same (though more extended) material in Isaiah 40–66 (of course, again, if these earlier six chapters are not from Isaiah, that would change the nature of this conclusion).[49]

In addition to this, in Isaiah's own day, the northern kingdom was already in Assyrian exile, and "Sennacherib claimed to have conquered forty-six walled cities in Judah and deported more than two hundred thousand of its citizens."[50] In view of this, together with the fact that Babylon was already on the ascendancy (see Isaiah 39), does it not make sense that Isaiah would have seen the captives as belonging eventually to Babylon (which he says in chapter 39) and that the future distant restoration must be from Babylon?

In this respect, the appeal to "Isaiah" as the author of Isaiah 40–66 by early Judaism and the New Testament is to underscore, at least in part, that God can predict the end from the beginning (God can make long-range prophecy). The best explanation of this is that they were following the original intention of Isaiah 40–66 itself, written by Isaiah long before

---

48. For support of the ideas offered in this paragraph, see Young, *The Book of Isaiah*, 2:59–75.

49. The most specific and alarming prophecy is that about "Cyrus" (Isaiah 44–45), but this is not as much of a problem for an exilic prophet as for a pre-exilic prophet (i.e., Cyrus may not have been reigning at the time of the purported exilic prophet's writing). You may recall that Harrison, *Introduction to the Old Testament*, 794, attributes this to a later scribal gloss (which does not *necessarily* compromise a "unity of Isaiah" view), but if genuine prophecy is allowed for, then why cannot such a prophecy be made, especially since (1) the Messiah is specifically prophesied, (2) the "Medes" have already been prophesied about in chapters 13 and 21, and (3) predictive prophecy is often referred to throughout all parts of Isaiah as evidence of God's sovereignty?

50. Schultz, "How Many 'Isaiahs'?" 164.

the exile and restoration. To claim that these were not prophecies at all but history written to appear as prophecy does not appear to do justice to the polemic that Isaiah 40–66 is conducting, since if those to whom this section of Isaiah was originally addressed knew that it was not prophecy, then the polemic against the idols' inability to predict becomes vapid and impotent. Even to say that an anonymous prophet living during the exile issued actual short-term prophecies, while still technically affirming real predictions, comes too close to affirming that such predictions were like weather forecasts or political prognostications. The author was living so close to the events about which he prophesied that he was able from the human perspective to predict what was going to happen. The fact that these events did occur demonstrates the divine inspiration of the prophecies (i.e., according to an unusual conservative view of such an anonymous exilic prophet). It would appear to be special pleading to say that though the prophecies came from an exilic anonymous prophet, that it was in the prophetic mind of God a few hundred years earlier. Even such short-range prophecy dilutes the polemic against the idols, that they cannot make long-range prophecies. While short-range prophecy can occur in the Old Testament and New Testament, the Isaianic statements support a long-range perspective, as the following texts appear to support. These following prophecies are specifically of restoration from Babylonian exile and are to be understood as long-range prophecies that were issued before even the Assyrian exile, most likely by Isaiah the prophet:

> Do you not know? Have you not heard?
> Has it not been declared to you from the beginning?
> Have you not understood from the foundations of the earth?
>> (Isa. 40:21)

> Who has performed and accomplished it,
> Calling forth the generations from the beginning?
> "I, the Lord, am the first, and with the last. I am He." (Isa. 41:4)

> Who has declared this from the beginning, that we might know?
> Or from former times, that we may say, "He is right!"?
> Surely there was no one who declared,
> Surely there was no one who proclaimed,
> Surely there was no one who heard your words. (Isa. 41:26)

Thus says the Lord, the King of Israel and his Redeemer, the Lord of hosts:

"I am the first and I am the last,
And there is no God besides Me.
Who is like Me? Let him proclaim and declare it;
Yes, let him recount it to Me in order,
From the time that I established the ancient nation.
And let them declare to them the things that are coming
And the events that are going to take place.
Do not tremble and do not be afraid;
Have I not long since announced it to you and declared it?
And you are My witnesses.
Is there any God besides Me,
Or is there any other Rock?
I know of none." (Isa. 44:6–8)

Declaring the end from the beginning,
And from ancient times things which have not been done,
Saying, "My purpose will be established,
And I will accomplish all My good pleasure";
Calling a bird of prey from the east,
The man of My purpose from a far country.
Truly I have spoken; truly I will bring it to pass.
I have planned it, surely I will do it. (Isa. 46:10–11)

I declared the former things long ago
And they went forth from My mouth, and I proclaimed them.
Suddenly I acted, and they came to pass. . . .
Therefore I declared them to you long ago,
Before they took place I proclaimed them to you,
So that you would not say, "My idol has done them,
And my graven image and my molten image have commanded them."
You have heard; look at all this.
And you, will you not declare it?
I proclaim to you new things from this time,
Even hidden things which you have not known. (Isa. 48:3, 5–6)

See also Isaiah 43:9–19.[51]

51. Though cf. the following text that uses the same language as the above Isaiah texts and affirms that the king of Assyria's recent victories over other nations were planned long ago by God:

The New Testament perspective is that Old Testament prophets made long-range predictions. For example, 1 Peter 1:10–12 affirms,

> As to this salvation, the prophets who prophesied of the grace that *would come* to you made careful searches and inquiries, seeking to know what person or time the Spirit of Christ within them was indicating as He predicted the sufferings of Christ and the glories to follow. It was revealed to them that they were not serving themselves, but you, in these things which now have been announced to you through those who preached the gospel to you by the Holy Spirit sent from heaven—things into which angels long to look.

This underscores not only that prophets from the Old Testament made long-range prophecy, but that they knew they were predicting things that would occur well after their contemporary audiences' generations. This is just the opposite of the presupposition noted above by so many in the contemporary Old Testament guild that prophecy had to include primarily material that was relevant for the contemporary audience of the prophet. Other New Testament passages make the same point (e.g., Matt. 13:16–17; John 8:56; Heb. 11:13).

What is also interesting about the 1 Peter text is that among the Old Testament prophets within Peter's purview is the prophet who made the restoration prophecies of Isaiah 40:6–8 (1 Peter 1:24–25) and Isaiah 53 (1 Peter 2:22–25, where repeated references are made to Isaiah 53[52]). These "Isaiah" texts are in the portion typically attributed to "Second Isaiah," not to the prophet Isaiah himself, because of the guild's presupposition about the relevance and fulfillment of prophecy before the prophet's contemporary audience. Yet these very texts are connected to the programmatic statement about long-range prophecy in 1 Peter 1:10–12! And, indeed, the New Testament writers understand that Isaiah 53 was fulfilled in Christ, which means that Isaiah 53 predicted it seven

---

"Have you not heard?
Long ago I did it,
From ancient times I planned it.
Now I have brought it to pass,
That you should turn fortified cities into ruinous heaps" (Isa. 37:26).

52. See D. A. Carson, "The Old Testament in the General Epistles," in *Commentary on the New Testament Use of the Old Testament*, ed. G. K. Beale and D. A. Carson (Grand Rapids; Baker, 2007), in loc.

centuries before the Messiah's coming (e.g., Matt. 8:17; Mark 15:28; Acts 8:28–35). If this be so, why is it so hard to believe that Isaiah could have predicted two centuries before Israel's return from Babylonian captivity, and even the specific prophecy about Cyrus being instrumental in that restoration (Isa. 45:1–13)?[53]

The typical response to this preceding paragraph and, indeed, most of the evidence of this chapter, is that the New Testament did not have the same perspective as the Old Testament and that this issue about Isaiah must be settled only by studying the book of Isaiah itself. This response is fueled typically by two notions: (1) the accepted idea that because Old Testament studies is a separate discipline that the New Testament's perspective on and interpretation of the Old Testament is not only secondary, but often enough does not reflect the true state of things in the Old Testament. Rather, the New Testament reflects only the evolved beliefs and traditions of first century Judaism. (2) The Bible is not fully inspired, so that there is not an ultimate divine author of the whole, which means that the New Testament's commentary on the Old (e.g., the authorship of Isaiah) is not reliable. The plea of this chapter, however, is that there are also reasonable and cogent arguments within Isaiah itself that have viability for its unity. Furthermore, this chapter contends that the New Testament should also be considered as part of the evidence of the authorship issue and that it confirms the argument for unity of authorship in Isaiah.

The degree of "intratextuality" (some would say "intertextuality") between Isaiah 1–39 and 40–66 has become so recognized that the apparent trend is that many Isaiah scholars who hold to diversity of authorship, nevertheless recognize a "final literary unity."[54] The line between "unity of authorship" and "final literary unity" is becoming thinner and thinner.

I also find Schultz's following conclusion pointing in the right direction:

> Rather, the issue is whether we legitimately can posit a series of inspired authors or editors when the involvement of multiple "prophets" is *not* acknowledged in the text and when one of the reasons for positing such a complex compositional process is the claim that the Spirit of God *could*

53. Following Schultz, "How Many 'Isaiahs'?" 162–63.
54. E.g., Ibid., 169.

not (or at least probably *did* not) reveal the diversity of contents identified in the book of Isaiah to just one individual.[55]

If Isaiah 40–66 were written by an unknown prophet, why include it in the canon together with Isaiah's book (Isaiah 1–39)? Why not make it a separate book following Isaiah's, without any attribution of authorship, which is the case elsewhere in the Old Testament? There is no precedent in the Old Testament for such an extended segment (27 chapters) being attributed to a pseudonymous author (though I realize that a number of higher critics would take exception to this statement).

DOES MINOR UPDATING OR EDITING OF ISAIAH NULLIFY THE NEW TESTAMENT'S WITNESS TO THE SINGLE AUTHORSHIP OF ISAIAH?

One of the well-known contenders for the single authorship of Isaiah was Oswald Allis, who was referred to earlier. A recent writer, J. H. Wood, has criticized Allis for allowing that the account of Moses's death at the end of the Pentateuch was not written by Moses but by some subsequent editor. That is, Allis acknowledged that not every word was actually written by Moses. Why did not Allis allow for the same thing in Isaiah? Specifically, the argument has been made that "if the NT authors assert that the Pentateuch is from Moses even though he did not write every word, then is it possible that NT ascriptions of Isaianic origin do not necessarily imply that the eighth-century prophet wrote every word?"[56] The assumption in this critique of Allis is that the New Testament ascriptions of Mosaic and Isaianic authorship are so diluted by allowing for some statements not being originally from Moses or Isaiah that the notion of the traditional authorship of these two books must be seriously questioned. But this is a legalistic view of authorship, which Wood also assumes in his critique.[57]

55. Ibid., 161.
56. J. H. Wood, "Oswald T. Allis and the Question of Isaianic Authorship," *JETS* 48 (2005): 256–57.
57. Wood's article contains several such flawed assumptions and illogical leaps. For example, Wood says that Allis was inconsistent since he acknowledged that Moses used and edited earlier sources about prior biblical history up to his own time but would not allow the notion that there were editors who used Isaiah as an earlier source and built on him within the book of Isaiah. This is comparing apples and oranges. First, Moses was writing his own work, not editing an earlier source with an author's name and writing in that earlier author's name (though whether he was editing earlier sources, oral or written, we do not know, and we

A viable understanding of single authorship of any writing can be held without assuming that every word is verbatim from that author. Two examples will suffice. It is clear that much of what Moses said in the Pentateuch was written down by scribes (or secretaries in contemporary parlance) and that this scribal record is what became part of the written Pentateuchal record.[58] Such scribes may have used some liberty in their recording, but it is unlikely that Moses and other Israelite officials would have let such scribal records continue to circulate if they did not genuinely reflect what Moses said. Likewise, Paul likely did not write any of the Epistle to the Romans. Romans 16:22 explicitly says that Tertius was his secretary and wrote down what he dictated. Yet it has always been called Paul's Epistle to the Romans because it is really from him, not Tertius. There were at least two ways to take dictation in the first century: by having a whole segment read and the secretary write it down, or having a scribe copy syllable by syllable.[59] We do

---

certainly do not know whether there were authors' names attached to those sources). Second, there is no problem with a later biblical writer's using earlier sources when writing his own works. This occurs throughout biblical literature (e.g., note the New Testament's use of the Old Testament, sometimes with interpretative paraphrases). Third, Moses was not primarily taking earlier prophecies and editing them but prior history and editing it, whereas in Isaiah the critical view is that later editors built significantly on Isaiah's earlier prophecies, not historical narratives, and even created many prophecies that did not emanate from Isaiah. With respect also to Moses's use of sources, Wood says that "Allis allowed for the possibility of a historical discrepancy between the original situation of Moses' source . . . and the situation in which Moses wrote" (ibid., 257). Why Wood believes that Moses's use of prior sources means that there could be a "discrepancy between" Moses's situation and that of Moses's source is a mystery, since he gives no reason for this conclusion. The use of earlier sources does not indicate the probability of discrepancies, unless the one using the source does the distorting, and this Wood does not even attempt to show in the case of Moses. Likewise, Wood confuses the nature of the prophecy in Deuteronomy 18 with that of the Servant in Isaiah 53, but there is not space to elaborate on this hermeneutical fallacy (Ibid., 258–59), except to say that partial fulfillments of earlier Old Testament prophecies do occur within the Old Testament epoch itself, with the climactic fulfillment in the New Testament era, which we believe to be the case of the prophecy of a prophet like Moses in Deuteronomy 18 (see G. P. Hugenberger, "The Servant of the Lord in the 'Servant Songs' of Isaiah," in *The Lord's Anointed: Interpretation of Old Testament Messianic Texts*, ed. P. E. Satterthwaite, R. S. Hess, and G. J. Wenham [Grand Rapids: Baker, 1995], 105–40, who sees the Isaiah 53 Servant as modeled on Moses, which is partly based on the Deuteronomy 18 forecast of a prophet like Moses). Oswald Allis could certainly acknowledge near and distant fulfillments in the Old Testament, but precise exegesis of each prophecy in particular, together with surveying subsequent recorded redemptive history, will show whether a prophecy concerns near or distant fulfillment. Allis believed, correctly, that Isaiah 53 prophesied a distant time.

58. On this, e.g., see Daniel I. Block, "Recovering the Voice of Moses: the Genesis of Deuteronomy," *JETS* 44 (2001): 385–408.

59. See Cicero, *ad Att.* 13.25.3.

not know which method Tertius followed. The former mode of dictation may well have allowed for some creative composition on the part of the secretary. Even if Tertius copied in this manner, the letter would have been read back to Paul to make sure that everything was what Paul intended. So it is possible that at various points we do not have the exact words of Paul, but we certainly have his clear conceptual "voice." For example, Paul starts by saying the letter is from him to the Romans (Rom. 1:1–7), not from Tertius to the Romans (the same thing is true with 1 Peter, where Peter says that Sylvanus is his secretary [1 Peter 5:12]).

It is for this reason that Oswald Allis could still see that Moses was the ultimate author of the Pentateuch, even if every word was not written by him. Even the record of his death, which may well have been intended to serve as a transition to the book of Joshua, may have been commissioned by Moses for someone else to record, perhaps one of his scribes or even Joshua.[60] But the New Testament writers can say that Moses wrote the Pentateuch because it is ultimately from him, even if he did not write it all. His handprint is all over the book.

It is certainly possible that there were scribes of Isaiah who wrote down some of his discourses, so that literary style may vary within the book. Furthermore, later inspired editors could have done some minor editing of Isaiah's prophecies. But the conceptual essence of each prophecy should be seen as stemming from what the historical Isaiah said or wrote in his lifetime; each prophecy is like a footprint left by Isaiah, even if later scribes or editors may have filled in a little tread here and there. This is not very different than the situation in the Gospels, where writers may have paraphrased Jesus' sayings, giving them various kinds of interpretative nuance, perhaps not explicit when Jesus spoke them. Nevertheless, the later evangelists bring out Jesus' true intention without altering the conceptual essence of what Jesus said. This is also not much different than the kind of creative secretarial activity spoken of above with respect to Paul.

Thus, along the same lines as we have shown with Moses, the gospel writers, Paul, and Peter, the other New Testament writers can attribute

60. Joshua is an excellent candidate in light of the repeated mention that he was commissioned (by Moses or God) to have the authority Moses had possessed in leading Israel (Num. 27:18–23; Deut. 3:27–28; 31:7–23; 34:9; Josh. 1:1). How appropriate would it have been for Joshua, having had Moses's prophetic mantle passed on to him, to have recorded Moses's death to complete the book that Moses wrote.

prophetic sayings throughout Isaiah to the prophet Isaiah, even if he did not write down every word of his book. Isaiah's historical conceptual handprint is over the whole book. We noted earlier that there are some who believe that Isaiah 40–66 has an Isaianic core upon which later editors built and expanded, but that no one is able to say precisely what belongs to Isaiah and what to his editors.[61] This position is too loose. Rather, the likelihood is that each prophecy is entirely from what the historical Isaiah said in a conceptual sense, but that some of the words and phrases may have been later altered for interpretative purposes. Further refinements and elaborations need to be made to the position just laid out, but space does not allow for this.[62]

CONCLUSION

None of the above views is sufficiently compatible with the use of Isaiah in the New Testament except the perspective that understands that these are references to the actual prophet Isaiah, who wrote the entire book that goes by that name. Neither do these other views comport with the traditional evangelical notion of the inspiration of Scripture. In one way or another, all of these other views understand the repeated mention of Isaiah to be the ultimately irrelevant husk that contains the "true" message of the particular Isaiah passages being quoted. Accordingly, this irrelevant husk is really not a significant part of what Scripture *intends* to say. This is just what I have argued against throughout this chapter. I think that this amounts to the "insignificant part" of Scripture not being inspired, and thus this leads to a limited view of the inspiration of the Bible and of Christ himself, who accordingly could make errors even in his affirmations about holy Scripture itself. Though those with whom I disagree might cry foul and say that I am mischaracterizing their view at this point, it is difficult for me to see that this is not what their view entails.

Packer's conclusion about proposals concerning pseudonymity of New Testament books applies just as much to Old Testament books: the

---

61. In this respect, see the earlier reference to Ridderbos, "Isaiah: Book of," 513–16. Similarly R. Schultz, "How Many 'Isaiahs'?" 158–59.

62. E.g., further work would need to be done on how the genres of the Pentateuch, the Gospels, and the epistolary literature bear on the issue of secretarial/scribal/editorial work.

position, that their canonicity cannot be affirmed if their authenticity is denied, thus seems to be the only one possible; and we may lay it down as a general principle that, when biblical books specify their own authorship, the affirmation of their canonicity involves a denial of their pseudonymity. Pseudonymity and canonicity are mutually exclusive.[63]

The overall intent of this chapter has been to demonstrate that the New Testament's repeated affirmation of Isaiah as the personal author of the entire book with that name is so clear and probable that to maintain multiple authorship of this Old Testament book should unavoidably take a person down one path: that the New Testament writers and Christ were mistaken in their conviction about the authorship of the book. For some scholars this may not be a problematic conclusion, but for those of a more conservative persuasion, this should be a difficult position to hold. Nevertheless, the clear New Testament stance on this topic confirms the long-established arguments within the book of Isaiah itself that the prophet Isaiah authored the complete book. The New Testament view of one author also explains quite well the different kinds of unity that a variety of Old Testament scholars over the past two decades have proposed but have credited to a final redactor(s). Should the authorship of Isaiah be a litmus test for a biblical view of the inspiration of Scripture? No more so than any other aspect of Scripture that is not being affirmed as true. One's position on this issue, especially in recent times, can be an indicator of one's overall view of the authority of Scripture, and this is why a whole chapter is being dedicated to this subject in this book.

Most of the same kinds of arguments offered for Isaiah in this chapter are applicable to the Mosaic authorship of the Pentateuch (though there is more abundant testimony for this in the Old Testament itself) and, to a lesser degree, Davidic authorship of the Psalms attributed to David in the superscriptions.

63. Packer, "Fundamentalism," 184.

6

Christology in Colossians 1:15–20 and Hebrews 1:1–4: An Exercise in Biblico-Systematic Theology

Lane G. Tipton

BIBLICO-SYSTEMATIC THEOLOGY in the Reformed tradition has grappled with the issue of how to distinguish, yet relate, the personal preexistence of the eternal Son of God (i.e., his pretemporal existence as the second person of the ontological Trinity) in regard to his so-called "postexistence" (i.e., the redemptive-historical mode of existence associated with Jesus' exaltation).[1] Working within this tradition, Richard B. Gaffin Jr. has demonstrated the pivotal importance of the resurrection of Christ in Pauline soteriology, noting that a redemptive-historical

---

1. See, for example, Herman Ridderbos, *Paul: An Outline of His Theology*, trans. John Richard de Witt (Grand Rapids: Eerdmans: 1987), 44–90; Geerhardus Vos, "The Range of the Logos Title in the Prologue to the Fourth Gospel," in *Redemptive History and Biblical Interpretation: The Shorter Writings of Geerhardus Vos*, ed. Richard B. Gaffin Jr. (Phillipsburg, NJ: P&R, 2001), 59–90.

emphasis on resurrection in Paul's thought does not compromise a vibrant theology of the Son's preexistence.[2] Yet much work remains in mapping out more precisely how the Son's preexistence relates to, and bears upon, his postexistence.

The exegetical section below will investigate the literary structure and theological significance of Hebrews 1:1–4 and Colossians 1:15–20 in order to map out the proper relationship between the personal preexistence and postexistence of the eternal Son of God. Careful exegesis turns up several intriguing parallels, as well as unique emphases, in the Christologies of Paul and the author of Hebrews, so that correlations specific to the systematizing process arise from the biblical texts themselves.[3] By carefully developing the exegesis of the biblical texts and drawing from those texts orthodox theological implications for *loci* as diverse as bibliology and trinitarian theology, we can offer a corrective to contemporary theological proposals that deviate in significant ways from biblical teaching and Reformed confessional orthodoxy.

HEBREWS 1:1–4

Chiastic Structure of Hebrews 1:1–4

Various proposals have arisen regarding the literary structure of the prologue contained in Hebrews 1:1–4. Most notable is William Lane's suggestion in his Word Biblical Commentary on Hebrews.[4] He proposes the following literary structure:

A (1–2a) Long ago, at many times and in many ways, God spoke to our fathers by the prophets, but in these last days he has spoken to us by his Son

    B (2b)—whom he appointed the heir of all things,

        C (2c)—through whom he made the world.

---

2. Richard B. Gaffin Jr., *Resurrection and Redemption: A Study in Paul's Soteriology* (Phillipsburg, NJ: Presbyterian & Reformed, 1987).

3. This way of speaking presupposes that inherent in biblical revelation, as an activity of the triune God in covenant history, there is a "correlation among elements of truth in which the beginnings of the systematizing process can be discerned." Geerhardus Vos, *Biblical Theology: Old and New Testaments* (Grand Rapids: Eerdmans, 1948), 25.

4. William L. Lane, *Hebrews 1–8*, WBC 47A (Waco, TX: Word Books, 1991), 6–7.

C' (3a-c)—He is the radiance of the glory of God and the exact imprint of his nature, and he upholds the universe by the word of his power.

B' (3d)—After making purification for sins, he sat down at the right hand of the Majesty on high,

A' (4)—having become as much superior to angels as the name he has inherited is more excellent than theirs.

Lane's proposal yields a central focus on 2c–3c, which admirably underscores the relationship between the Son's eternal status (C/C') and redemptive historical function (AB/B'A'), and lays the christological foundations for Hebrews' realized eschatology. His work along these lines is commendable and insightful.

However, there are problems with Lane's proposed arrangement of the chiasm. First, Lane's suggested structure lacks symmetry at C and C'. C is much more terse than its extended counterpart in C'. Insofar as *chiasmus* is characterized by symmetry, Lane's proposed structure seems somewhat deficient, particularly if the structure can be improved upon (as I suggest below). Second, as I will argue at some length below, C (2c) focuses on the Son's eternal person *with reference to creation* (i.e., what systematic theologians refer to as the *opera Dei ad extra* or economic aspect of the Trinity), whereas the only reference to the Son's relation to the created order in C' appears in the participial clause of 3c (i.e., "sustaining all things by the word of his power"). This construction leaves 3a-b, which is a reference to the eternal Son prior to and apart from creation, uncomfortably located in C'.

Put a bit differently, C and C' can be arranged better both in terms of chiastic symmetry and theological substance by adding a D and D' to the *chiasmus*. Consider a refinement of Lane's proposal as follows:

A (1–2a)—Long ago, at many times and in many ways, God spoke to our fathers by the prophets, but in these last days he has spoken to us by his Son

B (2b)—whom he appointed the heir of all things,

C (2c)—through whom he made the world.

D (3a)—He is the radiance of the glory of God

D' (3b)—and the exact imprint of his nature,

C' (3c)—and he upholds the universe by the word of his power.

B' (3d)—After making purification for sins, he sat down at the right hand of the Majesty on high,

A' (4)—having become as much superior to angels as the name he has inherited is more excellent than theirs.

Regarding the revised chiastic structure, notice two primary refinements to Lane's otherwise useful proposal.

First, observe greater symmetry in the revised structure. On Lane's proposal, C' contains one brief clause (2c), whereas C' contains everything in 3a-c. But by adding D and D', the symmetry of the prologue becomes more pronounced, which is clear below:

Lane's Chiastic Structure:

C (2c)—through whom he made the world.

C' (3a-c)—He is the radiance of the glory of God and the exact imprint of his nature, and he upholds the universe by the word of his power.

Revised Chiastic Structure:

C (2c)—through whom he made the world.

D (3a)—He is the radiance of the glory of God

D' (3b)—and the exact imprint of his nature,

C' (3c)—and he upholds the universe by the word of his power.

Second, notice that the revised structure allows us to discern something foundational to the christocentric eschatology of Hebrews. The covenant-historical activity of the Son of God, whether in his incarnate state (B/B') or preincarnate state (C/C'), manifests the fullness of glory and essential deity of the eternal Son of God (D/D').

D and D', when properly understood, therefore express the glory and deity that belong to the eternal Son of God prior to and apart from any economic activity at all. In this sense, then, the revelatory and redemptive work of Jesus Christ—his eschatological significance in redemptive history—derives ultimately from his eternal ontic status as the Son of God. What the Son *does* in redemptive history has significance because of who he *is* from all eternity.

The chiastic structure in Hebrews 1:1–4 therefore moves from the eschatological significance of the Son of God in redemptive history (AB/A'B'), to his significance prior to and apart from the incarnation (C/C'), to the eternal status the Son possesses prior to and apart from any economic activity whatsoever (D/D')—what theologians call the ontological Trinity or the *opera Dei ad intra*.

Consider in a bit more detail the theological thrust of the chiastic structure. A and A' accent the Son's revelatory supremacy with respect to prophets and angels in the old covenant, respectively. Old covenant prophets and angels were bearers of divine revelation and were instrumental in the mediation of the old covenant (cf. Ex. 18:15–18; Jer. 1:9; Heb. 2:2). Second, B and B' focus on the economic activity of the Son in redemptive history, with reference to his kingly exaltation (2a) and priestly mediation (3d). The emphasis here falls on what the Son has obtained in terms of death and resurrection and made available to his people who are united to him by faith (cf. Heb. 9:28; 11; 12:1–4). He is heir of all things, and the one who has provided purification of sins. Third, C and C' take us one step deeper into the *pre-redemptive* economy, describing the preincarnate Son's relation to creation (2b) and providence (3c). Fourth, and finally, D and D' form the central focus of the chiasm and accent the eternal glory (3a) and full deity (3b) of the Son of God.

The point in context is that the deity of the Son grounds the eschatological character of his prophetic/priestly/kingly functions in the new covenant order. The Son's eternal status decisively conditions his economic significance, whether prelapsarian or postlapsarian context comes into view. A closer examination of the passage will bear out these general conclusions.

Hebrews 1:3a-b: Elaboration and Analysis

Hebrews 1:3a begins a relative clause (*hos ōn apaugasma tēs doxēs*) that follows immediately after a reference to the Son's agency regarding creation at the end of verse 2. The relative pronoun *hos*, followed by the present participle *ōn*, denotes a timeless dimension to the Son's status. If 2c deals with the economic aspect of the Son's preexistence with respect to *creation*, 3a-b deals with the ontological aspect of the Son's preexistence in relation to the *Father*.

The movement of the chiasm, then, is from preexistence understood economically in 2c (i.e., with regard to the economy of creation) to preexistence understood ontologically in 3a–b (i.e., with regard to the deity of the Son and his coequality with God the Father). The movement is quite natural. An immediate level of explanation regarding the Son's role with respect to creation is his essential deity and coequality with the Father (i.e., the *homoousios*).

Looking at 3a–b in more detail, note that *apaugasma* can have either an active sense (i.e., radiance, effulgence) or passive sense (i.e., reflection). The active sense does convey more appropriately the fullness of deity, in the form of glory, present in the Son. The Son need not reflect glory, because glory resides in him and flows from him as the eternal Son.[5]

Isaiah 42:8 proves axiomatic for the singularity and uniqueness of Yahweh's identity. Isaiah 42:8 in the LXX reads: "I am the LORD [*kyrios ho theos*], that is My name; I will not give My glory [*tēn doxan mou*] to another, nor My praise to graven images" (NASB). But the author of Hebrews tells us that the Son is the *apaugasma*, radiance, or fullest expression of *tēs doxēs*. Hebrews 1:3a offers a virtual ascription of Isaiah 42:8 to the Son of God. The effulgence of the glory of the Lord God, which will not be shared with another, is essential to the identity of the eternal Son of God.

That the Son is the radiance of divine glory with unique reference to his divine essence becomes clear in light of the coordinate conjunction (*kai*) that amplifies and specifies what is in view in 3a. And what follows *kai* in 3b is a strenuous affirmation of the Son's essential divine nature as Son of God. *Charaktēr* denotes an exact representation of something (Louw-Nida), and can also be used with reference to something impressed on a coin or stamp to demonstrate authenticity (Lidell-Scott). What is in view is a precise, essential reproduction in every respect (Thayer).

And it is of the *hupostaseōs* of God that the Son is a precise reproduction. Thus, in addition to being the agent of creation (2c), the bearer of the

---

5. Cf. Geerhardus Vos's discussion of this issue in *The Teaching of the Epistle to the Hebrews*, ed. Johannes G. Vos (Grand Rapids: Eerdmans, 1956), 79–83.

radiance of the divine glory (3a), the Son is also an exact representation of God's nature or being (3b). The Son of God possesses the radiance of God's glory specifically as the *charaktēr* of God's nature. William Lane notes that this very language occurs in Philo, where Philo argues that there is nothing and no one who is an exact representation of God's nature (*charaktēr tēs hupostaseōs autou*).[6]

For this reason, I think Lane overstates when he sees 3a as a reference to the Son's outward display of God's glory, but 3b to the Son's essential identity with God. Rather, Wilckens is correct in noting a virtual parallelism between *charaktēr* and *apaugasma*.[7] This parallelism can be supported by the fact that *ōn* applies equally to 3a and 3b, that is, the Son as *charaktēr* and *apaugasma*. This parallelism is also suggested by the chiastic structure, with D and D' forming the center of the structure.

Geerhardus Vos on *apaugasma* and *charaktēr* in 1:3a-b

Geerhardus Vos offers significant insight on 3a-b. Vos says that the two terms that require intensive discussion are *apaugasma* and *charaktēr* and the two questions to ask are: "(1) What figure of speech is involved in each?; (2) For what purpose are they employed?" The main issue turns on whether we take these terms to denote a "cosmical" (i.e., economic) or "theological" (i.e., ontological) aspect of the Son's existence.[8]

Vos offers several lines of argument that offer support for taking D and D' in the theological sense. First, the author speaks in 3a and 3b of being (*ōn*), not doing (cf. *epoiēsen* and *pherōn* in 2c and 3c, respectively).[9] Second, since the world is not mentioned in either 3a or 3b, the theological sense fits better. Third, the Son is called "the [*charaktēr*] of the divine substance; to take this cosmically would imply a communicating of the divine substance to the world, which is too pantheistic a conception for the rest of the epistle."[10] Fourth, Vos observes, "Even if we accept the cosmological interpretation, we still cannot get rid of the theological background . . . the

---

6. Lane, *Hebrews 1–8*, 13.

7. Wilckens, *Theological Dictionary of the New Testament*, vol. 9, *Phi–Omega*, ed. Gerhard Kittel and Gerhard Friedrich, trans. Geoffrey W. Bromiley (Grand Rapids: Eerdmans, 1974), 421.

8. Vos, *Hebrews*, 79.

9. Ibid., 82.

10. Ibid.

theological idea is a necessary implication in the background, even if we accept the cosmical interpretation."[11] He adds,

> if we take them in a theological, trinitarian sense, then the first phrase expresses the essential unity of the Godhead by reason of the identity of the Father and the Son; we cannot think of the Son without the Father; and the second phrase indicates the result, namely, the *likeness* of the Son to the Father. In theological language, then, the expression *the effulgence of his glory* assures us of the Son's being *homoousios* with the Father, and the expression *the very image of his substance* assures us of the Son's being the *monogonese* of the Father.[12]

Vos's argument can be strengthened by the chiastic structure outlined above. D and D' help us avoid a pantheistic, or even panentheistic, concept of the Son of God in relation to creation, because D and D' do not bring into view the Son's relation to creation at all. Rather, D and D' accent the Son's relation to the Father—his *homoousios* and *monogonese*. Therefore, 3a-b forms the center of the chiasm and yields the conclusion that the most basic category that accounts for the realized eschatology of Hebrews rests in the interface between eternal/ontic and redemptive-historical aspects of Christology.

To use Vos's language, it is in the Son's *homoousios/monogonese* that we find the ultimate explanation for his "cosmic" or "functional" significance. This means that the "theological" understanding of D/D' provides the proper frame of reference for the "cosmical" implications that reside on either side of the chiastic center. Whether we think in terms of creation and providence (C/C') or redemption and realized eschatology (AB/B'A'), the eternal Son is central. And the Son is centrally significant in redemptive history ultimately in terms of his eternal status as *homoousios* with and *monogonese* from the Father (D/D'). Stated in summary form, *the preexistence of the eternal Son supplies the ultimate rationale for the eschatological significance of his postexistence.*

COLOSSIANS 1:15–20

Colossians 1:15–18 complements and expands the basic christological perspective found in Hebrews' prologue, while operating with slightly dif-

11. Ibid.
12. Ibid., 83.

ferent polemical concerns. The text is an early Christian hymn that offers praise to Christ in light of his full deity and redemptive-historical attainment. This hymn is appropriated polemically by Paul to avoid what has come to be known as the Colossian heresy—most likely a hybrid of gnostic and Judaizing thought.[13]

The passage is arranged in terms of two strophes (vv. 15–16 and 18b–20), with a transition midway through (17–18a). The arrangement appears as follows:

> Strophe 1:15–16—He is the image of the invisible God, the firstborn of all creation. For by him all things were created, in heaven and on earth, visible and invisible, whether thrones or dominions or rulers or authorities—all things were created through him and for him.

> Transition: 17–18a—And he is before all things, and in him all things hold together. And he is the head of the body, the church.

> Strophe 2:18b–20—He is the beginning, the firstborn from the dead, that in everything he might be preeminent. For in him all the fullness of God was pleased to dwell, and through him to reconcile to himself all things, whether on earth or in heaven, making peace by the blood of his cross.[14]

Each strophe is characterized by recurring phrases and ideas. Regarding the first strophe, notice *hos estin* begins verse 15, *prōtotokos* follows in 15b, followed by *hoti en autō* and *ta panta* in verse 16. The second strophe also begins with *hos estin* (18b), has a recurring *prōtotokos* (18b) and *en autō* (v. 19a), along with cosmic language *en pasin autos prōteuōn* (v. 18b). There is therefore marked symmetry between the two strophes. The transition in 17–18a has similar syntactical markers (e.g., *autos estin* in 17a, *pro pantōn kai ta panta* in 17b, *en autō* in 17b).

Previewing the theological significance of the strophes, it is important to note that the content in the first strophe accents the preexistence of

---

13. For some useful treatments of this difficult issue, see Clinton E. Arnold, *The Colossian Syncretism: The Interface Between Christianity and Folk Belief at Colossae* (Grand Rapids: Baker, 1996), and Troy W. Martin, *By Philosophy and Empty Deceit: Colossians as Response to a Cynic Critique* (Sheffield: Sheffield Academic, 1996).

14. For one example of another organizational scheme that maintains the two-strophe structure, see Gordon D. Fee, *Pauline Christology: An Exegetical-Theological Study* (Peabody, MA: Hendrickson, 2007), 300.

the Son of God, particularly his eternal ontic-status and role in *creation*, whereas verses 18b–20 accent the redemptive-historical activity of the Son of God, specifically his resurrection/exaltation and role in *redemption*. This means that the transition point in verses 17–18a, and the theology of the poem as a whole, bring into view both the Son's preexistence and his postexistence in a way that *the former is manifest in the eschatological significance of the latter.*

Preexistence and Creation (vv. 15–16)

Hos estin in 15a introduces a relative clause that refers back to "his beloved Son" in verse 13. The context in verse 13 clearly brings into view the work of Christ in redemptive history. This follows from at least two considerations. First, in verse 10, Paul refers to a walk that is "worthy of the Lord" (*peripatēsai axiōs tou kyriou*), language that typically denotes the exalted Christ in the Pauline corpus (1 Cor. 8:6; Phil. 2:11). Second, the reference in verse 13 to the Son is elaborated immediately in verse 14 as follows: *hō echomen tēn apolutrōsin, tēn aphesin tōn hamartiōn* (in whom we have redemption, the forgiveness of sins). The antecedent for *hō* is *tou huiou* and brings into view the redemptive activity of the incarnate Son of God. It is best to take *tēn aphesin tōn hamartiōn* as epexegetical of *echomen tēn apolutrōsin*, which means that the redemption in view consists in the forgiveness of sins (cf. Eph. 1:7, "we have redemption *through His blood*, the forgiveness of our trespasses").

Clearly, then, redemptive-historical concerns are at the forefront of Paul's thought. Taking these insights together, we must grant that the reference to "the kingdom of his beloved Son" (*tēn basileian tou huiou tēs agapēs autou*) in verse 13 denotes the present, eschatological reign of the crucified and exalted Savior. At present, in terms of realized eschatology, the incarnate Son of God, by virtue of his humiliation and exaltation in redemptive history, has inaugurated a heavenly kingdom for his saints in the light.

Because the antecedent of *hos* in 15a is "His beloved Son" (v. 13), and because of the reference to the redemptive benefit of forgiveness of sin given to those in Christ (v. 14), it is tempting to take the reference to "the image of the invisible God" (*eikōn tou theou tou aoratou*) in 15a as a reference to

186

the fact that Jesus, as the incarnate Son of God, is the outward and visible manifestation of the Father's image.

As plausible as the arguments for this view may seem, they are misleading in at least three significant ways. First, *estin* immediately following the relative pronoun *hos* can be taken as a timeless/atemporal present,[15] which would mean that the Son is eternally the image of the invisible God and would imply his eternal generation.

Second, closely coordinate with "image of the invisible God" is "firstborn over all creation" in 15b. This "firstborn" language, as we will see confirmed in verse 16, brings into focus the prelapsarian activity of the eternal Son with reference to creation,[16] lending support to taking *estin* as a timeless/atemporal present.[17]

Third, this position seems confirmed beyond dispute by verse 16, which tells us the Son is the image of the invisible God and firstborn over all creation (v. 15), "*hoti en autō ektisthē ta panta*" (16a). The *hoti* clause that begins verse 16 ("because by him all things were created") further explains the import of the Son's identity as image of God (and firstborn over all creation).[18] Verse 15 therefore cannot be taken as a reference to the Son *as incarnate*, since creation *precedes* the incarnation. The import of verse 16, indeed the import of the entire first strophe of the poem, is the eternal dignity of the Son's person and his role in creation. Only if we were to erase, or radically conflate, the categories of creation and redemption, and alter the notion of incarnation beyond recognition, could we understand the references in 15a as being to the Son of God in his incarnate state. Hence, these arguments demand that 15a denote the preexistent Son, prior to and apart from his incarnation in redemptive history.[19]

15. Cf. Murray J. Harris, *Colossians and Philemon* (Grand Rapids: Eerdmans, 1991), 43.

16. Ridderbos, *Paul*, 71; Fee, *Pauline Christology*, 298–300.

17. Complementing these insights, J. B. Lightfoot notes that Col. 1:17 teaches the personal preexistence of the eternal Son of God. He argues that "the present **is** declares that this preexistence is absolute existence. The **he** is as necessary for the completeness of the meaning as the **is**. The one emphasized the personality; the other declares the preexistence." J. B. Lightfoot, *Colossians and Philemon*, The Crossway Classic Commentary Series (Wheaton, IL: Good News, 1997), 76 (bold original). His observations cohere well with the previous arguments for the timeless/atemporal *estin* in 15a.

18. Harris, *Colossians and Philemon*, 44.

19. For a radical recasting of the notion of preexistence that denies personal preexistence to the eternal Son and speaks instead of "the preexistence of divine Wisdom" that the church came to confess resides in the resurrected Messiah, see James D. G. Dunn, *The Theology of the Apostle Paul* (Grand Rapids: Eerdmans, 1998), 274. Larry W. Hurtado pinpoints the problem

Verse 15b, however, relates the eternal Son in his preincarnate mode of existence to the created order; he is "firstborn over all creation" (*prōtotokos pasēs ktiseōs*). The word *prōtotokos* denotes superiority in rank or dignity, illustrated by its usage in LXX Psalm 89:27, "I will appoint him my firstborn [*prōtotokov* in the accusative], the *most exalted* of the kings of the earth." To be the firstborn of all the kings of the earth is to be the most exalted of all kings of the earth. As a result, *prōtotokos* in conjunction with *pasēs ktiseōs* indicates that the Son of God possesses a preeminence of rank with respect to creation. Whether the genitive *ktiseōs* is taken objectively, yielding the sense that the Son is *superior* over all of creation, or comparatively, underscoring *priority* (ontologically) over all of creation,[20] what is critical to grasp is that the priority admits of no degree; it is qualitative. Nothing less than the absolute, ontological distinction between the Creator and the creature hangs in the balance.

Therefore, the distinction between the Son of God as the image of the invisible God and the firstborn over all creation becomes clear. The image of God language clarifies the Son's consubstantial relation to the *Father* (cf. 1:19 and 2:9),[21] and the firstborn language clarifies the Son's fundamental relation to *creation*.[22] While there is a meaningful way to distinguish what

---

with Dunn's exegesis. He says, quite bluntly, "The problem is that is not what the Pauline passage says" (Larry W. Hurtado, *Lord Jesus Christ: Devotion to Jesus in Earliest Christianity* [Grand Rapids: 2005], 126). He continues by observing that passages such as Col. 1:15 "directly attribute to Jesus personally a preexistence and central role in creation" (Ibid., 126). Another cogent criticism of Dunn's mistreatment of preexistence passages in Paul emerges in the astute observations of Richard Longenecker, *Contours of Christology in the New Testament* (Grand Rapids: Eerdmans, 2005), 178–79. For a similar criticism of Dunn on his questionable exegesis of Heb. 1:3, see Dan O. Via, *What Is New Testament Theology?* (Minneapolis: Fortress, 2002), 56. For a helpful treatment of the preexistence of the eternal Son of God in the Synoptic Gospels, buttressing the reality of a strong doctrine of the personal preexistence of the eternal Son in the Pauline corpus and Hebrews, see Simon J. Gathercole, *The Pre-existent Son: Recovering the Christologies of Matthew, Mark, and Luke* (Grand Rapids: Eerdmans, 2006).

20. Harris, *Colossians and Philemon*, 43–44.

21. Murray J. Harris succinctly summarizes the import of "in him dwells all the fullness of deity bodily" (*en autō pan to plērōma tēs theotētos sōmatikōs*) in 2:9. He says, "Since [*pan*] is pleonastic with [*plērōma*] and [*en autō*] is emphatic by position, the whole statement is probably polemical: it is in Christ, and Christ alone, that the sum total of the fullness of the Godhead, no part or aspect excepted, permanently resides in bodily form" (Harris, *Colossians and Philemon*, 99).

22. All of this moves Herman Ridderbos to say that "(I)t can even be maintained that by the name Image of God in the passages in question Paul intended to elucidate the eternal relationship of the Father to the Son" (*Paul*, 71). Yet he goes on to observe that firstborn over all of creation implies a definite priority of the uncreated Son with reference all things created (Ibid., 82).

comes into view in 15a and 15b, namely, relationship to God and world respectively,[23] both phrases denote the personal preexistence of the eternal Son of God.

Preexistence and Eschatology/Redemption (vv. 18b–20)[24]

Strophe two (vv. 18b–20), as noted above, pertains to the Son's redemptive-historical status as resurrected and ascended. And Jesus' status as "firstborn from among the dead" in 18b (*prōtotokos ek tōn nekrōn*) hearkens back to the "*prōtotokos pasēs ktiseōs*" in 15b. Paul's *ek tōn nekrōn* alerts us to the fact that, as resurrected, Christ is first of many—the dead. Firstborn from among the dead is therefore conceptually similar to firstfruits (cf. 1 Cor. 15:20–23) in the sense that a solidaric bond exists between the resurrected Christ and those he represents.[25] Yet, *prōtotokos* singles out the resurrected Christ as unique in dignity and rank in a manner corresponding to what we already discussed in Col. 1:15b. Just as the eternal Son is firstborn over all creation, so also he is firstborn from among the dead.[26]

Put another way, the resurrection of the Son of God not only effects a transition from humiliation to exaltation in history, but it also unveils something of his eternal ontic status. Just as the eternal Son of God is before all things (17a), so also, as the ascended Son, Christ is preeminent in everything (v. 18c). Just as the eternal Son originates all things (v. 16), so also as resurrected he is "the beginning" (*hos estin archē*, 18b) of the new creation, the firstborn from among the dead, "so that in everything he might be preeminent" (18c). Just as he is the firstborn over all creation (15b), so also he is firstborn from among the dead (18b). In other words, Jesus' unique dignity as firstborn from among the dead manifests his prior uniqueness as firstborn over all creation.

Woven tightly into the fabric of Paul's argument, then, is the additional notion that Christ, as the eschatological beginning, rises as the firstborn from the dead "that he might be preeminent in all things" (*hina genētai en*

---

23. Lightfoot, *Colossians and Philemon*, 72.

24. This section deals predominantly with verse 18. Verses 19–20 introduce aspects of Paul's theology worth pursuing but would take us beyond the scope of the somewhat narrow focus of this section of the essay.

25. Gaffin, *Resurrection*, 36–39.

26. Ridderbos, *Paul*, 53–57.

pasin autos prōteuōn, 18c).[27] The *hina* clause, along with subjunctive aorist deponent *genētai*, invites us to see in this resurrection that Christ becomes something he was not—preeminent in all things *as firstborn from the dead*. This *genētai* stands in sharp contrast with the timeless *estin* in 15a/17a. The implication is that while the preexistent Son remains forever the one who is before all things as the eternal image of God and firstborn over all creation, he nonetheless comes to possess preeminence in all things by virtue of his exaltation in redemptive history.

For this reason, then, Jesus' coming to have something in his resurrection that he did not have previously marks a change in his redemptive-historical mode of existence with reference to his human nature.[28] The Son of God comes to possess no greater preeminence as resurrected than he always had as the eternal Son of God, when we consider only his eternal person and divine nature. Yet, the Son of God comes to possess preeminence as resurrected that he did not possess when we consider his human nature in the estate of humiliation. The preeminence that the Son of God comes to possess as resurrected involves not merely a transformation of his assumed human nature, but also a redemptive-historical expression (that is genuinely new!) of what is perennially true of his eternal person.

These observations in no sense minimize what Jesus becomes in terms of his resurrection (and ascension). But while we want to give full weight to the resurrection of Christ and all that his exaltation means for his present dominion and glory, we must also insist that the dominion and glory Christ enjoys as resurrected cannot for a moment be divorced from the significance of his eternal person as such.[29] Put in summary form, then, *the eschatological outcome of Jesus' resurrection is driven, at least in*

27. The *hina* clause can be taken either as a purpose or result clause, but the result clause best fits the context (cf. Harris, *Colossians and Philemon*, 48–49).

28. This parallels what Gaffin observes with regard to the exegesis of Romans 1:4, "The eternal Son of God, who was born, lived, and died [*kata sarka*], has been raised [*kata pneuma*] and so, in his messianic identity (of the seed of David), *has become what he was not before*: the Son of God in power" (Gaffin, *Resurrection*, 111 [emphasis added]).

29. Ridderbos says, "However much Paul's Christology finds its point of departure in Christ's death and resurrection and to whatever degree he draws the lines from thence on the one hand to the incarnation on the other to the future of the Lord, all this does not alter the fact that the whole of his preaching of the historical and future revelation of Christ is supported by the confession of Christ as the Son of God in the supra- and prehistorical sense of the word . . . this exaltation Christology is at the same time not for a moment to be divorced from Christ's person as such . . . one cannot, *precisely because of the preexistence of the Son*, permit the being of the Son to be lost in his revelation as the son of God. *And this means that one will have to judge the*

part, by the ontology of his eternal person, so that, as a result, Jesus' resurrection/exaltation reveals aspects of his eternal glory in a mode conditioned by redemptive history.[30]

SYSTEMATIC-THEOLOGICAL IMPLICATIONS

Significant theological and hermeneutical implications follow from Hebrews 1:1–4 and Colossians 1:15–20, which together allow us to promote Chalcedonian Christology (and ward off erroneous christological constructions) and expand the vistas of Reformed biblico-systematic theology with its special interest in redemptive history. The correlations of doctrines in these texts in the nature of the case demonstrate the reality of a biblico-systematic theology that derives directly from the biblical text.

Preexistence, Eschatology, and the *Communicatio Idiomatum*

The preexistence of the Son of God in Hebrews 1:3 and Colossians 1:15 relates core concerns of Chalcedon to christocentric eschatology. The Son's preexistence, particularly his *homoousios* with the Father and *monogonese* from the Father (Heb. 1:3), supplies the deepest christological rationale for the realized eschatology in the book of Hebrews. In this connection we can discern from these texts the deepest possible relationship between Chalcedonian orthodoxy and biblical theology.

In a complementary way, Paul's Christology in Colossians 1:15–18 enables us to articulate the *communicatio idiomatum*[31] in categories derived from the interface between the preexistence and postexistence

---

postexistence of the Son in the light of what is elsewhere so clearly stated of his preexistence." Ridderbos, *Paul*, 68–69 (emphasis added).

30. This way of understanding the bearing of preexistence on the eschatology of Jesus' resurrection entails that the event of resurrection in redemptive history has both a noetic function with respect to revealing the Son's deity, as well as a transforming significance that introduces the incarnate Son into an eschatological mode of glorified existence (cf. Gaffin's discussion in *Resurrection*, 103–5). See in the following section how this formulation helps us articulate the *communicatio idiomatum* in light of the interface between the preexistence and postexistence of the eternal Son of God.

31. Charles Hodge incisively summarizes the *communicatio idiomatum* when he says, "the one Person is the . . . partaker of the attributes of both natures; so that whatever may be affirmed of either nature may be affirmed of the person." *Systematic Theology*, Part 2 (Original from Oxford University, 1872), 392.

of the Son of God.[32] For instance, the Son of God is both the one by whom all things were created (16), as well as the beginning of the new creation as resurrected (18a); he is both the firstborn over all creation and the firstborn from among the dead (15b and 18b). How do these observations enable us to articulate the *communicatio idiomatum*? When we predicate something of Jesus' person, such as creation (15b–16), we do so with special reference to the Son's divine nature as the eternal Son of God. And when we predicate of his person a new state into which he entered as resurrected (18), we do so with special reference to his transformed human nature as Second Adam (cf. 1 Cor. 15:44bff.).[33] This is a distinctively redemptive-historical way of expressing Chalcedonian Christology that relates the implications of the unipersonality and dual natures of the Son of God to the eschatological outcome of his resurrection.

The christological formulations in Hebrews 1:1–4 and Colossians 1:15–20 therefore express Chalcedonian Christology in distinctive ways, while focusing our understanding of the preexistent Son's eschatological significance in redemptive history.

Preexistence and Hermeneutics

The preexistence theology in Hebrews and Colossians also contains a wealth of material that proves hermeneutically suggestive. First, the *most basic* hermeneutical reference for understanding the person and work of Christ must lie in eternity, not in time.[34] Whatever we predicate of the Son's

32. Standard accounts of the *communicatio idiomatum* explain the implications of the hypostatic union itself (cf. a good example is the heading to Hodge's discussion that introduces his exposition of the *communicatio idiomatum*, namely, "Consequences of the Hypostatical Union"). In a complementary way, the *communicatio idiomatum* can also be expressed in terms of the consequences that obtain in light of the resurrection of the eternal Son of God.

33. Perhaps the *communicatio idiomatum* is, at least in part, what motivates Ridderbos to observe that "exaltation Christology is at the same time not for a moment to be divorced from Christ's person as such" (cf. n21 above).

34. Along these lines, Ridderbos observes that, "Paul's eschatology is entirely determined by the realized and still-to-be realized redemptive work of God *in Christ* [italics original]. However much he gives expression to the significance of Christ's advent with the help of the conceptual materials of the Old Testament and Jewish eschatology, this does not mean that the eschatological 'setting' in which he describes this advent and significance can simply be reduced to an Old Testament or Jewish 'schema' lying ready to hand, from which Paul's Christology may be said to have borrowed its composition and from which it would thus be easy to extract this from. What is so remarkable about Paul's eschatology is that although he avails himself of all kinds of

activity in creation, providence, or redemption is not intelligible apart from his more basic identity as the eternal Son of God, coequal with the Father, yet hypostatically distinct from him. This implies that as important as history may be for understanding the person and work of Christ, *history is not the ultimate hermeneutical horizon*. If history were the most basic category when it comes to interpreting the person and work of Christ, then the *homoousios* and *monogonese* of the eternal Son would have no hermeneutical function.

Second, both the Hebrews and Colossians texts invite us to see the glory of the preexistent Son displayed in various ways prior to his incarnation, yielding rich hermeneutical insights. For instance, Paul clearly intends the language in Colossians 1:15–16 to supply a christological framework for interpreting Genesis 1, including Adam as the created image of God (cf. Gen. 1:26–28). Adam, as an image bearer created in covenant with God (Gen. 2:15–17; Luke 4:1–13; Rom. 5:12–19; 1 Cor. 15:45–49), was a *creaturely replica* of the eternal Son of God, who is himself the archetypal image of the invisible God (Col. 1:15a). By the very nature and function of his person as image of God, Adam manifested something of the glory of the eternal Son.

The preexistent Son as the archetypal pattern after which the historical Adam was created suggests that a properly christological hermeneutic does *not* begin with Genesis 3:15ff. A redemptive Christology—one that has to do with redemptive history—begins with Genesis 3:15, but the sort of christocentrism suggested by Hebrews 1:1–4 and Colossians 1:15ff. locates the significance of the Son of God as a basic *prelapsarian* reality, rooted in his personal preexistence.

Hebrews invites us to explore similar vistas, but with a slightly different focus. Rather than the emphasis lying on the relation of the eternal Son to prelapsarian Adam, Hebrews offers a christological frame of reference for understanding the typico-symbolic aspects of redemption and revelation

---

traditional terms and ideas, yet is distinguished from all forms of the contemporaneous Jewish eschatological expectation and bears a *completely independent character* [italics added]. Now this has its origin in the fact that Paul's eschatology is not determined by any traditional eschatological schema, *but by the actual acting of God in Christ*. This is the fundamental christological character of his eschatology." Ridderbos, *Paul*, 52. To the extent that the eschatological significance of Christ's advent in redemptive history derives *most basically* from his preexistence, the *ultimate* hermeneutical frame of reference for Paul's christocentric eschatology has its location in eternity, not in time.

in the Mosaic economy. Moses's transformed countenance (Ex. 34:29ff., 2 Cor. 3:13–18), the priestly garments for glory and beauty (Ex. 28:40), the tabernacle and land as microcosmic replicas of heaven inhabited by a holy priest/people (Heb. 8:5; 9:24; 11:10–17)—all of these are phenomena that manifest realities in the Mosaic covenant that both reflect the glory of the eternal Son of God (Heb. 1:3; Col. 1:15–17) and anticipate the manifestation of his glory as the resurrected and exalted Son of God (Heb. 1:1–4; Col. 1:18f.; 1 Cor. 15:45–49; Rev. 1:12–20).

Finally, we can discern that the functional identity of the Son and Spirit in the resurrection, and particularly the ascension, of Christ (cf. 1 Cor. 15:45 and 2 Cor. 3:18) finds its economic ground in the functional identity of the Son and Spirit in the prelapsarian context. Thinking along lines suggested in this essay, M. G. Kline observes the following,

> [T]he eternal, firstborn Son furnished a pattern for man as a royal glory-image of the Father. It was in his creative action as the Son, present in the Glory-Spirit, making man in his own son-image that the Logos revealed himself as the One in whom was the life that is the light of men. *Not first as incarnate word breathing on men the Spirit and re-creating them in his heavenly image, but at the very beginning he was quickening Spirit, creating man after his image and glory.*[35]

While Kline's concerns lie with the development of the image of God theme, we can still observe something germane to our investigation. Given the parallels between the function of the Glory-Spirit as covenant witness in both creation and redemption, and given the comment above, Kline argues for a functional identity of the Logos-Son as the Glory-Spirit in Genesis 1:2. Kline also reasons that 2 Corinthians 4:4 (and by implication Col. 1:15) furnishes a distinctively christological interpretation of Genesis 1[36]—a conclusion shared by Ridderbos.[37] Christ's functional identification with the Spirit in the redemptive economy finds its pre-redemptive analogue in the original creation of man in the image of the eternal Son of God.

---

35. Meredith G. Kline, *Images of the Spirit* (Eugene, OR: Wipf and Stock, 1998), 24 (emphasis added).

36. Reference the longer discussion in Kline's *Images*, 19–25.

37. Ridderbos, *Paul*, 71.

Preexistence and the Incarnational Analogy: The Primacy of the Divine Person of the Son and the Divine Authorship of Scripture[38]

The previous implication turned up the functional identification of the Son and Spirit in the prelapsarian era, which, in turn, supplies the foundation for their functional identification in the redemptive economy (cf. 2 Cor. 3:17; 1 Cor. 15:45). The close correlation of the Son and Spirit turns up a still further analogy between the Son and Spirit, namely, the correlation of the person and work of the Son in incarnation and the person and work of the Holy Spirit in inspiration/inscripturation. That conclusion can be summarized as follows: the divine and human in incarnation and inspiration/inscripturation are not equally ultimate. Put in summary form, *the divine persons of the Trinity (i.e., the Son and the Holy Spirit) remain primary, and the human nature/persons, while real, remain subordinate to the divine persons, in the events of both incarnation and inspiration/inscripturation.*

At least the following implications follow from the notion of preexistence sketched above in the exegetical sections. First, the divine person of the Logos remains the primary theological category when speaking of the incarnate Son. Not only does the divine Logos preexist the act of incarnation, but the incarnate Son of God remains, even in the incarnation, a divine person.[39] Second, the humanity of the Son

---

38. For a fuller discussion of this topic, see my forthcoming "Incarnation, Inspiration, and Pneumatology: A Reformed Incarnational Analogy," in *Ordained Servant: A Journal for Church Officers*. In this essay I explain more extensively the proper way to formulate an incarnational analogy. This is important in light of attempts by Smyth and Enns to apply the analogy in a way that denies, at least in function, divine authorship and its theological/hermeneutical implications (cf. Patterson J. Smyth, *How God Inspired the Bible: Thoughts for the Present Disquiet* [New York: James Pott, 1892], and Peter Enns, *Inspiration and Incarnation: Evangelicals and the Problem of the Old Testament* [Grand Rapids: Baker Academic, 2005]). For a critical analysis of some of the main problems with Enns's doctrine of Scripture, consult Peter A. Lillback's insightful essay in this volume, "'The Infallible Rule of Interpretation of Scripture': The Hermeneutical Crisis and the Westminster Standards."

39. Cf. Westminster Shorter Catechism, Q. 21: "Who is the Redeemer of God's elect? A.: The only Redeemer of God's elect is the Lord Jesus Christ, who, *being the eternal Son of God, became man*, and so was, and continueth to be, God and man in *two distinct natures*, and *one person, for ever*" (emphasis added). The Westminster Confession of Faith, 8.2, elaborates even more along these lines, as follows, "The Son of God, the second person in the Trinity, *being very and eternal God, of one substance and equal with the Father, did, when the fulness of time was come, take upon Him man's nature* (emphasis added), with all the essential properties and common infirmities thereof, yet without sin; being conceived by the power of the Holy Ghost, in the womb of the Virgin Mary, of her substance. So that two whole, perfect, and distinct natures, the Godhead and the

of God, while true humanity, is nonetheless subordinate to the divine person who assumes it in the act of incarnation. It is not adequate to say that Jesus is both fully God and fully man, leaving the impression that nothing more need be said.[40] Much more than this should be said, lest we think (mistakenly) that the divine person and human nature in the God-man are on some sort of equal footing. The divine person is primary; the assumed humanity, while real, is subordinate to the eternal person who assumed it in the event of the incarnation (cf. Phil. 2:6–8).[41]

How might we go about relating the incarnation of the preexistent Son of God to a theology of inspiration and inscripturation? At the outset we must recognize that while there may be analogies between incarnation and inspiration, there certainly can be no identity regarding the relationship between the divine and human in the incarnation of Christ, on the one hand, and the divine and human in the inspiration of Scripture, on the other hand.[42] But, assuming that an analogy is possible, what is the starting point for such an analogy?

Second Timothy 3:16, the *locus classicus* for the doctrine of inspiration, offers a concept of Scripture that is essentially *pneumatic*, focusing on the *divine authorship* of Scripture. When read in conjunction with 2 Peter 1:19–21, another foundational New Testament text regarding the nature of Scripture as the Word of God, the biblical witness attests that Scripture is the "expiration" (or out-breathing) of the eternal Spirit of God, the third person of the ontological Trinity. This pneumatic qualification supplies the most basic category in terms of which we must proceed in our understanding of the divine origin and nature of Scripture. What we understand Scripture, as a whole, to be proceeds

---

manhood, were inseparably joined together in one person, without conversion, composition, or confusion. Which person is very God, and very man, yet one Christ, the only Mediator between God and man" [cf. Luke 1:27, 31, 35; John 1:1–14; Rom. 1:3, 4; 9:5; Gal. 4:4; Phil. 2:6; Col. 2:9; 1 Tim. 2:5; 3:16; Heb. 2:14, 16–17; 4:15; 1 Pet. 3:18; 1 John 5:20].

40. See, for example, Enns, *Inspiration and Incarnation*, 17.

41. For an excellent treatment of Phil. 2:6–8, with special reference to the personal preexistence of the eternal Son of God, along with a cogent rejection of kenotic christologies that are mistakenly inferred from the passage, consult Moisés Silva, *Philippians*, 2nd ed., Baker Exegetical Commentary on the New Testament (Grand Rapids: Baker Academic, 2005), 98–108.

42. B. B. Warfield, *The Inspiration and Authority of the Bible* (Philadelphia: Presbyterian & Reformed, 1948), 162.

in terms of Scripture's own self-witness to its pneumatic origin—it is God-breathed, the product of the Holy Spirit.[43]

It is at this point that the incarnational analogy seems warranted and useful. Just as Christ's person remains divine in the act of incarnation, so also the Spirit's Word remains divine in the act of inspiration and inscriptura- tion. Notice that the primary locus for our discussion of both incarnation and inspiration is the *divinity* of the second and third persons of the Trin- ity, respectively. The primacy of the divine persons, the close and insepa- rable correlation of Christology and pneumatology, does not deny human authorship of Scripture any more than it denies the assumed humanity of Christ. But it does deny that divinity and humanity are *equally basic*, or share some sort of ontological parity, when it comes to either incarnation or inspiration/inscripturation. The divine persons are always primary in matters pertaining to incarnation and inspiration, since the divinity of the Son and the Holy Spirit supplies the presuppositions for the very possibility of incarnation and inspiration/inscripturation.

Gaffin distills the essence of this point with his characteristic clarity when he observes,

> The basic thrust . . . is plain: Scripture, like Christ, is both truly human and truly divine. Yet in the case of Scripture, as for Christ, these two factors are *not equally ultimate*; the priority and originating initiative belong to the divine, not the human. Specifically, the Word, in his antecedent identity as the Word, became flesh; and God is the primary author of the Bible, in distinction from the secondary human authors. This specifies the "related mysteries" of Christ and the Bible.[44]

In short, then, an orthodox incarnational analogy turns on the fact that both in Christ and in Scripture, the divine and human are *not* equally ulti- mate. Rather, the priority and originating initiative belong to the divine, not the human. This entails that God the Holy Spirit is the primary author of Scripture, with human authorship being a real, yet subordinate, reality. This analogy follows from a proper understanding of the preexistence of the Son of God and the primacy of his eternal person in relation to his

43. For an outstanding discussion of these issues, consult Edward J. Young, *The God-Breathed Scriptures*, with a foreword by Richard B. Gaffin Jr. (Willow Grove, PA: The Com- mittee for the Historian of the Orthodox Presbyterian Church, 2007).

44. Richard B. Gaffin Jr., "Old Amsterdam and Inerrancy?—I," *WTJ* 44 (1982): 267.

assumed humanity (cf. John 1:1–14; Rom. 1:3–4; 9:5; Phil. 2:5–11; Col. 1:15–17; Heb. 1:3).

Preexistence and the Trinity

The exegesis above also warrants the classical distinction between the ontological and economic aspects of the Trinity. The ontological Trinity designates God as the self-contained being who exists apart from and prior to his relation to the world. The economic Trinity, on the other hand, pertains to the works of God with reference to the world.

Theologians attempting to develop in various ways Rahner's rule (i.e., that the ontological Trinity is the economic Trinity, and *vice versa*), and operating in the shadow of neo-Hegelian philosophy, deny a meaningful distinction between the ontological and economic aspects of the Trinity. Catherine Mowry LaCunga[45] and Ted Peters[46] represent two attempts virtually to obliterate the distinction between the ontological and economic aspects of the Trinity, as understood within orthodox Reformed theology.

More recently, and with greater sophistication, Bruce McCormack inquires along lines suggested by Karl Barth and asks if there is any sense in which God's saving activity could be understood as *constitutive* of God's triunity. McCormack's answer is an astounding yes.

45. Catherine Mowry LaCugna, *God For Us: The Trinity and Christian Life* (San Francisco: HarperCollins, 1992). For instance, she boldly asserts that "the life of God—precisely because God is triune—does *not* belong to God alone"(1). In fact, "Because of God's outreach to the creature, God is said to be essentially relational . . . ."(1). Therefore, "Divine life is also *our* life"(1). She argues that on account of God's outreach to the creature, it is inappropriate to posit "*intradivine relations, God in Godself* (sic.)" (222). Instead of affirming the classical distinction between ontological and economic aspects of the Trinity, LaCugna says that the two are "aspects of *one* reality: the mystery of *divine-human communion*" (222). In other words, to speak of God as ontological Trinity is *already* to speak of divine-*human* communion. What Reformed theology would identify as God's eternal, self-contained existence, LaCugna would conceptualize merely as an aspect of a single "divine-*human*" relationship. In LaCugna's theological perspective it is illegitimate to speak of intradivine relations or of God as a self-contained, eternal being.

46. Peters speaks of "the divine process of self constitution with the world's history" in *God as Trinity: Temporality and Relationality in Divine Life* (Louisville: Westminster John Knox, 1993), 145. In Peters's construction, the very being of God is constituted by interaction with the created order, and this means that the features that pertain to the created order, such as process, change, and temporality pertain to God's own being. This Hegelian notion of God's being as constituted by interaction with the created order effectively undermines the Creator/creature distinction by placing God and creation within a single continuum of space-time reality. Paul D. Molnar offers trenchant criticism of Peters in *Divine Freedom and the Doctrine of the Immanent Trinity* (New York: T&T Clark, 2002), 138–44.

McCormack asserts that while Barth rejected the idea that God was triune only for the sake of his revelation in *Church Dogmatics* I/i, this previously rejected thinking seems to be implied by Barth's later doctrine of election. In other words, McCormack believes Barth was inconsistent in denying that God is triune only for the sake of election. The very nature of God as triune is logically dependent upon God's decision to establish a covenant of grace, along with the corollary notion of God's self-determination to be God for us in Jesus Christ.

This means that God's decree to be for us in Christ Jesus entails that the events of the incarnation and outpouring of the Spirit are constitutive of God's eternal being by way of anticipation. McCormack argues that "Barth either did not fully realize the profound implication of his doctrine of election for the doctrine of the Trinity, or he shied away from drawing them for reasons known only to himself."[47]

McCormack elaborates that "God's triunity is logically a function of divine election."[48] According to McCormack, this means that,

> The eternal act of Self-differentiation in which God is God a second time in a very different way (generation) . . . and a third time as well (spiration), is *given in* the eternal act in which God elects himself for the human race. The decision for the covenant of grace is the ground of God's triunity and, therefore, of the eternal generation of the Son and of the eternal procession of the Holy Spirit from the Father and the Son. The works of God *ad intra* (the trinitarian processions) find their ground in the first of the works of God *ad extra* (viz. election). And that means also that the eternal generation and procession are willed by God; they are not natural to him if 'natural' is taken to mean a determination of being fixed in advance of all actions and relations.[49]

The consequences of this formulation are as destructive as LaCugna and Peters, although perhaps more subtle. The eternal act of trinitarian self-differentiation is free as a *consequence* of God's freedom in election. The decision with regard to the covenant of grace, which easily could be

47. Bruce McCormack, "Grace and Being: The Role of God's Gracious Election in Karl Barth's Theological Ontology," in *The Cambridge Companion to Karl Barth*, ed. John Webster (Cambridge: Cambridge University Press, 2000), 102.

48. Ibid., 103.

49. Ibid.

otherwise, because it is free, is therefore the ground for the triunity of God. Therefore, it appears that had God not decided to be for all of humanity in the covenant of grace, God would not be triune.

If McCormack is willing to affirm that God's triunity is constituted by his saving activity, located in God's eternal self-determination to be for us in election, what stops McCormack from falling into the problems found in LaCugna and Peters, who argue that God's eternal being is constituted by his engagement with the world in history? Put differently, if God's triunity is constituted by his economic activity, why stop with the decree of election as the event that constitutes his triunity? McCormack seems hard pressed to avoid the problems associated with the approaches of LaCugna and Peters, who, more consistently, allow the full scope of economic activity to constitute God's being as such.

Robert Jenson, moving beyond Barth and McCormack and attempting to appropriate Rahner's rule, has gone so far to say that "we may say that the resurrection is the Christian God's *ousia*."[50] The redemptive-historical event of the resurrection of the Son of God, according to Jenson, is the eternal *ousia* of the Christian God. Regarding the preexistence of the eternal Son of God, he argues that,

> What in eternity precedes the Son's birth to Mary is not an unincarnate *state* of the Son, but a pattern of movement within the event of the incarnation, the movement to incarnation, as itself a pattern of God's triune life.[51]

Jenson is explicit that he intends to deny the preexistent divine Logos—the *Logos asarkos* of Chalcedonian and Reformed orthodoxy. He says that "the way in which the triune God is eternal is by the events of Jesus' death and resurrection."[52] This point leads Jenson to assert that the events of the redemptive economy that occur in history comprise the eternal being of God in such a way that an orthodox doctrine of the Son's personal preexistence vanishes within the monolith of history.

The most basic criticism of Jenson's proposal, in a manner that echoes Hurtado's critique of Dunn,[53] is its utter lack of exegetical support. His notion

---

50. Robert Jenson, *The Triune Identity: God According to the Gospel* (Philadelphia: Fortress, 1982), 168.

51. Robert Jenson, *Systematic Theology: The Triune God* (Oxford: Oxford University Press, 1997), 141.

52. Ibid., 219.

53. Cf. n19 above.

of preexistence strains Hebrews 1:3 and Colossians 1:15a, understood in context, beyond recognition. The resurrection of the Son of God does not constitute the Son's eternal *ousia*. Rather, it is just the reverse: the resurrection expresses in redemptive historical categories the preexistent glory of the eternal Son of God.

Another, more philosophical, criticism of Jenson's line of thinking is summarized nicely by Colin Gunton, who, objecting to LaCugna and Peters, makes the charge that applies equally to all who, like Jenson, deny the biblical (and orthodox) distinction between the *Logos asarkos* and the *Logos ensarkos*. He observes, "the question [which] must be asked therefore is whether Peters's and LaCugna's approaches finally escape the pantheism which results from any attempt to bring God and the world too close. The danger is particularly manifest in the latter."[54] Gunton's criticism penetrates to the heart of the matter.

The errors of LaCugna, Peters, Barth/McCormack, and Jenson derive in various ways from a perennial problem that confronts systematic theologians—the tendency toward abstraction and philosophical speculation.[55] The most basic problem with the proposals outlined in this section arises from the speculative, and essentially unbiblical, categories proposed by each theologian. It is faithful biblical exegesis that checks the errors in speculative, philosophical proposals that betray recalcitrance to the theological categories that emerge from the inscripturated Word of God.

CONCLUSION

Biblico-systematic theology, at its best, is an exegetical discipline regulated by the sole authority of the inscripturated Word of God and militant in its defense of Reformed orthodoxy. Biblical truth offers not merely a path of exploration that allows us to expand the vistas of biblico-systematic theology, but a fortress to be defended against the onslaught of heterodox hermeneutical and theological proposals that owe much more to Athens than Jerusalem.

54. Colin Gunton, *The Promise of Trinitarian Theology* (Edinburgh: T&T Clark, 1997), xviii.
55. For an excellent reminder that the lifeblood of systematic theology remains redemptive-historically regulated exegesis, which helps to ward off unbiblical speculation in the theological task, consult John Murray's insightful article, "Systematic Theology, Second Article," *WTJ* 26 (November 1963), 44ff.

This implies that Reformed biblico-systematic theology operates both in constructive and polemical ways. The constructive task without the polemical function is blind; the polemical function without the constructive task is empty. Both aspects of biblico-systematic theology need all the emphasis we can give them, so that we avoid the Scylla of Post-Conservative Evangelicalism, which casts a contemptuous eye at confessional Reformed orthodoxy,[56] on the one hand, and the Charybdis of Reformed traditionalism, resolute in polemics against heterodox innovations, yet resistant to authentic advancements within the Reformed tradition based on faithful biblical exegesis,[57] on the other hand.

This study merely scratched the surface of what lies before those interested in developing biblico-systematic theology in the Reformed tradition—a tradition that has been vastly enriched by the pioneering work of Dr. Richard B. Gaffin Jr., whose labor in the Lord is surely not in vain (1 Cor. 15:58).

---

56. See, for example, John R. Franke, *The Character of Theology: A Postconservative Evangelical Approach* (Grand Rapids: Baker Academic, 2005).

57. D. G. Hart, "Systematic Theology at Old Princeton: Unoriginal Calvinism," in *The Pattern of Sound Doctrine: Systematic Theology at the Westminster Seminaries* (Phillipsburg, NJ: P&R, 2004), 3–26.

7

God's Speech in These Last Days: The New Testament Canon as an Eschatological Phenomenon

C. E. HILL

In many and various ways God spoke of old to our fathers by the prophets; but in these last days he has spoken to us by a Son. (Heb. 1:1–2 RSV)

The academic study of the formation of the biblical canon, Old and New Testaments, is enjoying a resurgence of interest. Two large anthologies published recently signal this renewed interest,[1] though they form, as it were, the tip of the iceberg. Common to the vast majority of studies is the assumption that the critical port of entry for the subject of the NT canon is from a point or points outside the history and witness of the documents in question, that the rise of a NT canon is a historical phenomenon of the later church. That is, while the NT documents (along

---

1. Lee Martin McDonald and James A. Sanders, eds., *The Canon Debate* (Peabody, MA: Hendrickson, 2002); J. M. Auwers and H. J. De Jonge, eds., *The Biblical Canons*, BETL 163 (Leuven, Netherlands: Leuven University Press, 2003).

with similar writings) are acknowledged to be products of first- or in some cases second-century Christianity, the impetus for constructing from them a new set of Christian Scriptures to parallel the ancient Scriptures—including the formulation of criteria for their selection (whether loose or strict), and the ends to be served by such a collection—is to be found in the circumstances of the church of the second through the fourth centuries.[2] As Lee McDonald summarizes, "the NT canon process began in the second century with the recognition of Christian literature as scripture that was useful for the teaching and mission of the church," and, "for whatever reasons, the literature that best suited the needs of the church is the literature that survived in its traditions and became of [sic] a part of its sacred scriptures."[3]

If one locates the starting point for the study of the formation of the NT canon outside Scripture's self-testimony and virtually confines oneself to a set of historical phenomena outside these writings, one may be inclined to conclude with Harry Gamble that, "During the first and most of the second century, it would have been impossible to foresee that such a collection [of NT Scripture] would emerge. Therefore, it ought not to be assumed that the existence of the NT is a necessary or self-explanatory fact. Nothing dictated that there should be a NT at all."[4]

It is customary, when approaching from this angle the individual writings that constitute the NT, to describe them as *ad hoc* and "occasional," and thus as restricted in important ways by their particularity. Gamble observes that

> None of the writings which belong to the NT was composed as scripture . . . "the scriptures" for earliest Christianity were invariably the Jewish scriptures. The documents which were eventually to become distinctively Christian scriptures were written for immediate and

---

2. L. M. McDonald, *The Formation of the Christian Biblical Canon* (Peabody, MA: Hendrickson, 1995), 319. Craig D. Allert, *A High View of Scripture? The Authority of the Bible and the Formation of the New Testament Canon* (Grand Rapids: Baker Academic, 2007), wants us to consider "how the church judged and appropriated the very writings that the church included in its canon" (51); "even the Christian writings eventually included in the New Testament canon were subjected to this Rule of Faith" (55).

3. McDonald, *Formation*, 319.

4. H. Y. Gamble, *The New Testament Canon: Its Making and Meaning* (Minneapolis: Fortress, 1985), 12.

practical purposes with the early churches, and only gradually did they come to be valued and to be spoken of as "scripture."[5]

Robert Funk asks and answers his own provocative question, "Are the particular solutions proposed by Paul of Tarsus to particular problems of Christian living in the first century binding for all time on Christian communities? The answer nearly all theologians give to that question is negative."[6] This view conceives of the collecting of the NT writings and their eventual attainment of Scriptural eminence as unanticipated, fortuitous, and certainly "unnecessary" historical developments, as one of the "fateful accidents" of history. Some historians of the canon then lament the ultimate results, a fixed, twenty-seven-book canon of NT writings, separated and exalted above all others. Robert Funk even maintains that

> to regard the New Testament writings as authoritative guides for Christian belief and practice in all times and places is to rob them of their particularity and plurality and hence their historicity. To retain the traditional New Testament and understand it as a canon is to condemn it to progressive irrelevance with each passing century.[7]

Who would deny the difficulty felt by many Christians of a Holy Scripture that preserves the travel plans of Paul and his companions, along with his individual greetings to people now long dead and forgotten, and that addresses situations in the churches that can never again have an exact parallel? But these indications of historically conditioned particularity, after all, present no worse a difficulty than the numerous extended genealogical lists; detailed descriptions of tabernacle construction and cultic procedures; and geographical, military, and historical accounts that fill column after column of the scrolls of the Old Testament. Yet by everyone's agreement, these scrolls were considered Holy Scripture by Jews and early Christians alike,

---

5. Gamble, *The New Testament Canon*, 18. Elsewhere he states, "Of course, virtually all the writings which now stand in the canon were, in fact, composed for special groups of recipients and therefore fell short of the ideal of catholicity, but this was not always obvious to the ancient church. . . ." (*Canon*, 69).

6. Robert Funk, "The Once and Future New Testament," in Lee Martin McDonald and James A. Sanders, eds., *The Canon Debate* (Peabody, MA: Hendrickson, 2002), 541–57, at 542.

7. Funk, "Once and Future," 544.

who obviously did not believe they were thereby robbing those Scriptures of their particularity, plurality, or historicity.

But more importantly, one must judge that the views cited above have not been formed from a careful consideration of the New Testament's conception of its own origin and nature as divine revelation. It has been, in this writer's opinion, part of the genius and saving grace of a conscientiously Reformed approach to Scripture that it refuses to divorce the study of the formation of the biblical canon from the Scripture's own self-testimony, and indeed, retains its focus on Scripture's self-authenticating quality. At its best, the Reformed approach resists the temptation to make Scripture first into something it is not before judging what Scripture is. As a consequence, it recognizes, as Richard Gaffin says, that "The origin of the New Testament canon is not the same as its reception by the church. We must avoid confusing the existence of the canon with its recognition, what is constitutive (God's action) with what is reflexive (the church's action)."[8]

The history of the church's struggles to find unity on the literary boundaries of its Scriptures is fascinating and of great importance in its own right. Close study of this history ought to temper immoderate assertions from both ends of the theological spectrum. But as necessary as it is to recognize the role of the early church in the "ins and outs" of the collection and pronouncement process, the Reformed have always maintained that the primary locus for the legitimacy of a NT canon is God's self-attesting Word itself.[9] And the legacy of Reformed writers such as Geerhardus Vos, Herman Ridderbos, and Richard Gaffin[10] has been to develop and clarify the fully redemptive-historical character of that self-attestation.

Far from leading to an ahistorical attitude, this approach instead should promote the deepest concern for history, for God's revelation has always been given in history and bears providentially the ineradicable stamp of its

8. Richard B. Gaffin Jr., "The New Testament as Canon," in Harvie M. Conn, ed., *Inerrancy and Hermeneutic: A Tradition, A Challenge, A Debate* (Grand Rapids: Baker, 1988), 171.

9. Herman Ridderbos, *Redemptive History and the New Testament Scriptures*, 2nd rev. ed., trans. H. De Johngst, rev. Richard B. Gaffin Jr. (1955; Phillipsburg, NJ: P&R, 1988), 9, "The principle of the self-attestation of Scripture as the real ground or source of its recognition as a rule for faith and life is reiterated again and again by subsequent Reformed authors," that is, after Calvin.

10. The huge contribution of Dick Gaffin to this tradition is evident not only in his writing and teaching on the subject of the NT canon but in the tenor of his entire exegetical/theological corpus. It is also seen in his dedicated editorial involvement in the publishing of the works of both Vos and Ridderbos, making them accessible to wider audiences.

historical circumstances. But the history most critical to the understanding of the rise of a NT canon is not the history of the church past A.D. 100, but the redemptive history in which God's acts of redemption and his attendant acts of revelation take place. According to Ridderbos,

> . . . we cannot understand the significance of Scripture, of its canonicity and authority apart from the context in which it arose, the history of redemption. In other words, it is necessary to examine more closely *the connection between the history of redemption and the canon.*[11]

In contrast with Gamble and others, we shall argue that the rise of a NT Scripture, a NT canon was "inevitable," not because the church at some point decided it needed a companion volume to the OT, not because it decided it needed a permanent written form of its message for its preaching or to ward off heresy, not because it wanted to codify readings it had already adopted in liturgical settings—as important as these historical factors were in themselves. We maintain that the rise of a NT canon was inevitable because of the very nature of the eschatological redemption accomplished by God's anointed Son and Servant, Jesus of Nazareth, that the eventual appearance of a new Scripture was an organic development of the Messiah's redemptive work, fully consistent with, and in fact authorized by, the OT expectation. If one does not recognize, and indeed begin with, the truth and relevance of Jesus' redemptive work, it is only natural that one will fail to regard the New Testament as a necessary phenomenon. But the early church, including the writers of the NT documents, *did* believe in the reality of Jesus' redemptive work in fulfillment of OT expectation. To dismiss or downplay this fact is to place oneself on an outlying plateau from which one cannot hope to view closely the internal forces that inevitably gave rise to a new set of Christian Scriptures.

A New Messianic Message "in These Last Days"

Luke records that on the day of his resurrection Jesus gave his disciples crucial instruction about the Scripture's witness to him. The risen Lord gently

---

11. Ridderbos, *Redemptive History and the New Testament Scriptures*, 12, emphasis his. He continues by observing that the NT Scripture "is usually treated and judged as a phenomenon that belongs to the history of the church, rather than to the history of redemption. But that is only a half-truth" (12).

upbraided two disciples on the road to Emmaus by saying, " 'O foolish ones, and slow of heart to believe all that the prophets have spoken! Was it not *necessary* that the Christ should suffer these things and enter into his glory?' And beginning with Moses and all the Prophets, he interpreted to them in all the "Scriptures the things concerning himself" (Luke 24:25–27).[12]

The two major poles of Messianic prophecy identified by Jesus here, that the Christ should suffer and that he should enter into glory, received greater explication later that day when Jesus appeared to a larger group of his disciples in Jerusalem.

> Then he said to them, "These are my words that I spoke to you while I was still with you, that everything written about me in the Law of Moses and the Prophets and the Psalms must [*dei*] be fulfilled." Then he opened their minds to understand the Scriptures, and said to them, "Thus it is written, that the Christ should suffer and on the third day rise from the dead, and that repentance and forgiveness of sins should be proclaimed in his name to all nations, beginning from Jerusalem." (Luke 24:44–47)

A comparison of the language in 24:25–27 and 46 suggests that Messiah's "glory" (24:26) be defined in verses 46–47 as including both his rising from the dead on the third day *and* the preaching of repentance and forgiveness of sins in his name to all nations. The structure of 24:46–47, in any case, clearly indicates that the preaching of repentance and forgiveness of sins in the name of the Messiah to all nations beginning from Jerusalem is viewed as constituting a major aspect of the prophetic testimony concerning the Messiah, written beforehand in Scripture.[13] Because this was announced through the prophets, its fulfillment is "necessary" (*edei*, Luke 24:26, 44),[14] just as necessary in this sense as the Messiah's suffering and his resurrection.

We are evidently to suppose that the Scriptures of the Law of Moses, the Prophets, and the Psalms expounded by Jesus on the day of his resur-

---

12. Biblical quotations, unless otherwise noted, will be from the English Standard Version.

13. Joel Green, *Luke*, NICNT (Grand Rapids: Eerdmans, 1997), 856n19, "This structure is difficult to represent in English, but obvious in Greek: [*houtōs gegraptai pathein*] ... [*anastēnai*] ... [*kēruchthēnai*] ...."

14. Charles H. Cosgrove, "The Divine *Dei* in Luke-Acts: Investigations into the Lukan Understanding of God's Providence," *NovT* 26 (1984), 168–90, finds in Luke-Acts "at least fifteen instances of [*dei*] ... employed specifically in connection with Scripture proof. Furthermore, a number of other texts fall within the purview of these Scripturally-grounded 'musts' according to content" (173–74).

rection included prophetic testimonies not only to his suffering, as for instance Psalm 22:1–21 and Isaiah 52:14–53:12; and not only to his resurrected glory, as for instance Psalm 16:8–10, Psalm 22:22–31, and Isaiah 52:13 and 53:10–12, but also testimonies to the spread of a particular message of repentance and forgiveness in his name to the nations. Whether Luke's tradition preserved any of these testimonies or not, he does not relate any of them explicitly, though one, as we shall see, is present by allusion in Jesus' words that Luke does record. In any case, throughout the rest of the Lucan writings and elsewhere in the NT, a handful of interrelated Isaianic texts[15] in particular figure prominently, texts that the apostles and the early Christian communities understood to provide much of the prophetic foundation for the apostolic preaching/teaching mission in the last days, texts that therefore are also foundational for the appearance of a New Testament canon.

Isaiah 2:2–3

Already in Jesus' statement in Luke 24:47, "that repentance and forgiveness of sins should be proclaimed in his name to all nations, beginning from Jerusalem," there appears to be an allusion to one of the texts in question. Near the beginning of the prophecy of Isaiah is the proclamation,

> It shall come to pass in the latter days that the mountain of the house of the LORD shall be established as the highest of the mountains, and shall be lifted up above the hills; and all the nations shall flow to it, and many peoples shall come .... For out of Zion shall go the law, and the word of the LORD from Jerusalem. (Isa. 2:2–3; cf. Mic. 4:1–2)

This picture of the Word of the Lord going out from Jerusalem in Isaiah 2:3 is amplified at several points later in the prophecy, including 40:9;[16]

---

15. When we begin to see how interrelated these several texts are, and how allusion is made to them and to other portions of the book of Isaiah by the NT writers, we also appreciate that these Isaianic texts are not isolated "proof-texts," but simply the visible peaks of a unified reading of the prophet. Richard Bauckham, *God Crucified: Monotheism and Christology in the New Testament* (Grand Rapids: Eerdmans, 1999), 48, points to what he calls "an integrated early Christian reading" of Isaiah 40–55 lying behind many NT texts. The theme with which we are concerned here, however, transcends this portion of Isaiah and pertains to sections of the entire book.

16. "Get you up to a high mountain, O Zion, herald of good news [*ho euangelizomenos*]; lift up your voice with strength, O Jerusalem, herald of good news [*ho euangelizomenos*]; lift it up, fear not; say to the cities of Judah, 'Behold your God!' " (Isa. 40:9).

51:4–5;[17] and 59:20.[18] This picture also seems to provide a prophetic foundation for Jesus' claim in Luke 24:47 that the prophets predicted the preaching of forgiveness in his name to all nations, beginning from Jerusalem. This same Isaianic text also appears to lie behind Jesus' post-resurrection instruction to the eleven in Acts 1:8, "But you will receive power when the Holy Spirit has come upon you, and you will be my witnesses[19] in Jerusalem and in all Judea and Samaria, and to the end of the earth [*kai heōs eschatou tēs gēs*]."[20] Indeed, the rest of the book of Acts may be seen as the record of the onward march of the "word of the Lord" (see 6:7; 8:14; 12:24; 13:48–49; 19:20; 20:32) beginning from Jerusalem (1:1–6:7), then into all Judea and Samaria (6:8–8:40), then, beginning with the calling of the apostle to the Gentiles, to the end of the earth (9:1–28:31). Even Paul regarded his own mission as having its geographical starting point in Jerusalem (Rom. 15:19).

The eschatological setting for the going forth of the new "law," the "word of the LORD from Jerusalem" is announced at the beginning of Isaiah's prophecy, "It shall come to pass in the latter days" (Isa. 2:2). This sense of eschatological fulfillment, of course, pervades the consciousness of the NT writers,[21] pertaining even and especially to their understanding of the new speech that God had given, as the author of Hebrews says, "Long ago, at many

17. "Give attention to me, my people, and give ear to me, my nation; for a law will go out from me, and I will set my justice for a light to the peoples. My righteousness draws near, my salvation has gone out, and my arms will judge the peoples; the coastlands hope for me, and for my arm they wait."

18. " 'And a Redeemer will come to Zion, to those in Jacob who turn from transgression,' declares the LORD." As cited by Paul in Rom. 11:26, and therefore as probably understood by Luke, the LXX's *heneken Siōn* (on account of Zion) is taken to imply or include the meaning *ek Siōn* (out of Zion), and therefore it agrees with Isaiah 2:2–3. "Paul's quotation depicts the Lord's coming in person *from* a restored Zion to bring deliverance to his people who are scattered among the nations" (J. Ross Wagner, "Heralds of the Good News: Isaiah and Paul 'In Concert' in the Letter to the Romans," NovTSup 101 [Leiden: Brill, 2002], 284). Wagner relates Paul's "out of Zion" to Isaiah 2:3–4; Joel 3:16 (LXX; 4:16 MT); Ps. 13:7 LXX and Ps. 109:2 LXX.

19. "You will be my witnesses," echoes his earlier speech in Luke 24:48, both of which seem to draw upon the Isaianic proclamations of God, that his servants are his witnesses, in Isa. 43:10, 12; 44:8.

20. The phrase "to the end of the earth" is not found in Isaiah 2 but comes from Isaiah 45:22; 48:20, and especially 49:6, the latter being quoted later in Acts by Paul (13:47). See below.

21. See Geerhardus Vos, *The Pauline Eschatology*, foreword by Richard B. Gaffin Jr. (1930; Grand Rapids: Baker: 1979), 11, "[Paul's eschatology] draws within its circle as a correlated and eschatologically-complexioned parts practically all of the fundamental tenets of Pauline Christianity . . . to unfold the Apostle's eschatology means to set forth his theology as a whole. Through a conceptual retroversion the end will be seen to give birth to the beginning in the emergence of truth."

times and in many ways, God spoke to our fathers by the prophets, but in these last days he has spoken to us by his Son . . . ." (1:1–2). The implication of Jesus' allusion to Isaiah 2:2 is that he is announcing to his disciples the commencement of this eschatological mission of "the word of the Lord" in the latter days, and that this mission would commence with them. Thus Isaiah 2:2–3 (Mic. 4:1–2) should be seen as a critical part of the Scriptural foundation for the apostolic mission.

This understanding of the prophecy must have been widespread in the early church. It surfaces a hundred years later in the words of Justin Martyr, who narrates the fulfillment of Isaiah 2:2–3 in this way: "For from Jerusalem there went out into the world men, twelve in number, and these illiterate, of no ability in speaking: but by the power of God they proclaimed to every race of men that they were sent by Christ to teach to all the word of God" (1 Apol. 39.3; cf. *Dial.* 24.1, 3).[22] The same understanding of Isaiah 2:2–3 is presupposed in Melito of Sardis, *Peri Pascha* 7, developed by Irenaeus, *Against Heresies* 4.34.1, 4; *Proof of Apostolic Preaching* 86 and then adopted in Christian tradition generally, even providing an important motif in Christian art, the *traditio legis*.[23]

However, this Isaianic text should be regarded not only as part of the foundation for the apostolic mission; by natural extension, the prophecy of a new law, a new word of the Lord going forth out of Jerusalem, is part of the old covenant foundation for a new "canon" of Scripture wherein the new word-revelation is preserved and from which it will be continually propagated. Additionally, the allusions to Isaiah 2:2–3 in these two speeches by the resurrected Christ recorded by Luke (Luke 24:44–49; Acts 1:7–8)

22. See C. E. Hill, "Justin and the New Testament Writings," in E. Livingstone, ed., *Studia Patristica* 30 (Leuven, Netherlands: Peeters, 1997), 42–48, at 46. Justin also sees the preaching ministry of the apostles predicted in Ps. 110:2 (*1 Apol.* 45.5); Ex. 28:33 (*Dial.* 42.1), and Ps. 19:2 (*Dial.* 64.8).

23. Commenting on Oskar Skarsaune's observation that Isaiah 2:3–4 "is *the* testimony on the apostolic mission in Justin" (in Oskar Skarsaune, *The Proof from Prophecy: A Study in Justin Martyr's Proof-Test Tradition: Text-Type, Provenance, Theological Profile*, NovTSup 56 [Leiden, Netherlands: Brill, 1987], 160; cf. also 356ff.), Reidar Hvalvik writes that "In my opinion this statement can be expanded to include a majority of patristic writers from the second through the fifth centuries. In other words, in the early church Isa 2:3 (Mic 4:2) is the central proof-text for the apostolic mission" (Reidar Hvalvik, "Christ Proclaiming his Law to the Apostles: The *Traditio Legis*-Motif in Early Christian Art and Literature," in John Fotopoulos, ed., *The New Testament and Early Christian Literature in Greco-Roman Context: Studies in Honor of David E. Aune*, NovTSup 122 [Leiden: Brill, 2006], 419). Hvalvik discusses the motif in early Christian art and cites more instances of the patristic exegesis that supports it. Among these is Augustine, *City of God* 10.32, which directly links Isa. 2:2–3 to Jesus' words in Luke 24:44–47.

provide an interpretive setting for the appearance of other Isaianic texts in Luke-Acts and elsewhere, texts that further establish the centrality of the new *message* associated with the eschatological appearance of the suffering and now glorified Messiah.

Isaiah 61:1–2a; 52:7

One of these texts had appeared on the lips of Jesus in Luke's account of Jesus' preaching in Nazareth (4:18–19):[24] Jesus read that day from Isaiah 61:1–2a,[25]

> The Spirit of the Lord is upon me, because he has anointed me to proclaim good news to the poor [*echrisen me euangelisasthai ptōchois*]. He has sent me to proclaim liberty [*aphesin*] to the captives and recovering of sight to the blind, to set at liberty those who are oppressed, to proclaim the year of the Lord's favor.

The two main verbs in the quotation (he has anointed me; he has sent me) are completed in each case by one or more infinitives (to proclaim good news; to preach; to set; to preach). Three of the four infinitives have to do with the proclamation of a message.[26]

In this way Jesus inaugurated his public ministry by citing God's purpose in anointing him with the Spirit, to "bring good news" (*euangelisasthai*)

---

24. In Luke, Jesus' reading of this passage and application of it to himself form the basis for his words later to the followers of John the Baptist in Luke 7:22 (cf. Matt. 11:15), *tuphloi anablepousin . . . ptōchoi euangelizomai* ("the blind receive their sight . . . the poor have good news preached to them").

25. Actually, as Fitzmyer says, "a conflation of 61:a,b,d; 58:6d; 61:2a," Joseph Fitzmyer, *The Gospel according to Luke (I-IX)*, AB 28 (New York: Doubleday, 1970), 532.

26. Luke 4:18–19 (infinitives in bold)

pneuma kyriou ep eme
hou heineken
    echrisen me
        euangelisasthai
            ptōchois
    apestalken me
        kēruxai
            aichmalōtois aphesin
            kai tuphlois anablepsin
      aposteilai
            tethrausmenous en aphesei [this clause from Isa. 58:6]
      kēruxai
            eniauton kyriou dekton

to the poor. The proclamation of a message of good news is presented as belonging to the core of his mission as God's anointed. This is augmented by the affirmation that the Lord had sent him to preach "liberty" (*kēruxai . . . aphesin*) and to "set at liberty" (*aposteilai . . . en aphesei*). The word *aphesin* is often translated "liberty" or "release," as it pertains to captives and the downtrodden. Yet very likely even here the word was understood by Luke and his early readers with the overtones of its dominant sense in the NT, that of "forgiveness,"[27] that is, release to those spiritually held captive (just as spiritual sight would be given to the spiritually blind).[28] This is probably indicated by the fact that forgiveness is repeatedly proclaimed by Jesus, Peter, and Paul in the speeches recorded in Luke-Acts as having been promised by the prophets (Luke 24:47; Acts 10:43; 13:38; 26:18).

Jesus' Nazareth proclamation that the prophecy was being fulfilled in the hearing of his listeners (Luke 4:21, cf. 7:22) identifies him not only as "final eschatological prophet" (cf. 4:24–27), but as the divinely appointed eschatological "evangelist" who brings good news to the poor. This relates then to other Isaianic passages in which the "evangelist" is referred to, beginning with Isaiah 40:9. These texts that use the word *euangelizomai* then become the major source of the use of the word among NT writers, also therefore providing them with the noun *euangelion*.[29] Mark will introduce his written account of Jesus' life and ministry with the words, "The beginning of the gospel [*tou euangeliou*] of Jesus Christ, the Son of God" (1:1). All this serves to point to the prophetic basis for the "gospel" ministry of Jesus and his apostles.

In Acts 10:38–43, after reviewing the salient elements of the life of Jesus, his death and resurrection, and his commission to his disciples, Peter tells

---

27. "Although the word *aphesis* is used in these two verses in the sense of 'release,' it should be recalled that Luke also uses it in the sense of 'forgiveness' (especially of sins)," Fitzmyer, 533.

28. Such a spiritual reference does not, of course, invalidate a reference to those who are in a physical sense poverty-stricken, blind, maimed, or held prisoner.

29. Bauckham, *God Crucified*, 48, observes that "the very word 'Gospel' was taken by the earliest Christians from Deutero-Isaiah (Isa. 40:9)." This is despite the fact that the LXX translation of Isaiah uses only the verb and not the noun (the cognate feminine *euangelia* is used four times in 2 Samuel and once in 2 Kings). Since the time of Deissmann, some scholars have seen the origins of the Christian use of the terms *euangelizomai* and *euangelion* in the idiom of the Greco-Roman ruler cult. The famous Priene inscription (ca. 9 B.C.) announcing the good news of the birthday of the divine Caesar played a part. Many now recognize, however, that this background is only ancillary to the primary biblical source. See W. Horbury, " 'Gospel' in Herodian Judaea," in *The Written Gospel*, ed. M. Bockmuehl and D. A. Hagner (Cambridge: Cambridge University Press, 2005), 7–30.

those gathered at Cornelius's house that "all the prophets" bore witness to Jesus. And the witness they bore to him was, "That every one who believes in him receives forgiveness of sins through his name." What the prophets predicted is here asserted to be not simply Jesus the Messiah's death, or his glorious resurrection, but that people would receive forgiveness of sins through faith in Jesus. This echoes the summary of Jesus in Luke 24:47. A hint about one of the sources of that prophetic witness is probably to be recognized in the immediately preceding record of Peter's words, where we find embedded allusions to probably two of the Isaianic "good news" texts: "As for the word that he sent [*apesteilen*] to Israel, preaching good news of peace [*euangelizomenos eirēnēn*] through Jesus Christ (he is Lord of all), you yourselves know what happened throughout all Judea . . . ." (10:36–37). Not only is God's action of "sending" a word to Israel, a "preaching of good news," reminiscent of the words of Isaiah 61:1 as read by Jesus in Luke 4:18,[30] Jesus' activity of "preaching good news of peace" (*euangelizomenos eirēnēn*) is here couched in the terminology of Isaiah 52:7, "How beautiful upon the mountains[31] are the feet of him who brings good news, who publishes peace (*euangelizomenou akoēn eirēnēs*), who brings good news of happiness (*euangelizomenos agatha*), who publishes salvation, who says to Zion, 'Your God reigns.'"[32] This same verse is cited interpretatively by Paul in Romans 10:15 when establishing the necessity of preaching the *Christian gospel* to elicit the response of faith and calling on the name of the Lord.

While Peter's echo of Isaiah 52:7 in Acts 10:36 pertains properly only to *Jesus' own* preaching (cf. Jesus' claim in Luke 4:18–19 to being the eschatological, anointed prophet and evangelist of Isa. 61), Peter's statement that all the prophets foretold a message of forgiveness in Jesus' name implies that the "preaching of good news" spoken of by the prophet would not be completed by Jesus himself, but would require the ministries of others. Paul displays the same understanding in his citation of Isaiah 52:7 in Romans

30. Where both *euangelisasthai* and *apestalken* are used.

31. The reference to mountains ties this text to Isa. 40:9, "Get you up to a high mountain, O Zion, herald of good news," and even to the initial Isaianic, eschatological good-news text, Isa. 2:2, "It shall come to pass in the latter days that the mountain of the house of the Lord shall be established as the highest of the mountains, and shall be lifted up above the hills; and all the nations shall flow to it."

32. This verse looks back to the introduction of the theme in Isa. 40:9 at the outset of Isaiah's prophecy of restoration (chs. 40–55), and just after the prophecy that heralded the preparation of the way of the Lord (40:3–5), which was understood to signal the ministry of John the Baptist.

10:15 when he changes the singular participle to a plural, "How beautiful are the feet of those who preach the good news[33] [*tōn euangelizomenōn [ta] agatha*]!"[34] Both appropriations of Isaiah 52:7, by Peter and by Paul, then, view the text of Isaiah as authorizing not only the Messiah's preaching in person, but also the preaching of those commissioned to bring the good news about Jesus to Jew and Gentile, specifically the preaching of the apostles Peter and Paul.[35] This apostolic self-consciousness of representing Jesus is visible in the next Lucan text to be considered as well.

Isaiah 42:6–7; 49:6

Speaking to a crowd in Pisidian Antioch during their first missionary journey, in Acts 13, Paul and Barnabas reveal another of the OT prophetic testimonies understood to have predicted this message of forgiveness in Jesus' name. They justify their decision to turn to the Gentiles by telling their detractors, "Since you thrust it aside and judge yourselves unworthy of eternal life, behold, we are turning to the Gentiles. For so the Lord has commanded us, saying, 'I have made you a light for the Gentiles, that you may bring salvation to the ends of the earth'" (13:46–47).

Paul and Barnabas, then, in relating for the first time in Acts their own understanding of their mission,[36] do so in terms of Isaiah 49:6,[37] where the result of Jesus becoming a light to the Gentiles is said to be that salvation is brought to the uttermost parts of the earth. The phrase "to the uttermost parts of the earth" (*heōs eschatou tēs gēs*) is obviously taken to imply the widest geographical ministry, and extending not only to Jews but to Gentiles.

---

33. This abbreviated form which omits a phrase from the LXX of Isa. 52:7, *tōn euangelizomenōn eirēnēn*, is the main reading of the Alexandrian tradition, including P[46] ℵ* A B C 811739 cop Clem. Al, Origen, while ℵ[2] and "Western" and Byzantine witnesses, including D F G Ψ K L P vg Marcion (Irenaeus[lat]), have the missing phrase.

34. J. Ross Wagner, "Heralds of the Good News: Isaiah and Paul 'In Concert' in the Letter to the Romans," NovTSup 101 (Leiden: Brill, 2002), 173–74, "By means of this subtle modification to the text, Paul makes explicit his identification of the heralds of Isaiah 52:7 [*hoi euangelizomenoi*] with the Christian preachers [*kērussontes*] mentioned in Romans 10:8, 14–15." Wagner also notes the correspondence with the LXX of Joel 2:32, the first part of which Paul had just cited in Rom. 10:13—which mentions preachers of the good news (*euangelizomenoi*)—that "everyone who calls on the name of the Lord will be saved."

35. Irenaeus, *Against Heresies* 3.1.1 (hereafter cited as *AH*), paraphrases Isa. 52:7 in describing the departure of the apostles "to the ends of the earth, preaching the glad tidings of the good things from God to us, and proclaiming the peace of heaven to men."

36. Cosgrove, "Divine *Dei*," 175.

37. Cf. Isa. 42:6; also 9:1–2, cited in Matt. 4:15–16.

The same phrase (*heōs eschatou tēs gēs*) had appeared on the lips of the risen Jesus on the day of his ascension in Acts 1:8, when he commissioned his witnesses in terms reflective of Isaiah 2:2–3 and, as now appears reasonable to conclude, of Isaiah 49:6.

At a later stage of Paul's ministry recorded by Luke, the apostle again confirms how this Isaianic text and its earlier parallel in Isaiah 42:6–7 became programmatic for his calling: the wording of these texts was reflected in Christ's original commission to him on the occasion of his conversion. Having been, by way of a powerful, ironic, living symbolism, struck blind himself by a great heavenly light, Paul was told that Christ was sending him to the Gentiles "to open their eyes [*anoixai ophthalmous autōn*], so that they may turn from darkness to light and from the power of Satan to God, that they may receive forgiveness of sins and a place among those who are sanctified by faith in me" (26:17–18). The echoes of Isaiah 42:6–7, "I will give you as a covenant for the people, a light for the nations [*phōs ethnōn*], to open the eyes that are blind [*anoixai ophthalmous tuphlōn*]," were certainly not lost on this blinded man.[38] That he understood the Scriptural allusion is made clear in his declaration to Agrippa in 26:22–23 that he taught "nothing but what the prophets and Moses said would come to pass: that the Christ must suffer, and that, by being the first to rise from the dead, he would proclaim light [*phōs mellei katangellein*] both to the people and to the Gentiles."[39]

Paul understood that the risen Christ would make the proclamation, though he would do it through Paul (cf. Acts 15:12; 21:19). Paul's apostolic self-conception as the agent of Christ, as one commissioned to carry on Christ's own ministry,[40] is notable also at various places in his epistles: "For

---

38. On the continuation of the theme of light in Paul's ministry, see 2 Cor. 4:6; Eph. 5:7–14, etc. Another indication of the significance of Isa. 49 for Paul is seen in Gal. 1:15 where he mentions God's setting him apart from his mother's womb, corresponding to the experience of the servant in Isa 49:1, 5. This is only part of the evidence that Paul read the latter part of the prophecy of Isaiah in particular as setting the program for his calling to bring the gospel to the Gentiles. In Rom. 15:16–24 he speaks of his missionary strategy in geographical terms, and in doing so makes unmistakable reference to Isa. 66:18–21. Rainer Riesner, *Paul's Early Period: Chronology, Mission Strategy, Theology*, trans. Doug Stott (Grand Rapids: Eerdmans, 1998), 241–63, has argued that even the geographical specifications mentioned by Isaiah in this passage were regarded by Paul as providing the geographic framework for his mission.

39. Note the same categories of Messianic prophecy mentioned by Jesus in Luke 24: the Christ's suffering, his resurrection, and the proclamation of forgiveness (here "light") to both the people of Israel and the Gentiles.

40. Eckhard J. Schnabel, *Early Christian Mission*, vol. two, *Paul & the Early Church* (Downers Grove: InterVarsity, 2004), 942, rightly observes, "The accounts of Paul's conversion and other

I will not venture to speak of anything except what Christ has accomplished through me to bring the Gentiles to obedience—by word and deed" (Rom. 15:18); "Therefore, we are ambassadors for Christ, God making his appeal through us. We implore you on behalf of Christ, be reconciled to God" (2 Cor. 5:20). In Galatians 4:14 he attests that the Galatians "did not scorn or despise me, but received me as an angel of God, as Christ Jesus"; that is, they received him as an apostle who represented Christ.[41] This, of course, in another sense simply showed Paul's awareness of being called "out of time" and placed among the number of the apostles of Jesus, his chosen witnesses personally commissioned, according to all the Gospels and Acts, to represent him in a unique way.[42]

Summary

The prophetic announcement of a salvation to be accomplished "in the last days" by the Lord, a salvation extending beyond his covenant people to the nations, necessarily would entail a new message, new law, a new word of the Lord, a gospel preaching of forgiveness, of light to those who sat in darkness. Jesus becomes the evangelist, and also the subject of his own evangel: he is the new law, the Word of God made flesh, and a light to the nations. That Jesus appointed a limited number of apostles to be his representatives, such that it is Jesus who is making his appeal through them in a unique and non-repeatable way, is a basic assumption of the NT record, being well attested in other early Christian sources as well.

We have learned from this section that this apostolic appointment to bear witness to Jesus and be his mouthpieces arises not only from Jesus' personal commission, but is grounded in the prophetic literature of the Old Testament, the same prophetic literature that grounded the mission of Jesus himself to suffer on behalf of his people and then enter into his glory.

We have gained a glimpse of how this fund of prophetic testimony was understood from the beginning as establishing the function of Jesus' commissioned witnesses to bear authoritatively the *word* of the Messiah to the nations. Such prophetic texts therefore lay the foundation not only for a Christian mission to the ends of the earth, but, as we shall see below, also

---

texts show that Paul understood his missionary work among the nations as a continuation of the ministry of the Servant of God of Isaiah's prophecy."

41. Gaffin, "The New Testament as Canon," 173.

42. Matt. 10:40; Luke 10:16; 24:48; John 13:20; Acts 1:8, 21–27; etc.

for a new collection of written documents which authoritatively preserve and continually proclaim that word, with a living and active voice.

The significance of the new word of the Lord, coming to Israel and the nations "in these last days" (Heb. 1:2; cf. Isa. 2:2) in fulfillment of eschatological promises connected directly to the work of the Christ, is not simply because it comes "late in time." Rather, it is a new message that by its nature carries greater consequence, greater ultimacy than even the totality of the message revealed hitherto in the Scriptures. It is of a piece with Jesus' pronouncements, "behold, something greater than Jonah is here . . . something greater than Solomon is here" (Matt. 12:41, 42). The author of Hebrews asks, "since the message declared by angels proved to be reliable and every transgression or disobedience received a just retribution, how shall we escape if we neglect such a great salvation?" (Heb. 2:3). Elsewhere he warns, "Therefore, while the promise of entering his rest still stands, let us fear lest any of you should seem to have failed to reach it. For good news came to us (*esmen euēngelismenoi*) just as to them, but the message they heard did not benefit them . . ." (4:1–2). A similar consciousness of the elevated importance, the ultimate significance of the word concerning Christ, befitting its eschatological character, is apparent throughout the NT writings.

Eschatology and Inscripturation

In the context of prophetic expectation as understood by Jesus, Paul, Luke, and the NT writers generally, then, the new revelation from God about Jesus the Messiah is an intrinsic aspect of the "latter days" salvation (Isa. 2:2) inaugurated by Jesus' own teaching, death, resurrection, and ascension. The book of Acts and the NT letters give us glimpses of the preaching ministries of the apostles and their companions. And at a certain point, just as with many of the prophets of old, some of those Spirit-endowed apostles and prophets began to do an extraordinary thing. They began to write. They began to write not as a leisure pursuit, as some lighthearted distraction from their commission to be witnesses of Jesus to the nations, but precisely in the pursuit and fulfillment of that commission. This last point must be emphasized, because of popular misunderstanding.

A particular legacy of Adolf von Harnack and then of the neoorthodox movement is the notion that any attempt at writing down the NT *kerygma* represents a qualitative loss or diminishment, in some sense a failure of the word of God. Any thought that such a notion would have run its course with the passing out of fashion of neoorthodoxy, however, is premature. Very recently Robert Funk said,

> The transition from oral to written goes together with the move away from the free expression of the spirit to the controlled expression of bishops in an institution. It marks the transition from word *of* God to word *about* God.[43]

Some scholars still speak of the written word as an "unworthy mode of transmission,"[44] as if a spoken word may have an inherent authority and power that only fades or evaporates altogether once the ink hits the page, as if the Spirit finds in the spoken word a vehicle well-suited to his work, but finds in the written word a dead letter which can only hinder him.

Despite the persistence of such a view, the rigid dichotomy it assumes between the oral and the written word can only be seen as bizarre. For one thing, it has only to be recalled that the most common experience of the *writings* of Christian leaders on the part of most early Christians would have been the experience of hearing them read aloud. It is hard to imagine an absolute dichotomy between oral and written communication arising in such a culture where illiteracy, whatever its actual rate, was undoubtedly high by modern Western standards and the illiterate or semiliterate relied heavily on the oral "performance" of written texts. But even more important, Christianity, like the general Hebrew culture from which it sprang, treasured the written Scriptures of the Law, the Prophets, and the Writings as the very Word of God. Josephus speaks of the esteem in which the Scriptures were held, "it is an instinct with every Jew, from the day of his birth, to regard them as the decrees of God [*theou dogmata*], to abide by them, and, if need be, cheerfully to die for them" (*Against Apion* 1.42).

Yet some maintain that all this changed with the new religion. Funk claims that an "aversion to writing persisted in the early movement well into the second century. Although Paul writes to his churches, he promises in letter after letter to assert his real authority when he comes to them in

---

43. Funk, "Once and Future," 544.
44. J. Barr, *Holy Scripture: Canon, Authority, Criticism* (Philadelphia: Westminster, 1983), 12, cited by McDonald, *Formation*, 139.

person. It has frequently been pointed out that several of the church fathers preferred oral tradition to written as late as the middle of the second century C.E."[45] The "several" church fathers to which he alludes, however, turn out to be the one man, Papias of Hierapolis, writing in the early second century. And, as has now been amply demonstrated, this assessment is based on a misunderstanding of Papias's words.[46] But regardless what Papias might or might not have meant, we shall see in what follows that a view that divorced Christian preaching from writing in such a way as to deprive the latter of the authority of the former was far from the minds of Paul and other early Christian writers.

The New Covenant and Writing

It must be said, nonetheless, that the dichotomy mentioned has often been seen in Paul's words in 2 Corinthians 3, which appear at first blush to distance the "new covenant" from any notion of writing. Here the apostle says God "has made us competent to be ministers of a new covenant, not of the letter but of the Spirit. For the letter kills, but the Spirit gives life" (2 Cor. 3:5–6). Of this passage Harry Gamble has written,

> ... if the old covenant was thus seen as having a literary component, this was not true of the new covenant, and Paul is concerned to emphasize precisely this dissimilarity, among others, when he contrasts the written code and the Spirit. It may be added that in the only other early Christian text where the conception of Christianity as a new covenant receives any

---

45. Funk, "Once and Future," 544.

46. On the interpretation of Papias's statement, see L. Alexander, "The Living Voice: Scepticism towards the Written Word in Early Christian and in Graeco-Roman Texts," in D. J. A. Clines, S. E. Fowl, and S. E. Porter, eds., *The Bible in Three Dimensions: Essays in Celebration of Forty Years of Biblical Studies in the University of Sheffield*, JSOTSup 87 (Sheffield: Sheffield Academic Press, 1990), 221–47; C. E. Hill, "What Papias Said about John (and Luke). A 'New' Papian Fragment," *JTS* NS 49 (1998), 582–629, at 622–24; Richard Bauckham, *Jesus and the Eyewitnesses: The Gospels as Eyewitness Testimony* (Grand Rapids: Eerdmans, 2006), 21–38. The recent statement of Larry Hurtado is appropriate, "Papias' profession simply echoes the sort of claims that ancient historians regularly made for their works, claims that they either were eyewitnesses themselves or had learned of the events they narrate from witnesses. That is, Papias' words do not really represent a preference for oral tradition, but instead reflect the *literary* conventions of his time, in which one sought authority for one's *written* reports through claiming that they rested on authentic witnesses" (L. Hurtado, "The New Testament in the Second Century: Text, Collections and Canon," in J. W. Childers and D. C. Parker, eds., *Transmission and Reception: New Testament Text-Critical and Exegetical Studies*, Texts and Studies 3.4 [Piscataway, NJ: Gorgias, 2006], 3–27, at 26).

elaboration—namely, the Epistle to the Hebrews—it is apparent that the phrase does not entail any thought of written materials.[47]

But the "written code" (*grammatos*) with which the Spirit is contrasted in 2 Corinthians 3:6 is specifically the Mosaic legislation, and more specifically the Decalogue, for it is said to be "carved in letters on stone" (2 Cor. 3:7; cf. "tablets of stone" in 3:3). It is not written Scripture *per se*, which Paul, who instinctively attributed Scripture's words to God himself (Rom. 1:2; 9:25, etc.), could hardly have characterized as a letter that "kills"! It is the ministry of condemnation and therefore of death, associated with a particular function of the Law of Moses,[48] that is contrasted with the ministry of Spirit and of reconciliation. This simply cannot be read as a denial that the Spirit can be associated with writing, or with Scripture.[49] And when Paul says in 1 Corinthians 2:13, "And we impart this in words not taught by human wisdom but taught by the Spirit, interpreting spiritual truths to those who are spiritual," are we to think that this specifically would *not* apply to the words he is imparting to them in the letter he is writing?

Nor can we say that Paul meant that the new covenant could have no written component. Paul indicates in 2 Corinthians 3:6 that he is a minister of a new covenant (*diakonous kainēs diathēkēs*), a ministry he subsequently calls the ministry of the Spirit (*hē diakonia tou pneumatos*, 3:8), the ministry of righteousness (*hē diakonia tēs dikaiosunēs*, 3:9), and the ministry of reconciliation (*tēn diakonian tēs katallagēs*, 5:18). Is he not engaged in this ministry of the new covenant, of the Spirit, of righteousness, and of reconciliation as he writes the letter? Most certainly he is, as he indicates in 5:19–20: "in Christ God was reconciling the world to himself, not counting their trespasses against them, and entrusting to us

---

47. Gamble, *Canon*, 19.

48. The idea is further explained in Rom. 7:6, "But now we are released from the law, having died to that which held us captive, so that we serve not under the old written code (*palaiotēti grammatos*) but in the new life of the Spirit"; Rom. 7:9–11, "I was once alive apart from the law, but when the commandment came, sin came alive and I died. The very commandment that promised life proved to be death to me. For sin, seizing an opportunity through the commandment, deceived me and through it killed me."

49. Referring to what is written in Psalm 110:1, Jesus says, "David, in the Spirit, calls him Lord" (Matt. 22:43). The author of Hebrews, referring to what is written in the Law (9:8), in the Prophets (10:15–17) and in the Psalms (3:7), attributes words written in Scripture to "the Holy Spirit." And referring to prophecies of Scripture, 2 Peter 1:20–21 indicates that the prophets who spoke the now-written words were carried along by the Spirit.

the message of reconciliation [*ton logon tēs katallagēs*]. Therefore, we are ambassadors for Christ, God making his appeal through us. We implore you on behalf of Christ, be reconciled to God."

Earlier in the same epistle he had asserted "as men of sincerity, as from God, in the sight of God, we speak in Christ," where he is surely not excluding his "speaking" in this letter. Later in the same epistle he affirms "that Christ is speaking in me," as he writes (13:3). To think that Paul in 2 Corinthians 3:6 would be dismissing his own epistolary teaching, warnings, and consolations, characterizing them as the letter that kills, to be contrasted with the Spirit who gives life, would be absurd. In his writing ministry he is most energetically engaged (Col. 1:29) in the ministry of the new covenant which was given to him. This subject will gain further attention at a later point.

Gamble's reference to the new covenant in Hebrews not entailing "any thought of written materials" can also be misleading. It is true that the author nowhere points to a written form of the new covenant mediated by Jesus. But he certainly regards this new covenant as expressed and carried out through words, spoken by God himself "by his Son" (1:2), and spoken "by the Lord" (2:3). He speaks of the "word of God" (*ho logos tou theou*, 4:12; 13:7; *theou hrēma* in 6:5), the "oracles of God" (*tōn logiōn tou theou*, 5:12), the "word of righteousness" (*logou dikaiosunēs*, 5:13), the "word (or doctrine) of Christ" (*tou Christou logon*, 6:1). And it would be wrong to force a dichotomy between spoken and written words with regard to Hebrews. This is because the author of Hebrews constantly treats even the OT written Scriptures as "spoken" speech.

Geerhardus Vos, commenting on the fact that the author of Hebrews refers to God's revelation in terms of speech and not in terms of writing, observes,

> The speech is an organic, living process, a part and function of the speaking person, whereas the written communication is only a picture or symbol of the life-process it reproduces. But God's word, even when written, has this peculiarity that it retains the character of inspired, vitalized speech, opening up the depths of the divine mind and addressing itself in the most direct face-to-face way to the inner personality of the hearer. So vividly does the author realize this, that in a well-known passage it leads him to a formal personification of the [*logos tou theou*] in which attributes and activities are predicted of the word, belonging, strictly speaking, to God

Himself only, and in which a remarkable transition is made from the word to God as coordinate subjects in the same sentence [4:12–14] . . . God acts in and through His word, thus the word has the same power and effect that belong to God Himself.[50]

The author of Hebrews thinks in this way about his own letter: "Concerning him we have much to say [*polus hēmin ho logos*], and *it is* hard to explain, since you have become dull of hearing [*tais akoais*]" (Heb. 5:11). Again, this could be presupposing that the addressees will be literally hearing his words as they are being read in a congregational setting (Col. 4:16; Rev. 1:3). But there is obviously no thought here of a diminishing of power or authority because "the word of God" is written. It is either the written OT or the author's own words, or in my opinion most likely both, to which he refers when he speaks of the *logos tou theou* which is "living and active,[51] and sharper than any two-edged sword" (4:12).

Writing and the Apostolic Enterprise

By about AD 56, when Paul wrote 2 Corinthians, it is unclear how many written documents associated with the apostolic ministry of the new covenant might have been in existence, or how widely they had traveled. The ministry of the new covenant carried out by Paul and his associates and other apostles in their missions was primarily through preaching and oral teaching, and through example lived before other believers. But even by this time a written component of that ministry is forming, and as the apostolic history plays out, we receive clear indications of a continuity or

50. Vos, "Hebrews, the Epistle of the Diatheke," in Richard B. Gaffin Jr., ed., *Redemptive History and Biblical Interpretation: The Shorter Writings of Geerhardus Vos* (Phillipsburg, NJ: Presbyterian & Reformed, 1980), 190–91. He continues, "Owing to this permanent identification of God with His word, the lapse of time is not able to detract aught from the freshness and force that belonged to the self-disclosure of God at its first historic occurrence. It is not necessary to project one's self backward through the interval of the ages in order to feel near to the source of the revelation. The fountain of the living water flows close to every believer . . . although the epistle is addressed to Christians of the second generation, it none the less conceives of its readers as in the most immediate sense made recipients of the divine word spoken by Christ and through that word brought into no less direct communion with the supernatural world than the contemporaries of the earthly life of Jesus. God spake unto the fathers in the prophets: He spake in a Son unto *us* (191–92)."

51. Cf. 1 Peter 1:23, "the living and abiding word of God." As we shall see below, this description has particular reference to the new word of the gospel.

identity between the spoken, preached message as Word of God, and the written form of that word.

We noted above that the major movement in the book of Acts is that of the word of the Lord, brought by the appointed witnesses of Jesus, going forth from Jerusalem, to Judea and Samaria, and then to the ends of the earth, signified by Paul's preaching in Rome, all in fulfillment of the prophets. This shows coherence with Paul's understanding of the character of his preaching displayed already in the Thessalonian correspondence[52] in the early 50s. His conviction is clear that he had been entrusted with the gospel message (1 Thess. 2:4), and that his proclamation of the gospel is "not . . . the word of men but . . . the word of God" (1 Thess. 2:13). Like Luke, Paul too perceives the word of the Lord as on a journey, asking prayer for himself and his associates, Silvanus and Timothy, "that the word of the Lord may speed ahead and be honored" (2 Thess. 3:1). In this context he also makes it clear that he equates the authority of his written word in epistolary form with that of his spoken word:[53] "So then, brothers, stand firm and hold to the traditions that you were taught by us, either by our spoken word or by our letter" (2 Thess. 2:15). Thus at the end of the first letter he lays an unusually solemn charge on the church, "I put you under oath before the Lord to have this letter read to all the brothers" (1 Thess. 5:27). He regards refusal to comply with his written word as a choice of ultimate, spiritual consequence: "If any one does not obey *what we say in this letter*, take note of that person, and have nothing to do with him, that he may be ashamed" (2 Thess. 3:14). This sense of his apostolic authority being mediated through his epistles is constant throughout his epistolary ministry.

52. In what follows I shall be using 2 Thessalonians, Ephesians, Colossians, and the Pastorals as genuine writings of Paul. If the consensus of contemporary critical scholarship is correct and these are post-Pauline, they cannot postdate Paul by very many years and thus must still be regarded as reflective of the very early legacy of the apostle. The problems attending the judgment of inauthenticity, however, including the difficulties surrounding the "pious" production of pseudepigraphal letters so soon after the false author's death (on this, see, e.g., D. A. Carson and D. J. Moo, *An Introduction to the New Testament*, second edition [Grand Rapids: Zondervan, 2005], 337–50) and their early reception among Pauline churches as Pauline (cf. the witness of 2 Peter, 1 Clement, Ignatius, Polycarp, etc.) are to my mind much greater than the difficulties of style and content that face the assumption of authenticity. This is particularly the case given the implications of our greater understanding today of the possible role of Paul's writing associates and secretaries in the production of his letters for matters of style. See the informative book by E. Randolph Richards, *Paul and First-Century Letter Writing: Secretaries, Composition and Collection* (Downers Grove, IL: InterVarsity, 2004).

53. Cf. Ridderbos, *Redemptive History*, 15.

Again in 1 Corinthians he refers to his writing: "If anyone thinks that he is a prophet, or spiritual, he should acknowledge that what I am writing to you is a command of the Lord. If anyone does not recognize this, he is not recognized" (1 Cor. 14:37–38).[54] This is evidently the case even when he is forced (2 Cor. 12:11) to play the fool and say, in 2 Corinthians 11:17–18, "What I am saying with this boastful confidence, I say not with the Lord's authority[55] but as a fool. Since many boast according to the flesh, I too will boast"! We know this because near the end of the same epistle he looks back on his rhetorically charged boasting and asks, "Have you been thinking all along that we have been defending ourselves to you? It is in the sight of God that we have been speaking in Christ, and all for your upbuilding,[56] beloved" (2 Cor. 12:19); and then once again attests to the fact that "Christ is speaking in me" (2 Cor. 13:1–3) in the epistle he is writing. Paul obviously believes and expects the Corinthians to accept that Christ is speaking in him not only when he is present, but also when he is absent, and particularly by means of his letters (2 Cor. 13:10).

We are also fortunate to have the testimony of some contemporaries of Paul who both heard his preaching and read his letters, and who, contrary to what is often implied by writers today,[57] pronounced his letters to be "weighty and strong," more so than his personal presence (2 Cor. 10:10)!

In Ephesians, Paul momentarily reflects on his readers' experience of *reading* his letter. When he does so, he does not lament an inevitable loss of authority or submit a feeble plea that his readers simply make do until he can come to them with real insights, orally delivered. Rather he says, "*when you read this* [*anaginōskontes*] you can perceive my insight into the mystery of Christ, which was not made known to the sons of men in other generations as it has been revealed to his holy apostles and prophets by the Spirit . . . " (Eph. 3:4–5). Indeed, "to bring to light for everyone

---

54. Ridderbos, *Redemptive History*, 21–22, deals with the distinction in 1 Cor. 7 between commands from the Lord and commands not from the Lord. The distinction is not one of absolute and relative (moral) authority. It is rather "Jesus' own word that he has received as tradition and what he has to say to the church independently, on the basis of his apostolic authority, an authority that Paul claims from the Spirit of God (see v. 40, and cf. v. 25)" (21). So, "in some cases he could rest his appeal to apostolic authority on an express word of the Lord and in other cases he could not. Paul saw no difference between the authority of his own apostolic word and that of the words of the Lord that had been transmitted to him" (21).

55. Literally, "not according to the Lord" (*ou kata kyrion*).

56. "Upbuilding" is what Paul says is his commission from the Lord (2 Cor. 10:8; 13:10).

57. "Although Paul writes to his churches, he promises in letter after letter to assert his real authority when he comes to them in person," Funk, "Once and Future," 544.

what is the plan" of this "mystery" (Eph. 3:9) is precisely what Paul says is the purpose of his calling as a minister and apostle. He considers he is fulfilling this purpose in writing and sending them this epistle.

On this purpose he elaborates in Colossians 1:24–29, speaking of

> . . . the church, of which I became a minister according to the stewardship from God that was given to me for you, to make the word of God fully known, the mystery hidden for ages and generations but now revealed to his saints. . . . Him we proclaim, warning everyone and teaching everyone with all wisdom, that we may present everyone mature in Christ. For this I toil, struggling with all his energy that he powerfully works within me.

Are we to conclude that Paul was taking a leisurely break from this energetic "toil" as he wrote the Colossians this letter? The letter, by the way, was not dashed off and sent in a moment. A great deal of thought and labor went into its production,[58] not to mention the toil of Tychicus and Onesimus (4:7–9) who traveled the many miles to deliver Paul's letter. Richards points out that

> In the approximately 14,000 private letters from Greco-Roman antiquity, the average length was about 87 words . . . . The letters of the literary masters, like Cicero and Seneca, were considerably longer. Nonetheless, Paul stands apart from them all.[59]

The average length of Cicero's letters is 295 words; the average length of Seneca's is a whopping 995. But the average length of Paul's letters is 2,495! Even Colossians, short by Paul's standards, is (by my count, according to the N/A27 text) 1,416. No, the writing and sending of this letter, as with all his known letters, is most certainly an exercise of Paul's toilsome ministry "to make the word of God fully known," to proclaim, warn and teach every person in all wisdom.

---

58. We may assume that, as was typical, Paul kept at least one copy of each of his letters. E. Randolph Richards estimates that, after whatever time it took for Paul and Timothy (Col. 1:1) to produce the letter (including pre-writing discussion and possibly note-taking and the production of one or more drafts), each copy of Colossians would have consumed about half a day of a scribe's work and that Paul would have incurred, conservatively, a cost in today's figures of about $502 in papyrus and secretarial labor for producing his letter to the Colossians (cf. Richards, *Paul and First-Century Letter Writing*, 165, 169). Colossians is a relatively short Pauline letter. The longer letters would have been more time- and cost-consuming.

59. Richards, *Paul and First-Century Letter Writing*, 163.

It is also significant that Paul's "stewardship from God [*tēn oikonomian tou theou*]" had to do not merely with an initial "preaching of the gospel" to unbelievers, such as would garner conversions. Rather it was a ministry "to make the word of God fully known" (1:25, cf. Rom. 15:19) in such a way as to present each person "mature" in Christ. As Luke records him saying to the Ephesian elders in Acts 20:27, Paul did not shrink from declaring to them "the whole counsel of God." This is relevant to the charge that Paul's epistles are either too "particular" or too expansive, and to the idea that what is relevant to the church in an ongoing way as canon ought to be restricted to some short slogan or another.[60] Paul, however, had a rather more expanded and personal view of his apostolic stewardship of bringing people to maturity through the whole counsel of God. His epistles reflect the character of that stewardship.

More could be gleaned from other epistles, Pauline and non-Pauline,[61] but the point, I think, is sufficiently clear. While letters may have been in many social respects less preferable than the personal presence of the author (cf. 2 John 12; 3 John 13–14), writing was not viewed as merely a pallid substitute for oral delivery by the author himself. A letter written by an authority figure was viewed as bearing the authority of that person. Moreover, with Paul, and presumably with others who believed the new message they preached was the very Word of God and carried with it the call to be obeyed, letters bearing that message were likewise considered the Word of God. In short, the letter-writing ministry of Paul represented in his NT letters was viewed by him as an integral exercise of his apostolic commission.

Scriptures of the Apostolic Mission (The Canon Closed in Principle)

The authorization and eventual existence of a NT canon thus is implicit in and guaranteed by the very act of redemption accomplished by Jesus. His

---

60. J. D. G. Dunn believes that the church today ought to restrict the notion of "canon" to some short summary of Christian belief such as "Jesus-the-man-now-exalted," or, "The whole Christ-event," or some other reductionistic phrase (J. D. G. Dunn, "Has the Canon a Continuing Function?" in *The Canon Debate*, ed. Lee Martin McDonald and James A. Sanders [Peabody, MA: Hendrickson, 2002], 558–79 at 561–62).

61. In 1 Peter 1:10–12, Peter identifies the "grace" that the prophets predicted with the message of the gospel preached to the readers. At the end of the letter he seems to identify his own letter with this grace predicted by the prophets: "By Silvanus, a faithful brother as I regard him, I have written briefly to you, exhorting and declaring that this is the true grace of God. Stand firm in it" (5:12).

redemptive mission, as predicted in Israel's Scriptures, included the spread of a message of redemption to the nations, and Jesus set this in motion by commissioning his apostles to speak in his name and to be his witnesses to the ends of the earth. The conscientious use of writing in the execution of this mission is not viewed as an impediment to the word of the Lord but as a medium by which it could be further spread, and preserved. The foundation for the NT canon is thus laid in redemptive history, and its constituent parts are a direct result of the redemption wrought by Jesus.

Recognizing the character of this new revelation goes a long way toward explaining why this implicit authorization of a new body of Scriptures nowhere predetermines the precise number or identity of the documents that will make up a new set of Scriptures. The problem created by an absence of explicit apostolic fixing of a number of books is tempered by the eschatological, that is, the redemptive-historical, nature of the revelation. As Ridderbos says,

> The closed nature of the canon thus rests ultimately on the once-and-for-all significance of the New Testament history of redemption itself, as that history is presented by the apostolic witness.[62]

The unique position of the apostles, and closely aligned to this, revelations made to NT prophets (Eph. 2:20), not only set forth in the NT writings themselves but widely acknowledged in the post-apostolic period,[63] establish an inherent limit on what could be considered as belonging to this original mission and what therefore could be part of that apostolic word. Only a limited number of writings could conceivably be described as such, and it is by no means an uninformed credulity that confesses these writings are the ones we possess in the New Testament.

This is not the same, of course, as claiming that all NT documents were written by apostles. The apostles, as we learn through the book of Acts and the NT epistles, engaged a number of co-workers in their ministries. That apostolic companions were thus participants in the apostles' ministries and could legitimately write in service of this mission is seen in the recogni-

---

62. Ridderbos, *Redemptive History*, 25.
63. See, e.g., C. E. Hill, "Ignatius and the Apostolate: The Witness of Ignatius to the Emergence of Christian Scripture," in *Studia Patristica*, ed. M. F. Wiles and E. J. Yarnold (Leuven, Netherlands: Peeters, 2001), 36:226–48.

tion of the Gospels written by the apostolic co-workers Mark and Luke.[64] In addition, God continued for a time speaking through prophets, who, in their role as recipients of divine revelation, could function as part of the church's foundation along with the apostles (Eph. 2:20).

The redemptive-historical or eschatological authority of the new Messianic word, moreover, grounded in the prophetic Scriptures and in Jesus' commission, is not a "criterion" of canonicity in the usual sense, understood as what Gaffin calls an Archimedean point outside the canon[65] employed by the church to determine what is Scripture. It is rather an internal authority by which these relatively few writings validate themselves as divine and as canon. It may be said that we possess no other early Christian documents that establish themselves as belonging to the apostolic word from the original apostolic mission. The church of the second through fourth centuries, geographically scattered and not receiving at the same time all writings of the apostolic deposit, subject also to the incursions of literature that in some ways imitated or sought to supplement the apostolic writings, developed corpuses of new Christian Scriptures that diverged somewhat from one another in various locales. But it is significant that all the documents that for a time or in a given locality approached, or may have enjoyed, the status of Scripture (1 Clement, *The Shepherd* of Hermas, Ps. Barnabas,[66] Apoc. Peter) held some ostensible claim to being productions of apostles or of close associates of the apostles.[67]

This eschatological grounding of the NT canon also has a bearing on the book of Hebrews. It is often observed that the authorship of Hebrews was debated in the early centuries and that the epistle was apparently recognized by churches only when they accepted it (mistakenly, as most today would say) as Paul's. But this has much relevance only when canon is perceived as

---

64. E.g., Irenaus calls Luke "not merely a follower, but also a fellow-labourer of the apostles, but especially of Paul" (*AH* 3.14.2).

65. Gaffin, "The New Testament as Canon," 171.

66. See, e.g., Clement of Alexandria, *Strom.* 5.10, "Barnabas, too, who in person preached the word along with the apostle in the ministry of the Gentiles, says . . . ."

67. Of those mentioned, the first three were by some viewed as written by men who knew Paul. The church eventually concluded, as modern scholarship does, that *Shep.* and Ps. Barn. were not authentic productions of these companions of Paul. See the treatment of Hermas and Apoc. Pet. in the *Muratorian Fragment*. Several fathers mention variously titled Gospels written in Aramaic, *Gospel of the Hebrews*, *Gospel of the Ebionites*, *Gospel of the Nazoreans*. These are not attributed by title but were often viewed as being Aramaic versions (of varying fidelity) of Matthew's gospel.

the creation of the church. Hebrews, even if not penned by an apostle, still shows itself to belong to that original apostolic mission not only because of its early date (it was used by 1 Clement in the first century) and display of profound "apostolic" teaching,[68] but by the author's self-identification as a traveling companion of Timothy (13:23), marking him out as an apostolic co-worker. It is not like, for instance, the letter of Clement of Rome, who looks back to the age of Peter and Paul and is conscious of a gap of apostolic authority between himself and the apostles (1 Clem 5.3–7; 42.1–5; 44.1–3; 47.1–4).[69] Though the name of Hebrews' author is unknown, the letter, it would seem, could only have been written by one of a very small circle of apostolic companions.[70] Writings that look back on the apostolic mission, such as 1 Clement or the letters of Ignatius, obviously did not arise in any direct way from that apostolic mission by the hand of a commissioned apostle or an apostolic co-worker. The only document in the NT that ostensibly might seem to transgress this boundary would be the epistle of Jude, which recalls to readers' minds the predictions of the apostles (Jude 17–18). But these predictions are clearly of recent vintage, as his readers were personally addressed by them (18), and Jude, as the brother of James (1) and therefore of Jesus, was like James a leader in the original apostolic mission (cf. Acts 1:14; 1 Cor. 9:5).[71]

The Conscious Construction of a Written Legacy: The Seeds of "Canonization"

The picture generally given by scholars is that by the beginning of the second century, a mass of undifferentiated writings had emerged from the fledgling Christian movement. Many gospels or written collections of Jesus' words were circulating, as were letters of Paul, and by now letters of his imitators or successors, other letters claiming to be from other apostles or brothers of Jesus, church manuals (the *Didache*), official church correspondence (*1 Clement*), apocalypses claiming to reveal God's plans for

---

68. See Origen's assessment in Eusebius, *HE* 6.25.13–14.

69. Even though he believes he is writing "through the Holy Spirit" (63.2).

70. These would include Luke, Barnabas, Mark, Apollos, and Silas (Silvanus). In my view, the best case can be made for Silas, who was known to the church in Judea to which the epistle was addressed.

71. See the defense of Jude's authenticity by Richard J. Bauckham, *Jude, 2 Peter*, WBC 50 (Waco, TX: Word, 1983), 8–17: "once one has cast off the spell of the early Catholic and antignostic reading of Jude, the letter does give a general impression of primitiveness" (13).

church and empire (Revelation, perhaps *The Shepherd*). The differentiation process, if it has begun at all by this point, has begun on an *ad hoc* basis as each local church begins to cull from the multifarious literature then circulating some that it is experiencing as particularly useful for its ministries and controversies. Naturally, a great deal of variation exists from church to church in this matter. Without a central authority in Christendom, each church or perhaps local group of churches comes to prefer its own written account of Jesus' life and ministry, perhaps some churches using more than one, to function alongside the oral transmission of Jesus' sayings and stories about him. Some churches, perhaps especially those that received an authentic letter from the apostle Paul, have begun to build collections of Paul's letters, as they find occasion to do so.

Other epistolary literature from earlier days is used, perhaps updated, and pious ecclesiastical minds compose other letters in the names of Paul, Peter, and others of the first generation, for the sake of edification. As time passes, the reputations of apostles, as church founders who claimed to have known Jesus, rise in eminence, and writings associated with their names appreciate in value. Local or regional traditions begin to build, cross-regional communication leads to the exchange of books and letters, discussions of the authenticity of newly acquired sources take place. In debates with those on the margin of the Christian tradition(s), it is found useful to appeal to "authoritative" sources connected to Jesus and the apostles. Gradually, by the second century, some of these sources attain a status as high as the OT Scriptures. All of this, we are told, was happening in a free environment, and while most churches within the mainstream tended to hark back to many of the same resources, the idea that they all ought to adhere to the same ones seems hardly to have crossed anyone's mind—anyone, that is, with the exception of Irenaeus of Lyons, a man far ahead of his time, and even he was concerned only with the four Gospels. Wide concern for marking out or limiting the number of new Scriptures to be recognized as such is said not to have arisen until the third or even the fourth century.

Individual historians would modify this picture in various ways, but in broad strokes it seems to represent the opinion of the majority of scholars writing in this area today. Indeed, looking at the surviving documents of early Christianity outside those that make up the NT, one will find much to commend the above sketch. Yet there is also more than a little conjecture mixed in, and, more importantly, much too much of the self-witness of the NT authors left out.

Naturally there is no apostolically approved list of books that ought to function in an ongoing way as the church's new covenant Scriptures. The point seldom observed, however, is that throughout the NT writings there are what could be called signs of the deliberate construction of a written legacy, a deposit of faith, intended to be preserved and passed on to the faithful. This is important in light of statements such as the following by Harry Gamble,

> The immediacy of Christian experience and the fervor of its eschatological hopes made superfluous even the composition of Christian writings, and there is no intimation at all that the early church entertained the idea of Christian scriptures, much less a collection of them. Therefore, the NT as we think of it was utterly remote from the minds of the first generation of Christian believers.[72]

To whatever extent eschatological hopes produced any anti-scribal prejudices in early Christianity, these would have stemmed from a narrow eschatological focus on the imagined immediate return of the Lord. But any such inhibition did not last particularly long. (It is an irony that the only way we know about eschatological expectation that supposedly inhibited early Christian writings is through early Christian writings.) And it is precisely the larger, grander eschatological consciousness of the apostles which, one might say, engendered the writing and publishing impulse.

That the process of preserving and passing on this new word was not intended to be limited to oral means seems implicit in the very decision to utilize writing in the service of the apostolic ministry. The eschatological word of the Lord predicted in Isaiah and other Scriptures and realized in the words of Jesus and his apostles naturally assumes the preservation of that word for the entire duration of the last days. As we saw in the last section, writing soon came into service as an integral part of the apostolic enterprise of bringing the light of the world to all nations, of laying the foundation for the church. The choice to employ writing must have had something to do with the sense of permanency that was endemic to the

72. Gamble, *The New Testament Canon*, 57.

eschatological, apostolic mission by nature of its message, which was to last until the end of the age.

When the author of Hebrews 1:2 writes that "in these last days he has spoken to us by his Son," he surely implies that this filial revelation is valid throughout "these last days" in a way that shall be pertinent as long as the last days last, or "as long as it is called 'today' " (3:13). Paul has this sense in 2 Corinthians 6:2 in his citation of Isaiah 49:8, "For he says, 'In a favorable time I listened to you, and in a day of salvation I have helped you.' Behold, now is the favorable time;[73] behold, now is the day of salvation." The new word of the Lord naturally holds good for the entire "day of salvation." In the words of the Great Commission, Jesus tells his disciples to make disciples of all nations, imparting to them all he had commanded them, and promises to be with them in this endeavor "to the end of the age" (Matt. 28:19–20). This presupposes that his commandments will be preserved for that duration.

Indeed, Jesus was conscious of the permanence of the new word of the Lord, the gospel he preached, even his very words. All three Synoptic Gospels record an apparent allusion to Isaiah 40:6–8 in the context of the Olivet Discourse, Matthew 24:35/Mark 13:31/Luke 21:33, when Jesus proclaims, "Heaven and earth will pass away, but my words will not pass away [*hoi de logoi mou ou mē pareleusontai*]." Jesus' claim is astounding. It is no longer merely the grass of the field that withers away, as in Isaiah 40:7, but heaven and earth themselves are fleeting and temporary compared with the everlasting nature of Jesus' own words. If he is indeed alluding to Isaiah 40:8, he is plainly identifying his words as Yahweh's own words which will not pass away.[74]

Is it conceivable that the perpetuation of Jesus' words should be done wholly through memorization and oral transmission, "to the end of the age" and till "heaven and earth pass away?" Notwithstanding the greater emphasis on memorization in antiquity and the great feats of memorization achieved by certain trained adepts in antiquity, this ought to strike us as inherently unlikely. But the thought is in fact dispelled by the simple

---

73. *Kairō dektō*, cf. *eniauton kyriou dekton* ("year of the Lord's favor") in Isa. 61:2, cited by Jesus in Luke 4:19.

74. D. A. Hagner, *Matthew 14–28*, WBC 33B (Dallas: Word, 1995), "the words of Jesus . . . are thereby made the equivalent of the word of God, which is the usual contrasting element in such statements (e.g., Isa. 40:8)."

historical reality that many of the words of Jesus were set down in writing. Indeed, the only ones that survived the transmission process very long with integrity were the ones that were put down in writing. And these were put down not just in ephemeral notebooks but in substantial literary creations now known as the Gospels. The mere decision to publish written Gospels for the church must be seen in this light, and when it is, these decisions on the parts of those who published them may be regarded as claims that the books ought to function with religious authority, like Scripture, in the life of the new people of God.

Writing of the Gospels and Acts

The first words of the Gospel according to Mark are most instructive: "The beginning of the gospel of Jesus Christ, the Son of God." Scholars often labor to make the point that the word "gospel" here does not denote a written document *per se*, one of the "Gospels," as we think of them,[75] but simply the good news about Jesus. Even if so, the significance of Mark explicitly identifying that good news with *what he is now setting down in writing* cannot be brushed aside.[76] Indisputably, the "gospel of Jesus Christ" is not something capable only of oral expression or transmission. Mark, by common consent publishing his gospel within the lifetime of many who had heard Jesus' preaching, was obviously conscious of Jesus' proclamation, "Heaven and earth will pass away, but my words will not pass away," at the time he recorded this saying in a book (13:31), and naturally would have interpreted his own actions of writing and publication in its light.[77] These deliberate actions, whatever complex historical and literary processes may lie behind them, show that the "transition" to writing had something to do

75. "As a result, [*tou euangeliou*] carries the connotation of good news as preached, not just good news as such, much less good news as written in a book," Robert H. Gundry, *Mark: A Commentary on His Apology for the Cross* (Grand Rapids: Eerdmans, 1993), 33. The "much less" is hard to comprehend, as Mark is quite clearly setting forth a written account of the "good news preached."

76. "It has become common consensus that [*euangelion*] in 1:1 refers to at least the content of the literary work that follows. Drawing on other common mission terminology of his day, the evangelist makes reference to the 'gospel' as the proclaimed message six times and designates his work as such at the outset," Robert A. Guelich, *Mark 1–8:26*, WBC 34A (Dallas: Word, 1989), 9.

77. Mark is also certainly aware that what Jesus said would be told "wherever the gospel is preached in the whole world" (14:9), he was now writing in a book. Mark is conscious of his readers in his parenthetical comments, "Thus he declared all foods clean" (7:19), "let the reader understand" (13:14).

with the desire to provide for ongoing access to the accurately preserved words and deeds of Jesus.

Whether or not Matthew is dependent, as most think, on a written version of Mark, its author too is conscious of setting down the prophetically predicted gospel in written form, and of preserving in written form Jesus' words which "will not pass away" (24:35). Perhaps more than any of the other gospel writers, Matthew is conscious of his task of recording the fulfillment of prophecies about the Messiah,[78] not least of which are important Isaianic predictions about the coming of a new message. He cites Isaiah 9:1–2 about the land of Zebulun and Naphtali, Galilee of the Gentiles, seeing a great light, a text with strong affinities with Isaiah 42:6–7; 49:6. The "light" that "has dawned" must have to do with what Matthew immediately goes on to record, "From that time Jesus began to preach, saying, 'Repent, for the kingdom of heaven is at hand'" (Matt. 4:17).[79] That is, the light has to do with the message Jesus brought and which the author is now recording for posterity. Thus it coheres with the use of Isaiah's other predictions of "light to the nations" as interpreted by Paul in his epistles and in his speeches in Acts.[80] What Matthew adds to Mark's narrative (or to the common memorized material at some point set down in Mark) includes Jesus' repeated contrasts, "You have heard that it was said . . . but I say to you . . . ." (Matt. 5:21–22, 27–28, 31–32, 33–34, 38–39, 43–44). Not content with leaving Jesus' words (24:35) and deeds (11:2) and "all that I have commanded you" (28:20) to oral transmission, the evangelist commits them to writing.

Luke's short apologetic for his writing is likewise instructive. He writes and publishes his gospel in confidence that Theophilus, by reading his "orderly account," would be able to "have certainty [*tēn asphaleian*] concerning the things you have been taught" (Luke 1:3–4). Theophilus had already been taught (*katēchēthēs*) about Jesus. The verb as used by Luke elsewhere (Acts 18:25; 21:21, 24) seems to require that he means Theophilus had been taught at least mainly through oral instruction.[81]

---

78. Richard C. Beaton, "How Matthew Writes," in *The Written Gospel*, ed. M. Bockmuehl and D. A. Hagner (Cambridge: Cambridge University Press, 2005), 116–34, at 127–28.

79. Warren Carter, "Evoking Isaiah: Matthean Soteriology and an Intertextual Reading of Isaiah 7–9 and Matthew 1:23 and 4:15–16," *JBL* 119 (2000), 503–20, at 519.

80. See the first part of this essay.

81. Because Luke mentions other written accounts (1:1), it is certainly possible that Theophilus had been exposed to one of more of these. On the other hand, they may not have reached

Yet Luke deems it necessary and appropriate to write an orderly account which could impart to Theophilus and others a secure grasp of the "things that have been accomplished among us" and "delivered . . . us" (Luke 1:2, 3).

John, publishing his gospel, I believe, later than the other three, is even more explicit about his purpose and expectation for his writing: "but these are written so that you may believe that Jesus is the Christ, the Son of God, and that by believing you may have life in his name" (20:31). John, like the other evangelists, obviously was not content to leave this world with his own testimony (John 21:24) to Jesus preserved and handed down *only* in oral form.[82] He writes with confidence that the written form of his account will place no obstacle in the way of true and authentic belief in Jesus as the Christ, the Son of God; on the contrary, it was intentionally written to be a vehicle for such belief. This is indicated in another way in John 10:16, where Jesus says, "And I have other sheep that are not of this fold. I must bring them also, and they will listen to my voice. So there will be one flock, one shepherd." It is Jesus who will bring these sheep, and they will heed his voice. But this is problematic, for they will never hear his voice as his disciples did, from Jesus' own mouth.

The matter is resolved later when Jesus prays to his Father for the apostles and also for "those who will believe in me through their word" (17:20). It is Christ's voice that his sheep hear in the words of his apostles (17:8, "I have given them the words that you gave me"), those he commissioned as "my witnesses" (15:27). John, therefore, in his task of bringing the words of the Shepherd to his sheep scattered abroad (11:52) so that they might believe, thought it fitting in the execution of this task to set down permanently the words of Jesus and the signs which he accomplished "in this book" (20:30).

Theophilus. Luke, in any case, has become privy to information about Jesus that presumably was not contained in the other accounts. Luke's reference to the "many" is "a known rhetorical device, and its meaning is perhaps not to be pressed for this reason" (Joseph Fitzmyer, *The Gospel according to Luke (I-IX). Introduction, Translation, and Notes*, AB28 (New York: Doubleday, 1979), 291). Joel B. Green, *The Gospel of Luke* (Grand Rapids: Eerdmans, 1997), 30, makes the same point. Fitzmyer posits that Luke may have had three such sources, Mark, Q, and another hypothetical source he calls L, though he believes L might not have been solely written. Others believe Luke had Matthew's gospel in mind.

82. Generations of scholarship have been consumed with the attempt to obviate the natural meaning of John 21:24 and to separate the Beloved Disciple's witness from the written gospel. See the treatment of Bauckham, *Jesus and the Eyewitnesses*, 358–83.

The first part of this study catalogued many indications of Luke's awareness that the apostolic mission was the fulfillment of particularly Isaianic prophecies of the word of the Lord going to the nations. Luke therefore was more than simply aware of the import of these prophecies. We may reasonably suppose he received an impetus from them to write an authoritative account of the coming of the Word of God to the nations. It is precisely his understanding of the continuation of the words and works of Jesus in the words and works of his appointed witnesses, as we saw earlier, that "legitimizes" his decision to publish his second volume. Another way of saying this is that he sees the going forth of the new word of the Lord from Jerusalem to the end of the earth (Isa. 2:2–3; 42:6–7; 49:6; 55:11; 66:19), first through Jesus' personal, earthly ministry, then through the ministries of his appointed apostolic witnesses, as the subject of his Scripture. This is seen in his introduction to his second volume, "In the first book, O Theophilus, I have dealt with all that Jesus began to do and teach, until the day when he was taken up, after he had given commands through the Holy Spirit to the apostles whom he had chosen" (Acts 1:1–2). The implication is that this second volume is the continuation of what Jesus did and taught, but now through "the apostles whom he had chosen."[83]

Writing and Collecting Epistles

We have seen that Paul, like presumably all the apostles of Jesus, was convinced of the permanent validity of Jesus' words and of the message of salvation he and others had been commissioned to bring to the nations. In keeping with this, the durability of writing must have been a factor in Paul's decision to employ writing in the execution of his ministry to make the Word of God fully known. He could have sent messengers with memorized oral communications. Or he could have sent with his messengers notes written on wax tablets to jog their memories. We know that wax tablets were used in this way for the communication of ephemeral information which could

---

83. There is also the possibility that Luke saw as part of his motive the service of providing for the reader of the Pauline (and possibly other) epistles a historical context for understanding them. The relationship between Acts and the letters of Paul has a long and rocky history in scholarship, but it has become increasingly evident to me that there is a conscious attempt on the part of Luke to establish some historical background for the letters. I believe this is seen particularly in regard to Galatians, in the record of the first missionary journey and the events leading up to the Jerusalem council, and Romans, by mentioning in chapters 19 and 20 many of the names that occur in Romans 16.

then easily be rubbed out and the tablets used again.[84] Erasable parchment was also available. But these methods would have left no permanent record for later reference (2 Thess. 3:14; 1 Tim. 3:14–15; cf. 2 Peter 1:12–15), and for sharing with other churches (Col. 4:16; Rev. 1:11).

Paul's perception of the permanent validity of his message is seen also in his concern for handing on what he had himself received. Writing from Corinth in 51 or 52, he tells the Thessalonians to "stand firm and hold to the traditions that you were taught by us, either by our spoken word or by our letter" (2 Thess. 2:15). This is plain again in the Corinthian correspondence (1 Cor. 11:2, 23; 15:3; cf. 2 Peter 2:21). Paul is aware of what he "received" and is already attentive to the preservation of his teaching as *paradosis*, as tradition to be passed on, and this tradition is being preserved in part in his letters. So it is no surprise that he tells Timothy to guard what had been entrusted to him (1 Tim. 6:20; 2 Tim. 1:13–14). Jude too is concerned for the preservation of "the faith that was once for all delivered to the saints" (Jude 3), as is the author of 1 John, whose proclamation of what was from the beginning (1:1–4) is now expressed in *writing*.[85] He goes on to exhort, "Let what you have heard from the beginning abide in you. If what you heard from the beginning abides in you, then you too will abide in the Son and in the Father" (1 John 2:24, cf. 2 John 9).

Paul and these other *writers* obviously did not believe that the crucial task of handing down to succeeding generations the good news entrusted to them should be done solely by oral methods.[86] We can thus recognize that the concern for preserving the legacy of the apostolic testimony and preaching did not originate in the second century, but is apparent in the documents of the apostolic mission themselves. As Gaffin says, "The New Testament itself, then, anticipates and initiates a trend; it fixes the coordinates of a trajectory."[87]

---

84. "The thinly cut wood, its surfaces smoothed and whitened, could be written on with pen and ink. More often the surface of the wood was slightly hollowed and filled with wax, which was often colored, and could be written upon with a metal stylus. . . . Tablets could be reused after they were washed or smoothed and were handy for recording ephemera of all sorts—school exercises, accounts, notes, first-drafts, and so forth," Harry Y. Gamble, *Books and Readers in the Early Church: A History of Early Christian Texts* (New Haven, CT: Yale University Press, 1995), 50.

85. The *Muratorian Fragment* takes him to be referring here to his writing of the gospel. While John is probably not speaking directly about the gospel, the same concern manifested in 1 John 1:1–4 no doubt lies behind the writing of the gospel.

86. Luke wrote down what had been "delivered [*paredosan*] . . . to us" (Luke 1:2).

87. Gaffin, "The New Testament as Canon," 177.

A sense of the lasting significance of Paul's letters is at least reflected at the point at which a number of them were collected and circulated together among the churches. There is little reason to assume that this happened only gradually, sporadically, and long after his death. Many scholars recognize that 1 Peter already shows evidence of the knowledge of several Pauline epistles (at least Romans and Ephesians).[88] Second Peter 3:16, of course, knows an unspecified number of Pauline letters[89] which it identifies as "Scripture." Clement of Rome probably in the 90s and Ignatius and Polycarp before 110 all make it clear that they are working with multiple Pauline letters,[90] and they each assume knowledge of multiple Pauline letters on the part of their addressees throughout Asia Minor, Macedonia, and Achaia. While we do not know the full extents of these collections, the casual way each author assumes that his addressees in various churches may have access to Pauline letters seems most compatible with the assumption that they all knew a more-or-less standard collection. It is significant that Ignatius and Polycarp show knowledge of the Pastoral Epistles and Ephesians.

If Paul's letters were only gradually and haphazardly gathered together from the churches, one would expect that different collections with different

88. Helmut Koester, *History and Literature of Early Christianity*, 2nd ed., 2 vols., vol. 2, *Introduction to the New Testament* (New York/Berlin: Walter de Gruyter, 2000), 296, goes to the extreme of calling it "a deutero-Pauline letter." Even some who doubt that the author of 1 Peter shows any literary dependence on the Pauline epistles may acknowledge that "the letter undoubtedly arose in a Church tradition influenced by the terminology and concepts of Paul" as known to us through his letters (L. Goppelt, *A Commentary on I Peter*, ed. Ferdinand Hahn, trans. and augmented John E. Alsup [German original 1978; Grand Rapids: Eerdmans, 1993], 30).

89. Jerome Neyrey, *2 Peter, Jude: A New Translation with Introduction and Commentary*, AB 37C (New York: Doubleday, 1993), 134, tentatively concludes "that our author knows at least Romans and 1 Thessalonians, and possibly 1 Corinthians." See pages 133–34 for the use of Pauline words and themes.

90. Estimates vary as to the number of Pauline epistles that can be identified behind these three authors' citations, allusions, and echoes. A recent collection of essays aiming at "minimal but assured results that can be achieved on the basis of methodologically rigorous close readings of particular texts" (Gregory) finds virtually certain or probable knowledge of 1 Corinthians, Romans, and Hebrews in Clement (Gregory); 1 Corinthians, Ephesians, and 1 and 2 Timothy in Ignatius (Foster); 1 Corinthians, Ephesians, 1 and 2 Timothy, Romans, Galatians, and Philippians in Polycarp's letter to the Philippians (Holmes). See A. Gregory, "1 Clement and the Writings That Later Formed the New Testament," P. Foster, "The Epistles of Ignatius of Antioch and the Writings That Later Formed the New Testament," and M. W. Holmes, "Polycarp's *Letter to the Philippians* and the Writings that Later Formed the New Testament," chapters 6, 7, and 8, respectively, in A. Gregory and C. Tuckett, eds., *The Reception of the New Testament in the Apostolic Fathers* (Oxford: Oxford University Press, 2005). These would be minimum lists, as it is unlikely that their full knowledge of the extent of Paul's letters would be reflected.

orders and contents would have survived in the tradition. But instead the tradition is very regular, suggesting an early collection of the 13 letters of Paul.[91] In antiquity, when an author's letters were collected and published it was normally the author himself who edited and published them. Trobisch thus argues that it was Paul himself who issued the first collection of his epistles.[92] If it was not Paul, we may reasonably surmise it was the work of his immediate circle of co-workers such as Luke who, according to 2 Timothy 4:11, was with Paul in Rome near the end of his life, and Timothy, who was instructed in that letter to come to Paul in Rome and bring "the parchments" (2 Tim. 4:13), i.e., parchment notebooks in codex form.

E. Randolph Richards argues, plausibly in my opinion, that these note-books contained Paul's personal copies of his letters.[93] He maintains that "the first collection of Paul's letters was probably his personal set, which he had with him when he died," and reasonably suggests "that published collections of Paul's letters arose from this set and retained the notebook format (codex) of the original, thus explaining the early Christian preference for the codex."[94] If it was Paul who authorized copies of his collected letters for individual churches, even if this was the idea of his immediate circle of followers, the omission of one or more of Paul's original letters would not have been because of loss, but would have been intentional.[95] Paul's "lost"

91. See David Trobisch, *Paul's Letter Collection: Tracing the Origins* (Minneapolis: Fortress, 1994), a popular summary of his *Die Entstehung der Paulusbriefsammlung: Studien zu den Anfängen christlicher Publizistik*, NTOA 10 (Freiburg: Vandenhoeck & Ruprecht, 1989).

92. Trobisch, *Paul's Letter Collection*, 54, suggests Paul published an edition of Romans, 1–2 Corinthians, and Galatians, and that the 13-letter edition was put together after Paul's death.

93. Richards, *Paul and First-Century Letter Writing*, 218, 223, 231. Richards agrees with Gamble and against Trobisch in thinking that Paul did not publish the first edition of his letters, but rather that upon Paul's death, "These letters, along with his other personal effects, fell into the hands of a disciple" (223) and were published later. Richards even suggests that "At the time of his death, it is possible no one but Paul valued his letters" (219). If so (and I think there is reason to doubt this), all the more reason for Paul to want his collected letters published!

94. Richards, *Paul and First-Century Letter Writing*, 231. The notion that the Christian use of the codex grew out of a supposed notebook/codex collection of Paul's epistles had been advocated previously, particularly by Gamble, *Books and Readers*, 49–66.

95. Richards, *Paul and First-Century Letter Writing*, 220–21, theorizes that our possession of 1 and 2 Corinthians but not the two other letters (see next note) is not because of the predilection of the churches but because Paul may not have made copies of these letters before they were dispatched, and therefore they were not among his personal set when he died. In this case, or if Paul himself oversaw or gave instructions for the first edition, the cause for their non-inclusion will rest with Paul himself.

letter(s) to the Corinthians[96] and possibly his letter to the Laodiceans (Col. 4:16, if it is not essentially identical to Ephesians) are not a problem for the concept of canon, any more than the "loss" of many of the prophets' words or of Jesus' own words (cf. John 21:25). These letters may be affirmed to have been authoritative, but not canonical and never intended to be included (by decision of Paul or of his successors) in the authoritative edition for the churches.

In any case, the act of collecting and publishing a corpus of Paul's letters may have had other repercussions. It is interesting that besides making reference to a collection of Paul's epistles (2 Peter 3:15–17), 2 Peter links itself to an earlier Petrine letter (3:1), which most agree is 1 Peter, as no other letter under the name of Peter is known to have existed in the early period. Jude links himself to his brother James (1), at least plausibly linking his letter to one known to be from James, referring as well to apostolic words (17–18) recorded elsewhere now only in 2 Peter. The author of 3 John 9 refers to an earlier letter he wrote "to the church," either 2 John or 1 John. All these letters of prominent early Christian leaders seem to show an interest in maintaining *corpora* of their letters.

The book of Revelation is classifiable as an apocalypse by genre, but it is also in form a letter, and so may be considered here as well. It is a letter to seven churches, and incorporates seven individual letters addressed to these seven. It is an epistolary corpus in itself.[97] In Revelation, John is told specifically by the risen Christ not merely to preach but to *write* what he sees and hears into a book (1:11, 19)! The word *graphō* is used 29 times in Revelation, and John is commanded to write no less than 12 times. John also pronounces a blessing on those who *read*, those who *hear*, and those who *keep* the words of the *book* (1:3). The author of this book most certainly expected that his work would be copied multiple times, as he records in the colophon at the end Christ's curses on anyone who would attempt to add to or subtract from its words (22:18–19). Revelation is the single book of the NT that McDonald considers to be consciously written to be "Christian

---

96. See 1 Cor. 5:9; 2 Cor. 2:3–4, 9; 7:8, unless this last letter is now preserved, as some have suggested, in 2 Cor. 10–13.

97. The *Muratorian Fragment*, anachronistically but intriguingly, regards John's letters to seven churches as prototypical for Paul's letters to seven churches. Perhaps it is the other way around, and the sending of the seven letters of Revelation in a single letter reflects an existing exemplar of a Pauline letter collection.

scripture."[98] Yet this might be a premature judgment, given the several signs in other NT documents of the concern for constructing and preserving a written legacy from the apostolic age.

One way we might describe what we have been observing is by saying that a "testamentary aura" surrounds the writings of the NT, particularly the later ones. The apostles and their assistants are taking care to provide for the churches when the apostles depart from the scene. This is done, of course, by teaching and training of others, but it is also being done by the preparation of written materials to function in an ongoing way for the life of the church. In individual writings, this testamentary aura is seen most clearly in 2 Peter, though it is also visible in the Pastoral Epistles, Jude, and, I would say, the entire Johannine corpus. It should not be thought that the sense of a written legacy evident in these books requires a late date (that is, beyond the lifetimes of the attributed authors) or a fictional setting. We have noted that the concern for preserving and handing down the tradition existed from the first. As the apostle witnesses draw near the ends of their lives they are, naturally, increasingly aware of this need, and of the implications of their eventual departure for the ongoing life of the churches (it is noted already for Paul in Acts 20:25–32 at the end of his third missionary journey in about A.D. 57.)

Second Peter offers valuable reflection on its writing:

> Therefore I intend always to remind you of these qualities, though you know them and are established in the truth that you have. I think it right, as long as I am in this body, to stir you up by way of reminder, since I know that the putting off of my body will be soon, as our Lord Jesus Christ made clear to me. And I will make every effort so that after my departure you may be able at any time to recall these things. (2 Peter 1:12–15)

The desire to leave a permanent form of his message is explicitly Peter's motivation for producing the letter. The contents of the epistle are set down so that they should always (*aei*) function as a reminder, even after Peter's approaching death. Since Peter attests that the readers know and are established in the truth present with them, one might have supposed (on Funk's view) that they should have been able to stir each other up well enough without the aid of anything written. But Peter determines there is

---

98. McDonald, *Formation*, 42.

a need to leave them a permanent reminder of his teaching in this letter.[99] Later he alludes to his first letter in the same vein: "This is now the second letter that I have written to you, beloved, and in both of them I have aroused your sincere mind by way of reminder (*en hupomnēsei*); that you should remember (*mnēsthēnai*) the predictions of the holy prophets and the commandment of the Lord and Savior through your apostles" (2 Peter 3:1–2 RSV).

Though most scholars today reject the authenticity of 2 Peter, there is nothing about the letter that demands a date later than the first century.[100] Bauckham observes that "2 Peter has been widely recognized to be intended as a 'testament of Peter.'"[101] But the tendency among scholars is then to associate 2 Peter with other ancient documents that exhibit certain elements of a "genre" and then to dismiss these elements in 2 Peter as indications of pseudepigraphy. If this is the case, it will at least have to be realized that 2 Peter is an extraordinary example of the "genre" in that it was written and successfully promoted extremely close to the supposed author's death. Peter Davids has shown how much 2 Peter in fact differs from the other examples claimed for the testamentary form—particularly in that Peter's death is not recorded in this "testament."[102]

But Bauckham's thesis is also too facile in that it avoids the fact that real people in antiquity actually did, as they do today, seek to make provisions for others in advance of their approaching deaths. Any relic of such a concern cannot simply be dismissed as meaningless stock elements. The epistle of Jude manifests many of the same elements noted for 2 Peter: concern for passing on the faith, including its ethical components, to succeeding generations (3); "reminding" of the traditional or apostolic teaching (twice in this short epistle, 5, 17); and the cautionary prediction of the rise of false teachers in the last days (4–19).[103] The only significant difference is that Jude is not written with a strong self-awareness of the author's impending death. And yet, while Bauckham regards these in 2 Peter as rather formal elements of a "genre," he does not seem to notice that Jude, which he finds to be authentic, contains them as well.

---

99. See the similar train of thought in Paul already in Rom. 15:14–16.

100. See Michael J. Kruger, "The Authenticity of 2 Peter," *JETS* 42 (1999), 645–71.

101. Bauckham, *Jude, 2 Peter*, 132.

102. Peter H. Davids, *The Letters of 2 Peter and Jude* (Grand Rapids: Eerdmans, 2006), 145–49.

103. Compare the list of features of the testamentary "genre" as applied to 2 Peter by Bauckham, *Jude, 2 Peter*, 132–33.

The two main points here are that, a) given the foundational importance of the apostolic mission as both predicted by the prophets and established by Jesus' personal commission, it is a natural thing that a testamentary concern present itself in the documents that should be passed down as the permanent form of the apostolic teaching, and, b) that this concern is found not simply in certain stock elements in one or two of the later letters of the NT, but rather characterizes other features of the collection. In the weighty undertaking to preserve Jesus' "eternal" words and deeds in substantial books, based on the testimony of eyewitnesses, in the ubiquitous concern in the NT documents for maintaining the authoritative tradition handed down by the apostles, in the collecting and publishing of a corpus of the letters of Paul and other authors, we see signs of the deliberate construction of a written legacy, one might even say a canonical consciousness.

We close this section with the observation of one more phenomenon pertinent to the New Testament's self-attestation. By some time in the second century, church leaders were already defending their collections of Christian scriptures and doing so, in part, by seeking attestation or ratification for them from authoritative, apostolic sources. Peter is said to have "ratified" Mark's gospel personally, and his mention of Mark in 1 Peter 5:13 was also taken as an endorsement of Mark's gospel (Eusebius, *HE* 2.15.2).[104] Luke's gospel was being ratified by reference to Paul (Eusebius, *HE* 3.4.7; 3.24.15). Here we suggest that the roots of this practice are already visible in the later NT writings.

There are two places in the New Testament where another part of the NT is apparently referred to as "Scripture." One is 2 Peter 3:16 which places a group of Paul's letters in the category of "the Scriptures." This is usually seen as a sure indication of the lateness and inauthenticity of 2 Peter. But as we have observed, many scholars see signs of Peter's knowledge of some Pauline epistles already in 1 Peter.[105] And, as with 2 Peter's testamentary char-

---

104. Eusebius is not entirely clear as to whether this tradition goes back only to Clement of Alexandria, or further back to Papias at the beginning of the second century (*HE* 2.15.2), though Eusebius definitely tells us elsewhere (3.39.17) that Papias used 2 Peter. In the same context he says Papias used 1 John. It may be that Papias, like the author of the *Muratorian Fragment*, saw 1 John as a ratification of John's gospel. See C. E. Hill, *The Johannine Corpus in the Early Church* (Oxford: Oxford University Press, 2006), 411–16.

105. Richards, *Paul and First-Century Letter Writing*, 221–22, theorizes that since Paul died in Rome, Peter, if writing from Rome, would have had access there to Paul's personal copies of his letters. Alternatively, he or the church in Rome, as well as some of the Pauline churches, could have had copies of an early edition of his collected letters by the mid–60s.

acter, its high appreciation of Paul's letters cannot be regarded as requiring an extended period of time to develop. All it requires is the equation of the apostolic preaching with the Word of God and its valuation alongside OT scripture, and the assumption that this pertained to written epistles as well as to oral ones, and we have in principle already arrived at the view of Paul's epistles presupposed in 2 Peter. And, as we have already seen, this position was possible quite early, for it is apparently Paul's own. Canonical and, as long as 2 Peter is allowed as genuine, apostolic approval of a collection of Paul's letters as Scripture has to be recognized.

But the significance goes even further. An author who attests his regard for the epistles of one apostle as Scripture, and who does so in an epistle that he is writing as an apostle, in which he also links his epistle to an earlier epistle of his own, surely is making an implicit claim for these epistles as well.

The other NT passage that possibly refers to another NT passage as Scripture is 1 Timothy 5:18, where one of Jesus' sayings recorded precisely in this way only in Luke 10:7 (par. Matt. 10:10) is joined to a citation from Deuteronomy 25:4 under the introductory formula, "for the Scripture says." This in itself is not proof that Luke is being referred to as Scripture; for it could be that a non-scriptural saying is being appended here to a scriptural one.

Yet a comparison with Paul's earlier practice in 1 Corinthians 9:8–14 is highly suggestive. Here Paul, in defending his right to financial support as a minister of the gospel, cites the same saying from Leviticus 24:5 (referred to as "the Law" and "the Law of Moses") and then supports this by attesting, "In the same way, the Lord commanded that those who proclaim the gospel should get their living by the gospel." Though the import of the Lord's commandment is clear, there is no specific saying of Jesus quoted.[106] This would appear to come from Paul's fund of oral tradition about Jesus. But when teaching on the remuneration of elders in 1 Timothy, instead of referring to an unspecified command of the Lord, he supplements his quotation of Deuteronomy 25:4 this time with another quotation, "the laborer deserves his wages." This saying we know only from Luke 10:7, where it occurs as a pronouncement of Jesus. It thus would appear the saying Paul had in mind in 1 Corinthians 9:14 when he said that the Lord commanded "that

---

106. It would have applied equally well to Matthew's version, "the laborer deserves his food" (10:10).

those who proclaim the gospel should get their living by the gospel." Now, however, Paul subsumes both Deuteronomy 25:4 and Luke 10:7 under the formula, "for the Scripture says." The change from a general reference to Jesus' teaching in 1 Corinthians to a specific quotation seems to indicate that Paul is well aware of what he is doing in 1 Timothy 5:18.[107] It may well be that between the writing of 1 Corinthians and 1 Timothy, the Gospel of Luke was completed and was being used by Paul.[108] Paul's first letter to Timothy most likely indicates that Luke's gospel was at the time of writing being used as Scripture.

This apparent reference to Luke as Scripture in 1 Timothy opens up other possibilities,[109] including the potential enhancement of our understanding of what Paul means in 2 Timothy 3:16. It is rightly emphasized that when Paul declares that "all Scripture is breathed out by God," he has in mind the sacred writings, the OT, which he had mentioned in the previous verse. These are the sacred writings that Timothy had known since childhood and that are able to make one wise unto salvation. But given his reference to Luke as Scripture in his earlier letter, it is plausible that the emphatic "all" in "all Scripture is breathed out by God" signifies that Paul has in mind not only the ancient sacred writings but new ones as well.

THE ESCHATOLOGICAL WORK OF THE WORD

While the church functioned without official agreement on the boundaries of its new Scriptures for centuries, as consensus varied and shifted, the church was never without its new word from the Lord. In this final section we note certain important aspects of the new eschatological word that show

107. See George W. Knight III, *The Pastoral Epistles: A Commentary on the Greek Text* (Grand Rapids: Eerdmans, 1992), 234, who also notes, "Elsewhere in 1 Corinthians Jesus' teaching on marriage and divorce (7:10) and Jesus' institution of the Lord's Supper (10:23–24) are as authoritative for Paul as any word of OT scripture. Thus it would not be surprising that Paul refers here to Jesus' words under the rubric [*legei hē graphē*] . . . ."

108. That Luke's gospel was completed before or during Paul's two-year Roman imprisonment mentioned at the end of Acts is the most natural conclusion to draw from Acts and is held by many interpreters. Bo Reicke, *The Roots of the Synoptic Gospels* (Philadelphia: Fortress, 1986), 166–74, 180, holds that Luke was completed in Caesarea during Paul's imprisonment there, ca. A.D. 60. E. Earle Ellis believes Luke assembled materials for his gospel in 58–60 and published it in 63–64 (see Ellis, *The Making of the New Testament Documents* [Leiden: Brill, 2002], 252, 390n68, 402–3).

109. When he shortly thereafter refers Timothy to "the sound words of our Lord Jesus Christ" (6:3), does he have in mind a written account of those words?

why it is and has remained central to the life of the people of God ever since it arose in oral and then written form.

The eschatological preaching and, eventually, writing of the new word was attended by and is thereafter wedded to another uniquely eschatological phenomenon, the *parousia* of God's Spirit.

The New Word and the Spirit

In his Nazareth sermon, Jesus declared that he had been anointed with the Spirit of God for the purpose of bringing good news to the poor. This equipping of the Messiah, "the stump of Jesse, and a branch from his roots," with the Spirit of God, was forecast early in Isaiah's prophecy (11:1–2). The pouring out of the Holy Spirit on God's people "in the last days" (Acts 2:16–21), in fulfillment of the prophecy of Joel, is an eschatological act of the risen Messiah in his glorification (John 7:39). Thus the Spirit is given to individual believers as a guarantee (2 Cor. 1:22; 5:5; Eph. 1:14) and as the firstfruits (Rom. 8:23) of the coming age. Vos says the Holy Spirit, in passages such as Romans 8:23; Galatians 3:14; 2 Corinthians 5:5,

> is viewed as pertaining specifically to the future life, nay as constitut-ing the substantial make-up of this life, and the present possession of the Spirit by the believer is regarded in the light of an anticipation. The Spirit's proper sphere is according to this the world to come; from there He projects himself into the present, and becomes a prophecy of Himself in His eschatological operation.[110]

But besides the "common" operations of the eschatological Spirit in all believers, there was a special work that pertained to Jesus' commissioned witnesses. The Davidic Branch, himself endowed with the Spirit of the Lord (Isa. 11:2; 61:1–2; Luke 4:18–19), specially endowed them with the Spirit for their unique task: "But you will receive power when the Holy Spirit has come upon you, and you will be my witnesses in Jerusalem and in all Judea and Samaria and to the end of the earth" (Acts 1:8, cf. Luke 24:48). Their power for witness-bearing would be that of the Holy Spirit, whose special coming they awaited and then received at Pentecost.

110. Geerhardus Vos, "The Eschatological Aspect of the Pauline Conception of the Spirit," in Richard B. Gaffin Jr., ed., *Redemptive History and Biblical Interpretation: The Shorter Writings of Geerhardus Vos* (Phillipsburg, NJ: Presbyterian & Reformed, 1980), 91–125, at 103.

In John's gospel, Jesus' apostolic commission is recorded in 20:21–22, where again it is clear that the Spirit's special working would be necessary for carrying out their mission: "'As the Father has sent me, even so I am sending you.' And when he had said this, he breathed on them and said to them, 'Receive the Holy Spirit.'" Earlier, Jesus had told these disciples what the Spirit would do in and for them: "He will teach you all things and bring to your remembrance all that I have said to you" (John 14:26); "He will guide you into all the truth, for he will not speak on his own authority, but whatever he hears he will speak, and he will declare to you the things that are to come" (John 16:13).

That these were promises given directly only to a select group of his disciples designated as his witnesses, as in Luke-Acts, is plain from 15:26–27, "But when the Helper comes, whom I will send to you from the Father, the Spirit of truth, who proceeds from the Father, he will bear witness about me. And you also will bear witness, because you have been with me from the beginning." Because the Spirit equips these sent ones, the apostles themselves will bear witness to and glorify Jesus (John 15:26–27; 16:14). The author of the Johannine literature is clearly conscious of this special commission to bear witness when he writes in 1 John 1:1–3, "That which was from the beginning, which we have heard, which we have seen with our eyes, which we looked upon and have touched with our hands, concerning the word of life . . . we proclaim also to you . . . ."

These texts from John and Acts indicate that the apostolic preaching depends on a special equipping by the Spirit for the task of proclamation, of bearing verbal witness to Jesus—ensuring their faithful recollection of Jesus' words, their knowledge of (certain) future events, and the truth of their words, and that their message will glorify Jesus. Throughout the time of their mission, the apostles were conscious of this work of the Spirit. Peter refers to "those who preached the good news to you by the Holy Spirit sent from heaven" (1 Peter 1:12), the same Spirit who spoke by the prophets (1:10–11).[111] Paul speaks of his mission "to bring the Gentiles to obedience—by word and deed, by the power of signs and wonders, by the power of the Spirit of God—so that from Jerusalem and all the way around to Illyricum I have fulfilled the ministry of the gospel of Christ" (Rom. 15:18–19).

---

111. In the second letter he speaks of the prophets as "carried along" by the Holy Spirit as they spoke "from God" (2 Peter 1:21). This has to be understood as pertaining not only to the preached word of the prophets, which Peter could not have known firsthand, but also to their writings.

Paul refers to this link between the eschatological Spirit and the word when he tells the Ephesians that the mystery of Christ, formerly hidden, "has now been revealed to his holy apostles and prophets by the Spirit" (Eph. 3:5).[112] In 1 Thessalonians 1:5, he tells the Thessalonians that "our gospel came to you not only in word, but also in power and in the Holy Spirit and with full conviction" (cf. 1:6, with joy inspired by the Holy Spirit). The role of the Holy Spirit both in guiding and empowering the apostolic witness, and in giving understanding to spirit-filled believers, is reiterated again in 1 Corinthians 2:13, "And we impart this in words not taught by human wisdom but taught by the Spirit, interpreting spiritual truths to those who are spiritual" (1 Cor. 2:13).

This is what the Reformed have called the *testimonium Spiritus Sancti.* Because of the connection between eschatological word and eschatological Spirit, it is fitting that in Ephesians 6:17, when Paul gives a symbolic representation of the Word of God, that he should call it "the sword of the Spirit."

The Eschatological Word and the New Birth

The connection between this new word of the Lord and the new work of the Spirit is apparent not only in the equipping of the apostles and prophets to proclaim and write the word, but also in the critical act that effects the believer's entry into eschatological experience.

Regeneration is that work of the Spirit (John 3:5) which conveys the believer into a proleptic enjoyment of the benefits of heaven while still on earth. "Unless one is born again," Jesus says, "he cannot see the kingdom of God" (John 3:3) or enter into it (3:5). In his first letter, Peter links the new birth to the accomplishment of an unmistakably eschatological event, Jesus' resurrection (1 Peter 1:3; cf. John 11:25–26). This eschatological new birth thus also links believers to future enjoyment of "an inheritance that is imperishable, undefiled, and unfading, kept in heaven" for us (1 Peter

---

112. Josephus explicitly connects the writing and early custody of the "sacred books" (*Ap.* 1.1) with prophets, those who obtained their knowledge through inspiration (*Ap.* 1.37, 40). The later works of Jewish history, such as the *Maccabeean* books, Josephus says have "not been deemed worthy of equal credit with the earlier records, because of the failure of the exact succession [*diadochēn*] of the prophets" (*Ap.* 1.41). This shows the connection in the minds of at least some prominent first-century Jews between the prophetic office and the authoritative production and custody of "books."

1:3–4). What we must notice is that when Peter returns to the subject of the new birth later in chapter 1, he says we were "born anew, not of perishable seed[113] but of imperishable, through the living and abiding word of God." He then cites Isaiah 40:6–8 (LXX), "All flesh is like grass and all its glory like the flower of grass. The grass withers and the flower falls, but the word of the Lord abides for ever" (1 Peter 1:24–25).

Peter then identifies what he understands by this life-giving word: " ... this word is the good news that was preached [*to hrēma to euangelisthen*] to you" (1 Peter 1:23–25). That is, he identifies it as the word of the gospel of Jesus, predicted but not fully comprehended by the prophets (1 Peter 1:10–12), the good news preached by himself and the others appointed as witnesses of Jesus (1 Peter 1:12; Luke 24:48; Acts 1:8, etc., and particularly Acts 13:32; 19:10), who brought this good news "by the Holy Spirit sent from heaven" (1 Peter 1:12). The very next verse of the Isaianic passage Peter cites as predicting this word of the Lord uses the verb *euangelizomai*. Isaiah 40:9 is one of the great gospel texts which, as we saw in the first part of our study, inform the preaching ministry of Jesus and the apostles as recorded especially in Luke-Acts: "Get you up to a high mountain, O Zion, herald of good news [*ho euangelizomenos*]; lift up your voice with strength, O Jerusalem, herald of good news [*ho euangelizomenos*]; lift it up, fear not; say to the cities of Judah, 'Behold your God!'" This is the "gospel," the word brought by Jesus and by his witnesses. It is *this* word which, Peter says, effects the new birth, translating the believer into the eschatological existence, which is also the result of Jesus' resurrection and entry into the heavenly state.

A similar concept is found in James: "Of his own will he brought us forth[114] by the word of truth, that we should be a kind of firstfruits of his creation" (James 1:18). Here, God's sovereign will is cited as the cause of the new birth, but again the means for that regeneration is "the word of truth." The result is that born-again believers are the firstfruits of God's creatures. Interestingly enough, earlier in the chapter (1:11) James had alluded to Isaiah 40:6–8 as well.[115] Though James draws from this passage explicitly only the comparison of human flesh (in this case, the rich man) fading away

---

113. 1 John 3:9 says that God's seed abides in the believer. Is this not the seed of the word?
114. *apekuēsen*—this is birth terminology.
115. See, e.g., R. P. Martin, *James*, WBC 48 (Waco, TX: Word, 1988), 23–24.

like the withering "flower of the grass," the clear allusion to Isaiah 40:6–8 suggests that it forms part of the background for James's understanding of the "word of truth" (1:18) and the "implanted word" (1:21),[116] as it did for Peter's understanding of the word of "good news."

This all may be said to go back to the teaching of Jesus himself, who, in what is preserved for us, did not directly quote Isaiah 40:6–8, but who appears to have alluded to it. As noted earlier, in a saying recorded in all three Synoptic Gospels in the context of the Olivet Discourse (Matt. 24:35/Mark 13:31/Luke 21:33), he proclaims, "Heaven and earth will pass away, but my words will not pass away [*hoi de logoi mou ou mē pareleusontai*]." Elsewhere, Jesus speaks of "the word" (Mark 4:14; "the word of God," Luke 8:11; "the word of the kingdom," Matt. 13:18) yielding fruit "thirtyfold and sixtyfold and a hundredfold" (Mark 4:8) when people hear the word and receive it.

The Eschatological Word and the Full Attainment of Life

Besides being the means of the new birth, this word of the gospel of Jesus Christ is said by Peter also to be a means of growth in the Christian life along the path to ultimate salvation: "Like newborn babes," he says, "long for the pure milk of the word [*to logikon adolon gala*], that by it you may grow [*auxēthēte*] in respect to salvation" (1 Peter 2:2).[117] Having been born anew, Christians are to long for the pure word as newborn babies long for milk. And that milk is nourishment indeed, to give the believer growth unto salvation, a salvation predicted by the prophets (1 Peter 1:10) and thus conceived of in its full eschatological significance.

Peter's emphasis on the saving work of the word parallels James's charge to "receive with meekness the implanted word, which is able to

116. Behind James 1:10–11, 18, and 21 appears to be reflection on Jesus' Parable of the Sower, in which the sower plants the word (the "word of the kingdom," Matt. 13:18), which proves unfruitful among the "rich" and others who fall away when the sun rises (Mark 4:6/Matt. 13:6, cf. James 1:11), but others who receive the implanted word bear much fruit.

117. *Logikos* could mean "reasonable" or "spiritual" here, as in most recent translations. See the extended discussion in Ramsey Michaels, *1 Peter*, WBC 49 (Waco, TX: Word, 1988), 86–89. But "Since Peter has just been describing the living *logos* by which Christians are given new birth, it would seem that he is using *logikon* in the sense: 'the milk of the word,' as the AV has it" (Edmund P. Clowney, *The Message of 1 Peter: The Way of the Cross*, BST [Downers Grove, IL: InterVarsity, 1988], 78–79). Not only this, but Peter in 2:2 is continuing the metaphor begun in 1:23, where Peter assumes the believers' new birth, by now addressing them in the likeness of newborn babies. They have been born again through the living and abiding word of God, and now they are to be nourished by that same word to grow up to salvation. So also Goppelt, *I Peter*, 131–32.

save your souls" (James 1:21). This salvific function of the word of Christ is echoed also in the words of Paul spoken to the Ephesian elders, whom he commended "to God and to the word of his grace, which is able to build you up and to give you the inheritance [*klēronomian*] among all those who are sanctified [*hēgiasmenois*]" (Acts 20:32).[118] Here Paul strikingly attributes the edification of the saints and their delivery into their inheritance not to God directly, but rather to "the word of his grace,"[119] that is, to the word of God which Paul preached and taught, by mouth and by letter.

Thus again Paul, in his great letter to the Romans, declares that the gospel is the power of God unto salvation (*eis sōtērian*) for everyone who believes (Rom. 1:16, cf. 1 Cor. 15:1–2). Here "the gospel" is no truncated "gospel presentation," but encompasses the full apostolic message concerning the Christ promised by the prophets (Rom. 1:1–3). Here in fact is another connection to 2 Timothy 3:15–16, where Paul attests that the sacred writings, i.e., the OT Scriptures, are able to make one wise "for salvation [*eis sōtērian*]." In Romans, this ability to lead to salvation also belongs to the gospel, certainly capable of both oral and written expression, such as Paul goes on to deliver in his letter to the Romans (15:14–16). This is another reason for suspecting that Paul's statement in 2 Timothy 3:16 that "all Scripture is breathed out by God" may well contemplate not only the OT Scriptures but also Luke's gospel, and whatever else Paul might consider to be Scripture.

Thus there is an organic continuity between the two vital roles of the word. On the one hand, the word—the Christian message of salvation in Jesus—has a role as the seed by which the believer is born anew, imbued with life in the Spirit. On the other hand, the word has a role in nourishing and edifying the soul unto salvation. In this way we gain an appreciation of the critical, indispensable importance of the new word of the Lord, the good news which has Christ and his kingship as its focus. New life in the new age, "in these last days," would be impossible apart from this word. And that new word, authorized by the prophets and by Jesus, has been graciously bequeathed to the church in a new Scripture.

118. Paul is echoing the words Jesus spoke to him on the road to Damascus, Acts 26:18, "that they may receive forgiveness of sins and a place [*klēron*] among those who are sanctified [*hēgiasmenois*] by faith in me."

119. Cf. Rom. 12:3; 15:15; Eph. 3:4. In 1 Peter 5:12 Peter attests that what he has written in that letter is "the true grace of God."

CONCLUSION

Much of the recent focus on the subject of the NT canon approaches it *ab extra*, tending to view it as a somewhat arbitrary and certainly unanticipated, slowly developing brainchild of the church of the late second through fourth centuries. But the church, at least in the first centuries, did not see itself as empowered to select the books it wanted for its Bible, but only to recognize those provided by God through the apostles of Jesus. The eventual agreement of the majority of churches on the contents of the NT canon should rather be seen as the product of an organic process that began even before the arrival of Jesus on the scene of history, with the prophetic announcements of a Messiah. The NT gospel message and, by extension, the ultimate emergence of a written NT canon, is an aspect of Jesus the Messiah's eschatological glory—from the OT perspective, as much a part of his glory as his defeat of death by resurrection and his exaltation to the Father's right hand. For the Messiah's mission included his work of bringing light, the message of forgiveness, to the nations. In the execution of this mission he appointed a number of apostles to represent him as his unique witnesses, to speak in his name to the people and to the Gentiles. These apostles were conscious of their commission to speak and write in Jesus' name in the fulfillment of their ministries of making the word of God fully known (Rom. 15:19; Col. 1:25).

The key impetus for the eventual appearance of a NT canon, then, should not be seen as originating in the church of the second through fourth centuries. The concern for preserving and passing down the apostolic teaching to succeeding generations of the church was present from the beginning, in Jesus' own instruction. The intention of leaving the church with a *written* deposit of the Spirit-directed, apostolic witness is apparent in the very decision to publish the earliest written Gospels and Acts, in the decision to utilize writing as a major form of instruction and discipline in the accomplishment of the apostolic foundation-laying ministry, and particularly at the stage of collecting and publishing Paul's letters, and then other didactic letters from leaders of the original apostolic mission. This mindset is perhaps most clearly apparent in 2 Peter, which endorses a collection of Paul's letter and, in principle, other apostolic works, as Scripture. But it is also apparent in the book of Revelation, and may be said to characterize especially the later books of the NT.

In these writings are "words not taught by human wisdom but taught by the Spirit, interpreting spiritual truths to those who are spiritual" (1 Cor. 2:13); in them are "the words of eternal life" (John 6:68). As they are both read and preached, they are the living, active, and abiding Word of God (Heb. 4:12; 1 Peter 1:23), the seed by which those dead in sins are born anew unto a living hope (1 Peter 1:23–25). They were *written* that we might "believe that Jesus is the Christ, the Son of God, and that, believing, [we] might have life," life of the age to come, "in his name" (John 20:31). They are also the means of growth, by which we are nourished, like a newborn is nourished with milk, by which we grow up to a salvation ready to be revealed in the last time (1 Peter 2:1–2; 1:3–4).

In the canon of the NT, the church has its eschatological equipment, with the Spirit's attending presence and power, for life in the "already/not-yet." In it the church still has the voice of the apostles, delivering the voice of the Good Shepherd himself, whose sheep hear his voice, and they know him, and they follow him.

It is a joy to be able to dedicate these thoughts to one of this generation's premier expositors of the New Testament canon, Richard B. Gaffin Jr.

8

The First and Last Son: Christology and Sonship in Pauline Soteriology

DAVID B. GARNER

CAPTURING THE SWEEPING theological significance of the Pauline juxtaposition of Christ and Adam, John Murray writes, "What belongs to the essence of Paul's soteriology rests upon the parallel and contrast between Adam, the first man, made 'living soul,' and Christ, the second man and last Adam, made 'life-giving Spirit.' "[1] Put otherwise, the parallel and contrast between these two Adams bears a determinative function in Paul's doctrine of salvation, elucidating its thoroughly covenantal and redemptive-historical substructure.[2] This dual-Adam construct engages the prelapsarian

---

1. John Murray, *The Collected Writings of John Murray* (Edinburgh: Banner of Truth Trust, 1977), 1:11.

2. Cf. Oscar Cullmann, *Salvation in History*, trans. Sidney G. Sowers (London: SCM, 1967), 260–62; Herman Ridderbos, *Paul: An Outline of His Theology*, trans. John Richard DeWitt (Grand Rapids: Eerdmans, 1975), 333–41; Richard B. Gaffin Jr., " 'Life-Giving Spirit': Probing the Center of Paul's Pneumatology," *JETS* 41 (1998): 576–78; Herman Bavinck, *Our Reasonable Faith: A Survey of Christian Doctrine*, trans. Henry Zylstra (Grand Rapids: Eerdmans, 1956), 79–94; F. F. Bruce, *Paul: Apostle of the Heart Set Free* (Grand Rapids: Eerdmans, 1977), 188–202.

context of Genesis 1–2 with the postlapsarian of Genesis 3 and following,[3] uniting both pre-redemptive and redemptive history by *covenant*.[4] As Paul expounds in Colossians 1, Romans 8, and 1 Corinthians 15, redemption is an eschatological re-creation (cf. Eph. 1:10), and the full realization of creation's *telos*.[5] This eschatological realization is centered in the humiliation and exaltation of the Last Adam: the eternal Son of God incarnate is also the firstborn from the dead. Hence, Paul points up the uniqueness and supremacy of Christ in both creation and redemption.

For Paul, soteriology is exhaustively christological, a fact that he expresses unambiguously in the opening of his letter to the Romans. In his reflections on Romans 1:3–4, Richard Gaffin builds on Murray's biblical theology, challenging the traditional ontological interpretation (cf. e.g., Calvin, Hodge) of this formative passage. With regard to Romans 1:3, Calvin insists, "two things must be found in Christ, in order that we may obtain salvation in him, even divinity and humanity."[6] Following in the footsteps of more recent Reformed biblical scholarship, Gaffin defends his mentors' redemptive-historical interpretation (cf. e.g., Vos, Ridderbos, Murray), where the christological entrée to this epistle unveils the *messianic* sonship of Jesus Christ. In other words, this text does not unpack the hypostatic union, as Calvin proposed; instead, it advances a transitional, redemptive-historical point: Christ's own adoption,[7] or in characteristic Gaffin-esque clarity, Jesus' "judicially constitutive declaration of sonship."[8] According to Gaffin, Christ

---

3. Herman Bavinck, *In the Beginning: Foundations of Creation Theology*, ed. John Bolt, trans. John Vriend (Grand Rapids: Baker, 1999), 197–225.

4. Though Murray, in *The Covenant of Grace: A Biblico-Theological Study* (Phillipsburg, NJ: Presbyterian & Reformed, 1953), does not view the Adamic administration as a covenant, it is precisely Adam's role as head and representative of his posterity that makes the Adamic administration covenantal. "As Adam was head and representative of his posterity, so Christ is the head and representative of his people. And as God entered into covenant with Adam so He entered into covenant with Christ," Charles Hodge, *Systematic Theology* (Grand Rapids: Eerdmans, 1979; repr., Peabody, MA: Hendrickson, 1999), 2:360. Cf. Meredith Kline, *Kingdom Prologue: Genesis Foundations for a Covenantal Worldview* (Overland Park, KS: Two Age, 2000), 40.

5. See Geerhardus Vos, *The Eschatology of the Old Testament*, ed. James T. Dennison Jr. (Phillipsburg, NJ: P&R, 2001), 1–2, 73.

6. John Calvin, *Calvin Commentaries*, ed. David W. Torrance and Thomas F. Torrance, trans. Ross MacKenzie, vol. 8, *The Epistles of Paul the Apostle to the Romans and to the Thessalonians* (Edinburgh: Oliver & Boyd, 1960), 44.

7. This adoption of Christ is to be fully distinguished from the second-century heresy, adoptionism, which denies the deity of Christ.

8. Richard B. Gaffin Jr., *Resurrection and Redemption: A Study in Paul's Soteriology*, 2nd ed. (Philipsburg, NJ: Presbyterian & Reformed, 1987), 118.

in his resurrection begins a "new and unprecedented phase of divine sonship. The eternal Son of God, who was born, lived and died [*kata sarka*], has been raised [*kata pneuma*] and so, in his messianic identity (of the seed of David), has become what he was not before: the Son of God in power."[9]

While stressing the historical, Gaffin does not eliminate the metaphysical; he does not preclude the pre-temporal sonship of Christ. In fact, the contrary is true. Gaffin carefully asserts the redemptive-historical sonship of Christ in the context of eternal sonship. Christ's redemptive-historical transition presupposes pre-temporal, ontic reality. Gaffin contends that it is the "eternal Son of God" who became the Last Adam, and whose obedience to the prelapsarian covenant of works accomplished the great historical transition from the natural and fleshly aeon to the aeon of the Spirit (2 Cor. 3:1–11). Raised from the dead by the Father through the Spirit (Rom. 1:3–4), this adopted, messianic Son ushered in the cosmic eschatological age anticipated by generations of Adam's sons[10] according to the *protoevangelium* (Gen. 3:15).

Such interplay between pre-temporal, metaphysical, and messianic categories stimulates further analysis. How do a decisively redemptive-historical understanding of Christ and the onto-theological nature of eternal sonship relate to the first Adam and his progeny? How do these critical elements inform the fundamental nature of the Last Adam and the adopted sons? It is our task to investigate what particular ways these ontological, filial, and redemptive-historical notions are tethered in Pauline soteriology.

The Archetypal Son

The ontological nature of the triune God underlies the entirety of his economic activity in creation and redemption. Paul asserts this eternal, ontological confession in Colossians 1:15, showing that Jesus Christ is the perfect image of God eternally (cf. 2 Cor. 4:4): "in him the nature and being of God have been perfectly revealed."[11] While Colossians 1:15–20 has

---

9. Ibid., 111.

10. Our choice of the term "sons" is intentionally reflective of Paul's familial language, and unless contextually necessitated otherwise, is, as for Paul, inclusive of males and females.

11. F. F. Bruce, *The Epistles to the Colossians, to Philemon, and to the Ephesians*, NICNT (Grand Rapids: Eerdmans, 1984), 57. Cf. John G. Gibbs, "The Relation Between Creation and Redemption According to Phil. II.5–11," *NovT* 12 (1970): 275–76; Allen Mawhinney, "Yiothesia in the Pauline Epistles: Its Background, Use, and Implications" (PhD diss., Baylor University,

received inveterate literary criticism,[12] the likelihood of it being a pre-Pauline hymn[13] does not mitigate its theological value. In fact, by employing this Jewish (pre-Pauline) monotheistic poem,[14] Paul deliberately and consciously upholds Christ's eternal ontological sonship; and by incorporating extant Jewish psalmody, Paul is confessing *Jesus Christ* as this self-same eternal Son of God. This monotheistic poem, with its new christological referent, Jesus Christ, tactically buttresses the Pauline confession.[15] This poem then indicates two things. First, that Christ is *prōtotokos pasēs ktiseōs* ("the first-born of all creation") indicates not only his antecedence, but also his unique preeminence, authority, and prototypical influence over creation.[16] Christ's eternal ontological substance must always be viewed as archetypal in the created order, defining and framing the nature of the creation itself, most explicitly in the creation of mankind. "He is absolutely, not comparatively, superior. . . . He simply *is*, necessarily and underivatively."[17]

Second, that Jesus Christ is the *eikōn tou theou* ("the image of God") is reminiscent of Genesis 1:26–27, where Scripture expresses the creation

---

1982), 131–33. Among other inferences, this archetypal sonship of Christ is clearly attested by the author of Hebrews (1:1–4), by John (1:1–18; 14:9), and even by Ezekiel (1:26). Cf. Samuel J. Baird, *The Elohim Revealed in the Creation and Redemption of Man* (Philadelphia: Parry & McMillan, 1860), 139; Thomas F. Torrance, *The Christian Doctrine of God: One Being Three Persons* (Edinburgh: T&T Clark, 1996), 49.

12. This text is "one of the most debated passages in the history of New Testament interpretation," Robert W. Wall, *Colossians and Philemon*, IVP New Testament Commentary Series (Downers Grove, IL: InterVarsity, 1993), 61. Cf. C. K. Barrett, *From First Adam to Last: A Study in Pauline Theology* (London: Adam & Charles Black, 1962), 83–87; Otto Piper, "The Saviour's Eternal Work: An Exegesis of Col. 1:9–29," *Interpretation* 3 (1949): 287–98; Samuel G. Shepard, "The Pauline Doctrine of Sonship" (PhD diss., Southern Baptist Theological Seminary, 1951), 104–6.

13. See Bruce, *Colossians, Philemon, Ephesians*, 55n73; James D. G. Dunn, *The Epistles to the Colossians and to Philemon: A Commentary on the Greek Text*, New International Greek Testament Commentary (Grand Rapids: Eerdmans, 1996), 83–84, n5–n6.

14. N. T. Wright, *The Climax of the Covenant: Christ and the Law in Pauline Theology* (Minneapolis: Fortress, 1993), 107–19.

15. Cf. Gaffin, " 'Life-Giving Spirit,' " 575n6.

16. See Dunn, *Colossians and Philemon*, 87–90; Torrance, *Christian Doctrine of God*, 204; Geerhardus Vos, *The Teaching of the Epistle to the Hebrews*, ed. Johannes G. Vos (Eugene, OR: Wipf and Stock, 1998), 81–83; Robert Alexander Webb, *The Reformed Doctrine of Adoption* (Grand Rapids: Eerdmans, 1947), 99; Geerhardus Vos, *The Self-Disclosure of Jesus: The Modern Debate about the Messianic Consciousness*, ed. Johannes G. Vos (Grand Rapids: Eerdmans, 1954), 141–42, 225–26; Edward A. Robson, "A Biblical-Theological Exposition of Psalm 2:7 Considering the Sonship of the Messiah" (Th.M. thesis, Westminster Theological Seminary, Philadelphia, 1963), 35–60.

17. John Webster, "Resurrection and Scripture," in *Christology and Scripture: Interdisciplinary Perspectives*, ed. Andrew T. Lincoln and Angus Paddison (New York: T & T Clark, 2007), 141.

of man in God's image. In this creation account, the *eikōn tou theou* is the finite, historical replica of the eternal Son of God. As F. F. Bruce puts it, "The image of God in humanity . . . is a copy or reflection of the archetypal image—that is to say, of God's beloved Son."[18] This assertion has its detractors. Herman Bavinck resists the notion that man is created in the image of Jesus Christ, insisting rather that he is created in the image of the triune God.[19] Such a distinction, however, fails to do justice to the archetypal implications of Colossians 1:15 and to the explicit parallels of the first and Last Adam (Rom. 5:12–21; 1 Cor. 15:20–49), the filial implications of which we will consider later.

Adam's creation, therefore, is derivative of Christ's eternal sonship, but maintains radical distinction from it because, as second person of the Trinity, Christ is eternally transcendent and independent. The first and Last Adam interplay does not compromise this critical demarcation. As God, "even in the incarnation Christ could not commingle the eternal and the temporal. The eternal must always remain independent of and prior to the temporal."[20] Hence, the ontological and eternal preeminence of Christ underscores his determinative function for all creation, and in particular fashion for Adam and Eve. At the same time, the inviolable Creator/creature distinction, and the requisite function the archetypal Son plays in *all* creation, make the specific fiber of Adamic ectypal sonship less conspicuous. The actual character and theological significance of sonship for the first Adam and his progeny then necessitate further investigation.

THE SON OF GOD AND THE ECTYPAL SON

Sons of Adam as Sons of God

In the mid-nineteenth century, Robert S. Candlish, in debating the work of Thomas J. Crawford, found the adoptive sonship of believers to rest exclusively in the incarnate sonship of Jesus Christ. Insistent on the parallels

18. Bruce, *Colossians, Philemon, Ephesians*, 58. Cf. Mawhinney, "Yiothesia," 132; Edmund P. Clowney, *The Unfolding Mystery: Discovering Christ in the Old Testament* (Phillipsburg, NJ: Presbyterian & Reformed, 1988), 22, 28; Barrett, *From First Adam to Last*, 7; Donald Macleod, *The Person of Christ*, Contours of Christian Theology, ed. Gerald Bray (Downers Grove, IL: InterVarsity, 1998), 54–57.

19. Bavinck, *In the Beginning*, 186.

20. Cornelius Van Til, *The Defense of the Faith*, 3rd ed. (Phillipsburg, NJ: Presbyterian & Reformed, 1967), 16–17.

between adoptive sonship and the begotten sonship of Christ, Candlish dismissed the creative fatherhood of God as theological impossibility: "I do not think that there is in either [natural religion or in the Word of God] any trace of sonship constituted at creation." Candlish insists that to define God's fatherhood in terms of origination "evacuates the idea of fatherhood altogether of any precise or definite meaning; making the name little more than a euphonious synonym, or figurative personification, for causation; and in truth denying that there is any paternal relation on the part of God at all!"[21] In view of the manner in which Jesus speaks of it, Geerhardus Vos also denies the idea of God's universal fatherhood, insisting that God's fatherhood is an entirely *redemptive* concept: "In the Old Testament both the Fatherhood and the love are confined to the chosen people."[22]

Such a conclusion is not universally shared. Bavinck, for example, avers, "As a human being a man is the son, the likeness, or offspring of God (Gen. 1:26; 9:6; Luke 3:38; Acts 17:28; 1 Cor. 11:7; James 3:9)."[23] Thornton Whaling puts it more bluntly, "The natural Paternity of God and the natural sonship of man are immutably and eternally fixed and not even hell itself can alter or modify this unchangeable relation."[24] Meredith Kline fleshes out the same argument in view of the *imago Dei*, "Since the Spirit's act of creating man is . . . presented as the fathering of a son and that man-son is identified as the image-likeness of God, it is evident that image of God and son of God are mutually explanatory concepts."[25] As Reformed theology has

21. Robert S. Candlish, *The Fatherhood of God Being the First Course of the Cunningham Lectures Delivered Before the New College, Edinburgh, in March 1864*, 5th ed. with a suppl. vol. (Edinburgh: Adam and Charles Black, 1870), 21, 24–25.

22. Geerhardus Vos, *Biblical Theology: Old and New Testaments* (Grand Rapids: Eerdmans, 1948; repr., Edinburgh: Banner of Truth Trust, 1996), 367. While his argument is ambiguous, it appears that J. I. Packer also resists God's creative fatherhood; he states, "The idea that all men are children of God is not found in the Bible anywhere," *Knowing God* (Downers Grove, IL: InterVarsity, 1973), 181. Though he concedes a narrow element of truth, Murray is reluctant to speak of universal fatherhood. See Murray, *Collected Writings*, 2:224–25.

23. Bavinck, *In the Beginning*, 186. Cf. Clowney, *Mystery*, 20–21; Kline, *Kingdom Prologue*, 42–46; Meredith G. Kline, *Images of the Spirit* (n.p.: 1986), 23; Webb, *Adoption*, 41–69; Leon Morris, *The Gospel According to John*, NICNT, rev. ed. (Grand Rapids: Eerdmans, 1995), 87; Mawhinney, "Yiothesia," 207–8. Webb (*Adoption*, 58) contends, "The very essence of the filial relation consists in the production of one person by another in the likeness of himself with providence and exuberant love and care of the first person for the second. This is here [in Gen 1] precisely the case."

24. Thornton Whaling, "Adoption," *PTR* 21 (1923): 225.

25. Kline, *Kingdom Prologue*, 45–46. He states elsewhere (*Images*, 23), "As Genesis 2:7 pictures it, the Spirit-Archetype actively fathered his human ectype . . . . This reading of that event

taught for centuries, that man does not simply *bear* or *possess* the image of God, but truly *is* God's image, further attests to his sonship status, however corrupted such sonship might be through solidarity with Adam's sin. Man does not forfeit the *imago Dei* entirely, but only in a narrow sense.[26]

Through the fall then, man has no more lost his *entire* sonship character than he has lost his *entire* image. Just as depravity has distorted the divine image, it has distorted the created sonship; universal depravity through solidarity with Adam in his sin has not eradicated the divine filial imprint, but has ruined it. Adam and his posterity remain sons, but created sonship is intractably perverted.

Hence, as fallen sons the *obligation* to their Creator/Father is not annulled, but the *ability* of those sons to obey in filial and ectypal reflection has been irretrievably compromised. Sonship image—in both prelapsarian *and* postlapsarian contexts—compels obedience,[27] the obedience of the created son to his Creator/Father. Truly, the tyranny of sin obviated obedience for the Adamic posterity, but did not extricate the sons of Adam from moral and spiritual responsibility. Forfeiting all spiritual/filial privilege and anticipated eschatological glory by original sin, Adam and his posterity faced the consummate judgment of this Creator/Father. Only the second

---

in terms of a father-son model and the conceptual bond of the image and son ideas are put beyond doubt by the record of the birth of Seth in Genesis 5:1–3. There, a restatement of Adam's creation in the likeness of God is juxtaposed to a statement that Adam begat a son in his own likeness. Unmistakably, the father-son relationship of Adam and Seth is presented as a proper analogue for understanding the Creator-man relationship and clearly man's likeness to the Creator-Spirit is thus identified as the likeness of a son derived from his father." Put simply, "if we wish to understand what man was intended to be, we need to think of him as a son of God. If, in turn, we ask what it means to be a son of God, the answer must be found in terms of being God's image and likeness," Sinclair B. Ferguson, *Children of the Living God* (Colorado Springs: NavPress, 1987), 23.

26. "The whole being, therefore, and not *something in man* but *man himself*, is the image of God. Further, sin, which precipitated the loss of the image of God in the narrower sense and spoiled and ruined the image of God in the broader sense, has profoundly affected the whole person, so that, consequently, also the grace of God in Christ restores the whole person," Bavinck, *In the Beginning*, 186. John Murray (*Collected Writings*, 2:39) insightfully notes that the perpetuation of God's image in fallen man actually underscores total depravity: "Man conceived of as in the image of God, so far from toning down the doctrine of total depravity, points rather to its gravity, intensity, and irreversibility."

27. Murray's thoughts on the *imago Dei* are extremely fitting here. He (*Collected Writings*, 2:38) writes, "It is the metaphysical likeness to God that grounds obligation, and the fulfillment of obligation consists in conformity to the image of God." Kline (*Kingdom Prologue*, 62) agrees, "Man's likeness to God is a demand to be like God; the indicative here has the force of an imperative."

Son, the Last Adam, could restore unqualified familial access and impart constitutive glory by succeeding federally where Adam failed federally. The gospel message for Paul and the New Testament writers focuses precisely here: the messianic Son, as vindicated and confirmed by his transforming resurrection, has taken the cursed sons of Adam (*fallen* sons of God) and not only restored to them Edenic status, but also conferred to them the *telos* of Adamic sonship (1 Cor. 15:44–45).[28]

Many in modern scholarship, however, have eclipsed the eschatological, redemptive character of Christ's work as messianic Son. Expressly, under the tutelage of Adolf von Harnack, Protestant liberalism adulterated the notion of the fatherhood of God. Harnack, the modern father of this false conception of God, summarizes his inclusivistic scheme: "In the combination of these ideas—God the Father, Providence, the position of men as God's children, the infinite value of the human soul—the whole Gospel is expressed."[29] In Harnack's proposal, God's universal fatherhood and the universal brotherhood of man liquidate biblical soteriology of its *sine qua non*—the wrath to grace dynamic (in both *historia salutis* and *ordo salutis*), and thereby rob the gospel of redemptive integrity. Accordingly, orthodoxy rightfully seeks to maintain theological distance from the liberal sense of the universal fatherhood of God and the universal brotherhood of man propounded by Harnack. However, any reactive resistance toward created sonship, particularly of postlapsarian man, necessitates further comment on Adamic sonship. As will shortly become apparent, the fear of conflating created and redeemed sonship evidences a misapprehension both of Christ's archetypal sonship and of Adam's finite, ectypal sonship in its covenantal, prelapsarian, and postlapsarian contexts.

---

28. See Brian A. Gerrish, *Grace and Gratitude: The Eucharistic Theology of John Calvin* (Edinburgh: T&T Clark, 1993), 89; John Calvin, *Institutes of the Christian Religion*, ed. John T. McNeill, trans. Ford Lewis Battles (Philadelphia: Westminster, 1960), 2.12.2; Sinclair B. Ferguson, "The Reformed Doctrine of Sonship," in *Pulpit and People: Essays in Honour of William Still on His 75th Birthday*, ed. Nigel M. DeS. Cameron and S. B. Ferguson (Edinburgh: Rutherford House, 1986), 86–87.

29. Adolf von Harnack, *What Is Christianity?* trans. Thomas Bailey Saunders (Philadelphia: Fortress, 1986), 68. Harnack derives universalism from this construct, concluding, "man is seen to be on the side of the Eternal. This was certainly Jesus' meaning, and to take anything from it is to destroy it. In applying the idea of Providence to the whole of humanity and the world without any exception; in showing that humanity is rooted in the Eternal; in proclaiming the fact that we are God's children as at once a gift and a task, he took firm grip of all fumbling and stammering attempts and brought them to their issue . . . . A man may know it or not, but a real reverence for humanity follows from the practical recognition of God as the Father of us all" (69–70).

Paul himself plainly establishes universal, created sonship in his sermon to the Athenians in Acts 17:22–31. In order to expose the foolishness of idol worship, Paul calls the Athenians to consider their Creator. In so doing, he uses *filial* language to express their origins by the Creator God: mankind is the "offspring of God." Paul argues that the obligation of mankind to God is based on the *relationship* established at creation—created sons are to seek and to obey their Creator/Father. God is the One who has made all things (Creator), governs all things (Sovereign Ruler), sustains and directs all things (Providential Governor), and is the self-sufficient Source of all life (Progenitor/ Father). Summarily, with God as the Creator of humanity in his image, "A brute ancestry was denied; a divine paternity was affirmed."[30] As the "offspring of God," men must not foolishly cling to stony idols—the "image formed by the art and thought of man" (Acts 17:29) but respond to the One in whose image they have been created. Implicit in Paul's argumentation is the creative fatherhood of God; man as a creature—the "offspring" in God's image—is by virtue of creation the *son* of God. As son, man has an obligation to respond to this Father according to his paternal directives. Paul argues further that the *divine nature* cannot be construed as a non-filial creation of man because the *human nature* surpasses such abstraction: it is the imitative creation of the Father who birthed Adam and Eve in the likeness of his own image—the image of the archetypal Son.

More broadly, while some would assert that the image/likeness of God includes the physical phenomenon,[31] the Scriptures specifically reveal how God's agency in the creation of man is not limited to Adamic, fleshy, material existence. In fact, according to Hebrews 12:9, God is the *Father* of the spiritual aspect of humanity (cf. Zech. 12:1; Num. 16:22; 27:16.).[32] Biblical language never promotes Platonic dualism—a dichotomy of the

---

30. Webb, *Adoption*, 54. Justifying his claim by pointing to the absence of the repetition of such a statement in the Pauline corpus, Samuel Shepard ("Pauline Sonship," 81) contends that Paul erred in his preaching to those in Athens by citing God as the Father of all mankind. Throughout the rest of his ministry Paul changed his view and taught that God is only "the Father of his spiritually-changed children." Luke gives no indication whatsoever of theological error in Paul's preaching here, and to assert such divulges theological bias, not careful exegesis.

31. Bavinck (*In the Beginning*, 192) suggests, "The human body is a part of the image of God in its organization as instrument of the soul, in its formal perfection, not in its material substance as flesh (*sarx*)." Cf. Murray, *Collected Writings*, 2:39; Calvin, *Institutes*, 1.15.3–4.

32. We do not claim Paul as the author of Hebrews, but rather recognize how the language of Hebrews underscores an ontological reality which both Paul and the author of Hebrews recognize.

human spirit from the human body, but rather indicates that man's sonship is derived not merely of *physical* generation through Adam. Man is a psychosomatic whole, and God as Father creates man in his (Son's) image and likeness with a *spiritual* aspect. F. F. Bruce resists this interpretation, claiming that the author of Hebrews is not promoting any metaphysical implications for man. While Bruce is correct in resisting a stark metaphysical dichotomizing of man, he adds an interpretive word to his translation of the Greek text in order to fortify the statement of God being a spiritual Father *for believers*.[33] It is more likely that this language reflects Numbers 16:22 and 27:16, where God is called "the God of spirits of all flesh" (*theos tōn pneumatōn kai pasēs sarkos*, LXX). These passages in Numbers and Hebrews point not only to the transcendence and veritable authority of God, but to the reality that his *fatherhood* is expressed in the spiritual characteristic of man. "The contrast between [*tous tēs sarkos hēmōn pateras*] and [*tō patri tōn pneumatōn*] denotes God as the author of man's spiritual being."[34]

Just as a human son *looks* like his father, he often noticeably *acts* like, *sounds* like, *thinks* like, and *responds* like his father: his immaterial aspect is also like his human father's. In the likeness of God then, man the son is a spiritual, moral being, made in God's image. As Paul implicitly contends in Acts 17, as long as man remains a descendant of Adam in his material and immaterial aspects, he is in a created sense a *son* of God, and possesses intrinsic obligation to obey him. In summary, just as a human child "instrumentally derives existence from his earthly parent, so may it be held that God, as the primary source of our being, is in the truest and highest sense our Father."[35]

Man's created sonship is attested by the *imago Dei* as it concerns created dominion, the relational intimacy of Adam and Eve with their Creator, and

---

33. F. F. Bruce, *The Epistle to the Hebrews*, NICNT (Grand Rapids: Eerdmans, 1964), 360.

34. James Moffatt, *A Critical and Exegetical Commentary on the Epistle to the Hebrews*, ICC (Edinburgh: T&T Clark, 1968), 203. Cf. William L. Lane, *Hebrews 9–13*, WBC 47B (Waco, TX: Word, 1991), 423–24.

35. Thomas Crawford, *The Fatherhood of God Considered in Its General and Special Aspects and Particularly in Relation to the Atonement with a Review of Recent Speculations on the Subject* (Edinburgh: William Blackwood and Sons, 1867), 34. Thomas Houston wrote shortly after Crawford, "In an extensive sense, God is a Father, and is so revealed in His works as well as His word. The paternal relation among men aids us in contemplating the loving relation in which God stands to His creatures—it is a shadow and representation of the Divine Fatherhood," *The Adoption of Sons, Its Nature, Spirit, Privileges and Effects: A Practical and Experimental Treatise* (Paisley: Alex. Gardner, 1872), 42.

the analogy of marriage with the church. This ectypal sonship, furthermore, is the intrinsic familial impetus for redemption accomplished by the Last Adam, and is of ontological necessity because of the eternal ontological nature of God. To these explicit and implicit issues of sonship in biblical theology we now turn.

The *Imago Dei* and Ectypal Sonship

Having discussed the *imago Dei* briefly above, a few substantiating comments concerning man in the image of God will augment the notion of man's created sonship. In seeking to describe the manner in which man is in God's image, Berkouwer notes that the biblical witness does not stress "ontological qualities—though they may indeed exist—but rather emphasizes the concepts of *conformitas* and child-father relation to God as basic to image."[36] Reacting against philosophical attempts to dichotomize man, Berkouwer underscores the psychosomatic wholeness of man.[37] While he fails to identify with clarity what the *imago Dei* actually is, he appropriately relates the image of God with the Father-son relationship introduced at creation. In the Garden of Eden, the relationship with God, vis-à-vis the *image*, and the intrinsic roles expected of the son by God, typify man's created familial relation to the Father/Creator. One of these intrinsic role-expectations stated explicitly by the Father/Creator is for man to exercise dominion over creation.

Whether dominion is an intrinsic aspect of the *imago Dei* or is derivative of it, Genesis 1:26–28 clearly links the two.[38] As God has absolute authority over his creation, man's responsibility to the earth is commanded by the Creator himself. This bestowal of dominion accentuates the sonship of

36. G. C. Berkouwer, *Man: The Image of God*, vol. 8, *Studies in Dogmatics*, trans. Dirk W. Jellema (Grand Rapids: Eerdmans, 1962), 60–61. Cf. Anthony A. Hoekema, *Created in God's Image* (Grand Rapids: Eerdmans, 1986), 60.

37. John Laidlaw concurs, "It [is] characteristic of these Scriptures to assert the *solidarité* of man's constitution,—that human individuality is of one piece, and is not composed of separate or independent parts," *The Bible Doctrine of Man*, new rev. and rearranged edition (Edinburgh: T&T Clark, 1895), 56.

38. While Socinianism equated the *imago Dei* with dominion, John Murray (*Collected Writings*, 2:41) contends that dominion is not specifically "an element of the divine image. It would appear preferable . . . to regard dominion as a function or office based upon the specific character defined as the image of God." In other words, one of Adam's responsibilities as son was dominion over the earth as his home. Such caretaking and authority are implicit aspects of sonship responsibility. Cf. Berkouwer, *Image*, 70–72.

Adam. A slave would be given only commands to *work* in the garden; the son is given the privilege of *oversight* and *dominion*. Just as God demonstrated his paternal sovereignty over all things by *speaking* creation into existence and by *naming* his creation (cf. Gen. 1:9–10), Adam, in obedience to his familial assignment, exercised his derived sonly authority by naming the animals. "Adam's dominion over the creatures and the intelligence necessary for its exercise are clearly evidenced by this prerogative—'Whatever Adam called any living creature that was its name' (Gen. 2:19)."[39] Only one created in God's image and as his son could rightfully carry out such an important father-like function in creation. The question remains, however, does this prelapsarian function of the created son carry over into the postlapsarian context?

Though the fall compromised man's image and sonship, and brought the "offices God gave to man . . . into disrepute as he disqualified himself from exercising them,"[40] it did not overturn *all* of man's essential responsibilities for oversight. Man still retained many responsibilities in creation, but his reoriented role approximated slavery more than sonship. After the fall, the created son remained a son in alienated fashion, but was burdened by the curse in his call to fulfill the cultural mandate. Now skewed from his original image, fallen man subsists in slave-like estrangement, with the inaccessible freedom and full privileges of sonship engendering only a longed-for glory. While full sonship privileges and intimacy vacated the sons of Adam through sin, remnants of the created sonship/image persist through all the descendants of Adam. Banishment from Eden does not preclude the cultural mandate, since the *imago Dei*, in its prelapsarian and postlapsarian states, irretractably perpetuates the sons' full accountability to carry on their oversight responsibilities. In its biblical formulation, sonship is a prerequisite for dominion.

Not all, however, have accepted this dominion responsibility as constitutive of sonship and the *imago Dei*. Consider, for instance, a viewpoint representative of neoorthodoxy. The *imago Dei* according to Karl Barth is exclusively confrontational:

---

39. Murray, *Collected Writings*, 2:10.

40. Ferguson, *Children*, 25. Though the general fatherhood of God over mankind continues after the fall, "there are no privileges attached . . . . The relationship which the word properly describes is missing," James Montgomery Boice, *Foundations of the Christian Faith: A Comprehensive & Readable Theology*, rev. ed. (Downers Grove, IL: InterVarsity, 1986), 443.

> Could anything be more obvious than to conclude from this clear indi-
> cation that the image and likeness of the being created by God signifies
> existence in confrontation, i.e., in this confrontation, in the juxtaposition
> and conjunction of man and man which is that of male and female, and
> then to go on to ask against this background in what the original and
> prototype of the divine existence of the Creator consists?[41]

With a perceptibly patronizing tone, Barth asserts his interpretation as
obvious and *exhaustive*.[42] He views man as a "special creature of God's
special grace,"[43] a distinction expressed at least in part by the fact that
"he has been honoured by the grace of God to be the image of God
in the uniqueness of his plurality as male and female."[44] Expressed in
maleness and femaleness, the image of God is therefore explicitly *relational* and (post-lapse) *confrontational*. In response, while we renounce
Barth's unjustifiably truncated exegetical analysis,[45] his theological
insights prove helpful.[46] The image of God must extend beyond the
breathing of the breath of God into man's nostrils making him a *nefesh
khayyah* ("living being"); this same phrase is used of the animals in
Genesis 1:21, 24; and 2:19. Instead, man's uniqueness is distinguished
from the lower creation, for it resides in the *imago Dei*, which contextually and implicitly encompasses a relational notion: man is uniquely
formed to glorify God by imitating the relational character of intra-
Trinitarian fellowship.

41. Karl Barth, *The Doctrine of Creation*, ed. G. W. Bromiley and T. F. Torrance, trans. J. W.
Edwards, O. Bussey, and Harold Knight; vol. 3, bk. 1, *Church Dogmatics* (Edinburgh: T&T Clark,
1958), 195.

42. Reiterating his point in his comments on Gen. 1:26, Barth (*Creation*, 183) suggests that
the concept of *imago Dei* "means to be created as a being which has its ground and possibility in
the fact that in 'us,' i.e., in God's own sphere and being, there exists a divine and therefore self-
grounded prototype to which this being can correspond; which can therefore legitimate it for all
that it is a heterogeneous imitation; which can justify its existence; and by which, when existence
is given to it, it will in fact be legitimated and justified." To Barth, this relational essence of man
is the *imago Dei*. Cf. Kline, *Images*, 33.

43. Barth, *Creation*, 186.

44. Ibid., 188.

45. Cf. Paul Helm, "Image of the Spirit and the Image of God" in *Creator, Redeemer, Consummator: A Festschrift for Meredith G. Kline*, ed. Howard Griffith and John R. Muether (Greenville,
SC: Reformed Academic, 2000), 203–14.

46. Meredith Kline's resistance (*Images*, 34) to the relational character of man as an aspect
of the *imago Dei* is unfounded. Just as Barth's relational notion does not exhaust the *imago Dei*,
neither does Kline's "glory-image."

Acknowledging then that the *imago Dei* assumes relational dimensions, and recalling the decisive archetypal function of the eternal Son, how else may we define those relational dimensions of the created being with his Creator than in terms of Father/son language? Men and women, created as children in God's image, are at least partly so formed, in view of their ability beyond that of other creatures—to relate profoundly with one another and with their Father/Creator. As discussed above, the intimacy of the garden setting and vocation indicates an intensely deeper attachment than the slave/Master relationship. The original description of Adam and Eve's intimacy with the Creator is notably familiar, and even *familial* in nature (cf. Gen. 3:8). Further, the fall from intimacy with the Creator, which required banishment from his holy presence in Eden (Gen. 3:23–24), indicates that the intimacy once shared is now compromised, and what was once precious closeness with their Creator/Father becomes disastrous segregation from him.

In God's image, man enjoyed relationship with the Creator in a *familial* fashion; now under the curse of sin, a relational reality still exists but only in the sense of *banished* remoteness. This relational remoteness returns to relational intimacy only by God's grace through Jesus Christ the Son and the fellowship of his Holy Spirit (2 Cor. 13:14). Relying on the *imago Dei* in creation, the apostle Paul unveils this eschatological restoration of this relational dimension of sonship with his marriage analogy: the union of the husband and wife is analogous to the union of Christ and his church (Eph. 5:21–33). Accordingly, in Ephesians 5, Paul's mind turns to God's creation and to the divine institution of marriage pictured in Genesis 2. Under inspiration of the Holy Spirit, Paul assesses that the intimacy to be enjoyed in Christian marriage, with an admitted level of inscrutability (cf. Eph. 5:32), is explicated by analogy to the intimacy enjoyed in the union of the messianic Son of God and his bride, the church.

How does this marriage metaphor relate to created sonship and the *imago Dei*?[47] As specified earlier, Jesus Christ is the *eikōn tou theou tou aoratou prōtotokos pasēs ktiseōs* ("the image of the invisible God, the firstborn of all creation," Col. 1:15). This passage unpacks the connection of the perfect image, Jesus Christ as head in creation, with his function as head of the church, his bride. The eternally glorious Son, in whom full deity

---

47. Cf. Clowney, *Mystery*, 35–42.

resides (Col. 2:9), took on the likeness of the skewed image of God at his incarnation ("sinful flesh," Rom. 8:3), and came to restore to the Father the sons of Adam, those ruined by their sin-smitten image—sons for whom sonship is marked by radical alienation from the Father (cf. Col. 1:19–20). Hence, Jesus Christ—the image of God and the only-begotten Son, took on the likeness of humanity—the image of God created and fallen, to restore those who had by treasonous sin sought to rob the Father/Creator of his rightful glory. While the Scriptures demonstrate his covenantal solidarity with *prelapsarian* Adam (1 Cor. 15:44–45) and his absolute sinlessness, it was Jesus' restoration accomplished by his identification with *fallen* Adamic sonship (Rom. 8:3 and Gal. 4:4) that qualified him as the messianic Son, and enabled the full restoration of the progeny of Adam. In the Son *par excellence*, the image marred was substitutionarily restored; the One who became the perfect human image of God restores the relationship of man-kind with his Creator/Father.

Returning to Paul's marriage metaphor, the first Adam, created in God's image, wed Eve—who was also created in God's image. As the first institu-tion established by God the Creator, Edenic marriage reflected the nature of intra-Trinitarian fellowship; Adam and Eve's interpersonal relationship reflected the intimacy of the social Trinity. Through the fall, not only was the image of God grossly compromised, and the Father/son relationships tragically ruined, but further, human interrelationship—most agonizingly, the marriage relationship—became irreversibly non-intimate (Gen. 3:12–13). It was only when the Last Adam, the perfect image of God, became the substitutionary sacrifice for fallen sons, that this relational image was restored. Two relational realities flow from Christ's redemptive-historical restoration of the divine image: (1) Father/son intimacy is restored because of Father/Son intimacy,[48] and (2) brother/brother (marital and general human) intimacy is also restored only on the basis of Father/Son intimacy (cf. Eph. 2:11–22; 4:1–6; 5:18–6:9).

Hence, it is in view of the *imago Dei* that Paul is able to assert this marriage/church analogy. Since the restoration of the bride through redemp-tion rested on the Son who was the perfect image, the marriage relation-ship in Genesis 2 must likewise rest on the original relational image of God imprinted on God's sons. The analogy of the precious and intimate

---

48. See M. M. B. Turner, "The Significance of Spirit Endowment for Paul," *VE* 9 (1975): 65.

relationship of the bride of Christ, the church, with the groom, Jesus Christ, is based on God's creation of the marriage institution as a reflection of himself. The re-created *daughter* of God is fit to wed the incarnate Son;[49] the bride in whom his image is restored is thereby qualified to wed the *perfect Image Son* who gave up his life for her. Summarily, the relational makeup of humanity, as an aspect of the *imago Dei*, exists within the context of created and redeemed sonship. Just as the Father has fellowship with the Son, so, too, the children of God have fellowship with one another, by the restoration of relational purity in the messianic Son himself (see chart below). The relationship of Christ to his church attests to this analogy and to the ectypal sonship of created man.

Marriage and Sonship

	First Adam	*Second Adam*	**Eve/Church**
Creation	Created Son	*Eternal Son*	Created Bride
Fall	Alienated Son	*Eternal Son*	Alienated Bride
Redemption	Restored Son	*Incarnate Son*	Restored Bride
Eschaton	Realized Son	*Wedded Son*	Consummated Bride

Put summarily, derivative of the ontological realities of the eternal order, the image of God in man is markedly expressed by man's creation as God's son: the ectypal son presupposes and finitely reflects the archetypal Son. In view of God as Progenitor, man's derived familial dominion over creation, and his relational capacities, God's creative fatherhood and man's embedded sonship are confirmed.

The Father and the Redemption of the Sons

Since Martin Luther's sixteenth-century resurfacing of salvation by grace through faith, justification has taken prominence in a Reformational understanding of salvation. In the heavenly tribunal, God the Judge declares the sinner *righteous* on the basis of the substitutionary death of Jesus Christ.[50] Sin is a legal violation against a holy God, and God's justice must be met

49. Macleod, *The Person of Christ*, 71–73.

50. With Gaffin, we accept the Reformation understanding of justification, and more specifically, classical Reformed soteriology. See Richard B. Gaffin Jr., *By Faith, Not By Sight: Paul and the Order of Salvation* (Bletchley, UK: Paternoster, 2006). The so-called New Per-

forensically. In view of this juridical focus, some would rebut the notion of God's creative fatherhood. For example, Candlish rejects the creative fatherhood of God on the basis of the remedial work of Christ, which he claims "is always represented in Scripture,—in exact consistency with its representation of the evil to be remedied,—as purely and wholly legal, forensic, and judicial."[51] This statement is grossly one-sided. While it is true that Christ's sacrifice accomplished legal justification because of man's legal accountability, is it not true that the Son's sacrifice also restored familial privilege in view of the *imago Dei* and ectypal sonship? Is not the grace included in the exacting of the curse on Adam and Eve reflective not only of the judicial consequences of their actions, but of the gracious longsuffering of God as their *Father*? Moreover,

> The parental character of God, no less than His rectoral character, is concerned in the atonement; and it is only by combining these with one another that this great remedial provision for the salvation of a lost world can be satisfactorily accounted for. If it be because God is a King and Judge that the atonement was *required*; it is, on the other hand, because God is a Father that the atonement is *provided*.[52]

Even in propitiation, man's created sonship is implicitly affirmed. Any suggestion short of God as eternal Father and man as created son compromises not only the underlying categories of Pauline soteriology, but also the very nature of God in the accomplishment of redemption.[53] It is the Father's love for his created sons that motivates his redemptive, eschatological work:

spective on Paul is articulated by N. T. Wright in *What Paul Really Said: Was Paul of Tarsus the Real Founder of Christianity?* (Oxford: Lion, 1997).

51. Robert S. Candlish, *The Fatherhood of God Being the First Course of the Cunningham Lectures Delivered Before the New College, Edinburgh, in March 1864* (Edinburgh: Adam and Charles Black, 1865), 128.

52. Crawford, *Fatherhood of God*, 66.

53. "We are just as much entitled to infer the existence of such a relation from the evidences of fatherly kindness observable in His dealings with us, as to infer His *magisterial* relation towards us from the like evidences of His sovereign rule and moral government," Crawford, *Fatherhood of God*, 14–15. J. Scott Lidgett, who wishes to make God's fatherhood the primary organizing principle for theology, adds, God's "Fatherhood does not set aside the necessity that penal conditions should enter into His dealings with a sinful world, or even into His dealings with His Son acting on its behalf. The Fatherhood of God strengthens rather than weakens this necessity, for of all relations the fatherly can least throw off its jurisdiction. The difference, which is brought about when Fatherhood is seen to be behind and within sovereignty, is simply to give a larger meaning, more salutary and necessary ends, to the infliction of penalty, than would otherwise

"The love of the Father as the source of the atonement is the love from which the whole plan of salvation takes its origin."[54]

First and Last Adam

While the impetus for the atonement clearly entails sonship, another vital Pauline formulation seals this filial conclusion. In his theology, redemption is accomplished in parallel to and in fulfillment of the prelapsarian context. Specifically, Paul uses the first Adam/Last Adam parallel construction (Rom. 5:12–21; 1 Cor. 15:21–49) to express the accomplishment of redemption in view of the failure of the first man. Though this determinative paradigm has been discussed in various ways already in our argument, it is critical to accentuate how the two-Adam construction necessitates the created sonship of Adam. If the Last Adam is the Son of God, and his redemptive incarnation amounted to solidarity with created mankind, then the first Adam and his progeny must also be sons of God for the establishment of genuine solidarity. Paul expresses Christ's solidarity with humanity in terms of messianic sonship (cf. Gal. 4:3–4), and therefore, the parallel Adams, in their parallel covenantal functions, are parallel sons, even as both are the image of God.[55] Redemption, as Paul perceives it, is a redemption of adoptive sonship (Gal. 4:1–6; Eph. 1:4–5), and this pre-temporally ordained redemption occurs in the messianic *Son* whose perfect transformation at his adoption/resurrection accomplished the restoration of failed Adamic sonship. Thus, as attested by the two-Adam construction and the fatherly nature of God in atonement, the entire work of redemption confirms the created, restored, and consummated sonship of mankind in the sonship of Christ. Even as the first Adam is the first created son, the Last Adam in his solidarity with the first Adam is the first of many eschatological sons.

God the Eternal Father

At the outset, we established the ultimacy of Christ's eternal sonship for Pauline theology. Expressly, Christ's eternal sonship provides the archetypal representation of the actual character of all created sonship. We

---

be the case," *The Fatherhood of God in Christian Truth and Life* (Edinburgh: T&T Clark, 1902), 391.

54. Murray, *Collected Writings*, 2:144.

55. See Whaling, "Adoption," 223–24.

assume, therefore, the prototypical character of the ontological Trinity in creation and redemption, and as Van Til and others have demonstrated, the context of intra-Trinitarian relationship (*pactum salutis*) establishing the covenantal character of God's dealings in the created order.[56] In brief, Trinitarian ontology determines Trinitarian activity. With this chief ontological principium in mind, we will consider God's sovereignty in election, and by analogy consider the eternal reality of God's fatherhood as it transcends man's created and redeemed sonship.

Scripture suggests at least three applications of God's sovereign elective decree: creative, theocratic, and redemptive. First, whether one accepts supralapsarianism or infralapsarianism, Reformed theology concurs that election is implicit in the creative work of God. While election generally bears soteriological overtones, it is only *created* sons on whom this election is applied. Thus, divine election for special grace presupposes divine sovereignty over birth. "The purpose to create, to permit the fall, to elect some to everlasting life, while others are left, to send his Son to redeem his people, and to give the Spirit to apply that redemption, are purposes which harmonize one with all others, and form one consistent plan."[57] In other words, that he chose to create certain individuals and not to create others evidences the absolute sovereign elective authority of God.[58] In his wisdom, God chose to create man in his image, as his son. Second, God elected the nation of Israel (a corporate election)—again by his sovereign will (Gen. 12, 15, 17).[59] Third, God elected certain individuals for redemptive grace (personal and specific), and this redemption is one of *restored* sonship by adoption in Christ (cf. Rom. 9–11; Eph. 1:3–14). The creative election is universal in scope, but contains no abiding individual guarantee of redemptive re-creation. The theocratic election of Israel was narrower in scope, and yet contains no abiding guarantee of redemption simply by genetic

---

56. See Kline, *Kingdom Prologue*, 15–16. Cf. Herman Witsius, *The Economy of the Covenants between God and Man Comprehending a Complete Body of Divinity*, trans. William Crookshank (London: Printed for T. Tegg and Son, Cheapside, 1837), 31; Cornelius Van Til, "Nature and Scripture," in *The Infallible Word: A Symposium by the Members of the Faculty of Westminster Theological Seminary* (Philadelphia: The Presbyterian Guardian, 1946), 259; Greg L. Bahnsen, *Van Til's Apologetic: Readings and Analysis* (Phillipsburg, NJ: P&R, 1998), 66.

57. Hodge, *Systematic Theology*, 2:334. Cf. Louis Berkhof, *Systematic Theology*, 4th rev. and enl. ed. (Grand Rapids: Eerdmans, 1941), 100.

58. Cf. Torrance, *Christian Doctrine of God*, 131.

59. Berkhof, *Systematic Theology*, 114. Cf. Mark W. Karlberg, "Israel and the Eschaton," *WTJ* 52 (1990): 126–27.

connection to Abraham (Rom. 9) or national participation in cultic ritual. As determined within the *pactum salutis*, however, redemptive election is explicitly narrow and redemptively secure: adopted sons are eternally chosen sons who through the messianic Son attain their sonship *telos*. Hence, while election manifests its implications differently in history, it is a metaphysical necessity *because God is inherently the Sovereign Ruler* of the universe. The ontological essence governs the economic activity.

The fatherhood of God possesses three analogous and related components: creative fatherhood, theocratic fatherhood, and adoptive (redemptive) fatherhood. First, God's very creation of mankind, the imprint of his image on man, and his providential care over all his creation, demonstrate his *fatherly* origination and care for humanity. Since God *is* Father, those whom he created in his image are his *sons*. Second, the theocratic fatherhood of God appears in his corporate adoption of Israel as his chosen people. As demonstrated by the exposition in Romans 9, this covenant people is definitively recognized by God as his *son* (cf. Ex. 4:22–23). In establishing the sonship of Israel, God elucidated his sovereign expectations of his people (Ex. 4:23), but also his particular and *paternal* care for his chosen ones.[60] In this elevated position as corporate son, Israel typologically foreshadowed the exclusive privileges of those adopted under the provisions of the new covenant, and affirmed the intended teleology of covenantal sonship. Third, the adoptive fatherhood of God restores the original blessings of intimacy established in the Garden of Eden, and advances these blessings to their glorious dénouement in solidarity with Christ the Son *par excellence* (cf. Rom. 8:12–17) by the eschatological Spirit. In view of this development of the filial interactions of God with humanity in history, we must say that God acted in a fatherly fashion throughout Scripture, *because he is a Father by nature*.[61] More specifically, the ontological character of God as Father is

60. Through God's fatherly provision in the exodus, "Israel was to be set free; for they were sons of God, the LORD, who graciously had adopted them as his special inheritance and had set them apart from the nations to be his instrument for bringing blessing to all the nations of the earth," Walter C. Kaiser Jr., *Exodus*, Expositor's Bible Commentary 2 (Grand Rapids: Zondervan, 1990), 332.

61. The ontological fatherhood of God provides the legitimate basis by which we can genuinely assert sonship as a primary redemptive-historical organizing principle. See Ferguson, "Doctrine of Sonship," 86–87. "Behind the creation of 'all things' stands the living God, *who has always existed as Father*, but has not always been Creator," Douglas F. Kelly, *Creation and Change: Genesis 1.1–2.4 in the Light of Changing Scientific Paradigms* (Ross-shire: Christian Focus, 1997), 45. Torrance (*Christian Doctrine of God*, 57) adds, "This means

determinative of the creative and the redemptive; God's fatherly actions in creation and redemption are derivative of his eternal ontological character. Presupposed by God's eternal fatherhood, created men are sons, who alone are redeemed to intended sonship privileges and constitution by the messianic Son himself. Adoptive sonship realized in Christ is grounded for Paul in the eternal reality of God's fatherhood, and is in direct continuity with the created reality of Adamic sonship as a finite replica of the archetypal sonship of Jesus Christ.

To reiterate, Jesus' eternal sonship explicitly attests to God's eternal fatherhood and man's created sonship.[62] Though some theologians have attempted to restrict Jesus' sonship to post-incarnation, Scripture militates against this understanding (cf. Heb. 1:1–4; John 3:17; 17:5; Col. 1:15). Jesus Christ did not *become* the Son of God at the incarnation; he became the *incarnate* Son of God.[63] For our purposes, we may say that Jesus Christ's sonship is eternal as the eternally generated Son,[64] and his eternal sonship exists *because* of the eternal fatherhood of God. Vos puts it well, "Beginning . . . with the order in the sphere of being, we note that the highest thing is the pre-temporal, pre-mundane sonship of the Second Person of the Trinity with reference to the First."[65]

Hence, when God is seen as Father of all mankind, when he is called the Father of the nation of Israel (Ex. 4:22), when he is addressed as Father by his incarnate Son, and when he is called the Father of his adopted children (Rom. 8:15–17), he is so-called ultimately because he is *fatherly* by eternal nature. The familial title unveils the metaphysical truth: God is the Father generationally, creatively, theocratically, and adoptively, *because he eternally is Father*. Hence, to insist that God is the Father of Israel *only* in a collective sense (Ex. 4) and of his adopted children *only* in a redemptive and eschatological sense is to abandon the ontological basis for this fact. The essential reason God acts fatherly and bears the title "Father" is

---

that God is to be acknowledged as eternally Father in himself, as Father of the Son, before the foundation of the world and apart from the creation, and so is Father in a sense that is absolutely unique and transcendent." Cf. 207–9, 237.

62. See Vos, *The Self-Disclosure of Jesus*, 142.

63. Given to God over two hundred times in the Scriptures, the title "Father" is the most common appellation and Jesus' most-used name for the first person of the Trinity.

64. Cf. Vos, *The Self-Disclosure of Jesus*, 148–49; Robert Reymond, *A New Systematic Theology of the Christian Faith* (Nashville, TN: Thomas Nelson, 1998), 324–30.

65. Vos, *The Self-Disclosure of Jesus*, 189.

because he essentially and eternally *is* Father; as such, he "*owes it to Himself to act . . . a father's part*,"[66] a part he carries out in eternal generation, in creation, and in redemption for his sons.

THE ADOPTED SON AND THE ADOPTED SONS

Using the term *huiothesia* in five formative passages, Paul conceives of redemption as adoptive sonship. In his theology, adoption possesses a vast biblico-theological scope, a scope which originates in pre-temporal intra-Trinitarian decree (Eph. 1:5) and consummates in the eschatological realization of redemptive sonship at the resurrection (Rom. 8:23). Associated with each stage of adoption revealed in redemptive history is a christological thrust, precisely commensurate with the christological focus in the *historia salutis*. A focused summary of the biblico-theological examination of *huiothesia* in its redemptive-historical perspective proves the thoroughgoing christological cast of it. As Calvin has put it, "the promise, by which God adopts us to himself as his sons, holds the first place among . . . [all the promises]. Now the cause and root of adoption is Christ."[67] While space limitations prevent us from traversing each of the texts fully,[68] James Cook's comments on four of the texts containing *huiothesia* highlight adoption's christocentricity:

> The four texts (and their contexts) which deal with Christian adoption manifest Paul's customary emphasis on the essential role of Christ and the Spirit. Romans 8 makes plain that adoption (v. 15) means that Christians are both children and heirs of God (v. 16); and that to be heirs of God . . . is at the same time to be fellow-heirs . . . with Christ (v. 17). This christological connection is carried through to the end of the paragraph

66. Crawford, *Fatherhood of God*, 25, emphasis added.

67. John Calvin, *Calvin's Commentaries*, trans. John Pringle, vol. 20, *Commentaries on the First Book of Moses Called Genesis* (Edinburgh: The Calvin Translation Society, n.d.; repr., Grand Rapids: Baker, 1989), 138. Cf. John Owen, *The Works of John Owen*, ed. William H. Goold (n.p.: Johnstone & Hunter, 1850–53; repr., Edinburgh: Banner of Truth, 1988), 2:207; Tim J. R. Trumper, "An Historical Study of Adoption in the Calvinistic Tradition" (PhD diss., University of Edinburgh, 2001), 18.

68. For fuller treatments of biblical adoption, see Trevor Burke, *Adopted into God's Family: Exploring a Pauline Metaphor*, New Studies in Biblical Theology 22, ed. D. A. Carson (Downers Grove, IL: InterVarsity, 2006); David B. Garner, "Adoption in Christ" (PhD diss., Westminster Theological Seminary, 2002).

by the verbs *sympaschomen* and *syndoxasthomen.* As was noted above, v. 23 of the same chapter links adoption with "the redemption of our bodies." Once again the christological connection is made, albeit more subtly. For apart from the resurrection of Christ there would, of course, be no Christian expectation of the redemption of the body. In Gal. 4:4f. the place of the work of Christ in the adoption of his people is made perfectly clear. The purpose for which God sent forth his Son, the goal of the incarnation itself, is "that we might receive adoption as sons." And in Eph. 1:5 it is emphasized that just as all the blessings described in that doxology are received in Christ, so also God predestined Christians for adoption "through Jesus Christ." The cumulative testimony of these passages asserts forcefully that Christians do not receive adoption apart from Jesus Christ.[69]

Cook correctly assesses these passages; however, he fails to round out his discussion, neglecting the critical Pauline text that explicitly coordinates *huiothesia* in the old and new covenants through *Christ,* the messianic Son. Such an oversight weakens the conclusion that christocentricity pervades Paul's theology of adoption. Yet, Romans 9:4 equally accentuates this christological focus, leaving any question of christocentricity in *huiothesia* no longer moot.

When Paul explains the covenantal blessings enjoyed by those under the old covenant in Romans 9:1–5, he details several illustrative blessings of the old covenant. In his explication of these divine blessings, Paul crowns his argument with the antitype of them *all:* "Christ according to the flesh" (9:5).[70] Demonstrating that not all biological descendants of Abraham were *ever* children of Abraham in the truest sense (Rom. 9:8), and that God has not rejected his people (Rom. 11:1), Paul proclaims that any perceived failure of God to fulfill his promises to Israel represents not a failure on God's part, but a failure of the Jews to understand the heart of the covenant of grace (Rom. 11:28–32)—now revealed in Jesus Christ. The substantive link between old covenant and new covenant, according to Paul, is the incarnate

69. James I. Cook, "The Conception of Adoption in the Theology of Paul," in *Saved by Hope: Essays in Honor of Richard C. Oudersluys,* ed. James I. Cook (Grand Rapids: Eerdmans, 1978), 141–42.

70. John Murray, *The Epistle to the Romans: The English Text with Introduction, Exposition and Notes,* repr. as single book (Grand Rapids: Eerdmans, 1997), 2:6; Joseph A. Fitzmyer, *Romans: A New Translation with Introduction and Commentary,* AB 33 (New York: Doubleday, 1993), 547.

Son of God;[71] the christological culmination of the covenant serves as the explicit basis for the continuity of blessing between the dispensations. Old covenant provisions, while evidence of God's blessing under the Mosaic administration, were temporary provisions with a forward-look, anticipating divine fulfillment, exclusively *in Christ*.[72]

More particularly, it is Jesus Christ according to the flesh (cf. Rom. 1:3) who serves as the antitype for Israel's corporate *adoption*. From a redemptive-historical perspective then, inter-covenantal adoption abides in perfect continuity through the true Israel—Christ himself, who alone fulfills old covenant typology. Christ, the Son *par excellence*, the prophesied Prophet, Priest, and King, efficiently accomplishes redemptive sonship for those old covenant and new covenant spiritual sons of Abraham. It is exclusively in the Son of God that this redemption is accomplished: typological adoption and eschatological adoption unite in messianic adoption, in the person of Jesus Christ.

Summarizing then the replete christological cast to adoption, it was Christ as eternal Son of God who participated in the pre-temporal decree for adoptive sonship (Eph. 1:5) and carried out the decree as Son in redemptive history, Christ as messianic Son who fulfilled the character of Israelite, typological sonship (Rom. 9:4–5), Christ as incarnate Son—made in the likeness of the sons of Adam—who in his humiliation and exaltation inaugurated the eschatological and pneumatic age for adoptive sonship (Gal. 4:5; Rom. 8:15), and Christ as consummate Son whose resurrection grounds the resurrection/adoption of the believer (Rom. 8:23). In view of this christological saturation in adoption, the character of *Christ's* eternal and messianic sonship bears immediately and exhaustively upon the character of adoption.

In short, in view of the centrality of union with Christ, redemptive sonship occurs through critical solidarity of the adopted sons with the Adopted Son. *Christ's adoption* (Rom. 1:3–4) is the "cause and root" (Calvin) of the believer's adoption. In solidarity with the resurrected, messianic Son, the redeemed son of Adam enjoys his "judicially consti-

---

71. Vos, *The Self-Disclosure of Jesus*, 149.

72. Cf. O. Palmer Robertson, *The Christ of the Covenants* (Phillipsburg, NJ: Presbyterian & Reformed, 1980), 296–97. Because of the perfect coalescence of the eschatological Son and the eschatological Spirit (2 Cor. 3:17), Willem A. VanGemeren's insight concerning the new humanity as "the community of the Spirit" in continuity with old covenant blessing (Rom. 9:4–5) further attests to the christological coordination of old covenant and new covenant. See "The Spirit of Restoration," *WTJ* 50 (1988): 92.

tutive declaration of sonship" (Gaffin). Created sons are adopted sons because they are united to the Son of God.

Conclusion

Behind the creation of the cosmos—and most relevantly here, behind the creation of man—exists the archetypal, eternal sonship of Christ. Man, made in the image of God, a finite replica (ectype) of the eternal, ontological Son (archetype), is, at creation, necessarily a son of God. While the fall skewed sonship and alienated the relationship of the created son with the Father, just as man did not completely lose the divine image, he likewise did not lose the broad sense of his sonship. Still sons, but alienated and depraved, the first man and his progeny stood under the curse of their Creator/Father, and were in need of the judicial declaration of God to rectify their sonship status, and the redemptive power of God to restore their sonship constitution, indeed to vouchsafe their eschatological familial *telos*. In view of the failure of the first son of God, the realization of this declaration and redeeming power by God's grace came through the Last Adam, the Son of God *par excellence*, whose redemptive work provided the reversal of the curse on man and the attainment of adoption for the fallen sons of Adam. In Christ, created sons of Adam become the adopted sons of God.

While the entire redemptive-historical development and realization of redemptive sonship organically derive from his messianic sonship, Christ's pre-temporal constitution plays the prior, ultimate role. In fact, all biblical sonship flows from an anterior, ontological *principium*—the eternal Son of God, in whom the ectypal, typological, and antitypical sonships find their *raison d'être*. This *principium* of christological sonship unites the sonships of Adam, of Israel, of the incarnate Christ, and of the eschatologically adopted believer in covenantal, redemptive-historical continuity. The first Adam finitely replicates the First Son; the Last Adam fulfills the *telos* of the first created son. In this way, Christ is not only the eternal Son, he is also the archetypal Adam. Further, by his covenantal obedience as the Last Adam, he became the glorious, exalted, eschatological Son of God in power (Rom. 1:4). We see therefore in Pauline soteriology an exhaustively christological cast, wherein the filial, ontological, and redemptive-historical are securely tethered in Christ the Son of God, the Source, Epicenter, and Consummator of all reality. He is the Alpha and the Omega, the Beginning and the End, the First Son *and* the Last.

PART 2

Studies in Historical and Polemical Theology

9

"The Infallible Rule of Interpretation of Scripture": The Hermeneutical Crisis and the Westminster Standards[1]

PETER A. LILLBACK

A "CONTROVERSIAL BIBLE,"[2] the "Battle for the Bible,"[3] the "Problem of the Old Testament,"[4] and the "messiness of the Old Testament"[5] are a few of the shibboleths revealing the strained relationship between recent

1. It is a privilege to offer this article in honor of Professor Richard B. Gaffin Jr.'s long and illustrious career at Westminster Theological Seminary. In seeking to honor his labors, I have selected themes that have been close to his life's work—the theology of biblical inspiration and the Westminster Standards. Consider, for example, his soon-to-be-republished articles, "Old Amsterdam and Inerrancy?—I," *WTJ* 44 (Fall 1982): 250–89; and "Old Amsterdam and Inerrancy?—II," *WTJ* 45 (Fall 1983): 219–72. They will be published with the new title, *God's Word in Servant Form* (Greenville, SC: Reformed Academic Press, 2008). Consult also his "Biblical Theology and the Westminster Standards" in *The Practical Calvinist* (Fearn, Ross-shire: Mentor/Christian Focus, 2002), 425–42.

2. G. C. Berkouwer observes that "Holy Scripture has become in Claus Westermann's words, a "controversial Bible . . . ," *Holy Scripture*, Studies in Dogmatics (Grand Rapids: Eerdmans, 1975), 9. For cogent critiques of the "controvesial Bible" occasioned by Rogers/McKim thesis, see Gaffin, "Old Amsterdam and Inerrancy?" and John D. Woodbridge, *Biblical Authority: A Critique of the Rogers/McKim Proposal* (Grand Rapids: Zondervan, 1982).

3. Cf. Harold Lindsell, *The Battle for the Bible* (Grand Rapids: Zondervan, 1976). The "battle for the Bible" has focused especially on inerrancy.

4. Peter Enns, *Inspiration and Incarnation: Evangelicals and the Problem of the Old Testament* (Grand Rapids: Baker Academic, 2005), 15–16.

5. Ibid., 108, 110.

biblical studies and the historic evangelical theology of Holy Scripture. Indeed, for some, "reading the Bible has already become a serious theological problem—perhaps even a crisis."[6] Berkouwer explains:

> A crisis has arisen in the hearts and minds of many people concerning this knowledge and certainty. There is a very close connection between this crisis and the development of the so-called historical criticism of Scripture, which drew attention to the nature of these scriptures as *human* writings.[7]

> It was inevitable that this radical question—and many others implied in it—should have a profound effect upon the life of the church, which until then had unquestioningly accepted the trustworthiness of Holy Scripture.[8]

> When the radical critics concluded from the "human character" of Scripture that they had a right to criticize it—and many of them claimed that an honest historical examination left little or nothing of the nimbus of infallibility, supernaturalness, and uniqueness—their opponents were tempted to present the divine character of Scripture in such a manner that the human character could be of little significance.[9]

As we engage the hermeneutical crisis, it behooves us to remember Berkouwer's appeal to the astute observation of Bavinck where he avers that opposition to Scripture can arise from both within as well as from without orthodoxy.

> There are different kinds of opposition to the real authority of Scripture that are not precluded or conquered by any kind of theory. When Bavinck reflects on the attack upon Holy Scripture, he sees this attack first of all as enmity of the human heart, which can manifest itself in various ways: It is by no means only, and maybe not even most, prominent in the criticism to which Scripture is subjected in our day. Scripture as the Word of God meets with opposition and unbelief from every psychic human being. In the period of dead or-

6. Ibid., 15.
7. Berkouwer, *Holy Scripture*, 12.
8. Ibid., 13.
9. Ibid., 17.

thodoxy unbelief in Scripture was in principle just as powerful as in our historico-critical age.[10]

Similarly, the hermeneutical crisis that wrestles with "the real authority of Scripture" can be found not only at the fault line between orthodoxy and secular biblical criticism, but also within the boundaries of those who openly profess a sincere commitment to Scripture as divine self-revelation.

THE HERMENEUTICAL CRISIS, THE WESTMINSTER STANDARDS, AND WESTMINSTER SEMINARY

In this crisis context, what should we think of the Westminster Confession of Faith, the climactic statement of Reformed theology, as it developed its theology during the period of High Orthodoxy?[11] The confession, having defined the canon of Scripture, says of the canonical books, "All which are given by inspiration of God, to be the rule of faith and life."(I.2). Can this high and historical view of Scripture, championed by the Westminster Divines[12] as well as by Calvin,[13] Kuyper,[14] the Princetonian forerunners[15] and

10. Ibid., 34–35.

11. Philip Schaff says of the Westminster Assembly and its influence, "Whether we look at the extent or ability of its labors, or its influence upon future generations, it stands first among Protestant councils," *Creeds of Christendom* (Grand Rapids: Baker, 1983), 1:728. Richard A. Muller defines the epoch of 1640–1700 as the period of "High Orthodoxy" for Reformed theology (see *Post-Reformation Reformed Dogmatics*, vol. 1, *Prolegomena to Theology* [Grand Rapids: Baker, 1987], 46). The Westminster Assembly met from 1643 to 1649.

12. Westminster Confession of Faith Chapter 1 is titled "Of the Holy Scripture," and is a classic statement of the Reformed understanding of Scripture. This succinct summary of the doctrine of Scripture touches many themes including Scripture's necessity, the definition of its canon, its divine authority, the divine source of human assurance concerning its infallibility, its sufficiency and perspicuity, the authority of its original languages, its preservation and propriety of its translation, its interpretation, and its finality for controversy.

13. J. I. Packer notes, "It seems obvious from what has been said that Calvin could never have consciously entertained the possibility that human mistakes, whether of reporting or of interpreting facts of any sort whatever, could have entered into the text of Scripture as the human writers gave it. Nor did he," "John Calvin and the Inerrancy of Holy Scripture," in *Inerrancy and the Church*, ed. John D. Hannah (Chicago: Moody, 1984), 178. Summarizing Calvin, John Murray writes, "God speaks in Scripture. In it he opens his sacred mouth." *Calvin on Scripture and Divine Sovereignty* (Philadelphia: Presbyterian & Reformed, 1960), 50.

14. Kuyper's views are well summarized by Gaffin, "Old Amsterdam—I," 272-75.

15. Benjamin B. Warfield, *The Inspiration and Authority of the Bible* (Philadelphia: Presbyterian & Reformed, 1948), 173; Archibald A. Hodge and Benjamin B. Warfield, *Inspiration* (Grand

founders of Westminster such as Geerhardus Vos,[16] John Murray,[17] Cornelius Van Til,[18] and E. J. Young,[19] remain in force in the face of the hermeneutical crisis confronting the church?

Westminster Seminary Professor E. J. Young believed it could. As a keen advocate of the relevancy of the confession's teaching on Scripture, Young declared:

> We do not believe that the "facts" which the modern "scientific" study of the Bible has brought to light compel us to change or modify or abandon the historic doctrine of inspiration which finds such a

---

Rapids: Baker, 1979); Benjamin B. Warfield, *Revelation and Inspiration* (New York: Oxford University, 1927), 74. Paul D. Feinberg writes in "The Meaning of Inerrancy," "As has already been indicated, for at least a fair number of biblical and theological scholars of former days inspiration was synonymous with inerrancy. To say that the Bible is inspired was to say that it is absolutely accurate or inerrant. Two men among those who held such a view were B. B. Warfield and Charles Hodge." *Inerrancy*, 287.

16. Geerhardus Vos, the founder of Reformed biblical theology, issued a clarion call for inerrancy as a *sine qua non* in the principles of biblical theology. On May 8, 1894, Vos delivered his inaugural address as professor of biblical theology entitled, "The Idea of Biblical Theology as a Science and as a Theological Discipline." (Originally published in 1894 by Anson D. F. Randolph and Company, this essay is now in the public domain.) In this historic address, Vos elucidates the dual nature of Scripture, simultaneously underscoring the primacy of divine authorship and the indispensably human and historical nature of revelation. Vos emphasizes the critical point that the historical character of biblical truth is not in any way antithetical to, but throughout subordinated to, its *revealed* character. The historical setting of Scripture has been employed by God for the very purpose of revealing *absolute* truth. Vos also warns against historicist presuppositions, present in the critical tradition of biblical theology that Vos himself self-consciously opposed, that deny the absolute character of biblical truth as a revelation from the triune God. Vos' warning is perhaps more relevant today than in 1894.

17. John Murray, "The Attestation of Scripture," in *The Infallible Word: A Symposium by the Members of the Faculty of Westminster Theological Seminary*, ed. Ned B. Stonehouse and Paul Woolley (Phillipsburg, NJ: Presbyterian & Reformed, 1978), 6–9.

18. Cornelius Van Til, "Introduction" to Benjamin B. Warfield, in *The Inspiration and Authority of the Bible* (Philadelphia: Presbyterian & Reformed, 1948), 66–68. A change in one's doctrine of Scripture impacts one's theological apologetics, as Van Til notes in the preface to his *An Introduction to Systematic Theology*, ed. William Edgar (Phillipsburg, NJ: P&R, 2007), 12.

19. Edward J. Young, *Thy Word Is Truth: Some Thoughts on the Biblical Doctrine of Inspiration* (Grand Rapids: Eerdmans, 1957). The front cover of the ninth printing in 1976 declares, "A forthright defense of the Bible as the infallible and inerrant Word of God, with explanations of apparent contradictions, based on the evidence of the Bible itself; and a pointed refutation of some modern theories that reject a verbally inspired Bible." See also Edward J. Young, *The God-Breathed Scripture*, The Bauman Memorial Lectures for 1966 delivered at Grace Theological Seminary and College. Foreword by R. B. Gaffin Jr. (The Committee for the Historian of the Orthodox Presbyterian Church, 2007).

classic expression, for example, in the first chapter of the Westminster Confession of Faith.[20]

Similarly, Moises Silva declares that the confession's teaching on Scripture is intact even in the face of the advance of biblical studies.[21]

Harvie Conn, however, concerned for cultural contextualization in hermeneutics and the hermeneutical spiral,[22] was less sure, at least in terms of

---

20. Young, *Thy Word Is Truth*, 17.

21. "Referring again to the Westminster Confession of Faith, perhaps the most comprehensive theological statement arising from the Reformation, we may ask: Is there any chapter in that document that needs revision because we now conclude that, say, the Song of Solomon was written, not as an allegory, but as a description of human love? Is there even a paragraph that must now be excised because of advances in textual criticism or philology? The answer is a *definitive and unequivocal no*." Moises Silva, *Has the Church Misread the Bible? The History of Interpretation in the Light of Current Issues* (Grand Rapids: Zondervan, 1987), 92 (italics added).

22. Harvie M. Conn asks, "Can one believe in the Bible as the only infallible rule of faith and practice and, at the same time, affirm its culturally oriented particularity? . . . Will our current sensitivity to the New Testament as a word addressed to our century relativize our parallel commitment to it as a word addressed also to the first century?" (185). He continues, "Following the lead of Hans-Georg Gadamer, scholars associated with what has been called the New Hermeneutic have described this process of understanding as a hermeneutical circle. But the model has its problems. Evangelicals have feared that to bind text and exegete into a circle is to create a relationship of mutuality where 'what is true for me' becomes the criterion of 'what is true.' Instead, it has become more popular among evangelicals to speak of a hermeneutical spiral. Behind the idea of the spiral is the idea of progress in understanding; it is closer to the biblical image of sanctification, of growth in grace. Within the spiral, two complementary processes are taking place. As our cultural setting is matched with the text and the text with our setting, the text progressively reshapes the questions we bring to it, and in turn, our questions force us to look at the text in a fresh way" (194). He then adds, "At the same time, our participation in hermeneutics is real also. And as we have noted, that is not a neutral participation without theological, cultural, or psychological presuppositions. We cannot escape the influence of our preunderstandings in looking for meaning and significance. How, then, does my specific sociocultural and psychological background aid or distort my reading of Scripture?" (203). Berkouwer also addresses the "hermeneutical circle" in *Holy Scripture*, "This leads us to what is now commonly called the 'hermeneutical circle.' The term usually describes the relationship of the understanding of the whole of Scripture to its parts and *vice versa*. It is understandable that the circle has also been invoked in opposition to the 'pre-understanding' (i.e., the interpreter is no *tabula rasa*). The idea is that understanding though it focuses on the text, is yet not the sum total of variously understood parts, since the 'pre-understanding' cannot be eliminated. The part which subjectivity plays in the process of understanding must be recognized. In all of this the circle itself is not at stake, inasmuch as it demands attention to the particular involvement of the interpreter, who does not approach the text of Scripture with a clean slate. The critical question in regard to this is whether or not the 'encounter,' the positing of the *a priori* of the text over against all of the interpreter's baggage and presuppositions, is completely recognized. Only then does the circle avoid being a necessarily vicious one. Only when the aim is a correlation between kerygma and existence, in which existence itself, despite every accent on the text, is made the final 'canon' for

287

the use of the confession. Thus Conn specified the dangers of "gnosticizing" culture and "remythologizing" the confession. [23] He expressed his worries over "the evangelical's perception of theology as some sort of comprehensively universal science . . . the Queen of the sciences, the watchdog of the academic world, the ultimate universal Confessional theology." He believed that "our creedal formulations, structured to respond to a sixteenth-century cultural setting and its problems," would "lose their historical character as contextual confessions of faith and become cultural universals, having comprehensive validity in all times and settings." What was the resulting danger in Conn's mind for this view of the Westminster Confession? He explains: "The possibility of new doctrinal developments for the Reformed churches" would be " . . . frozen into a time warp that gnosticizes the particularity of time and culture." The cure for these dangers was the "contextualization" of the creeds and the recognition of "how we have diminished their historical, contextual character." [24]

The Reformed confessions, to be sure, have a historical context. Consequently it can be claimed, as Conn implies, that the Reformed confessions

---

its understanding, will such a peculiarly vicious circle be created." "Normativity, Relevance, and Relativism," in *Inerrancy and Hermeneutic: A Tradition, a Challenge, a Debate*, ed. Harvie M. Conn (Grand Rapids: Baker, 1988), 185–209.

23. In his inaugural address as professor of missiology at Westminster, Harvey Conn, for example, expresses his concern of a perceived "gnosticizing" of culture that impedes missiological and doctrinal advances: "Related to this struggle is the evangelical's perception of theology as some sort of comprehensively universal science. Theology becomes functionally the Queen of the sciences, the watchdog of the academic world, the ultimate universal. Combined with Western ethnocentrism, it produces the tacit assumption 'that the Christian faith is already fully and properly indigenized in the West.' Our creedal formulations, structured to respond to a sixteenth-century cultural setting and its problems, lose their historical character as contextual confessions of faith and become cultural universals, having comprehensive validity in all times and settings. The possibility of new doctrinal developments for the Reformed churches of Japan or Mexico is frozen into a time warp that Gnosticizes the particularity of time and culture. The Reformation is completed and we in the West wait for the churches of the Third World to accept as their statements of faith those shaped by a Western church three centuries before in a *corpus christianum*. In all this, there is no desire to diminish the place of the creed as the expression of the progressive understanding of truth conveyed by the Holy Spirit. Nor do we want to minimize or question the system of doctrine found in the Reformed creeds of these centuries. Our concern is over how we have diminished their historical, contextual character. The creed as a missionary document framed in the uniqueness of an historical moment has too often been remythologized by white paternalism into a universal essence for all times. Contextualization, as a missionary demand of theologizing, is relegated to the non-Western 'mission field.'" *WTJ* 45 (1983), 16–17.

24. Ibid.

are time bound, because they were primarily aiming at Roman Catholic/anti-Protestant apologetics. Yet it is important also to keep in mind what Turretin[25] recognized: "in every age the enemies of true religion and of Scripture have thought that they had found contradictory passages in Scripture. . . . various libertines, who, although living in the bosom of the church, never stop calling attention to some 'irreconcilable differences' and 'contradictions,' so as to erode the authority of Scripture."[26] This latter group extends far beyond the compass of Roman Catholic theology.

Under Conn's lead, a faculty symposium was published addressing the interplay between inerrancy and hermeneutics,[27] reflecting a breadth of opinions within Westminster's confessional tradition.[28] The essays in general,

25. Critics of inerrancy see philosophical motivations rather than biblical concerns at work in Turretin's development of his doctrine of Scripture. Jack B. Rogers and Donald K. McKim claim, "Falling back on the philosophy of Aristotle and the theological categories of Thomas Aquinas, Turretin produced a scholastic theology that placed great emphasis on precise definition and systematic, scientific statement." *Authority and Interpretation*, 235.

26. Turretin writes, "When the divine quality of Scripture, which was argued in the preceding question, has been accepted, its infallibility follows of necessity. But in every age the enemies of true religion and of Scripture have thought that they had found contradictory passages in Scripture, and have vigorously presented them in order to overthrow its authority; for example, Porphyry, Lucian, and Julian the Apostate among the pagans of antiquity, and today various atheists, who in hostile fashion declare that there are contradictions and irreconcilable differences which cannot be harmonized in any way. Therefore this particular question must be discussed with them, so that the integrity of Scripture may be upheld against their impiety by a completed fabric and covering. Our controversy is not with open atheists and pagans, who do not recognize Holy Scripture, but with others who although they seem to accept it, yet indirectly deny it in this manner; for example, the enthusiasts, who allege the imperfection of the written word in order to attract people to their esoteric word or special revelations . . . and finally, various libertines, who, although living in the bosom of the church, never stop calling attention to some 'irreconcilable differences' and 'contradictions,' so as to erode the authority of Scripture." *The Doctrine of Scripture*, ed. and trans. John W. Beardslee III (Grand Rapids: Baker, 1981), 57–58.

27. Conn's introductory article is "A Historical Prologue: Inerrancy, Hermeneutic, and Westminster," which surveys the development of the views of Scripture held by Westminster Seminary's faculty. He concludes on page 34, "The chapters in this volume are, as stated in the preface, only bridge building in intention. They attempt to sketch the agenda changes over four decades. They are catch-up exercises for the evangelical, concerned with affirming the reliability of our fundamental commitment to the inerrant Word of God in the face of new questions. The problems shift and move; the Word of our God abides forever."

28. Silva writes, "The hermeneutical flexibility that has characterized our tradition would probably come as a surprise to many observers who view Westminster as excessively rigid. Ironically, our Confessional documents, the Westminster Confession and Catechisms, are far more extensive and detailed than those found in most evangelical institutions. Our theological parameters are indeed very clearly defined, and yet those parameters themselves have made possible a diversity of viewpoints that would not have been tolerated in some other institutions." Moises Silva, "Old Princeton, Westminster, and Inerrancy," in *Inerrancy and Hermeneutic*, 78.

however, made minimal explicit reference to the confession's implications for the task of hermeneutics.[29]

More recently, Professor Peter Enns, professor of Old Testament and hermeneutics at Westminster Theological Seminary,[30] has published a hermeneutical study that repeatedly calls for a reconsideration of the evangelical doctrine of Scripture.[31] Enns seeks a "Reassessment of doctrine on the basis of

29. In the fourteen essays presented in *Inerrancy and Hermeneutic* edited by Harvie Conn, there are only eight references to the Westminster Standards. Two are general references to the Westminster Confession. Five are specific citations of the confession, one is a reference to the first question of the Shorter Catechism, and none refers to the Larger Catechism. The five specific citations of the confession are all to the first chapter, namely 1.2–3, 4, 5, 7, 8. The salient point is that there is no citation of 1.9 of the confession, the central text that directly links infallibility and hermeneutics! This relevant passage defines "the only infallible rule of interpretation of Scripture." And specifically, Professor Conn's extensive citations of literature in his two articles in *Inerrancy and Hermeneutic* do not include any citation of the Westminster Standards. Ironically, *Inerrancy and Hermeneutic* references Bultmann eight times.

30. Enns once references Westminster Seminary but does not refer to the Westminster Standards: "Also influential has been my own theological tradition, represented by my colleagues at Westminster Theological Seminary, past and present, and the wider tradition of which that institution is a part. This is not to imply that I speak for that institution or tradition. Nevertheless, I am thankful for being part of such a solidly faithful group, that does not shy away from some difficult yet basic questions and with whom I am able to have frank and open discussions." *Inspiration and Incarnation*, 9.

31. Enns emphasizes this point: "My focus . . . to look at these data (data that biblical scholars work with every day) with a clear view toward discussing their *implications for an evangelical doctrine of Scripture*" (9, emphasis added). He indicates that, "The purpose of this book is to bring *an evangelical doctrine of Scripture* into conversation with the implications generated by some important themes in modern biblical scholarship—particularly Old Testament scholarship—over the past 150 years. To put it this way is to suggest that such a conversation has not taken place, at least not to the degree that it could have" (13, emphasis added). He explains, "In my view, however, what is needed is not simply for evangelicals to work in these areas, but to engage *the doctrinal implications* that work in these areas raises. Without wanting to overstate the matter, I know or hear of a fair number of Christians who conclude that the contemporary state of biblical scholarship makes an evangelical faith unviable. These are the primary readers I envision for this book, those who desire to maintain a vibrant and reverent doctrine of Scripture, but who find it difficult to do so because they find familiar and conventional approaches to newer problems to be unhelpful" (13, emphasis added). Elaborating, he says, "On the one hand, I am very eager to affirm that many evangelical instincts are correct and should be maintained, for example, the conviction that the Bible is ultimately from God and that it is God's gift to the church. Any theories concerning Scripture that do not arise from these fundamental instincts are unacceptable. On the other hand, *how the evangelical church fleshes out its doctrine of Scripture* will always have somewhat of a provisional quality to it. This is not to say that each generation must disregard the past and start afresh, formulating ever-new doctrines, bowing to all the latest fads. But it is to say that at such time when new evidence comes to light, or old evidence is seen in a new light, we must be willing to *engage that evidence and adjust our doctrine accordingly*" (13–14, emphasis added). Then he boldly asserts that, "*Reassessment of doctrine on*

external evidence.... My concern is that, at least on a popular level, a defensive approach to the evidence tends to dominate the evangelical conversation."[32]

This appears to be a significant step beyond the perspective of Professor Conn. Conn concluded his essay, " . . . in the face of new questions. The problems shift and move; the Word of our God abides forever."[33] But Professor Enns begins his study by connecting "the problems" directly with the Bible, with the Old Testament, as seen in his provocative title: *Inspiration and Incarnation: Evangelicals and the Problem of the Old Testament.*

For Enns, the external evidence about the Bible that has accumulated since the 1800s requires a new synthesis of doctrine and data. He writes:

> My aim is somewhat more foundational . . . . I want to contribute to a growing opinion that what is needed is to move beyond both sides [i.e., liberal v. conservative] by thinking of better ways to account for some of

---

the basis of external evidence, therefore is nothing new. To state it differently, our topic is the age-old question of the relationship between special revelation (the Bible) and general revelation (creation, i.e., everything else). My concern is that, at least on a popular level, a defensive approach to the evidence tends to dominate the evangelical conversation. . . . the terms are familiar, liberal v. conservative, modernist v. fundamentalist, mainline v. evangelical, progressive v. traditionalist.... My aim is somewhat more foundational . . . I want to contribute to a growing opinion that what is needed is to move beyond both sides by thinking of better ways to account for some of the data, while at the same time having a vibrant, positive view of Scripture as God's word. . . . To put it another way, *my aim is to allow the collective evidence to affect not just how we understand a biblical passage or story here and there within the parameters of earlier doctrinal formulations. Rather, I want to move beyond that by allowing the evidence to affect how we think about what Scripture as a whole is*" (14–15, emphasis added). He then reasons that, "The end result, I truly hope, will be to *provide a theological paradigm* for people who know instinctively that the Bible is God's word, but for whom reading the Bible has already become a serious theological problem—perhaps even a crisis" (15, emphasis added). Fleshing out his argument, he says, "Regardless of how we organize the data, the issue before us is not how we handle this verse or this issue, one at a time. Rather, what needs to happen is that we take a step back from the details and allow these issues to challenge us on a more fundamental level. What is needed is a way of thinking about Scripture where these kinds of issues are addressed from a very different perspective—where these kinds of problems cease being problems. . . . It is not enough simply to say that the Bible is the word of God or that it is inspired or to apply some other label. The issue is how these descriptions of the Bible bear fruit when we touch down in one part of the Bible or another. How does the study of Scripture in the contemporary world affect *how we flesh out descriptions such as 'word of God' or 'inspired'?*" (16–17, emphasis added). The result is that, "The *doctrinal implications* of these discoveries have not yet been fully worked out in evangelical theology" (25, emphasis added). According to Enns, this means that "the *doctrinal implications* of the Bible being so much a part of its ancient contexts are still not being addressed as much as they should" (47, emphasis added).

32. Enns, *Inspiration and Incarnation*, 14.

33. Conn, "A Historical Prologue: Inerrancy, Hermeneutic, and Westminster," 34.

the data, while at the same time having a vibrant, positive view of Scripture as God's word. . . . To put it another way, my aim is to allow the collective evidence to affect not just how we understand a biblical passage or story here and there within the parameters of earlier doctrinal formulations. Rather, I want to move beyond that by allowing the evidence to affect how we think about what Scripture as a whole *is*. . . .

But to those who struggle to synthesize their own doctrinal commitments with what we have learned about the Bible over the past 150 years, these ways of handling the evidence can be both frustrating and even debilitating. . . .

The findings of the past 150 years have made extrabiblical evidence an unavoidable conversation partner. The result is that, as perhaps never before in the history of the church, we can see how truly provisional and incomplete certain dimensions of our understanding of Scripture can be. On the other hand, we are encouraged to encounter the depth and riches of God's revelation and to rely more and more on God's Spirit, who speaks to the church in Scripture.[34]

There is indeed a hermeneutical crisis, one whose magnitude, if we accept Peter Enns's phrase, is monumental in proportion: "perhaps never before in the history of the church."[35] Given that such is the case, even after

---

34. Enns, *Inspiration and Incarnation*, 14–15, 48, 49, respectively.

35. There is some confusion as to the audience that Enns is addressing: the troubled evangelical or the historic evangelical. D. A. Carson (at the online e-zine *Reformation 21*, May 2006), writes, "Who are the intended readers? The answer to that question, in the case of this book, must be an integral part of the evaluation. Enns himself, it must be recalled, states that his envisaged readers are the 'fair number of Christians who conclude that the contemporary state of biblical scholarship makes an evangelical faith unviable' (13). In other words, granted the historical/literary/archaeological/historical difficulties cast up by 'biblical scholarship,' how can 'evangelical faith'—presumably what evangelical faith says about the Bible—be viable? Taking this at face value, the difficulties should be the 'given' in the minds of the envisaged readers, and the book would then either challenge some of those 'difficulties' in order to maintain evangelicalism's stance on the Bible, or it would accommodate the difficulties and provide a more sophisticated understanding of 'evangelical faith,' or perhaps a revision of it. Yet in the three substantive chapters, most of the space is devoted instead to convincing the reader that the difficulties Enns isolates are real, and must be taken more seriously by evangelicals than is usually the case. In other words, despite his initial claim that he is writing the book to comfort the disturbed, as it were, the actual performance aims to disturb the comfortable. This makes the book rather difficult to evaluate. Moreover, Enns's ambitions are vaulting: the evidence cast up by biblical scholarship, we are told, is of the sort that requires that an 'adjustment' be made in how we think of Scripture, akin to the re-interpretation generated by the Copernican revolution (13). Wow. So are we explaining how evangelical faith accommodates biblical scholarship, or are we asserting that a Copernican revolution must take place within evangelical faith so as to

the hyperbole is taken into account, it seems appropriate to borrow Harvie Conn's language and embellish his desire "to sketch the agenda changes over four decades."[36] To do so, let us contrast two OT faculty members of Westminster, namely, E. J. Young and Peter Enns. By doing so, the changed OT hermeneutical agenda fueling this crisis and impacting the historic confessional view of Scripture and hermeneutic taught at Westminster will thereby come into sharper relief.

Reflecting, then, on the same "data" and "extrabiblical evidence" impacting OT scholars and their doctrine of Scripture referenced by Enns, Young, earlier Westminster professor of OT, wrote:

> In the face of this constant demand for a new doctrine of inspiration, what attitude is the Christian man to adopt? . . . Have the findings of "scientific" biblical study actually demonstrated the untenability of the traditional attitude toward inspiration? There are some evangelical Christians who apparently think that such is the case.[37]

> When we have once grasped the idea that we must derive our doctrine of inspiration from the Bible, we may begin to understand what the real issue before the Church is. The real issue is not whether we are to substitute one doctrine of inspiration for another. That is at the most a somewhat secondary question. The real issue before the Church today, and for that matter before every individual Christian, is whether the Bible is any longer to be regarded and accepted as a trustworthy teacher of doctrine. In other words, when the Bible testifies as to its own nature, are we to pay heed to what it has to say?[38]

> The Bible, therefore, whether we will or not, is constantly being thrust into the forefront of discussion and one can only be amazed, to say nothing of being saddened, at the glibness with which many speak of the old-fashioned view of inspiration as being out of date and not relevant for the present age.[39]

---

accommodate biblical scholarship?" D. A. Carson, "Three Books on the Bible: A Critical Review" [accessed January 8, 2008]. Online: http://www.reformation21.org/Past_Issues/2006_Issues_1_ 16_/2006_Issues_1_16_Shelf_LIfe/May_2006/May_2006/181/vobId__2926/.

36. Conn, "A Historical Prologue: Inerrancy, Hermeneutic, and Westminster," 34.
37. E. J. Young, *Thy Word Is Truth*, 16.
38. Ibid., 28.
39. Ibid., 15.

> To understand the present demand for a new doctrine of inspiration and a new attitude toward the Bible one must know something about the background and soil from which much of our modern religious life and thought has sprung. ... [40]

Clearly, the hermeneutical crisis is real and has impacted Westminster Seminary. There are two theologies of Scripture wrestling in the faculty room. The question before us, to use an OT image, is whether the elder theology shall serve the younger. In answering this, the role of the Westminster Standards and the faculty vow to those standards take on high importance.

THE HERMENEUTICAL CRISIS AND THE HISTORIC PRESBYTERIAN SUB-SCRIPTION TO THE CONFESSION

The importance of the question of the relationship between the confession and biblical studies is especially important in the context of biblically oriented Presbyterian churches in general and Westminster Theological Seminary in particular. This is because subscription to these standards is required. The subscription made by ordained Presbyterian officers in the Orthodox Presbyterian Church (OPC) and in the Presbyterian Church in America (PCA) is well known.[41] Perhaps less well known, the faculty and board of Westminster Theological Seminary make an extensive and even more explicit *ex animo* commitment to the Westminster Standards.[42]

---

40. Ibid.

41. See, *Book of Church Order*, OPC, 23.8, "(2) Do you sincerely receive and adopt the Confession of Faith and Catechisms of this Church, as containing the system of doctrine taught in the Holy Scriptures?"; *Book of Church Order*, PCA, 21–25, "2. Do you sincerely receive and adopt the *Confession of Faith* and the *Catechisms* of this Church, as containing the system of doctrine taught in the Holy Scriptures; and do you further promise that if at any time you find yourself out of accord with any of the fundamentals of this system of doctrine, you will on your own initiative, make known to your Presbytery the change which has taken place in your views since the assumption of this ordination vow?"

42. Westminster Theological Seminary's constitution prescribes the following pledge for every voting member of the faculty: "I do solemnly declare, in the presence of God, and of the Trustees and Faculty of this Seminary, that (1) I believe the Scriptures of the Old and New Testaments to be the Word of God, the only infallible rule of faith and practice; and (2) I do solemnly and *ex animo* adopt, receive, and subscribe to the Westminster Confession of Faith and Catechisms in the form in which they were adopted by this Seminary in the year of our Lord 1936, as the confession of my faith, or as a summary and just exhibition of that system of doctrine and religious belief, which is contained in Holy Scripture, and therein revealed by God to man for his salvation; and I do solemnly, *ex animo*, profess to receive the fundamental principles of the

Alongside this confessional subscription, OPC and PCA officers as well as Westminster faculty and trustees have also specifically subscribed to the infallibility of the Scriptures. The language of the seminary's subscription is identical to that of the OPC and nearly so to the PCA. The only difference of the OPC and Westminster subscriptions from that of the PCA is that the PCA's text adds a phrase indicating commitment to the inerrancy of the *autographa*:

> Westminster: I believe the Scriptures of the Old and New Testaments to be the Word of God, the only infallible rule of faith and practice. (See note 43.)

> OPC: Do you believe the Scriptures of the Old and New Testaments to be the Word of God, the only infallible rule of faith and practice? (Book of Church Order, OPC, 23.8, [1].)

> PCA: Do you believe the Scriptures of the Old and New Testaments, as originally given, to be the inerrant Word of God, the only infallible rule of faith and practice? (Book of Church Order, PCA, 21–5, 1.)

Clearly, the historic Presbyterian commitment to the authority of the Westminster Standards and to the infallibility of the Scriptures has been maintained by Westminster Seminary, the OPC, and the PCA as evidenced by these explicit vows.[43]

Presbyterian form of church government, as agreeable to the inspired oracles. And I do solemnly promise and engage not to inculcate, teach, or insinuate anything which shall appear to me to contradict or contravene, either directly or impliedly, any element in that system of doctrine, nor to oppose any of the fundamental principles of that form of church government, while I continue a member of the Faculty in this Seminary. I do further solemnly declare that, being convinced of my sin and misery and of my inability to rescue myself from my lost condition, not only have I assented to the truth of the promises of the Gospel, but also I have received and rest upon Christ and His righteousness for pardon of my sin and for my acceptance as righteous in the sight of God and I do further promise that if at any time I find myself out of accord with any of the fundamentals of this system of doctrine, I will on my own initiative, make known to the Faculty of this institution and, where applicable, my judicatory, the change which has taken place in my views since the assumption of the vow."

43. Cf. Peter A. Lillback, "Confessional Subscription among the Sixteenth Century Reformers," in *The Practice of Confessional Subscription*, ed. David W. Hall (Lanham, MD: University Press of America, 1995), 33–66. In regard to the nature of the authority of the Protestant confessions, Schaff writes,

"The value of creeds depends upon the measure of their agreement with the Scriptures. In the best case a human creed is only an approximate and relatively correct exposition of revealed truth, and may be improved by the progressive knowledge of the Church, while the Bible remains perfect

Given the criticisms of the primacy afforded to the Westminster Standards, both from without and from within the Westminster tradition,[44] a significant question arises concerning the Westminster Standards' impact on the interpretation of the "infallible" Scriptures. In light of the hermeneutical crisis, the question to be considered here is: what are the hermeneutical

---

and infallible. The Bible is of God; the Confession is man's answer to God's word. The Bible is the *norma normans*; the Confession the *norma normata*. The Bible is the rule of faith (*regula fidei*); the Confession the rule of doctrine (*regula doctrina*). The Bible has, therefore a divine and absolute, the Confession only an ecclesiastical and relative authority. The Bible regulates the general religious belief and practice of the laity as well as the clergy; the symbols regulate the public teaching of the officers of the Church, as Constitutions and Canons regulate the government, Liturgies and Hymn-books the worship of the Church. Any higher view of the authority of symbols is unprotestant and essentially Romanizing. Symbololatry is a species of idolatry, and substitutes the tyranny of a printed book for that of a living pope. It is apt to produce the opposite extreme of a rejection of all creeds, and to promote rationalism and infidelity." *The Creeds of Christendom*, 1:7–8.

But if the Westminster Standards are a norm that is normed by Scripture, to what *extent* can they be considered authoritative? Are they to be subscribed because *(quia)* they are scriptural or are they to be subscribed as far as *(quatenus)* they are scriptural? Klotsche explains,

"To decide this question we must remember that the object of a confession is, not to find out what God teaches, for this we find in the Scriptures, but to show what we believe. A quatenus-subscription is no real confession, but an evasion and leaves it to a person's subjective judgment what to accept and what to reject. The church must ask for a quia-subscription, for she must know where her ministers and teachers stand. A confession of faith is to the church what a constitution is to a society, and no one has a right to enter or remain in any Christian church except as its terms of membership give him that right.

"Not only the heretical sects connected with Protestantism but also the liberal theologians of the church have raised an outcry against the authority of symbols as inconsistent with 'the right of private judgment.' They style the church's attitude in respect to symbols 'symbololatry,' worship of symbols, and see in the symbols only a yoke of human authority, a new popery in the form of printed documents. Making all due allowance for the prejudice which many of the opponents of the church's confessions have displayed, and for their ignorance which lies behind most of their comments on the subject, nevertheless, we cannot in the least support such a tirade against the symbols of the church, for the church does not *compel* anyone to accept her doctrines. A candidate for the ministry offers himself to the church for service, and his offer is accepted by the church on the ground that he is one with her in faith. If he cannot subscribe to the confessions of his church, he should not seek her ministerial office; or if, as a minister of the church, he has abandoned the faith of his church, he will, if he is at all sincere, leave that church and join another with which he is one in faith." E. H. Klotsche, *Christian Symbolics or Exposition of the Distinctive Characteristics of the Catholic, Lutheran and Reformed Churches as well as the Modern Denominations and Sects Represented in this Country* (Burlington, IO: The Lutheran Literary Board, 1929), 15–16.

Thus the Protestant confessional tradition simultaneously recognizes the subordinate character of its standards with respect to the Scriptures and the superiority of its standards with respect to the qualifications of its ministers and officers.

44. Harvie M. Conn, as noted above, expresses his concern for a "gnosticizing" of culture as well as a fear of a "remythologized" confession. *WTJ* 45 (1983), 16–17. In this context consider Berkouwer's criticisms of Edmund Clowney's critique of the United Presbyterian Church's proposed confession in *Holy Scripture*, 163–65.

parameters the Westminster Standards establish for the interpreters of Holy Scripture who have subscribed to these standards?

THE REGULATIVE PRINCIPLE OF HERMENEUTICS: THE WESTMINSTER STANDARDS' PARAMETERS AND "INFALLIBLE" HERMENEUTICAL PRINCIPLE

Moises Silva, writing at the time as a professor of New Testament at Westminster, notes that there are significant theological parameters established by the Westminster Standards that are vital for hermeneutics:

> The hermeneutical flexibility that has characterized our tradition would probably come as a surprise to many observers who view Westminster as excessively rigid. Ironically, our Confessional documents, the Westminster Confession and Catechisms, are far more extensive and detailed than those found in most evangelical institutions. Our theological parameters are indeed very clearly defined, and yet those parameters themselves have made possible a diversity of viewpoints that would not have been tolerated in some other institutions.[45]

Westminster's discussion of the doctrine of Scripture under the lead of Richard B. Gaffin Jr. has identified deeply with the Reformed tradition reflected by Abraham Kuyper and Herman Bavinck,[46] and

45. Moises Silva, "Old Princeton," 78. Berkouwer affirms the inescapable connection of theology and hermeneutic, *Holy Scripture*, 106, "The fact that hermeneutics is continually busy with rules for the exposition of Scripture shows a desire to oppose the arbitrariness which, despite the recognition of Scripture as God's Word, neglects its concrete authority. It is impossible for any theological study to bypass these questions. For in every hermeneutical question lies an aspect which is intrinsically tied to the confession of scriptural authority." See also Silva, *Has the Church Misread the Bible?* 38, "The first item listed above—the Bible as both divine and human—constitutes the most basic question of all. Strictly speaking, it is not so much a hermeneutical question as it is one of theology, even though, as we shall see in the course of our discussions, one can hardly divorce doctrine from interpretation."

46. See for example, "Old Amsterdam—I," where the point emerges that "the biblical records are impressionistic; that is, they are not marked by notarial precision or blue-print, architectural exactness.... This understanding of 'impressionistic' is echoed at a number of places elsewhere in Kuyper's writings.... Whoever in reading Scripture thinks that everything was spoken precisely as it stands in the text, is 'totally mistaken.' Again, he points to the differences between the four Gospels and the NT use of the OT as sufficient to show that as a rule the *lalia* of God has not come to us 'in its original form ....' In typical fashion, Kuyper illustrates his point by recalling an aspect of modern European parliamentary practice. Both the French and English parliaments keep two kinds of records; one is

has thereby avoided the conundrums created by the theology of fundamentalism.[47]

---

a verbatim account of what a speaker says (a 'proces-verbal'), the other a brief resume or summary account (a 'proces-analytique').... It would be a mistake, Kuyper continues, to suppose that the verbatim report is better or more desirable.... In a similar vein, we ought not to think that the speeches in Job are given precisely as Bildad spoke them. Rather they provide a 'romantic representation' or 'free rendering' of what was said. But because this happens 'under guarantee of the Holy Spirit,' they express what was said 'not only not inaccurately [onjuist], but more accurately [juister] and, besides that, more elegantly.... On the one hand, the biblical narratives do not record the past with stenographic preciseness or photographic exactness. Yet as historical records they are completely accurate and do not at all mislead.... The distinguishing mark of inspiration, however, above everything else is that it guarantees absolute accuracy [absolute juistheid]. The singular character of the writers of the Old and New Testaments lies in the fact that the stamp of truth and certainty is impressed upon their writings. The Holy Spirit so leads their spirit that in them the results of sin are cut off and prevented. This distinguishing mark is not relative, but absolute. . . . Biblical narrative is absolutely accurate without being notarially exact...." (278–79).

47. Cf. Berkouwer, who says in *Holy Scripture*, "It is true that fundamentalists do not deny the human element in Scripture, but they allow their apologetics to be determined by the fear that emphasis on the human witness may threaten and overshadow Scripture's divinity" (24). "Fundamentalists allowed themselves, however, to be guided by the 'wholly divine or wholly human' dilemma, and thus they allowed the camp they opposed to force a problem on them" (25). "Bavinck points to the self-witness of Scripture, which is unalterable, and he acknowledges moreover that the examination of Scripture in recent years comes up with 'phenomena and facts that can hardly be reconciled with this self-witness.' The difference between fundamentalism and Bavinck is not that his confession regarding Scripture is less positive than fundamentalism's, but that he gives much more attention to the manner in which Scripture came to us as *human* witness. Because of the divine nature of Scripture, the human witness does not become less important to Bavinck; rather, it receives special significance. This does not result from a relativizing of Scripture, but from his great respect for the manner of revelation that itself compels us to reflect on the nature of Scripture's authority" (26). "Bavinck did not capitulate in any way to the criticism of Scripture of his day. Instead, he analyzed this criticism and arrived at the conclusion that the critics had totally lost sight of the purpose of Holy Scripture.... he calls attention to what the *intent*—the specific and emphatic objective—of Scripture is. The important thing to notice is that Bavinck's rejection of biblical criticism takes the form of a positive contribution to the understanding of the nature of Scripture. It goes without saying that here many new questions could be raised. For example, what exactly is this 'goal' (*scopus*) of Scripture?" But Gaffin rightly points out that Berkouwer is not a completely faithful expositor of Kuyper and Bavinck. In "Old Amsterdam—I," 279–80, he observes, "Accordingly, when Kuyper speaks of the possibility of 'innocent inaccuracies' in historical records (*Principles*, 457), this expression ought not simply to be lifted out of context and enlisted without further qualification against efforts at harmonization, as Berkouwer does. If we are not to distort Kuyper's meaning, we must not fail to note the specific terms of the contrast that serves to define these 'innocent inaccuracies': they 'so far from doing harm, rather bring to light the free expression of life above notarial affectation.' " "Perhaps the deepest perspective on the sense of the quotation under examination in this section is provided by reflecting further on the distinction, already noted, between divine and human errorlessness.... What is the difference, Kuyper asks, between 'divinely errorless' and 'humanly errorless'? ... Divine errorlessness, in contrast, is like the work of a painter.... In summary, divine errorlessness, like art, gives the essence without error, but without maintaining precisely the same form.... The errorlessness of Scripture, then, is divine, not human."

Nevertheless, the question before us in Silva's words is whether the "diversity of viewpoints that . . . have been tolerated" and "made possible" at Westminster by these "theological parameters" have begun to erode or even breach the parameters that sheltered and enabled them in the first place?

In this context, it appears significant that Enns's expressed desire is to "move beyond" the "parameters of earlier doctrinal formulations."

> . . . my aim is to allow the collective evidence to affect not just how we understand a biblical passage or story here and there within the parameters of earlier doctrinal formulations. Rather, I want to move beyond that by allowing the evidence to affect how we think about what Scripture as a whole *is*.
>
> The end result, I truly hope, will be to provide a theological paradigm for people who know instinctively that the Bible is God's word, but for whom reading the Bible has already become a serious theological problem—perhaps even a crisis.[48]

What then are the confession's theological parameters and presuppositions concerning Scripture? Are there confessional hermeneutical parameters and principles for interpreting Scripture? Young believed that these existed and identified them when he placed the entire first chapter of the Westminster Confession as an appendix to his defense of inerrancy,[49] while Enns leaves his understanding of what is intended by the "parameters of earlier doctrinal formulations" vague and undefined.[50]

---

48. Enns, *Inspiration and Incarnation*, 14–15.

49. Young, *Thy Word Is Truth*, 277–80.

50. The closest statement of theological disclosure that Enns provides is: "Also influential has been my own theological tradition, represented by my colleagues at Westminster Theological Seminary, past and present, and the wider tradition of which that institution is a part. This is not to imply that I speak for that institution or tradition" (*Inspiration and Incarnation*, 9). The lack of theological clarity in Enns's theological position has been expressed by the *OPC Mid-Atlantic Presbytery's Report*: "This general neglect of any detailed interaction with the classical Reformed treatments of Inspiration is notable. He seems to embrace Warfield's concept of concursus but does not tell us how he differs from Warfield. He is able to simultaneously place Warfield and J. Patterson Smyth in his 'Further Reading' section (*Inspiration*, 22) seeming to commend Smyth for 'honesty and spiritual sensitivity.' Yet Warfield was not so favorable to Smyth's work. While reviewing it along with two other works (*Presbyterian and Reformed Review* 5, 1894), Warfield states: 'These are therefore three very instructive little books. They exhibit to us the working of the new leaven in its mildest form; and advertise to us what is the least change in our attitude towards the Bible which will satisfy the most moderate adherents of the new views. As such, they are not reassuring. It becomes evident at once not only that an entire revolution in the doctrine

Although not directly addressed in *Inerrancy and Hermeneutic* nor by Enns in *Inspiration and Incarnation*, it is evident that the confession in chapter one, "Of the Holy Scripture," establishes an overarching hermeneutical parameter or hermeneutic principle when it declares:

> The infallible rule of interpretation of Scripture is the Scripture itself: and therefore, when there is a question about the true and full sense of any Scripture (which is not manifold, but one), it must be searched and known by other places that speak more clearly. (WCF 1.9)

Thus the principle of Scripture interpreting Scripture is declared to be of foundational importance. The confession's mandate for this hermeneutical method is patent and principial: it is an "*infallible* rule of interpretation." Further, it is sweeping in its impact since it relates to the "true and full sense of *any* Scripture." In fact, this interpretive method is not optional, but obligatory, since the meaning of any Scripture "*must* be searched and known." The *canonical* self-interpreting character of this scriptural hermeneutic is captured in the words, "by *other places* that speak more clearly."[51] Finally, all of these words substantiate what is intended by the word *rule*—a *rule* is to be observed.

---

of sacred Scripture incorporated in our creeds, and held indeed by the whole Christian past, will be required of us (which is a comparatively small matter); but also that on the new ground we can no longer occupy the same attitude towards Scripture that our Lord and His apostles occupied. The attempts of these books being taken as samples, it becomes equally evident also that no consistent doctrine of inspiration, conservative of the detailed divine authority of the Scriptures, can be framed on the basis of the new views.'"

If we are to open a new trajectory in our understanding of inspiration, it would at least be helpful to gain some sense of where and why the boundaries suggested by Warfield—or perhaps better yet Bavinck—are not adequate. If Enns is not saying anything that Bavinck has not said, he should acknowledge his debt. If he is saying something new, he should step forward and show the Reformed community—not just broad evangelicals—where they need further reformation.

51. Cf. Turretin: "It is not a question of whether matters necessary for salvation are presented clearly everywhere in Scripture. Indeed we grant that there are many passages that are difficult to understand, by which God wills to exercise our effort and the skill of the scholar. The question is whether these necessary matters are presented somewhere in such a manner that a believer can recognize their truth when he has given them serious consideration, because nothing is learned from the more obscure passages that is not found most plainly taught elsewhere. As Augustine says, 'the Holy Spirit has arranged the Scriptures in such a wonderful and wholesome manner, that hunger is remedied by the plainer passages and pride by the more obscure . . . ,' and, 'We feed on the clear passages, and are disciplined by the obscure; in the one our appetite is overcome, in the other our pride.'" *Doctrine of Scripture*, 187.

As Larger Catechism question 99 says, "For the right understanding . . . these rules are to be observed. . . ." Hence, the confession's hermeneutical principle is given an importance that cannot be ignored or diminished if the Scripture's authority as the "only infallible rule of faith and practice" is consciously recognized with the seriousness that an *ex animo* subscription requires. This confessional rule for the interpretation of Scripture might well be denominated, *the regulative principle of hermeneutics.*

The historic understanding of this principle of comparing Scripture with Scripture is enunciated by Turretin:

> Comparison matches one passage of Scripture to another (Acts 9:22), by comparing the more obscure with the more understandable, similar or parallel ones with those like them, and the dissimilar with the dissimilar. The analogy of the faith (Rom. 12:6) means not only a measuring standard for the faith, or a measure given to each of the believers, but also the constant harmony or agreement of all the articles of faith in the most glorious words of the revealed Scripture, to which all expositions must conform, lest anything be taught contrary to the articles of faith or the commandments of the Decalogue.[52]

Turretin reasons that this method is required since we must recognize that God possesses the authority to interpret His own words.

> Just as a ruler is the interpreter of his own law, so also God is the interpreter of his own Scripture, which is the law of faith and conduct. And the privilege which is proper for other writers that each one is the interpreter of his own words, should not be denied to God when he speaks in Scripture.[53]

Westminster NT professor Vern Poythress well illustrates this principle:

> At a fundamental level, there is no such thing as a passage in and of itself. John 2:16 is part of the Bible, and God intends that we read it and understand it in relation to all the other parts of the Bible. When he caused these words to be written in the Gospel of John, he already intended that

52. Ibid., 207.
53. Ibid., 215.

they should be seen as we are seeing them, namely, in connection with other passages that together unfold the purpose of God.[54]

Moreover, this is the teaching of the confession in 1.5, where it speaks of "the consent of all the parts" that "doth abundantly evidence itself to be the Word of God."

Sola Scriptura: Scripture, Science, and the "Infallible Rule of Interpretation"

In the midst of the hermeneutical crisis, the importance of the reformational principle of *Sacra Scriptura sui ipsius interpres* (Sacred Scripture is its own interpreter) must again be affirmed. For what is at stake is nothing less than the Reformation's commitment to *sola Scriptura*. As Berkouwer explains, the principle of Scripture interpreting Scripture is the logical outgrowth of a full and deep commitment to *sola Scriptura*. Berkouwer, who also is concerned not to miss the human dimension of Scripture, underscores this point.

> Nowhere was the relationship between authority and interpretation so clearly expressed as in the Reformation confession of Scripture, which, based on *sola Scriptura*, offered a perspective on the real relationship between authority and interpretation, and expressed it in its hermeneutical rule: *Sacra Scriptura sui ipsius interpres* (Sacred Scripture is its own interpreter).[55]

The principle might appear to be primarily an apologetic for the Reformation. "Calvin," for example, "spoke of the Holy Spirit as 'a unique self-interpreter,' since he spoke by the prophets."[56] Berkouwer declares, however, that this hermeneutical principle actually emerges from Scripture.

> On hearing this rule, one can react that it is polemically understandable but really not a concrete and fruitful notion for the present interpretation of Scripture. The formula is indeed a polemical focusing of the

54. Vern S. Poythress, *God-Centered Biblical Interpretation* (Phillipsburg, NJ: P&R, 1999), 45.
55. Berkouwer, *Holy Scripture*, 127.
56. Ibid., 127–28.

sola Scriptura on interpretation. This already excludes the possibility of speaking of a purely formal rule without diverse perspectives. It contains a concrete rejection of other interpretations which are foreign to the nature of Scripture. By so doing it naturally reminds us of the scriptural message that no prophecy of Scripture is a matter of one's own interpretation (2 Pet. 1:20).[57]

And so in the context of the current hermeneutical crisis, what happens to the Reformation's hermeneutical principle flowing from *sola Scriptura* when the issues of modern science[58] or scholarship in their many forms enter this discussion? Berkouwer pointedly asks this question:

> It has been repeatedly pointed out that behind many of the questions presently related to the interpretation of Holy Scripture looms the important presence of science. . . . The way in which this relationship is usually discussed is by maintaining that certain results of science, be it natural science or historical research can provide the "occasion" for understanding various aspects of Scripture in a different way than before. If this is indeed the case, then what is the relationship between such an "occasion" and the authoritative power of "Sacred Scripture is its own interpreter"?[59]

---

57. Ibid., 127.

58. "Science" in Berkouwer's mind is broader than what is often intended in the American use of the word. Jack B. Rogers, translator of *Holy Scripture*, 133n80, explains, "The word 'science' is used throughout this book in a much broader sense than is usual in the U.S.A. Berkouwer's concept of a science is equivalent to our notion of an academic discipline. Thus, studies done in the humanities and social sciences as well as the natural sciences are included. Theology is also a science, since it proceeds by orderly academic research and reflection."

59. Berkouwer, *Holy Scripture*, 133–34. The Reformed theologians Kuyper and Bavinck also wrestled with the findings of science and their impact on the theology of the inspiration of the Bible. See Gaffin, "Old Amsterdam," 281–82: "The classic, rational apologetic for graphic inspiration is not only inappropriate but counterproductive, because it places the demands of mechanical preciseness on Scripture, which by its nature demands organic precision; Scripture is forced into a mold which is not suited to its organic character. . . . Kuyper observes that the full, multifaceted character of Scripture cannot be exhausted by the finite grasp of our logical, mathematical thinking. One result is that according to intellectual demands and on the flat terrain of logic, everything in Scripture is not in harmony. But certainly that harmony is there, and we see it when, in faith, we view it 'from the standpoint of the Holy Spirit.' . . . Kuyper and Bavinck held that Scripture does not intend to give us 'technically correct scientific information.' That is right. But at the same time what Kuyper would also want to point out is that in its undeniably impressionistic, not notarially precise, not scientifically exact, fashion, Scripture gives information that is directly relevant to science."

Berkouwer asks, "Does it mean that science has become a fellow interpreter, or is it impossible to state the problem in such a way?"[60] Enns seems to answer affirmatively: "the findings of the past 150 years have made extrabiblical evidence an unavoidable conversation partner."[61] Yet for Berkouwer, if science becomes part of biblical hermeneutics, the principle of *sola Scriptura* is lost. Berkouwer explains:

> It is not true that, as far as the Reformation was concerned, Scripture alone was its own interpreter and that now we see a second interpreter being added. If that were the case, it might be better to recognize that the Reformation scriptural principle now appears insufficient and out of date.[62]

> When, however, the *sui ipsius interpres* receives increasingly concrete attention, it also becomes apparent that science cannot become an "interpreter" alongside Scripture itself. This is one pretension not found in the circles of science itself, except for odd cases of vain scientific idealism which are convinced that the light of Scripture has been permanently extinguished by that of science. Not just to spite science, but rather because of its totally different nature and of the secret of Scripture—the secret of the gospel—we will have to continue on the basis of the "is its own interpreter" and thus continue to honor Scripture as canon.[63]

Indeed, for Berkouwer, the "trustworthiness" of Scripture denies the legitimacy of the "new hermeneutic," which coercively forces concessions on the canonical hermeneutical principle of the Reformation.

> The discussion about Scripture, its God-breathed character and authority, cannot take place via a coerced concession to a new hermeneutical method and the "occasion" of science. It can only take place in the perspective of that trustworthiness of Scripture which enables us to abandon ourselves in complete trust to its authority and to preach its message.[64]

60. Berkouwer, *Holy Scripture*, 133–34.
61. Enns, *Inspiration and Incarnation*, 49.
62. Berkouwer, *Holy Scripture*, 134.
63. Ibid.
64. Ibid., 138

To fail to see the uniqueness of Scripture in this regard has but one end in Berkouwer's mind—being "seized by irresolute doubt."

> Those who, because of the complicated questions of interpretation, the dangers of projection and twisting, of subjectivism and objectivism, want to give up trying to understand Scripture in accordance with its divine intent, have been seized by irresolute doubt. . . . To overcome doubt of this kind, we must not allow any questions of interpretation, including those arising from newly disclosed knowledge, to hinder new essays into scriptural understanding from the vantage point of the *sui ipsius interpres*. On these voyages we will be aware that no single postulate that circumvents this dictum can in fact block our way. There is no single technique able to provide the key to the secret of Scripture, not even a perfected hermeneutics.[65]

We can scarcely summarize Berkouwer's point here more cogently than by reaffirming his declaration of the uniqueness of Scripture that he denominates "the secret of Scripture":

> Not just to spite science, but rather because of its totally different nature and of the secret of Scripture—the secret of the gospel—we will have to continue on the basis of the "is its own interpreter" and thus continue to honor Scripture as canon.[66]

Given the infallibility, extensiveness, and mandatory character of the Westminster Confession's hermeneutical rule (WCF 1.9), all other "scientific" considerations for interpreting Scripture must be viewed as having secondary importance. Whether they are historical, archaeological, linguistic, or extra-biblical phenomena, as helpful as they may be to reflect the historical milieu of Scripture and to provide insights into the nature and meaning of biblical language, they must be considered subordinate and not equivalent in interpretive force to the self-interpreting character of Scripture.

Moreover, as Kuyper argued, there are two kinds of science—that which operates within the Christian worldview and that which comports

---

65. Ibid., 135.
66. Ibid.

with a naturalistic philosophy.[67] Consequently, the "canon"[68] for biblical hermeneutics as opposed to naturalistic hermeneutics is and must be the canon of Scripture.[69] This alone preserves *"sola Scriptura."* At this point it is interesting, perhaps even ironic, to observe that the "modern" Berkouwer is in sympathy with the "Protestant orthodox" Turretin. The latter writes,

> The purpose of Scripture requires this perfection, for it was given that we might have salvation and life from it (John 20:31; 1 John 5:13; Rom. 15:4). How could this purpose be accomplished, unless Scripture were perfect,

67. Abraham Kuyper explains, "Our proposition that there are two kinds of science is, from the nature of the case, merely the accommodation to a linguistic usage. The two sciences must never be coordinated with each other. In fact, no one can be convinced that there is more than one science, and that which announces itself as science by the side of, or in opposition to, this can never be acknowledged as such in the absolute sense. As soon as the thinker of palingenesis has come to that point in the road where the thinker of naturalism parts company with him, the latter's science is no longer anything to the former but 'science falsely so called.' Similarly the naturalistic thinker is bound to contest the name of science for that which the student of the 'wisdom of God' derives from his premises. That which lies outside of the realm of these different premises is common to both, but that which is governed, directly or indirectly, by these premises comes to stand entirely differently to the one from what it does to the other. Always in this sense, of course, that only one is right and in touch with actual reality, but is unable to convince the other of wrong. It will once be decided, but not until the final consummation of all things." Abraham Kuyper, *Principles of Sacred Theology*, trans. J. Hendrik de Vries (Grand Rapids: Baker, 1980), 176.

68. For a helpful summary of the development of the meanings of "canon" see *Nicene and Post-Nicene Fathers*, vol. 14, *The Seven Ecumenical Councils of the Undivided Church: Their Canons and Dogmatic Decrees, Together with the Canons of All the Local Synods Which Have Received Ecumenical Acceptance*, ed. Henry R. Percival (Peabody, MA: Hendrickson, 1995), 14:9–10.

69. In Reformed theology, the Holy Spirit's ministry was not absent from the creation of the canon of Scripture, cf. Gaffin, "Old Amsterdam," 268, where he says, "The apostles themselves believed in a predestined Bible and saw inspiration as extending to the individual words and letters (2.177). The scriptural attire (*het Schriftgewaad*) of the Word is woven by God according to the pattern that he has drawn up for it (1.86). Graphic inspiration in the narrower sense is the operation of the Holy Spirit in the various human authors, "whereby they wrote in just the way and at such a time and in such a form as was necessary for the delivery of that part of Scripture for which each was responsible, finished and adapted to the canonical linking together of all the parts, to that one harmonious whole which the Lord God had foreseen and foreordained for Holy Scripture." This graphic inspiration concerns "the production of the autograph in the form intended by God, at the moment it enters the canon (2.127) . . ." (270). "The Holy Spirit directed them, brought to their knowledge what they were to know, sharpened their judgments in the choice of documents and records, so that they should decide aright, and gave them a superior maturity of mind that enabled them always to choose exactly the right word. . . . But whether He dictates directly, as in the Revelation of St. John or governs indirectly, as with historians and evangelists, the result is the same: the product is such in the form and content as the Holy Spirit designed, an infallible document for the Church of God." (Cf. R. Laird Harris, *Inspiration and Canonicity of the Scriptures* [Greenville, SC: A Press, 1995]).

containing all that is necessary for salvation? It was given to be canon and rule of faith but a rule which is not full and sufficient is no rule; a rule is a standard from which nothing can be taken and to which nothing can be added, "an inviolable law and infallible measure, allowing no addition or substitution," as Favorinus says.[70]

The vows of the OPC, the PCA, and Westminster all reflect Turretin's "canon and rule of faith" and "inviolable law and infallible measure" when they unitedly declare belief in "*the only infallible rule of faith and practice.*"[71] Such an "infallible rule" would appear to be "a rule" or "standard from which nothing can be taken and to which nothing can be added."

"A MODERN DOCTRINE OF SCRIPTURE"? "PROVISIONAL THEOLOGIZING" AND THE CONFESSION'S "INFALLIBLE RULE OF INTERPRETATION"

As we turn from this consideration of the Reformers', Turretin's, and Berkouwer's understanding of *sola Scriptura* to the views of Professor Enns, we must engage Professor Enns's emphasis on the humanity of Scripture and his concomitant insistence that the doctrine of Scripture be developed without "blissful isolation" from extrabiblical evidence. Do the archaeological discoveries of scholars require a mere provisional confession of our doctrine of Scripture?

Professor Enns has strongly pressed these issues and has here given his views in unmistakable terms. His "two assumptions," his stated presuppositions, clarify his perspective:

1. I assume that the extrabiblical archeological and textual evidences should play an important role in our understanding of Scripture. . . . I reject the notion that a modern doctrine of Scripture can be articulated in blissful isolation from the evidence we have.

2. All attempts to articulate the nature of Scripture are open to examination, including my own. I firmly believe . . . that the Spirit of God is fully engaged in such a theological process and at the same time that our attempts to articulate what God's word

---

70. Turretin, *Doctrine of Scripture*, 175.

71. See "The Hermeneutical Crisis and the Historic Presbyterian Subscription to the Confession" above.

is have a necessarily provisional dimension. To put it succinctly: The Spirit leads the church to truth—he does not simply drop us down in the middle of it. To say this is not a low view of Scripture or of the role of the Holy Spirit. It is simply to recognize what has been the case throughout the history of the church, that diverse views and changes of opinion over time have been the constant companions of the church and that God has not brought this process to a closure.[72]

Here Enns assumes the view that both Berkouwer and Turretin have just rejected. Thankfully, Enns does not advance in place of the confession's "infallible rule of interpretation" the "irresolute doubt" identified by Berkouwer. But he does overtly confess a "provisional" doctrine of Scripture:[73]

If even God expresses himself in the Bible through particular human circumstances, we must be very ready to see the necessarily culturally limited nature of our own theological expressions today. I am not speaking of cultural relativism, where all truth is up for grabs and the Bible ceases being our standard for faith. I simply mean that all of our theologizing, because we are human beings living in particular historical and cultural moments, will have a temporary and **provisional**—even fallen—dimension to it. In other words, there is no absolute point of reference to which we have access that will allow us to interpret the Bible stripped of our own cultural context.[74]

The theme of the provisional doctrine of Scripture is a repeated element of his study:

On the one hand, I am very eager to affirm that many evangelical instincts are correct and should be maintained, for example, the conviction that the Bible is ultimately from God and that it is God's gift to the church. Any theories concerning Scripture that do not arise from these fundamental instincts are unacceptable. On the other hand, **how the evangelical church fleshes out its doctrine of Scripture** will always have somewhat of a **provisional** quality to it. This is not to say that

72. *Inspiration and Incarnation*, 48–49.

73. In the following quotations, Professor Enns's use of "provisional" and related concepts is highlighted by bold type.

74. Enns, *Inspiration and Incarnation*, 168–69.

each generation must disregard the past and start afresh, formulating ever-new doctrines, bowing to all the latest fads. But it is to say that at such time when new evidence comes to light, or old evidence is seen in a new light, we must be willing to **engage that evidence and adjust our doctrine accordingly**.[75]

The findings of the past 150 years have made extrabiblical evidence an unavoidable conversation partner. The result is that, as perhaps never before in the history of the church, we can see how truly **provisional** and incomplete certain dimensions of our understanding of Scripture can be. On the other hand, we are encouraged to encounter the depth and riches of God's revelation and to rely more and more on God's Spirit, who speaks to the church in Scripture.[76]

Perhaps, then, it makes more sense to speak of the incarnational *parallel* between Christ and the Bible. This should lead us to a more willing recognition that the expression of our confession of the Bible as God's word has a **provisional** quality to it. By faith, the church confesses that the Bible *is* God's word. It is up to Christians of each generation, however, to work out what that means and what words work best to describe it.[77]

. . . it would be very difficult for someone holding to such a view to have a meaningful conversation with linguists and historians of the ancient world. To argue in such hypothetical terms can sometimes become an excuse for maintaining a way of thinking that is otherwise unsupportable. It is just such explanations that some readers might find problematic, for they **seem motivated by a desire to protect one's theology rather than to engage the available evidence**. . . . regardless of when Genesis was written and in what language, it still reflects an ancient Near Eastern worldview that clearly is significantly older.[78]

Because our theologies are necessarily limited and **provisional**, the church today must be open to listening to how other Christians from other cultures read Scripture and live it out in their daily lives. . . . The incarnational

75. Ibid., 13–14.
76. Ibid., 49.
77. Ibid., 168.
78. Ibid., 52.

analogy helps us to see it differently: diverse expressions of God's one, but multidimensional gospel are precisely what he wanted.[79]

This provisional nature of the churches' confessions results in a process without "clear rules or guidelines to prevent us from taking this process too far." Professor Enns acknowledges that this results in a kind of uncertainty with regard to the Scriptures given the questions that may be raised by evidence yet to be discovered:

> There do not seem to be any clear rules or guidelines to prevent us from taking this process too far. But again, this is why the metaphor of journey or pilgrimage is so appealing. The path we walk may contain risks, unexpected bumps, twists, and turns. We do not always know what is coming around the corner—we were not able to anticipate the discovery of ancient Near Eastern creation texts or the Dead Sea Scrolls for example. But yet, we have turned a few important corners over the past several generations. It is always an option, I suppose, to halt the journey and stand still, or perhaps turn around and walk back a few hundred yards, so as to stand at a safe distance from what lies ahead. We should continue the journey, however; not because we are sure of our own footing, but because we have faith in God who placed us on this journey to begin with.[80]

Is Enns really saying by his word "provisional" that *sola Scriptura* and the "infallible rule of interpretation" can no longer be the foundational hermeneutic of the Reformed tradition? If so, the stakes are high indeed. Simply put, the hermeneutical crisis has brought us to a major crossroads of theology.

Young would agree.

> The Church is indeed at the crossroads. Shall she listen to God or to man? Will she receive what the Spirit says concerning inspiration, or, turning her back upon Him, will she cleave unto man? This is the choice to be made. Sad is it, however, that many do not realize the necessity for making a choice. Having their vision obscured by the dense fog that modern theology is casting over the way, many do not realize that there is a crossroad. They are not aware that they must decide which road they will follow. Unless

79. Ibid., 169.
80. Ibid., 171.

something is done, they will travel on, taking the wrong turning, until the road leads them at last into the valley of lost hope and eternal death.[81]

But this is not merely the "traditionalist" view of Young the "conservative." Even Berkouwer the "progressive" agrees:

> Those who see the *lamp* of the Word of God on a continuum with the new and increased *light* of science, lit before all the world, inevitably arrive at a dangerous crossroads. They will either follow a course condescending to Scripture and its message, or they will tend to abandon every new question about interpretation because of the danger involved. Both paths must be avoided.[82]

Yet Enns unflinchingly writes, "In other words, there is no absolute point of reference to which we have access that will allow us to interpret the Bible stripped of our own cultural context."[83] But in saying this, does he not strip the church of *sola Scriptura* and the hermeneutical principle afforded us by the Bible which the confession declares to be the "infallible rule of interpretation"?

The crossroads is now clear.[84] We must either confess an "infallible rule of interpretation" (WCF 1.9) reflecting the hermeneutical rule of *sola Scriptura*, or confess a "provisional" (168) theology subject to the "bumps, twists and turns" (171) of the unanticipated discoveries of "extrabiblical evidence" (48). Moreover, all of this occurs on a "journey or pilgrimage" (171) led by Professor Enns and others who assure us that we walk no "slippery slope" (172) on this "appealing" (171) journey. Nevertheless, we are not "sure of our footing" (171), and "there do not seem to be any clear rules or guidelines to prevent us from taking this process too far" (171). Consequently, all Enns leaves for the church is "faith in God who placed us on this journey" (171). The "infallible rule of interpretation" (WCF 1.9) that emerges from divine "infallible truth" (WCF I.5) is nowhere to be found since "there is no absolute point of reference to which we have access that will allow us to interpret the Bible . . ." (169).

---

81. Young, *Thy Word Is Truth*, 35.
82. Berkouwer, *Holy Scripture*, 135.
83. Enns, *Inspiration and Incarnation*, 168–69.
84. The quoted phrases in this paragraph can be found in *Inspiration and Incarnation* on the identified pages.

Consequently, Enns also seems to dismiss or redefine another type of "evidence" that the confession affirms. Referring to Holy Scripture, the confession says that it abundantly provides "**evidence** . . . to be the Word of God: yet notwithstanding, our full persuasion and assurance of the infallible truth and divine authority thereof, is from the inward work of the Holy Spirit bearing witness by and with the Word in our hearts" (WCF 1.5).

To be sure, Enns does not deny "the role of the Holy Spirit" in relationship to human understanding of Scripture.

> I firmly believe . . . that the Spirit of God is fully engaged in such a theological process and at the same time that our attempts to articulate what God's word is have a necessarily provisional dimension. To put it succinctly: The Spirit leads the church to truth—he does not simply drop us down in the middle of it. To say this is not a low view of Scripture or of the role of the Holy Spirit.[85]

But what Enns affirms here does not appear to cohere with the confession's explanation of the Spirit's intimate "witness **by and with the Word** in our hearts." He confesses that "The Spirit leads the church to truth—he does not simply drop us down in the middle of it." Although he claims that " . . . this is not a low view of Scripture or of the role of the Holy Spirit," this does not appear warranted when it is compared with the affirmations of the confession: " . . . the Word of God . . . full persuasion and assurance . . . infallible truth and divine authority . . . the Holy Spirit bearing witness by and with the Word in our hearts. . . . the Holy Spirit speaking in the Scripture" (WCF 1.5, 10).[86] The confession binds together Word and Spirit far more closely than Enns appears willing to do.

85. *Inspiration and Incarnation*, 48–49.

86. There is a clear epistemological emphasis in the Westminster Standards. The Westminster Confession of Faith 1.1 states, "Although the light of nature, and the works of creation and providence do so far manifest the goodness, wisdom, and power of God, as to leave men unexcusable; yet are they not sufficient to give that knowledge of God, and of his will, which is necessary unto salvation. Therefore it pleased the Lord, at sundry times, and in divers manners, to reveal himself, and to declare that his will unto his church; and afterwards, for the better preserving and propagating of the truth, and for the more sure establishment and comfort of the church against the corruption of the flesh, and the malice of Satan and of the world, to commit the same wholly unto writing: which maketh the Holy Scripture to be most necessary; those former ways of God's revealing his will unto his people being now ceased." Larger Catechism question 192: "What do we pray for in the third petition? Answer: In the third petition (which is, Thy will be done in earth, as it is in heaven), acknowledging, that by nature we and

Indeed, Enns's phrases are a stunning contrast with those in the confession. His phrases are as follows: "the word of God," "not sure of our footing," "provisional," "The Spirit leads the church to truth—he does not simply drop us down in the middle of it," "no absolute point of reference to which we have access that will allow us to interpret the Bible...." These statements are difficult to reconcile with the union of Word and Spirit reflected by Larger Catechism Q. 2: "How does it appear that there is a God? Answer: The very light of nature in man, and the works of God, declare plainly that there is a God; but his Word and Spirit only do sufficiently and effectually reveal him unto men for their salvation." Enns's uncertainty seems inconsistent with the knowledge of God claimed by Larger Catechism Question 6, which asks: "What do the Scriptures make known of God? Answer: The Scriptures make known: What God is, the persons in the Godhead, his decrees, and the execution of his decrees."

At the heart of the hermeneutical crisis there is an epistemological crisis[87] that denies to men the certainty of divine knowledge.[88] Thus Helm critiques Enns's theological method,

---

all men are not only utterly unable and unwilling to know and do the will of God, but prone to rebel against his Word, to repine and murmur against his providence, and wholly inclined to do the will of the flesh, and of the devil: we pray, that God would by his Spirit take away from ourselves and others all blindness, weakness, indisposedness, and perverseness of heart; and by his grace make us able and willing to know, do, and submit to his will in all things, with the like humility, cheerfulness, faithfulness, diligence, zeal, sincerity, and constancy, as the angels do in heaven." Harvie Conn agrees with D. A. Carson in "Normativity, Relevance, and Relativism," *Inerrancy and Hermeneutic*, 191, in calling attention to the non-neutrality of all interpreters: "In short, we are all biased already in our thinking and knowing, bringing assumptions structured by our cultural perceptions, even by the language symbols we use to interpret reality. We are, that is, 'interested' before we begin to read a text and remain active as we read it. We belong, to a great extent through language, to the theological, social, and psychological traditions that have moulded us as subjects and without whose mediation we could understand nothing. D. A. Carson puts it bluntly: 'No human being living in time and speaking any language can ever be entirely culture-free about anything.' In sum, the idea that the interpreter is a neutral observer of biblical data is a myth. How then do we avoid hermeneutical discoveries based largely on what we have assumed? If what we hear from the text, and how we act upon what we have heard, is so heavily influenced by the baggage we carry with us in the process, how do we avoid the relativism of selective listening and selective obedience?"

87. For a representative study of the deep commitment of the Reformed faith to an epistemology built upon the accessibility by revelation of divine knowledge for the Christian in spite of man's metaphysical agnosticism given the noetic effects of sin and his autonomous rebellion from the Creator, see Cornelius Van Til, *An Introduction to Systematic Theology*.

88. Enns defends God's own lack of divine knowledge, *Inspiration and Incarnation*, 103–7. Although ostensibly distancing himself from the "openness of God" theology (106), he ultimately cannot fully do so because he rejects the confession's "infallible principle" of Scripture

We see now that Enns' problems have little or nothing to do with the discoveries and claims of Old Testament scholarship. Instead, they are due to two basic failures. A failure in theological method, that of starting from difficulties instead of from dogma. And a failure in epistemology, a commitment to the idea of universal cultural bias that makes objectivity and finality about our faith impossible.[89]

When we consider Professor Enns's repeated statements in this regard, it seems as if a believer can trust God, but he may not necessarily be able to trust Scripture:

We are to place our trust in God who gave us Scripture, not in our own conceptions of how Scripture ought to be.[90]

---

interpreting Scripture. He writes, "*In this story*, God did not know until after the test was passed" (103). "Any attempt to force the God *of Genesis* 6 into a mold cast by certain theological commitments or to reconcile this description to other biblical passages simply amounts to reading past this story" (104). "The Bible really does have authority if we let it speak, and not when we—intentionally or unintentionally—suspend what the Bible says about God in some places while we work out our speculations about what God is 'really' like, perhaps by accenting other portions of the Bible that are more amenable to our thinking" (106). This appears to be a denial of WCF 1.9, "The infallible rule of interpretation of Scripture is the Scripture itself: and therefore, when there is a question about the true and full sense of any Scripture (which is not manifold, but one), it must be searched and known by other places that speak more clearly." Perhaps Enns's insistence on the primacy of the specific narrative over the theological metanarrative of the Scripture's system of doctrine as well as its infallible hermeneutic reflects the hermeneutic of Lyotard, the postmodern whose dictum is "narrative not metanarrative." Jean-Francois Lyotard has been a leader in postmodern thought, a contemporary form of skeptical philosophy. Postmodernism questions and critiques all claims for certainty. Lyotard dismissed the claim for universal theories of truth, claiming that arguments defending "grand narratives" were no longer credible. Thus Lyotard's opposition to the grand narrative, as well as its inherent authority, led him to defend the idea of the "little narrative," namely the stories of individual human beings, which require no foundational or epistemological defense. His summary of postmodernism declares, "I define postmodern as incredulity toward metanarratives. This incredulity is undoubtedly a product of progress in the sciences: . . . To the obsolescence of the metanarrative . . . corresponds, most notably, the crisis of metaphysical philosophy. . . . The narrative function is losing . . . its great goal. It is being dispersed in clouds of narrative language. . . ." Postmodernism in general claims that a correct description of reality is impossible, reflecting the skepticism of Nietzsche, Wittgenstein, Popper, and Kuhn. The core beliefs of postmodernity include: 1. Truth is limited, approximate, and is constantly evolving; 2. No theory can ever be proved true (a theory can only be shown to be false); 3. No theory can ever explain everything; 4. Thus absolute and certain truth that explains all things is unobtainable.

89. Paul Helm (in the e-zine *Reformation 21*, April 2006), a "Review of *Inspiration and Incarnation* [Accessed January 8, 2008]." Online: http://www.reformation21. org/Reformation_21_Blog/Reformation_21_Blog/58/vobId__2801/.

90. Enns, *Inspiration and Incarnation*, 169.

This should lead us to a more willing recognition that the expression of our confession of the Bible as God's word has a provisional quality to it. By faith, the church confesses that the Bible is God's word. It is up to Christians of each generation, however, to work out what that means and what words work best to describe it.[91]

The second concerns the Bible's integrity, its trustworthiness. It is a common expectation that the Bible be unified in its outlook, be free of diverse views, if we are being asked to trust it as God's word (does not God have just one opinion on things?).[92]

There are many ways of asking these questions, but they all boil down to this: Is the Bible still the word of God?[93]

If anything, would we not expect the Bible, which records God's revelation, to "get it right" by not allowing authors to be biased like all the other histories of the surrounding cultures, but instead just giving us the objective and neutral facts? No evangelical can consider this issue and not feel the force of this argument. If the Bible does not tell us what actually happened, how can we trust it about anything?[94]

My intention below is to explore how the biblical and extrabiblical evidence can affect these assumptions. If, in full conversation with the biblical and extrabiblical evidence, we can *adjust our expectations* about how the Bible should behave, we can begin to move beyond the impasse of the liberal/conservative debates of the last several generations.[95]

Lacking in Enns is the insistence of Berkouwer on the trustworthiness of Scripture.

The discussion about Scripture, its God-breathed character and authority, cannot take place via a coerced concession to a new hermeneutical method and the "occasion" of science. It can only take place in the perspective of that trustworthiness of Scripture which enables

91. Ibid., 168.
92. Ibid., 16.
93. Ibid., 39.
94. Ibid., 45.
95. Ibid., 48.

us to abandon ourselves in complete trust to its authority and to preach its message.[96]

At the core of the hermeneutical crisis there is a contrast of great importance. The Westminster Confession presents an "infallible rule of interpretation" while Enns proposes a hermeneutic that embraces a method without "clear rules." When Young and Berkouwer can agree on the gravity of what is at stake in the hermeneutical crisis, should we not heed their warnings before we "blissfully" embrace the "modern doctrine of Scripture"[97] advocated by Professor Enns?

THE STARTING POINT: A UNIQUE OR NON-UNIQUE SCRIPTURE?

The hermeneutical crisis is born at the intersection of the question concerning the nature of Scripture and the consideration of the starting point for its interpretation. Does one begin the interpretation of Holy Scripture viewing it primarily as divine revelation or instead as a human book?[98]

Bavinck's description of the eternal and yet human relevance of Holy Scripture helps to set the stage for this discussion:

> In a human manner it always speaks of the highest and most holy, of the eternal and invisible things. Like Christ, it considers nothing that is human strange. But that is why it is a book for mankind and lasts until the end of the ages. It is old, without ever aging. It always remains young and flourishing; it is the language of life. *Verbum Dei manet in aeternum.*[99]

Should not this high view of Scripture flow from Enns's view of Christ's incarnation? This would seem to be so, particularly when he writes,

---

96. Ibid., 138.

97. Ibid., 48–49.

98. Other important hermeneutical issues raised by Professor Enns cannot be addressed here since they are beyond the purview of this study. For significant discussions of how the NT writers quote the OT, consider the following: Enns, *Inspiration and Incarnation*, 113–65; G. K. Beale, *The Right Doctrine from the Wrong Text? Essays on the Use of the Old Testament in the New* (Grand Rapids: Baker, 1994); Walter C. Kaiser Jr., "Legitimate Hermeneutics," in *Inerrancy*, 117–47; Dan G. McCartney, "The New Testament's Use of the Old Testament," in *Inerrancy and Hermeneutic*, 101–16; Dennis E. Johnson, *Him We Proclaim: Preaching Christ from All the Scriptures* (Phillipsburg, NJ: P&R, 2007), 137–64; Young, *Thy Word Is Truth*, 143–61.

99. Cited in Berkouwer, *Holy Scripture*, 27.

The starting point for our discussion is the following: as Christ is both God and human, so is the Bible. . . . Jesus is 100 percent God and 100 percent human—at the same time. . . . In the same way that Jesus is—must be—both God and human, the Bible is also a divine and human book.[100]

But when Enns moves beyond the starting point for his "discussion" and elaborates his starting point for engaging *Scripture*, it becomes clear that he does not believe that the starting point is the Bible's full divinity or its uniqueness. Instead, his starting point for hermeneutics is the Bible's non-uniqueness given its full humanity:

It is essential to the very nature of revelation that the Bible is not unique to its environment. The human dimension of Scripture is essential to its being Scripture. This, I argue, is the proper starting point for looking at the relationship between the Bible and the issues we will discuss in this book. That the Bible is so easily situated in its ancient context is a source of difficulty for many modern readers.[101]

The "100 percent divine" of Christ's incarnation seems here in the context of the Bible to have little relevance and seems to have been eclipsed by the "100 percent human."

Accordingly, Enns finds the Genesis stories mirrored in the Babylonian texts as evidence of the Bible's humanity and apparent dependence on other human and pre- or non-Hebrew sources.[102] But when Young reviews

100. Enns, *Inspiration and Incarnation*, 17.

101. Ibid., 20. Enns repeatedly affirms the non-uniqueness of Scripture. See, for example, 15, 16, 18, 20, 21, 31, 32, 42, 43, 46, 47, 168.

102. Enns writes, "In both their oral and written versions, the stories of Genesis seem to be younger than the stories of other ancient Near Eastern cultures. If pressed, one could attempt to mount the argument that the Israelite stories are actually older than all the Ancient Near Eastern stories but were only recorded later in Hebrew. Such a theory—for that is what it is, a theory—would need to assume that the biblical stories are the pristine originals and that all the other stories are parodies and perversions of the Israelite original, even though the available evidence would be very difficult to square with such a conclusion. But could it have happened this way? Yes, I suppose one could insist on such a thing, but it would be very difficult for someone holding to such a view to have a meaningful conversation with linguists and historians of the ancient world. To argue in such hypothetical terms can sometimes become an excuse for maintaining a way of thinking that is otherwise unsupportable. It is just such explanations that some readers might find problematic, for they seem motivated by a desire to protect one's theology rather than to engage the available evidence. . . . regardless of when Genesis was written and in what language, it still reflects an ancient Near Eastern worldview that clearly is significantly older. It

these Babylonian texts in light of Scripture he instead proclaims the Bible's uniqueness[103] and the divine origin and inerrancy of Scripture.[104] In fact

---

stretches logic and common sense to try to protect the uniqueness of the Genesis accounts by arguing that Mesopotamian peoples, who existed long before Israel came on the scene and who were the dominant cultures of the day, had no creation myths for hundreds of years and simply waited for Israelite slaves to provide the prototype, which they then corrupted." *Inspiration and Incarnation*, 52. In engaging Enns's claims here, one should consider Herman Bavinck's concept of "primitive revelation" or "original revelation" in *The Philosophy of Revelation* (Grand Rapids: Baker, 1979), 171, 188–89, "Both in earlier and later times in the Christian church the truth and wisdom found among the heathen have been generally derived from a primitive revelation, from the continuous illumination by the Logos, from acquaintance with the literature of the Old Testament, or from the operation of God's common grace. . . ." "All these fundamentals are given from the beginning in human nature; they are transmitted from generation to generation, and are at the same time grounded in the very nature of man, so that dependence and independence work together here. And they all point back to a divine origin: 'all knowledge is,' at least so far as principles and foundations are concerned, 'of divine origin.' Knowledge in this sense flows from revelation. To this original revelation is joined on that revelation which according to the Old Testament was bestowed upon Israel. The latter is built upon the former and rests upon it, and is at the same time the continuation, the development and completion of it. The distinction between what has come to be called general and special revelation does not begin until the call of Abraham; before that the two intermingle, and so far have become the property of all peoples and nations. Special revelation certainly is set antithetically over against all the corruption which gradually entered into the life of the peoples, but it takes up, confirms, and completes all that had been from the beginning put into human nature by revelation and had been preserved and increased subsequently in the human race."

103. Young explains, "When compared with other literature from the ancient Near East, the Bible stands out like a fair flower in a dreary, barren desert. We read the crude polytheism of the Babylonian documents, and then open the pages of Holy Scripture and learn of Him who is good and true and holy. We read the pseudo-creation accounts of the ancient world and then listen to the majestic account of true creation given in the Bible. We read of the struggles and strivings of men to atone in one way or another for sins. How dark was the light of ancient religion! Then we learn from the Bible that man cannot save himself, but that God has provided the one Lamb that taketh away the sin of the world. How unspeakably grand is the doctrine of salvation by grace! . . . Many and convincing are these evidences whereby the Scriptures reveal their Divine origin. Yet, despite their clarity, not all men are willing to accept these evidences, and the reason for this unwillingness is not far to seek. Is it because there is some defect in the evidences themselves? Are not they of sufficient clarity and cogency to convince all men? The answer is that the evidences are clear enough; indeed so clear are they that he who is not convinced by them has no excuse." *Thy Word Is Truth*, 33.

104. Young writes, "If then we may arrive at the position (and it is the only position at which one may legitimately arrive) that the early chapters of Genesis purport to be history let us next ask the question whether, as a matter of actual fact, they are filled with the errors which inescapably accompany a pre-scientific age. The answer to this question must be in the negative. In their statements these chapters are scientifically accurate. They do not teach anything that is not in accord with the facts. Can anyone point out an actual error, for example, in the first chapter of Genesis? Particularly interesting does this question become when one compares the first chapter of Genesis with the so-called Babylonian account of creation. Are there errors in the Babylonian account? To ask this question is to give the answer. No one

the uniqueness of Scripture in Young's mind is a foundational perspective that necessarily flows from the doctrine of providence affirmed by the Westminster Confession.[105]

In this context, consider D. A. Carson's critique of what he believes to be the one-sided use of the incarnational analogy in Enns's hermeneutic:

----

would think seriously of defending the Babylonian narrative from the charge of error, for the simple reason that it is so full of it. In the midst of the polytheism and superstition of that ancient world the first chapter of the Bible, on the other hand, stands out like a fair flower in a barren wilderness. The Genesis account differs completely from the cosmogonies of the ancient world. In it there is a robust and vigorous monotheism; the Creator is glorified and His wondrous work in creation exalted. Here God is honored in such a way that the reader may come to marvel at the greatness of Him who by the word of His mouth brought all things into being. Are there errors in the first chapter of the Bible? Let us say without fear of contradiction that no one has been able to demonstrate the presence of error in this majestic opening chapter of Scripture." *Thy Word Is Truth*, 167.

105. Young writes, "There is of course no question but that the events of the Bible are unique events. We may very legitimately speak of the uniqueness of these things which God wrought in history for the salvation of sinners. We are saved from our sins, not by the exploits of Alexander the great, but by the death of Jesus Christ upon the cross. For the believer, the latter event is rich with meaning that is lacking in the former. The Christian is naturally more interested in those events in history by means of which his redemption was obtained. When all this is granted, however, we must insist that the events of Biblical history took place in history. They were, in other words, historical events. As such, they are related to all other events of history. Since the sovereign God in His providence upholds all things, we may be assured that all events of history are related. The matter has been accurately stated—accurately, because it is in agreement with the teaching of the Bible—by the Westminster Confession of Faith: 'God the great Creator of all things doth uphold, direct, dispose, and govern all creatures, actions, and things from the greatest even to the least, by His most wise and holy providence, according to His infallible fore-knowledge, and the free and immutable counsel of His own will, to the praise of the glory of His wisdom, power, justice, goodness and mercy.' All things that occur, according to the Confession's statement are ordained of God. They occur because he has decreed that they should occur. All are parts of His over-all plan. All are parts of His one all-embracing eternal purpose and decree. Inasmuch as this is the case, all events of history in the very nature of the case, are related. With the words of Pascal, we may well agree, 'If the nose of Cleopatra had been shorter, the whole face of the earth would have been changed.' The events of Biblical history are parts of this eternal purpose of God. As such they occur in the realm of history. They cannot be removed or separated from their historical context and background. Our salvation was wrought by the Lord of Glory when He died upon the cross and rose again from the dead. . . . Christianity, therefore, is rooted and grounded in history. At the same time it is true, as we noted above, that there is indeed a uniqueness about biblical history. This uniqueness has been expressed in the words of the Westminster Confession as follows: 'As the providence of God doth, in general reach to all creatures, so, after a most special manner, it taketh care of His Church, and disposeth all things to the good thereof.' Jesus Christ is, without controversy, the center of history. There is a *Before Christ* and an *In the year of our Lord*. The distinction is perfectly legitimate. There is a certain sense in which all things may be said to subserve the purposes of God in salvation." *Thy Word Is Truth*, 254–57. Also compare how differently Young handles the Nuzi tablets, 201ff., from Enns, 29–31.

Using the incarnational analogy, the "human dimension" of the God/man not only places him in the human environment, but leaves him unique in that environment since only he is without sin. And even more strikingly, of course, what makes Jesus most strikingly unique to the human environment is that, without gainsaying his thorough, perfect, humanness for an instant, he is also God, and thus the perfect revealer of God, such that what Jesus says and does, God says and does. But when Enns speaks of "the very nature of the revelation of the Bible" as "not unique in its environment," he looks only at its "human dimension" and integrates nothing of what else must be said if we are to understand what the Bible is in this "human environment."[106]

Moreover, Paul Helm's assessment of Enns's incarnational hermeneutical methodology finds that a non-unique Bible results in a "disturbingly new" approach that moves Enns ever "farther away" from an "orthodox doctrine of Scripture."

However what is new, disturbingly new, is the claim that Enns makes about this cultural embeddedness. We discover that the Bible itself is far from unique: it's a diverse, culturally-biased product, which we can only ever hope to understand provisionally. It'll be best to assess the book by considering a set of answers from Enns to three questions: Is our interpretation of the Bible provisional? Is the Bible unique? And finally, and most importantly, Is the Bible objective? These are among the central questions the author himself raises. My argument in this review is that in his answers to such questions Professor Enns has not gone too far—as he occasionally fears, perhaps—but that he has not gone far enough. The book is troubling not because of the profundity of the treatment but rather because of its superficiality. We shall find that Enns's answers to each of these questions take him farther and farther away from being able to maintain an orthodox doctrine of Scripture.[107]

Whether one agrees or disagrees with Carson's and Helm's critiques of Enns, one thing is clear. The methodology of Enns is to express concern for previous "doctrinal formulations" but not to quote those "formulations" as he develops his own doctrine of Scripture.

---

106. Carson (*Reformation 21*, May 2006).
107. Helm (*Reformation 21*, April 2006).

A summary of Professor Enns's doctrine of Scripture manifests that he assiduously avoids the traditional theological terminology that hitherto has articulated the evangelical and Reformed doctrine of Scripture. Conspicuous by their absence are: "infallible," "verbally inspired," "verbal plenary inspiration," "God-breathed," and "inerrant." Nevertheless, Professor Enns does employ specific phrases to develop his doctrine of Scripture.

Enns begins[108] by speaking of "a vibrant and reverent doctrine of Scripture" (13) and affirms that "the Bible is ultimately from God and that it is God's gift to the church" (14). Thus he can speak of "a vibrant positive view of Scripture as God's word" (15), and he declares that "the Bible is God's word" (15). However, "It is not enough simply to say that the Bible is the word of God or that it is inspired" (17), because "the Bible is also a divine and human book" (17). Thus Enns asks, "How does Scripture's full humanity and full divinity affect what we should expect from Scripture?" (18). His desire for "a high and healthy view of Scripture as God's word" (46), and for "a sound doctrine of Scripture" (56), leads him to emphasize extrabiblical evidence and incarnation: "A doctrine of Scripture that does not think through this incarnational dimension is inadequate in light of the evidence we have" (67). Hence for Enns's doctrine of Scripture, " . . . the bottom line is this: how we conceive of the normativity or authority of the Old Testament must be in continual conversation with the incarnate dimension of Scripture" (67–68). And this "incarnate dimension" means "our confession of the Bible as God's word has a provisional quality to it" (168).

What then are the consequences of Enns's "provisional" doctrine of God's Word as incarnate Scripture? There seem to be four. First, there is a new definition of the uniqueness of Scripture: "Its uniqueness is seen not in holding human cultures at arm's length, but in the belief that Scripture is the only book in which God speaks incarnately" (168). Second, there is no longer any basis to place our trust in our confession of Scripture: "We are to place our trust in God who gave us Scripture, not in our own conceptions of how Scripture ought to be" (169). Third, the Bible's significance for ethics is significantly redefined: so from now on we are to consider ". . . the Bible not as a timeless rule book or owner's manual for the Christian life—so that we can lift verses here and there

---

108. The quoted phrases in these paragraphs can be found in *Inspiration and Incarnation* on the identified pages.

and apply them" (169–70). Finally, "It is in the person and work of Christ that Christians seek to read the Old Testament, to search out how it is in Christ that the Old Testament has integrity, how it is worthy of trust, how the parts cohere. . . . A christotelic coherence is not achieved by following a few simple rules of exegesis" (170).

Does this summation of Professor Enns's teaching on Scripture substantiate Helm's claim that Enns's approach moves him away from an orthodox doctrine of Scripture? Perhaps a more specific and precise question is this: does Professor Enns's doctrine of Scripture reveal that he is departing from the Westminster Standards' teaching on Holy Scripture?

We conclude this study by a comparison of Enns's doctrine of Scripture and hermeneutics as summarized above with the teachings of the Westminster Standards. As we do, the following seven questions will be briefly addressed:

1. Is the confession therefore "inadequate" in that it has not thought "through this incarnation dimension" that incorporates "extra-biblical evidence"?
2. Is the confession's view of biblical "authority in continual conversation with the incarnate dimension of Scripture"?
3. Does the confession argue for the uniqueness of the Scriptures because God therein uniquely speaks "incarnately"?
4. Does the confession view itself as a "provisional" confession and thus not a trustworthy guide for how we understand what "Scripture ought to be"?
5. Does the confession prohibit viewing the Bible as a "timeless rule book . . . for the Christian life"?
6. Does the confession teach that the only dimension of the Scripture's trustworthiness is in its specific focus on Christ, i.e., a "christotelic coherence"?
7. Does the confession reject the idea that there are a few basic rules of exegesis?

If we discover that these elements do not "cohere" with the confession, then we must conclude that Professor Enns's doctrine of Scripture is out of accord with the Westminster Standards.

INSPIRATION AND INCARNATION CONTRA THE WESTMINSTER STANDARDS

Since Professor Enns has stated, "All attempts to articulate the nature of Scripture are open to examination, including my own,"[109] let us now examine his doctrine of Scripture in light of the confession. To do so, we will assess the principles we have just distilled from his doctrine of Scripture.

1. Is the confession therefore "inadequate" in that it has not thought "through this incarnation dimension" that incorporates "extra-biblical evidence"?

In making this claim, Enns is actually taking a position not contained in the confession, since the Reformed confessions do not use the incarnational analogy to explain the doctrine of Scripture. As Berkouwer declares, " . . . it is useful to remember that the church did not adopt this parallel in its confessions."[110]

As we have seen above, the confession rejects the notion of a required extrabiblical criteria for biblical hermeneutics given its expressed hermeneutical principle of *sola Scriptura* in 1.9. Indeed, it calls this canonical hermeneutic the "infallible rule of interpretation." This rule is consistent with and emerges from the high view of Scripture as the Word of God summarized in Chapter One of the confession. The confession declares that the Scriptures are *necessary* given mankind's inability to know God truly in any other way.[111] While the Reformed tradition has valued archaeological findings and ancient discoveries, it has held them to be historically relevant, linguistically fruitful, and potently illustrative

---

109. Enns, *Inspiration and Incarnation*, 48–49.

110. Berkouwer, *Holy Scripture*, 199.

111. WCF 1.1. "Although the light of nature, and the works of creation and providence do so far manifest the goodness, wisdom, and power of God, as to leave men unexcusable; yet are they not sufficient to give that knowledge of God, and of his will, which is necessary unto salvation. Therefore it pleased the Lord, at sundry times, and in divers manners, to reveal himself, and to declare that his will unto his church; and afterwards, for the better preserving and propagating of the truth, and for the more sure establishment and comfort of the church against the corruption of the flesh, and the malice of Satan and of the world, to commit the same wholly unto writing: which maketh the Holy Scripture to be most necessary; those former ways of God's revealing his will unto his people being now ceased."

for interpretation, but not ultimately determinative for the meaning of the text.[112] For the confession, Holy Scripture is the "Word of God written."[113] So if this principle of Professor Enns is true, the Westminster Standards must be declared to be "inadequate." But this raises the question whether one can take an *ex animo* subscription to an "inadequate" confession. This principle is immediately incompatible with the confession because its demand for equivalent consideration for extrabiblical evidence violates the confession's "infallible rule" (1.9) of Scripture interpreting Scripture.

2. Is the confession's view of biblical "authority in continual conversation with the incarnate dimension of Scripture"?

Since the Scriptures are self-interpreting, their authority is not based on anything outside of Scripture. From the confession's perspective, the *authority* of the Scriptures does not depend upon men but upon God[114] who is Truth itself and has given his Word.[115] Although "the many other incomparable excellencies and the entire perfection" of Holy Scripture are

---

112. Cf. for example Young, *Thy Word Is Truth*, 201ff; Meredith G. Kline, *Treaty of the Great King* (Grand Rapids: Eerdmans, 1963); Herman Bavinck, *The Philosophy of Revelation* (Grand Rapids: Baker, 1979), 170–202.

113. WCF 1.2: "Under the name of Holy Scripture, or the Word of God written, are now contained all the books of the Old and New Testaments. . . . All which are given by inspiration of God to be the rule of faith and life."

WCF 1.3: "The books commonly called Apocrypha, not being of divine inspiration, are no part of the canon of the Scripture, and therefore are of no authority in the church of God, nor to be any otherwise approved, or made use of, than other human writings."

WSC A.2 "The Word of God, which is contained in the Scriptures of the Old and New Testaments, is the only rule to direct us how we may glorify and enjoy him." Cf. Gaffin, "Old Amsterdam," 261: "The immediate context is the section on the testimony of the apostles to the inspiration of the OT. His third and last major point is the apostolic conviction that the OT is 'the predestined transcript of God's counsel, of which the instrumental author has, often unconsciously, produced the record, and which, as being of a higher origin, has divine authority' (446). Not only do we find that 'there is no hesitancy in announcing God the Holy Spirit as the subject speaking in the Old Testament' (447), but the stringing together of quotations from different books (e.g., Acts 1:20; Rom 15:9–12; 1 Tim 5:18) 'shows equally clearly, that in the estimation of the apostles the human authors fall entirely in the background' (447f.)."

114. Cf. Poythress, *God-Centered Biblical Interpretation*, 33–45, for an excellent extended discussion of "The Divinity of the Word."

115. WCF 1.4: "The authority of the Holy Scripture, for which it ought to be believed, and obeyed, dependeth not upon the testimony of any man, or church; but wholly upon God (who is truth itself) the author thereof: and therefore it is to be received, because it is the Word of God."

evidences of its being the Word of God, "assurance of its infallible truth and divine authority" comes only from the "inward work of the Holy Spirit."[116] The "whole counsel of God" is found in Scripture and is understood only by the "inward illumination of the Spirit of God."[117] Hence the idea of an "infallible rule" that flows from these foundational truths of Scripture along with its attendant divine authority does not comport with the vicissitudes and variability implied by Professor Enn's principle of "continual conversation." Hence, this principle of Professor Enns is also incompatible with the Westminster Confession's doctrine of Scripture.

3. Does the confession argue for the uniqueness of the Scriptures because God therein uniquely speaks "incarnately"?

We have already seen that this cannot be viewed as a confessional position, since the Reformed confessions do not utilize the incarnational analogy. However, the literature in this context reveals there is substantial disagreement over the propriety of using the incarnational analogy to present the doctrine of Scripture. Great Reformed theologians take positions both in favor of and in opposition to the analogy's value for developing the doctrine of Scripture.[118]

We must therefore ask how Enns can make this controverted principle the definition of the Bible's uniqueness? It clearly is less convincing when

116. WCF 1.5: "We may be moved and induced by the testimony of the church to an high and reverent esteem of the Holy Scripture. And the heavenliness of the matter, the efficacy of the doctrine, the majesty of the style, the consent of all the parts, the scope of the whole (which is, to give all glory to God), the full discovery it makes of the only way of man's salvation, the many other incomparable excellencies, and the entire perfection thereof, are arguments whereby it doth abundantly evidence itself to be the Word of God: yet notwithstanding, our full persuasion and assurance of the infallible truth and divine authority thereof, is from the inward work of the Holy Spirit bearing witness by and with the Word in our hearts."

117. WCF 1.6: "The whole counsel of God concerning all things necessary for his own glory, man's salvation, faith and life, is either expressly set down in Scripture, or by good and necessary consequence may be deduced from Scripture: unto which nothing at any time is to be added, whether by new revelations of the Spirit, or traditions of men. Nevertheless, we acknowledge the inward illumination of the Spirit of God to be necessary for the saving understanding of such things as are revealed in the Word: and that there are some circumstances concerning the worship of God, and government of the church, common to human actions and societies, which are to be ordered by the light of nature, and Christian prudence, according to the general rules of the Word, which are always to be observed."

118. See, for example, Gaffin, "Old Amsterdam"; Silva, *Has the Church Misread the Bible?* 38–45; Berkouwer, *Holy Scripture*, 195–212.

this theological principle is not accepted by many in the Reformed tradition, and when it is a theological paradigm that is not employed in any Reformed confession, let alone the Westminster Standards.

If we seek the uniqueness of the Scriptures according to the confession, however, it is clear that the Scriptures are unique because they are divine,[119] even though Scripture is very available to men in human form.[120] Hence the Bible's uniqueness is discovered in what the confession calls its "infallibility."[121] This unique reality of the Scriptures has led the church to speak of the Scripture's inerrancy[122] or "errorlessness."[123] This uniqueness or high

---

119. Cf. Gaffin, "Old Amsterdam—I," 276: "Rogers and McKim, for one, cite this passage to show Kuyper's support of their view that the authority of Scripture is located in its divine content in distinction from its human form." Yet Gaffin points out (277), "What graphic inspiration effects, then, is divinely authoritative certification. Concerning this certification Kuyper immediately adds the qualification that it happens 'always impressionistically,' in the NT as well as the OT.... The point of the passage in question, then, is that the differences between the four Gospels (along with the NT use of the OT) exemplify the 'impressionistic' character of the biblical records.... Concerning the activity of the human writers the sum of the matter is that 'the Holy Spirit worked effectively as a leading, directing and determining power; but their subjectivity was not lost.... This is how biblical history lives on. It gives no notarial acts, but reproduces what has been received in the consciousness, and does this not with the precision of outline which belongs to architecture, but with the impressionistic certainty of life."

120. Compare here, Kuyper's view of the divinity of Scripture in Gaffin, "Old Amsterdam," 266, "This authority derives from the fact that the speaker in the Holy Scripture is not a creature but God himself. That speech in Scripture to his church could come to pass by God immediately, i.e., without instruments (*sine instrumento*).... But this has not been the way of the Lord: As in the work of redemption he does not continue to confront us transcendently as God, but immanently in Jesus Christ he has united the divine and human natures in such a way that the divine life has appeared in a man, so also the Lord God has given us H. Scripture not transcendently but immanently, because he has so intimately united the divine factor with the human factor that the divine word has come to us, always from a human pen, mostly from a human mind, and not seldom from a human heart.... In the union of both these factors now lies the mystery of Holy Scripture. Parallel with the mystery of the incarnation runs the mystery of inscripturation. In both cases the Word of God comes to us, in the manger as Emmanuel in the world where we live, in H. Scripture as Emmanuel in the world of our thoughts and ideas. Both revelations of the word belong together, just as our living and the consciousness of that living belong together. Thus both mysteries must either be rejected together or confessed together and if confessed, then on the same ground."

121. WCF 1.5, 9.

122. Cf., for example, Young, *Thy Word Is Truth*, 113–85.

123. See Young, *Thy Word Is Truth*, 185, where he argues for the need to reserve judgment about errors in the Bible given its divine character. See also Gaffin, "Old Amsterdam," 281, "It bears emphasizing, as Kuyper notes in this context, that the Bible's divine errorlessness ultimately roots in its divine authorship, formally considered. If I transmit an authoritative message from someone else, then I must do so literally and may not change the wording.... But since ultimately it is the Holy Spirit who everywhere speaks in Scripture, formally and materially, he is

doctrine of Scripture is also evidenced in the Westminster Standards when it speaks of Scripture as "the Word of God,"[124] and God's "revealed will."[125]

Along with the confession's emphasis on the divine character of Scripture, it also recognizes Scripture's human form. Scripture was originally in Hebrew and Greek, and was committed wholly to writing.[126] Divine revelation has come into human history in various ways which have now ceased with the finality of Scripture.[127] Since divine revelation in Scripture came into human history with specific purposes, some parts of Scripture no longer carry authority, as the abrogation of the laws of Israel attests.[128] All parts of

---

free to make the variations we observe, without any detriment to its divine errorlessness. . . . By means of free quotations, in graphic inspiration the Holy Spirit maintains himself as the author of underlying material inspiration. . . . In fact, the Holy Spirit, who alone is able to convince us of graphic inspiration, enables us to perceive that the many incongruities in Scripture could not be left standing in a human author but are in fact a mark of its divinity. . . . There are two sorts of precision: mechanical and organic. A mechanically molded statue or piece of artillery precisely resembles from every angle all others cast from the same mold; among ice floes or winter flowers, however, there are great dissimilarities. The edges of a piece of wood fashioned by an artisan are completely smooth and even; the bark of a tree is quite coarse. And yet, if someone asks, where is the greatest precision, in the mechanical or the organic, everyone feels that it is not in the mechanical but in the organic that there is the greater precision and most perfect beauty."

124. Larger Catechism question 3: "What is the Word of God? Answer: The Holy Scriptures of the Old and New Testaments are the Word of God, the only rule of faith and obedience." Larger Catechism question 4: "How does it appear that the Scriptures are the Word of God? Answer: The Scriptures manifest themselves to be the Word of God, by their majesty and purity; by the consent of all the parts, and the scope of the whole, which is to give all glory to God; by their light and power to convince and convert sinners, to comfort and build up believers unto salvation: but the Spirit of God bearing witness by and with the Scriptures in the heart of man, is alone able fully to persuade it that they are the very Word of God."

125. The answer to Shorter Catechism question 39 speaks of "obedience to his revealed will." The answer to Shorter Catechism question 40 states, "The rule which God at first revealed to man for his obedience, was the moral law." Larger Catechism question 11 asks, "How does it appear that the Son and the Holy Ghost are God equal with the Father? Answer: The Scriptures manifest that the Son and the Holy Ghost are God equal with the Father . . . ." Larger Catechism question 157 speaks of " . . . the will of God revealed in them."

126. WCF 1.1, 8.

127. WCF 1.1

128. WCF 19.4. See also John H. Gerstner, Douglas F. Kelly and Philip Rollinson, *A Guide to the Westminster Confession Faith*, ch. 19, "Concerning the Law of God": "19.4 In addition to these CEREMONIAL LAWS for the church in her former state GOD ALSO GAVE THE ISRAELITES, AS A POLITICAL BODY, VARIOUS JUDICIAL LAWS. These traditional laws EXPIRED when that state of the church changed. While the moral law never changes, other laws not only change but actually EXPIRE. For example, the sixth commandment against killing remains, but the judicial law that *certain violators* of the moral law should be executed has not. Since capital punishment for such a violation as breaking the sabbath is not part of the moral law but only of the judicial, it EXPIRES with the end of the Israelite church-state."

Scripture are not equally plain to all and not all parts are equally clear.[129] It is not exhaustive and so requires human logic, the light of nature, and Christian prudence to interpret and apply.[130] Its written texts have faced the vicissitudes of transmission requiring God's providential care.[131] Engagement with the Scriptures can generate controversies of religion.[132] The Scriptures must be translated.[133] The canon itself has not been easily or fully recognized as seen by a canonical listing that excludes the apocryphal books.[134] The idea of "general equity" in interpreting relevance of the laws of Israel for the NT era also affirms the humanity of Scripture.[135] Because the Bible is a human book, it welcomes human means to interpret its message.[136]

129. WCF 1.7.

130. WCF 1.1, 6.

131. WCF 1.8

132. WCF 1.10.

133. WCF 1.8.

134. WCF 1.2, 3.

135. WCF 19.4. For a consideration of the notions of equity and general equity, see the "Report of the OPC Concerning Women in the Military." Cf. Robert Shaw, *An Exposition of the Westminster Confession of Faith*, ch. 19, "Of the Law of God" (Fearn, Ross Shire: Christian Focus, 1973): "The *judicial* law respected the Jews in their political capacity, or as a nation, and consisted of those institutions which God prescribed to them for their civil government. This law, as far as the Jewish polity was peculiar, has also been entirely abolished; but as far as it contains any statute founded in the law of nature common to all nations, it is still obligatory." See also George S. Hendry, *The Westminster Confession for Today*, ch. 21, "Of the Law of God" (Richmond: John Knox, 1960): "While God's law is the fundamental determination of man's being, and is, as such, absolutely and permanently binding upon all men, it involves obligations which are relative to the concrete situations in which it has to be obeyed . . . judicial laws were involved in the fact that Israel was at once a church and a state ('a body politic'), and they were necessary for the regulation of its life in its political aspect; since they were formulated in view of the peculiar historical conditions and geographical circumstances of the life of Israel as a primitive agrarian society, they are no longer obligatory, except in so far as they reflect general principles of equity."

136. Larger Catechism question 157: "How is the Word of God to be read? Answer: The Holy Scriptures are to be read with an high and reverent esteem of them; with a firm persuasion that they are the very Word of God, and that he only can enable us to understand them; with desire to know, believe, and obey the will of God revealed in them; with diligence, and attention to the matter and scope of them; with meditation, application, self-denial, and prayer." Larger Catechism question 159: "How is the Word of God to be preached by those that are called thereunto? Answer: They that are called to labor in the ministry of the Word, are to preach sound doctrine, diligently, in season and out of season; plainly, not in the enticing words of man's wisdom, but in demonstration of the Spirit, and of power; faithfully, making known the whole counsel of God; wisely, applying themselves to the necessities and capacities of the hearers; zealously, with fervent love to God and the souls of his people; sincerely, aiming at his glory, and their conversion, edification, and salvation." Turretin writes, "It is not a question of a perspicuity that excludes necessary means for interpretation, such as the inner light of the Spirit, the attention of the mind, the voice and ministry of the church, lectures and commentaries, prayers and vigils.

Consequently, Professor Enns's view that the Bible's uniqueness is in its human incarnate form is the opposite emphasis of the confession, which instead highlights its divine character. Hence his view appears to be incompatible with the Westminster Confession's emphasis on the priority of the divine infallibility of Scripture.

4. Does the confession view itself as a "provisional" confession and thus not a trustworthy guide for how we understand what "Scripture ought to be"?

It is important to recognize here that the confession never calls for acceptance for its own sake.[137] Instead, it points all to Holy Scripture, as when it identifies in 1.9 the "infallible rule of interpretation":

> The infallible rule of interpretation of Scripture is the Scripture itself: and therefore, when there is a question about the true and full sense of any Scripture (which is not manifold, but one), it must be searched and known by other places that speak more clearly.

Since this hermeneutical principle is "infallible"—as "infallible" as "the Word of God . . . the infallible truth" (1.5) from which it is drawn, there is consequently no "provisionality" about what the Word of God is.

The confession, consistent with its claim to present an infallible Scripture that gives to the church an infallible hermeneutical rule, seeks to focus on and exclusively to present the teaching of the Scriptures by its vast, consistent and insistent appeal to the Scriptures.[138] There are many who criticize the confession's alleged "proof text" method. Yet, what the confession seeks to do is to interpret Scripture with Scripture.[139] Hence the confession could

---

We acknowledge such means are not only useful but also normally are necessary, but we want to deny any obscurity that keeps the common people from reading Scripture, as if it were harmful or dangerous, or that leads to a falling back on traditions when one should have taken a stand on Scripture alone." *Doctrine of Scripture*, 187–88.

137. For a discussion of the confession as a subordinate standard to Scripture, see notes 44 and 45 above.

138. The scriptural citations in the Westminster Standards number well over two thousand.

139. Cf. here Berkouwer, *Holy Scripture*, 279–85, concerning "the so-called proof from Scripture," and Young, *Thy Word Is Truth*, 219–21. Young writes, "On all sides one hears it asserted that we must not use the Bible as a book of proof texts. To use the Bible in such a way is, we are told, to betray a profound misunderstanding of its nature. . . . One thing,

best be described as a subordinate standard making a consistent, albeit fallible, attempt to apply an infallible hermeneutical rule derived from an infallible written divine revelation.

The point here is that Professor Enns's principle of provisionality with regard to the Westminster Standards *per se* is not ultimately incompatible with the Westminster Standards' teaching since the standards are in fact subordinate standards. Yet his perspective of provisionality becomes incompatible with the historic Presbyterian vows to Scripture and confession discussed above when it is remembered that the "infallible rule" itself is not provisional. It is instead the mandated method established by the infallible truth of Scripture, which is the Word of God in human form. Hence Professor Enns's principle of provisionality is incompatible with the confession's teaching on the nature of Scripture and in regard to the confession's "infallible rule of interpretation of Scripture."

5. Does the confession prohibit viewing the Bible as a "timeless rule book . . . for the Christian life"?

Contrary to Professor Enns's desire for a doctrine of Scripture that removes the notion of timeless rules for the Christian life, the confession consistently affirms that there are important "rules that are to be observed" by the Christian, whether in interpreting the Scriptures, or observing the Ten Commandments—which are the standards or rules for the Christian life—or engaging in prayer and worship. The places in the standards where timeless scriptural rules for the Christian life are directly stated are listed below.

> Shorter Catechism Q. 2: The Word of God, which is contained in the Scriptures of the Old and New Testaments, is the only rule to direct us how we may glorify and enjoy Him.

---

however, may be said about this practice. It was employed by none other than our Lord Himself" (219). Berkouwer writes, "Many of these 'proofs from Scripture' stem from a deep awareness of the humanity and coherence of Scripture. . . . Clearly there is room for 'therefores' and 'so that's' in conclusions and counter arguments within the realm of the gospel (II Tim. 3:16). . . . Anselm's question 'Why did God become man?' should not automatically be rejected as rationalism. For we read everywhere of the coherence, centrality and depth of God's actions," 280, 282–83.

Shorter Catechism Q. 24: What is sin? Answer: Sin is any want of conformity unto, or transgression of, any law of God, given as a rule to the reasonable creature.

Shorter Catechism Q. 40: What did God at first reveal to man for the rule of his obedience? A. The rule which God at first revealed to man for his obedience, was the moral law.

Shorter Catechism Q. 99: What rule hath God given for our direction in prayer? The whole Word of God is of use to direct us in prayer; but the special rule of direction is that form of prayer which Christ taught his disciples commonly called *The Lord's Prayer.*

All which [the canonical books] are given by inspiration of God to be the **rule** of faith and life. (WCF 1.2).

According to the general **rules** of the Word, which are always to be observed. (WCF 1.6).

The infallible **rule** of interpretation of Scripture is the Scripture itself. (WCF 1.9).

The Law . . . continued to be a perfect **rule** of righteousness. (WCF 19.2).

The Law . . . a **rule** of life informing them of the will of God, and their duty.(WCF 19.6)

To set down **rules** and directions for the better ordering of the public worship of God. (WCF 31.2)

All synods or councils since the apostles' times, whether general or particular, may err, and many have erred; therefore they are **not** to be made the **rule** of faith or practice, but to be used as a help in both. (WCF 31.3).

Larger Catechism Q. 3: The Old and New Testament are the Word of God, the only **rule** of faith and obedience.

Larger Catechism Q. 24: Or transgression of any law of God given as a **rule** to the reasonable creature.

Larger Catechism Q. 92: The **rule** of obedience revealed to Adam in the estate of innocence, and to all mankind.

Larger Catechism Q. 97: Their greater care to conform themselves thereunto as the **rule** of their obedience.

Larger Catechism Q. 186: But the special **rule** of direction is that form of prayer which our Saviour Christ taught his disciples.

Most significantly here, Larger Catechism question 99 must be noted, as this answer teaches, "For the right understanding of the Ten Commandments, **these rules are to be observed.**"

Beyond this, the very vows of Westminster, the OPC, and the PCA recognize the "only infallible rule of faith and practice" that everyone taking the vow is to believe and so to obey. Therefore Professor Enns's principle of a Bible without timeless rules for the Christian life is incompatible with the Westminster Confession.

6. Does the confession teach that the only dimension of the Scripture's trustworthiness is in its specific focus on Christ, i.e., a "christotelic coherence"?

Professor Enns writes,

Not only do we no longer share the conventions of the ancient Near Eastern world, but we also live in union with the crucified and risen Christ, in whom all of the Old Testament finds its completion. All this to say that the central function of the Old Testament may not be there to "tell us what to do." It may be more a part of a larger story that God brings to an end many hundreds of years later in Christ.[140]

Clearly the christological focus of the Bible is one of the major theological paradigms advanced by the confession.[141] This can be seen in the

---

140. Enns, *Inspiration and Incarnation*, 67–68.

141. There are a number of theological and interpretive paradigms or theological constructs offered by the Westminster catechisms. These include: a decretal theology: Larger Catechism question 6; a theology of union with Christ: Larger Catechism question 79; a covenant theology that focuses on the history of redemption: Shorter Catechism question 59, Larger Catechism

history of the covenant of grace outlined by the Westminster Standards in chapters 7 and 8 that reflect the history of salvation in the covenant of grace in Christ.[142] Moreover, the idea of the Bible having a goal or "scope" is also referenced by the confession.[143]

But what does the confession declare the "scope" of Scripture to be? In 1.5 it says, " . . . the scope of the whole (which is to give glory to God). . . ." Larger Catechism question 4 says, " . . . the scope of the whole, which is to give all glory to God. . . ." Larger Catechism question 157, discussing how the Word of God is to be read, states " . . . with diligence and attention to the matter and scope of them. . . ." What all of this seems to be saying is that the "scope" of the Word of God is God's glory, while the "matter" of the Bible is Christ and His saving work. Thus the Westminster Standards present the doxological purpose of Scripture[144] that fits not only with the famous first question of the

---

questions 33, 34, 35, 36 101, 121; a covenant theology structured on theological covenants: Larger Catechism questions 30, 31, 32; a theology of kingdom and eschatology: Shorter Catechism question 102; and a theology of the offices and estates of Christ: Larger Catechism questions 42, 43, 44, 45.

142. Turretin, *Doctrine of Scripture*, 204–5, reflects an implicit appreciation for christocentric interpretation, or the historical redemptive nature of Scripture when it is interpreted in light of Christ. He says, "Since Scripture, which contains much more than words, is very rich in meaning, it is not absurd to say that the Holy Spirit wanted to give many teachings to us in the same word, but always one subordinated to the other so that one is the sign and figure of the other, or that they have some connection and dependency. Thus the promise given Abraham concerning his descendants refers both to Isaac as type and to Christ as antitype (Gal. 3:16). The oracle forbidding the breaking of the bones of the lamb (Ex. 23:46) refers both to the paschal lamb as a figure and to Christ in mystery (John 19:36). The promise given David, 'I will be a father to him' (II Sam. 7:14), refers both to Solomon and to Christ (Heb. 1:5). The prediction in Psalm 16:10 that the holy one will not see corruption applies both to David, although incompletely, and to Christ, completely (Acts 2:29–30). There are any number of such texts in Scripture, which have various aspects which must be held together in order to have the full meaning of the oracle, and they are fulfilled not all at once, but in stages over a period of time. Thus many of the ancient oracles had three aspects: for the dispensation of the law in the Jewish church, for the dispensation of grace in the Christian church, and for the dispensation of glory in heaven. Thus Isaiah 9:1, about the people who walked in darkness and saw a great light, has three stages of fulfillment: the liberation from Babylon, the proclamation of the gospel (Matt. 4:14–16), and the final resurrection, through which those who were living in the valley of the shadow of death will see the great light of the glory of God. Likewise in Ezekiel 37, it can be observed concerning the dry bones that the oracle had already been fulfilled when the people went out from their most bitter captivity in Babylon as from the tomb (v.12), it is being fulfilled today in the spiritual resurrection (Eph. 5:14), and it will be perfectly fulfilled in the final resurrection (John 5:25)."

143. Cf. Berkouwer, *Holy Scripture*, 124–37.

144. Francis R. Beattie, *The Presbyterian Standards: An Exposition of the Westminster Confession of Faith and Catechisms*, ch. 34, "Summary and Conclusions" (Richmond:

Shorter Catechism, but also parallels other passages of the standards that refer to God's glory such as Larger Catechism Questions 112, 113, and 190.

If the christotelic principle of Professor Enns is arguing for a christo-centricity to Scripture, this is consistent with the Westminster Confession. But this understanding of his term may not be accurate or sufficient. His further explication of christotelic seems to make the Scripture's focus so much on Christ as the ultimate fulfillment of Scripture that the ethical dimension is diminished or removed.[145] In that case, there is a loss of the Shorter Catechism's emphasis on the dual teachings of the Scriptures—"what we are to believe concerning God and what duty God requires of man" (Shorter Catechism Q. 3).

If this de-emphasis of the Christian duty to obey God's law is an inherent aspect of a christotelic hermeneutic, it would then be inconsistent with the confession. A commitment to christomonism, that is, a scriptural hermeneutic where only Christ is found in Scripture, without the concomi-tant pursuit of Christ's glory through the new obedience of the believer, is a perspective that is incompatible with the theology and ethic of the confession. The potential for christotelic exegesis to devolve into christo-monism seems possible, since it appears to be a group quest for biblical meaning by an exclusive focus on Christ in the Bible. Moreover, there does

---

Presbyterian Committee of Publication, 1896): "The inquiry now raised may be consid-ered from a twofold point of view: *First*, A general view of the principle upon which the entire Standards are constructed may be taken. Here what may be termed the theocentric principle rules. Everything is from God, is subject to God, and is for the glory of God. The absolute sovereignty of God in creation, in providence, and in grace, is the fundamental idea of the Standards. He is sovereign in the sphere of natural or physical government, and in the realm of moral government, as well as in the domain of his spiritual redemptive gov-ernment. Thus the sovereignty of God, rightly regarded and applied, is the root idea of the generic Calvinism of the Standards, and it supplies their constructive principle. The first question in the Catechisms strikes the key-note, and the entire contents of the Standards are in harmony with this view. God is the ruler of nature, and he is the Lord of the head, the heart, the conscience, and the life of all men. He is also King of kings and Lord of lords, as well as the king and head of his church. The theocentric principle is the constructive principle of the Standards as a whole, and it gives great majesty and remarkable complete-ness to the doctrines, ethics, and polity which they contain."

145. "Not only do we no longer share the conventions of the ancient Near Eastern world, but we also live in union with the crucified and risen Christ, in whom all of the Old Testament finds its completion. All this to say that the central function of the Old Testament may not be there to 'tell us what to do.' It may be more a part of a larger story that God brings to an end many hundreds of years later in Christ." Enns, *Inspiration and Incarnation*, 67–68.

not appear to be a clear sense of when this goal is achieved, according to Professor Enns.[146]

If a christotelic hermeneutic necessitates a christomonism such as summarized here, then this perspective is incompatible with the Westminster Standards' christocentricity, which is the heart of the confession's teaching on the covenant of grace and which calls for a saving faith in Christ that also seeks to bring glory to God by obedience to his law. The doxological end of the Christian life is simply portrayed by Shorter Catechism questions one and two, which declare,

> Q. 1. What is the chief end of man?
> A. 1. Man's chief end is to glorify God, and to enjoy him for ever.
> Q. 2. What rule hath God given to direct us how we may glorify and enjoy him?
> A. 2. The Word of God, which is contained in the Scriptures of the Old and New Testaments, is the only rule to direct us how we may glorify and enjoy him.

7. Does the confession reject the idea that there are a few basic rules of exegesis?

Berkouwer writes,

> The fact that hermeneutics is continually busy with rules for the exposition of Scripture shows a desire to oppose the arbitrariness which, despite the recognition of Scripture as God's Word, neglects its concrete authority. It is impossible for any theological study to bypass these questions. For in every hermeneutical question lies an aspect which is intrinsically tied to the confession of scriptural authority.[147]

It appears, then, that the notion of *rule* is intrinsic not only to the confession, but also to hermeneutics. Thus this proposed principle of Professor Enns seems to be not only anomalous to the confession, but

---

146. "I am very intentional here in saying that this is something we seek after. A christotelic coherence is not achieved by following a few simple rules of exegesis. It is to be sought after, over a long period of time, in community with other Christians, with humility and patience. Biblical interpretation is . . . a path we walk rather than a fortress we defend." Enns, *Inspiration and Incarnation*, 170.

147. Berkouwer, *Holy Scripture*, 106.

strangely inconsistent with the science of hermeneutics itself. We have already considered the confession's "infallible rule" of hermeneutics above. We have also seen that Westminster, the OPC, and the PCA each affirm a belief in the "only infallible rule of faith and practice."

But finally, there are other significant hermeneutical rules for living the Christian life presented in the standards. Perhaps most directly, let us cite Larger Catechism Question 99:

> Question 99: For the right understanding of the Ten Commandments, these rules are to be observed:
>
> 1. That the law is perfect, and binds everyone to full conformity in the whole man unto the righteousness thereof, and unto entire obedience forever; so as to require the utmost perfection of every duty, and to forbid the least degree of every sin.
>
> 2. That it is spiritual, and so reaches the understanding, will, affections, and all other powers of the soul; as well as words, works, and gestures.
>
> 3. That one and the same thing, in divers respects, is required or forbidden in several commandments.
>
> 4. That as, where a duty is commanded, the contrary sin is forbidden; and, where a sin is forbidden, the contrary duty is commanded: so, where a promise is annexed, the contrary threatening is included; and, where a threatening is annexed, the contrary promise is included.
>
> 5. That what God forbids, is at no time to be done; what he commands, is always our duty; and yet every particular duty is not to be done at all times.
>
> 6. That under one sin or duty, all of the same kind are forbidden or commanded; together with all the causes, means, occasions, and appearances thereof, and provocations thereunto.
>
> 7. That what is forbidden or commanded to ourselves, we are bound, according to our places, to endeavor that it may be avoided or performed by others, according to the duty of their places.
>
> 8. That in what is commanded to others, we are bound, according to our places and callings, to be helpful to them; and to take heed of partaking with others in what is forbidden them.

These eight rules that "are to be observed" cohere with Shorter Catechism Question 2,[148] but also prohibit the development of a christomonism. Thus, they stand as a critique of the potential christomonism in Professor Enns's christotelic hermeneutics, which admits that it has no "clear rules or guidelines to prevent us from taking this process too far."[149]

Given this emphasis on these rules for interpreting the Ten Commandments, as well as the other references to the rules of interpretation considered above, it is clear that Enns's hermeneutic is incompatible with the Westminster Standards.

CONCLUSION: CROSSROADS, SLIPPERY SLOPE, AND WATERSHED

To use Young's and Berkouwer's metaphor, the hermeneutical crisis has brought us to a crossroads. Since Professor Enns's hermeneutical proposals are not compatible with historic Reformed hermeneutics, they lead in a direction that the evangelical and Reformed churches ought not to travel, or if they do, to do so at their own risk. Although Professor Enns denies that he has led the church to a "slippery slope of unbelief,"[150] the crossroads has in fact brought us to a watershed as well.

Francis Schaeffer some years ago wrote about the "watershed" issue of inerrancy.

> We must say that if evangelicals are to be evangelicals, we must not compromise our view of Scripture. There is no use in evangelicalism seeming to get larger and larger, if at the same time appreciable parts of evangelicalism are getting soft at that which is the central core—namely, the Scriptures. We must say with sadness that in some places, seminaries, institutions and individuals who are known as evangelical no longer hold to a full view of Scripture. The issue is clear: is the Bible truth and without error wherever it speaks, including where it touches history and the cosmos, or is it only in some sense revelational where it touches religious subjects? That is the issue. The heart of neoorthodox existential theology is that the Bible gives us a quarry out of which to have religious experience, but that the

---

148. Shorter Catechism question 2. "What rule hath God given to direct us how we may glorify and enjoy him? Answer: The Word of God, which is contained in the Scriptures of the Old and New Testaments, is the only rule to direct us how we may glorify and enjoy him."

149. Enns, *Inspiration and Incarnation*, 171.

150. Ibid., 172.

Bible contains mistakes where it touches that which is verifiable—namely, history and science. But unhappily we must say that in some circles this concept now has come into some of that which is called evangelicalism. In short, in these circles the neoorthodox existential theology is being taught under the name of evangelicalism. The issue is whether the Bible gives propositional truth (that is, truth that may be stated in propositions) where it touches history and the cosmos, and this all the way back to pre-Abrahamic history, all the way back to the first eleven chapters of Genesis, or whether instead of that it is only meaningful where it touches that which is considered religious.[151]

The evangelical church stands again at a watershed, but this time it is the precipice of a hermeneutical watershed. Lest we are swept away by the flow of the hermeneutical crisis, we must once again stand fast on the infallible Scriptures and interpret them by the "only infallible rule for the interpretation of Scripture" which "is Scripture itself."

When Schaeffer summoned the church to a recommitment to inerrancy, he quoted a statement attributed to Luther,

If I profess with the loudest voice and clearest exposition every portion of the truth of God except precisely that little point which the world and the Devil are at that moment attacking, I am not confessing Christ, however boldly I may be professing Christ. Where the battle rages, there the loyalty of the soldier is proved, and to be steady on all the battle front besides, is merely flight and disgrace if he flinches at that point.[152]

In this context of the hermeneutical crisis I would like to appeal to Luther as well. But as I do, I wish to note that there are strong parallels between the Germanic courage of Martin Luther and Peter Enns. Both have been willing to take on their known world about what they believe to be true about the Bible. Both have stood strongly for their views in the face of disagreements by colleagues and criticisms from theological authorities. Both have written down their beliefs and have been unwilling to change. But there is a difference and it is an important one. Luther boldly affirmed his commitment to *sola Scriptura* when he declared at the Diet of Worms, "My

---

151. *The Complete Works of Francis A. Schaeffer*, vol. 2, *A Christian View of the Bible As Truth, No Final Conflict* (Wheaton, IL: Crossway, 1982), 121–22.

152. Ibid., 122.

conscience is bound by the Word of God. Here I stand, I can do no other." In stark contrast Enns boldly affirms that "our confession of the Bible as God's word has a provisional quality to it"[153] and declares that he is bound by "the trajectory of flexibility set out in Scripture itself."[154]

If Luther's motto—*sola Scriptura*—is now to be replaced, what should take its place? Should the new motto be *Scientia et scriptura*, to reflect the new hermeneutic that calls for the "adjustment" of "the evangelical doctrine of Scripture" in light of "extrabiblical evidence"?

But rather than walk with Enns on his theological "journey" of "bumps, twists and turns," let us instead continue to stand with Luther on God's Word and sing,

> That Word above all earthly powers,
> No thanks to them, abideth;
> The Spirit and the gifts are ours,
> Thru him who with us sideth.
> Let goods and kindred go,
> This mortal life also;
> The body they may kill;
> God's truth abideth still;
> His kingdom is forever.

Only thereby can we truly keep our historic vow to believe the "only infallible rule of faith and practice" and at the same time keep our footing before the crossroads, the watershed, and the slippery slope created by the hermeneutical crisis of our generation.

---

153. Enns, *Inspiration and Incarnation*, 168.
154. Ibid., 170.

IO

Reason, History, and Revelation:
Biblical Theology and the Enlightenment[1]

WILLIAM D. DENNISON

IN MY JUDGMENT, until recently, respect and peace have existed
between the proponents of biblical theology and her critics within Reformed
confessional churches and seminaries. In recent years, however, this spirit
of tolerance has begun to crumble. Although mystery surrounds what has
triggered this deteriorating spirit, three popular criticisms have intensified
with respect to Reformed biblical theology. First, biblical theology fails to
apply the biblical text to the lives of God's people; often the analogy is used
that it flies like an airplane over the earth, never touching the ground. Sec-

---

1. This article is a revised edition of an address given at the Kerux Conference (1999) at
Westminster Seminary California. This article should be viewed as the first in a trilogy by the
author. It originally appeared under the same title in *Kerux: The Journal of Northwest Theological
Seminary* 18 (May, 2003) 3–25. It appears here by permission. If one wishes to read the trilogy
in sequence, he should read next "Biblical Theology and the Issue of Application," in *Reformed
Spirituality: Communing with Our Glorious God*, ed. Joseph A. Pipa Jr. and J. Andrew Wortman
(Taylors, SC: Southern Presbyterian Press, 2003), 119–51. The third article is "The Redemptive-
Historical Hermeneutic and Preaching," *Kerux: The Journal of Northwest Theological Seminary*
21 (May, 2006), 11–39. Permission has been granted for this third article to appear on the Gaffin
website, www.richardgaffin.info.

ond, the redemptive-historical genre of Holy Scripture (biblical theology) is only one perspective of many genres that appear throughout the biblical narrative (for example, there are the genres of wisdom literature, parabolic literature, apocalyptic literature, etc.). Third, the origin of the theological discipline of biblical theology is within the critical-liberal theological tradition, specifically the German Enlightenment (*Aufklärung*), and for this reason the discipline must be viewed as destructive to the purity of Reformed theological orthodoxy.

From my point of view, the first two criticisms (applicational and perspectival) are the most persistent on today's theological landscape. The third criticism is not, however, without its vigorous adherents, and for that reason this essay will address the third area of criticism—the relationship between Reformed biblical theology and the Enlightenment. In the current air of criticism, it is common to hear the more strident opponents of biblical theology simply attempt to discredit the discipline because it arose in the critical-liberal thought of the Enlightenment. A deductive argument is employed: biblical theology arose in the context of liberalism; therefore, it is liberal.

Although logicians would tell us that these critics have employed a logical fallacy in their argument (the "genetic fallacy," i.e., attacking the source rather than the person or position), we must not dismiss their criticism so quickly. After all, we cannot overlook the fact that Reformed scholars as well as critical-liberal scholars hold that biblical theology arose during the German Enlightenment. Specifically, whether we are reading Geerhardus Vos or Bernhard Weiss, Richard B. Gaffin Jr. or Brevard Childs, there is agreement that the modern development of the discipline of biblical theology occurred on March 30, 1787, with the inaugural address of Johann Philipp Gabler at the University of Altdorf.[2] On that day, Gabler addressed his audience on

2. Cf. Geerhardus Vos, *Biblical Theology: Old and New Testaments* (Grand Rapids: Eerdmans, 1954), 17–18; Bernhard Weiss, *Biblical Theology of The New Testament*, trans. from 3rd revised edition by David Eaton (Edinburgh: T & T Clark, 1892), 1:26; Richard B. Gaffin Jr., "Systematic Theology and Biblical Theology," in *The New Testament Student and Theology*, ed. John H. Skilton (Phillipsburg, NJ: Presbyterian & Reformed, 1976), 3:34; Brevard S. Childs, *Biblical Theology of the Old and New Testaments: Theological Reflection on the Christian Bible* (Minneapolis: Fortress, 1993), 4–5. An English translation of Gabler's address appeared in John Sandys-Wunsch and Laurence Eldredge, "J. P. Gabler and the Distinction Between Biblical and Dogmatic Theology: Translation, Commentary, and Discussion of His Originality," *Scottish Journal of Theology*, 33, no. 2 (1980), 133–58. A partial English translation appears also in W.G. Kümmel, *The New Testament: The History of the Investigation of Its Problems*, 98–100. A more

the subject: "An Oration on the Proper Distinction Between Biblical and Dogmatic Theology and the Specific Objectives of Each." Gabler's title demonstrates that he wished to define the distinction between the new discipline of biblical theology and the traditional rendering of dogmatic theology. In light of the attack on theological dogma in the universities as well as in the churches, Gabler called for a return to the Bible. He mapped out before his audience the formulation and distinctive path for biblical theology that he felt would alleviate the tensions surrounding dogmatic theology.

As Reformed and critical scholars have reflected on the content of Gabler's address, both sides have recognized that his project was steeped in the complex nuances of the Enlightenment. To be sure, such recognition creates an uneasy atmosphere around Reformed biblical theology since the Enlightenment expounds the fundamentals of modernity, that is, exalting human reason over against the revelation of God's work in history.[3] Leading intellectuals of the era of the Enlightenment have been described as "modern pagans."[4] These intellectuals served as the inquisitors, placing the God of the Bible on the stand in their court of human reason—demanding that God tell the truth, the whole truth, and nothing but the truth.[5] They demanded that the god they had fashioned by their own mind forsake the lies found in the Bible. In other words, it was time that their god of reason tell the

---

recent German translation appeared in Otto Merk, *Biblische Theologie des neuen Testaments in ihrer Anfangszeit* (Marburg: Elwert, 1972), 273–84. Also compare Hans W. Frei, *The Eclipse of the Biblical Narrative: A Study in Eighteenth and Nineteenth Century Hermeneutics* (New Haven, CT: Yale University Press, 1974), 165–67.

3. Geerhardus Vos admitted that "her [biblical theology's] very birth took place under an evil star" ("The Idea of Biblical Theology as a Science and as a Theological Discipline (1894)," in *Redemptive History and Biblical Interpretation: The Shorter Writings of Geerhardus Vos*, ed. Richard B. Gaffin Jr. (Phillipsburg, NJ: Presbyterian & Reformed, 1980), 15. Herein, Vos wrote of the modern use of the term; however, recent discussions have placed the conception in the context of the Reformation (see O. Betz, "History of Biblical Theology," in *The Interpreter's Dictionary of the Bible: An Illustrated Encyclopedia* [New York: Abingdon, 1962], 1:432, and Charles H. H. Scobie, "History of Biblical Theology," in *New Dictionary of Biblical Theology*, ed. T. Desmond Alexander, Brian S. Rosner, D. A. Carson, Graeme Goldsworthy, Steve Carter [Leicester: InterVarsity, 2000], 12). In fact, Robert Morgan states that the expression "biblical theology" is "first found in 1629, has its roots in Christian discussion, intensified by the Reformation, of the relationship of theology to its biblical bases" ("Biblical Theology," in *A Dictionary of Biblical Interpretation*, ed. R. J. Coggins and J. L. Houlden [London: SCM, 1990], 86).

4. See Peter Gay, *The Enlightenment: An Interpretation: The Science of Freedom* (New York: W.W. Norton, 1977), 2:125.

5. Carl L. Becker describes the climate of opinion well: "What we have to realize is that in those years [Enlightenment] God was on trial" (*The Heavenly City of the Eighteenth-Century Philosophers* [New Haven, CT: Yale University Press, 1932], 73).

truth: serpents do not speak, seas do not part, miracles do not occur, and men do not rise from the dead. Furthermore, the religion presented from Genesis through Revelation is not the sole religion that brings redemption to a fallen creature. Many religions can direct us to the essence of a credible religious experience of freedom, fraternity, and life.

In light of the Enlightenment worldview, the question may be asked of Reformed biblical theologians: why would we even entertain the prospect of enriching the theological enterprise with anything that sets before us blatant unbelief and rebellion against Christian orthodoxy? Let me provide a tentative response to this question as I also reveal my thesis. Although Reformed theologians such as Vos and Gaffin commend Gabler's address for making the distinction that biblical theology is a historical discipline and that dogmatic theology is a didactic (teaching) discipline, at this point their approval of Gabler ends. After all, in compliance with the critical mood of his era, Gabler's enlightened mind and "pious" heart scrutinized the historical and revelatory character of the biblical narrative in order to make it relevant to his generation. For this reason, as Vos unfolds his conception of biblical theology, it can be said that the discipline formulated by Gabler was *not* biblical theology at all. Rather, Gabler's conception of biblical theology was merely a critical hybrid of the grammatical-historical hermeneutical method. He adapted his exegetical method to the spirit of the Enlightenment while attempting to sustain stability for less than orthodox Christian beliefs in an era of transition and confusion.

THE MOOD OF THE GERMAN *AUFKLÄRUNG*

The thesis of Immanuel Kant's famous 1784 essay titled "What is Enlightenment?" captured not only the spirit of the age, but also its theological and hermeneutical landscape.[6] His dictum was clear: "Enlightenment is man's release from his self-incurred [self-caused] tutelage [immaturity].... Have courage to use your own intelligence!"[7] As Kant defended his thesis, he

6. Frei made a similar point: "Hermeneutical theory, like all other theory in the latter part of the eighteenth century, obeyed the slogan: 'Dare to think.'" (*Eclipse*, 94). Further insight into the sentiment of Kant's thesis can be found in the essay by Thomas P. Saine, "Who's Afraid of Christian Wolff?" in *Anticipations of the Enlightenment in England, France, and Germany*, ed. Alan Charles Kors and Paul J. Korshin (Philadelphia: University of Pennsylvania Press, 1987), 107.

7. "What is Enlightenment?" [1784], *The Philosophy of Kant: Immanuel Kant's Moral and Political Writings*, ed. and trans. Carl J. Friedrich (New York: Modern Library, 1949), 132.

encouraged both scholar and cleric within the German ecclesiastical setting to use their minds in order to free themselves and the laity from the tutelage of traditional creedal church dogma. Kant tempered his evangelic spirit of freedom with the consciousness of German culture; he had to be sensitive to the submissive character of the church to the state as a German way of life. The state finalized, and on occasion initiated, ecclesiastical appointments and dismissals; likewise, on occasion, the state employed censors who approved or disapproved all books about religious subjects.[8] In this environment, Kant believed that enlightenment and liberation could be achieved by aligning what many leading German intellectuals had come to distinguish as the private and public use of reason.[9] As a pastor, the clergyman carried out his ministry with the private use of reason in mind. He followed his obligation to teach his congregation and pupils according to the doctrine of the church since he was accepted into the pastorate on the basis of compliance to the teachings of the church. On the other hand, as scholars, the clergy were free and even obligated to carry out their scholarly task with the public use of reason in mind. In this case, the scholar must demonstrate to his listeners and students all the erroneous points in church dogma as well as his proposals to improve on the religion presented in the church. Herein, within the public use of reason, the scholar exercised the courage and boldness of enlightened wisdom to go beyond the tutelage of traditional church dogma, and yet the continual exercise of the private use of reason provided the appearance of a cautious movement.

Although Kant's essay has left its mark on the history of ideas, its substance was not really new. Some sixty years prior to the appearance of Kant's essay, Christian Wolff (1679–1754), a disciple of Leibniz, had declared the Enlightenment motto—"that freedom consists in this, that in judging truth

8. Kant experienced the problems with both the academic and literary oversight of the German state. In 1786, Kant was denied the opportunity to teach philosophy at Marburg University because of the ruling of Frederick the Great and his government. Even so, in September of 1786, Kant was singled out by Frederick's administration and was elected a member of the Berlin Royal Academy. Later, in 1792, he had a book rejected for publication by the censor in Berlin.

9. The distinction between private and public use of reason did not originate with Kant. We know that it goes back to Leibniz (1646–1716), and is also found in Gotthold Ephraim Lessing (1729–81) and Hermann Samuel Reimarus (1694–1768). Concerning the connection between Leibniz and Lessing, see Henry Chadwick's essay, "Introduction," in *Lessing's Theological Writings*, trans. Henry Chadwick (Stanford: Stanford, 1956), 11. Concerning Reimarus, see Charles H. Talbert's essay, "Introduction," in *Reimarus: Fragments*, ed. Charles H. Talbert, trans. Ralph S. Fraser (Philadelphia: Fortress, 1970), 6.

one depends not on what others say, but on one's own mind."[10] Wolff was emphatic; for one to be under the tutelage of another—whether a teacher or a creed—was to be in a state of slavery. For Wolff, freedom had to be realized through the continuing Cartesian renaissance of rationalism, and its attack on the dominant status of theology as the queen of the sciences. Wolff demanded that the theologians carry out their discipline by using the rules of logic and reason as uncovered by the philosopher.[11] He did not find this demand inconsistent with freedom; rather, the unimpaired activity of the human mind was its liberating effect. In this context, Wolff asserted two basic premises which had a profound influence during the eighteenth century: "1) that revelation may be above reason but not contrary to reason, and 2) that reason establishes the criteria by which revelation may be judged."[12] Although Wolff's synthesis of reason and revelation influenced the eighteenth century, during the fourth decade of the century the popularity of the pure structure of his philosophy began to wane in light of the new demand to reassess the relationship of philosophy and history.[13] Even so, Wolff's position that reason is judge was solidly in place, assisting the emerging discussion between philosophy and history. For not only was the faculty of reason being employed to liberate modern man from the dogma of the church, but in view of the widening influence of Benedict Spinoza's (1632–77) *Tractatus Theologico-politicus* (1670), the discipline of history under the direction of philosophy began to liberate theological dogma from what history conceived as the errors of theology.[14]

In light of our focus, the German pietistic movement, from which the modern discipline of biblical theology emerges, operated in the midst of this complex discussion of reason, history, and revelation. Sometimes referred to as neologians, S. J. Baumgarten (1706–57) and J. S. Semler (1725–91)

10. This quote is an analysis of Wolff's position by Thomas P. Saine ("Christian Wolff," 107).

11. See ibid., 105.

12. Talbert, "Introduction," 5; cf. Saine, "Christian Wolff," 109–11.

13. Wolff's seeming synthesis of reason over revelation can be seen in the following statement: "The natural way, as the superior way, must always be preferred over the way of miracles, and therefore miracles cannot occur except where God cannot achieve his goal in the natural way. And in such a case miracles derive not only from God's power, but also at the same time from his wisdom, for he uses them as a means for achieving his end, which he afterward connects to natural ends; whereby the miracles are integrated into the natural order of things" (quote appears in Saine, "Christian Wolff," 111).

14. See Hans-Georg Gadamer, "On the Problem of Self-Understanding (1962)," *Philosophical Hermeneutics*, trans. and ed. David E. Linge (Berkeley: University of California, 1977), 46.

employed a historical-critical approach to the Bible.[15] They held, in different degrees, that the Bible revealed religious truth and that the Bible was imperative for the religious life; they also held that its content was not different from that of natural religion in general. Furthermore, following Wolff's lead, reason was to eliminate those individual doctrines of Christian revelation that were not identical with the reader's view of reason.[16] Perhaps more noteworthy is the fact that as rational and historical criticism performed its operation on the pages of Scripture, the basic tenet of seventeenth-century German pietism remained intact. The pietistic movement established by Philip Spener (1635–1705) and his disciple, August Francke (1663–1727) continued to maintain that the inner religious experiences of the soul ranked above the dogma and external authority of the church.[17] In fact, Spener expressed this distinction with interesting terminology: he contrasted the devotional "biblical theology" (*theologia biblica*) with the dogma of the prevailing Protestant "scholastic theology" (*theologia scholastica*).[18] In this context, our principal figure, Johann Philipp Gabler, emerged.

BIBLICAL THEOLOGY IS RECOGNIZED

I have noted that Gabler's inaugural address (1787) has been viewed by many scholars as the turning point in the discipline of biblical theology. When the address was delivered, however, its immediate historical importance was not apparent. According to John Sandys-Wunsch and Laurence Eldredge, it was not until D. G. C. von Cölln's reference to the address in 1836 (about fifty years afterward) that Gabler received such patriarchal

15. See Frei, *Eclipse*, 111; Chadwick, "Introduction," 13; and Kümmel, *The New Testament: The History of the Investigation of Its Problems*, trans. S. McLean Gilmour and Howard C. Kee (Nashville: Abingdon, 1972), 62–68.

16. See Talbert, "Introduction," 5. Concerning the term "neologian," John Sandys-Wunsch and Laurence Eldredge write: "This term has been used by modern historians since Wilhelm Mauer to designate the theologians who steered a middle way between defending the whole of orthodox theology on rational principles and those who denied that there was any revelation apart from reason alone. In the eighteenth century 'neologian' was usually a term of abuse. The development of this term has not been adequately chartered by historians; however, Gabler appears to have been one of the first to use 'neologian' in a purely descriptive sense free from pejorative overtones" ("J. P. Gabler," 147n1).

17. See Talbert, "Introduction," 4. Halle was founded in 1694 as a pietistic university.

18. See Scobie, "History of Biblical Theology," 13. This particular contrast became part of the theological environment of the Enlightenment as evidenced in the title of A. F. Büsching's work, *Advantage of Biblical Theology over Scholasticism* (1758).

status concerning biblical theology.[19] In fact, there is no evidence that his inaugural address had a broad influence on those who attended the address or on his theological contemporaries throughout the German provinces. Rather, it seems that the theological climate at the time was "slow to accept biblical theology itself as a discipline."[20] Moreover, until the appearance of Gotthilf Traugott Zachariä's (1729–1777) five-volume set on *Biblical Theology*, which appeared from 1771–86 (1771, 1772, 1774, 1775, 1786), the modern description of biblical theology was extremely vague, and its popularity had not emerged. Even after the publication of Zachariä's first four volumes in the first half of the 1770s, the next book that included the phrase "biblical theology" in its title was Hufnagel's *Handbook of Biblical Theology* in 1785. The discipline remained so obscure that J. A. Noesselt's work, *Direction to the Knowledge of the Best General Books in All Subjects of Theology* (1779), which was a standard guide for theology students of his day, did not include a section on biblical theology, and Zachariä's work on *Biblical Theology* was mentioned only among those works "recommended" for reading. Even Noesselt's last edition in 1800 failed to include a section on biblical theology.

Finally, in 1813, the succeeding volume to Noesselt's own last edition included a section on biblical theology in the theological handbook for students. Although in the 1790s there was an increased appearance of the phrase "biblical theology" in books and articles, there still seemed to be confusion about what the term meant and how the discipline should be understood. Even so, Gabler and a few others (e.g., C. F. von Ammon's *The Design of a Pure Biblical Theology*, 1792, and G. L. Bauer's four volumes on biblical theology, 1800–1802) attempted to keep the theological world abreast of issues associated with biblical theology. Although we do not know to what extent they were effective, we do know that W. M. L. de Wette's *Biblical Dogmatic of the Old and New Testaments* (1813) and von Cölln's *Biblical Theology* (1836) publicized Gabler as the figure who did the most to launch biblical theology as a separate discipline.[21] For this reason, Weiss, Vos, Childs, Gaffin, and others (e.g., Kümmel and Frei)

19. See "J. P. Gabler," 149.

20. Ibid.

21. It is believed that Gabler influenced Bauer (see Kümmel, *New Testament*, 104). Also, it is believed that de Wette was the first writer to mention Gabler's work explicitly in his own work on biblical theology (see Sandys-Wunsch and Eldredge, "J. P. Gabler," 149n2).

regard Gabler as the distinguishing figure of modern biblical theology. Sandys-Wunsch and Eldredge argue that Zachariä was probably the one who laid the foundations for Gabler's pivotal position in the history of the discipline.[22]

GABLER'S ADDRESS

As Kant's essay revealed, the last half of the eighteenth century may be viewed as a period of theological unrest in the churches as well as in theological institutions. Things were not going smoothly. Sandys-Wunsch and Eldredge seem to be on target as they present the two basic problems.

> First, how could the Bible still be the final authority in Christian doctrine when so many critical studies seemed to be destroying its believability and its unity of doctrine? Secondly, even if the Bible were assumed to be the basis for Christian faith, could there be a role for any further development of Christian ideas, namely dogmatic theology?[23]

Hence Gabler set out to maintain that the Bible is the final authority for Christian doctrine as he also attempted to reestablish a legitimate place for dogmatic theology. Gaffin summarizes Gabler's position correctly:

> The gist of Gabler's position is that biblical theology is an historical, and for him that means, a purely descriptive discipline, concerned to discover what in fact the biblical writers thought and taught; dogmatics, on the other hand, is a didactic or normative discipline, concerned to provide a contemporary statement of faith based ultimately not on the Bible but on philosophy and the use of reason.[24]

Although Gabler held that there is a distinction between the historical origin of biblical theology and the didactic (teaching) origin of dogmatic theology, his address depicts a synthesis of the grammatical-historical method of biblical interpretation with the historical-critical and rationalistic approach of his own era.[25]

22. Sandys-Wunsch and Eldredge, "J. P. Gabler," 151–58.
23. Ibid., 145.
24. Gaffin, "Systematic Theology and Biblical Theology," 34.
25. Hans Frei also made this observation (*Eclipse*, 103).

In light of bold attacks on the integrity of the Bible in his day, Gabler's address invoked the grammatical-historical hermeneutic of the Reformation.[26] He must have sounded like a breath of fresh air as he demanded that his peers return to the Bible and its grammatical-historical character. Indeed, he echoed the Reformers by maintaining that the exegete is to *study* and *classify* the text according to its historical period (time and place), viewing the authors as well as the words and grammatical constructions from within its immediate historical environment. After recognizing this basic proposition of agreement, however, his adaptation of the grammatical-historical hermeneutic begins to dissolve. Like Kant, Wolff, and the liberating mind of the Enlightenment, Gabler's call to get "back to the Bible" was filtered through modern rational-empirical and pietistic lenses. As Gabler proceeds with the exegetical task, these lenses become apparent.

After studying and classifying the historical and grammatical context of the biblical authors, the exegete must *collect* and *classify* the ideas of each author throughout the biblical narrative as well as clearly distinguish between what belongs to the Old and New Testaments, while at the same time (in pietistic fashion) giving higher relevance to the New Testament text. As the New Testament takes its exalted position in the biblical text, Gabler pushed his synthetic hermeneutic toward its final goal. He told his audience in 1787 that the "careful and sober comparison" of each author as well as each testament was to enable the exegete to understand what is of *temporal value* and what is of *universal value* in the Bible. Specifically, in rational-empirical fashion, the opinions of the authors of Holy Scripture are to be "carefully collected" and "suitably digested" in order to see what "universal notions" emerge in comparing them.[27] For Gabler, what seems to be culturally conditioned by a particular time, place, or human idea is the temporal element, whereas what emerges as being universal is the divine element. As Gabler proceeded in his address, it became apparent that the litmus test concerning the universal was typical of the pietistic genre. The truly universal—that which is truly divine—is "the unchanging idea of the doctrine of salvation" for all men.[28] Herein, we are to find true *religion* as

---

26. Kümmel defends this point (*New Testament*, 112).
27. Sandys-Wunsch and Eldredge, "J. P. Gabler," 142.
28. Ibid., 143.

opposed to theology.[29] For Gabler, then, true religion and the doctrine of salvation "is every-day, transparently clear knowledge" concerning "what each Christian ought to know and believe and do in order to secure happiness in this life and life to come."[30] Simply put, it is an enlightened *moral universal religion* clothed with Christian nuances. Furthermore, in his mind, this true understanding of biblical *religion* releases Christianity from the traditional dogmatic and creedal propositions of church doctrine.[31]

In this context, Gabler advocated his view of biblical inspiration: he maintained that the doctrine of inspiration must be viewed merely as conveying the *universal* notion of salvation. In other words, the biblical authors are inspired only as they bear the divine message of salvation. On the other hand, if the message of the biblical authors is viewed as being relevant only to a *particular* time or place, then that specific message is not to be viewed as inspired.[32] Here, Gabler is following the lead of his fellow neologian, J. S. Semler (1721–91), and his landmark work on the biblical canon, *A Free Investigation of the Canon* (1771).[33] Semler had come to believe that since the application of scriptural interpretation should take place in accordance with universal moral and religious principles, one may no longer believe that all sections in the Bible are equally inspired.[34] Gabler was simply following suit.

What cannot be overlooked, however, is how the distinction between the eternal and the temporal, the spiritual and the worldly, the universal and the particular in union with his view of biblical inspiration affected his own distinction between biblical and dogmatic theology. In summary,

29. Gabler's conception of the universal here is not that far detached from the twentieth-century distinction between *Geschichte* and *historie* in German critical-liberal theological thought. Gabler is defending a trans-historical position, a supra-temporal notion, of the universal in distinction from the temporal—admittedly without the transcending twentieth-century existential element of going beyond the subject-object relationship. Indeed, we have here the notion of a canon within a canon—the Bible within the Bible.

30. Sandys-Wunsch and Eldredge, "J. P. Gabler," 136.

31. Gabler's method and moral religion were typical of the Enlightenment project (see Becker, *The Heavenly City*, 100).

32. There is no plenary view of inspiration found in Gabler. In contrast, the Reformed biblical theologian Geerhardus Vos will strongly defend plenary inspiration. See his "The Nature and Aims of Biblical Theology," *The Union Seminary Magazine* (February-March, 1902), 198; this article has been republished under the same title in *Kerux: A Journal of Biblical-Theological Preaching* (May, 1999), 3–8, esp. 7.

33. See Frei, *Eclipse*, 111; cf. also Kümmel, *The New Testament*, 68.

34. See Ibid.

Gabler told his audience that biblical theology "deals only with those things which holy men perceived about matters pertinent to religion, and is not made to accommodate our point of view."[35] Such a goal is accomplished by the empirical-grammatical-historical-critical hermeneutic, which for Gabler simply meant biblical theology. On the other hand, dogmatic theology is varied according to the "variety both of philosophy and of every human point of view of that, which is subtle, learned, suitable and appropriate, elegant and graceful."[36] Simply put, dogmatic theology is a discipline whose chief task is to adapt its material to "our own times."[37] Specifically, dogmatic theology takes the universal principle as extracted by biblical theology and applies it to a whole theological system that accommodates the philosophical nuances to one's own time. Herein, dogmatic theology was transformed into an immediate contemporary theology.

ANALYSIS OF GABLER'S ADDRESS

As previously stated, Gabler was in tune with the spirit of his enlightened age: he was committed to employing the public use of human reason as a vehicle for liberation from traditional theological authority. Specifically, he was committed to a modern empirical-scientific method which maintained that biblical theology is "of historical origin, conveying what the holy writers felt by divine matters."[38] The key term is "felt"; however, his use of the term was not a romantic-existential concept of feeling of a shared consciousness between the biblical writers and the reader. Rather, for the exegete to know what the biblical writers *felt* by "divine matters" would require a rigorous scientific investigation. Specifically, Gabler held that we are to proceed chronologically as we *observe, collect, classify,* and *compare* (empirical method of modern science) the data that each author wrote (grammatical) in his own historical context (historically) as the authors conveyed what they *felt* about divine matters. If the author's ideas "shape" men's "souls," then he is writing as a "sacred author," but if his ideas are attempting to "shape" the "needs of his time," then he is versing only human opinion. But how does one reach such a distinction? What is being observed, collected, classified,

---

35. Sandys-Wunsch and Eldredge, "J. P. Gabler," 144.
36. Ibid.
37. Ibid.
38. Ibid., 137.

and compared? Simply, one is analyzing the biblical text in order to extract the moral ethos of the Enlightenment: goodness, happiness, the natural, innocence, pleasure over pain, tolerance, duty, liberty, equality, fraternity, etc. Herein, we discover that Gabler's critical method is a means to an end; that is, the method is used in order to authenticate Gabler's preconceived conception of a universal moral world, or more specifically, a universal moral religion. Such a presupposition and a methodological analysis of the biblical narrative reveal a conception of a canon within a canon. Analogous to the mind-body dualism of antiquity and the Cartesian mind-body problem, he has employed a method that makes a judgment between the eternal (essential to the human spirit) and the temporal (relative to the immediate culture) in the biblical text.

Besides recasting the grammatical-historical hermeneutic of the Reformation into the empirical-rational framework of modern science, Gabler in his view of biblical theology also demonstrated a methodological difference with his Enlightenment predecessor, Christian Wolff. Although an examination of the structure of his thought reveals that he agreed with Wolff's assertion that reason is to judge revelation, nevertheless, when Gabler analyzed the historical and grammatical context of the biblical narrative, he began with language in its environmental context and not logic. In other words, unlike Wolff, Gabler held that language precedes concepts (logic); or, to put it another way, history precedes philosophy.[39] For Gabler, however, history is merely the sequence—the progress—of the biblical narrative, written by inspired authors at various places and times in a contextual world, using the language of the culture. Herein, Gabler incorporated the position of the later Enlightenment period in distinction from Wolff, i.e., that history must liberate us from philosophy and logic. For him, biblical theology, as a historical discipline, secured such liberation. On the other hand, in the area of dogmatics, Gabler maintained the Cartesian and Enlightenment directive that reason or philosophy informs one's theological dogmas. In the arena of dogmatics, therefore, Gabler continued to find Wolff's method relevant; reason will continue to judge what had previously been believed.

Gabler was committed to his enlightened hermeneutical procedure: "if I judge of anything, everything must be accomplished by exegetical observation only, and that with constant care, and compared with the things spoken

---

39. Cf. Frei, *Eclipse*, 103.

of and promised by our Savior in this matter."[40] However, in order to hold on to the notion of eternal or universal religion, Gabler employed a Stoic philosophical paradigm that he attributed to the influence of the German scholar, Tiedemann.[41] As to what this meant, Gabler was not clear. Perhaps, if we take our cue from Stoic philosophy, the universal will be defined in Stoic fashion as moral worth, justice, and duty. In principle, this is what we find when Gabler states that the religion of the Bible is "teaching what each Christian ought to know and believe and do in order to secure happiness in this life and in the life to come."[42] Herein, man is pictured as securing his own salvation through what he knows, believes, and does; he is showing himself to be of moral worth. Unlike Stoicism and more like Platonism, however, the universal becomes transcendent for Gabler; it is able to take us beyond the world of appearance into a world that is unchanging in all its ideas and notions.

As the universal principle is grasped by means of an empirical-scientific investigation of the biblical text, it should not be overlooked that Gabler's method includes an empirical historiography driven by a comparable conception of reason. During the Enlightenment, the faculty of reason went through a conceptual change: no longer is it merely a static faculty that possesses, acquiesces, and judges information; rather, it also has an inherent power to control, change, and overcome the terrain of its world. This transition is a continuation of the authority and the autonomy of reason in secular western thought. In my judgment, the impetus for this movement was implicit in the construction of the nature-grace dualism (scholasticism) in which reason was presented as a neutral foundational category, and yet complementary to revelation, faith, and grace. In the context of this dualism and the sinful state of man, reason will only press for its own liberation—liberation not only of its own faculty but also as a power unto itself. In Gabler, we are observing reason as a power unto itself.

Through the empirical and rational procedure of observation, classification, collection, and comparison in the sequence of historical events, the inherent power of reason moves to the forefront of the enterprise. Through the empirical process, reason lifts off the pages of the biblical narrative the universals that are to be believed from those things that are merely cultural.

---

40. Sandys-Wunsch and Eldredge, "J. P. Gabler," 143.
41. Ibid., 142.
42. Ibid., 136.

Reason judges and affirms within its own power what is to be received as divine and what is to be received as human. As one can guess, Gabler's view of "reason" teaches that we have access only to the *effects* of biblical inspiration and not the *cause*.[43] Gabler held that an exclusive empirical approach to biblical inspiration excluded an *a priori* understanding of the supernatural status of the Word of God. His point should be evident: we have only the record of sacred authors (the *effects* of biblical inspiration). Reason reveals that on occasion the sacred authors were conveying a human teaching and at other times a divine message. Reason has the inherent power to extract from the grammatical-historical-empirical investigation of the sacred authors the universal message that is relevant for the salvation of men's souls. Moreover, reason also has the inherent power to extract from its scientific method what is left as mere human instruction from the biblical author. In essence, Gabler's biblical theology was constructing a new moral religion. Simply stated, it is a religion extracted from the Bible by the later Enlightenment view of human reason. For this reason, the religious product of Gabler's biblical theology is different from the supernatural revelation presented by the entire biblical corpus. Specifically, the power of reason shaped biblical historiography into its own moral universal religion.

GABLER AND VOS

Gabler's notion of biblical theology is merely the transformation of the grammatical-historical hermeneutic of the Reformation into the empirical method of modern science and its fraternal companion, the liberating effect of enlightened reason. In terms of Gabler's synthesis, his notion of biblical theology is far removed from the kernels of biblical theology found in Calvin and others during the Reformation, and it is also far removed from what would emerge within the confines of modern Reformed orthodoxy in the work of Geerhardus Vos (1862–1949).[44] Simply put, Vos's biblical theology did not begin by isolating the empirical landscape of history in order to find how "holy writers felt about divine matters."[45] Vos began with God as the Creator and sustainer of his creation and with the God of

---

43. Ibid., 143.

44. Recently, Scobie has argued that Reformers such as Calvin and Luther "practiced a form of Biblical Theology" ("History of Biblical Theology," 12).

45. Sandys-Wunsch and Eldredge, "J. P. Gabler," 137.

the Bible who reveals himself in providential history. The entire canon of Scripture records the condescending activity and deeds of the living God on the plain of his own created history. The knowledge and understanding of God is unfolded within the historical revelation of his activity. For Vos, the process of God's self-disclosure is apparent: event precedes word, deed precedes interpretation.[46] God's revelatory activity precedes man's comprehension of that activity in his whole existence (including heart, soul, mind, senses, etc.).

In God's inscripturated Word, God's activity and God's interpretation of that activity cannot be separated. One must start with God and his revelatory activity in order to know, understand, and interpret God and his revelatory activity correctly. The hermeneutical approach to the canon includes the eschatological identity of God—one must begin with God (deed), and one must end with God (interpretation) in one's understanding of his Word. Such an eschatological structure of biblical revelation cannot be found in Gabler's address; rather, his hermeneutical approach falls into its own eschatological structure. As an Enlightenment rationalist, Gabler begins with an empirical-rational religion and he ends with an empirical-rational religion; specifically, he begins with reason taking on the investigation toward uncovering truth, and he ends with reason uncovering the universal principle of religious truth. Sandys-Wunsch and Eldredge are correct when they conclude: "Gabler has perhaps a better claim to be considered the father of the study of biblical religion than the father of biblical theology."[47] Although this observation is correct, it should not be overlooked that the "biblical religion" presented by Gabler is *not* the religion of the Bible at all. Moreover, it brings into question whether Gabler, the so-called father of biblical theology, should be viewed as a true participant in the discipline itself.

---

46. See Vos, *Biblical Theology*, 13; idem., "The Idea of Biblical Theology," 7. Further insight on this point is provided by Richard B. Gaffin Jr.'s essay, "The Vitality of Reformed Dogmatics," in *Vitality of Reformed Theology: Proceedings of the International Theological Congress, June 20–24, 1994* (Kampen, Netherlands: Kok, 1994), 16–50. James T. Dennison Jr. also captures Vos's position: "He [Vos] emphatically declares the revelatory character of the mighty acts of God in history. The act is *identified* with revelation in history. Moreover act is further explicated by word. Hence the mighty acts of God are not abstract moments—they are followed by words of explanation and interpretation. And in the organic continuum of redemptive history, act and word progressively unfold. Acts recapitulate one another; words additionally exegete one another" ("What is Biblical Theology? Reflections on the Inaugural Address of Geerhardus Vos," *Kerux: A Journal of Biblical-Theological Preaching* [May, 1987] 38).

47. Sandys-Wunsch and Eldredge, "J. P. Gabler," 158.

Perhaps in light of the connecting link to biblical and Reformed orthodoxy, Vos is the father of modern biblical theology. Indeed, new elements were brought to mind by the critical-liberal biblical theologians, e.g., the position that biblical theology is a historical discipline. Since facts have meaning only within their given context, the connection between critical and orthodox biblical theology ends. Gabler's view of history was shaped by the dynamic of empirical reason and not by the authority of God and his Word. In what had become customary and fashionable during the Enlightenment, his view of reason stripped history of its supernatural character, and thus constructed another natural religion—a universal moral religion based on the Christian *ethos*. It was not a coincidence, therefore, that Vos frequently used the terminology of "supernatural religion" to describe the revelation of biblical religion. Such terminology was used purposely to contrast the natural or rational religion of the critical-liberal Christian theologians who preceded him. As far as Vos was concerned, their view of history was antithetical to the God who acts and interprets the whole story of biblical history.

Even in light of this tainted past, Vos was able to place the new discipline consistently within the confines of biblical and Reformed orthodoxy. One may ask why the Reformation tradition of the sixteenth and seventeenth centuries did not advance to Vos's understanding of the discipline? Vos's teacher at the University of Berlin, Bernhard Weiss, provides some insight for answering that question. He highlights three points. First, the Reformation brought to the forefront the difference between the authority of the church and the authority of the Bible, and demanded a renovation of theology in accordance with the sole authority of Holy Scripture.[48] Second, although the Reformers were dominated by the consciousness of *sola Scriptura* against Roman Catholic doctrine, nevertheless at this time the Reformers continued to accept the system of theology passed down to them, that is, the scholastic systematic arrangement of theological rubrics.[49] Third, by means of the exegesis of Scripture, the Reformers imported a new and more biblically informed interpretation into the doctrines of theology without examining

---

48. See Weiss, *Biblical Theology*, 22.

49. See Ibid., 22–23. Richard A. Muller has made the same observation (*Post-Reformation Reformed Dogmatics: Prolegomena to Theology* [Grand Rapids: Baker, 1987], 1:63, and "The Problem of Protestant Scholasticism—A Review and Definition," in *Reformation and Scholasticism: An Ecumenical Enterprise*, ed. Willem J. van Asselt and Eef Dekker [Grand Rapids: Baker, 2001], 53–54.

or questioning the system of theology at all.[50] Simply put, the Reformers were changing the substance of the various theological rubrics without transforming the system of theology.

I would suggest that this directive makes sense; we must remember first things first. First, the Reformers had to change the substance of theological formulations, and then, perhaps, they would see the need of addressing the system of theology. In their day, however, and even by the late nineteenth century, the need to address the formulation of the system of theology was not clearly perceived by most Reformed theologians. In my judgment, Vos was the person who not only continued to address the substance of theology (e.g., Christ's resurrection is the primary subject of Paul's soteriology, not the atonement), but also attempted to transform the system of theology (e.g., eschatology moves from the end of systematics to the beginning). Vos's project should not be viewed as an attempt to upstage or truncate the position of the Reformers; rather, he was simply attempting to apply more consistently a Reformed view of hermeneutics to the whole spectrum of the theological enterprise. In other words, in terms of the subject of our study, the roots of Vos's biblical theology are not to be found in Gabler and the Enlightenment; rather, the roots of his theology are to be found in the Reformers. Let me be specific, although not comprehensive.

Although the Reformers were still operating with the rubrics of medieval Roman Catholic theology, the seeds were being planted for understanding the structural flow of biblical revelation in a whole new way. The emphasis was on the authority of God and the sovereign control of whatsoever comes to pass. Specifically, God's own providential dealings in the course of history are pervasive in the Reformers and the Reformed confessions. This view of God and history came to expression in what the Reformers saw as the continuity element in biblical revelation—the idea of the covenant. Unlike some Lutherans or the Anabaptists, the Reformers understood the Bible as a whole. The Reformers did not elevate some portions of Scripture in comparison with others (as the Lutherans did), and they did not view the New Testament as eradicating the Old Testament (as the Anabaptists did). Rather, with Augustine, the Reformers proclaimed that the Old is contained in the New and the New is contained in the Old.

---

50. See Weiss, *Biblical Theology*, 23.

In this context, one must not forget that for Calvin, typology became a hermeneutical principle he employed to attack the allegorical interpretation of medieval hermeneutics, i.e., Old Testament persons as well as certain institutions (e.g., priesthood, temple) were types of Christ.[51] Even among the Reformers, the expanse of the grammatical-historical method was not limited to the language, historical context, and sequence of the narrative. Rather the grammatical-historical method appeared in the context of the sovereign God of heaven and earth revealing himself in history, i.e., through the covenant unfolding in Christ.[52] In Reformed theology, therefore, the covenant and christocentric typology provided a fundamental link in understanding and stressing the unity of Scripture; they are at the core of the meaning of Scripture. This same understanding is found at the heart of Vos's biblical theology.

Furthermore, one cannot overlook the hermeneutical principle of the Reformation, i.e., "that Scripture interprets Scripture." The Reformed view of the historical continuity of Scripture testifies specifically to the hermeneutical principle of the Reformers; this hermeneutical principle is nonsense without the unfolding history of revelation. For this reason, Richard B. Gaffin Jr. has stressed that the analogy of Scripture is implicitly biblical theological; this hermeneutical principle depicts the essence of the discipline of biblical theology.[53] In light of Gaffin's observation, it is easy to conclude that Vos's work was a consistent outworking of the Reformed principle of hermeneutics. On the other hand, it takes great strain to connect Gabler to this Reformed principle. If anything, Gabler teaches us the

51. See John Calvin, *Commentaries on the First Book of Moses Called Genesis*, trans. John King (Grand Rapids: Eerdmans, 1948), 1:114, and his *The Epistles of Paul the Apostle to the Galatians, Ephesians, Philippians, and Colossians*, ed. David W. Torrance and Thomas F. Torrance, trans. T. H. L. Parker (Grand Rapids: Eerdmans, 1965), 84.

52. See Scobie, "History of Biblical Theology," 12; Muller, *Post-Reformation Reformed Dogmatics*, 37; and Vos, "The Doctrine of the Covenant in Reformed Theology," in *Redemptive History and Biblical Interpretation*, 234–67.

53. John Murray made this same observation about the relationship between the analogy of Scripture in the Westminster Confession of Faith and the discipline of biblical theology (see his "Systematic Theology," in *The New Testament Student and Theology*, ed. John H. Skilton [Nutley, NJ: Presbyterian and Reformed, 1976], 3:26n20. Gaffin's comment is worth noting: "It does not appear to be going too far to say that in 'biblical theology,' that is, effective recognition of the redemptive-historical character of biblical revelation, the principle of context, of the analogy of Scripture, the principle that Scripture interprets Scripture, so central in the Reformation tradition of biblical interpretation, finds its most pointedly biblical realization and application" ("Systematic Theology and Biblical Theology," 45). Gaffin made almost the same statement in 1994 (cf. his "The Vitality of Reformed Dogmatics," 26n19) in *Theology: Proceedings of the International Theological Congress, June 20–24, 1994* [Kampen, Netherlands: Kok, 1994], 26n19).

danger of the grammatical-historical method of exegesis if not properly placed within Reformed orthodox parameters.

Conclusion

If one truly believes that Reformed biblical theology is tainted merely because modern biblical theology arose in the Enlightenment, then one has failed seriously to do his homework. As students of God's Word and the history of western thought, it is our duty to uncover and expose the philosophical presuppositions that underlie the critical-liberal construction of biblical theology, especially as formulated in its so-called father, Johann P. Gabler. Furthermore, we are to examine and investigate those presuppositions in order to see how they conform to the revelation of God's Word. In our study, we have seen that the critical-liberal formulation of biblical theology appeared in the context of the Enlightenment and its presupposition of an empirical-rational worldview. Its proponents interpret the "facts"—the grammatical-historical construction of the Bible—in light of their scientific method. Such an approach begins with man and not with God. It has no integrative stance between the biblical text and the sovereign God who is the author of the entire canon of Scripture. Rather, it proceeds exclusively on the empirical grounds of the liberating effects of public, practical, and enlightened reason in order to extract a divine moral religion in the pursuit of everlasting happiness. The liberal-critics are freeing themselves from supernatural revealed religion and returning to a world that resembles Greek mythology and how the muse "felt about divine matters" (to use the language of Gabler).

When this humanistic religion is exposed through uncovering its presuppositions, then we are confronted with the full force of the antithetical nature of liberal-critical biblical theology in respect to Vos and his faithfulness to the hermeneutic of the Reformed tradition. We must realize that the common features between Vos and Gabler dissolve in light of the presuppositions, structure, and content of their respective views on biblical theology. The holistic construction of Vos's biblical theology is antithetical to the holistic construction of Gabler's formulation.[54] The

54. Interestingly, Vos provides the church with one of the most succinct critical analyses of Enlightenment biblical theology that one will find within the bounds of orthodoxy (see "Idea of Biblical Theology," 7–8, and his *Biblical Theology*, 17–23).

idea that biblical theology is a historical discipline and dogmatics is a didactic discipline, or that the discipline of history precedes the disciplines of philosophy and dogmatic theology does not reveal much substantive continuity between Vos and Gabler. For Vos, these observations as well as biblical "facts" occur in a context—the context in which the one true God, that is, the ontological Trinity, gives meaning to the facts. The Bible records the actual activity of God, and the Bible provides God's own interpretation of those acts. Such a position is not found in Gabler. For Vos, God revealing himself in history is integrated with a grammatical-historical approach to the Bible; it is a holistic approach. In this approach, any empirical and rational investigation of the biblical text is integrated with the authority and person of God, who must control the investigation by the exegete submitting to the structure of biblical revelation. Thus, Vos would endorse the fact that history precedes philosophy because of the nature and character of God's revelation of himself, not because of the necessity to liberate man from rationalism. Hence, the Enlightenment is the enemy; it is not a friend! As we hold passionately to the God of the Bible and the unfolding of his revelation, we will not allow Gabler and the Enlightenment to define the terms on which we stand. Gabler's biblical theology is not biblical theology at all, in light of God's true revelation of himself recorded on the pages of Holy Scripture. The roots of an orthodox biblical theology are not found in the Enlightenment; rather, in the final analysis, they are found in God himself! Indeed, we are not declaring ourselves to be children of modernity (Enlightenment); rather, by the sovereign grace of God, we are children who hold passionately to the whole counsel of God as revealed to us from Genesis through Revelation. We are to preach, teach, and proclaim the full-orbed message as God has given it to his church in his infallible Word!

II

"Something Much Too Plain To Say": A Systematic Theological Apologetic[1]

K. Scott Oliphint

IN THEIR RECENT anthology titled *The Impossibility of God*, Michael Martin and Ricki Monnier note that there are "basically two kinds of arguments for the nonexistence of God: arguments for the improbability of God and arguments for the impossibility of God."[2] Arguments for the improbability of God deal, in the main, with the notion of evidences. The

---

1. I count it a privilege to contribute to this festschrift for my teacher and colleague, Richard B. Gaffin Jr. This article is an edited version of "Something Much Too Plain To Say," *WTJ* 68/2, Fall 2006: 187–202. If the reader will permit a short autobiographical note . . . When I was a young-ish student at Westminster, I had the privilege of hearing Dr. Ed Clowney present what was, in my opinion, the best thing he would ever write, "Preaching the Word of the Lord: Cornelius Van Til, V.D.M." (subsequently published in the *WTJ* 46, no. 2 [1984]: 233–53). After that presentation, I vividly remember Dr. Clowney emerging from the auditorium and receiving an enthusiastic hug from Dr. Gaffin. And I remember thinking as a student that, from a human perspective, such an expression would be the ultimate in affirmations. This essay began as my inaugural lecture to the position of professor of apologetics and systematic theology. After it was given, I received from Dr. Gaffin the ultimate affirmation. It is with this in mind that I submit it to this well-deserved expression of appreciation for Dr. Gaffin's ministry to me, and to the church of Jesus Christ.

2. Michael Martin and Ricki Monnier, eds., *The Impossibility of God* (Amherst, NY: Prometheus Books, 2003), 14.

anthology that Martin produced is meant to address and support the latter kinds of arguments, that is, arguments for the impossibility of God.

In that anthology, Martin and Monnier arrange arguments for the impossibility of God into five categories: there are *definitional disproofs* based on an inconsistency in the definition of God; there are *deductive evil disproofs* based on an inconsistency between the existence of God who has certain attributes and the existence of evil; there are *doctrinal disproofs* based on an inconsistency between the attributes of God and a particular religious doctrine; there are *multiple attributes disproofs* based on an inconsistency between two or more divine attributes; and finally there are *single attribute disproofs* based on an inconsistency within just one attribute. While Martin is clear that this categorization is not written in stone, it should be noted here that in *every case* the disproofs for the existence of God have to do with God's attributes, and with how a God who is supposed to have certain attributes can, at the same time, relate to his creation or to other attributes he might have by virtue of creation. Since Martin's contributors—call them Martin's Minions—argue that there are insuperable contradictions between a God who has these attributes and creation, this kind of God simply cannot exist. Clearly, according to Martin, since the traditional concept of God provides nothing but "an ocean of contradictions,"[3] God cannot exist. Or, to put it in the common philosophical vernacular, given certain agreed attributes of God, there is no possible world in which he can exist. His existence is, therefore, impossible.

As most of us realize, attacks on the attributes of God are not reserved for unbelievers. The history of the church is replete with examples of many within the church who have attempted to deny what have traditionally been seen as essential attributes of God. Open theism is perhaps the most recent example; Karl Barth's theology is perhaps the most extensive modern example.

My purpose in this chapter is, first of all, apologetic; it is a defense of Christian theism. We will not be dealing with every specific argument for the impossibility of God offered by Martin's Minions, but will, instead, offer a corrective that any philosopher or theologian worth his salt would have to take seriously if objections to God's existence based on his attributes are to be taken seriously by a Christian audience. (And it should be noted here that, in lodging objections against God's existence, Martin's Minions attempt

3. Ibid.

to stand on the ground of theism; they attempt to argue their points *on the basis* of certain attributes of God that theism affirms.)

My second purpose, however, and more central in the overall scheme, is that I want to use the tools and methods of philosophy, incorporated with Reformed systematic theology, to develop a response to these objections to God's existence, based as they are on a supposed incompatibility of properties. I will attempt as well to respond to many, if not most, of the discussions of God's existence and attributes in Martin's anthology that seek to undermine a biblical, and by that I mean Reformed, understanding of who God is and how he relates to his creation. I should say here that what I am attempting to do in responding to Martin's Minions is to lay out different strands of an argument that will resolve itself only in the conclusion. So, while you might think at times that our discussion is not related to Martin's objections, the relationship, I hope, will be more obvious and explicit when these strands are brought together at the end.

Two methodological notes of importance to remember in this discussion:

1) I will not be moving from exegetical to theological to philosophical considerations. I will rather be presupposing that, since no significant exegetical or theological refutations have been forthcoming concerning the central elements of a Reformed doctrine of God, those efforts in the history of the church remain in place and intact.

2) Secondly, note that I will be using the *tools and methods of philosophy* in order to respond to the objections given. In using those tools, please note carefully what I am *not* saying. I am *not* saying that philosophical tools are the best, certainly not that they are the most efficient, way to discuss these matters. And I am *not* saying that *the* way to discuss the doctrine of God is by way of philosophy. All of the doctrinal points that I will make here have exegetical and theological support behind them, and those are primary when discussing who God is.

But we should note here that, in using philosophy's own language and tools, not only is this in keeping with Van Til's approach to apologetics, but it has a rich and deep tradition that itself was at the heart of Reformed and post-Reformation developments in systematic theology. Without belaboring details here, we can simply note that in such cases where philosophy is used in the service of theology, it can be a useful handmaiden, especially when objections to Christianity are lodged within that context. And it should not escape us that, in using such language and tools, there is a persuasive value that would not be present otherwise.

So, in response to Martin's Minions, we can begin with the question, "Is the existence of God really impossible?" How would we go about answering such a question? One rather dismissive, though fundamentally correct, answer might be Hamlet's response to Horatio—"There are more things in heaven and earth, Horatio, than are dreamt of in your philosophy."[4] Perhaps one, and even one legitimate response would be to say that philosophy is just not able to imagine who the true God is and what he is able to do. But, true as it is, there is little of persuasive value in such a response. Is there a way to respond that would contain something of a persuasive element in that it would seek to discuss such objections within the context in which they are given? Maybe so.

In the vast majority of arguments given by Martin's Minions for the impossibility of God, the problem that these authors set out is *not*, in the first place, that there is no evidence for God's existence. That approach has a rich history as well, but it is not the one these authors take. *Rather, and this is all-important for our purposes here, the problem is that God, as he is traditionally thought of, cannot exist because of an inherent incompatibility or inconsistency either between his own attributes, or between his attributes and the properties of creation.* Thus, there is no possible world in which this kind of God can exist. So, the proper response to such objections is not to turn to evidential proofs for God's existence, but rather it is to provide a context in which the existence of God as he is traditionally understood can be articulated consistently, though, of course, not and never exhaustively.

One response, therefore, to Martin's Minions might be this: Suppose we assume the notion of essentialism in our discussions about God. Essentialism goes back at least as far as Aristotle, and has been part and parcel, in one form or another, of Christian theology from its earliest days to the present. Not only so, but along with a revival of discussions about God in philosophy has come a revival, through Saul Kripke and others, of a state-of-the-art notion of essences. Put simply, essentialism affirms that there are such things as essences, and that some things are essential and some contingent. But then just what is an essence? Typically, an essence has been defined as that which something *must* be, in contrast with that which a thing *might* be. An essence is that which is *necessary* to something.

---

4. *Hamlet*, Act 1, Scene 5.

But then how do we understand this notion of *necessity*? Again, one of the ways that philosophers and theologians have understood "necessity" is as a basic "mode" of truth or of existence. Modes of truth deal with propositions and are called *de dicto* modalities; modes of existence deal with those things to which propositions point, and are called *de re* modalities. Our interest here is in *de re* modalities, modalities of things rather than propositions. And whenever modes of existence are discussed, the primary modes articulated are necessity, contingency, possibility, and impossibility. Something is necessary if it *must* be; something is impossible if it *cannot* be; something is contingent if it *may or may not* be, and something is possible if it is necessary or contingent, but not if it is impossible. In discussions about God relative to essentialism, the modal notions that will occupy us are primarily the necessary and the contingent. In order to understand what we mean by these modes of existence, a couple of definitions are in order.

Modal notions are routinely discussed in terms of possible worlds semantics. Though there are a number of definitions available, to keep matters simple we will define a "possible world" as a "possible state of affairs." This is important in the discussion. We should not think of a possible world as a "thing" like our world or like the universe. It is simply a possible state of affairs. Given our understanding of possibility, i.e., that it includes both the necessary and the contingent, a possible state of affairs, or possible world, may exist either necessarily or contingently. That is, a possible world includes (1) a state of affairs that may not exist but could, (2) a state of affairs that *must* exist, or (3) a state of affairs that *may* exist. So, a possible world can include the actual, the contingent, the necessary, as well as the non-actual. Further, if we define essence as "a property, or set of properties, which something has necessarily," we can readily see that entailed in the concept of essence is a notion, or a *mode*, of necessity. Part of the design of possible worlds semantics is to help us see just what we mean when we ascribe modalities, such as necessity (and contingency), to things.

In "possible worlds speak," something has a property necessarily if it has that property in every world in which it exists. Or, to put it another way, necessity, in the way that we're discussing it here, is about essential properties. That is, if W equals "a possible world," then we could define essence as

E_{df} = For any thing x and any possible world, W, in which x exists and any property P, x has P in W.[5]

Since, therefore, x has P at any possible world in which it exists, P is essential to it; it does not exist at any world at all unless its existence includes the property P (this entails, of course, that it is impossible that x exist without P). Contrast this with properties that are not essential to a thing—contingent properties. In such cases, we could define these properties as

C_{df} = For any thing x and any possible world, W, in which x exists and any property P, x has P in W and x does not have P in W_1.

There are some worlds, W, at which x has P and some worlds, W_1, at which x does not have P.[6] This means that P is a contingent property of x.

In virtually all of Martin's anthology, the notion of God as a necessary being is assumed. It is just *that* assumption that causes problems for most of his contributors. But, for the most part, the authors understand that if there is such a being who is in every way perfect and in no way lacks anything good, then this being must exist necessarily. The problems, therefore, revolve around the fact that this perfect and necessary being either cannot co-exist with other attributes he is supposed to have, or cannot have a particular attribute, given what we know of the universe.

So, let's begin to address this problem by applying essentialism to the traditional understanding of God. Within the domain of possible worlds, the argument for the necessity of God's existence entails the fact that God exists at every possible world. If there was a possible world, *per impossibile*, at which there was no God, then God's existence would be merely possible, and he could not be One without lack or privation, since his existence would be reduced to a contingency. That is, there would be a

---

5. Assumed in this discussion, without argument, is a notion of the actual such that only those things that exist have properties. See, for example, Alvin Plantinga, "Actualism and Possible Worlds," *Theoria* 42 (1976): 139–60.

6. This account of contingent or accidental properties depends for its cogency on the S5 system of modal logic. The details of the various systems are beyond the bounds of our discussion here. Suffice it to say at this point that, to the extent that modal logic and possible worlds semantics is useful, S5, including (and advancing) as it does its lesser cousins, S4 and T, seems to make the most sense. For a helpful summary of the differences in these systems, see Jay Wesley Richards, *The Untamed God: A Philosophical Exploration of Divine Perfection, Simplicity, and Immutability* (Downers Grove, IL: InterVarsity, 2003), 53–54n14.

possible world at which God did not exist. If that were true, then it would be the case that his existence was dependent on a certain possible world obtaining, in which case he would be dependent on something that was independent of his own existence, i.e., a possible world, or the notion of possibility itself.

Now entailed in the notion of God's necessary existence is God's essence. Assuming for the moment that existence is a property, p, the proposition, (1) God has p in every world, extends not only to his existence but (remembering E_{df} above) to anything else that God has (or *is*) essentially.[7]

Without rehearsing the exegetical material here, one further point must be understood. Reformed theology has historically often made its way to the attributes of God by way of the *names* that he gives to himself in Scripture. And prominent among God's given names in Scripture (used more than 5,000 times) is the "I Am" name, or Yahweh, which gives rise to the focus of our understanding of God as *a se*.

With this in mind, how do we begin to understand certain attributes of God as essential attributes? One way, though admittedly not the only way, would be to take those attributes that are entailed by his character as the "I Am," attributes that are necessarily exemplified at every possible world, attributes, we could say, that are related strictly to God (quite apart from anything else), and affirm them to be of the essence of who he is. In other words, given that God is essentially *a se*, we could begin to posit attributes or properties that are entailed by his essential independence, which would themselves, therefore, also be exemplified at every possible world.

For example, is it the case that God is essentially infinite? If we affirm that God is a perfect and necessary being who lacks nothing, if we affirm his character as *a se*, then it cannot be the case that he is in any way limited by anything outside himself, since to be limited would, by definition, be a lack; it would be a constraint placed on God by something else, be it space, or time, or human choices, or . . . . We can affirm, then, that God is essentially infinite. Entailed in his independence and his perfection is infinity itself.

---

7. We should note here that to say that God *has* a property is not to undermine the biblical doctrine of simplicity. It is simply to say *what kind of* God we are talking about, without pronouncing, at this point, on the relationship of his properties, or of him to his properties. The doctrine of simplicity, together with an essentialist understanding of God's properties, would affirm that whatever properties or attributes are essential to God are, themselves, identical to him. They are not parts or properties in some way added to or divisible from him.

On the other hand, is the property of "being Creator" of the essence of God? One way to answer this question is to ask whether there is a possible world in which God is not the Creator.[8] Or, to put it another way, is it possible that God not create anything? The orthodox answer to this question is, of course, yes. To answer no would mean that God *had to* create the world, in which case there is no possible world in which God is not the Creator, in which case, therefore, the creation of the world would itself be a necessary property of God.[9] But then God would have a necessary property that (1) was not entailed by his independence (since the necessity of God's creative activity would entail a dependence on something besides God) and (2) implied some kind of lack in God (since the necessity of something *ad extra* would mean that God was in need of it in order to be who he essentially is). So "being Creator" is not an essential property of God.

It would seem, then, that God has essential properties, and others that are not essential to him. How should we delineate between these two? What is it that helps us to see God's essential properties as essential, and what is it that helps us to see God's other properties as nonessential? According to our definition of essential properties, E$_{df}$, essential properties are essential if they are exemplified at every possible world. Not only so, but that which is exemplified at every possible world (and thus necessary) is anything that is entailed by the fact that God is the "I Am."

That is, God's essential properties are properties which God has that in no way depend on anything but himself in order to obtain at every world. Since God has these properties in every possible world, they are essential properties; they are necessary attributes of his. It is not possible, then, that God not have these properties (i.e., there is no possible world in which God does not have these properties).

We can say as well that God is essentially omniscient; he knows himself exhaustively. There is nothing hidden from his understanding of himself. Unlike us, God has exhaustive knowledge of his triune character. He is also eternal; there is nothing constraining God's essential character such that he is subject to the passing of moments or is in some essential way

---

8. We may be tempted to say there is no possible world in which God is not Creator, since for any possible world to exist at all, God has to create it. However, this is to think of a world as something actualized, rather than as a maximal state of affairs.

9. The Reformed scholastic notion of hypothetical necessity, as pertaining to creation, is not denied here, because contained in that notion is the possibility of no creation at all.

bound to a past, present, and future. But it is precisely at these points, to use just two examples, where philosophers of religion, atheistic philosophers, and many Christian theologians have problems. Examples could be multiplied almost endlessly, but since I began with Martin's Minions, let me give just one example from that anthology. In his survey of what he calls "incompatible-properties arguments," Theodore Drange offers the following argument:

1. If God exists, then he is immutable.

2. If God exists, then he is omniscient.

3. An immutable being cannot know different things at different times.

4. To be omniscient, a being would need to know propositions about the past and future.

5. But what is past and what is future keep changing.

6. Thus, in order to know propositions about the past and future, a being would need to know different things at different times (from 5).

7. It follows that, to be omniscient, a being would need to know different things at different times (from 4 and 6).

8. Hence it is impossible for an immutable being to be omniscient (from 3 and 7).

9. Therefore, it is impossible for God to exist (from 1, 2 and 8).[10]

In offering a response to this kind of argument, and any other argument that seeks to deny God's aseity, or to show an inherent conflict in God's essential character by virtue of his creation, we can sum up our initial response by considering the Westminster Confession of Faith's initial and thus more general notion of *covenant*:

The distance between God and the creature is so great, that although reasonable creatures do owe obedience unto Him as their Creator, yet they could never have any fruition of Him as their blessedness and reward, but by some voluntary condescension on God's part, which He hath been pleased to express by way of covenant. (WCF 7.1)

10. Theodore M. Drange, "Incompatible-Properties Arguments: A Survey," in *The Impossibility of God*, 189.

In other words, the confession recognizes that there is an ontological distance between God and man. The distance here is not, of course, spatial. It is a distance of *being*: a distance that comes about by virtue of the fact that God creates something, some *being*, that is ontologically different from himself. How, then, does God bridge the gap between himself and those he has created in his image? "By some voluntary condescension" the confession says. It is this condescension that I would like for us to think about in light of what we have said thus far, and in light of the objections of Martin's Minions.

Just what is this condescension? It is *not*, we should make clear, God's attempt to fit into an otherwise hostile, or perhaps neutral, context. It is not God coming down to take to himself habits and customs that are foreign to him in order to blend in with a particular culture. God's condescension is much broader and deeper than that. But just what does this voluntary divine condescension entail? We should note that, *as far as God's relationship to that which he creates*, it entails everything that he does, says, and is *with respect to that relationship*.[11] For example, the very fact that God brings into existence something to which he is in some way related entails, automatically, an act of condescension.

It entails an act of condescension because of who God is essentially. Given that God is supremely perfect and without need or constraint, to begin to relate himself to that which is limited, constrained, and not perfect is, in sum, to condescend.[12] For example, the very fact that Scripture tells us "the Spirit of God was hovering over the face of the waters" (Gen. 1:2) is evidence of God's own condescension; he had to "come down" to hover over the waters. God, as infinite spirit, has no need to constrain himself by hovering over the face of the waters. He is altogether infinite, without constraint. But he does hover, and he condescends to do so.

Not only so, but, just after Adam and Eve sinned, "they heard the sound of the LORD God walking in the garden in the cool of the day" (Gen. 3:8).[13]

11. When we say that God's condescension involves everything that he *is*, we are not saying that all that he is becomes exhausted in this act of condescension; that would be to deny what we have already affirmed with respect to God's essential character.

12. To say that creation is not perfect is not to say that it was not good, as God declared it to be. It is simply to say that it was inherently dependent and thus not in any way necessary, as a perfect being would be.

13. For an analysis of this "theophany," see James A. Borland, *Christ in the Old Testament* (Chicago: Moody, 1978), 83–86.

God condescends to his creation in order to maintain a relationship with those creatures whom he has made in his image. Evidence of (something of) the extent of that condescension is found in the next verse as well: "But the LORD God called to the man and said to him, 'Where are you'" (Gen. 3:9)? In condescending to relate to Adam and Eve, he is, like them (not essentially, but covenantally), restricted in his knowledge of where they might be hiding in the garden.

In order to see this condescension in its clearest light, however, it should be obvious to all of us—though it seems almost universally to escape the notice of most philosophers and many theologians—that we need to turn to that supreme example of condescension as given to us in the person of Christ. As with our discussion of theology proper, we will not enter into the exegetical material here, but will have to content ourselves with the traditional, Reformed understanding of Christ, resting as it does on the historic creeds and on the thus far irrefutable exegetical work that produced it.

And here we will need to be all too brief and must presuppose a rudimentary understanding of Christology as we proceed. Any doctrinal discussion of the person of Christ must begin with the Chalcedonian Creed. In that creed, you will remember, the relationship between the person of the Son of God and his human nature is laid out in a series of four negatives. The creed affirms that the Son of God, as God, is to be "acknowledged in two natures inconfusedly, unchangeably, indivisibly, and inseparably." It goes on to affirm, concerning this hypostatic union, that with regard to these two natures,

> the distinction of natures [is] by no means taken away by the union, but rather the property of each nature [is] preserved, and concurring in one Person and one Subsistence, not parted or divided into two persons, but one and the same Son, and only begotten, God the Word, the Lord Jesus Christ.

And here is the crucial and profound truth of the matter. While there are careful distinctions that must be maintained with respect to God (e.g., that God's essence is identical with God himself), there is no question that what orthodox Christology has always taught is that God *came down*, in the second person of the Trinity, who was, is, and remains fully God, and he took on a human nature without thereby in any way changing his essential nature as God. To think that because God interacts with creation he must necessarily change or in some way limit his essential deity is, in effect, to fail to see the incarnation for what it is. It is to fail to see Christian theism for what it is. It is, to use the standard ecclesiastical jargon, heresy. It is, we could say, to fail to see the most basic truth of Christianity as in any way relevant to philosophical discussions of theism. A truly Christian theology, a truly Christian philosophy or philosophy of religion, will take seriously the principle that God came down; while remaining who he is essentially, he condescended, in order, first, to create something other than himself, and then also to relate to that creation by taking on that which is and was in no way essential to him.

Here again, certain theological categories that have been useful in helping us expand the truth of the Chalcedonian Creed can be helpful in our discussion. Let's think first of all about the *communicatio idiomatum*. The basic notion of *unio personalis* was and is noncontroversial in the history of the church. Orthodox theology has always affirmed the basic hypostatic union with respect to the person of Christ. From this basic agreement, however, matters become a bit more complex. Once the personal union is affirmed, the next obvious question is just how we should think about the relationship of the divine person to his assumed human nature. Even if the heresies of Nestorianism and Eutychianism are avoided, as they are in the Chalcedonian Creed, there are still questions looming about the relationship of the divine person of the Son of God to the human nature that he has taken on.

The question is: is there any sense in which we can speak about a *communication of properties* in the person of Christ, while at the same time affirming all that the Chalcedonian formulation says? John Murray suggests that this notion of a communication of properties is not a Reformed one. It seems to me that Murray suggests this because, over time, the *communicatio* came to mean, primarily at least, the communication of properties from the divine person to his human nature. Indeed, if that is what is meant by the *communicatio*, then Reformed theology would reject that notion. This is not, however, what Calvin meant:

> It is equally senseless to despise the "communication of properties," a term long ago invented to some purpose by the holy fathers. Surely, when the Lord of glory is said to be crucified [1 Corinthians 2:8], Paul does not

mean that he suffered anything in his divinity, but he says this because the same Christ, who was cast down and despised, and suffered in the flesh, was God and Lord of glory. In this way he was also Son of man in heaven [John 3:13], for the very same Christ, who, according to the flesh, dwelt as Son of man on earth, was God in heaven.[14]

The sense of the *communicatio* that is affirmed by Calvin, and the Reformed after him, is that properties of each nature, and both together, may be ascribed to the *one person*. The *communicatio*, therefore, has to do with the relationship of the human nature to the divine person. So, we can affirm the *communicatio idiomatum* just so long as what we are denying is that the properties of one nature are communicated to the other, and we are affirming that the properties of either nature are rightly referred to the one person of Christ. In that regard, we should note as well the usefulness of what has been called the *extra Calvinisticum*.

The notion of the "*extra Calvinisticum*" or the "Calvinistic 'outside'" is another label that surfaced in the context of Lutheran theology. It is a label given by the Lutherans to try to show the error in Reformed Christology. As most note, however, even though this notion of the "*extra*" arose out of the controversy with the Lutherans over the Lord's Supper, the concept itself is not restricted to Calvin. Some have argued, rightly in my opinion, that it could be better labeled the "*extra catholicum*" in that it represents the majority view of the church in history. The supposed error, according to Lutheran theology, is this: the person of the Son of God is not contained within the person of Christ as the God-man, but rather the *Logos* transcends, in his deity, Christ in the flesh. There is, then, an "outside" (*extra*) aspect to the Son of God, even as incarnate. But this view is not erroneous from a Reformed perspective. Part of what motivated this "*extra*" was the standard dictum: *Finitum non capax infiniti*—the finite cannot contain the infinite. But there was more to it than that. One other (lengthy) quotation from Calvin summarizes the position well:

> But some are carried away with such contentiousness as to say that because of the natures joined in Christ, wherever Christ's divinity is, there also is his flesh, which cannot be separated from it. As if that union had compounded

---

14. John Calvin, *Institutes of the Christian Religion,* ed. John T. McNeill, trans. Ford Lewis Battles (Philadelphia: Westminster, 1960), 4.17.30.

from two natures some sort of intermediate being which was neither God nor man! So, indeed, did Eutyches teach, and Servetus after him. But from Scripture we plainly infer that the one person of Christ so consists of two natures that each nevertheless retains unimpaired its own distinctive character. And they will be ashamed to deny that Eutyches was rightly condemned. It is a wonder they do not heed the cause of his condemnation; removing the distinction between the natures and urging the unity of the person, he made man out of God and God out of man. What sort of madness, then, is it to mingle heaven with earth rather than give up trying to drag Christ's body from the heavenly sanctuary? . . . They bring forward these passages for their side: "No one has ascended into heaven but he who descended from heaven, the Son of man, who is in heaven"; and again: "The Son, who is in the bosom of the Father, he has made him known." In this manner, he is said to have descended to that place according to his divinity, not because divinity left heaven to hide itself in the prison house of the body, but because even though it filled all things, still in Christ's very humanity it dwelt bodily, that is, by nature, and in a certain ineffable way. There is a commonplace distinction of the schools to which I am not ashamed to refer: although the whole Christ is everywhere, still the whole of that which is in him is not everywhere. And would that the Schoolmen themselves had honestly weighed the force of this statement. For thus would the absurd fiction of Christ's carnal presence have been obviated.[15]

The primary reason Calvin gives for affirming the "*extra*" is that without it, we cannot say that Christ became like we are in every way, yet without sin. If the omnipresence of God is communicated to the human nature, for example, then Christ became like us in every way, except for sin *and omnipresence*. This is why Calvin thinks that not affirming the "*extra*" produces a third thing, neither man nor God.

The point that we must recognize here, in light of our discussion above, is that God, in the second person of the Trinity and in his condescension to us, was able to take on the entirety of human nature (without sin) and he was able to do so without in any way compromising, contravening, or undermining his essential deity. Paul Helm, speaking of Calvin's *extra*, puts it this way:

According to the Chalcedonian view of the Incarnation . . . , whatever is essential to the divine nature cannot be yielded up in the Incarnation. That

15. Calvin, *Institutes*, 4.17.30.

is, if there are properties that are essential to God being God . . . then in becoming incarnate God cannot cease to be omnipotent or omniscient . . . . By insisting on the *extra*, Calvin is arguing that the Son of God is God, and therefore has God's essence. In other words, the Son has all of God's essential properties . . . . Therefore, if the Incarnation is truly the Incarnation of the Son of God, then it must preserve the divinity of the Son of God unaltered or unimpaired.[16]

One further point on the *extra* before we move on, a point relevant to our entire discussion here. Although it is impossible to do justice to the complexity of Karl Barth's theology in this chapter, it is worth noting that a Reformed doctrine of God is compromised, not just in philosophy but in neoorthodoxy as well.

As is the case with most of the doctrines of historic Christianity, Karl Barth has a problem with the historic Christian notion of the *extra*. And his problem relates directly to his unusual ontology. Barth's ontology has been labeled "actualistic." Included in that label is an opposition to any "essentialistic" ontology. Barth is adamantly opposed to any notion that would not identify God with his revelation. He argues as well that God's freedom, which itself is ultimate, is the determining condition for God's being. In other words, it is God's absolute freedom, his absolute will, which is and must be free, that determines exactly who and what God is like.

The problem that Barth seems to have with the *extra*, given this ontology, is precisely the point that we are trying to support, i.e., that there is a notion of God's essence that defines, and is presupposed by, everything else that God is and does. That notion of essence carries with it at least two theological problems for Barth.

1. The first problem is this: how can one relate the essence of God, in this case of God in Christ, to the Christ of history? On Barth's view, if there is a *Logos asarkos* "outside" the *Logos ensarkos*, then this *Logos asarkos* is an indeterminate state of being which is above and prior to the determination to enter time. And if indeterminate, then there is or can be (who can really know?) a radical discontinuity between the *Logos asarkos* and the *Logos ensarkos*.

2. The second problem for Barth is related to the first. If there is a *Logos asarkos* that transcends, and even "predates" the *Logos ensarkos*,

---

16. Paul Helm, *John Calvin's Ideas* (Oxford: Oxford University Press, 2004), 61–62.

then, in the words of Bruce McCormack, "the decision to assume flesh in time could only result in something being added to that already completed identity; an addition which has no effect upon what he is essentially. Being the Redeemer, in this view, tells us nothing about who or what the Logos is in and for himself. It is merely a role he plays, something he does; but what he does in time has no significance for his eternal being."[17]

Barth's "solution" to this problem is what McCormack calls a "covenant ontology." This is identical to what he elsewhere calls an "actualistic ontology." What it means is that the *act* of God incarnating himself is of the essence of God himself. So, says Barth:

> We have consistently followed the rule, which we regard as basic, that statements about the divine modes of being antecedently in themselves cannot be different in content from those that are to be made about their reality in revelation . . . . The reality of God in His revelation cannot be bracketed by an "only," as though somewhere behind His revelation there stood another reality of God; the reality of God which encounters us in His revelation is His reality in all the depths of eternity.[18]

The important point to note here is that Barth denies the *extra* because, at least in part, he can think of no way in which God can determine to relate himself to his creation except by being *essentially* related to that creation. There is then, in Barth, no distinction between God as he is essentially and God as he is covenantally. That is, God *is* essentially revealed; and this, I hope you can see, erases the Creator/creature distinction. God is dependent on his revelation to be who he is; to put it another way, he is *essentially* incarnate, which is to say, essentially dependent on that which is created. If that is the case, then it is difficult to see how Barth could hold to any orthodox Christology at all.

It should also be said, though we cannot develop it here, that Barth's actualistic ontology, including his notion of God, either requires that God's freedom is who he "essentially" is, so that his freedom just *is* his essence, or as we have said, it makes God as dependent on creation as creation is on him. If Barthians would reply by saying that God's free decision is the only

17. Bruce McCormack, "Grace and Being: The Role of Gracious Election in Karl Barth's Theological Ontology," in *The Cambridge Companion to Karl Barth*, ed. John Webster (Cambridge: Cambridge University Press, 2000), 97.

18. Quoted in McCormack, "Grace and Being," 100.

reason he is *essentially* "for us," then that free decision stands behind and above—it transcends—who God is and thus becomes an "essence" in and of itself. Thus, Barth's actualism is either essentialism in disguise, with the unhappy consequence of an arbitrary and capricious God, or it is another version of a God whose "godness" is defined by who we are, rather than the other way around.

In terms of our main consideration, and in stark contrast with Barth, we should note that in the incarnate Christ, the essential precedes and determines the covenantal (this provides the "link" between the essential and covenantal that Barth cannot find). With respect to the hypostatic union, the theological point that has been important historically to emphasize is that the human nature of Christ was both *anhypostatic* and *enhypostatic*. That is, the human nature is *anhypostatic* in that it has no existence in and of itself; it is *enhypostatic* in that it can exist or subsist only by virtue of the person of the Son of God. The reason this is crucial is that it properly and biblically safeguards the Creator/creature distinction in that it affirms that between the divine and human natures in Christ, the divine is, in every way, primary and foundational. This is an important point to realize any time we discuss the incarnation (and, parenthetically, any time we discuss the nature of Scripture). To put it another way, in the incarnation we do not have two natures coming together to produce a new person. Rather, the incarnation is the person of the Son of God assuming human flesh, so that the person of Christ just *is* the person of the Son of God, but now with a human nature added.

This is important because it highlights again to us that the ontological precedes, determines, guides, and regulates the historical and the temporal. Or to put it in Van Tilian vernacular, the ontological Trinity is the presupposition behind everything else, including history, and including redemptive history. In both the *communicatio* (in its Reformed mutation) as well as in the *extra Calvinisticum*, note that it is the *person*, the *person* of the Son of God, who takes precedence over any notion of human nature or of properties. That is, in the *communicatio*, both human and divine properties are rightly ascribed to the person; so also in the *extra Calvinisticum* the *person* of the Son of God is not constrained by the nature assumed. To put it more generally, it is the ontological and essential that determines and defines the contingent and covenantal, *and not vice versa*.

In the same way, it is God's essential character—complete with his aseity, immutability, omniscience, etc.—that is the presupposition behind

377

his contingent—what I prefer to call his "covenantal"—character, *and not vice versa*. There is, in this sense, an *asymmetrical* relationship between the divine nature of Christ, which itself is identical to the person of the Son of God, and the human nature, depending as it does on the *Logos* himself. And the glory of God is manifested in the fact that the weakness of the incarnate Christ is understood and interpreted only against the backdrop of the glory that is his as the Son of God. The glory of God in his covenantal character is what it is—and here we should recognize the historic faithfulness of Reformed orthodoxy—only against the backdrop of the glory of the fullness of his essential deity. Give up one iota of that deity, and his glory begins to recede into oblivion, only to be replaced by a perverse glory that we seek for ourselves. Give up one iota of that deity, and the incarnation cannot be seen in all its humility and in all of its glorious mystery.

Much more could be said in this regard—but we are now in a position to respond to Martin's Minions, and to the charge of the Impossibility of God. And here we need think only of the incarnation, without taking away from its uniqueness and its "once-for-all-ness," as the consummation and climax of God's dealings with his creation, dealings which commenced at the point of creation. That is, in line with our definition and distinction between E_{df}—that which is essential—and C_{df}—that which is contingent, we can say, as we have said with respect to the incarnation, that God possesses both kinds of properties as a result of his decision first to create and then to redeem. There are essential properties or attributes of God, and there are properties or attributes that God has by virtue of his free decision to create and redeem, properties that are contingent and that, as in the incarnation, effect no change whatsoever in his essential deity.

In other words, just as the Bible is christocentric with respect to the *work* of Christ, it is also, in this important sense, christocentric with respect to the *person* of Christ who himself is the substance of the covenant. All too briefly, then, we may note that with respect to the *communicatio idiomatum* as well as the *extra Calvinisticum*, what is true uniquely and supremely of the Son of God in the flesh, is *also true* generally, historically, and typologically of God himself from creation and into eternity. If by virtue of the *communicatio* we are able to ascribe the properties of both the divine and the human natures of Christ to the one person without fear of inconsistency, *so also* are we able to ascribe essential properties and contingent or covenantal properties to God himself without fear of inconsistency. Scripture itself does this. It will speak of God relenting or repenting. And theologians have argued over whether this requires that we give up on the notion of God's sovereign control, or whether it is simply a figurative way of speaking, or some other kind of attempt to reconcile, or, in a post-conservative context, no attempt at all. But the fact of God relenting no more requires that we give up on his aseity than does the fact of Christ being hungry require that we give up on his full deity. We can ascribe the properties of both to the one person, realizing all the while that some properties are essential—they exist in every possible world—and thus are foundational, and other properties are contingent—they exist in only some possible worlds—and thus they depend on the essential to be what they are.

Or to use another example, one orthodox Calvinistic philosopher, in an attempt to explain Calvin's ideas, articulates the gospel transition from wrath to grace in this way:

> So the truth about atonement, about reconciliation to God, has to be represented to us as if it implied a change in God, and so an inconsistency, an apparent contradiction, in his actions towards us. But in fact there is no change in God; he loves us from eternity. There is however, a change in us, a change that occurs as by faith Christ's work is appropriated. The change is not from wrath to grace, but from *our belief* that we are under wrath to *our belief* that we are under grace.[19]

This philosopher can see no way to reconcile the notion that God's disposition toward us changes, given his immutability. In good orthodox fashion, he is attempting to safeguard the aseity of God. In doing so, however, his solution comes closer to neoorthodoxy than to orthodoxy. Why not affirm that there is indeed a change with respect to God, specifically in his disposition toward us in history, but that such a change in no way obtains with respect to God's essential character? It only obtains with respect to God's covenantal character. Thus, there is no essential change in God, only a covenantal one, and one that depends on the essential in order to "be" at all. To think in the way this philosopher does, more typical than not in many Calvinistic contexts, is to attempt to map the dealings of God with man directly to his essential character. This would be similar

---

19. Helm, *Calvin*, 395.

to attempting to map Christ's humanity onto his deity—a practice that no orthodox theology has entertained.

So also with the *extra Calvinisticum*. Just as we affirm that Christ's actions here on earth in no way constrained the essential attributes of his deity as the Son of God, *so also* do God's acts here on earth in no way constrain the essential attributes of his deity. He is and remains essentially God, all the while, *really and truly*, interacting with us in creation. Since that is the case, then, we can say that God, in dealing with his creation covenantally, has, from the point of creation, taken to himself characteristics, attributes, and properties of his creation in order to interact covenantally with his human creatures. While we agree with the Westminster Confession that Christ is *the substance* of the covenant (WCF 7.6), we should also be ready to affirm that the nature of condescension, which has been a part of God's dealings with his creation from the outset, is that God takes to himself created properties, all the while remaining who he is, in order to relate himself to man. We can look at the incarnation, then, redemptive-historically, as the climax and culmination of the way in which God has, since creation, interacted with that which he has made.

This, of course, has the effect of radically altering our notion of compatibility and consistency. Is it the case that the nature of God in the fullness of his deity is compatible or consistent with the nature of creation in the fullness of its dependence? Only if and when God is able, by virtue of his condescension, while remaining God, to bring the two together. And he *does* bring the two together in his dealings with man, but supremely in one person, the Lord Jesus Christ. (Perhaps you can see that this notion of compatibility has ramifications across the entire spectrum of God's dealings with his creation, including such things as his control over us, his causality, his presence, etc. In each case, God can bring together his own "godness" with respect to these things and relative to creation in such a way that the two—his control and our choices, for example—are brought together into a unity-with-diversity, and thus are compatible and consistent.) But isn't this the way God has always acted? Isn't God making two otherwise incompatible things compatible part of his glorious design for creation? The two becoming one flesh, the union of the church with Christ—these things are analogous to the incarnation itself, and they show us that God is not hindered by our limited, creaturely, perhaps even sinful, notions of compatibility.

In closing, we come back to Martin's Minions. Is it the case, as Drange argues, that God cannot be both immutable and omniscient because to be omniscient would be for him to know different things at different times? This would be the case only if it were impossible for God to condescend. It would be the case only if the essential deity of God would be compromised if he took on contingent or covenantal properties. But we have already seen that there is no inherent incompatibility between that which is essential to God and that which is contingent. The person of Christ is the supreme testimony to that. And here is the good news for Martin and his Minions. There is a possible world in which the triune God takes to himself properties of his creation, all the while remaining fully God, in order not simply to interact with us, but to redeem a people for himself. And that possible world just happens to be the actual world.

The title of this chapter is taken from a poem by G. K. Chesterton, titled "The Wise Men," a part of which is this:

> Oh, we have learnt to peer and pore
>   On tortured puzzles from our youth,
> We know all the labyrinthine lore,
> We are the three wise men of yore,
>   And we know all things but truth.
>
> The gods of violence took the veil
>   Of vision and philosophy,
> The Serpent that brought all men bale,
> He bites his own accursed tail,
>   And calls himself Eternity.
>
> The world grows terrible and white,
>   And blinding white the breaking day;
> We walk bewildered in the light,
> For something is too large for sight,
>   *And something much too plain to say.*
>
> The Child that was ere worlds begun
>   (. . . We need but walk a little way,
> We need but see a latch undone . . .)
> The Child that played with moon and sun
>   Is playing with a little hay.

381

Something much too plain to say—"the Child that played with moon and sun is playing with a little hay." God is only impossible in a possible world where he is incapable of condescending to come to us to save us from ourselves and our sin. And thanks be to God that a possible world that God cannot redeem —*that kind* of possible world—*is*, as a matter of fact, impossible.

12

Geerhardus Vos and Culture

W I L L I A M E D G A R

ON THE SURFACE there would appear to be an enormous distance between the trends in contemporary culture studies and any robust theology of culture represented in the venerable tradition of Reformed theology. Literary critic Terry Eagleton examines the state of culture studies today and concludes, not without alarm, that we are in the midst of culture wars. There are at least three sides: culture as civility, culture as identity, and culture as commercial or postmodern.[1] What he means by "civility" is the view that culture is an ethos, a standard of excellence to which a society should aspire. It's an Arnoldian call to the finer life of civilization. By "identity" is meant using culture to characterize any cause to which one is tied, be it NASCAR dads or soccer moms, old-world Europeans or romantic rebels from the 1960s. By "commercial" or "postmodern" is meant the consumerist culture of late capitalism, the fragmented world of anti-foundationalism, or even the mores of "libidinous gratification."

---

1. Terry Eagleton, *The Idea of Culture* (Oxford: Blackwell, 2000), 64. These "culture wars" bear no resemblance to the notion set forth by James Davison Hunter in *Culture Wars: The Struggle to Define America* (New York: Basic Books, 1992) and subsequent works, which pits the "orthodox" v. the "progressive" poles in America.

What, we may ask, do these concepts have to do with what H. Richard Niebuhr calls "Christ the transformer of culture" in the Reformed tradition? Niebuhr argues, over against dualism—which so longs for the end that it downplays the present—that "the conversionist, with his view of history as the present encounter with God in Christ, does not live so much in expectation of a final ending of the world of creation and culture as in awareness of the power of the Lord to transform all things by lifting them up to himself."[2] Or what do these warriors have to do with the Kuyperian expression of cultural engagement? One of many articulations of this view is by Albert Wolters in *Creation Regained*. This view holds that every area of life is subject to the lordship of Christ. Discussing Colossians 1:20 and the comprehensiveness of the reconciliation of *ta panta* (all things), Wolters concludes, "The obvious implication is that the new humanity (God's people) is called to promote renewal in every department of creation." He adds, "we have a redemptive task wherever our vocation places us in his world."[3]

At one level we have such a difference in paradigms, between the three trends noted by Eagleton and the Reformed tradition's concern for the great transformative work of Christ in every realm of the created order, that there appears to be nothing in common. The major difference is in the underlying presuppositions that inform the one and the other. Succinctly stated, whereas we must begin from below in much of contemporary culture studies, the intention of the Reformed view is to begin from above. To elucidate the former, we could go back to the Enlightenment and the Romantic roots of the contemporary view and cite the work of E. B. Tylor (1832–1917). He is perhaps the first to look at culture as learned behavior, that is, as customs or habits that could be passed on. Indeed, he famously defined it this way: "[Culture is] that complex whole which includes knowledge, belief, art, law, morals, custom, and any other capabilities and habits acquired by man as a member of society."[4] By saying these habits are acquired, he shows his

2. H. Richard Niebuhr, *Christ and Culture* (New York: Harper & Row, 1951), 195. By quoting Niebuhr I do not mean to endorse his general approach to the subject, fascinating and lucid though it be. With various critics I agree that his definitions of both "Christ" (somewhat neoorthodox) and "culture" (a somewhat static view appropriated from Malinowski) are in need of revision.

3. Albert M. Wolters, *Creation Regained: Biblical Basics for a Reformational Worldview* (Grand Rapids: Eerdmans, 1985), 60.

4. E. B. Tylor, *Primitive Culture* (London: John Murray, 1871), 1.

commitment to an evolutionary approach to culture. A well-known characteristic of Tylor's position is the disparagement of faith. For him, expressions of religious belief in his own day meant holding up progress. These were remnants of a more superstitious age. They survived by carrying the vestiges of "primitive religion"; that is, the "belief" part of ancient culture was passed down and uncritically expressed in an age which ought to have gone beyond the earlier stages. According to Tylor, primitive people had developed a belief system based on a mistaken notion: that a vital force (or the soul) present in living organisms is detachable and capable of independent existence in its own mode. Perhaps because of dreams, he thought, they surmised that detached and detachable vital forces make up a suprahuman, or supernatural realm of reality that is just as real as the physical world of rocks, trees, and plants. We now know better, he argued, but we're still haunted by the ancients. This view has had significant influence, albeit with many variants, right up to the present.

Thus, attempts to build bridges between culture studies and a Reformed approach are difficult at best, some would say impossible. Lest we be too hasty, however, we ought to recognize certain signs of rapprochement. In ways that do not appear to participate in Eagleton's "culture wars," we do find some commentators at least attempting to rescue culture from its hibernation into nonrelevance. Recent trends reflect a move from a rather parochial view of culture to a more healthy recognition of culture's role. A rediscovery of culture in various quarters wants to connect us with history and to allow a better understanding of people as people. Part of such a rediscovery has been forced on us by the sea change that occurred at the end of the Cold War. Considering the major transformation in the world's geopolitical configuration since the "miracle year" of 1989, David Brooks, commentator for the *New York Times*, said this not too long ago:

> Events have forced different questions on us. If the big contest of the 20th century was between planned and free-market economies, the big questions of the next century will be understanding how cultures change and can be changed, how social and cultural capital can be nurtured and developed, how destructive cultural conflict can be turned to healthy cultural competition.[5]

5. David Brooks, *International Herald Tribune*, February 21, 2006, 9, available online at http://www.iht.com/protected/articles/2006/02/20/opinion/edbrooks.php (accessed March 3, 2008).

He is not alone. Recently Nassrine Azimi of the United Nations described nation-building in the contemporary world as missing one critical ingredient.

> Some weeks ago at a gathering in Hiroshima of managers of cultural heritage from Asia, the soft-spoken and thoughtful Afghan participant read to us the sign that stands at the entrance of Kabul Museum: "A nation is alive if its culture is alive." The far-reaching implications of these simple words should become the mantra of all aspiring nation-builders.[6]

Thus, culture is being revived because tried-and-true explanations for world events seem both dated and shallow. This does not mean that we are moving toward a fully biblical view of culture as renewal in every realm of creation. And it certainly does not mean that there is a new longing for the lordship of Christ. But it does mean we are in a good place to offer our insights into the true nature of culture to a world dearly in need of both.

Perhaps less ambitiously, but no less urgently, I would submit, this is a good time to look carefully at the biblical teaching on culture and on the lordship of Christ over all the spheres of creation, if only that we may move beyond the culture wars and beyond cultural hibernation to something much more theologically responsible. To get at this, what I propose here is an examination of the views of Geerhardus Vos on the matter. In part this is to honor Dick Gaffin, in whose honor this is written, and whose great love for the man is patent. And in part, it is because Vos's reflections on culture have never been fully explored, though he has much to contribute to the conversation.

It happens that Vos did not say much about culture, at least directly. First, though, he is not altogether silent. And second, we will argue, his entire theological scheme represents a marvelous defense of cultural engagement.

Vos did state his views quite plainly in *The Kingdom of God and the Church*, where he says that the kingdom of God is broader in outreach than the state. Human life reaches far beyond the exclusive domain of church life, and into every realm of legitimate creation activity. Here is a fascinating passage from that work, one which has a decidedly Kuyperian ring to it:

6. Nassrine Azimi, *International Herald Tribune*, May 8, 2007, available online at http://www.iht.com/articles/2007/05/08/opinion/edazimi.php?page=1 (accessed March 6, 2008).

> From this [that all authority exercised within the church is Christ the King's], however, it does not necessarily follow, that the visible church is the only outward expression of the invisible kingdom. Undoubtedly the kingship of God, as his recognized and applied supremacy, is intended to pervade and control the whole of human life in all its forms of existence. This the parable of the leaven plainly teaches. These various forms of human life have each their own sphere in which they work and embody themselves. There is a sphere of science, a sphere of art, a sphere of the family and of the state, a sphere of commerce and industry.

He goes on to clarify what these things mean for the lordship of Christ over all things:

> Whenever one of these spheres comes under the controlling influence of the principle of the divine supremacy and glory, and this outwardly reveals itself, there we can truly say that the kingdom of God has become manifest.[7]

As Vos continues, he mentions that in Christ's earthly ministry he did not take the time to spell out the explicit details of what this might look like. Still, there is no doubt about his intention. On the one hand, Vos says, his doctrine of the kingdom was so comprehensive that everything that is normal and pertains to human life pertains to Christ's kingdom. Then Vos makes the all-important statement that, on the other hand, this result should not be reached by making human life and its spheres subject to the visible church.[8]

This point is crucial in view of the many forms of church-centered approaches to culture in the evangelical world, both in Vos's times and in ours. This is not the place to investigate such views in any detail. Typically, such an approach refuses to give much countenance to various spheres of social life outside the church. The state, in one outlook, is more or less a necessary evil, one which accommodates our fallen estate, but which in no way represents the heart of God's concerns, and would not have been necessary in Adam's administration. To single out one notable representative, we could cite Richard Hays, the influential New Testament scholar, an

---

7. Geerhardus Vos, *The Kingdom of God and the Church* (Phillipsburg, NJ: Presbyterian & Reformed, 1979), 87–88. Henceforth cited as *KGC*.

8. *KGC*, 88.

ethicist coming broadly out of an Anabaptist tradition. In his magisterial book, *The Moral Vision of the New Testament*, Hays argues that the heart of ethics involves "embodying Scripture's imperatives in the life of the Christian community."[9] The church is the "new community" which so identifies with Jesus that it manifests a "glad and generous heart," the sure sign of God's presence, making God's power in the world palpable.[10] The reason the church could "turn the world upside down," Hays says, is not only that it concentrated on witnessing, but that it could be defiant of Roman authority. Not violently, of course, but in its refusal to accommodate.[11] The only theology of the state here is rather negative.

Indeed, for Hays, neither the state, nor any other sphere except the church, can truly display the power of God in a lost world. For him, the Sermon on the Mount is where we must live. This message is so important that it represents "Jesus' programmatic disclosure of the kingdom of God and of the life to which the community of disciples is called." Basically, according to Hays, we are to live in a "counter-cultural polis," which Matthew, who records the longest version of the sermon (chapters 5–7), understood as a fulfillment of the Torah. Accordingly, for example, Hays proclaims that all violence is out of bounds. He cites a number of cases from Jesus' life where the Lord is shown as choosing the way of "suffering obedience" rather than the way of violence. Nonviolent love of enemy is both the eschatological reality and the way of Jesus, he proclaims. Matthew, in this view, managed to undermine the *lex talionis* of the Torah (Deut. 19:15–21).[12]

This approach faces a problem when it comes to understanding the authority of the state, and particularly the right of the state to exercise violence when the occasion calls for it. A dualistic scheme is the answer. Here is how it works. Hays cites Romans 12:14–21 approvingly. The passage forbids vengeance, and tells us to bless those who persecute and live peaceably with others. Then he turns to Romans 13, which is quite different. He argues that though there may be a sort of necessity for the existence of the state, he cannot condone any Christian participation in the state's call to rule for justice. Astonishingly, he says, "Though the governing authority

9. Richard B. Hays, *The Moral Vision of the New Testament* (San Francisco: HarperSanFrancisco, 1996), 7. Henceforth cited as *MV*.
10. *MV*, 125.
11. *MV*, 128–31.
12. *MV*, 324–25.

bears the sword to execute God's wrath (13:4), *that is not the role of believers.* The church is a community of peace.[13] He argues against just war theory, because it fails to recognize that violence begets only violence, and because it is based on the hope that we can approximate God's justice by killing.[14] This, of course, is far removed from the tradition that goes by the name of just war. But it is what Hays understands.

The fundamental struggle in such a dualistic approach is that there is no overarching worldview in which a sphere of authority such as the state could be a legitimate entity in itself, and not dependent on the church. This view leads Hays into some strange conclusions. For example, he admits soldiers in the New Testament are not condemned for their profession, but he says the purpose of their being singled out is to show how the gospel reaches the most unlikely people! He cannot fathom a legitimate calling into statecraft. The military is not a Christian option. He adds that good soldiers "weigh negligibly" in a synthetic statement of the New Testament's witness.[15]

While it is not our purpose to provide either a full repudiation of this view or a defense of the just war tradition, a couple of thoughts related to our central purpose are appropriate. Romans 12 is not as isolated from Romans 13 as Hays makes it sound. Both chapters are addressed to Christians. Romans 12 forbids believers as believers to exercise private vengeance. God will judge. And he does judge even now, Romans 13 tells us, through the civil magistrate, who is "God's servant," operating in an authority structure duly instituted by God. It is perfectly legitimate for a person, believer or not, to aspire to the profession of soldiering. The state is a legitimate sphere for human life, established not because of the fall, but because of the requirements of good order in the world of creation.

Contrary to Hays's radical view, the point of the Sermon on the Mount is not to set up a special ethic for the church, but to proclaim a new world order, one where the kingdom of God has come, one where the blessedness of its members is for now, not just later. True enough, the sermon tells us about God's radical love in Christ, a love that forgives enemies and gives good gifts to its children. But the sermon is neither ascetic nor revolutionary. There is no section of life to which it does not speak. The key to the sermon is Matthew 5:17, in which Jesus proclaims he has not come to abolish

13. *MV*, 331.
14. *MV*, 342.
15. *MV*, 335–37.

the law but to fulfill it. His teaching explains the full extent of God's law, and puts an end to casuistry. To understand how the ethics of the sermon work, one can benefit from navigating the wisdom literature of the Bible. Like the Proverbs, the teachings in the sermon are cumulative. And as in the wisdom literature, there is not a single, comprehensive application of one part of the law that is not meant to be kept in balance with the rest. For example, in 5:16 Jesus tells us to let our light shine before men, whereas in 6:1 he warns against doing our righteousness before men. Again, in 7:1, he forbids judging another, whereas in 7:6 he tells us to identify dogs and swine. These are not contradictions. Only when we understand the depths of God's love, and the radical claims of his kingdom, can we know when to make one application or another. Therefore, to "turn the other cheek" is not a blanket rule for all of life, nor a better way for believers, as Hays would have it, but exactly the right response in the particular situation where one is tempted to enact vigilante violence.

Herman Ridderbos confirms this view in his wonderful book, *When the Time Had Fully Come*. In the chapter on the sermon he states:

> There is no contradiction, no difference of level, between Matthew 5 and Romans 13. Kingdom of God does not mean the abolition of God's previous ordinations for the natural and social life. . . . On the contrary, social life, political order, international justice as such belong just as well to the righteousness in all sectors of life and that they have to do that in the light of the whole revelation of God to which the Sermon on the Mount refers.[16]

Put thus, we can understand that any attempt to dichotomize between the church as the most spiritual location for Christian living, and the world as a necessary holding pattern, is not helpful. Believing that the different realms of creation in which we must somehow navigate are temporary support systems in which we must be careful not to overinvest, is simply sub-biblical. The best of the Reformed tradition, albeit with significant variants, has acknowledged a more holistic worldview approach which sees the state, and every other legitimate sphere of activity, as a place to live out the full reality of the kingdom of God.

16. Herman N. Ridderbos, *When the Time Had Fully Come* (Grand Rapids: Eerdmans, 1957), 42.

It is our understanding that Geerhardus Vos confirms this view, and helps us counter the narrow trends in culture studies and in evangelical dualism. Where should we begin in order to find out how he looks at culture? The first place, quite logically, is in his considerations about the creation and its original purpose. In the marvelous collection of notes which became *Biblical Theology*, Vos stresses the importance of four great principles at work in the pre-redemptive "primeval revelation."[17] The first he calls "the principle of life in its highest potency," which he says is sacramentally symbolized by the Tree of Life. Much could be said here, but what is significant for our purposes is that by placing man in the garden of God, the Lord intends to state at the dawn of creation that human beings are in fellowship with God, the God of life. Indeed, life is virtually synonymous with the call, and the very meaning of humanity. By reiterating the life-giving purpose of placing man in a garden, the prophets, the psalmists, and many authors right up to John's Revelation (2:7) tell us that to be God's people is to have life.

As is well recognized, Vos has a strong eschatological understanding of the first creation. While beautiful and satisfying, there was more to come, as indicated by the Tree of Life. The second principle is that of "probation," which is also symbolized by a tree, the Tree of the Knowledge of Good and Evil. After discussing various views, Vos decides that the purpose of this unique test, not to eat of the fruit of this particular tree, was meant to lead to a higher state, beyond even the perfection of the garden. What is the central idea of this progress? It is the call to greater ethical strength, and thus "to that state of religious and moral maturity wherewith its highest blessedness is connected."[18] He argues that greater knowledge of good and evil is not a bad thing, because it could have happened without guilty disobedience.

The point for us to notice is that there was a plan for human development, a project for historical unfolding. The third and fourth principles develop these points. They are the temptation and sin and the principle of death. Each of these illustrates God's intention to lead the human race to a higher place. The importance of such an eschatology for understanding culture cannot be missed.

---

17. Geerhardus Vos, *Biblical Theology: Old and New Testaments* (Grand Rapids: Eerdmans, 1948) 37ff. Henceforth cited as *BT*. Vos had originally wanted these studies to be called "the history of special revelation."

18. *BT*, 41.

As we know, man fell, and death and dissolution ensued. Vos makes the point that this death was every opposite of life. We know, too, that God in his mercy promised life again to our first parents. The seed of the woman would overcome the seed of the serpent. Again, when he describes death, Vos is in fact concentrating on the reality of life. In his sermon, "The Spiritual Resurrection of Believers," based on Ephesians 2:4–5, he eloquently describes the death which is presupposed in Paul's promise of life. To reckon with the damage done by death is one way to grasp the extent of the principle of life.[19] Life, he says, is an attribute of God, who alone has it truly. Life for the creature is only to be had in fellowship with God. Just as at the beginning, darkness covered the earth until the Spirit of God hovered over it, so we are lifeless until God breathes into our nostrils the breath of life. "As long as love and God's fellowship lived in him, they controlled all lower forces and led them in the right direction so that they could not harm him."[20] But when God's life-power is no longer active, then everything goes wrong.

Thus far, we see that "culture" must be connected to the great original principles set down by God for the government of the world. By living with God, we live. And life characterizes everything we do in this place which God has made. While sin corrupts everything, it is not allowed to abrogate the entire world fabric, nor human exercise of culture. The narrative leading up to the flood proceeds in three stages, according to Vos. First, it describes the degeneration in the line of Cain. Even here, though, there is a "working of common grace in the gift of invention for the advance of civilization in the sphere of nature."[21] Sin comes and prostitutes God's common grace gifts, so that what would have been there to protect and enrich people, becomes twisted into arrogant usage. Thus, cattle-raising, music, metallurgy, and so forth are good in themselves, but are eventually used for belligerent boasting (Gen. 4:23–24). Next, the narrative describes another line, the Sethites, about which nothing pertaining to culture is said, but that they issued in those who walked before God. Vos is quick to add, though, that "God sometimes chooses families and nations standing outside the sphere of redemption to carry on the progress in secular culture."[22] He then, rather like Calvin, cites

19. Geerhardus Vos, *Grace and Glory* (Edinburgh: Banner of Truth, 1994), 209–32. Henceforth cited as *GG*.

20. *GG*, 220.

21. *BT*, 56.

22. *BT*, 58.

the Greeks for their art and the Romans for their jurisprudence. Finally, he says that the contrast of the two lines is only relative, since both would perish. Third, then, the text shows an intermarriage which ends the distinction.

When the Lord does judge, with the great flood, he then saves one family and begins the creation dynamic all over again. There is the promise of life, and its protection. There is "the echo of some of the original creative ordinances," including the command and blessings of fruitfulness. There are differences between the original creation and this re-creation. In the beginning, nature, including the animal world, submitted willingly to human rule, but now they do so out of fear. Reciprocally, man must show reverence for life by not eating animals as wild beast do their prey.[23] What is significant for our purposes is to note that what we call culture, the rule, the fruitfulness, the development of humanity, are restored and blessed, even in a fallen world.

Looking at the progress of redemptive history and its coordinate revelation, one would rightly conclude that the climax of world events is in the coming of Jesus Christ. In his comments on Galatians 4:4, Vos asserts that it is "a phrase which certainly means more than that the time was ripe for the introduction of Christ into the world: the fullness of the time means the end of that aeon and the commencement of another world-period."[24] What should not be missed, however, is that most often Vos considers this culmination, the change of eras, not just as an end point, but as the introduction of the final reality into the present. As he puts it in the same place, the resurrection of Jesus anticipates and secures the general resurrection. And his death, which is an atonement, is also "the securing and embodying in advance the judgment and destruction of the spiritual powers opposed to God," in other words, the final judgment. This "other great eschatological transaction" is thus brought within the scope of Christ's present activity, *and* the present activity of the believer.[25]

So for Vos the reality of heaven is already upon us. That maturing into consummate bliss anticipated in the garden is now made a reality, thanks to the grace of God in Christ. In what is possibly his most important con-

---

23. *BT*, 64.

24. "Paul's Eschatological Concept of the Spirit," in *Redemptive History and Biblical Interpretation: The Shorter Writings of Geerhardus Vos*, ed. Richard B. Gaffin Jr. (Phillipsburg, NJ: Presbyterian & Reformed, 1980), 93. Henceforth cited as *SW*.

25. *SW*, 93.

tribution to our understanding of the ways of the Lord with human affairs, Vos discusses the "already" and "not yet" of the new world order. There is hardly a text from his pen that does not articulate this in some way. To call the "already" presence of the last estate an "intrusion" is perhaps accurate as far as it goes, but it is more exact to speak of the "provisionally-realized final state."[26] Particularly for the apostle Paul, but most assuredly for other authors of Scripture, including especially the letter to the Hebrews, this present reality is not divided from the future consummation in any simple way. Nor does it mean lowering the expectation of a world to come. It does mean we live in the reality of the heavenlies (Eph. 1:3, 20; Col. 1:1, 2, 13; 2 Tim. 4:18; etc.).

In the eschatology of the Old Testament, events of the end times had been considered successively, Vos reminds us. Thus we live in the times of anticipation until the judgment, the ushering in of the new heaven and the new earth, together with the coming of the Messiah, which are telescoped into one great final event. But now, with the coming of Christ, and especially the pouring out of the Spirit, two worlds are superposed: "If the second world has received its actual beginning through Christ, and if nevertheless, as cannot be denied, the first world, this present world, is still continuing in its course, then it is clear that both now exist contemporaneously."[27] Put another way, the eschatological state is no longer only future, but is present, although, as he puts it, "in a higher way."[28] Or, again, "the Christian things are not a new product of time; they are rather the descent into time of the essence of eternity."[29]

Regarding our concerns about cultural life, a basic question does arise. How do we know that Vos is not somehow dualistic himself, when he appears to deny the importance of this first or present world, by calling the second one higher, or calling it eternal v. temporal? At least two constant themes in Vos's output would confirm his opposition to any wrong-minded dichotomizing.

The first is his constant reminder that the world of grace does not override the world of nature, but informs it and recasts it. We see this in

26. Geerhardus Vos, *The Pauline Eschatology* (Grand Rapids: Eerdmans, 1952), 38–39. Henceforth cited as *PE*.

27. "Hebrews, the Epistle of the Diatheke," in *SW*, 197–98.

28. *SW*, 198.

29. *SW*, 199.

his treatment of the "psychical man" and the "pneumatic man." We find it in many places. Take, for example, his review of Von D. Wilhelm Bousset's important book at the time, *Kyrios Christos*.[30] Vos faults Bousset for finding Paul to erect a dichotomy between *sarx* and *pneuma*. As Bousset would have it, "The Christian state is said to destroy the continuity in the life of man, because in making him pneuma it does not restore or develop what was originally given in nature, but supplants the latter by something altogether new." For Vos, this amounts to an opening for Gnosticism and a split between nature and grace. For Paul does not use the term *sarx* to represent the original natural condition of man. Rather, it is synonymous with sin, and therefore is not the product of creation. Christ came to reverse what *sarx* destroyed. Certainly, alongside that, the world of the Spirit lifts us to a higher stage which even Adam did not possess. But, as Vos insists, "Still, it would be incorrect to find in this a suspension of the continuity or identity of life."[31]

---

30. Book review, Von D. Wilhelm Bousset, *Kyrios Christos: Geschichte des Christusglaubens von den Anfängen des Christentums bis Irenaeus*, orig. in *PTR* 12 (1914): 636–45, reproduced in *SW*, 534–43.

31. *SW*, 541.

13

A Millennial Genealogy: Joseph Mede, Jonathan Edwards, and Old Princeton[1]

JEFFREY K. JUE

CONTEMPORARY EVANGELICAL SYSTEMATIC theologies present three options for interpreting the millennium found in the apostle John's vision in Revelation 20: pre-, post-, or amillennialism. Premillennialism is the view that the millennium will be a future earthly event, inaugurated by Christ's second advent and lasting for a literal one thousand years. Postmillennialism is the view that understands the millennium to begin either sometime within the present church age, or in the future, and conclude with the second advent of Christ. Finally, amillennialism is the view that interprets the millennium as the entire church age, the period between the first and second advents of Christ. Now these definitions are very basic and general, and there are nuances and subtleties within each of the three positions, but in general these are the three most popular options.

In comparing the interpretive options, modern theologians from all three camps have noted the closest affinity between the postmillennial and

1. Material from this essay was presented at the Kerux Conference in Lynnwood, WA, in 2001. At that conference I had the pleasure of meeting for the first time Dr. Richard B. Gaffin Jr.

amillennial positions. In his book *Millennialism: The Two Major Views*, Charles Feinberg (a premillennialist) limits his critique to the amillennial position because "there will be many points of similarity to be seen between the postmillennial and amillennial positions."[2] Likewise, Lorraine Boettner (a postmillennialist) writes, "[t]here is comparatively little difference between postmillennialism and amillennialism, at least when either of these is compared with historic premillennialism or dispensationalism."[3] Finally, O. T. Allis subsumes both of these positions under the traditional Augustinian interpretation. He writes,

> it is to be noted that all forms of the Augustinian view, by which we mean, all views which discover the millennium in the inter-advental period or in some part of it, whether that part be past, present, or future, may properly be called both amillennial and postmillennial.[4]

Clearly, modern theologians, regardless of their own millennial preferences, observe the closest association between the postmillennial and amillennial positions. While the modern consensus seems unanimous, however, is it entirely legitimate? Does the evidence justify this conclusion? These are the questions that this study will seek to answer. By closely examining the historical roots of millennial thought we will be able to understand properly and accurately the relations between the various eschatological interpretations, as well as some of the theological implications for these relations.[5]

JONATHAN EDWARDS (1703–58)

The obvious place to examine the roots of postmillennialism is with Jonathan Edwards. C. C. Goen comments that Edwards holds the "distinction

2. Charles L. Feinberg, *Millennialism: The Two Major Views*, 4th ed. (Chicago: Moody, 1980), 27.

3. Lorraine Boettner, "A Postmillennial Response," in *The Meaning of the Millennium: Four Views*, ed. Robert G. Clouse (Downers Grove, IL: InterVarsity, 1977), 199.

4. O. T. Allis, *Prophecy and the Church* (Philadelphia: Presbyterian & Reformed, 1945), 4.

5. It is important to point out that modern categories of pre-, post- and amillennialism cannot be unilaterally imposed on different historical periods. The positions of theologians must be understood in their own languages and the categories of their own eras. For the purposes of clarity and simplicity I have tried to use modern categories as much as possible, but traditionally it would be better to speak of an Augustinian view (similar to amillennial) and a millenarian view.

of being America's first major postmillennial thinker."[6] For many historians and sociologists, Edwards's postmillennialism provided the intellectual roots for the idea of progress, manifest destiny, and a distinct triumphalism that supposedly helped to shape American identity.[7] Likewise the title of Goen's article is, "Jonathan Edwards: A New Departure in Eschatology." This "new departure," by which Goen means postmillennialism, was in contradistinction to the premillennialism that was pervasive in preceding generations of New England Puritans.[8] At this point Goen's thesis must be questioned: was Edwards's eschatology really a new departure?

If we follow the thesis proposed by modern theologians, we would expect Edwards to be thoroughly versed in and citing with regularity those commentators who stood firmly within the Augustinian tradition. Following Augustine's interpretation found in his *magnum opus*, *The City Of God*, Augustinian apocalypticists described the millennium as a spiritual symbol representing the entire church age between Christ's first and second advents.[9] In the sixteenth century, this tradition would include commentaries by two Genevans who were members of Calvin's inner circle: Antonie Du Pinet and Nicolas Colladon (who co-edited Calvin's biography with Theodore Beza).[10] Likewise the seventeenth century produced a massive commentary by David Pareus, professor of theology at Heidelberg.[11] But Edwards's sources tell a different story. The sources that Edwards consulted were not written in the Augustinian tradition, but instead were steeped in the millenarianism of the seventeenth century. Contrary to what modern

6. C. C. Goen, "Jonathan Edwards: A New Departure in Eschatology," *Church History* 29 (1959): 38.

7. See Alan Heimert, *Religion and the American Mind: From the Great Awakening to the Revolution* (Cambridge, MA: Harvard University Press, 1966); Ernest Lee Tuveson, *Redeemer Nation: The Idea of America's Millennial Role* (Chicago: University of Chicago Press, 1968).

8. A list of New England premillennialists includes: John Cotton (1584–1652), John Davenport (1597–1670), Thomas Shepherd (1605–49), John Eliot (1604–90), Increase Mather (1639–1723), and Cotton Mather (1663–1728).

9. See Augustine, *The City of God against the Pagans*, book XX, chapter 7.

10. For details and Du Pinet's and Colladon's apocalyptic interpretations see Irena Backus, *Reformation Readings of the Apocalypse: Geneva, Zurich and Wittenberg* (New York: Oxford University Press, 2000), 37–66; Erik de Boer, "The Book of Revelation in Calvin's Geneva," in *Calvin's Books: Festschrift Dedicated to Peter de Klerk on the Occasion of His Seventieth Birthday*, ed. W. H. Neuser, H. J. Selderhuis, and W. van't Spijker (Heerenveen, Netherlands: J. J. Groen, 1997).

11. On Pareus see Irena Backus, "Apocalypse 20.2–4 et le millennium protestant," *Revue d'histoire et de philosophie religieuses* 79 (1999): 101–18; Howard B. Hotson, *Paradise Postponed: Johann Heinrich Alsted and the Rebirth of Calvinist Millenarianism* (Dordtrecht, Netherlands: Kluwer Academic, 2000), 115–16.

theologians have surmised, during Edwards's day—the era of the birth of postmillennialism—premillennialism and postmillennialism shared a common foundation and tradition over against the Augustinian or broadly amillennial position. In his critique of C. C. Goen's article, John F. Wilson writes, "A rigid distinction between premillennialism and postmillennialism cut against the grain of how thinking about 'last things' [during the seventeenth and eighteenth centuries] was carried on."[12] The evidence suggests that Edwards viewed his eschatological position as closely in line with the millenarian commentators of the post-Reformation period and not with the Augustinian or amillennial tradition.

In order to establish this thesis, we must first understand Edwards's eschatological position. The majority of Edwards's writings on eschatology are found in four sources. Three of these sources are private notebooks titled "Notes on the Apocalypse," "Notes on Scripture," and "Theological Miscellanies."[13] The fourth is a series of sermons preached and later published under the title "A History of the Work of Redemption."[14] These four sources comprise Edwards's lifetime of reflection on the Apocalypse, both public and private.

In regard to the millennium, Edwards placed the period entirely in the future. He concluded that history would follow the sabbath-week pattern of seven days. Citing 2 Peter 3:8, Edwards symbolically interpreted each day of the week to represent one thousand years. Thus the world would continue for six periods, each of which were a thousand years, with the last being the millennium.[15] Additionally, this final period of a thousand years had not yet been manifested, but was rapidly approaching. Edwards writes,

> And what further confirms that the sabbath of the world will begin near about the beginning of the seventh thousand years of the world, is because

12. John F. Wilson, "History, Redemption, and the Millennium," in *Jonathan Edwards and the American Experience*, ed. N. O. Hatch and H. S. Stout (New York: Oxford University Press, 1988), 138.

13. Published in the Yale editions as *The Works of Jonathan Edwards* (New Haven, CT: Yale University Press, 1957–2000), vol. 5, *Apocalyptic Writings*, ed. S. J. Stein (1977); vol. 13, *The "Miscellanies," Entry Nos. a-z, aa-zz, 1–500*, ed. T. A. Schafer (1994); vol. 15, *Notes on Scripture*, ed. S. J. Stein (1998); vol. 18, *The "Miscellanies," 501–832*, ed. A. Chamberlain (2000).

14. *The Works of Jonathan Edwards*, vol. 9, *A History of the Work of Redemption*, ed. J. F. Wilson (New Haven, CT: Yale University Press, 1989).

15. Edwards, *Apocalyptic Writings*, 130.

> we are sure, it cannot be far from it. For we are come near it already; so that the beginning of this glorious time, cannot be far on this side.[16]

Not only was the millennium a future event, but Edwards's adherence to the sabbath-week pattern also limited the duration of the millennium to a thousand years. Now there is some reservation as to whether or not Edwards held to a literal thousand-year millennium. In the twenty-seventh sermon from *A History of the Work of Redemption*, Edwards described the "prosperous state of the church" as "a long time," without further details on its duration.[17] While his ambiguity in this sermon might open the possibility for alternative readings, the sabbath-week paradigm does not support this. Edwards argued that Abraham was called in the two-thousandth year of the world, the settlement of Solomon's kingdom and the completion of the temple in the three-thousandth year, Christ's birth in the four-thousandth year, and finally the millennium to begin in the six-thousandth year.[18] Following the literal interpretation of the first six periods of the world, it is more than likely that, for Edwards, the seventh period of the millennium would be literal as well.

What events would precede the arrival of the millennium? Edwards noted three specific events. First, the downfall of the kingdom of Satan and the Antichrist.[19] "The visible kingdom of Satan shall be overthrown and the kingdom of Christ set up on the ruins of it everywhere, through out the whole habitable globe," writes Edwards.[20] The kingdom of Satan included: the Antichristian kingdom or the papacy, the Mahometan kingdom or the Turks, and the heathen kingdoms—the pagan inhabitants of America, the East Indies, and Africa.[21] Prophetically, these three kingdoms are represented by the beast, the false prophet, and the dragon found in the visions of the Apocalypse.

The second event preceding the millennium would be the conversion of the Jews. Edwards proclaims,

16. Ibid.
17. Edwards, *A History of the Work of Redemption*, 485.
18. Edwards, *Apocalyptic Writings*, 135.
19. Edwards, *A History of the Work of Redemption*, 456.
20. Ibid., 473.
21. Edwards, *Apocalyptic Writings*, 174. Also see Reiner Smolinski, "Apocalypticism in Colonial North America," in *The Encyclopedia of Apocalypticism*, ed. S. J. Stein (New York: Continuum, 1998), 3:36–71.

And then shall all Israel be saved. The Jews in all their dispersions shall cast away their old infidelity, and shall wonderfully have their hearts changed, and abhor themselves for their past unbelief and obstinacy; and shall flow together to the blessed Jesus, penitently, humbly, and joyfully owning him as their glorious king and only savior.[22]

Edwards emphatically believed that the eleventh chapter of Paul's Epistle to the Romans teaches a future national conversion of Israel.[23] This would occur concurrently with the overthrow of the kingdom of Satan and inaugurate the millennium. Edwards continues, "and this last event must doubtless be before the millennium begins."[24] It must be pointed out that Edwards's understanding of a future conversion of Israel is not unique to his eschatology. In the sixteenth, seventeenth, and eighteenth centuries, theologians of various eschatological persuasions held to this same belief—from Peter Martyr Vermigli to Johannis Cocceius.[25] However, what is distinctive about Edwards is his insistence that this event will occur immediately before the millennium—serving as a prophetic sign heralding the dawn of the millennial age.

The third event preceding the millennium would be the gradual success of the gospel in converting large numbers to Christianity, and contributing to the destruction of the kingdom of Satan. Edwards writes, "But this is a work that will be accomplished by means, by the preaching of the gospel, and the use of the ordinary means of grace, and so shall be gradually brought to pass."[26] Two implications can be drawn from this event. First, Christians who are actively involved in the advancement of the gospel are likewise participants in ushering in the millennium. Thus Edwards's emphasis on prayer, and his great interest in what he called the "pouring out of God's Spirit" in the revivals of the first Great Awakening, are all framed within his eschatological program.[27] Second, the expectation of this gradual success of the gospel and the destruction of Satan encouraged a sense of optimism. Edwards determined that the church would grow exponentially in

22. Edwards, *A History of the Work of Redemption*, 469.
23. Ibid., 469–70.
24. Edwards, *Apocalyptic Writings*, 196.
25. For Johannis Cocceius's view see W. J. van Asselt, "Structural Elements in the Eschatology of Johannes Cocceius," *CTJ* 35 (2000): 100.
26. Edwards, *A History of the Work of Redemption*, 459.
27. Ibid., 461.

her understanding of the Scriptures, propagate religion and advance Christ's kingdom, and prevail over all enemies—what more could a suffering church ask?[28] The hope for the latter-day glory created a positive sentiment that the dark days were over, and only better days lay ahead.[29]

Moreover, Edwards's understanding of the millennium itself included a number of additional interpretive points. Most obvious was the placing of Christ's second coming at the conclusion of the millennium—hence the term "postmillennialist." This, of course, would void any notions of an earthly millennial reign of Christ. Edwards concludes,

> It is a greater privilege to the church on earth to have Christ, her head and Redeemer, in heaven at the right hand of God, than for him to be in this lower world: for Christ in heaven is in his glorious throne. For him to come down to this earth to dwell here, would be a second humiliation, a descending from an higher glory to a lower.[30]

Similarly the reign of the martyred saints during the millennium would not be on earth. Edwards interpreted the "first resurrection" of Revelation 20:4–5 as a "spiritual resurrection" or regeneration.[31] He determined that because of their union with Christ, the saints who were slain in Revelation 20:4 would reign through those saints who were still alive during the millennium. The souls of the slain saints would be revived on earth through their communion with the living, "as if their souls descended from heaven and lived in them"—for Edwards this will be the first resurrection.[32] Therefore, since the first resurrection would not be corporeal but instead spiritual, these martyrs would in actuality be reigning in heaven with Christ.[33]

---

28. Edwards, *The "Miscellanies," Entry Nos. a-z, aa-zz, 1–500*, 426–27.

29. Additional evidence for this optimism is found in Edwards's interpretation of the slaying of the two witnesses in Revelation 11. The majority of previous commentators placed this event in the future. Edwards, however, concluded that this event had already passed. Such a catastrophic event did not match the anticipated victory for which Edwards hoped. Edwards, *Apocalyptic Writings*, 385ff. For previous interpretations of the two witnesses, see Rodney L. Petersen, *Preaching in the Last Days: The Theme of 'Two Witnesses' in the 16th & 17th Centuries* (New York: Oxford, 1993).

30. Edwards, *The "Miscellanies," 501–832*, 537.

31. Edwards, *The "Miscellanies," Entry Nos. a-z, aa-zz, 1–500*, 167–68; idem, *Apocalyptic Writings*, 144–45.

32. Edwards, *The "Miscellanies," Entry Nos. a-z, aa-zz, 1–500*, 167.

33. Edwards, *The "Miscellanies," 501–832*, 537.

Furthermore, Edwards described the period of the millennium as "the most glorious state of the Church on earth."[34] This would be a time of great knowledge and learning where the Bible would be published in Africa and the East, and where difficult doctrines and apparent inconsistencies would be reconciled.[35] Additionally, global communication would improve dramatically through the "art of navigation" (Edwards was probably referring to massive improvements in shipping and navigation during the eighteenth century). Even more, both the church and the world would experience great prosperity, peace, and love.[36] Intensive harmony would probably be the best way to describe Edwards's millennium. Nevertheless, near the end of the millennium Satan would be released and allowed to instigate one last apostasy. Finally, Edwards declares, the "wickedness of the world will remarkably call for Christ's immediate appearing."[37]

Christ's return would mark the universal resurrection and the last judgment. The conclusion would be a great conflagration that would melt and consume all the elements of the earth (from 2 Peter 3).[38] Edwards speculated that the earth would then be hell and the new heaven and new earth "will be some glorious place in the universe prepared by God, removed at an immense distance from the solar system."[39] While this interpretation might seem extremely peculiar, Edwards's intent was to demonstrate the radically different constitution of the state of the new heaven and new earth in comparison with the age that preceded it. In light of the consummated state, the millennium would display a closer resemblance to the previous church age than to the succeeding final age.

THE ROOTS OF POSTMILLENNIALISM

Completing our survey of Jonathan Edwards's eschatology, we must now assess the position and uniqueness of his postmillennialism within the Protestant tradition of apocalyptic interpretation. In order to accomplish this, we must first examine the sources that influenced Edwards's eschatology.

---

34. *The Works of Jonathan Edwards*, vol. 4, *The Great Awakening*, ed. C. C. Goen (New Haven, CT: Yale University Press, 1989), 354.

35. Edwards, *A History of the Work of Redemption*, 480–81.

36. Ibid., 484.

37. Ibid., 490.

38. Edwards, *The "Miscellanies,"* 376.

39. Edwards, *Apocalyptic Writings*, 141.

One important source for Edwards was Matthew Poole's (1624–79) *Critical Synopsis of the Interpretation of Holy Scripture.*[40] Poole began this work in 1666, and it was eventually published in four volumes. It was a massive commentary containing Protestant, Roman Catholic, and Jewish sources. Poole was educated at Emmanuel College, Cambridge, and later served as a minister until he resigned following restoration of the monarchy and the passing of the Act of Uniformity in 1662.

In the section on Revelation in his *Synopsis*, Poole presented various interpretive options for each chapter. The millenarian or premillennial interpretation was represented equally alongside various positions that agreed with the Augustinian tradition. David Pareus and Franciscus Junius were cited frequently. By simply reading Poole's *Synopsis* one would not be able to determine which position he favored, yet it is certain that he considered the premillennial interpretation a viable option, and well within the bounds of orthodoxy. The *Synopsis* included interpretations of the place of the millennium, the first resurrection, and the reign of Christ and the saints.

Not surprisingly, Poole's commentary was an invaluable resource for Edwards. It provided not only a quick summary of interpretive options, but also exposure to a wide range of apocalyptic commentators.[41] As a reference tool for biblical studies it was unrivaled in its day.[42]

At times it is difficult to determine whether Edwards was consulting the original text, or simply using Poole as a secondary source reference. Nevertheless, in regard to Edwards's eschatology, Poole's work is worth noting because it increased the accessibility and exposure of alternative apocalyptic positions.

Another influential source for Edwards was a commentary by Moses Lowman (1680–1752) titled, *Paraphrase and Notes on the Revelation*, first published in 1737. Lowman was an English minister with dissenting sympathies. He studied at both the universities of Leiden and Utrecht, under tutelage of a number of eminent Protestant scholastics including Herman Witsius, Peter Von Mastrict, and Melchoir Leydecker. Although none of these theologians were persuaded by millenarian doctrines, Dutch theology was exploding with millenarian interest in the late sixteenth and early sev-

---

40. I have translated the title for this essay. The original is *Synopsis Criticorum aliorumque Sacrae Scripturae Interpretum* (London, 1669–76).

41. Edwards, *Apocalyptic Writings*, 61.

42. Ibid., 60.

enteenth centuries. This explosion can be judged not only by the increased publication of millenarian writings, but also the critical response deemed necessary by non-millenarians.[43] It is reasonable to suggest that Lowman was at the very least aware of the heightened apocalyptic interest that surrounded him during his education in the Dutch Republic.

More specifically, Lowman's commentary revealed his definitive break with his non-millenarian professors in Leiden and Utrecht. Lowman placed the millennium entirely in the future. He expressed his dissatisfaction with previous interpreters who began the millennium at the time of the Emperor Constantine, and instead concluded that the time of the millennium must be "very distant."[44] The millennium would not only be in the future, Lowman argued, but it would extend for a literal one thousand years.[45] Concerning the first resurrection, Lowman did not understand this event to be a bodily rising, but simply the restoration of the church.[46] Furthermore, the reign of the martyrs should be taken symbolically since Lowman could not fathom the thought that these saints should return to earth and be subjected to Satan's attacks during his release at the end of the millennium.[47]

We can recognize with little difficulty the similarities between Lowman and Edwards's exegesis of Revelation 20. Both held to a future, literal thousand-year millennium, and both interpreted the first resurrection as non-corporeal. Still, Lowman's influence on Edwards extended beyond mere similarities. Edwards frequently cited Lowman in his notes on the *Apocalypse*, and his notebook contained a number of extracts from Lowman's commentary along with Edwards's comments.[48] Clearly Edwards saw Lowman's book as an important reference when beginning his own study on Revelation.

A final source for Edwards's eschatology was Sir Isaac Newton. The impact of Newton's scientific discoveries has fueled volumes of scholarly

---

43. Ernestine van der Wall surveys the interest in apocalyptic thought in the Netherlands in the late seventeenth century in her article, " 'Antichrist Stormed': The Glorious Revolution and the Dutch Prophetic Tradition," in *The World of William and Mary: Anglo-Dutch Perspectives on the Revolution of 1688–89*, ed. D. Hoak and Mordechai Feingold (Stanford, CA: Stanford University Press, 1996), 152–64. Also see Jeffrey K. Jue, *Heaven Upon Earth: Joseph Mede (1586–1638) and the Legacy of Millenarianism* (Dordtrecht, Netherlands: Springer, 2006), 211–43.

44. Moses Lowman, *Paraphrase and Notes on the Apocalypse* (London, 1737), 64.

45. Ibid., 239.

46. Ibid., 244.

47. Ibid., 246, 248.

48. Edwards, *Apocalyptic Writings*, 219–52.

articles and books, but few scholars have explored the importance of Newton's eschatology.[49] One such scholar, Sarah Hutton, writes, "Newton's study of the apocalypse is, arguably, a point of intersection for his apparently diverse interests, be these mathematics or alchemy, astronomy or ancient religions, chronology or bible-study."[50] Edwards was familiar with Newton's scientific works, but he also consulted his writings on Revelation.[51] Citations of Newton are found in Edwards's notebook on the *Apocalypse*.[52] Newton's writings on Revelation were published posthumously in 1733 under the title, *Observations upon the Prophecies of Daniel and the Apocalypse of St. John*.

Newton's eschatological position contains various millenarian or premillennial conclusions. Like earlier commentators, he placed the millennium entirely in the future, extending for one thousand years, and inaugurated by Christ's second advent. Newton states,

> He [the apostle John] goes on to describe their destruction more fully, and the future kingdom. He saith, that because the coming of Christ should be long deferred, they should scoff, saying where is the promise of his coming? Then he describes the sudden coming of the day of the Lord upon them, as a thief in the night, which is the Apocalyptic phrase; and the millennium, or thousand years, which are with God but as a day; the passing away of the old heavens and earth, by a conflagration in the lake of fire, and our looking for new heavens and a new earth, wherein dwelleth righteousness.[53]

Newton anticipated that the destruction of the kingdom of the Antichrist would precede the millennium.[54] He also interpreted the first resurrection

49. The most helpful studies are: Frank E. Manuel, *The Religion of Isaac Newton* (New York: Oxford, 1974); J. E. Force and R. H. Popkin, eds., *Essays on the Context, Nature, and Influence of Isaac Newton's Theology* (Dordtrecht, Netherlands: Kluwer Academic, 1990); idem, *The Books of Nature and Scripture: Recent Essays on Natural Philosophy, Theology, and Biblical Criticism in the Netherlands of Spinoza's Time and the British Isles of Newton's Time* (Dordtrecht, Netherlands: Kluwer Academic, 1994); idem, *Newton and Religion: Context, Nature, and Influence* (Dordtrecht, Netherlands: Kluwer Academic, 1999); Jue, *Heaven Upon Earth*, 169–73.

50. Sarah Hutton, "The Seven Trumpets and the Seven Vials: Apocalypticism and Christology in Newton's Theological Writings," in J. E. Force and R. H. Popkin, eds., *Newton and Religion: Context, Nature, and Influence* (Dordtrecht, Netherlands: 1999), 165.

51. See C. C. Goen, "Jonathan Edwards: A New Departure in Eschatology," 35; Perry Miller, *Errand into the Wilderness* (Cambridge, MA: Harvard University Press, 1956), 228–29.

52. Edwards, *Apocalyptic Writings*, 230, 244, 250.

53. Isaac Newton, *Observations upon the Prophecies of Daniel and the Apocalypse of St. John* (Dublin, 1733), 241.

54. Manuel, *The Religion of Isaac Newton*, 99.

as a literal one in which Christian martyrs would rise up and reign with Christ. Newton writes,

> For when the Martyrs and Prophets live again they may reign here with Christ a thousand years till all the nations Gog and Magog be subdued and the dominion of the new Jerusalem be established and death be vanquished by raising the rest of the dead (those who do not live again untill the thousand years be finished,) and all this time they may be in the same state of happiness in or neare these regions as afterwards when they retire into the highest heavens.[55]

However, Newton does distinguish between the reign of the martyrs and those who are alive on earth when the millennium begins. The martyrs would not reign in a terrestrial New Jerusalem; instead, these "Children of the Resurrection" would abide in a heavenly realm.[56] Subsequently, the earthly millennial kingdom will be occupied by converted Jews and others who are alive at Christ's second coming.[57] Finally, Newton believed that the millennium would end with the Petrine conflagration.

Again the similarities between Edwards and Newton are significant. Both interpreted the millennium as a future, literal, thousand-year period. Both believed the end of Satan's dominion would precede the millennium, with the end of the present world marked by a great consuming fire, and both anticipated a national conversion of the Jews. Yet one distinctive feature of Newton's eschatology was not reflected in Edwards. As a traditional premillennialist, Newton placed the second coming of Christ at the beginning of the millennium, and not—like Edwards—at the end. It is interesting to observe that regardless of Newton's denial of the divinity of Christ (he was a Unitarian), he still placed great importance in the second coming in

55. Newton, "Of the Day of Judgment and World to Come," included in F. E. Manuel, *The Religion of Isaac Newton*, 136.

56. Quoted from Reiner Smolinksi, "The Logic of Millennial Thought: Sir Isaac Newton among His Contemporaries," in Force and Popkin, *Newton and Religion*, 284–85.

57. Newton writes, "The rest of his kingdom are the nations of them which are saved: and they are mortals remaining on earth, because Christ has a kingdom there which he now begins to rule with a rod of iron, and tis only out of this kingdome which the wicked could be gathered. Conceive therefore that when Christ comes to judge the dead he judges also the living and that as many as are found written in the Book of life are adjudged to life and saved by being either caught up into the air to be with the Lord or left below on earth in the Kingdome of mortals which he thenceforth rules with a rod of iron and the rest are adjudged to death and cast into the Lake of fire," Newton, "Of the Day of Judgment and World to Come," 132.

prophetic history. Still, although Newton held to a corporeal first resurrection, he and Edwards both maintained that the martyrs would not be confined to an earthly reign during the millennium.

JOSEPH MEDE (1586–1638)

Thus far we have demonstrated that the sources Edwards consulted can all be categorized broadly as millenarian, because all of these apocalyptic commentators—Edwards included—understood the millennium to be a future earthly period, lasting for a thousand years. Yet this millennial genealogy, from Poole, Lowman, and Newton down to Edwards, is incomplete. There was another individual who stood behind these commentators and inspired their collective millennial imaginations. The primogeniture for post-Reformation Protestant millenarian thought was born a century before Jonathan Edwards.

In 1627 a book was published that radically changed the landscape of eschatological thought in the post-Reformation era: Joseph Mede's *Clavis Apocalyptica* (later translated as *The Key of the Revelation*).[58] The publication of Mede's book marked the rebirth of millenarianism or premillennialism. Not since the chiliasm of the ante-Nicene church fathers had an individual with orthodox credentials held to a premillennial interpretation of Revelation 20.[59] Mede spent his entire academic career in the quiet confines of early seventeenth-century Cambridge University. The isolation and freedom of the academy allowed him to devote himself to his scholarly pursuits. Mede was regarded by his contemporaries as one of the foremost biblical scholars in England, and his primary area of expertise was the book of Revelation.[60]

Aside from his view on the millennium, Mede's most significant contribution to apocalyptic studies was his structural analysis of the book of Revelation. For Mede, Revelation was not to be read as a strict chronology (as modern premillennialists would advocate). He developed a complex system whereby he determined that certain visions were contemporaneous based

58. I recognize that the rebirth of millenarianism is also attributable to Johann Heinrich Alsted. However, his impact was felt less in Britain and in North America than in Alsted's home of Germany. For details on Alsted's millenarianism, see Howard B. Hotson, *Paradise Postponed*.

59. Before Alsted and Mede, millenarianism was a doctrine espoused only by some on the radical fringes of Protestantism.

60. Jue, *Heaven Upon Earth*, 7–16.

on similar symbolic details contained within each vision.[61] For instance, the visions of the woman fleeing into the wilderness for 1,260 days (Rev. 12), the seven-headed beast ruling for 42 months (Rev. 13), the trampling of the outer courts of the temple for 42 months (Rev. 11), and the prophesying of the two witnesses in sackcloth for 1,260 days would all occur at the same time (Rev. 11).[62] He called these contemporaneous visions "synchronisms." When rigorously applied, this method would serve as a key for unlocking the mysteries of the Apocalypse.

It was this method of "synchronisms," along with one other important interpretation, that convinced Mede that the millennium would be in the future. Likewise, Mede applied a thorough historicist approach to his interpretations. Once he established a chronology for the visions, he then attempted to assign particular events in history to each vision. Now sixteenth-century writers such as Heinrich Bullinger and Franciscus Junius (whose comments on the Apocalypse were incorporated in the Geneva Bible) both placed the millennium in the earlier history of the church. They dated it roughly from the conversion of Constantine to the Reformation.[63] Mede rejected that interpretation, and instead declared that this thousand-year period did not reflect the blessed millennium, but actually was the time of great apostasy prophesied in 1 Timothy 4:1. The evidence for this apostasy was the rise of the cult of saints established on the teaching of the first popes—an idolatry of the greatest offense. For Mede this was the reign of Antichrist, not the glorious millennium.[64] Consequently, if the millennium could not be located in the past, then it must be projected into the future. Mede applied the sounding of the sixth trumpet to his own day and synchronized the seventh with the millennium—thus logically placing it entirely in the future. With regard to the duration of the millennium, Mede employed the same creation-week paradigm: the seventh day or thousand years would constitute the millennial kingdom.[65]

61. Mede's method should not be confused with the amillennial understanding of recapitulation. He did maintain a historical chronology within Revelation based on his synchronisms.

62. Mede, *The Key of the Revelation* (London, 1643), Parts 1 and 2. Also see Jue, *Heaven Upon Earth*, 100–106.

63. See Heinrich Bullinger, *A Hundred Sermons upon the Apocalips* (London, 1561); and Franciscus Junius, *The Apocalyps or Revelation of S. John the Apostle and evangelist of our Lord Jesus Christ* (Cambridge, 1596).

64. Joseph Mede, *The Apostasy of the Latter Times* (London, 1641).

65. Jue, *Heaven Upon Earth*, 89–108.

The events leading up to the millennium, for Mede, were literal as well. He anticipated the fall of the Antichrist—even speculating that the victories of the Swedish Lutheran King Gustavus Adolphus during the Thirty Years' War could possibly be the pouring out of the fourth vial. Mede also was convinced that there would be a mass conversion of the Jews prior to the millennium. This conversion would have a supernatural element similar to the apostle Paul's experience on the road to Damascus, where a "Vision and Voice from Heaven" would call out to the Jews.[66] For Mede this interpretation also solved the geographical problem posed by the Jewish Diaspora. In waiting for such monumental events, Mede's millenarianism was not overtly pessimistic. The unfolding of prophetic history bore a hint of optimism as he awaited the impending victory of the Lord over the forces of the Antichrist.

Indeed the interpretation of the events within the millennium revealed Mede's distinctive millenarianism. With great reluctance, he admitted that the first resurrection should be taken as literal. Mede writes,

> Thus I yet admit the First Resurrection to be Corporal as well as the Second, though I confess I have much striven against it; and if the Text would admit another sense less free of Paradox, I had yet rather listen unto it; but I find it not.[67]

Mede asks: who would participate in the first resurrection? He answers,

> The Rising of the Martyrs is that which is called the First Resurrection, being as it seems, a prerogative to their sufferings above the rest of the Dead; who as they suffered with Christ in the time of his patience, so should be glorified with him in the Reign of his Victory before the Universal Resurrection of all.[68]

Participation in the first resurrection will be the reward for the slain martyrs. Mede also elevated their status during the millennium above the

---

66. Joseph Mede, *The Works of The Pious and Profoundly-Learned Joseph Mede* . . . (London, 1677), 761.

67. Ibid., 603. Again Mede writes, "But howsoever when at first I perceived that Millennium to be a State of the Church consequent to the times of the Beast, I was averse from the proper acception of that Resurrection, taking it for a rising of the Church from a dead estate; as being loth to admit too many Paradoxes at once: yet afterward more seriously considering and weighing all things, I found no ground or footing for any sence [sic] but the Literal." Ibid., 770.

68. Ibid., 604.

rest of the inhabitants. At first he argued that the reign of the martyrs would not be on earth, but that they would "resume their Bodies and reign in Heaven."[69] Their reward would include remaining in the constant presence of Christ, who Mede believed would reign in heaven and not on earth during the millennium. Mede, as a premillennialist, affirmed that Christ's second coming would inaugurate the millennium, yet Christ would not remain on earth to reign because the "Kingdom of Christ ever hath been and shall be *Regnum Caelorum*, A Kingdom whose throne and Kingly Residence is in Heaven."[70] So the sequence of Christ's return would be as follows: Christ would appear visibly for the first resurrection and the conversion of the Jews, and afterward return to heaven for his millennial reign. But later Mede reversed his opinion and agreed with Johann Heinrich Alsted that the saints of the first resurrection would indeed reign on earth.[71] However he still maintained a degree of privilege for these saints. They alone would inhabit the New Jerusalem, which would be an earthly city reflecting the characteristics of the final glorified state after the universal resurrection. The New Jerusalem will be "the Metropolis . . . of the New world," and those who dwell in it will be "*extra ominem mutatationis aleam* [beyond all possibility of change]."[72] Their inhabitance in the New Jerusalem will reflect their heavenly position, not a return to their previous mutable earthly existence. Finally, Mede agreed that the millennium and the world would undergo a great purifying fire. As the first world under Noah ended with water, so the second world would be consumed by fire.[73]

MILLENARIAN GENEALOGY

It is easy to see the similarities between Joseph Mede's eschatology and the views advocated by Matthew Poole, Moses Lowman, and Isaac Newton. Nevertheless, clear and substantial lines of influence can be determined. The most likely place for Poole's initial exposure to the teachings

69. Ibid.

70. Ibid., 603. "The Presence of Christ in this Kingdom shall not doubt be glorious and evident: yet I dare not so much as imagine (which some Ancients seem to have thought) that it should be a Visible Converse upon earth."

71. "I differ therefore from Piscator, and agree with Alstedius, That the Saints of the First Resurrection should reign on Earth during the Millennium, and not in Heaven." Ibid., 772.

72. Ibid.

73. Ibid., 613.

of Mede was in Cambridge. While Poole's student days were after Mede's death, the reputation of Mede should not be underestimated. Mede's scholarly abilities were renowned both within and beyond Cambridge.[74] Even more significant was the fact that Poole was tutored at Emmanuel College by John Worthington (1618–71). Worthington was a latitudinarian who shared ecclesiastical sympathies with Mede.[75] Moreover, Worthington was the editor of Mede's collected works, which underwent four editions. It was probably through Worthington that Poole was introduced to the works of Mede.

Poole's *Synopsis* also demonstrates his intimate knowledge of Mede's eschatology. In the section on Revelation 20, Poole almost exclusively uses Mede to represent the millenarian or premillennial interpretation. He points to Mede as one who understood the first resurrection to be a literal, corporeal resurrection.[76] In addition, Poole used Mede's later position to illustrate the millenarian view that the martyrs from the first resurrection would reign in the earthly New Jerusalem.[77] And of course he cites Mede's positions as teaching that this millennium would be entirely in the future, after the fall of the beast, when Satan would be chained and Christ would reign.[78] Thus, anyone consulting Poole's commentary would recognize that he owed a considerable debt to Mede for the premillennial interpretation of Revelation.

Out of the three—Poole, Lowman and Newton—Lowman demonstrated the greatest divergence from Mede's eschatology, yet Mede's influence is still traceable. Lowman disagreed primarily with Mede's structural

---

74. Jue, *Heaven Upon Earth*, 7–16.

75. Ibid., 38–39.

76. "Qu. 4. Qualis est haec vita & resurrectio? Resp.I. Literalis & propria . . . Sensus enim literalis non est deferendus sine necessitate, maxime in simplici & plana narratione, qualis haec est, paucis tantum interspersa figuris Propheticis, quas usus loquendi, vel alibi, vel etiam in hoc Libro, manifestas fecit." In the margin Poole cites p. 943 of Mede's *Works*. Poole, *Synopsis*, p. 1986. Also, "Cum ergo secunda Resurrectio sit corporalis, talem quoque primam esse necesse est," Ibid., 1987.

77. "Qu. 5 Quale & ubinam erit hoc regnum? . . . Resp.2. In terra sancta, & in Jerosolyma, in qua regnabunt Sancti in statu Beatitudinis & gloriae, Divina praesentia & visione Christi fruentes, quasi coelum in terra possidentes, sive novam Pradisum immutabilem," Ibid., 1998.

78. "Qu.7. Quodnam est tempus huius millennii? Ubi hi millen ani inchoantur & disinunt? Num praeterierunt prorsus, vel ex parte? Num vero adhuc futuri sunt? . . . [Sed videamus quomodo Cl. Medus sententiam suam & explicat & astruit.] Millenni ligati Draconis seu Satanae, Regnique Christi Augusti, contemporant Tubae septimae, seu intervallo ab Excidio Bestiae." Ibid., 1989, 1991.

divisions. He preferred a stricter chronological reading instead of Mede's synchronisms. Lowman writes,

> This natural Order will, I conceive, free us from that Intricacy and Difficulty which a Supposition of Synchronisms, and contemporary Events in the different Periods, have occasioned in the Interpretation of this Book; and it may greatly help us, in applying historical Events to the several Prophecies, to look only at such as fall within the time to which the Periods belong.[79]

Additionally, Lowman and Mede differed in their interpretation of the first resurrection. Yet even with their difference, both commentators shared the same intent—to preserve a higher degree of reward for the martyrs. Lowman situated them in heaven, while Mede eventually placed them in the New Jerusalem. Similarly, it is clear that Lowman was familiar with Mede's work, citing his various historical applications.[80] Regardless of their various exegetical disagreements, Lowman still relied on Mede for his fundamental millenarian premise—a literal, future, thousand-year millennium.[81]

The influence of Mede's eschatology on Newton has been documented in other studies.[82] Included in Newton's library was the 1672 third edition of Mede's works.[83] Newton enthusiastically subscribed to Mede's method of synchronisms, while occasionally modifying it to support what he thought was a more consistent reading:

> Mr Mede hath explained the Prophecy of the first six trumpets not much amiss: but if he had observed that the Prophecy of the pouring out of the

---

79. Lowman, *A Paraphrase and Notes*, xii.

80. Ibid., 31, 45, 49; "Extracts from Mr. Lowman," in Edwards, *Apocalyptic Writings*, 222.

81. The influence of Daniel Whitby (1638–1726) on Moses Lowman should be noted. Lowman depended on Whitby's interpretation of the first resurrection as "spiritual." Whitby is one of the first millenarians to place Christ's second coming at the end of the millennium rather than the beginning. See Daniel Whitby, *Paraphrase and Commentary on the New Testament* (1703).

82. Manuel, *The Religion of Isaac Newton*, 90–92; R. H. Popkin, "Newton as a Bible Scholar," in *Essays on The Context . . .*, ed. J. E. Force and R. H. Popkin, 103–18; S. Hutton, "More, Newton, and the Language of Biblical Prophecy," in *The Books of Nature and Scripture . . .*, ed. J. E. Force and R. H. Popkin, 39–45; idem, "The Seven Trumpets and the Seven Vials: Apocalypticism and Christology in Newton's Theological Writings," in *Newton and Religion*, ed. J. E. Force and R. H. Popkin, 165–78; M. Murrin, "Newton's Apocalypse," ibid., 203–20; R. Smolinski, "The Logic of Millennial Thought: Sir Isaac Newton Among His Contemporaries," ibid., 259–90.

83. M. Murrin, "Newton's Apocalypse," 209.

vials of wrath is synchronal to that of the sounding of the trumpets, his explanation would have been yet more complete.[84]

Like Mede, Newton believed the fall of the Antichrist and the conversion of the Jews would precede the second coming of Christ, which would be followed by a literal millennium. Newton's interpretation of the first resurrection reflected Mede's early position in which the martyrs would be raised to rule in heaven. Newton's understanding of the New Jerusalem was an attempt to occupy a middle ground between Mede's literal earthly city and the metaphoric heavenly city of other commentators. The New Jerusalem would be Christ's assembly of the saints, represented both in an earthly city and a heavenly city. Newton writes,

> This city must be understood to comprehend as well Christ and the children of the resurrection as the race of mortal Jews on earth. It signifies not a material city but the body politique of all those who have dominion over the nation whether they be the saints in heaven or their mortal viceregents on earth.[85]

Subsequently he agreed with Mede that the world would end with a great consuming fire. The Apocalypse as the "point of intersection"—as described by Sarah Hutton—for Newton's various interests was to a large extent shaped by the eschatology of Joseph Mede.

Having demonstrated the substantial influence of Mede on the eschatology of Poole, Lowman and Newton—whom Edwards consulted for his own apocalyptic studies—consequently we can trace the millennial genealogy from Mede down to Edwards. At the least, Edwards would have been exposed to Mede's eschatology through the filter of Poole, Lowman, and Newton—especially Poole's *Synopsis*. But Edwards was not reading Mede simply through these secondary sources. Mede's works were available to him in the Yale College library, among the books donated by Jeremiah Drummer.[86] From these books and the writings of Poole, Lowman, and Newton, Edwards became a student of the father of seventeenth-century millenarianism.

---

84. Newton, *Observations*, 334.

85. Yahuda MS 6, fol. 18r, at the Jewish National and University Library, Jerusalem. As cited in R. Smolinski, "The Logic of Millennial Thought," 284.

86. Edwards, *Apocalyptic Writings*, 61; Louise May Bryant and Mary Patterson, "The List of Books Sent by Jeremiah Drummer," in *Papers in Honor of Andrew Keogh*, ed. Mary Withington (New Haven, CT: Yale University Press, 1938), 423–92.

In evaluating Lowman's strict chronological reading of Revelation, Edwards rejected Lowman in favor of Mede's synchronized method. Edwards writes,

> That there are no SYNCHRONISMS, or resumings of things before proph- esied of more generally, to foretell them more particularly or in another manner, and declare something further concerning them, is contrary to the method of almost all the prophecies of Scripture, and plainly contrary to the manner of this prophecy of the Revelation.[87]

Mede's *clavis* or key to the Revelation provided Edwards the basic outline for reading the entire book. From this, Edwards followed a historicist approach that sought to demonstrate the fulfillment of the Apocalypse in events past, present, and future. Edwards clarifies by writing,

> The method of these visions is first, to give a more general representation of things, and then afterwards, a more distinct description of the particular changes and revolutions that are subjects of them.[88]

More specifically, Edwards's interpretation of events that would lead up to the millennium was similar to Mede's. Both anticipated the fall of the Antichrist and the conversion of the Jews, and both maintained that the duration of human history would follow the creation-week paradigm, with the final "day" or thousand-year period constituting the millennial kingdom ending in the Petrine conflagration.[89] It is imperative that we understand that Edwards agreed with Mede that the millennium would be a future, literal, earthly kingdom extending for a thousand years.

Nevertheless, Edwards did not adopt Mede's eschatology uncritically. Contrary to Mede, he held that the millennium would not begin with Christ's second coming and a corporeal first resurrection of the martyrs; Christ would return only at the end of the millennium. Yet even with these points of difference, a degree of continuity can be traced. For Mede, the abode of Christ during the millennium would be in heaven. Mede and Edwards agreed that the rightful place of Christ's rule is from his throne in heaven, not in an

---

87. Edwards, "Remarks on Lowman," in *Apocalyptic Writings*, 251.

88. Edwards, *Apocalyptic Writings*, 106.

89. Edwards also regarded the past as a time of great apostasy and not a period of millennial bliss and felicity.

earthly capital. Likewise Mede elevated the place of the martyrs, first putting them in heaven, but later assigning them to the New Jerusalem—fixed in their glorified state. Edwards, too, wanted to preserve a higher status for the slain martyrs by situating them in heaven during the millennium.

Another apparent distinction between Edwards and Mede follows what has been defined stereotypically as a fundamental difference between postmillennialists and premillennialists. Postmillenialism has been characterized as an optimistic eschatology, while premillennialism has been characterized as pessimistic. Postmillennial optimism is supposedly a result of the church's active involvement in the spread of the gospel, which would prepare for arrival of the millennium. Edwards believed that this would be a gradual process accomplished through the preaching of the gospel, arriving in a period of latter-day glory.[90] The church—individuals included—would play an active role in ushering in the millennium. For Edwards, the church was not waiting passively for the arrival of Christ to begin the millennium, but was fervently praying and working toward that end. This was Edwards's great hope for the revivals during the Great Awakening. Thus, without a monumental event such as the second advent, this gradual process would make it more difficult to determine when the millennium actually would begin. Still, Edward argued that the "end of Satan's visible kingdom" would mark the beginning of the millennium.[91]

Mede commented little about the church's involvement in the arrival of the millennium—probably because of mounting tensions within the early Stuart church, where Mede's apocalyptic opinions were not always received favorably.[92] However, Mede's millenarian successors supported the active involvement by the church and individuals in preparing for the millennium. John Dury, an irenicist and member of the Westminster Assembly, along with his colleagues Samuel Hartlib and Jan Amos Comenius, committed themselves to an effort to unify all Protestant churches in Europe. This project was pregnant with apocalyptic intentions, because they hoped that unification would help ring in the millennial age.[93] Similarly, many congregationalists, both in Britain and New England, labored to make the visible church reflect

90. Edwards, *A History of the Work of Redemption*, 459.
91. Ibid., 456.
92. Mede's *Clavis* was banned from re-publication by the Laudian establishment because it supported the identification of the pope with the Antichrist. Mede, *Works*, 798.
93. Jue, *Heaven Upon Earth*, 77–84.

more strictly the invisible church. Their labors were an attempt to present a more purified bride to her groom at Christ's return.[94] Finally, many of the seventeenth- and eighteenth-century millenarians also viewed their missionary efforts in the New World as preparation for the millennium.[95] While premillennialists marked the beginning of the millennium with the second advent, they still maintained an active and not passive role for the church in preparing for its arrival.

Subsequently, the eschatology of Jonathan Edwards was both indirectly and directly shaped by the millenarian thought of Joseph Mede—a millennial genealogy can be traced from Mede through Matthew Poole, Moses Lowman, and Isaac Newton down to Edwards. As a result, the postmillennialism of Edwards bore a stronger resemblance to the millenarianism or premillennialism of his apocalyptic predecessors. The defining character for distinguishing eschatological positions was not the place of Christ's second coming (either before or after the millennium), but rather the interpretation that the millennium would be a literal, future, and earthly event—extending for a thousand years. Thus the eschatology of Jonathan Edwards contradicts the assumption of modern theologians that postmillennialism is closer to amillennialism, when compared with premillennialism.

POSTMILLENNIALISM, DISPENSATIONALISM, AND OLD PRINCETON

If the modern assumptions are incorrect, then another question emerges: to what can we attribute the rise of such a prevalent misconception? There are two primary reasons for the shift in postmillennial perception. The first is the modification of Edwards's postmillennialism by theologians at Old Princeton. While many members of the Old Princeton faculty are considered "standard" postmillennialists, their eschatology was not identical to Edwards's. Charles Hodge (1797–1878), perhaps one of the most influential theologians of the nineteenth century, displayed a tension in his writings on the millennium, indicating a less-rigid millenarian interpretation. Hodge asserted that the millennial age would be included in the present age of the Spirit. Hodge writes, "it is evident that the Apostles considered the dispensation of the Spirit under which we are now living,

94. Ibid., 175–210.
95. See J. A. de Jong, *As the Waters Cover the Sea: Millennial Expectations in the Rise of Anglo-American Missions 1640–1810* (Kampen, Netherlands: Kok, 1970).

as the only one which was to intervene between the first advent of Christ and the end of the world."[96] For Hodge, the progressive improvements in the present age would continue until the glorious perfections of the millennium.[97] At this point it seems that Hodge is blurring any adamant distinction between the present church age and the future millennial age. This is not the postmillennialism of Edwards according to which the millennium would be explicitly marked by the accomplishment of certain events—the fall of the Antichrist, the conversion of the Jews, etc.

Nevertheless, traces of a millenarian heritage can be detected in Hodge. In interpreting Revelation 20, Hodge allowed for the possibility of a literal reading. He writes,

> There is to be a period of millennial glory on earth, and a still more glorious consummation in heaven. This period is called a millennium because in Revelation it is said to last a thousand years, an expression which is perhaps generally understood literally.[98]

It is uncertain as to whether this was Hodge's understanding, because he writes further, "Some however think it means a protracted season of infinite duration."[99] Yet, he concludes, "During this period, be it longer or shorter, the Church is to enjoy a season of peace, purity, and blessedness such as it has never yet experienced."[100] In the end we can best describe Hodge as a moderate postmillennialist.

A year before Charles Hodge's death, his son, A. A. Hodge (1823–1886), was appointed to the chair of didactic and polemical theology at Princeton. In his book *Outlines of Theology*, A. A. Hodge responds to the question, "What is the Scriptural doctrine concerning the millennium?"

> 1st. The Scriptures, both of the Old and New Testament, clearly reveal that the gospel is to exercise an influence over all branches of the human family, immeasurably more extensive and more thoroughly transforming than any it has ever realized in time past. This end is to be gradually attained through the spiritual presence of Christ in the ordinary dispensation of

96. Charles Hodge, *Systematic Theology*, 3:802.
97. Ibid., 2:94.
98. Ibid., 3:858.
99. Ibid., 3:858–59.
100. Ibid.

Providence, and ministrations of his church . . . 2nd. The period of this general prevalency of the gospel will continue a thousand years, and is hence designated the millennium—Rev. xx.2–7.[101]

Similar to his father, A. A. Hodge did not make it explicit whether the millennium would be a literal thousand-year period in the future. For him, it was not coterminus with the entire interadvental period, yet he did not indicate definitively that it was entirely in the future either. However, evidence of Edwards's eschatology can be seen in the younger Hodge as well. Unlike his father, Hodge did include the national conversion of Israel as an apocalyptic sign of the millennium. He gave two options, "The Jews are to convert to Christianity either at the commencement or during the continuance of this period" (referring to the millennium).[102] While for Edwards the conversion will mark the beginning of the millennium, for Hodge the conversion will indicate the presence of the millennium—either the beginning or some point therein. Subsequently, like Edwards and Mede, the national conversion of Israel will serve as a sign for the presence of the millennium.

The last prominent Old Princeton theologian was B. B. Warfield (1851–1921). In Warfield we have the most definitive break with the post-millennial tradition. Warfield rejected premillennialism, but was also convinced that, "though no doubt the extreme postmillennial view is equally untenable in view of the consistent Biblical teaching that we may not know when the Lord may come."[103] Warfield's interpretation of Revelation 20 rejects Edwards's view and the millenarian tradition. Warfield agreed with Augustine and understood the millennium to be coterminus with the entire period between Christ's first and second comings. Warfield states, "our own tendency is to return to Augustine in interpreting the thousand years . . . [as] the Christian dispensation looked upon from the standpoint of the saints in heaven."[104] Again he writes, the "thousand years, thus, is the whole

---

101. A. A. Hodge, *Outlines of Theology* (Grand Rapids: Zondervan, 1972), 568–69.

102. Ibid.

103. B. B. Warfield, "The Millennium and the Apocalypse," *PTR* 2 (1904): 599–617; reprinted in *Biblical Doctrines* (Grand Rapids: Baker, 1981), 643–64.

104. Warfield, "Review of Studies in Eschatology. The Thousand Years in Both Testaments, By Nathan West," *The Presbyterian and Reformed Review*, J1 (1890), 514. Likewise, Warfield displayed his familiarity with the Augustinian apocalyptic tradition by citing Nicholas Colladon and David Pareus in Warfield, "The Millennium and the Apocalypse," 645.

of this present dispensation, which is again placed before us in its entirety, but looked at now relatively not to what is passing on earth but to what is enjoyed 'in Paradise.'"[105] Strictly speaking, Warfield's exegesis of Revelation 20 followed an amillennial interpretation.

As we have observed, Warfield made the most significant break with the millennial tradition inherited from Edwards, yet aspects of previous commentators still manifested themselves in Warfield's thought. Lest we mistakenly identify Warfield as a consistent amillennialist, it should be noted that he did see differences between his own view and those of the Dutch amillennialists, including Abraham Kuyper and Herman Bavinck.[106] Additionally Warfield, like Edwards, anticipated a time of great prosperity for the church. Regarding his Augustinian interpretation, Warfield adds, "but this conclusion obviously does not carry with it the denial that a 'golden age' yet lies before the Church, if we may use this designation in a purely spiritual sense."[107] Warfield's anticipation of a "latter day glory" was a spiritualized version of the millennial tradition of Edwards.

In the eschatological positions of Charles Hodge, A. A. Hodge, and B. B. Warfield, we observe a diluted postmillennialism that plainly departed from Edwards, yet continued to exemplify various interpretations from the millenarian tradition. The confusion over the roots of postmillennialism can be attributed to this dilution. Definitions and distinctives are not so clearly demarcated within the views of Old Princeton, producing sympathies for postmillennialism that would never have been accepted in the previous centuries.[108] Even Geerhardus Vos, the quintessential amillennialist, at times seemed not to delineate between his position and Old Princeton postmillennialism.[109] Vos distanced himself only from the more "pronounced . . . post-millenarian" view.[110] Indeed the softening of postmillennial eschatology in the writings of Old Princeton

105. Warfield, "The Millennium and the Apocalypse," 649.
106. Samuel G. Craig, "B. B. Warfield," in B. B. Warfield, *Biblical and Theological Studies* (Philadelphia: Presbyterian & Reformed, 1952), xli.
107. Warfield, "The Millennium and the Apocalypse," 662.
108. Millenarianism was condemned in the Augsburg Confession of 1530, the English Forty-Two Articles of Religion of 1552, and the Reformed Second Helvetic Confession of 1566.
109. Geerhardus Vos, *Pauline Eschatology* (Grand Rapids: Baker, 1979), 226.
110. Vos, "The Second Coming of Our Lord and the Millennium," G. Vos, *Redemptive History and Biblical Interpretation: The Shorter Writings of Geerhardus Vos*, ed. Richard B. Gaffin Jr. (Phillipsburg, NJ: Presbyterian & Reformed, 1980), 419.

contributed to the misinterpretation of the roots of postmillennialism that modern theologians have accepted.[111]

The second reason for the modern misconception was the rise of Dispensational pre-millennialism in the mid-nineteenth century[112] —specifically, within Dispensationalism, the interpretation of the 70th week of Daniel 9. Dispensationalists disjoin the final week or 70th week of Daniel's prophecy from the previous 69, and place it in the future immediately preceding the millennium. That final week would be a tribulational period extending for seven years, where the Antichrist would reign and persecute the church. This interpretation encouraged an attitude of radical pessimism, because dark and evil days await with the rise of the Antichrist. One could see clearly the contrast between the pessimism of Dispensational premillennialism and the optimism so prevalent in the postmillennialism of Old Princeton. Yet at this very point it is not postmillennialism that breaks from the millenarian tradition, but Dispensationalism. No previous postmillennial or premillennial commentators interpreted such a radical break in the chronological succession of Daniel's prophecy. Joseph Mede understood the 70 weeks as a literal 490 years, following successively without a break, concluding with the destruction of Jerusalem in 70 A.D.[113] I suggest that the rise of such an aberrant premillennial eschatology contributed to the postmillennial confusion, as postmillennialists and even some premillennialists distanced themselves from Dispensationalism.

THE PRESENT MILLENNIAL MAZE

Historical studies have their own intrinsic academic value, but does this historical study of millennial interpretations have any further value for the church? I submit that this historical theological study complements the

---

111. Another question emerges on this point—if Old Princeton did shift its postmillennialism away from Edwards, are the observations of modern theologians now valid? Did they realign their postmillennialism with amillennialism? In Warfield, the observations of contemporary theologians have some validity. His interpretation of Revelation 20 is consistently Augustinian. With the elder and younger Hodge it is more difficult. They still interpreted Revelation 20 as a period—in some form or another—between the present church age and the consummation. This is not an amillennial position, only a variance which still can be placed under a broad millenarian umbrella.

112. Robert G. Clouse, Robert N. Hosack, Richard V. Pierard, *The New Millennium Manual: A Once and Future Guide* (Grand Rapids: Baker, 1999), 94.

113. Mede, *Works*, 697–709.

conclusions of other systematic and biblical theologians in their respective fields. The similarities between premillennialism and traditional postmillennialism have been observed and analyzed by others such as Richard B. Gaffin Jr. Gaffin writes, "like premillennialism, postmillennialism—distinguished from amillennialism—'de-eschatologizes' the present (and past) existence of the church."[114] What Gaffin is pointing out is that the assertion, made by pre- and postmillennialists, that another finite age (the millennium) will precede the eternal eschaton reduces the eschatological character of the present age. How so? If the present church age will be followed by another intermediate state, then the church's final eschatological hope is weakened and delayed. Likewise, Geerhardus Vos stated that an intermediate state "falling short of the perfect heavenly life would be of an anti-climax."[115] Even John Calvin, although specifically addressing millenarianism, made a similar observation:

> Those who assign the children of God a thousand years in which to enjoy the inheritance of the life to come do not realize how much reproach they are casting upon Christ and his Kingdom. For if they do not put on immortality, the Christ himself, to whose glory they shall be transformed, has not been received into undying glory. If their blessedness is to have an end, then Christ's Kingdom, on whose firmness it depends, is but temporary. In short, either such persons are utterly ignorant of everything divine or they are trying by a devious malice to bring to nought all the grace of God and power of Christ, the fulfillment of which is realized only when sin is blotted out, death swallowed up, and everlasting life restored![116]

Calvin argued that millenarianism destroyed the very foundation of the kingdom of Jesus Christ, because it rejected the certainty of the reward of the eternal state, secured by Christ. For Calvin, a temporary millennial kingdom would only reduce the consummate glory of the eschatological age. According to these systematic and biblical theological studies, it is important to recognize that any form of millenarian eschatology calls

---

114. Richard B. Gaffin Jr., "Theonomy and Eschatology: Reflections on Postmillennialism," in *Theonomy: A Reformed Critique*, ed. William S. Barker and W. Robert Godfrey (Grand Rapids: Zondervan, 1990), 202.

115. Vos, *Pauline Eschatology*, 236.

116. John Calvin, *The Institutes of the Christian Religion*, ed. John T. McNeill, trans. Ford Lewis Battles (Philadelphia: Westminster, 1960), 3.25.5.

into question the provisional character of the kingdom already inaugurated at Christ's first coming.[117] This critique applies equally to premillennialism and traditional postmillennialism, thereby again demonstrating that these two positions are in closer proximity than either with amillennialism. Therefore historical, systematic, and biblical theological studies ought to foster the church's hope in the advent of the eternal heavenly kingdom to be unveiled at Christ's glorious *parousia*.

117. Richard B. Gaffin Jr., "Theonomy and Eschatology: Reflection on Postmillennialism," 206.

14

Christ and the Spirit: The Meaning and Promise of a Reformed Idea[1]

MARK A. GARCIA

THOUGH A RATHER NARROW topic at first blush, the "economic identity" of Christ and the Spirit brings into view an impressive collection of the perennial questions with which theology continues to be engaged. I have chosen to come at this topic from the perspective of Calvin's theology, particularly as it informs his exegesis of Romans and opens up this vast theological expanse. Through a brief analysis of union with Christ and story in Calvin's theology, I will point to several of the more significant features in Calvin's model and raise some matters for reflection.

1. This is a lightly revised version of a paper read on March 26, 2007, at Westminster Theological Seminary, Philadelphia. It draws selectively from material in my *Life in Christ: Union with Christ and Twofold Grace in Calvin's Theology,* Studies in Christian History and Thought (Milton Keynes, UK: Paternoster, 2008). To aid the reader, I will point to places in *Life in Christ* where arguments in this paper are given more extensive attention. I am delighted to include this essay in a collection devoted to honoring my esteemed professor, Dr. Richard B. Gaffin Jr.

424

CHRIST WITHOUT HIS SPIRIT? MEDIEVAL MICE AND REFORMED THEOLOGY

The Objectivity of Christ's Eucharistic Presence

From one perspective, the theological tradition we call "Reformed" began with a mouse on a medieval church floor. The medieval tradition made official at the Fourth Lateran Council (1215) affirmed a presence of Christ in the eucharistic elements so objective that it is wholly independent of the worthiness of the communicant. This tradition was motivated by a concern to emphasize the objectivity of Christ's presence in the Mass in order to ensure God does not become dependent on the creature. For theologians, however, this also raised an immediate and pressing question. Is Christ's presence so definite, so *objective*, that his transubstantiated body and blood may be consumed not only by an unbeliever but even by an animal, say, a mouse?

Aquinas and the Mouse

Thomas Aquinas (ca. 1225–74) provided the definitive answer to this question (whether or not unbelievers partake of Christ in the Supper) as well as the related thought experiment (whether or not animals partake of Christ). He explained that Christ's bodily presence necessarily persists as long as the accidents of bread and wine remain. And so Aquinas grants the point of the thought experiment: if a crumb of consecrated bread should fall to the floor and be eaten by a mouse, then the body of Christ will in fact have been eaten by a mouse. However, though Christ's body will have been consumed, it will have been eaten *physically*, not *spiritually*. For to use the elements spiritually is to use them properly, that is, to one's spiritual benefit, something of which a mouse is naturally incapable.[2]

What is true for mice must then be true for unbelievers. In Aquinas's words, "Should even an unbeliever receive the sacramental species, he would receive Christ's body under the sacrament: hence he would eat Christ sacramentally . . . ." Or, put differently, both the pious and the impious share a real sacramental eating of Christ, one "perfectly" and the other "imperfectly."[3]

---

2. Thomas Aquinas, *Summa Theologica* (London: Burns, Oates & Washburne, Ltd., 1920–42), III q.80 a.3. Hereafter, the *Summa Theologica* shall be referred to as *ST.*

3. *ST* III. q.80 a.1; cf. a.4.

The Lutheran Version and Calvin's Response

But what do opportunistic mice have to do with Reformed theology? Even though the Lutheran model of eucharistic communion was joined to a rejection of transubstantiation, Aquinas's argument is the line of reasoning Calvin was convinced he encountered in his Lutheran opponents. In his *Second Defense* against the feisty Lutheran Joachim Westphal, Calvin addresses Westphal's conviction that communion in the sacramental *substance* (Christ) is common both to believer and unbeliever while the spiritual *effect* differs with respect to the presence or absence of faith. Hence both believer and unbeliever partake of the substance of Christ but with differing outcomes, one to life but the other to judgment.

Calvin objects to both Roman Catholic and Lutheran separations of the "substance" from the spiritual "effect" of Christ. He argues that, on this view, "Christ is rendered lifeless and is severed by sacrilegious divorce from his Spirit and all his virtue."[4] A careful reading of Calvin's argument, which appears with astounding frequency against Westphal and others, points to a consistent christological-pneumatological *sine qua non* in Calvin's theology: the economic identity of Christ and the Spirit. While on the one hand Christ must never be confused ontologically with the Spirit, on the other hand, in their functional or economic identity, Christ *must not* be separated from his Spirit. In fact, at one point Calvin framed his entire disagreement with the Lutherans in precisely these terms. Seeing Lutheran thinking on the Supper as but one revealing instance of a broader area of disagreement, Calvin writes: "The matter now disputed between us, that is, whether unbelievers receive the *substance* of the flesh of Christ *without his Spirit*, is peculiarly applicable to the Supper."[5]

---

4. John Calvin, *Secunda Defensio, Ioannis Calvini Opera Quae Supersunt Omnia*, 59 vols., ed. Wilhelm Baum, Eduard Cunitz, and Eduard Reuss. Included in the *Corpus Reformatorum*, 101 vols., ed. Karl G. Bretschneider et al. (Halle, Berlin, Leipzig, and Zurich: 1834–1962), 9:89. Hereafter this will be referred to as *CO*; *Tracts and Treatises: With a Short Life of Calvin by Theodore Beza*, ed. Thomas F. Torrance, trans. Henry Beveridge (Grand Rapids: Eerdmans, 1958), 2:303. Hereafter this will be referred to as *TT*.

5. Calvin, *Secunda Defensio, CO* 9:90; *TT* 2:305. The distinction is essentially the same as the distinction in later Reformed orthodoxy of a *manducatio sacramentalis* or *symbolica* from a *manducatio spiritualis* (Richard A. Muller, *Dictionary of Latin and Greek Theological Terms Drawn Principally From Protestant Scholastic Theology* [Grand Rapids: Baker, 1985], 183–84). "Sacramental" or "symbolical" eating pertains to all who eat the bread and drink the wine, believer or unbeliever; however, real, "spiritual" eating, i.e., a true partaking of Christ's flesh and blood by the operation of the Spirit, belongs exclusively to those with faith. This seemed to Calvin's Lutheran critics to entail a denial of the real presence of Christ, understood in the ordinary sense of presence, for if Christ is truly present he is present independent of the communicant's faith or unbelief. To argue otherwise is to make

The Locus of the Economic Identity of Christ and the Spirit

But why should we see Christ and the Spirit as economically one? If it is clear that Calvin argues strongly for the economic identity of Christ and the Spirit, we do not yet see where—or, better, when—he locates its origin or grounds. For this we should look to the memorable opening section to Book 3 added in the final revision of his *Institutes of the Christian Religion*.[6] Prefacing his famous exposition of saving grace, here Calvin introduces the Spirit as the "bond" of union with Christ. And it is here that Calvin ties the union-work of the Spirit to Christ's own *baptism* or anointing with the Spirit (3.1.1). Calvin explains that the Father bestowed the Spirit liberally upon the Son to be minister to us of his own liberality. He "laid up" the gifts of the Spirit in Christ in order then to give them to us (3.1.2). In short, Christ cannot be separated from his Spirit because, from the point of his baptism, he is always, as Mediator, the Spirit-anointed Christ and no other.

This conviction stems from Calvin's larger theology of Christ's person and work. As Calvin scholars have noted, Calvin's model reflects the Western christological perspective as rooted in Hilary, Ambrose, and Augustine, in which the distinction rather than inseparability of the natures is emphasized in contrast with the divinization idea of the East. From the start, this generally Western perspective carried with it a natural orientation into soteriological matters, and it certainly did in Calvin's case. In particular, Calvin's modification of the traditional person-work use of the Anselmic model, in the direction of a whole-person structure, functions to clarify that Christ as Mediator "must be considered in and through his office."[7]

Christ's promise and God's work entirely dependent on man, and thus to do dishonor to the glory of Christ. On their view, the unbeliever truly partakes of the flesh and blood of Christ (by way of a *manducatio oralis*, which is not a carnal eating but a *manducatio hyperphysica sive supernaturalis*), but to his condemnation rather than blessing (because the spiritual body and blood are not "digested" in a similar sense that bread and wine are not digested), while the believer by faith receives, through the *manducatio sacramentalis* or *spiritualis*, the merits and graces of Christ.

6. On the importance of the timing of his additions to Book 3, and its context in the ongoing eucharistic controversy, see Garcia, *Life in Christ*, 133, 210, et al., esp. 36–41.

7. Richard Muller, *Christ and the Decree: Christology and Predestination in Reformed Theology from Calvin to Perkins* (Durham: Labyrinth Press, 1986), 28, noting also François Wendel, *Calvin: Origins and Development of His Religious Thought*, trans. Philip Mairet (1963; repr. Grand Rapids: Baker, 1997), 216–20; Wolfhart Pannenberg, *Jesus—God and Man*, trans. Lewis L. Wilkins and Duane A. Priebe (Philadelphia: Westminster, 1968), 124, 221–23. Calvin's modification also points to the basically Scotist strain in his explanation of the necessity of a Mediator: it is not an absolute necessity but one resulting from God's ordained will regarding our salvation.

In connection with this "official" or "mediatorial" focus, Calvin's frequent emphasis on Christ's humanity concentrates specifically on his humanity *as sanctified by* or *as gifted with the Spirit.* As the Spirit-invested incarnate Son of God, however, Christ is anointed in his whole divine-human person, not only his humanity. For Calvin, the Spirit bestows upon the incarnate Son the gifts requisite to performing his mediatorial function or role, and these gifts then belong to the entire person by reason of the *communicatio idiomatum* (communication of properties).[8] So the *communicatio* is not made irrelevant by the accent on messianic baptism; far from it. While Calvin locates the economic identity of Christ and the Spirit at the baptism of Jesus, it is the *communicatio* that renders the full God-man the Spirit-anointed Mediator.

In this connection, it is important to notice that Christ and the Spirit are not economically identified simply because they are ontologically united in the Trinity. Their economic identity is not just another way of speaking of their sharing the divine essence. Instead of looking to the Trinity, Calvin looks to the baptism at the Jordan. It is as the baptized, anointed Messiah that Jesus Christ, not in his humanity alone but in his whole person, performs his work *in the power of the Spirit*, so that there is already, on this christological presupposition, no possibility of separating the intent and effect of Christ's redemptive work from the person and work of the Spirit. Christ, Calvin writes, "was filled with the Holy Spirit, and loaded with a perfect abundance of all his gifts, that he may impart them to us."[9]

Recalling his objection to his Lutheran counterparts, Calvin's chief contention was thus tied to his Mediator-focused theology of Christ as Redeemer. As the Spirit-anointed Mediator, there is no partaking of Christ that is not at the same time a partaking in his Spirit, no union with Christ that may be divorced from the life-giving Spirit. Not for the faithless, and especially not for a mouse.

From Sacrament to Salvation: No Justification without Sanctification

But the importance of the economic identity of Christ and the Spirit extended well beyond questions of mice and consecrated wafers. From

---

8. Muller, *Christ and the Decree*, 32. Muller notes (32) that this is not yet the twofold anointing subsequently described by Ursinus, Perkins, and Polanus, though Calvin's idea "does, however, contain the germ of the later conception."

9. Cf. Westminster Confession of Faith 8.3.

the start, it is important to recognize Calvin's theological objection to the Lutheran model (one cannot truly partake of Christ without partaking in his life-giving Spirit) as the sacramental form of Calvin's familiar soteriological argument that justification cannot be separated from sanctification (and *vice versa*).

It is only one theological parallel among many, but it is arguably the most important one. In both contexts, sacramental and soteriological, Calvin's argument rests on the presupposition that the nature of the Christ-Spirit relationship *requires* a life-giving, transformative effect in all who partake in or are truly united to Christ. As he does on many occasions, in his commentary on Romans Calvin makes this point with recourse to a particularly violent metaphor. In each case, he adds the metaphor in his final revision which, like his 1559 *Institutes*, reflects the ongoing eucharistic controversy.[10] In his comment on Romans 8:9:

> ... those *who separate Christ from His Spirit* make Him like a dead image or a corpse. We must always bear in mind the counsel of the apostle, that free remission of sins cannot be separated from the Spirit of regeneration. This would be, as it were, *to tear Christ apart.*[11]

Commenting on Romans 8:13, Calvin notes similarly that Paul adds a severe warning for those who think they are justified by faith but are sluggish in loving righteousness. "It is, indeed, true," he says, "that we are justified in Christ by the mercy of God alone, but it is equally true and certain, that all who are justified are called by the Lord to live worthy of their vocation." In 1556, Calvin adds a further note to this comment:

> Let believers, therefore, learn to embrace Him, not only for justification, but also for sanctification, as He has been given to us for both these purposes, that they may not *tear him to pieces* by their own mutilated faith.[12]

10. For an investigation of Calvin's use of this metaphor against the backdrop of classical rhetorical and sixteenth-century controversial-polemical usage, see Garcia, *Life in Christ*, 228–41.

11. Calvin, *Commentarius in epistolam Pauli ad Romanos*, ed. T. H. L. Parker and D. C. Parker (Genève: Librairie Droz, 1999), 160. Hereafter this will be referred to as *Comm. Epist. ad Romanos*; *Calvin's New Testament Commentaries*, ed. T. H. L. Parker (Grand Rapids: Eerdmans, 1971), 164. Hereafter this will be referred to as *CNTC*.

12. Calvin, *Comm. Epist. ad Romanos*, 163; *CNTC*, 166–67.

He also makes the same point, using the same metaphor, in the opening sentence of his commentary on Romans 6, again adding the metaphor in his 1556 revision in the heat of the christological-eucharistic controversy.

UNION WITH THE SPIRIT-ANOINTED CHRIST AND PAUL'S CONDITIONAL LANGUAGE

The Challenge of Romans 2

This general argument takes on a specific shape in his exegesis of challenging verses in Romans 2.[13] When Johannes Eck, vigorous opponent of Luther, criticized Luther's doctrine of justification, he did so by citing several Pauline passages (and one from Luke) as part of a brief discussion of how good, living works are acceptable to God and worthy of eternal life, as opposed to works done by the impious, which the apostle condemns. His discussion prominently features Romans 2:6, 7 and 13. Most importantly, in almost every case Eck points to *instances of conditional language*, that is, to places where eternal life is conditioned in some way upon obedience or good works, of which Romans 2 is arguably the most familiar example.

What This Passage Does Not Mean

Among Calvin's chief concerns, therefore, was the acutely felt obligation to account fully for Paul's conditional language, perhaps especially in Romans 2. Here the apostle makes the explicit statement that God "will render to every man according to his works" (v. 6 RSV), specifically "to those who by perseverance in doing good seek for glory and honor and immortality, [he will give] eternal life" (v. 7). The relationship of 2:13 ("for not the hearers of the Law are just before God, but the doers of the Law will be justified") to 3:20 ("because by the works of the Law no flesh will be justified in his sight") poses a similar interpretative challenge.

Keenly aware of the difficulties connected with the passage, Calvin still remarks both in his commentary and in a parallel passage in his 1539 *Institutes* that "this sentence, however, is not as difficult as it is generally assumed."[14] Calvin argues that Paul is not explaining the merit of good

---

13. For what follows, see the fuller discussion in Garcia, *Life in Christ*, 89–148.
14. Cf. Calvin, *Comm. Epist. ad Romanos*, 42; *CNTC*, 44. This important section from 1539 would remain in 1559 as *Inst.* 3.18.1–10. Cf. *Institutes of the Christian Religion*, ed.

works accruing to the zealously obedient but is exposing, of necessity, the instability before God of the pseudo-holy, those "unseeing pretenders to sanctity" who mask their wickedness with a veneer of good works. The purpose of Paul's statement is therefore not the commendation of meritorious works as a ground for divine acceptation, but the identification of the particular character of the righteousness of which God approves.[15] Therefore the reference to works is not positive but negative: "By punishing the wickedness of the reprobate with just vengeance, the Lord will repay them what they deserve,"[16] despite appearances to the contrary counterfeited by superficial holiness.

In his comment on Romans 2:13, the argument is similar. Calvin has little patience with those who use this passage to support justification by meritorious works: they "deserve universal contempt." Instead of supporting justification by works, this passage actually rules out the possibility inasmuch as no one can claim full obedience to the law. At these points, then, Calvin agrees with Melanchthon's basic identification of the statements as, one might say, law, not gospel.

The Bigger Picture: A Gospel Context for Conditional Language

But to leave it there, as some are inclined to do, would be a tragic misstep as it would neglect the bigger picture Calvin is concerned to keep in view. Hearing him thus far one might ask, "But Calvin, does not the apostle also teach that God will reward the works of the righteous with eternal life?" His subsequent comments on this passage confirm that Calvin would reply in the affirmative, and rather strongly at that, explaining how this idea is not in conflict with the doctrine of justification.

Quite to the contrary, the certainty of eschatological glory, included in God's election of believers, implies and ensures his progressive work of renewal within them: " . . . because He sanctifies those whom He has previously resolved to glorify, He will also crown their good works . . . ."[17] Still, against

---

John T. McNeill, trans. Ford Lewis Battles Library of Christian Classics 20–21 (Louisville: Westminster John Knox, 1960), 20:821–33. Hereafter this will be referred to as LCC 20–21.

15. Calvin, *Comm. Epist. ad Romanos*, 42; *CNTC*, 44. "He has, therefore, pointed out the true righteousness of works which God will value, in case they should confidently assume that it was enough to please Him by bringing words and mere trifles."

16. Calvin, *Comm. Epist. ad Romanos*, 42; *CNTC*, 44.

17. Calvin, *Comm. Epist. ad Romanos*, 42; *CNTC*, 44.

the view represented vigorously by Eck and the Sorbonne, Calvin argues that a *meritorious* "crowning" of believers' works is not the point in Romans 2:6 since Paul is affirming the reward but not the value due to good works.[18]

Importantly, however, this distinction does not preclude Calvin's linking of good works with the reward of eternal life, as his remarks on v. 7 make clear. Here, where the apostle says eternal life is granted to those who patiently pursue glory, honor, and immortality, Calvin states, summing up the apostle's argument: "The meaning, therefore, is that the Lord will give eternal life to those who strive to attain immortality *by endeavoring to do good works.*"[19]

Order, Sequence, and Pattern: The Hermeneutical-Theological Priority of Romans 8

To understand how Calvin is able to use such strikingly positive language about the place of good works in salvation, we need to observe his use of Scripture to interpret Scripture and, in connection with this, observe how the economic identity of Christ and the Spirit functions in his model. In brief, the ideas of *order*, *sequence*, and *pattern* are of the highest importance to Calvin in his handling of conditional language.

Through the Pursuit of Good Works

Calvin offers a few points of explanation for his take on Romans 2. We are first brought into fellowship or union with Christ by the faith-work of the Spirit. Only then does eternal life "begin" in us and then finally progress to fruition. So for Calvin it is, first, union with Christ by faith and the Spirit, and with this union the true beginning of eternal life, which leads finally to its consummation. The exegetical basis for Calvin's perspective, however, is six chapters later than his present concern, in the Pauline "order" he locates in Romans 8:29–30.

18. Calvin, *Comm. Epist. ad Romanos*, 42; *CNTC*, 44. Later, at 2:11, Calvin notes the positive place of regeneration and good works by describing a "twofold acceptance (*duplicem acceptionem*) of men before God." First, God elects us out of his unmotivated goodness alone, not because of anything attractive in our nature; second, the result of his work of regeneration within us and the bestowal of his gifts upon us is that he "shows favor" to the image of Christ which he sees in us (*Comm. Epist. ad Romanos*, 45; *CNTC*, 46). This *duplicem acceptionem* of election and image-favor has clear parallels to his more familiar *duplex gratia*, indicating his strong proclivity for the language of *duplex*.

19. Calvin, *Comm. Epist. ad Romanos*, 43; *CNTC*, 44.

That passage is crucial for understanding Calvin because it carries a *hermeneutical priority* over conditional passages, functioning very much as a lens through which Calvin reads, in this case, the conditional language of Romans 2. More specifically, Calvin understands the theology of Romans 8:29–30 as the large-scale framework within which Paul's conditional language must be located.

The point will be clearer when we look briefly at Romans 8, but the basic idea is already amply evident from Calvin's comment on 2:6 in which he makes a clear allusion to the language of 8:29–30. Calvin explains that God "sanctifies those whom He has previously resolved to glorify" and will, consequently, "also crown their good works . . . ."[20] We can perhaps think of it this way: Calvin affirms the reality of these conditions for eternal life because his perspective on this topic is fully governed or controlled by the end in view for all believers—not just chronologically, as in the end of time, but teleologically—the end result in view for our salvation. In other words, Calvin looks to what the church will *be* when grace gives way to glory and, on the basis of the Spirit's role in bringing about this certain end, and in light of the nature of his ministry in believers, he is able to claim a fully legitimate yet non-meritorious place for conditional language in the context of the gospel. As will soon become clear, this amounts to an eschatological redefinition of the traditional understanding of causation.

Calvin helpfully elucidates this emphasis on the positive place of Christian obedience in God's *ordo* or ordained pattern of salvation more fully in his 1539 revision of the *Institutes*, on which he was working the same time as he worked on his Romans commentary. Here Calvin is more expansive about the issue of "causation," stating that Paul in Romans 2:6

---

20. Calvin, *Comm. Epist. ad Romanos*, 42; *CNTC*, 44. Of note is Calvin's use of the Augustinian idea of the "crowning" of the believer's works. Peter Martyr Vermigli, in his 1558 commentary, would argue along similar lines: "But works are not of our selves, for they are called the gifts of God, which he works in us. Wherefore Augustine very wisely says: That God doth crown his gifts in us. Now if our works be due unto him (which thing we cannot deny) then undoubtedly the nature of merit is utterly taken away." More notable still is the parallel between aspects of Calvin's replication principle (defined below) and the way Vermigli relates works to the reward of eschatological life: "Eternal life is sometimes in the holy scriptures called a reward: But then is it not that reward, which Paul writeth to be given according to debt: but is all one as if it should be called a recompensation. Gods will and pleasure was, that there should be this connection, that after good works should follow blessedness: but yet not as the effect followeth the cause, but as a thing joyned with them by the appointment of God (*In Epistolam S. Pauli ad Romanos commentarii doctissimi . . .* [Basel, 1558], 40a)."

intends "an order of sequence rather than the cause." Setting the commentary beside the 1539 *Institutes* is revealing. Here are two statements, practically identical, in which Calvin makes a series of important theological points regarding Romans 2:6. The passage in the *Institutes* is slightly fuller, and reads:

> The statement that God will render to every man according to his works is explained with little difficulty. For the expression indicates an order of sequence rather than the cause. But, beyond any doubt, it is by these stages of his mercy that the Lord completes our salvation when he calls those chosen to himself; those called he justifies; those justified he glorifies. That is to say, he receives his own into life by his mercy alone. Yet, since he leads them into possession of it through the pursuit (*studium*) of good works in order to fulfill his own work in them according to the order that he has laid down, it is no wonder if they are said to be crowned according to their own works, by which they are doubtless prepared to receive the crown of immortality.[21]

This carefully constructed passage is like a well-oiled machine: every part works together. Two of these parts, the sequential and the "order" elements, are clearly important to Calvin's theology of good works. He sees that it is by "stages of mercy" that God, according to his own sovereign design, "completes our salvation" when he calls us to himself, justifies the called, and glorifies the justified. Indeed, "he leads them into possession of it [i.e., eternal life] *through the pursuit of good works* in order to fulfill his own work in them according to the order that he has laid down. . . ." Through this diligent obedience which characterizes the life of the Christian, one is thus "*prepared* to receive the crown of immortality."[22] Though Paul does not include sanctification in the Romans 8:29–30 series, Calvin appears to include it under the aegis of glorification as its preparatory and anticipatory precursor in the experience of the redeemed. In this divine sequence, good works are therefore indispensable to the ongoing restoration of the divine image in believers and their ultimate salvation and glory. Believers pass from calling to eschatological glorification and eternal life *through* the "pursuit of good works."

21. 1539 *Institutes*. In the margin next to this passage, Calvin (or possibly his editors) placed references to Romans 2 and 8 near the obvious allusions to these Pauline texts.
22. Calvin, *Institutes* (1539) 3.18.1; LCC 20:821.

Elsewhere, Calvin's dependence on this Pauline *ordo* is equally clear. For instance, he refers to works as "inferior causes," tying this to God's "order of dispensation," and says

> What goes before in the order of dispensation [God] calls the cause of what comes after. In this way he sometimes derives eternal life from works, not intending it to be ascribed to them; but because he justifies those whom he has chosen in order at last to glorify them, he makes the prior grace, which is a step to what follows, as it were the cause.[23]

Anticipating concerns, he adds a little later that this does not make believers the authors of their own salvation, or make salvation to stem from their good works. Rather, the good work that God has begun in his own he will certainly complete, but it is only complete when his people resemble their Father in righteousness and holiness, thus proving their identity as his children.

The Christ-Pattern: Suffering, Then Glory

This leaves us to add one last layer of detail in Calvin's portrait for a finished picture. And this last layer is also the most pastorally important. What we have observed in Calvin's exposition of Romans 2:6–7 is his concern for a particular sequence of obedience-then-eternal life. We have also seen, albeit briefly, that his perspective is fully controlled by the end in view: the certainty of the church's eschatological glory combined with the nature of the Spirit's work in his glory-producing ministry results in a contextualization of conditional language along the lines of sequence.

But what Calvin's comments on Romans 8 make clear is that this sequence is itself grounded in Christ, or more specifically the Spirit-anointed Christ with whom believers have been united. In short, the existential character of saving union with Christ is that of a replica, in the experience of believers, of the pattern of Christ's own historical experience. Baptized with

---

23. Calvin, *Institutes* (1539) 3.14.21; LCC 20:787. In 1559, Calvin made an additional clarification, again expounding on the relationship of sequence and cause: "In short, by these expressions sequence more than cause is denoted. For God, by heaping grace upon grace, from the former grace takes the cause for adding those which follow that he may overlook nothing for the enrichment of his servants. And he so extends his liberality as to have us always look to his freely given election, which is the source and beginning."

the same Spirit that brought Christ from death to resurrection, humiliation to exaltation, and suffering to glory, the church in union with Christ, by that same Spirit, also goes from death to resurrection, humiliation to exaltation, and suffering to glory. Here, in this Christ-sequence, one is able to discern the economic identity of Christ and the Spirit functioning to resolve a crucial exegetical and theological question.

It is this sequence that Calvin has in view in Romans 2, and which is unfolded strikingly in Romans 6 when he modifies the *imitatio Christi* tradition in his discussion of baptism into Christ's death and resurrection. But it comes more fully into view with his reflections on Romans 8.

In the apostle Paul's teaching in Romans 8, one encounters this Christ-pattern in connection with Christian suffering and the conditional nature of adoption. This is particularly important since, in this chapter, Paul states that the blessing of adoption entails becoming fellow-heirs with Christ of the eschatological reward of eternal life. For Calvin the key to Paul's point here is simple: only those who suffer like Christ are truly God's children. But this suffering is neither a cruel twist of fate nor a mere "imitation of Christ" effort on our part. It is in fact the Spirit's work of replication of the pattern of Christ, something Calvin regards as indispensable to salvation.

Perhaps surprisingly, this Christ-pattern is included in the content of predestination. When the apostle in Romans 8:28 points sufferers to the divine purpose, Calvin sees Paul's predestination language as specifically referring to suffering so that predestination is specifically predestination *to cross-bearing*. The source of election is (ultimately) the same as the source of suffering. In the divine decree, suffering in Christ is laid out as the path of conformity to Christ and as a prerequisite of heaven.[24] Predestination, one might say, has in view the means as well as the end of the church's story.

All of this comes together in the way Calvin interprets the conditional language in Romans 8:17, which reads: "If truly sons, then heirs, heirs of God and co-heirs with Christ—if indeed we share in his sufferings so that we will share his glory." Calvin explains that we are fellow-heirs of Christ only if we, with a view to our inheritance, follow the pattern of our Leader. Expanding on his point, Calvin sums up the apostle's chain of reasoning:

> Paul made this mention of Christ, because he intended to pass on to this exhortation by these steps: "The inheritance of God is ours, because we

24. Calvin, *Comm. Epist. ad Romanos*, 175–76; CNTC, 179–81.

have been adopted by His grace as His sons. To remove any doubt, the possession of it has already been conferred on Christ, with whom we are made partakers. But Christ went to that inheritance by the cross. *We, therefore, must go to it the same way.*[25]

Hence cross-shaped suffering is the ordinary path to the believer's inheritance. However, this should not suggest that our suffering-obedience causes our eternal glory in an unqualified sense. Scripture is identifying the "order" that God follows "in ministering salvation to us, rather than its cause."[26] The first cause of salvation in this divine order is God's sovereign act of adoption in Christ, but this act includes the real necessity that suffering conform us to his holy image.[27]

As Calvin puts it in his comment on 8:29, God has determined that his adopted children will bear the distinct image of the Christ of death and resurrection. Free salvation is thus inseparable from the calling to bear the cross. In fact, he says, "*No one can be an heir of heaven who has not first been conformed to the only begotten Son of God.*"[28] Indeed, "conformity to the humility of Christ *is* our salvation. In this [Paul] teaches that our participation in the cross is so connected with our vocation, justification, and finally our glory, that *they cannot in any way be separated.*"[29]

So Calvin is not opposed in principle to the language of *exemplar* or even imitation of Christ; nor is he uncomfortable with the idea of the believer's present sanctification (the pneumatic preparatory precursor to final glorification) as a true condition of eternal life. But the distinguishing mark of his doctrine is that this imitation-like process belongs to the Spirit's

25. Calvin, *Comm. Epist. ad Romanos*, 167; *CNTC*, 171.

26. Calvin, *Comm. Epist. ad Romanos*, 167; *CNTC*, 171. Note also Calvin's integration of the ideas of decree, adoption, and inheritance in his comments on 8:23.

27. Calvin, *Comm. Epist. ad Romanos*, 176; *CNTC*, 179–80. Also, his abiding concern with merit in Christian works leads Calvin immediately to add an important qualification to his note on Rom. 2:6: "but not on account of merit."

28. Calvin, *Comm. Epist. ad Romanos*, 177; *CNTC*, 181. More fully, " . . . Paul meant only that God had determined that all whom He has adopted should bear the image of Christ. He did not simply say that they should be conformed to Christ, but to the image of Christ, in order to teach us that in Christ there is a living and conspicuous example (*exemplar*) which is set before all the sons of God for their imitation. The sum of the passage is that free adoption, in which our salvation consists, is inseparable from this other decree: that He had appointed us to bear the cross. *No one can be an heir of heaven who has not first been conformed to the only begotten Son of God*" (emphasis mine).

29. Calvin, *Comm. Epist. ad Romanos*, 177–78; *CNTC*, 181 (emphases mine).

437

larger project of replication. It is indeed because of this principle that the works/sufferings/obedience of believers do not compromise the reality of a gracious justification *sola fide* as in the semi-Pelagian presuppositions of the "imitation of Christ" traditions. Instead they serve to confirm the truth that all of salvation must be sought in Christ as Head, and that all aspects of a believing response are ultimately the work of his Spirit.

SUMMARY

We may now restate these points in summary form before raising some matters for further reflection. In rejecting the Lutheran argument that the faithless truly partake of Christ but not his Spirit, Calvin argues that Christ is identified economically with his Spirit. And this economic identity of Christ and the Spirit has implications. Because by virtue of this economic identity Christ is never where his Spirit is not, no one or nothing—not even a medieval mouse nibbling on a consecrated wafer—truly partakes of Christ in the Supper without partaking of his life-giving Spirit. For the same reason, in a soteriological context, no one is truly joined to Christ for justification who is not sanctified by his Spirit. To divorce the reality and necessity of sanctification from justification is in effect to tear Christ from his Spirit.

This conviction finds expression in the way Paul's conditional language is to be understood. The certainty of final, eschatological glory informs the way we understand the means to that end. Because glorification is sure, and because the present sanctifying work of the Spirit is the ordinary prerequisite to the consummation of his work, we can speak properly of obedience, good works, or faithful suffering as conditions of eternal life. They are "conditions" because, in the divine sequence or pattern, "what goes before may be called the cause of what comes after," to use Calvin's language.

But we can also say something specific about this pattern: it is Christ-shaped. And this accentuates the economic identity of Christ and the Spirit. Because union with Christ is always union with the Spirit-anointed Christ who went from obedience to resurrection life, humiliation to exaltation, suffering to glory—and who did so in history—this is precisely what our union with Christ by the same Spirit looks like: obedience to eternal life, humiliation to exaltation, suffering to glory. The pattern that the church exhibits is the pattern fleshed out in her Head. Put simply, there is no other Christ than this Christ, and so there is no union with Christ apart from participation in his story.

REFLECTIONS

Inevitably these matters raise related ones, and I would like to tease out of Calvin's model the following points for consideration. First, a historical-theological point. What I have rehearsed here is only a snapshot of a much larger image of the emergence of the Reformed theological tradition. But it seems to me beyond question that, because what we call "Reformed" has its origins as a distinct perspective on eucharistic union with Christ, we need to appreciate that, with a view to its wide-ranging implications, the Reformed theology of union with Christ lies in significant ways at the theological heart of what it means to be Reformed.[30] Even more particularly, we should recognize that there is such a thing as a Reformed theology of union with Christ, one that has at its core a conviction regarding the economic identity of Christ and the Spirit. It is this christological-pneumatological infrastructure of union with Christ which was cross-applied in sacramental and soteriological contexts in Calvin's theology, and which in just two decades served to distinguish Reformed theology along more than eucharistic lines.

Beyond this general observation we can raise a second point, this time about Calvin's model itself. It is crucial to appreciate what Calvin accomplishes: his move toward a whole-person, threefold office theology of Christ as Mediator, which entails the baptism-to-resurrection story of this Mediator, is a strong affirmation of the indispensability of *history*. Because in contemporary theology it seems we cannot fully shake off the

---

30. However, this is not to say that union with Christ is the *central dogma* of Reformed theology, i.e., that it is the idea that governs all of the theological system and on which that system ought to be built. Neither do I intend to suggest here, nor have I ever suggested, that union with Christ is Calvin's *central dogma*, and certainly not on the basis of the *Institutes* alone. For an example of confusion on this question, see Thomas Wenger, "The New Perspective on Calvin: Responding to the Recent Calvin Interpretations," *JETS* 50 (2007): 311–28, who refers to several writers as representatives of this view who, to my knowledge, in fact do not argue for a union with Christ *central dogma* as this term has been understood in Calvin scholarship. Wenger confuses their approach with the Barthian-Torrancian (et al.) approach which puts Calvin in almost unqualified tension with his successors. In one of their many misrepresentations of my review article, W. Robert Godfrey and David VanDrunen use Wenger's mistaken thesis as a criticism of my own analysis of Calvin in their "Response to Mark Garcia's Review of *Covenant, Justification, and Pastoral Ministry*" in *Ordained Servant* (December, 2007). But see Garcia, *Life in Christ*, 15–19, where I discuss the *central dogma* theory and reject it, pointing out only some of its flaws. Further, despite Wenger's argument (and Godfrey and VanDrunen's assumption) that appreciation for the controlling prominence of union with Christ within Calvin's theology of salvation is somehow new, the reality is that this has long been a matter of common knowledge among both scholarly and non-scholarly readers of Calvin's works (cf. Garcia, *Life in Christ*, 11–45).

idea that history is in some sense less important than the communication of a message or idea, that revelation is identifiable not with *historie* but with *geschichte*, this alone makes his model very timely. To turn Cornelius Van Til's critique of Barth into a positive statement, Calvin's replication model clarifies further why there *must be* a transition from wrath to grace, from cross to resurrection, from humiliation to exaltation, from suffering to glory *in history*, or the church's life in union with Christ is without shape, meaning, or hope.

In light of theological construals that oppose metaphysics to story, we should also observe how Calvin makes this move without leaving behind the classic, ontologically oriented two-natures model. Instead, the threefold mediatorial office of Christ functions as an extension and enlargement of the classical two-natures model. As his persistent critique of the ontology of the Lutheran model makes clear, two-natures Christology hardly recedes into the background because of the threefold office. Calvin sees no need to choose between ontology and redemptive history. While for him the eternal, trinitarian status of the incarnate Son is clearly more ultimate and controlling, the office and, yes, the baptism-to-resurrection story that the incarnate Son assumed and lived out are far from marginalized. It is in fact in connection with Christ's eternal divine status, or perhaps better in extension from it, that an equally robust, redemptive-historically focused exposition of Christ's mediatorship and of his story emerges clearly into view.

This leads to a third observation. As we have seen, Calvin's model ordinarily focuses on baptism as the point of Spirit-investiture (there are exceptions but this is certainly typical). Now, there is a clear benefit to this: baptism-anointing accents the parallel of Christ's story to the church's story in terms of what one might call a common point of departure: baptism. But we also need to recognize a significant liability: put simply, identifying the baptism at the Jordan as the point of the economic identity of Christ and the Spirit *over-reads* the baptism. It does so as it ascribes to baptism what Paul clearly ascribes to the resurrection. To illustrate, Calvin rightly denies that the economic identity of Christ and the Spirit is exclusively ontological, but then pulls from Paul's writing on the resurrection to make a point he ordinarily makes by reference to the baptism. He writes, "He is called the 'Spirit of Christ' not only because Christ, as eternal Word of God, is joined in the same Spirit with the Father, but also from his character as the Mediator. . . . In this sense he is called *the 'Second Adam,' given from heaven as 'a life-giving spirit'* " (3.1.2). If Calvin is occasionally unclear on this point, we should not be unclear, because it is indeed the resurrection, not the baptism, which for Paul serves as the redemptive-historical, theological ground for the economic identity of Christ and the Spirit. To pull from the place Calvin himself used, it is at resurrection that Paul says Christ *became* life-giving Spirit (1 Cor. 15:45).

Now, in moving in this direction, I have in view the development of Reformed reflection on this topic, particularly as that development has taken place in the tradition of Geerhardus Vos and especially, of course, in the work of Professor Gaffin, to whom this volume is dedicated. And for this reason it is useful to highlight, albeit briefly, some striking comments in Vos's landmark lecture, "The Eschatological Aspect of the Pauline Conception of the Spirit." In his lecture Vos notes perceptively, in a discussion of the OT anticipation of the Messiah as bearer of the Spirit, that "[N]ot merely the ethical but also the eschatological life of the resurrection is derived from the Messiah" and, in this connection, that "What God did for Jesus, He will do for the believer also." Also, just as Calvin insisted, Vos adds that " . . . [W]e must take into account the Christological background of the soteriological process. The pneumatic life of the Christian is a *product and a reflex of the pneumatic life of the Christ*. It is a life . . . *to the same extent as* it is a life . . . ."[31] This awaits a fuller treatment, certainly, but we can appreciate that this "product and reflex of the pneumatic life of the Christ" to which Vos points is precisely what Calvin intuited from the same apostle Paul, and Vos, because of his understanding of Paul's eschatology, gives it a clearer, more exegetically grounded expression.

What might one say about this intriguing connection? We are familiar with the argument that, as a discipline, the covenant-historical hermeneutical and theological approach fathered in most respects by Vos is only the faithful application of the classical Reformed doctrine of Scripture as this doctrine is expressed, e.g., in the Westminster Confession of Faith, chapter 1. I completely agree with this assessment, though it is not possible to discuss the question here. But let me also suggest that Reformed biblical theology in this general tradition is, in terms of the concern in this paper, also the application of the classical Reformed *Christology*, particularly

31. Geerhardus Vos, "The Eschatological Aspect of the Pauline Conception of the Spirit," in *Redemptive History and Biblical Interpretation: The Shorter Writings of Geerhardus Vos*, ed. Richard B. Gaffin Jr. (Phillipsburg, NJ: P&R, 1990), 98, 101, and 113, respectively.

with a view to the relationship of Christ to the eschatological Spirit and in terms of the implications of this relationship for the shape of salvation in union with Christ. It would appear this is a connection which merits further sustained reflection.

On a fourth and final note, Calvin properly understands Paul's teaching on union with Christ to entail a commendation of Christ's own story for the church's self-understanding. As Calvin understands Paul, union with the resurrected Christ means, yes, that we are united to the One who is exalted beyond the cross and the grave, never more to be touched by the cold, deathly fingers of a cursed, fallen, and passing age. But it is much more than that. Union with the resurrected Christ means that the end of our story, as the church, is in these respects nothing less than the end of his story. Believers too have a present though provisional identity, and a certain future, which is imbued with glory and not with shame, life and not with death, rest and not suffering. To pull from Vos's lecture once more, "[T]he argument from the analogy between Jesus and the believer is further strengthened by the consideration that the instrument through which God accomplished this in Jesus *is already present* in the readers."[32] For the Christian sufferer, the one whose faith is sometimes shaken by the strong winds of temptation or discouragement, the gospel announces that the Spirit of the exalted, resurrected Lord – the Spirit of glory who produces glory – is already present in the church and active in bringing pilgrims to their inheritance.

CONCLUSION

This investigation started with a mouse on a church floor. Since then, that mouse has pointed the way to Calvin's rich teaching on Christ and the Spirit in the sacraments and in salvation. Here once again, as is so often the case, careful reflection on Calvin's theology has opened up wider and wider vistas of the theological terrain that we as Reformed theologians delight to traverse. In this respect, if what we have considered briefly uncovers some of the rich meaning of our Reformed theological identity, certainly we can appreciate it also holds much promise for the ongoing maturation and development of Reformed theology as well.

---

32. Vos, "The Eschatological Aspect of the Pauline Conception of the Spirit," 101.

15

On the Antiquity of Biblical Theology

J. V. FESKO

OVER THE YEARS the father of Reformed biblical theology, Geerhardus Vos (1862–1949), has received both praise and criticism.[1] There are those who hail him for great exegetical and theological insight, and others who view him with great suspicion. Vos himself may have contributed to the cloud of suspicion by writing of the discipline of biblical theology, "Her birth took place under an evil star." He goes on to write, "It was the spirit of Rationalism which first led to distinguishing in the contents of the Scriptures between what was purely human, individual, local, temporal—in a word, conditioned by the subjectivity of the writers—and what was eternally valid, divine truth."[2] These words have given some readers the impression that

1. This title has been applied to Vos by Richard B. Gaffin Jr., "The Vitality of Reformed Dogmatics," in *The Vitality of Reformed Theology: Proceedings of the International Theological Congress*, ed. J. M. Batteau (Kampen, Netherlands: Uitgeverij Kok, 1994), 21. For a similar characterization of Vos, see Richard Lints, "Two Theologies or One? Warfield and Vos on the Nature of Theology," *WTJ* 54 (1992): 236, 243.

2. Geerhardus Vos, "The Idea of Biblical Theology as a Science and as a Theological Discipline," in *Redemptive History and Biblical Interpretation: The Shorter Writings of Geerhardus Vos*, ed. Richard B. Gaffin Jr. (Phillipsburg, NJ: Presbyterian & Reformed, 1980), 15. For a similar description of the origins of biblical theology from Vos's colleague at Princeton for

biblical theology is a discipline that has its origins in classical liberalism and rationalism, and therefore the specter of the evil star hangs over all forms of biblical theology, conservative and liberal alike.

One can see the cloud of suspicion, for example, when Jay Adams writes about biblical theology that "Geerhardus Vos rescued it from the liberal theologians."[3] Or, coming from another corner of the Reformed community, D. G. Hart has written: "One hundred years ago BT was an infant science for conservative Presbyterians."[4] Again, Hart writes, "The problem for biblical theology is that it is a recent scholarly effort, originating only in the late nineteenth century."[5] The underlying assumption of many detractors of biblical theology is that it is a novel discipline originated by liberals.

It is the contention of this essay that biblical theology is not at all a novelty, but a discipline of great antiquity. Richard B. Gaffin Jr. has generally responded to the alleged or perceived novelty of biblical theology and the insights of Vos:

> Contrary to the impression occasionally left by some, it is not as if the church were stumbling about in interpretive darkness until he burst onto the scene, lightning-strike, toward the close of the nineteenth century. In fact, already in the second century in the first great struggle for its existence, the battle with Gnosticism, the church had impressed upon it indelibly the controlling insight, as much as any, of biblical theology, namely that salvation resides ultimately not in who God is or what he has

---

over twenty-five years, see B. B. Warfield, "The Century's Progress in Biblical Knowledge," in *Benjamin B. Warfield: Selected Shorter Writings*, vol. 2, ed. John E. Meeter (1973; Phillipsburg, NJ: P&R, 2001), 12.

3. Jay Adams, "Reflections on Westminster Theology and Homiletics," in *The Pattern of Sound Doctrine: Systematic Theology at the Westminster Seminaries. Essays in Honor of Robert B. Strimple*, ed. David VanDrunen (Phillipsburg, NJ: P&R, 2005), 263.

4. D. G. Hart, "Tradition-Challenged," *Nicotine Theological Journal* 9.1 (2005): 2.

5. Ibid., 4. During Vos's day, it was Abraham Kuyper (1837–1920) who was also critical of the idea of biblical theology and Vos's theological methodology (see Richard B. Gaffin Jr., "Geerhardus Vos and the Interpretation of Paul," in *Jerusalem and Athens: Critical Discussions on the Philosophy and Apologetics of Cornelius Van Til*, ed. E. R. Geehan [Phillipsburg, NJ: P&R, 1980], 228–37). At the same time, the disagreement between Vos and Kuyper was not of such a nature to keep Kuyper from inviting Vos to take the first chair of biblical theology at the Free University of Amsterdam (see Michael Horton, "What God Hath Joined Together: Westminster and the Uneasy Union of Biblical and Systematic Theology," in *The Pattern of Sound Doctrine*, 49–52, esp. 50n8). In fact, Vos's published correspondence with Kuyper is reflective of a cordial and friendly relationship despite whatever disagreements they might have had (see Geerhardus Vos, *The Letters of Geerhardus Vos*, ed. James T. Dennison [Phillipsburg, NJ: P&R, 2005], passim).

said, but in what he has done in history, once for all, in Christ. Virtually from its beginning on and more or less consistently, the church has been incipiently biblical-theological.[6]

In other words, it is the thesis of this essay that biblical theology has been a part of the church's interpretive history from the earliest years, not simply in the patristic period, but stretching back into the very formation of the Old Testament (OT) canon, evidenced in its own intra-canonical interpretation.

We will set about to demonstrate the antiquity of biblical theology by first defining the discipline, its nature and methodology. We must do this so we can contrast the views of Vos with those of Johann P. Gabler (1753–1826), who first proposed the separation of biblical from dogmatic, or systematic, theology. With our definition, nature, and methodology of biblical theology in hand, we will then proceed to survey the history of interpretation beginning with the OT on through the post-Reformation period, to demonstrate the existence and use of biblical theology. In recognizing the antiquity of biblical theology, we will see how fundamental the discipline is to the hermeneutical and theological process. As Brevard Childs has noted, we will see that, in the end, "The real question is not whether to do biblical theology or not, but rather what kind of biblical theology does one have."[7] We may therefore proceed to define the nature and methodology of biblical theology by comparing and contrasting the views of Vos and Gabler.

Johann Gabler on Biblical Theology

On the Distinction between Biblical and Dogmatic Theology

It is important to begin with Johann Gabler's understanding of biblical theology, as he is often credited with defining or even creating the discipline. In fact, Ben Ollenburger has written that "if philosophy is a series of footnotes to Plato, then Old Testament theology is a series of very expansive footnotes to Gabler."[8] Gabler offered his contribution to the definition of

6. Richard B. Gaffin Jr., "Biblical Theology and the Westminster Standards," *WTJ* 65 (2003): 166.
7. Brevard Childs, *Biblical Theology in Crisis* (Philadelphia: Westminster, 1970), 95.
8. Johann P. Gabler, "An Oration on the Proper Distinction between Biblical and Dogmatic Theology and the Specific Objectives of Each," in *The Flowering of Old Testament Theology: A Reader in Twentieth-Century Old Testament Theology, 1930–90,* ed. Ben C. Ollenburger, Elmer A.

biblical theology in his famous inaugural lecture at the University of Altdorf on March 30, 1787, which was titled, *De justo discrimine theologiae biblicae et dogmaticae regundisque recte utriusque finibus*, or "On the Proper Distinction Between Biblical and Dogmatic Theology and the Specific Objectives of Each." The lecture is quite brief, but as the title nonetheless indicates, Gabler wanted to sever biblical theology from dogmatic theology.

Gabler was distressed over the proliferation of theological opinions, divisions, and contention in his day. He argued that the theological chaos in his day arose "from an inappropriate combination of the simplicity and ease of biblical theology with the subtlety and difficulty of dogmatic theology."[9] In defining and distinguishing between biblical and dogmatic theology, Gabler argued that the former was of historical origin whereas the latter was of didactic origin. The former arose from the Bible and the latter from the opinion of theologians of the church.[10] Gabler wanted to strip away philosophical and theological layers that had accumulated over the centuries and distill the pristine and eternal religion of the Scriptures. The manner that he proposed for arriving at the distilled religion is found in his methodology of situating each biblical text in its historical setting. Gabler writes:

> We must carefully collect and classify each of the ideas of each patriarch—Moses, David, and Solomon, and of each prophet with special attention to Isaiah, Jeremiah, Ezekiel, Daniel, Hosea, Zachariah, Haggai, Malachi, and the rest; and for many reasons we ought to include the apocryphal books for this same purpose; also we should include the ideas from the epoch of the New Testament, those of Jesus, Paul, Peter, John, and James. Above all, this process is completed in two ways: the one is in the legitimate interpretation of passages pertinent to this procedure; the other is in the careful comparison of the ideas of all the sacred authors among themselves.[11]

Here we see, then, the historical nature of Gabler's approach. Nonetheless, we should note another key feature of Gabler's methodology.

Martens, and Gerhard F. Hasel (Winona Lake, IN: Eisenbrauns: 1992), 489. There are those who argue that Gabler does not deserve the credit for creating the discipline of biblical theology: see Charles H. H. Scobie, "The Challenge of Biblical Theology," *TynBul* 42.1 (1991): 34.

9. Gabler, "Biblical and Dogmatic Theology," 493.

10. Ibid., 495–96.

11. Ibid., 498.

Gabler was of the opinion that the authors of the various parts of Scripture were divinely inspired and armed with divine authority. It was the biblical-theological task, however, to discern "whether all the opinions of the Apostles, of every type and sort altogether, are truly divine, or rather whether some of them, which have no bearing on salvation, were left to their own ingenuity."[12] In other words, we see that Gabler believed that the biblical theologian had to evaluate the Scriptures and determine which belonged to divine revelation, which spoke of the eternal universal religion, and which belonged to the opinion, time, or culture of the biblical writer: "We must investigate what in the sayings of the Apostle is truly divine, and what perchance merely human."[13]

Another element that emerges in Gabler's understanding of the relationship between the testaments is the inherent superiority of the New Testament (NT) over the OT:

> All the sacred writers are holy men and are armed with divine authority; but not all attest to the same form of religion; some are doctors of the Old Testament of the same elements that Paul himself designated with the name "basic elements" [*stoicheia*]; others are of the newer and better Christian testament. And so the sacred authors, however much we must cherish them with equal reverence because of the divine authority that has been imprinted on their writings, cannot all be considered in the same category if we are referring to their use in dogmatics.[14]

In this statement, we find important contours of Gabler's understanding of biblical and dogmatic theology. Once again we should note that Gabler believed the Bible to be divinely inspired, but that it was the interpreter's task to determine where the divinely inspired message lay in the text. Moreover, it is important to see that he calls the NT the "newer and better *Christian* testament," which means that he saw the OT as inherently sub-Christian. For the task of biblical theology, one would collect, classify, and historically situate a particular text; however, not all of the collected data is necessarily of value for dogmatic theology. The worthiness of particular data for dogmatics is of use only if it is part of the universal and eternal

12. Ibid., 501.
13. Ibid., 500.
14. Ibid., 497.

religion. In other words, there is no unified, organic, historically unfolding divine revelation but only punctuated moments in history where the principles of the divine eternal religion are revealed, and even then the principles must be distilled to be of any use for dogmatics. As Gabler writes, "For only from these methods can those uncertain and undoubted universal ideas be singled out, those ideas which alone are useful in dogmatic theology . . . a dogmatic theology adapted to our own times."[15]

Analysis

As we stop and reflect for brief analysis it is important that we note how much Gabler is indebted to the Enlightenment project. Gabler was indebted to the Enlightenment idea that Christianity could be distilled to its very essence—universal moral and religious principles. In this regard Gabler was following in the footsteps of Johann Semler (1721–91), who argued in his work *A Free Investigation of the Canon* (1771) that not all portions of the Bible are equally inspired, and that the test of inspiration was whether a text testified to universal moral and religious principles.[16] Gabler and Semler, among others, were representatives of the *neologian* school of thought, which believed that "'revelation' was simply a rational reaffirmation of moral truths already available to enlightened reason."[17] Gabler's commitment to rationalism is therefore evident not only in his stated methodology, but especially in the absence of any mention of Christ, whether for his understanding of dogmatic or biblical theology.

In one sense, Gabler stood in continuity with historic Reformation exegetical principles, namely the need to interpret the Scriptures within their grammatico-historical contexts as well as to be vigilant against theological eisegesis. On the other hand, given his understanding of the inspiration and authority of Scripture and his commitment to Enlightenment rationalism, Gabler's understanding of biblical theology is significantly different than other manifestations throughout church history. One may

15. Ibid., 501.

16. See Hans Frei, *The Eclipse of Biblical Narrative: A Study of Eighteenth and Nineteenth Century Hermeneutics* (New Haven, CT: Yale University Press, 1980), 111–13; D. A. Carson, "Current Issues in Biblical Theology: A New Testament Perspective," *Bulletin for Biblical Research* 5 (1995): 20; William D. Dennison, "Reason, History and Revelation: Biblical Theology and the Enlightenment," *Kerux* 18/1 (2003): 14.

17. Alister E. McGrath, *The Making of Modern German Christology 1750–1990* (1987; Grand Rapids: Zondervan, 1994), 20.

speak of Gabler's understanding of biblical theology as merely a descriptive process concerned with discovering what biblical writers thought and taught, or presenting the theology of ancient Israel and early Christianity in a purely historical manner.[18] While Gabler created the way to distinguish and establish biblical theology as a separate discipline, his distinction also undermined the relationship between exegesis and dogmatics. No longer was dogmatic theology bound directly to Scripture through exegesis; now it was first passed through the filter of the universal and eternal religion. Doctrines such as Christology or the Trinity, which lie at the core of the biblical message, were in jeopardy. Gabler opened the way for an "increasingly independent dogmatic theology far less influenced by the results of exegesis, even as it reinforced the removal of exegesis from the theological patterning of the exegetical tradition of the fathers, the medieval doctors, and the interpreters of the Reformation and post-Reformation eras."[19] To say the least, this form of biblical theology is markedly different from that which we find from the pen of Vos.

VOS ON BIBLICAL THEOLOGY

It is immediately evident that Vos's understanding of biblical theology is qualitatively different from that of Gabler. Vos defines biblical theology as "that branch of Exegetical Theology which deals with the process of the self-revelation of God deposited in the Bible."[20] We can note here, in contrast with Gabler, that biblical theology for Vos is exegetical, which means it originates from the exegesis of the biblical text, which is authored ultimately by God; it is a process traced through history that deals not with the revelation of eternal timeless principles, but with the self-revelation of God. As Vos fills out his definition of biblical theology he explains that revelation does not stand alone—that is, special revelation—but is inseparably connected to the redemptive activity

18. Richard B. Gaffin Jr., "Systematic and Biblical Theology," in *The New Testament Student and Theology*, ed. John H. Skilton (Nutley, NJ: Presbyterian & Reformed, 1976), 3:34; also Dennison, "Biblical Theology," 12; Richard A. Muller, *Post-Reformation Reformed Dogmatics: The Rise and Development of Reformed Orthodoxy, ca. 1520 to ca. 1725* (Grand Rapids: Baker, 2003), 2:454.

19. Muller, *Post-Reformation Reformed Dogmatics*, 455.

20. Geerhardus Vos, *Biblical Theology: Old and New Testaments* (Carlisle, PA: Banner of Truth, 1996), 5.

of God. And, it is God's redemptive activity in Christ that is central to Vos's understanding of revelation, as, "the process of revelation is not only concomitant with history, but it becomes incarnate in history."[21] Vos, however, explains: "God has not revealed Himself in a school, but in covenant; and the covenant as a communion of life is all-comprehensive, embracing all the conditions and interests of those contracting it."[22] Hence, we see several key ideas emerge in Vos's understanding of biblical theology.

First, the biblical theologian does not treat the biblical text from merely a historical perspective. Vos explains:

> A Biblical Theology thus conceived ought to classify itself with Historical Theology, not with Exegetical Theology. It professes to be a History of Doctrine for Biblical times. It treats Isaiah as it would treat Augustine, the sole question being what was believed, not whether it was truth or not. Our conception of the discipline, on the other hand, considers its subject matter from the point of view of the revelation from God. Hence the factor of inspiration needs to be reckoned with as one of the elements rendering the things studied "truth" guaranteed to us as such by the authority of God.[23]

It is for this reason that Vos prefers the term *history of special revelation* in lieu of *biblical theology*.[24] Since the Bible is special revelation with God as its author, this therefore means that the entire corpus is an organic whole: "Biblical Theology, rightly defined, is nothing else than *the exhibition of the organic progress of supernatural revelation in its historic continuity and multiformity*."[25] Here, then, we find great disparity between Vos and Gabler. In fact, concerning the biblical theology produced by Gabler and similar-minded theologians, Vos calls it the "Biblical Theology of Rationalism" in which "the historical principle merely served to eliminate or neutralize the revelation-principle."[26] *Vos always saw the historical nature of biblical theology*

21. Vos, *Biblical Theology*, 6.
22. Vos, "Idea of Biblical Theology," 10.
23. Vos, *Biblical Theology*, 13.
24. Ibid., 14.
25. Vos, "Idea of Biblical Theology," 15. One should also note that for Vos, pre-redemptive special revelation was paradigmatic for all subsequent special revelation, particularly as it focused on the probation of the first and last Adams (see Vos, *Biblical Theology*, 27–40).
26. Vos, "Idea of Biblical Theology," 15.

subordinated to the principle of its revealed character.[27] Moreover, unlike many contemporary biblical theologians, Vos believed that the divine word preceded a divine act, which was then followed by a divine interpretive word.[28] By contrast, some biblical theologians often argue that the word is merely reflective of human ideas or symbols, not actual divine acts in history. Ultimately, therefore, Vos believed recognizing the inspired and authoritative character of special revelation was destructive to the critical Enlightenment-influenced biblical theology such as that of Gabler.[29]

Second, unlike Gabler's understanding of biblical theology, Vos believed the discipline focused on Christ and covenant, which is the manner in which the church learns of redemption accomplished and applied:

> From the beginning all redeeming acts of God aim at the creation and introduction of this new organic principle, which is none other than Christ. All Old Testament redemption is but the saving activity of God working toward the realization of this goal, the great supernatural prelude to the Incarnation and the Atonement. And Christ having appeared as the head of the new humanity and having accomplished His atoning work, the further renewal of the kosmos is effected through an organic extension of His power in ever widening circles.[30]

Here then we see the christocentric nature of biblical theology as Vos understands it in stark contrast with Gabler. Moreover, this means that all of biblical revelation, both OT and NT, is a unified, organic whole. Unlike Gabler, who saw the OT as sub-Christian and the NT as the Christian testament, Vos argues that the various stages of the historic, gradual, progressive unfolding of God's revelation in Christ are manifested through the various covenants where the theologian sees the Savior designated as the seed of the woman, the seed of Abraham, the seed of Judah, and the seed of David.[31] One of the key principles that demonstrate the organic unity of the Testaments is biblical typology. In particular, Vos writes that "the bond that holds type and antitype together must be a bond of vital continuity in the progress of redemption."[32]

27. Ibid., 19.
28. Ibid., 18; Vos, *Biblical Theology*, 7.
29. Vos, "Idea of Biblical Theology," 22.
30. Ibid., 12.
31. Ibid., 12.
32. Vos, *Biblical Theology*, 146.

Third, given the divinely inspired nature of special revelation, Vos therefore believed, in contrast with Gabler, that biblical theology is of the greatest importance to systematic, or dogmatic, theology. Vos notes:

> Dogmatic Theology is, when rightly cultivated, as truly a Biblical and as truly an inductive science as its younger sister. And the latter needs a constructive principle for arranging her facts as well as the former. The only difference is, that in the one case this constructive principle is systematic and logical, whereas in the other case it is purely historical. In other words, Systematic Theology endeavors to construct a circle, Biblical Theology seeks to reproduce a line.[33]

Vos believed that systematic theology, rightly conceived, was thoroughly exegetical and was "the crown which grows of all the work that Biblical Theology can accomplish."[34]

Given these basic characteristics, we may therefore describe biblical theology as that exegetical discipline that recognizes: (1) the whole of Scripture in both Testaments as special revelation both in word and act; (2) the progressive historic unfolding of God's self-revelation in Christ through covenant; (3) the primary interpretive principle of recognizing the organic unity of the Scriptures in typology, type, and antitype; and (4) recognizing that biblical and systematic theology are necessary counterparts—that one may distinguish but never separate the two disciplines.[35] That one finds these characteristics in Reformed theologians either contemporaneous with or subsequent to Vos is without question. Similar affirmations regarding the nature and characteristics of biblical theology can be found in the writings of B. B. Warfield (1851–1921), John Murray (1898–1975), Meredith G. Kline (1922–2007), and Richard Gaffin (1936–).[36] It is necessary to show, however,

33. Vos, "Idea of Biblical Theology," 23.

34. Ibid., 24.

35. For broad agreement on these defining characteristics of biblical theology see Craig Bartholomew, *Out of Egypt: Biblical Theology and Biblical Interpretation* (Grand Rapids: Zondervan, 2004), 3, 5, 23, 46, 149, 261, 313, 320, 329. For a survey of the various definitions of biblical theology, see Carson, "Current Issues in Biblical Theology," 17–41; Scobie, "The Challenge of Biblical Theology," 31–61; idem, "The Structure of Biblical Theology," *TynBul* 42.2 (1991): 163–94.

36. See B. B. Warfield, "The Idea of Systematic Theology," in *The Works of Benjamin B. Warfield*, ed. E. D. Warfield, vol. 9 (1932; Grand Rapids: Baker, 1981), 49–87, esp. 66–68, 73–75; John Murray, "Systematic Theology," in *Collected Writings of John Murray*, vol. 4 (Edinburgh: Banner of Truth, 1982), 1–21, esp. 9ff; Meredith G. Kline, *Kingdom Prologue: Genesis Foundations for a Covenantal Worldview* (Overland Park, KS: Two Age, 2000), 7; cf. Gaffin, "Systematic Theology

that Vos's understanding of biblical theology is not present only in those who consciously have thought to carry forward his insights, but rather has an ancient pedigree. This is not to say that we are searching for pre-incarnations of Vos or conducting eisegetical historical theology, but rather that one can find the same general interpretive and biblical-theological commitments from the earliest days of the church.[37] It is therefore to the OT that we turn to see biblical theology at work in its ancient, canonical setting.

BIBLICAL THEOLOGY THROUGHOUT THE AGES

As we survey the history of biblical interpretation we should first note that such a survey cannot be exhaustive, as it has often been the subject of entire monographs. Nevertheless, we can see how various interpreters throughout the centuries have employed the hermeneutics of biblical theology, which therefore demonstrates the antiquity of the discipline. However, we should note, undisputedly, that we will not find biblical theology as an independent formal discipline for very many years. Rather, by this survey we are looking for the use of the biblical-theological method. Or, stated in other terms, biblical theology does not formally exist until the eighteenth century; it is, however, materially manifest in the hermeneutics of the church for centuries before Gabler delivered his address. Keeping these things in mind, we may move forward to begin our survey with the OT.

The OT and Intra-Canonical Interpretation

Old Testament scholars have often noted that the Pentateuch is considered to be the old testament of the OT.[38] In other words, all OT revelation subsequent to the Pentateuch is built on themes and concepts found within the first five books of the Bible. This means, therefore, that one finds a hermeneutical relationship between the Pentateuch and the rest of the OT,

---

and Biblical Theology," 32–50; idem, "Reformed Dogmatics," 16–50. This is not to say that the aforementioned authors agree in every respect concerning the nature and definition of biblical theology. For analysis of the differences between Vos and Warfield, for example, see Lints, "Two Theologies or One," 235–53, esp. 250–52.

37. Cf. Hart, "Tradition-Challenged," 4. In this regard one should recognize that biblical theology can be equated with redemptive-historical exegesis (so Gaffin, "Reformed Dogmatics," 25).

38. E.g., R. W. L. Moberly, *The Old Testament of the Old Testament* (Minneapolis: Fortress, 1992).

one that is exhibited in the intra-canonical interpretation within the OT. While there are many examples from which one could pick, it is perhaps Daniel's vision of the four beasts that best exhibits a biblical-theological hermeneutic. In Daniel 7 the prophet has a vision where he sees four beasts rise out of the sea: a lion with eagle's wings (v. 4), a bear (v. 5), a leopard (v. 6), and a dreadful and terrible beast, exceedingly strong (v. 7). Daniel sees the dominion of the four ferocious beasts taken away (v. 12), and one like the son of man comes on the clouds of heaven and, "to him was given dominion and glory and a kingdom" (v. 14).

At first glance, Daniel's vision may not seem to exhibit anything vaguely resembling a biblical-theological hermeneutic, but on closer examination such hesitation quickly fades into the background. Daniel's vision describes the eschatological victory of Christ over those kingdoms that oppose him in protological terms, as in Genesis 1–2.[39] Daniel's vision is a repetition of Psalm 8, the completed creation and enthronement of man. Psalm 8 poetically echoes Genesis 1:26–28 with: "What is man that you are mindful of him, and the son of man that you care for him? . . . You have given him dominion over the works of your hands; you have put all things under his feet, all sheep and oxen, and also the beasts of the field, the birds of the heavens, and the fish of the sea" (vv. 4, 6–8).[40] Daniel's vision tells of the eschatological victory of Christ in terms of Psalm 8: the son of man comes and takes dominion from the beasts of the earth. The conclusion of all history is given in terms of the beginning of history; eschatology is recounted in protological terms. Or, the work of the second Adam is rooted in and mirrors the work of the first Adam (cf. Gen. 1:26–28; Ps. 8:4–8; Dan. 7; Rev. 13–14).[41] Stated simply, Daniel's prophecy is a visual rendition of Psalm 8.

39. E. J. Young, *Daniel* (Edinburgh: Banner of Truth, 1978), 155–56.

40. Joyce G. Baldwin, *Daniel*, TOTC (Downers Grove, IL: InterVarsity, 1978), 143.

41. John E. Goldingay, *Daniel*, WBC 30 (Dallas: Word, 1989), 188, 190. N. T. Wright comments that, "Daniel was a favorite with Jews of the first century AD. One of the climactic moments in this book, arguably, is the scene in which the true Israel, seen in apocalyptic terms as a human figure, is exalted to a position of glory and authority over the mythical beasts who have been oppressing God's people. Whatever referents may have been in the mind of the original authors, there should be no doubt that in the first century many would read such imagery as referring to Israel and the nations, and would hear in the background the overtones of Genesis 2. Divine order will be restored to the creator's garden, through a genuine Adam—i.e., Israel—who will renounce idolatry and so, in obedience to the creator, rule wisely over the creation" (N. T. Wright, *The New Testament and the People of God* [Minneapolis: Fortress, 1992], 266).

In this regard we see a definite pattern employed in Daniel's prophetic vision, namely, antecedent special revelation, through which Genesis 1–2 is organically and typologically connected with the eschaton and the person and work of Christ. Previous revelation, whether Genesis 1–2 or Psalm 8, anticipates the self-revelation of God in Christ, the Messiah. That self-revelation is communicated to the prophet in terms of preceding revelation. One should also note the inherently covenantal nature of this prophecy, namely the coming kingdom of God. Viewed against the wider redemptive-historical horizon, the book of Daniel begins to answer the questions of God's faithfulness to his covenant promises given to Israel in exile. It shows that God has not forgotten his people and that they will be protected from contamination (ch. 1), idolatry (ch. 2), fire (ch. 3), and wild beasts (ch. 4).[42] Hence, here we see the OT in its intra-canonical interpretation employing those characteristics that define biblical theology: the divine origin of special revelation, the organic unity of the whole, the typological relationship between foundational revelation and the coming eschatological revelation of God in Christ and covenant.

Second-Temple Judaism: The Dead Sea Scrolls

When we turn to the literature of second-temple Judaism, we undoubtedly enter upon non-revelatory literature. That the inter-testamental literature of Judaism was not of divine origin is something that has been acknowledged not only by a host of Reformed theologians and exegetes but even by first-century Jews such as Josephus (ca. AD 37–100).[43] Josephus writes:

> For we have not an innumerable multitude of books among us, disagreeing from and contradicting one another but only twenty-two books, which contain the records of all the past times; which are justly believed to be divine; and of them five belong to Moses, which contain his laws and the traditions of the origin of mankind till his death. This interval of time was little short of three thousand years; but as to the time from the death of

42. Stephen G. Dempster, *Dominion and Dynasty: A Biblical Theology of the Hebrew Bible*, New Studies in Biblical Theology (Downers Grove, IL: InterVarsity, 2003), 213.

43. See J. Gresham Machen, *The Origins of Paul's Religion* (1925; Eugene, OR: Wipf & Stock, 2002), 180; see also E. Earle Ellis, *Paul's Use of the Old Testament* (1957; Grand Rapids: Baker, 1991), 83.

Moses till the reign of Artaxerxes, king of Persia, who reigned after Xerxes, the prophets, who were after Moses, wrote down what was done in their times in thirteen books. The remaining four books contain hymns to God, and precepts for the conduct of human life. It is true, our history has been written since Artaxerxes very particularly, but has not been esteemed of the like authority with the former by our forefathers, because there has not been an exact succession of prophets since that time; and how firmly we have given credit to those books of our own nation, is evident by what we do; for during so many ages as have already passed, no one has been so bold as either to add anything to them, to take anything from them, or to make any change in them.[44]

Here we see a clear differentiation between the inspired OT canon and the non-inspired literature of inter-testamental Judaism. We do not turn therefore to the literature of second-temple Judaism without noting this significant difference. Even so, it is important that we see how certain strands of second-temple literature interpreted the Scriptures employing the patterns characteristic of biblical theology.

To be sure, second-temple literature was often severely misguided in its hermeneutics and theological conclusions. There have always been orthodox strands, however, within the body of literature that Reformed theologians have acknowledged since the Reformation. Regarding the following words from the apocrypha, "For it is not because of any righteous deeds of our ancestors or our kings that we bring before you our prayer for mercy, O Lord our God" (Bar. 2:18 NRSV), John Calvin could write that they are "very true and holy words."[45] We find similar orthodox theological ideas bound with a biblical-theological hermeneutical trajectory in the Dead Sea Scrolls. The Qumran community, at least as it is reflected in the Dead Sea Scrolls, believed that the patterns of pre-redemptive history would be the same ones that would emerge in the eschaton: "For God has chosen them for an

44. Josephus, "Against Apion," in *The Works of Josephus*, trans. William Whiston (Peabody, MA: Hendrickson, 1987), 1.8 (38), 776.

45. John Calvin, *Institutes of the Christian Religion*, ed. John T. McNeill, trans. Ford Lewis Battles, The Library of Christian Classics 20–21 (Philadelphia: Westminster, 1960), 3.20.8. Vos saw connections between second-temple Judaism's understanding of history in terms of two ages and the NT's use of the phrases *present age* and *age to come*. He surveyed the eschatology of the Similitudes of Enoch, 2 Maccabees, 4 Maccabees, Wisdom of Solomon, Book of Jubilees, the Assumption of Moses, and the Apocalypse of Ezra, among others (see Geerhardus Vos, *The Pauline Eschatology* [1930; Phillipsburg, NJ: P&R, 1994], 19–30).

everlasting covenant and all the glory of Adam shall be theirs" (1QS 4) and "Thou wilt cast away all their sins. Thou wilt cause them to inherit all the glory of Adam and the abundance of days" (1QH 4 [17] Hymn 1 [23]).[46] Here there is a clear hermeneutical trajectory—the Qumran community expected the eschaton to resemble the proton. Or, stated in terms of revelation, they expected there to be an organic connection between Genesis 1–2 and the eschatological revelation of redemption.

This biblical-theological trajectory is especially evident in other statements regarding the eschaton:

> I shall accept them and they shall be my people and shall be for them forever. I will dwell with them for ever and ever and will sanctify my [sa]nctuary by my glory. I will cause my glory to rest on it until the day of creation on which I shall created my sanctuary, establishing it for myself for all time according to the covenant which I have made with Jacob in Bethel. (2 QT = 2Q19, 20 19, ln. 7–10)

We should note that this eschatological redemption is conceived as covenantal, though there is the glaring misconception that the community would be redeemed by the Teacher of Righteousness rather than the incarnate covenant Lord. Moreover, the Qumran view of soteriology was based in a works-righteousness paradigm, one antithetical to the teaching of Scripture. We see a mixture of truth and error when we read: "He has commanded that a Sanctuary of men be built for Himself, that there they may send up, like the smoke of incense, the works of the law" (4 Q174). Here we see a proper biblical-theological insight, namely that the OT foreshadowed that God would build his eschatological temple, not out of bricks but out of living stones, his people. However, it is mixed with an error in soteriology, that the people would offer the Lord the sacrifice of the works of the law, which reflects a works-righteousness paradigm. Nevertheless, we still see biblical-theological patterns appear in the Qumran hermeneutics.

The NT and the Interpretation of the OT

When we return to the realm of special revelation, whatever mixture of truth and error that appears in the hermeneutics of the Qumran community

---

46. Geza Vermes, *The Complete Dead Sea Scrolls in English* (1962; New York: Penguin, 1996).

vanishes. One of the more hermeneutically significant passages to which one might turn is Christ's discourse on the road to Emmaus. Luke tells us that "beginning with Moses and all the Prophets, he interpreted to them in all the Scriptures the things concerning himself" (Luke 24:27). In the verses that follow, Luke says that Christ explained that everything written about him "in the Law of Moses and the Prophets and the Psalms" had to be fulfilled (Luke 24:44). Once again we see the characteristic patterns of biblical theology emerge in the ideas of the organic nature of special revelation, which is evident in Christ's appeal not just to select portions of the OT, but to the revelatory whole as echoed in the references to the Law, the Prophets, and the Psalms, the three parts of the Hebrew OT.[47] As Darrell Bock notes, "Jesus makes it clear that he is the subject of these Scriptures and that when it comes to God's promise, he is at the center of those events."[48] In one sense, we can say that Jesus is the theologian *par excellence* who exegetes the Scriptures employing a biblical-theological hermeneutic.[49] There is, of course, a universe of exegetical data in the NT's interpretation of the OT, particularly in its use of typology.

In fact, we may say that a typological hermeneutic governs the NT's interpretation of the OT.[50] This characteristic is especially prominent in the book of Hebrews. We find the organic nature of God's special revelation and its culmination in Christ in the opening verses of the book: "Long ago, at many times and in many ways, God spoke to our fathers by the prophets, but in these last days he has spoken to us by his Son" (Heb 1:1–2a). That Christ is the culmination and zenith of God's self-revelation in covenant is evident throughout the book, particularly as the author shows how the OT ceremonies and structures foreshadowed the person and work of Christ and have been superseded by him (Heb. 8–10). Concerning the nature of the book of Hebrews, Andrew Lincoln explains:

> The whole of Scripture can be seen as promise. The opening statement that in the past God spoke through the prophets is not to be inter-

47. E. Earle Ellis, *The Gospel of Luke*, NCB (1981; Grand Rapids: Eerdmans, 1996), 279.
48. Darrell L. Bock, *Luke 9:51–24:53*, BECNT (1996; Grand Rapids: Baker, 1998), 1937.
49. Cf. Danny E. Olinger, *A Geerhardus Vos Anthology* (Phillipsburg, NJ: P&R, 2006), 26–27; Geerhardus Vos, *The Teaching of Jesus Concerning the Kingdom of God and the Church* (Eugene, OR: Wipf & Stock, 1998), 191–94.
50. Leonhard Goppelt, *Typos: The Typological Interpretation of the Old Testament in the New*, trans. Donald H. Madvig (1939; Grand Rapids: Eerdmans, 1982), ix.

preted narrowly. In fact, of the thirty-one actual scriptural citations in Hebrews, seven are from the Prophets, twelve from the Pentateuch, and twelve from the Writings (eleven from Psalms, and one from Proverbs). This suggests that, for Hebrews, all of Scripture is being viewed as prophetic.[51]

In this sense, then, we can characterize the *type* as promise and the *antitype* as fulfillment.

One finds these same patterns in other portions of the NT. The NT authors write with an acute awareness of the dawning of the eschaton which has come with the first advent of Christ (e.g., 1 Cor. 15:45ff).[52] That Peter, for example, writes with a cognitive awareness that the eschaton has begun is evident in numerous places throughout his first epistle, for example, in his recognition of the flood (Gen. 6–8) as a *type* (*tupos*) and baptism as the *antitype* (*antitupos*) (1 Peter 3:21). As Leonhard Goppelt (1911–73) explains, "The manner in which baptism is the antitype of the OT event is expressed by [*antitupos*]. This word is probably being used already as a technical term, since through Paul [*tupos*] became in early Christianity a hermeneutical technical expression for OT pre-representations of the eschatological event beginning with Christ (1 Cor. 10:6, 11; Rom. 5:14)."[53]

Patristic Exegesis: Irenaeus

As we move into the post-apostolic church, these same hermeneutical patterns continue, though it goes without saying that we once again leave the sphere of divinely inspired special revelation. However, this is not to say that biblical-theological hermeneutics were dominant to the exclusion of other paradigms. Unfortunately, the hermeneutics of the apostolic fathers and the patristics were often colored by the use of allegory, which

---

51. Andrew T. Lincoln, "Hebrews and Biblical Theology," in *Out of Egypt: Biblical Theology and Biblical Interpretation*, ed. Craig Bartholomew et al. (Grand Rapids: Zondervan, 2004), 329. See also Gaffin, "Reformed Dogmatics," 25.

52. See Vos, *Pauline Eschatology*, 1–41, esp. 38n45.

53. Leonhard Goppelt, *A Commentary on 1 Peter*, ed. Ferdinand Hahn, trans. John E. Alsup (1978; Grand Rapids: Eerdmans, 1993), 266; idem, tupoj, in *Theological Dictionary of the New Testament*, ed. Gerhard Friedrich, trans. Geoffrey Bromiley (1982; Grand Rapids: Eerdmans, 2006), 8:251–59. See also Geerhardus Vos, "Hebrews, the Epistle of the Diatheke," in *Redemptive History and Biblical Interpretation: The Shorter Writings of Geerhardus Vos*, ed. Richard B. Gaffin Jr. (Phillipsburg, NJ: P&R, 1980), 201; also Henning Graf Reventlow, *Problems of Biblical Theology in the Twentieth Century* (Philadelphia: Fortress, 1986), 18.

was clearly a distortion of the biblical text.[54] Allegorical interpretation is much like astrology, in that it begins with a factual basis but then leaps into speculation that has no inherent connection to the factual base and depends almost entirely on the interpreter's own creative imagination.[55] Theologians have labored strenuously to differentiate typological from allegorical interpretation. Vos, for example, has explained:

> The bond that holds type and antitype together must be a bond of vital continuity in the progress of redemption. Where this is ignored, and in the place of this bond are put accidental resemblances, void of inherent spiritual significance, all sorts of absurdities will result, such as must bring the whole subject of typology into disrepute. Examples of this are: the scarlet cord of Rahab prefigures the blood of Christ; the four lepers at Samaria, the four Evangelists.[56]

Allegory, therefore, is not typology. Along similar lines as Vos, Goppelt notes that only historical facts—persons, actions, events, and institutions—are material for typological interpretation.[57] It is without question that the church fathers were given to the allegorical interpretation of Scripture. However, there were patristics in whom one can find the responsible use of a biblical-theological hermeneutic. While there are many patristic theologians among whom one might choose, such as Augustine (354–430) or Origen (185–ca. 254), we will explore the theology of Irenaeus of Lyons (ca. 115–ca. 202).

Irenaeus was engaged in theological battles against Gnosticism. It has been noted that he employed a biblical-theological hermeneutic in this battle.[58] Brevard Childs explains that in the battle with Gnosticism, Irenaeus sought to set forth a comprehensive summary of the Christian faith in terms of the testimony of Scripture as the written form of the *regula fidei*, or rule of faith. Irenaeus argued that God's order for salvation extended from creation to its fulfillment in Christ as God progressively made himself known in the creation, the giving of the law, and prophecy.[59] Irenaeus writes of God:

---

54. See Robert M. Grant with David Tracy, *A Short History of the Interpretation of the Bible* (1963; Minneapolis: Fortress, 1984), 52–62.

55. Gerald Bray, "The Church Fathers and Biblical Theology," in *Out of Egypt*, 31.

56. Vos, *Biblical Theology*, 146.

57. Goppelt, *Typos*, 17–18.

58. Bray, "The Church Fathers and Biblical Theology," 25.

59. Brevard Childs, *Biblical Theology of the Old and New Testaments: Theological Reflection on the Christian Bible* (Minneapolis: Fortress, 1992), 30–31.

He is always known through Him by whose means He ordained all things. Now this is His Word, our Lord Jesus Christ, who in the last times was made a man among men, that He might join the end to the beginning, that is man to God. Wherefore the prophets, receiving the prophetic gift from the same Word, announced His advent according to the flesh, by which the blending and communion of God and man took place according to the good pleasure of the Father, the Word of God foretelling from the beginning that should be seen by men, and hold converse with them, and should be present with His own creation. (4.20.4; cf. 4.9.3; 4.2.3)[60]

Here we see that for Irenaeus, God's self-revelation and his redemption of man center on Christ.

Irenaeus believed that Christ had been revealed throughout the Scriptures with both types and prophecies. Irenaeus writes that God called Israel's attention to things of

primary importance by means of those which were secondary; that is, to things that are real, by means of those that are typical; and by things temporal, to eternal; and by the carnal to the spiritual; and by the earthly to the heavenly; as was also said to Moses, "Thou shalt make all things after the pattern of those things which thou sawest in the mount." For during forty days He was learning to keep [in his memory] the words of God, and the celestial patterns, and the spiritual images, and the types of things to come; as also Paul says: "for they drank of the rock which followed them: and the rock was Christ." (4.14.3)

Likewise, concerning prophecy, Irenaeus explains that the OT scriptures prophesy of the advent and suffering of Christ, which is evidence that they were inspired by the same God (4.10.1). Another important factor is that Irenaeus saw that Christ was the one author and end of both covenants, old and new: "All things therefore are of one and the same substance, that is, from one and the same God" (4.9.1). Irenaeus elsewhere writes:

For the new covenant having been known and preached by the prophets, He who was to carry it out according to the good pleasure of the Father was also preached, having been revealed to men as God pleased; that they

---

60. Irenaeus, *Against Heresies*, in *Ante-Nicene Fathers*, vol. 1, ed. Alexander Roberts and James Donaldson (1885; Grand Rapids: Eerdmans, 1993).

might always make progress through believing in Him, and by means of the [successive] covenants, should gradually attain to perfect salvation. (4.9.3; cf. 4.11.3; 1.10.1–3; 4.13.1)

In all of these things we see the same characteristics defined by Vos: a unified organic understanding of God's revelation and redemption in Christ that comes progressively in the course of history through his covenantal dealings with his people. Given these points, it is no wonder Childs concludes that "Irenaeus was indeed a biblical theologian."[61]

The Middle Ages: Aquinas

When we approach the Middle Ages, it is Thomas Aquinas (1225–74) who stands head and shoulders above his peers. Yet, some people might scratch their heads in confusion at the suggestion that Aquinas employed the biblical-theological method in his theology, as he is known for his philosophically oriented theology. Aquinas is undoubtedly the author of a more philosophically minded theology, one, for example, that approaches the doctrine of God not from Christ and covenant, as Reformed theologians would do later, but in terms of the *via antiqua* approach, namely ontology.[62] Then again, this is not to say that Aquinas's theology was pure sophistry. On the contrary, while there are certainly many features about Aquinas's theology that should be questioned, he was nonetheless a *magister de sacra pagina* before he penned his famous *Summa Theologiae*. That he was a biblical interpreter is evident not only in the prolegomena of his *Summa*, but also in his commentaries on Job, Matthew, John, and the Pauline epistles.

When we turn to the pages of his *Summa*, we find that Aquinas not only set forth his theology, but implicitly developed rules for biblical hermeneutics as well.[63] In his theological exposition of the Decalogue, Aquinas turns to answer the question of whether the ceremonies of the old law ceased with the coming of Christ. To answer this question Aquinas materially appeals to the unity of the canon, which implies its inspiration, and also the typologi-

61. Childs, *Biblical Theology*, 32. For similar conclusions, see also Scobie, "Challenge of Biblical Theology," 37; J. Ligon Duncan, "The Covenant Idea in Irenaeus of Lyons: An Introduction and Survey," a paper given at the North American Patristic Society, national meeting, Thursday, May 28, 1998.

62. See Francis Turretin, *Institutes of Elenctic Theology*, 3 vols., ed. James T. Dennison Jr., trans. George Musgrave Giger (Phillipsburg, NJ: P&R, 1992–97), 1.5.4, 1:16.

63. Childs, *Biblical Theology*, 40.

cal relationship between the OT and NT. So, for example, concerning Col. 2:11–12 and the relationship between circumcision and baptism, Aquinas writes that the latter replaces the former. Concerning other types of the OT, Aquinas writes:

> As to the Sabbath, which was a sign recalling the first creation, its place is taken by the *Lord's Day*, which recalls the beginning of the new creature in the Resurrection of Christ.—In like manner other solemnities of the Old Law are supplanted by new solemnities: because the blessings vouchsafed to that people foreshadowed the favors granted us by Christ. Hence the feast of the Passover gave place to the feast of Christ's Passion and Resurrection: the feast of Pentecost when the Old Law was given, to the feast of Pentecost on which was given the Law of the living spirit: the feast of the New Moon, to Lady Day, when appeared the first rays of the sun, i.e., Christ, by the fullness of grace: the feast of Trumpets, to the feasts of the Apostles: the feast of Expiation, to the feasts of Martyrs and Confessors: the feast of Tabernacles, to the feast of Church Dedication: the feast of Assembly and Collection, to the feast of the Angles, or else to the feast of All Hallows.[64]

One can immediately identify many references to Roman Catholic beliefs and theology, particularly the connection Aquinas draws between the feast of the new moon (Ps. 81:3), which is identified by the Roman Catholic Church as vernal equinox, and what he calls *Lady Day*, which is the "feast of the annunciation of the blessed virgin Mary."

Protestants likely recoil at such "biblical" interpretation, as such a typology would draw disapprobation from all Reformed biblical theologians. While the conclusion he draws is certainly erroneous, though one that would perhaps draw the approval of an allegorist, nevertheless we should take note of the hermeneutical pattern. Aquinas sees a connection between OT type and NT antitype; he employs a biblical-theological methodology in his understanding of the unity of the Scriptures. This is not to say that he successfully and consistently employed this method. Nor should one ignore Aquinas's use of the medieval quadriga that the Reformation all but scuttled. Nevertheless, it is indisputable that one can find Aquinas using a biblical-theological hermeneutic at key points in his interpretation of Scripture.

---

64. Thomas Aquinas, *Summa Theologica*, 5 vols. (Allen: Christian Classics, 1948), Ia IIae q. 103 art 3 (vol. 2, 1085).

The Reformation: Calvin

During the Reformation, the likes of Martin Luther (1483–1546) and John Calvin (1509–64) sought to divest the church of whatever tendencies toward exegetical flights of fancy were common during the Middle Ages. Childs notes that "a great majority of the major theological issues involved in the modern enterprise of Biblical Theology were already adumbrated in Luther in a profound sense."[65] Of greater interest, especially for Reformed biblical theology, is the hermeneutics of Calvin.

While it is often acknowledged that Luther was a strong advocate of a christocentric interpretation of Scripture, many might be surprised to discover that Calvin believed in the same interpretive principle. Commenting on Luke 24:27 and Christ's appearance on the road to Emmaus, Calvin explains that the relationship between the Testaments is bound up in Christ as he is foreshadowed in the type and then revealed in the antitype. Calvin writes: "That Christ may be seen by us today through the Gospel, Moses and the Prophets must take their place as forerunners." He goes on to explain that "in what way passages are to be applied to Christ that are frequently written in the Scriptures, is not the task of the present book to explicate. It would be sufficient to hold, in brief, that not for nothing was Christ called the end of the law." Calvin explains that in the OT types, the visible rites of the law were shadows of spiritual things, and that Christ therefore was to be sought in the shadows of the priesthood, sacrifices, and order of the tabernacle.[66]

What is interesting about Calvin's analysis of Christ's teaching on the road to Emmaus is that he takes note of the OT's own intra-canonical interpretation. Beginning with the Shiloh prophecy of the preeminence of the tribe of Judah and the coming Messiah (Gen. 49:8–10), Calvin writes that the OT prophets sought to bring to remembrance the covenant and turn Israel's hope to the salvation that would come through the Mediator. He then writes: "Since it had pleased God to delay the full revelation to the coming of His Son, their interpretations were not unneeded."[67] These

65. Childs, *Biblical Theology*, 45; see also Scobie, "Challenge of Biblical Theology," 38.
66. John Calvin, *A Harmony of the Gospels: Matthew, Mark, & Luke and James and Jude*, ed. T. F. Torrance and David W. Torrance, trans. A. W. Morrison (1972; Eerdmans: Grand Rapids: 1995), 235–36. On Calvin's understanding of typology, see David L. Puckett, *John Calvin's Exegesis of the Old Testament* (Louisville: Westminster John Knox, 1995), 106–24.
67. Calvin, *Harmony*, 236.

points of exposition reveal key elements of Calvin's biblical-theologically minded hermeneutic. Namely, they show that he saw special revelation as a unified organic whole which centered on the covenantal and progressive redemptive revelation of God in Christ.

Therefore, Calvin believed that Christ was the goal of the Scriptures: "We must hold that Christ cannot be properly known from anywhere but the Scriptures. And if that is so, it follows that the Scriptures should be read with the aim of finding Christ in them. Whoever turns aside from this object, even though he wears himself out all his life in learning, will never reach the knowledge of the truth." Echoing his earlier comments on Luke 24:27, Calvin writes: "For Christ did not first begin to be manifested in the Gospel; but the one to whom the Law and the Prophets bore witness was openly revealed in the Gospel."[68] Periodically, Calvin would demure from finding Christ in various passages of Scripture, and was at times much more cautious than his peers in his use of typology.[69]

Nevertheless, what biblical-theological commitments that lay in seminal forms throughout the historical unfolding of the church's collective understanding of Scripture grew quite quickly in the fertile soil of the Reformation and germinated in a full-blown biblical theology in the post-Reformation period.

Post-Reformation

The Westminster Standards. In the post-Reformation period there are two sources where we find either implicit or explicit biblical-theological commitments, namely in Reformed confessions and in individual theologians. Turning first to the Westminster Standards (1647), we find for the first time specific attention given to the codification of key principles of Reformation hermeneutics. The Westminster divines expressed a commitment to the idea that the Scriptures in both the OT and NT were the authoritative and inspired revelation of God (WCF 1.1–2, 4). They also articulated the theological organic unity of the whole of Scripture in their articulation of its perspicuity:

> All things in Scripture are not alike plain in themselves, nor alike clear unto all: yet those things which are necessary to be known, believed, and observed for

68. John Calvin, *John 1–10, CNTC*, ed. T. F. Torrance and David W. Torrance, trans. T. H. L. Parker (1961; Grand Rapids: Eerdmans, 1995), 139.
69. Muller, *Post-Reformation Reformed Dogmatics*, 2:449, 470–71.

salvation, are so clearly propounded and opened in some place of Scripture or other, that not only the learned, but the unlearned, in a due use of the ordinary means, may attain unto a sufficient understanding of them. (WCF 1.7)[70]

In this statement which defines the nature of perspicuity, the underlying presupposition is that the Bible is an organic whole. In other words, the Bible is God's special revelation and is consistent in all its parts. Everything the divines believed about hermeneutics, however, is not restricted to the first chapter of the confession.

In other portions of the standards the divines also give key hermeneutical points that reveal their biblical-theological commitments, namely Christ and covenant. From the outset of the creation, the way in which God has condescended to his creation is through his covenants, first with Adam and then with fallen man (WCF 7.1–3). It is in their explanation of the relationship between the OT and NT, specifically the nature of the administration of the covenant of grace, where the divines state:

> This covenant was differently administered in the time of the law, and in the time of the gospel; under the law it was administered by promises, prophecies, sacrifices, circumcision, the paschal lamb, and other types and ordinances delivered to the people of the Jews, all foresignifying Christ to come, which were for that time sufficient and efficacious, through the operation of the Spirit, to instruct and build up the elect in faith in the promised Messiah, by whom they had full remission of sins, and eternal salvation; and is called the Old Testament. (WCF 7.5)

Like Calvin before them, the divines held this view as crucial for understanding the interpretive trajectory set forth in the standards. Given what we have seen thus far, we must recognize that not only did the divines believe that the Bible was a revealed organic whole, but that this redemptive revelation came through God's covenantal dealings with man and centered on the progressive revelation of God in Christ (cf. WCF 8). This is evident when they acknowledge that the same covenant of grace was administered, or revealed, in the OT in shadows and types, all of which foresignified Christ to come. One finds similar, if not more explicit, biblical-theological commitments in various post-Reformation theologians.

70. *Westminster Confession of Faith* (1646; Glasgow: Free Presbyterian Publications, 1995).

Cocceius and Witsius

In the history of doctrine from the earliest days of the church, the presentation of the teaching of Scripture has typically been synthetic, or following a logical, or topical, format. This is certainly true of Augustine's *De Doctrina* or the later developments in the Middle Ages with Peter Lombard's (1100–1160) *Sentences* or Aquinas's *Summa*.[71] Though, while Lombard or Aquinas employ a synthetic approach to their theological systems, one should not forget the historical pattern that they follow, namely: God, creation, redemption, sacraments, and eschatology.[72] The sixteenth-century Reformers did not follow the medieval format, specifically in its scholastic form, but instead pursued the *locus*, or topical, format which loosely followed the same historical-topical order, or they often structured their doctrinal works on the Apostles' Creed. In the post-Reformation period there was an explicit re-appropriation of the scholastic synthetic approach evident in the works of one such as Francis Turretin (1623–87). At the same time, however, there was also a significant flowering of a biblical-theological movement.

While the majority of theological works in the sixteenth and early seventeenth century were synthetic in presentation of their teaching of Scripture, there was the development of presenting the theological teaching of Scripture in an analytic, or historical, manner. The biblical-theological movement was nurtured by theologians such as Johannes Cocceius (1603–69) and Herman Witsius (1636–1708). Both Cocceius in his *Summa Doctrinae de Foedere et Testamento Dei* (1648), and Witsius in his *De Oeconomia Foederum Dei cum Hominibus* (1693), follow a historical presentation by use of God's covenantal dealings with man. The doctrine of the covenant is the architectonic principle of both works. In *Summa*, Cocceius does not begin with the doctrine of God or creation but with the covenant of works. He then demonstrates throughout the rest of his work how this covenant was abrogated. In this regard he traces the redemptive historical movement of the abrogation of the covenant of works through history to the eschaton.[73]

---

71. See Augustine, *Christian Doctrine*, in *Nicene and Post-Nicene Fathers*, vol. 2, ed. Philip Schaff (1886; Grand Rapids: Eerdmans, 1993); Peter Lombard, *Quatuor Sententiarum*, in *Patrologia Latina*, vol. 192, ed. J. P. Migne (Paris: 1854).

72. Karl Rahner, ed., "Scholasticism," in *Sacramentum Mundi: An Encyclopedia of Theology* (London: Burns & Oates, 1970), 6:26.

73. See Willem J. van Asselt, *The Federal Theology of Johannes Cocceius (1603–69)*, trans. Raymond Blackleter (Leiden: Brill, 2001), 37–53.

Similarly, Witsius explains in the preface to his work that the covenant of grace is the manner in which God has chosen to reconcile sinners to himself, but that this covenant has had manifold dispensations. He goes on to write:

> I have chosen to enter on this subject from its very beginning, and have endeavored, as far as I could, to explain it methodically and clearly, enlightening the obscurer passages of scripture, carefully examining the phrases used by the Holy Ghost, and referring the whole to the practice of faith and godliness to the glory of God in Christ.[74]

Once again we see the common elements of biblical theology present in this statement, namely Christ in covenant revealed progressively through history to man for his redemption. Moreover, evident in Witsius's hermeneutic of interpreting obscure passages by the clear, we also see his commitment to the revelatory and organic whole of Scripture.

These observations are not new. In fact, Vos wrote a key essay in historical theology tracing the history and development of covenant theology.[75] He saw classic Reformed covenant theology as an antecedent to his own biblical theology. Others, however have been even bolder in identifying the theology of Witsius and Cocceius as being explicitly biblical-theological. J. I. Packer, for example, in the introduction to Witsius' *Economy of the Covenants*, writes: "Today we name the Cocceian procedure 'biblical theology' and that which he opposed 'systematic theology.'"[76]

This opinion is not new, but is the way people often characterize the debate between Cocceius and Gisbert Voetius (1588–1676) and his disciples: systematic v. biblical theology. Frederic Farrar (1831–1903) captures as well as anyone the common misconception concerning the Cocceius-Voetius debate. Farrar explains that Cocceius' "theology became in fact a soteriology, a history of Redemption . . . and almost for the first time developed the correct and fruitful conception of the progressive-

---

74. Herman Witsius, *The Economy of the Covenants Between God and Man*, trans. William Crookshank (1822; Phillipsburg, NJ: P&R, 1990), 1:18.

75. Geerhardus Vos, "The Doctrine of the Covenant in Reformed Theology," in *Redemptive History*, 234–70.

76. J. I. Packer, "Introduction," in *Economy*, vol. 1, § 5; see similar comments in Charles H. H. Scobie, *The Ways of Our God: An Approach to Biblical Theology* (Grand Rapids: Eerdmans, 2003), 13.

ness of Revelation as the ruling principle of theological inquiry." Farrar goes on to write:

> He helped to expel the Aristotelian dogmatics which passed for orthodoxy, revived the original investigation of Scripture … taught his contemporaries to study the structure of the Bible, and to abandon the unfruitful method of splitting it into isolated texts.[77]

To say the least, this characterization makes for a good story, but it is ill-informed.

While space does not permit a full-blown treatment of this important debate, nevertheless it is important to note briefly its true nature. First, both Cocceius and Witsius were biblical theologians, but they were also scholastic theologians. As Richard Muller has ably demonstrated, scholasticism has never been bound to any one philosophy, let alone Aristotelianism.[78] Muller has clearly established from in-depth research into the vast sea of primary sources the exegetical nature of Reformed Scholastic theology.[79] Additionally, both Cocceius and Witsius produced traditional theological works following the *locus*, or common places method. In other words, both theologians saw no tension or antithesis between an analytic or synthetic presentation of the teaching of Scripture.[80]

Second, what few note is that there were significant doctrinal issues at stake that divided Cocceius and Voetius and their respective followers, such as Cocceius's at-times fanciful interpretation of Scripture, his rejection of the abiding nature of the fourth commandment, his peculiar understanding of the abrogations of the covenants, and most importantly that many of

---

77. Frederic W. Farrar, *History of Interpretation* (1886; Grand Rapids: Baker, 1979), 385. For a similar characterization of Cocceius' theology see Charles McCoy, "Johannes Cocceius: Federal Theology," *Scottish Journal of Theology* 16 (1963), 352–70. Though this portrait has been overturned by recent historical theological research, there are those in the field of biblical studies who continue to rely upon this outdated research (see, e.g., Scobie, "Structure of Biblical Theology," 154, 174).

78. See Willem van Asselt, "Cocceius Anti-Scholasticus?" in *Reformation and Scholasticism: An Ecumenical Enterprise*, ed. Willem van Asselt and Eef Dekker (Grand Rapids: Baker, 2001), 227–52; cf. idem, *Federal Theology*, 139–92.

79. See Muller, *Post-Reformation Reformed Dogmatics*, esp. 2:151–223.

80. See Johannes Cocceius, *Summa Theologiae ex Scripturis repetita* (Geneva: 1665); Herman Witsius, *Sacred Dissertations on the Apostles' Creed*, 2 vols., trans. Donald Frasier (1823; Phillipsburg, NJ: P&R, 1994).

his followers embraced a Cartesian epistemology.[81] In fact, in contours that anticipate current debates, Cocceians used more "biblical" language in their theology rather than the traditional scholastic or theological terminology which enabled them to mask their Cartesian epistemic commitments. Those of the Voetian school saw Cartesian epistemology as detrimental to the very heart of Reformed dogmatics because it rooted theological knowledge, not in the authoritative revealed word, but in the autonomous doubting individual. Ernst Bizer explains that "the remarkable fact is to be observed that the Cartesians at the same time were all Cocceians," which is undoubtedly an overstatement. Nevertheless, he gives us a window into the true nature of the debate when he writes:

> It was therefore natural that the Cartesians now also adopted the new "scriptural" theology of Cocceius and sought to adhere, within the inner theological domain, as much as possible to the terminology of the Bible. The development which can be observed among the late medieval Nominalists is here repeated: the more profane philosophy becomes, the more biblistic theology becomes.[82]

The debate, therefore, was not strictly about biblical theology *per se*; it only factored in the debate to the degree that theologians used biblical theology to mask their tendencies toward rationalism. The debate was consequently more about the abuse rather than the proper use of biblical theology.

Owen, Edwards, and Fairbairn

Moving beyond the Cocceius-Voetius debate, we should take brief note of other biblical-theological works that appeared in the post-Reformation period. While there are undoubtedly other noteworthy works, three deserve our specific attention. First, there is the work of John Owen (1616–83), published in 1661, *Theological Affirmations of All Sorts, or, Of the Nature, Rise, Progress, and Study, of True Theology*. At first glance the title might not

81. See Farrar, *History*, 385n1, 8; Willem van Asselt, "The Doctrine of the Abrogations in the Federal Theology of Johannes Cocceius (1603–69)," *CTJ* 29 (1994): 101–16; idem., *Federal Theology*, 81–94; Ernst Bizer, "Reformed Orthodoxy of Cartesianism," *Journal for Theology and Church* 2 (1965): 20–82.
82. Bizer, "Reformed Orthodoxy," 58–59.

seem all that significant, yet it is not until one burrows into the dense work to discover Owen's intention and structure:

> I decided, after a preliminary statement concerning the name and nature of theology, to record the advances made in various ways by divine revelation, paying particular attention to the historical order of events, splitting it into its important phases since the first appearance of true theology and, also, recording the defections of many from the truth and the errors resulting there from, the various corruptions in the worship of the church, judged by the standard set by revelation, the many falls of the ancient church, and its restorations by grace.[83]

It is quite easy to see how Owen's approach was not synthetic but rather analytical, historical, tracing the progressive unfolding of God's revelation throughout history. Now, while Owen does not directly characterize the progressive revelation of God as christocentric in this opening description, he does recognize that Christ is the substance of God's revelation. Concerning God's covenant promises to Abraham, Owen explains that "Christ began to 'look forth at the window, showing Himself through the lattice' (Song 2:9) . . . that is, He began to manifest himself more openly and sweetly to the faith, the longing, the love of His elect."[84] Hence, we see that Owen believed he was treating the historical progression of the unfolding of the revelation of God in Christ through the successive covenants God made with Abraham and his descendants. It should be no surprise, therefore, that the publishers of his translated work re-titled it, *Biblical Theology*.

A second work worthy of our attention is that of Jonathan Edwards (1703–58), *A History of the Work of Redemption* (1774). As one can see, the work was published well after Edwards's death. Nevertheless, one has the helpful words of the preface, written by Edwards's son, Jonathan Jr., where he explains:

> Mr. Edwards had planned a body of divinity, in a new method, and in the form of a history; in which he was first to show how the most remarkable

---

83. John Owen, *Biblical Theology or the Nature, Origin, Development, and Study of Theological Truth in Six Books*, trans. from Latin by Stephen P. Westcott (1661; Morgan, PA: Soli Deo Gloria, 1996), xlix.

84. Owen, *Biblical Theology*, 365–66.

> events in all ages from the Fall to the present times, recorded in sacred and profane history, were adapted to promote the work of redemption; and then to trace, by the light of Scripture prophecy, how the same work should be yet further carried on even to the end of the world.[85]

To be sure, we can see that Edwards's work extends beyond the OT and NT and into church history, a method that would likely draw disapproval in our own day. It is perhaps in this regard that Edwards believed his work was new or unique. Nevertheless, what is of particular interest to us is the way in which he expounds the unfolding revelation of God in Christ as he traces it through redemptive history. Edwards begins the work by interpreting the significance of Isaiah 51:8: "For the moth will eat them up like a garment, and the worm will eat them like wool; but my righteousness will be forever, and my salvation to all generations."

Edwards explains that ultimately God's righteousness and salvation relate to the covenant of grace: "For salvation is the sum of all those works of God by which the benefits that are by the covenant of grace are procured and bestowed."[86] Edwards also explains that the term *redemption* refers not only to the specific work of Christ, but also more broadly to everything that God has done to bring about Christ's work throughout redemptive history.[87] And, like other Reformed theologians before him, Edwards acknowledges that the revelation of God's redemption in Christ was progressive. Edwards recognizes the progressive nature of the revelation of redemption in the types that foreshadow Christ, such as the animal skins that God clothed Adam and Eve being a type of the righteousness of Christ that clothes the naked soul, or the translation of Enoch being a typical manifestation of the bodily resurrection of believers, or Joseph's descent into humiliation and ascent to exaltation being a type of the humiliation and exaltation of Christ. Edwards uses language evocative of progression when he writes that the redemption through Christ "began to dawn in the *types of it*."[88]

A third and final work worthy of mention is of course Patrick Fairbairn's (1805–74) *Typology of Scripture*. Fairbairn's work is an expansive two-volume

---

85. Jonathan Edwards, *A History of the Work of Redemption* (1774; Edinburgh: Banner of Truth, 2003), vii. The same work can be found in idem, *The Works of Jonathan Edwards*, ed. Edward Hickman (1834; Edinburgh: Banner of Truth, 1992), 1:532–619.

86. Edwards, *History*, 3; idem, *Works*, 1:533.

87. Edwards, *History*, 6–7; idem, *Works*, 1:534.

88. Edwards, *History*, 28–29, 30, 38, 68–69; idem, *Works*, 538, 540, 545.

study. As we have seen throughout our survey, typology is one of the critical elements of biblical theology because its use implicitly recognizes the organic unity of the Scriptures and spans redemptive history from creation to the consummation, from the proton to the eschaton. In the opening chapters of Fairbairn's work, where he sets forth the interpretive principles of typology, he illustrates its importance by drawing attention to the fact that in the NT "the eternal world comes constantly into view" but "nothing of this is to be found in the earlier portions of the word of God."[89] What explains the disparity? Fairbairn answers, "But let the typical element be duly taken into account—let it be understood that inferior and earthly things were systematically employed of old to image and represent those which are heavenly and divine."[90] We may state Fairbairn's point in contemporary nomenclature, namely typology, especially that which is antitypical, is eschatological. It is clear from Fairbairn's work that it was his intention not only to demonstrate the relevance of the whole of Scripture, especially the OT, but also to show how the OT speaks of the unfolding kingdom of Christ.[91] Once again, this is an inherently biblical-theological hermeneutic.

SUMMARY AND CONCLUSION

In the survey we have conducted stretching from the OT's own intra-canonical interpretation to the post-Reformation period in the nineteenth century which precedes Vos's own day, we have come full circle and have clearly seen a pattern that establishes the antiquity of biblical theology. Far from being a novelty or originating from the mind of Johann Gabler, biblical theology has been a part of the church's interpretive history from the very beginning when God revealed the shadows and types of his Son in the creation of man (cf. Rom. 5:14). To one degree or another, and admittedly it has waxed and waned through the centuries, the church has always sought to explain the unified and organic Scriptures as the inspired progressive revelation of God in Christ which has come to man through God's covenants. Given the antiquity of biblical theology, this leads us to some important observations.

89. Patrick Fairbairn, *The Typology of Scripture*, 2 vols. (1870; Grand Rapids: Zondervan, 1965), 173.
90. Ibid., 174.
91. Ibid., 177, 188.

First, for those who criticize biblical theology as a novelty, they seem to forget the scriptural maxim that there is nothing new under the sun (Eccl. 1:9).[92] While it is true that prior to Gabler's address, biblical theology did not exist as an independent discipline within the theological encyclopedia, nevertheless this is in no way a mitigating factor in terms of its essential and vital existence in the interpretive or theological process. Rather, it is simply a reflection of the development and specialization in the field of theology. There was a time when theologians studied the Scriptures, there were no OT, NT, biblical, or systematic theologians, neither were there textual critics, or theological ethicists. Yet as theologians began to distinguish and define the various categories that one finds in the teaching of theology, various sub-disciplines began to emerge. In this regard, Gabler no more created biblical theology as a discipline than Christopher Columbus created the Americas.

Moreover, there is a case to be made, especially concerning the antiquity of the discipline, that Gabler's own version has little if anything to do with biblical theology and more to do with Enlightenment rationalism.[93] In other words, Gabler's biblical theology is the bastard child of Enlightenment critical scholarship, not the legitimate offspring of historic exegetical theology. Therefore, Vos did not rescue biblical theology from the liberals but rather simply continued sharpening the post-apostolic biblical-theological interpretation of the Scriptures. It appears that Vos may have conceded too much ground by claiming that the discipline of biblical theology was born under a dark star; Vos mistakenly gave Gabler too much credit.

Moreover, it seems more accurate to say that Vos is not the father of Reformed biblical theology, but rather a contemporary contributor in a long line of those who have employed biblical theology. Or, one may say that Vos is the father of contemporary Reformed biblical theology.

Second, for those who see an inherent tension between biblical and systematic theology, it is helpful and instructive to see nearly two millennia of biblical theology standing side by side with dogmatic or systematic

92. Hart, "Tradition-Challenged," 2, 4; contra James Barr, *The Concept of Biblical Theology: An Old Testament Perspective* (Philadelphia: Fortress, 1999), 3; cf. Carson, "Current Issues in Biblical Theology," 19.
93. So Gaffin, "Biblical Theology," 34; Frei, *Eclipse*, 103; Dennison, "Biblical Theology," 12; cf. Reventlow, *Problems of Biblical Theology*, 7.

theology. Theologians such as Witsius or Owen saw no tension between biblical and dogmatic theology—the two ways of exploring the Scriptures are complementary.[94] Systematic and biblical theology are *synoptic*, at least defining the term etymologically. They are like stereo vision; apart from one another the Scriptures are two-dimensional, but together they appear three-dimensional. Without biblical theology, one might come to the conclusion that theology drawn from Scripture is an atemporal system of belief not necessarily rooted in space, time, or history.[95] Without systematic theology, on the other hand, one might come to the conclusion that the teaching of Scripture is not a unified and consistent organic body of doctrine.[96]

As Vos stated, whether one draws a line or a circle, systematic and biblical theology work together, their material cause the exegesis of Scripture. Or, as J. Gresham Machen (1881–1937) stated in the first convocation address at the newly founded Westminster Theological Seminary in 1929:

> It must not be thought that systematic theology is one whit less biblical than biblical theology is. But it differs from biblical theology in that, standing on the foundation of biblical theology, it seeks to set forth, no longer in the order of the time when it was revealed, but in the order of logical relationships, the grand sum of what God has told us in his Word. There are those who think that systematic theology on the basis of the Bible is impossible; there are those who think that the Bible contains a mere record of human seeking after God and that its teachings are a mass of contradiction which can never be resolved. But to the number of those persons we do not belong. We believe for our part that God has spoken to

---

94. Contra Wright, *New Testament*, 132; cf. Craig G. Bartholomew and Michael W. Goheen, "Story and Biblical Theology," in *Out of Egypt*, 158.

95. Gaffin, "Reformed Dogmatics," 29.

96. E.g. Peter Enns, *Inspiration and Incarnation: Evangelicals and the Problem of the Old Testament* (Grand Rapids: Baker, 2005), 71–112. It seems that Enns's view of the canon has more in common with a historical-critical understanding of biblical theology than that offered by historic Reformed biblical theology, especially as it is embodied in Vos's formulation of the discipline. Enns, for example, seems to state that the NT authors did not respect the original intent of the OT authors, which mitigates, if not outright materially denies, the divine inspiration and authorship of Scripture (cf., Enns, *Inspiration*, 113–66, esp. 115–16, 132–34, 136–38; G. K. Beale, "Positive Answer to the Question Did Jesus and His Followers Preach the Right Doctrine from the Wrong Texts," in *The Right Doctrine from the Wrong Text?: Essays on the Use of the Old Testament in the New*, ed. G. K. Beale [Grand Rapids: Baker, 1994], 387–404; idem, "Myth, History, and Inspiration: A Review Article of *Inspiration and Incarnation*," *JETS* 49/2 [2006]: 287–312).

us in his Word, and that he has given us not merely theology, but a system of theology, a great logically consistent body of truth.[97]

Machen's point is certainly evident, for example, in Irenaeus's doctrine—he wanted to demonstrate both its veracity and historicity. Hence, to borrow a famous illustration, while we may distinguish the rays of the sun from its heat, we cannot separate them. Likewise, we may distinguish biblical from systematic theology, but we must never separate them: the *ordo* and *historia salutis* are inseparably conjoined. Systematic theologians need not fear recognizing the biblical-theological, or redemptive-historical, character of their theology; neither, on the other hand, should biblical theologians fail to acknowledge the logical consistency, veraciousness, and divinely inspired character of their biblical theology.[98]

Third, and last, there are those who argue that biblical theology leads to liberalism or biblicism, as this has marked the discipline whether in the days of Cocceius, Gabler, or in our own contemporary setting vis-à-vis the new perspective on Paul. Aside from the fact that to make such a claim is to commit the genetic fallacy, perhaps the misguided nature of such a statement can be quelled by Carl Trueman's theological appeal to the National Rifle Association: "Doctrines don't kill people, people kill people."[99] Or, the abuse of biblical theology is no reason to abandon its use. Rather, as we observed from the pen of Childs, "The real question is not whether to do biblical theology or not, but rather what kind of biblical theology does one have."[100] If we discount biblical theology on the grounds that it has lead to liberalism, then we must also discount systematic theology because it has brought on far more heresies than her handmaid. Such a conclusion, however, is a self-referential absurdity.

97. J. Gresham Machen, "Westminster Theological Seminary: Its Purpose and Plan," in *J. Gresham Machen: Selected Shorter Writings*, ed. D. G. Hart (Phillipsburg, NJ: P&R, 2004), 191. For Vos's influence on the Orthodox Presbyterian Church, see Charles G. Dennison, *History for a Pilgrim People: The Historical Writings of Charles G. Dennison*, ed. Danny E. Olinger and David K. Thompson (Willow Grove, PA: Committee for the Historian of the OPC, 2002), 67–90.

98. Gaffin, "Reformed Dogmatics," 27. Cf. Walter Brueggemann, *Theology of the Old Testament: Testimony, Dispute, Advocacy* (Minneapolis: Fortress, 1997), 107.

99. I owe this reference to the NRA to Carl Trueman in his inaugural lecture, "Rage, Rage Against the Dying of the Light," as a full professor of historical theology and church history, Feb. 22, 2006, at Westminster Theological Seminary, Philadelphia, PA.

100. Childs, *Biblical Theology in Crisis*, 95.

In the light of the surveyed evidence, therefore, one may conclude that biblical theology is not of recent origins but is of the greatest antiquity. To ignore its proper use is to ignore the unfolding progressive revelation of God in Christ as he gathers a bride for his Son from every people, tribe, tongue, and nation. To ignore biblical theology is to chop off one's nose to spite one's face. Rather, all theologians, exegetes, and pastors must employ biblical theology in the interpretive process. To do so is to acknowledge the divinity and historicity of the Scriptures. Moreover, it helps the church see the relevance of the whole of the Bible in both its Testaments. In a day when ignorance or contemporary Marcionism abounds, a holistic view of Scripture is a much needed antidote to this cancer spread throughout the church. In the end, biblical theology is of great antiquity because the church, from its inception in the garden-temple of Eden on the heels of the rebellion and divine promise of the seed of the woman, has longed for the fulfillment of God's covenant promise, the revelation of God in Christ. Maranatha.

16

Jonathan Edwards's "Ambiguous and Somewhat Precarious" Doctrine of Justification?

JEFFREY C. WADDINGTON

RICHARD B. GAFFIN JR. has argued in several places for the integral connection between justification and union with Christ.[1] While this insight has been recognized by many as central to the Reformed tradition's understanding of redemption (it can be found in the writings of John Calvin, John

1. At several places in his corpus, Gaffin explains the nature of union with Christ and its relationship to justification. See his *Resurrection and Redemption: A Study in Paul's Soteriology* (Phillipsburg, NJ: Presbyterian & Reformed, 1987); "Biblical Theology and the Westminster Standards," *WTJ* 65, no. 2 (Fall 2003): 165–79, also found in modified form in *The Practical Calvinist: An Introduction to the Presbyterian & Reformed Heritage: In Honor of Dr. D. Clair Davis*, ed. P. A. Lillback (Fearn, Ross-shire: Christian Focus [Mentor], 2002), 425–41. More recently, see his "Union with Christ: Some Biblical and Theological Reflections," in *Always Reforming: Explorations in Systematic Theology*, ed. A. T. B. McGowen (Leicester: InterVarsity Press, 2006), 271–88; *By Faith, Not By Sight: Paul and the Order of Salvation* (Waynesboro, GA: Paternoster, 2006). Gaffin's insights have been furthered by both Lane G. Tipton, "Union with Christ and Justification," *Justified in Christ*, ed. K. Scott Oliphint (Fearn, Ross-shire: Christian Focus [Mentor], 2007), 23–49, and Mark Garcia, *Life in Christ: Union with Christ and Twofold Grace in Calvin's Theology*. Studies in Christian History and Thought (Milton Keynes, UK: Paternoster, 2003).

Owen, John Flavel, and James Ussher), some are unnecessarily confused by it.[2] Jonathan Edwards has been the subject of such misunderstanding himself. While one could beneficially examine several attempts to interpret Edwards on the relationship of justification and union with Christ, this chapter will focus on the work of one scholar in particular.

In 1951, the Edwardsian scholar Thomas A. Schafer penned an article in which he alleged that Jonathan Edwards had placed his doctrine of justification by faith in an "ambiguous and somewhat precarious position."[3] While Schafer recognized that Edwards had clearly affirmed his allegiance to the doctrine in two lectures delivered in 1734 and then published in revised form in 1738 as part of the *Discourses on Various Important Subjects*,[4] Schafer believes that Edwards failed to stress the doctrine as strongly later in his life, given its importance earlier in Edwards's career.

2. See, for instance, Tom Wenger's "The New Perspective on Calvin," *JETS* 50, no. 2 (June 2007): 311–28.

3. Thomas A. Schafer, "Jonathan Edwards and Justification by Faith," *Church History* 20 (December 1951): 55–67. Quotation is on page 57. Schafer is addressed in at least seven secondary sources. See Conrad Cherry, *The Theology of Jonathan Edwards: A Reappraisal* (Bloomington, IN: Indiana University Press, 1966 [1990]), 39–41; Anri Morimoto, *Jonathan Edwards and the Catholic Vision of Salvation* (University Park, PA: Pennsylvania State University Press, 1995); Morimoto's summary article "Salvation As Fulfillment of Being: The Soteriology of Jonathan Edwards and Its Implications for Missions," *PSB* 20, no. 1 (1999): 13–23; *The Works of Jonathan Edwards*, vol. 21, *Trinity, Grace, and Faith*, ed. Sang Hyun Lee (New Haven, CT: Yale University Press, 2003), 73, 101, and 104 (hereafter all references to volumes in the Yale edition of Edwards's works, following the first full citation, will be *WJE* followed by the volume number and pages). See also George Hunsinger, "Dispositional Soteriology: Jonathan Edwards on Justification," *WTJ* 66 (2004): 107–20, and the abbreviated form of the same in "An American Tragedy: Jonathan Edwards on Justification," *MR* 13/4 (July/August 2004): 18–21. The most recent treatment of Edwards and justification and its historical context is Michael McClenahan's excellent "Jonathan Edwards's Doctrine of Justification in the Period Up to the First Great Awakening," D Phil diss., Oxford University, 2006. Edwards addressed the issue of justification in his master's *Quaestio* at what is now Yale University, which can be found in Latin and English in *The Works of Jonathan Edwards*, vol. 14, *Sermons and Discourses, 1723–1729*, ed. Kenneth J. Minkema (New Haven, CT: Yale University Press, 1997), 55–64. See also the helpful introductory essay by George G. Levesque in the same volume on 47–53. Edwards ruminated on justification throughout his life in various "Miscellanies." A helpful listing of these can be found in the table of "Miscellanies" subjects in *The Works of Jonathan Edwards*, vol. 13, *The "Miscellanies" a–500*, ed. Thomas A. Schafer (New Haven, CT: Yale University Press, 1994), 139–40. My concluding unscientific count yields approximately 100 entries on justification in Edwards's private notebooks. For additional information about the historical context in which Edwards spoke, see George M. Marsden, *Jonathan Edwards: A Life* (New Haven, CT: Yale University Press, 2003), esp. 177–78.

4. These lectures were apparently aimed at a growing Arminianism in New England, and they were the human instrument that instigated the first series of revivals that Edwards would experience in his tenure as pastor of the congregational church in Northampton,

In view of the circumstances surrounding Edwards's discourse on justification and its prominence among his first publications, *the almost total
lack of emphasis on the doctrine in the great works of his last twenty years
needs some explanation.*[5]

Schafer admits that other concerns, such as defending doctrines that
actually *were* under attack in Edwards's day (such as original sin and freedom of the will), and the pressure of events (perhaps his deposition from
the Northampton pulpit) may account in some way for the perceived lack
of emphasis on justification in Edwards's later life, but he thinks there are
other things that provide further and perhaps more adequate explanation for
this phenomenon.[6] Schafer singles out three aspects of Edwards's theology,
especially related to the role of faith, that undermine or compromise the
doctrine of justification that Edwards ostensibly embraced.[7]

Massachusetts. The best version of this discourse can be found in the Yale edition of *The
Works of Jonathan Edwards:* vol. 19, *Sermons and Discourses, 1734–1738,* ed. M. X. Lesser
(New Haven, CT: Yale University Press, 2001), 147–242. Lesser offers a brief but helpful
introduction to the discourse on 143–45. See Ava Chamberlain's introductory comments on
the relationship of Edwards's discourse on justification to his "Miscellanies" in *The Works
of Jonathan Edwards,* vol. 18, *The "Miscellanies," 501–832* (New Haven, CT: Yale University
Press, 2001), 12–18 and 35–41. For a thorough discussion of the historical and theological
context surrounding the justification lectures, see McClenahan, *Justification in the Period.*

5. Schafer, "Edwards and Justification," 57. Emphasis added. One could ask two immediate questions of Schafer at this point: 1) Does Edwards, in fact, indicate an "almost total lack
of emphasis" on this doctrine in his later works? 2) Even if he does, does this evidence as such
demand *Schafer's* particular explanation? Our concern in this essay is with the second question.
Regarding the first question, John Gerstner tells us, "And yet there is no total loss of interest in
justification by faith in the sermons of the same period. In 1744 and 1757 Edwards preached
on Hos. 1:11, 'They that do truly believe in Christ do therein by their own act appoint Christ to
be their head.' In July 1750 there came the message on 1 John 5:1(1), 'Saving Faith Differs from
all Common Faith in its nature, kind, and essence.' From Gal. 5:6 (2) he preached, 'Tis a great
and distinguishing property of a saving faith that it worketh by love,' March 1751 and Jan 1752.
A sermon on 'Abraham's faith' (Romans 4:20), which justified him, was delivered in May 1753.
And there are many allusions to justification by faith in the body of late sermons. Finally, in
Original Sin, the doctrine of justification is very important to Edwards's exposition." Gerstner
quote is from *The Rational Biblical Theology of Jonathan Edwards* (Powhatan, VA, and Orlando:
Berea Publications & Ligonier Ministries, 1993), 3: 208n62. On the second question we should
keep the following question in mind as we look at this issue: does Edwards's concern with regen-
eration/sanctification/practice/disposition or transformational issues require that he *necessarily*
undermine the forensic nature of justification? We think that if the answer is yes, then the same
would have to be said for most Reformed theology on the matter.

6. Schafer, "Edwards and Justification," 57–58.

7. Ibid., 57. Schafer states that the concerns he explores will "cause the doctrine of justification to occupy an *ambiguous* and *somewhat precarious* place in his theology." Schafer, then, is

The three critical areas of compromise in Jonathan Edwards's formulation of justification, as divined by Thomas Schafer, are: 1) Edwards's grounding of the *legal* imputation of Christ's righteousness to the believer in the believer's *real* union with Christ; 2) Edwards's placement of sanctification *before* justification; and, 3) Edwards's use of the notion of *formed* faith, a notion rejected by the Protestant Reformers and more in line with Roman Catholic thinking.[8] As we examine these issues we will soon discover that they interrelate as though we were looking at a diamond through the various facets of the gem.

Questions & Thesis

Our questions are these: Does Schafer do justice to Edwards's doctrine of justification by faith within his own Reformed context as it relates to the three points mentioned above, and, Does he prove his case that Jonathan Edwards compromised his doctrine? The thesis in this essay is that Schafer has failed to make his case (despite its fruitfulness in contemporary Edwardsian studies) due to his apparent failure to understand or take into adequate consideration the Reformed context in which Edwards formulates his doctrine of justification and the specific nature of Edwards's formulations and the interrelations of his doctrines, specifically the relationship

---

not wanting to argue that Edwards knowingly repudiated the doctrine of justification, since he obviously maintained an interest in the doctrine throughout his life as evidenced in his personal notebooks (the so-called "Miscellanies") and in his preaching, but that he compromised the doctrine by embracing other views inconsistent, at least to Schafer, with a proper Protestant understanding of the doctrine of justification.

8. Schafer, "Edwards and Justification," 58–61. Interestingly enough, more recent scholarship has picked up on the observations of Schafer. Two inferences have been drawn from Edwards's supposedly compromised doctrine of justification: 1) Edwards's theology is more amenable to Roman Catholic theology in his doctrinal formulations than even he would have appreciated and, 2) While he would not have embraced the notion, his theology allows for the salvation of those outside the reach of Christianity or those without explicit faith in Christ. With regard to the first inference, see Jon O'Brien, *The Architecture of Conversion: Faith and Grace in the Theology of Jonathan Edwards* (Rome: Pontifical Gregorian University, 1967), and more recently, Morimoto's *Catholic Vision of Salvation*. With regard to the second inference, Gerald McDermott has stated that Edwards affirmed justification by faith "primarily." See his *Jonathan Edwards Confronts the Gods: Christian Theology, Enlightenment Religion and Non-Christian Faiths* (Oxford: Oxford University Press, 2000), 136. For a helpful counter-response to these two inferences in contemporary Edwardsian scholarship, see John Bombaro's "Beautiful Beings: The Function of the Reprobate in the Philosophical Theology of Jonathan Edwards," PhD diss., University of London, 2002, and his article "Dispositional Peculiarity, History and Edwards's Evangelistic Appeal to Self-Love," *WTJ* 66 (2004): 121–57.

between the forensic (justification) and the transformational (regenera-tion/sanctification).[9] While we readily grant that Edwards was a creative and unique theologian/pastor/philosopher, that his doctrinal formula-tions are often subtle and complex, and that his language is perhaps more fluid than what is found in other representatives of Reformed theology, we will find that he stands well within Protestant and specifically Reformed orthodox treatments of the subject. In fact, we believe, for the most part, that he brought particularly clear insight and depth to his discussion of the doctrine of justification and did not, in fact, compromise the doctrine or put it in a tenuous position.[10]

9. This is, of course, not to impune the scholarship of Schafer on the whole. Edwardsian scholars owe a huge debt of gratitude to Schafer, who is one of the editors of the Yale edition of Edwards's works, especially for his work on transcribing the Miscellanies.

10. This is not to say that we agree with every detail of Edwards's discussion of the doctrine, but that he falls within the bounds of Reformed or Calvinistic orthodoxy. Michael Horton, in his recent volume, *Covenant and Salvation: Union with Christ* (Louisville, KY: Westminster John Knox Press, 2007), 288–89, suggests that Charles Hodge criticized Edwards for "tinkering" with justification. However, he fails to reference Hodge on Edwards and justification. Hodge, in *Systematic Theology* (Grand Rapids: Eerdmans, 1971), 3:116–18 and 148, notes that Edwards has sometimes taken positions that have led to problems within the Reformed tradition. But with justification, Edwards is sound. Having said that, Edwards's formulations are sometimes overly subtle and speculative (his discussion of faith as an instrument, for instance). While we disagree with the way Chamberlain frames the discussion about Edwards's two models of "conversion," her discussion raises some interesting questions. Our problem with Chamberlain's remarks stems from her apparent desire to pit Edwards's forensic doctrine of justification against his con-cerns about transformation. Chamberlain says that Edwards employed "two different theological models to describe the transformation that occurs in the sinner at the conversion moment" (*WJE*, 18:37). According to the historic Reformed perspective, this is the wrong way to frame the issue. The forensic and transformational are not competing models for understanding conver-sion. In fact, justification is not about transformation or conversion *at all*. Justification, with its concern with imputation, addresses the question of how a sinner can stand before a righteous and holy God and be found acceptable by him. Sanctification has to do with the real change or transformation that occurs in the sinner's life. The one is concerned with a sinner's *standing* and the other with his *character*. One deals with the guilt of sin and the other with its power or pollu-tion. Justification and transformation are complementary, neither in opposition nor confusion. Clearly Edwards's concern is heavily weighted on the side of the transformational, but this does not negate his real and legitimate concern for the forensic. Justification involves the imputation of both Christ's negative righteousness, or pardon of sin, and his positive righteousness, the obedience of Christ that is credited to the account of the believer—and so the believer can be found acceptable in the sight of God as the believer is seen *in Christ*. Regeneration and sanc-tification provide real change in the character and life of an individual. Justification is always complete and perfect and satisfies the demands of a holy God. Sanctification, while real, is not perfect in the believer this side of the new heaven and the new earth. Justification is *not* about transformation. It always accompanies transformation but cannot be either *reduced to* or *con-flated with* transformation. See Lee, *WJE*, 21:72. Regarding Edwards's Calvinistic theology (and

Our method of enquiry will be to examine each of the three evidences of possible compromise and evaluate Schafer's reading in light of our own understanding of Edwards's formulation of the doctrine of justification, and then offer our alternative assessment of each area involving the grounding of imputation in union, the placing of sanctification before justification, and the acceptance of the notion of formed faith.

THOMAS SCHAFER ON JONATHAN EDWARDS'S DOCTRINE OF JUSTIFICATION

Preliminary Thoughts

Of the three evidences of compromise offered by Schafer, only the first and third can really be said to stem from Edwards's discourse on justification as such. Schafer primarily seeks to show compromise on the doctrine from material outside the discourse, or by the ostensible absence of appropriate emphasis. Ironically, Schafer offers what is probably the best summation of Edwards's discourse on justification:

> The "doctrine" of Edwards's discourse is unequivocal enough; "We are justified only by faith in Christ, and not by any manner of virtue or goodness of our own." The justified man is "approved of God as free from the guilt of sin and its deserved punishment, and as having that righteousness belonging to him that entitles to the reward of life." Justification is not merely the remission of sins, but a status of positive righteousness in God's sight. Christ's satisfaction of God's justice and righteousness of

---

his fluid use of language or theological terminology), he was happy to be called a Calvinist, but did not see himself as a slavish follower of Calvin. See his remarks on the subject in his *Freedom of the Will*, which is volume 1 of *The Works of Jonathan Edwards*, ed. Paul Ramsey (New Haven, CT: Yale University Press, 1957), 12 and 131, where Edwards states, " . . . yet I shall not take it at all amiss, to be called a Calvinist, for distinction's sake: though I utterly disclaim a dependence on Calvin, or believe the doctrines which I hold, because he believed them; and cannot justly be charged with believing everything just as he taught." We do not want to deny that Edwards had his own distinct emphases. For various assessments of his uniqueness *within* the Reformed orthodox tradition, see B. B. Warfield's fine article "Jonathan Edwards and the New England Theology" in *The Works of B. B. Warfield: Biblical and Theological Studies*, ed. Ethelbert Warfield (Grand Rapids: Baker Book House, 2000), 9:515–30; John Murray, *The Imputation of Adam's Sin* (Phillipsburg, NJ: Presbyterian & Reformed Publishers, 1957); and Gerstner, *Rational Biblical Theology*, 3:191–97. Even Alister McGrath, in his *Iustitia Dei*, Second Edition (Cambridge: Cambridge University Press, 1998), 306–7, puts Edwards well within the confines of Reformed orthodoxy on the very of issue of justification.

his active obedience constitute the only meritorious cause of justification; and these become the believers' only by imputation. Since every sin is infinitely heinous in God's sight, God in justifying does not consider any goodness, value or merit whatsoever in the sinner. Faith alone is the means or instrument of justification, because it is the act by which the soul receives and is united to Christ and which therefore makes possible the imputation of Christ's righteousness to the believer. All works are therefore destitute of merit, even those which flow from faith; it is only the element of faith in them that God accepts for justification. Hence, the believer is unconditionally and eternally justified upon his first act of faith. A saving faith is one which, by definition, perseveres; and all future acts of repentance and faith are *virtually* contained in the first act and are so regarded by God. There is no real conflict between Paul and James: Paul speaks of justification before God, which is by faith alone; whereas James deals with justification before men, which is by works as the *evidence* of faith.[11]

Our concern is not with a detailed exposition of Edwards's discourse on justification as such, but this faithful summation is included here to serve as an indication of Edwards's thought on the doctrine as a whole.

The Legal Grounded in the Real

The first piece of evidence that Schafer puts forward in his desire to demonstrate Edwards's compromise is that Edwards grounds the *legal* imputation of Christ's righteousness to the believer in the believer's *real* union with Christ by faith. "It is actual union with Christ which renders the soul acceptable to God and is the 'ground' of justification."[12] Edwards specifically tells us that "what is *real* in the union between Christ and his people, is the foundation of what is legal; that is, it is something really in them, and between them, uniting them, that is the ground of the suitableness of their being accounted as one by the Judge."[13]

11. Schafer, "Edwards and Justification." 58.
12. Ibid. George Hunsinger, in "Dispositional Soteriology," says that for Edwards, the believer's union with Christ is "merely legal" in contrast with the personal and communal form of union in the theology of Calvin, and so Edwards must posit a primary and secondary ground of justification. The primary ground is the imputation of the active obedience of Christ to the believer and the secondary ground is the virtue of faith. Unfortunately, we do not have space to interact with Dr. Hunsinger's article. Suffice it to say that we come to vastly different conclusions.
13. Edwards, "Justification by Faith," *WJE*, 19:158.

Schafer is apparently uncomfortable with the grounding of the legal in the real, as though this somehow compromises the forensic or gracious nature of justification.[14] "What then of the 'legal union' of the soul with Christ which is concerned in the imputation of Christ's righteousness?"[15] For Schafer, it appears as though the real union vitiates the external nature of imputation. "But the natural creates the legal, not vice versa; something *really existing in the soul precedes the external imputation.* . . . Justification from this point of view, is but the restatement in forensic terms of a fait accompli, for faith is the union, and the union effects the justification."[16]

What could be Schafer's problem with Edwards's fairly standard Reformed construal of justification as being grounded in union with Christ?[17] Has Schafer construed the union of the believer with Christ as vitiating the *external* nature of imputation? Does the very idea of an imputation of an external or alien (i.e., Christ's) righteousness require that the believer be "outside" or separated from Christ? Does the union of the believer with Christ, which for Edwards serves as the grounding of the imputation of Christ's righteousness, imply some kind of *innate* or *intrinsic* (i.e., "natural") holiness, virtue or other state or quality of the soul? The fact is, for Jonathan Edwards, the union of the believer with Christ does not produce a commingling of Christ and the believer (*a tertium quid*) so that the Christian then becomes divinized or, as he put it, the believer is *not* "godded."[18] Rather, the Holy Spirit (i.e., the Spirit of Christ) is directly active in the soul of a believer but not merged with him. While the believer is united to Christ, the righteousness that is accepted *on behalf of* the believer is really Christ's. Therefore, the imputation still involves an external righteousness as such.

Perhaps Schafer wants to offer a general criticism of the Reformed perspective while using Edwards as an example of that position? That is,

---

14. Schafer may be exhibiting the same problem as Ava Chamberlain here. That is, perhaps he assumes that concern with transformation negates or compromises a concern with forensics. We don't see this as a necessary conclusion. See *WJE*, 18:37. Another possibility is that Schafer (and others) have misunderstood Edwards at this point. That is, has Schafer equated the "real" with the transformational or renovative aspect (sanctification) of union? For Edwards, the "real" simply *is* the relation or union between the believer and Christ. See *WJE*, 19:155–56.

15. Schafer, "Edwards and Justification," 58.

16. Ibid.

17. See Bombaro, *Beautiful Beings*, n.p.

18. Jonathan Edwards, *The Works of Jonathan Edwards,* vol. 2, *Religious Affections,* ed. John E. Smith (New Haven, CT: Yale University Press, 1959), 203.

some see this Reformed emphasis on union with Christ as the "central soteric blessing"[19] as detrimental to the centrality of the doctrine of justification by faith. In his *Institutes of the Christian Religion*, John Calvin argues that "our whole salvation and all its parts are comprehended in Christ."[20] Stressing the need for union between the believer and Christ, Calvin says "as long as Christ remains outside us, and we are separated from him, all that he has suffered and done for the salvation of the human race remains useless and of no value for us."[21] What may be disturbing to some concerning Calvin's doctrine of *unio cum Christi* is that he holds to a *duplex gratia dei* in which justification and sanctification are concurrent blessings received, along with adoption, and so forth, all at once.[22] This could be seen to jeopardize the forensic and declarative nature of justification, but it need not necessarily do so. To receive all the blessings at once is not to merge or blur them. Justification and sanctification are to be distinguished but never separated.[23]

19. I owe this expression to Lane Tipton, associate professor of systematic theology at Westminster Theological Seminary in Philadelphia.

20. John Calvin, *Institutes of the Christian Religion*, ed. John T. McNeill, trans. Ford Lewis Battles (Louisville: Westminster John Knox, 1960), 2.16.19.

21. Calvin, *Institutes*, 3.1.1. I do not want to be understood as suggesting that there are no differences between Calvin and Edwards as to union with Christ.

22. Lutherans have historically made this criticism. In Theodore Mueller's *Christian Dogmatics* (St. Louis: Concordia Publishing House, 1934), 320, justification is *outside* of and *leads into* the union of the believer with Christ. "Justification effects the *mystical union (unio mystica).*" Schafer strikes us as exhibiting what we would consider Lutheran tendencies in this regard, although this is not made explicit. Another possibility is that Schafer has accepted the thesis of Albert Schweitzer in his *The Mysticism of Paul the Apostle*, trans. William Montgomery (Baltimore: Johns Hopkins University Press, 1998) that justification for Paul is a "subsidiary crater" and an ad hoc argument which the apostle used against his Judaizing opponents. For Schweitzer, the center of Paul's soteriology is a *participationist* form of union with Christ shorn of any forensic elements, thus making it purely transformative and so concerned with sanctification alone. As we will see, Edwards echoes the *duplex gratia dei* model of union with Christ formulated by Calvin. For a fuller treatment of this subject, see Kevin Woongsan Kim's "Justification By Faith: Jonathan Edwards's Doctrine of Justification in Light of Union with Christ," PhD diss., Westminster Theological Seminary, 2003.

23. Schafer, "Edwards and Justification," 59. This also tends to ignore just the issue we will look at next, namely the relationship between the *historia salutis* and the *ordo salutis*; that is, the foundation of all the blessings of union pertains to the ontological (or "predestinarian") union, whereas the experience of those same blessings in time relates to the temporal (or the "historical" or "federal" *and* "present faith") union. I owe a debt of gratitude to Richard B. Gaffin Jr., *Resurrection and Redemption: A Study of Paul's Soteriology* (Phillipsburg, NJ: Presbyterian & Reformed Publishers, 1981), for the terminology used here. I do not want to suggest that Gaffin agrees with Edwards at every point. See n29 below.

Regarding Jonathan Edwards in particular, his doctrine of justification must be understood within his overall theology and, as John Bombaro reminds us, must be seen in the context of inner-Trinitarian relations. It must be seen especially in terms of the purchase of the Holy Spirit in the *eternal* sphere within the *pactum salutis* as well as in the temporal accomplishment of redemption in the life and death of Jesus Christ and the application of redemption.[24] In other words, the

> ontological basis for forensic imputation, i.e., the transaction of Christ's faith and righteousness to the believer, fundamentally concerns the Spirit in an eternal arrangement. Indeed, in Edwards's soteriology, if the topic is faith, love or consent, *especially mutual consent*, then these ideas must be understood in terms of the Spirit; and the forensic arrangement for justification must be understood against the background of its eternal context, namely, the eternal "confederation," the *pactum salutis*.[25]

The *real* union of the believer in Christ involves the work of the Holy Spirit, which can be traced back to the eternal inner-trinitarian pact.[26] In other words, the "real" union that Edwards says grounds the legal imputation *is* the Holy Spirit bringing to bear on the individual believer the results of the eternal *pactum salutis* and the *historia salutis* involving the life and death of Christ, not some innate or intrinsic quality or state of the human soul.[27] The *real* or ontological union of the believer

24. Bombaro, "Beautiful Beings," n.p.

25. Ibid. For a very informative discussion of the role of the Holy Spirit with regard to the forensic nature of justification, see Geerhardus Vos, "The Eschatological Aspect of the Pauline Conception of the Spirit," in *Redemptive History and Biblical Interpretation*, ed. Richard B. Gaffin Jr. (Phillipsburg, NJ: P&R, 2001), 91–125.

26. Jonathan Edwards, *The Works of Jonathan Edwards*, vol. 9, *A History of the Work of Redemption* (New Haven, CT: Yale University Press, 1989), 119.

27. This relates to Edwards's understanding of the work of the Holy Sprit in the life of the believer. For Edwards, the disposition of love or faith *is* either the Holy Spirit or some mediating entity such as created grace (i.e., a disposition or habit); see *WJE*, 21:71–77. See also Lee, *Philosophical Theology*, 231, for the view that the new sense simply is the Holy Spirit. For an alternative reading that aims to read Edwards as upholding the creaturely integrity of a distinct human nature so that the new disposition is in fact a "created" grace and not the Holy Spirit himself, see McClenahan, *Justification in the Period*, 294. Unfortunately we do not have the space here to settle this dispute. Edwards's language is vague enough to allow for either reading. In either case, there is still a distinction between the Holy Spirit himself and the believer who is acted upon. See Edwards, "The Mind" 1 and 45, *The Works of Jonathan Edwards*, vol. 6, *Scientific and Philosophical Writings*, ed. Wallace Anderson (New Haven, CT: Yale University Press, 1980), 336–38 and 362–66.

with Christ, for Edwards, has been ordained in eternity and has been accomplished in redemptive history, and involves the purchase of the Holy Spirit by Christ for his people. The Holy Spirit in turn *is* the exercise of faith and love in the life of the believer. So imputation is ordained in eternity and is accomplished by Christ and applied in temporal history. But the ontological (or predestinarian) union must be distinguished from the temporal (historical-federal and present faith) union which is brought about through the work of Christ and the ministrations of the Holy Spirit. For Edwards, the believer is justified because Christ himself has been justified (or, as some translations have it, "vindicated") in his resurrection out from among the dead.[28] In the light of the foregoing, the legal union (i.e., imputation) is ordained in the eternal ontological union of Christ with his people that occurs in the *pactum salutis* and is accomplished in the redemption of the *historia salutis*, not in the temporal (or present faith) union that occurs in regeneration. That is, for Edwards, justification is not based on something innate or intrinsic in the soul. It is admittedly a real union, something that resides in the human soul, but it is the Holy Spirit, who is the vinculum between the eternal and the temporal unions.

Whether Schafer criticizes Edwards's doctrine of justification because union grounds forensics or because Schafer is critical of the general Reformed emphasis on union with Christ, we believe Edwards

---

For differing views about Edwards's acceptance or rejection of substance ontology, see Sang Hyun Lee, *The Philosophical Theology of Jonathan Edwards* (Princeton: Princeton University Press, 2001 Expanded Edition), 47–51, and portions of John Bombaro's "Beautiful Beings." Lee argues for a dispositional ontology and Bombaro differs only with applying that ontology to God and man. God and man are substantial ideas for Edwards according to Bombaro, although he agrees with Lee in his understanding of Edwards as far as the rest of creation is concerned. For a more critical reading of Lee's interpretation on this, see Stephen R. Holmes, "Does Jonathan Edwards Use a Dispositional Ontology: A Response to Sang Hyun Lee," *Philosophical Theologian*, 99–114.

28. Edwards, "Justification," *WJE*, 19:151, "But God when he justified him in raising him from the dead, did not only release him from his humiliation for sin, and acquit him from any further suffering or abasement for it, but admitted him to that eternal and immortal life, and to the beginning of that exaltation, that was the reward of what he had done. And indeed the justification of the believer is no other than his being admitted to the communion, or participation of the justification of this head and surety of all believers; for as Christ suffered the punishment of sin, not as a private person, but as our surety, so when after his suffering he was raised from the dead, he was therein justified, not as a private person, but the surety and representative of all who should believe in him; so that he was raised again not merely for his own, but also for our justification, according to the Apostle." Gaffin picks up on this theme in Edwards and notes it in his *Resurrection and Redemption*, 123n147 and 132n159.

has not, at least on this point, compromised his doctrine of justification by faith. In fact, with John Gerstner, we would argue that his especially clear emphasis on union with Christ only enhances his treatment of justification and gives it a rather solid foundation.[29]

Sanctification Precedes Justification

Thomas Schafer's second piece of evidence for Jonathan Edwards's compromised doctrine of justification is his perceived placement of sanctification before justification.[30] Typically in Reformed theology there have been two views of this relation. Sanctification has been seen either as a progressive work in the life of the Christian subsequent to effectual calling, regeneration, faith and repentance, and justification, or as a concurrent blessing received with justification in union with Christ.[31] Schafer

29. Gerstner, *Rational Biblical Theology*, 3:211–13.
30. Schafer, "Edwards and Justification," 59.
31. For a more contemporary standard treatment of this from within conservative Reformed theology, see John Murray's *Redemption Accomplished and Applied* (Grand Rapids: Eerdmans, 1955). Strictly speaking, there have been at least two major views on the relationship of justification and sanctification. The first is the view of John Calvin, which we have discussed already, that justification and regeneration/sanctification are *concurrent* blessings obtained in union with Christ. The second view, enunciated at the Synod of Dordt and exemplified in Francis Turretin, is that in the *ordo salutis*, regeneration precedes justification and is followed by sanctification. Interestingly, a tension may exist in Murray's book between the *ordo salutis* model of the application of redemption and his enthusiastic affirmation of the centrality of union with Christ, which ought not to be understood as a phase of the application of redemption coordinate with the others. Murray says, "There is, however, a good reason why the subject of union of Christ should not be coordinated with the other phases of the application of redemption with which we have dealt. That reason is that union with Christ is in itself a very broad and embracive subject. It is not simply a step in the application of redemption; when viewed according to the teaching of Scripture, in its broader aspects it underlies every step of the application of redemption. Union with Christ is really the central truth of the whole doctrine of salvation not only in its application but also in its once-for-all accomplishment in the finished work of Christ. Indeed the whole process of salvation has its origin in one phase of union with Christ and salvation has in view the realization of other phases of union with Christ" (*Redemption Accomplished*, 161). Does Murray, with his emphasis on both the *ordo salutis* and union with Christ exhibit necessary tension? Yes, if the benefits of redemption accruing from union with Christ stem from his resurrection. Redemption is, then, a single event with many facets (for instance, justification, adoption, sanctification, and glorification) rather than a logical-causal order or series of discrete events. For further discussion of this issue see Gaffin's *Resurrection and Redemption* as well as "Biblical Theology and the Westminster Standards." It should probably be noted that Calvin, Edwards, and Gaffin are *not* identical in their theological nuances. Calvin and Edwards appear to understand union as foundational to justification and sanctification, whereas Gaffin stresses the *concurrent* or *simultaneous* nature of union, justification, and sanctification arising from the single event of Christ's resurrection. Even here,

sees Edwards departing from Reformed orthodoxy at this point.[32] Conrad Cherry captures the central thrust of Schafer's criticism:

> The upshot of the argument appears to be an abandonment of the traditional Calvinist position that sanctification is a progressive struggle for holiness that *grows out of* faith, and the adoption of a view repugnant to the thrust of Reformation Protestantism, the view that faith is based upon man's becoming sanctified or holy-in-himself.[33]

What do we make of this contention that justification is made to rest upon sanctification (i.e., it rests upon some virtue or innate state or quality of the human soul possessed by the believer)? Is it a fair reading of Edwards? He does appear to add fuel to Schafer's criticism in a remark, cited by Schafer, made in one of his "Miscellanies," to the effect that "there must be the principle before there can be the action, in all cases. . . . Yea, there must be the principle of holiness before there can be the action, in all cases."[34] This principle of holiness would then be the basis for the first act of faith that ends in union with Christ that results in justification. This would then seem to make the exercise of faith by the believer rest upon some virtue in the soul.

As mentioned, Edwards self-consciously stood within the Reformed tradition in which regeneration either *preceded* faith and repentance (and therefore justification) in the logical-causal *ordo salutis* or was a concurrent blessing with justification obtained in union with Christ.[35] Regeneration

---

though, Edwards recognizes that the resurrection was Christ's own justification (per 1 Tim. 3:16) and, by virtue of the believer's union with Christ, the believer is also justified (see *WJE*, 19:150–51). While we see commonalities between Calvin, Edwards, and Gaffin, we must not flatten out their distinctives. In other words, we must recognize *both* their commonalities *and* their differences. They share a *central soteric structure*. There is, in their stress on union with Christ, a strong family resemblance. We must recognize continuity, development, and difference.

32. We should make it clear that Schafer, as far as we can tell, is not intending to defend or affirm Reformed orthodoxy in his criticisms of Edwards, but merely to pinpoint areas of Edwards's deviation from his own professed tradition.

33. Conrad Cherry, *The Theology of Jonathan Edwards: A Reappraisal* (Bloomington, IN: Indiana University Press, 1990), 41.

34. Edwards, "Miscellanies no. 77," *The Works of Jonathan Edwards,* vol. 13, *The "Miscellanies" a–500,* ed. Thomas A. Schafer (New Haven, CT: Yale University Press, 1994), 244–45.

35. But as mentioned above, the eternal *pactum* and *historia salutis* precede the present application. See Calvin's remark that "Christ cannot be known apart from the sanctification of the Spirit. It follows that faith can in no wise be separated from a divine disposition" (*Institutes,* 1:552–53 [3.2.8]). As already indicated, even though Edwards can be understood within either model of the *ordo,* he is best understood as standing closer to Calvin than to Dordt.

can be seen as a form of sanctification, perhaps as initial sanctification or as sanctification begun.[36] Looking at a larger segment of Edwards's Miscellanies 77 may help us in ascertaining Edwards's point in the last quotation:

> What is held by some, that none can be in a state of salvation before they have particularly acted a reception of the Lord Jesus Christ for a savior, and there cannot be sanctification one moment before the exercise of faith, as they have described it, cannot be true as they explain this reception of Christ. There must be the principle before there can be the action in all cases. There must be the alteration made in the heart before there can be action consequent upon this alteration. Yea, there must be a principle of holiness before holiness is in exercise. Yea an alteration must not only be before this act of faith in nature as the cause before the effect, but also in time, if this embracing Christ as a savior be a successive action, that is, an action when one thought and act of the mind in anywise follows another, as it certainly is. For first there must be an idea of Jesus Christ in the mind, that is an agreeable and truly lovely idea of him. But this cannot be before the soul is sanctified.[37]

It seems clear here that Edwards is talking about regeneration, even though he uses the words "holiness" and "sanctification." As Conrad Cherry says,

> It is perhaps best to call this action of the Holy Spirit which is the foundation of faith a *kind* of sanctification. Traditionally Reformed theologians held to "progressive" sanctification: it was the activity of God's Spirit in man's inward parts whereby regeneration, initiated by vocation, was continued and gradually completed as man struggled in the race of life and as the Spirit more and more cleansed man of his sin. Sometimes the

---

36. The terminology here is fluid. In the Reformed tradition, sanctification can be taken to embrace growth in grace subsequent to conversion and justification and as a synonym for "regeneration." "Regeneration" can also be used in a broad and narrow sense, similar to "sanctification." Broadly understood, regeneration can refer to the whole renovative process in the Christian life (i.e., akin to sanctification broadly conceived) or to the work of the Holy Spirit at the inception of the Christian life. See Peter Van Maastricht's "Regeneration," the only section of his *Theoretico-Practica Theologica* that has been translated from Latin into English (New Haven, CT: Thomas & Samuel Green, 1770), 16–17. This translation has been reprinted recently with an introduction and editing by Brandon Withrow as *A Treatise on Regeneration* (Morgan, PA: Soli Deo Gloria, 2002).

37. Edwards, "Miscellanies no. 77," *WJE*, 13:244–45. Original sin is a disposition, for instance, prior to any sinful acts. Edwards's argument against libertarian freedom in *Freedom of the Will* depends on this same line of reasoning, that acts depend on prior dispositions.

term "regeneration" was virtually identical with "sanctification" embracing the whole work of the Spirit in man. At other times "regeneration" designated the new birth of man in conversion which does not admit of degrees, while "sanctification" referred to the progressive cleansing by the Holy Spirit. Although Edwards applied "sanctification" to the gift of the principle which awakens the act of faith, and although he is not careful at all times to distinguish sanctification from regeneration and calling, he by no means fell away from his Reformed tradition in meaning.[38]

In the Reformed tradition, regeneration either *precedes* faith and justification or, at the very least, it is a concurrent blessing.[39] It is not possible for someone to exercise faith (an act of the soul) without the proper disposition, and this disposition we call regeneration. It is this regeneration (or for Edwards, sanctification or principle of holiness) that causes the believer to see the idea of Jesus Christ as "agreeable and truly lovely."[40]

Additionally, this disposition is not, as Schafer seems to think, an "inherent state" or quality of the soul.[41] Regeneration is either the direct, unmediated act of the Holy Spirit in the human soul, or the infusion of a new disposition resulting from that special work of grace (i.e., it is mediated).[42] Unless Schafer wants to affirm that Edwards held to some form of *theosis* or divinization, how could he think that Edwards was talking about innate or intrinsic states when he was talking about regeneration?[43]

As with the issue of the grounding of the legal imputation of Christ's righteousness to the believer involved in justification in union with Christ, Edwards has been found not to compromise his doctrine of justification by faith by putting sanctification as such before justification. Despite his admitted peculiarities, Edwards stands within the pale of Reformed orthodoxy. He

---

38. Cherry, *Theology of Edwards*, 42–43.

39. See n36 above about the broad and narrow uses of terms such as regeneration and sanctification.

40. Edwards, "Miscellanies no. 77," *WJE*, 13:244–45.

41. Schafer, "Edwards and Justification," 59. See Lee, *WJE*, 21:73. The Holy Spirit acts in the "manner" of a disposition. See Lee, *Philosophical Theology*, 231. See again the comments in n27.

42. Edwards, *Treatise on Grace and Other Posthumous Writings*, ed. Paul Helm (London: James Clarke, 1971), 51. See also Lee, *WJE*, 21:73, and *Philosophical Theology*, 231; also n27 above.

43. Bombaro, "Beautiful Beings," n.p. Remember, Edwards affirms the distinctiveness of the individual believer and the Holy Spirit. The believer is not "godded." However, Michael Horton, in his *Covenant and Salvation*, 288–89, following the lead of Michael McClymond, suggests (incorrectly, we might add) that Edwards can be read as affirming divinization or deification.

has not placed justification in a tenuous position by making it contingent on *innate* or *intrinsic* states or qualities in the soul.[44]

Formed Faith

The third piece of evidence of Jonathan Edwards's compromise of his doctrine of justification by faith is his apparent acceptance of the (traditionally Roman Catholic) notion of formed faith. As Schafer tells us, "According to the Catholic theologians, it is love which makes faith saving and meritorious, changing it from mere 'informal' assent to 'formal' and living faith."[45] Schafer rightly notes that love (or consent or affiance) is a central concern for Edwards.

> Here is the center of Edwards's piety: a direct intuitive apprehension, a "sight," a "sense," a "taste," of God's majestic beauty, a love of God simply because he is God, an exultant affirmation of all God's ways. *This, to Edwards, is the meaning of faith.* Upon this experience Edwards builds his doctrine of the "divine and supernatural light," which confers and is—this new sight and taste of the essential loveliness of God and divine things. Spiritual light does not reveal new articles of faith; it suffuses the familiar gospel with a glow that irresistibly draws the soul. True faith is its essence and fruit.[46]

Schafer here is reminding us about Edwards's central doctrine of the "sense of the heart" in which he distinguishes between two types of knowledge or understanding, *notional* or *speculative* knowledge and *spiritual* knowledge. All people, regenerate or unregenerate, possess notional or speculative knowledge but only the regenerate possess spiritual knowledge. According to Edwards, a man might be an exceptional theologian, understanding the intricacies of subtle philosophical distinction, and yet not be regenerate. He possesses speculative knowledge only. On the other hand, the regenerate believer possesses spiritual knowledge because he or she "has" a relish for God and divine things. You could have speculative knowledge without spiritual understanding, but you could not have spiritual understanding without

---

44. Again, we can recognize that Edwards's central concern was with the transformational aspects of salvation without negating his commitment to forensic justification.

45. Schafer, "Edwards and Justification," 59.

46. Ibid., 61. Emphasis added.

speculative knowledge. But what is the essence of this spiritual understanding or sense of the heart? Schafer offers this description:

> Speculative knowledge, including "historical" faith (the practical equivalent of the Catholic "informed" faith), belongs to the understanding alone; whenever the mind perceives in its object that which touches the self or its concerns, the will goes out of equilibrium and "consents" to or "dissents" from that object. The "consent" or "affiance" of the soul to Christ in faith is therefore an act of love—"love is the main thing in saving *faith*; the life and power of it."[47]

The difference between notional or speculative understanding and spiritual understanding, then, is the presence of love, which for Schafer means that Edwards may be (however unwittingly) affirming the Roman Catholic doctrine of formed faith, which would compromise the Protestant understanding of true faith having its own integrity. But is Schafer correct here? Does Edwards for all practical purposes embrace the doctrine of formed faith or has Schafer elided some significant differences, despite the apparent similarities? Schafer inquires:

> But one may fairly ask whether Edwards has retained a unique act of the soul called faith which becomes the condition of justification separately from all other acts of the soul. The Reformers, and their disciples after them, had felt it necessary to deny that the essence of justifying faith includes the idea of obedience or love since these are acts or at least "habits" in the soul, whereas justification respects no such possessions of the believer. According to the Catholic theologians, it is love which makes faith saving and meritorious, changing it from mere "informed" assent to "formal" and living faith.[48]

Love is surely central to Edwards's understanding of the "sense of the heart." But it is a mistake to confuse the presence of love accompanying true faith with the meritorious nature of love in the Roman Catholic doctrine of formed faith. In other words, Reformed theologians would not have separated true faith from love, although they would be clear to distinguish them.

47. Ibid.
48. Ibid., 59.

There may be a formal similarity between the Catholic understanding of "informal" or "unformed" faith and Protestant "historical" faith, but they are not the same. Historical faith is a faulty or incomplete faith as such whereas Roman Catholic theologians often spoke of a "true" but unformed faith that was indeed a real faith, but one that lacked its own integrity. What made this so-called true faith acceptable was the addition of *meritorious* love. While love always accompanies true faith for the Protestant, it is not meritorious in any sense of the word. But what is it that distinguishes true or saving faith from historical faith for Protestants? Traditionally, Protestants have distinguished three elements in true faith; knowledge (*scientia*), assent (*assensus*), and trust (*fiducia*).[49] Historical faith would appear to be a faith that stops with knowledge and assent, but fails to go on to trust. It is then this fiducial element that distinguishes true and saving faith from historical faith. While trust and love would seem to be natural allies or partners, they are not exactly the same. It may be this distinction that Schafer doesn't accept. It makes more sense, though, to interpret Edwards in line with *his own* Reformed tradition than to try to interpret him within an antithetical theological system such as that of Roman Catholicism, which was undoubtedly familiar to him and rejected by him.[50]

Edwards's distinction between notional and speculative understanding on the one hand and spiritual understanding on the other aligns better with the Protestant understanding of faith involving knowledge, assent, and trust. Historical faith and speculative understanding correspond to knowledge and assent, and spiritual understanding (consent or affiance) generally corresponds with trust. This trust, of course, is always accompanied by love, but love is neither the form for faith nor is it meritorious for Edwards as

49. Francis Turretin, *Institutes of Elenctic Theology,* ed. James Dennison, trans. George M. Geiger (Phillipsburg, NJ: P&R, 1993), 2:560–64, lists six acts involved in faith: the act of knowledge; theoretical assent; fiducial and practical assent; the act of refuge; the act of reception and union; the reflex act and the act of confidence and consolation.

50. Edwards certainly rejected Roman Catholicism as such. His critical remarks in *The Works of Jonathan Edwards,* vol. 5, *Apocalyptic Writings,* ed. John F. Wilson (New Haven, CT: Yale University Press, 1977), to the effect that the pope was the antichrist would certainly lead one to question Schafer's construal here. This is not to say that Edwards was ignorant of the discussions within Roman Catholic theology as modern conservative evangelicals often are concerning Catholic theology of our day. He was undoubtedly conversant, as Morimoto has pointed out in his *Jonathan Edwards and the Catholic Vision of Salvation.* Nor do our remarks fail to recognize that Edwards may have used concepts and language gained from Roman Catholic sources that he deemed usable.

it is for Roman Catholic doctrine.[51] For Edwards, in order for his stress on love to be the virtual equivalent of formed faith, he would have to have a notion of *true* faith that is both true and unaccompanied by love as such (which given Edwards's grounding of faith in regeneration or the "new sense" seems impossible) *and* he would have to hold some idea of love as meritorious so that this formed faith (true faith plus meritorious love) is what merits justification.[52] Given Edwards's discussion in his discourse on justification that faith as such is not even the instrumental cause (meritorious or otherwise) of justification, properly speaking, but the very act of unition of the believer to Christ (the vinculum), the idea that he came close to holding the doctrine of formed faith fails to make sense.

Related to the meritorious nature of love in formed faith is the relationship faith bears to good works or obedience. This arises since obedience is rightly seen as a correlate of love or its fruit. If obedience is meritorious as such it would compromise the nature of faith as the vinculum between the believer and Christ, and it would compromise the sufficiency of the imputation of Christ's righteousness to the believer. Pastorally, Edwards wanted to avoid the dangers of both legalism and antinomianism in his doctrine of justification by faith. For Edwards, then, justifying faith contains within it virtually all future acts of repentance and obedience. For Edwards, justifying faith is a faith that perseveres.

> Edwards sought for a way to articulate the importance of a faith that *perseveres*, even when parishioners did not. But this created a dilemma for him: a

---

51. Francis Turretin, a major influence on Edwards, tells us that Roman Catholicism errs in thinking that there can be a faith that is both true and unformed, and thus needing love to perfect it. Referring to the Roman Catholic theologian Durandus, Turretin says that Durandus put forward that "love is not the form of faith according to its natural being; yea, it can be separated from it. But it is the form of faith according to its meritorious being, inasmuch as it deserves eternal life because the act of faith is not meritorious, except insofar as it is commanded by love (without which it does not have the relation of merit and by which man pleases God)." *Elenctic Theology*, 2:581.

52. Edwards tells us in his discourse on justification that "when it is said that we are not justified by any righteousness or goodness of our own, what is meant is that it is not out of respect to the excellency or goodness of any qualifications, or acts, in us, whatsoever, that God judges it meet that this benefit of Christ should be ours; and it is not, in anywise, on account of any excellency or value that there is in faith, that it appears in the sight of God, a meet thing, that he who believes should have this benefit of Christ assigned to him, but purely from the relation faith has to the person in whom the benefit is to be had, or as it unites to that Mediator, in and by who we are justified." *WJE*, 19:155.

persevering faith, according to his reading of the Scriptures, is not dormant but active. His tradition reconciled Luther's difficulty with the Epistle of St. James by asserting that St. James and St. Paul were in complete agreement: faith alone justifies, but it is an active faith. Not only is "True Grace Distinguished from the Experience of Devils" in terms of "true" religious affections but also accompanying performance.... The difficulty of striking a balance is remarkable: antinomianism, neonomianism, nominalism, and legalism are all to be avoided, while at the same time there is the reality of *semper iustius peccator* to contend with. Edwards finds an innovative solution by proposing a theological doctrine that did not rest upon an evaluation of one's own "works," but Christ's: he (1) grounds initial justification in the conditional "first act of faith"; and (2) also makes the status of "justified" conditional upon perseverance; but then (3) declares that Christ has actually persevered in faith and practice for the believer.... According to Edwards, that first act of faith gives a "title" to salvation, because it does, virtually at least, "trust in God and Christ for perseverance among other benefits, and gives a title to this benefit with others, and so virtually contains perseverance."[53]

In other words, it is by our union with Christ that we enjoy the benefits of Christ's actual faith, obedience, and perseverance so that they become ours by virtue of being his intrinsically. This vital union between the believer and Christ brings with it many benefits among which obedience and perseverance are but two. This is not to deny that the Christian is to persevere to the end, but that the perseverance is not perfect in this life, given the fact that the Christian is always a justified sinner. The obedience in justifying faith is Christ's faith, obedience, and perseverance, and not some meritorious act of faith or innate quality in the believer's soul.

Neither love nor obedience is meritorious for Jonathan Edwards, so we find that Schafer's contention that Edwards compromised his doctrine of justification by faith by holding to something like formed faith or a faith plus obedience/good works scheme is not tenable. Edwards has once again made union with Christ the linchpin of his understanding of justification.

CONCLUSION

We have surveyed Thomas Schafer's 1951 article "Jonathan Edwards and Justification by Faith" and its evidence for Edwards's compromise of

---

53. Bombaro, "Beautiful Beings," n.p. See esp. Edwards, "Miscellanies" no. 729, *WJE*, 18:353–57.

the doctrine of justification by faith and found that we could offer what we think is a better, more plausible reading of the issues—a reading grounded within the riches of Edwards's own Reformed heritage. Edwards's grounding of legal imputation in the real union of the believer with Christ does not make justification an after-the-fact forensic declaration.[54] Nor does Edwards place sanctification before justification when we consider the fluid use of the word "sanctification" as covering the sense of regeneration or when we consider regeneration/sanctification as a concurrent blessing received with justification in union with Christ. Finally, Edwards does not embrace any kind of notion of either formed faith or a mixed faith plus obedience/good works scheme as such. On all points, Edwards falls within the confines of Reformed Protestant orthodoxy on the doctrine of justification by faith, especially within the union with Christ model of the application of redemption as articulated by John Calvin. This is not to deny any originality of expression or emphasis on Jonathan Edwards's part, nor is it to deny his theological creativity as such (his doctrine of the virtual perseverance of the believer by his union with Christ is one such example), but that very originality drew upon the richness of his own Reformed heritage.[55]

There does seem to be a tendency in recent Edwardsian scholarship (including Schafer's article under consideration here) to pit the forensic nature of the doctrine of justification against the transformational nature of regeneration/sanctification/practice/disposition as though they stood in opposition to one another. The Reformed tradition has never understood the matter this way. They are complementary. The problem has always been, so it seems, to either pit one against the other, as here, or to confuse the one with the other. We believe Edwards would have seen both the forensic nature of justification and the transformational nature of regeneration/sanctification as distinguishable but never separable. The forensic nature of justification by itself might appear to be a legal fiction and transformation by itself would always seem to fall short of the perfect righteousness demanded by a holy God. With this in mind, we believe that Jonathan Edwards did not compromise on the doctrine of justification by faith nor did he place it within a tenuous context.

54. We would grant that it is concurrent with "present faith" union, but the legal is grounded in the eternal or ontological union which is the result of the covenant of redemption or *pactum salutis*.

55. Sang Lee understands Edwards to stand within the contours of Protestant and Reformed tradition. Lee, *WJE*, 21:73. As mentioned in n29, Edwards shares a central soteric structure with Calvin and the majority of the Reformed tradition.

PART 3

Studies in Pastoral Theology

17

Oliver Bowles on the Life and Ministry of the Evangelical Pastor

---

TRANSLATED BY JONATHAN B. ROCKEY
AND PHILIP G. RYKEN

OLIVER BOWLES (ca. 1577–1646) was the oldest member of the West-minster Assembly. Following a brief teaching fellowship at Queens College, Cambridge, where he trained John Preston and other leading Puritans for gospel ministry, Bowles held a long and distinguished pastorate at Sutton in Bedford-shire. His ministry must have been highly regarded by his students and his colleagues in ministry, for he was asked to preach before Parliament on one of the fast days that marked the opening of the Assembly.[1] Indeed, Preston described his former professor as "a very holy & learned man, a noted & carefull Tutor."[2]

Bowles died before the Divines completed their work, yet his legacy was preserved through the posthumous publication of his long treatise on practical theology, *De Pastore Evangelico Tractatus*.[3] This work is divided into three main

---

1. Oliver Bowles, *Zeale for God's House Quickened; or, a Sermon preached before the Assembly of Lords, Commons, and Divines, at their solemn Fast, July 7, 1643, in Abbey Church, Westminster: expressing the Eminency of Zeale required in Church-Reformer* (London, 1643).

2. John Preston, as quoted in Thomas Ball, *The Life of the Renowned Doctor Preston*, ed. E. W. Harcourt (1628; repr. Oxford: Parker, 1885), 6.

3. Oliver Bowles, *De Pastore Evangelico Tractatus* (London, 1649). When translated in full, the book title reads: *A Treatise on the Evangelical Pastor: In Which the Whole Pastoral Office—Not Only the Calling and Preparation of the Pastor, but also the Exercise of the Office Itself—Is Carefully Set Forth.*

sections, which address a minister's spiritual and intellectual preparation for ordination, his public and private ministry of the Word, and his administration of the sacraments and conduct of pastoral prayer. Although it has yet to be published in English, *De Pastore Evangelico Tractatus* stands as a landmark volume in the history of pastoral theology and the Reformed tradition of gospel ministry.[4]

Oliver Bowles was esteemed by his contemporaries for many of the same virtues we treasure in Richard B. Gaffin Jr. As a man of exemplary piety and godliness, Bowles was fully committed to the supreme authority of Scripture, the accurate exegesis of the biblical text, the propositional statement of orthodox doctrine in systematic terms, and the practical application of biblical truth to daily life—qualities that are obvious hallmarks of Dr. Gaffin's vibrant ministry at Westminster Theological Seminary and in the Orthodox Presbyterian Church. The two men also have this in common: a passion for communicating spiritual truth with crystal clarity, carefully choosing exactly the right word to say precisely what needs to be said.

The following selections from *De Pastore Evangelico Tractatus* include translations of chapters on the minister as an example to his flock, on his expertise in the sacred Scriptures, and on his public ministry of the Word of God. In all likelihood, this material was first delivered to divinity students at Cambridge University. Anyone who has ever had the privilege of hearing Dr. Gaffin lecture will quickly recognize Oliver Bowles as a kindred spirit. Apparently there have been men like Dr. Gaffin before; we pray that there will be men like him again.

De Pastore Evangelico Tractatus: Book I, Chapter 5: Certain Particular Duties, in Which He Ought to Be an Example to the Flock

HE WILL BE AN EXAMPLE IF HE MANAGES HIS HOUSEHOLD WELL

The first particular requirement is that the pastor should manage his own household well (1 Tim. 3:4), first, because he must be judged unfit to

---

4. For further background, see Philip Graham Ryken, "Oliver Bowles and the Westminster View of Gospel Ministry," in *The Westminster Confession into the 21st Century: Essays in Remembrance of the 350th Anniversary of the Westminster Assembly*, ed. Ligon Duncan III (Fearn, Ross-shire: Christian Focus, 2004), 409–27.

govern the church of God (which is his household) who does not know how to manage his own household, which is (according to Seneca) "a mini-republic." He who does not know how to lead one company will hardly be able to command an entire legion; one who is not up to commanding a rowboat on a pond or stream will not be able to navigate a vast sea or lead his ship on the ocean into harbor. In addition, ordinary people are so impressionable that as failures in the pastor's household become widely known, people quickly take them for an example.

Pastors who slip up in this area contract greater guilt because they are counted in the number of those from whom God requires greater holiness than the common people. Hence the remarkable legal sanction concerning the daughter of a priest: if she prostituted herself, she was to be handed over to be burned alive (Lev. 21:9); yet the unengaged or unmarried daughters of other tribes were to be dealt with less severely. Therefore, let the evangelical pastor take every precaution that none of his own bring scandal upon the church or perpetrate the kind of deed by which God's name may be blasphemed.

In its totality, a household consists of three relationships: husband and wife, father and child, master and servant. It is for the head of the household to manage all of these relationships, not only by providing what is owed to each, but also by requiring what they owe.

How the Head Is to Manage His Household

Those things which contribute to the exercise of this household authority are owed either to the entire household or to individual members. Here are the things which the head of the home owes to the entire household:

First, he should lead them in the family worship of God, both pouring out prayers for them and instructing them from the Scriptures and from the works and judgments of God: "He will teach his sons and his household after him, so that they may guard the way of Jehovah" (Gen. 18:19); "I and my family will worship Jehovah" (Josh. 24:15).

Second, he should bring his whole household—as far as he is able—to the public assemblies of the church, and he should ask them for an account of their progress. The head of the household is commanded to see to it that everyone under his authority observes the Lord's Day with holiness (Ex. 20:10).

Third, he should give wise and wholesome care to the food, clothing, and security of all who are under his roof: "You will rejoice over every good thing that Jehovah your God gives to you and your household" (Deut. 26:11); "Anyone who does not provide for his household, and especially for members of his own family, has denied the faith and is worse than an unbeliever" (1 Tim. 5:8).

Fourth, if someone in his family has been delinquent, he should exercise discipline wisely and patiently. If there is hope of restoring a sinner to good fruit, he should either be admonished or chastised, in proportion to his wrongdoing. However, if there is no improvement after whatever remedies have been applied, a servant should be expelled from the household at the first opportunity (Gen. 21); whereas in the case of a son, the help of a magistrate should be sought (Deut. 21:18–21).

His Role as a Husband

Here is what the head of the household owes to individuals. First, as a husband, he must love and embrace his wife as a partner joined to him in the Lord for his assistance: "Let your wife be to you as a most beloved doe and graceful deer; may her breasts satisfy you at all times, and may you always wander within her love" (Prov. 5:19; cf. Eph. 5:25). Let this love drive away all harshness (Col. 3:19).

Second, let him wisely tolerate it whenever he sees her weakness: "Let men live together according to the knowledge of God, giving honor to the woman as a weaker vessel" (1 Pet. 3:7). A husband absorbs many of her mistakes by wisely overlooking them as foibles of her gender. At the same time, let him take care not to encourage them by his indulgence.

Finally, let him hold on to what is his: according to the Persian edict, "Let him be the master of his own house" (Est. 1:22). Let him be the leader of "the wife of his youth." "I do not permit a woman to usurp the authority of a man" (1 Tim. 2:12).

His Role as a Father

As a father, let the head of the household look after his children so that they are reared piously from tender infancy. In making and molding them, both cruelty and indulgence are to be avoided: "Fathers, do not exasperate your children, lest they become disheartened" (Eph. 6:4; Col. 3:21); "You must not withhold chastening from a child; when you beat him with a rod, he will not die. You will strike him with a rod, and you will free his soul from the sepulcher" (Prov. 23:13, 14). Finally, as soon as they give evidence of their God-given gifts and natural inclination, let them be appointed to some legitimate calling: "Instruct a man according to the purpose of his life" (Prov. 22:6; cf. Dan. 1).

His Role as a Master

As a master, let the head of the household take in servants who are either truly religious or who submit themselves to the exercises of religion and live without scandal: "He who walks in a blameless way will minister to me" (Ps. 101:6); "Cornelius called a devout soldier" (Acts 10:7).

Let him require tasks and services of them to which they are equal, not ones that exceed their mental or physical powers: "A righteous man cares for the life of his cattle" (Prov. 12:10). Yet, on the other hand, he should not allow them to grow lazy through idleness (2 Thess. 3:10).

Let him also reward their faithfulness, diligence, and effort by paying their due compensation: "Masters, give your servants what is right and fair" (Col. 4:1). Furthermore, when some servants distinguish themselves with diligent and faithful industry in doing their jobs, let us pay them more than we agreed and pay attention to promoting them: "He who attends to his master will be honored" (Prov. 27:18).

Now all of this is that art called domestic economy, briefly described, which a good pastor ought always to keep in view if he is to be an example to the flock. God has avenged those who have been negligent in their attention to this art with the most severe punishment, as the deadly disaster that swallowed the house of Eli testifies (see 1 Sam. 4:12ff.). Similarly, God became so angry at Moses for his failure promptly to circumcise his son that he was not far from destroying him with death on his journey (see Ex. 4:24–26).

LET THE PASTOR BE HOSPITABLE

The second particular requirement for the evangelical pastor is to be a lover of strangers, that is, he should be given to hospitality. In the days when tyrannical madness was raging against the church, this kindness was especially needful for the poor who were exiles for the sake of Christ's name. For when they were being driven away by the infidels, there was a danger that if they had found no comfort among their own people, they would have despaired, having been crushed under a mountain of calamities. But as soon as the heat from these persecutions cooled, this love of strangers was not quite so necessary, however highly it still should be praised.

At the very least, by the force of this precept, the Holy Spirit wishes the following. First, that we should receive hospitably those who suffer injustice for the cause of Christ and who flee to us for refuge. As Luther says, "He who receives an exiled brother for the sake of the Word, receives God in such a brother."[5] Second, as we are able, we should come to the aid of people who are driven to extreme need not by their own fault, but by God's chastisements or the injustice of the times: "The blessing of the dying man came upon me" (Job 29:13). Finally, when the poor, who are unequal to making a living, are placed in our neighborhood, we should bless them according to our means by feeding them, clothing them, and relieving them any way we can: "This is holy worship before God: to visit orphans and widows in their affliction" (James 1:27). For it is required not only that we minister as a doctor to souls, but also as an innkeeper to bodies. Christ himself, who had nowhere to lay his head, was still kindly to the poor.

LET THE PASTOR BE A LOVER OF THE GOOD

The third particular requirement is for the evangelical pastor to be an intimate lover of the good. Here there will be need of careful scrutiny to distinguish the sincerely good from the specter of hypocrisy. Whenever we find someone to be good without pretense, first, let us value him above others: "With an upright heart, he honors those who fear Jehovah" (Ps. 15:4). Second, to the good in particular (all other things being equal), let the pastor extend a helping hand (see Gal. 6:6). Third, let the pastor especially rejoice in the company of the good: "My whole delight is in the saints" (Ps. 16:3).

The apostle Paul's love of the good is attested by those frequent, love-filled salutations which he attaches to almost every one of his letters. The pastor will easily double the number of good people in his flock when those who have made more progress in piety than others sense that he loves them without limit.

5. Martin Luther, *Luther's Works*, vol. 8, *Lectures on Genesis*, ed. Jeroslav Pelikan (St. Louis: Concordia, 1966), 19.

Book I, Chapter 12: On Expertise in the Scriptures, and Other Things Required in a Pastor

Let the Pastor Be Very Well Versed in the Sacred Scripture

The one who would take this chair ought to be a "bibliophage"—that is, a devourer of that book which by reason of excellence we call The Book.[6] He should be very well versed in the Scriptures; he should understand them thoroughly, and if possible he should learn them by heart. Following the example of both Ezekiel and John, let him devour the book of God (see Ezek. 3:3; Rev. 10:10). There are four reasons for him to be very well versed in the Scriptures.

First, because men of God have always been celebrated by this encomium. Thus Ezra is called "a ready scribe in the law of Moses" (Ezra 7:6); Apollos, "mighty in the Scriptures" (Acts 18:24); Timothy, "nourished on the words of faith" (1 Tim. 4:6). Second, because the Scriptures are both the only and the first principles of faith, on which everything in theology rests; so let them consult "the Law and the Testimony" (Isa. 8:20). "You search the Scriptures, for in them you think that you have eternal life" (John 5:39). Whatever other writings exist should be examined according to this norm. What Ecclesiastes says of the sea is also true of the Scriptures: "all rivers go out from there, nor do they fail to return there" (Eccl. 1:7). So too all the volumes of the most learned come from Scripture as from a fountain; and to this place they return again, so that their opinions may be tested. Third, because the people are bound to seek the law from his mouth: "The lips of the priest should guard knowledge, and they should seek the law from his mouth, for he is the messenger of the Lord of the Hosts" (Mal. 2:7). Therefore, let the minister of the Word be like "the scribe instructed in the kingdom of God—like a master of the house who brings forth from his treasury things both new and old" (Matt. 13:52). Finally, he should be very well versed in the Scriptures because they render the man of God fully equipped for the work of ministry (2 Tim. 3:17). There is in them such self-sufficiency that

---

6. See Luther, *Genesis*, 16.

if every single book in the world were burned, and only these Scriptures were preserved safe and sound, then whatever truth is necessary for salvation would be safe with them. As much then as we place our apprenticeship in the knowledge of arts and languages, it is necessary for us not only to grow up in the Scriptures, but also to grow old with them. Let us first get a little taste of them and then soak our lips in their sacred fount. Let us give them every moment of our spare time; let us linger in them, meditating day and night.

Those who bypass the sacred oracles of God to immerse themselves completely in the broken cisterns of the Fathers, the Scholastics, and various other writers are like servants who deserve a good beating. In the Scriptures they are strangers and wayfarers, yet in the other writings they are thoroughly learned. Somewhere Luther wrote this worthy saying:

> I myself hate my own books, and often wish them destroyed, for I fear that they delay readers and draw them away from reading the Scripture itself, which alone is the fountain of all wisdom. I am also frightened by the example of the previous age, for after they encountered the commentaries of men who were devoted to sacred studies, not only did they consume a good deal of time reading the ancient theologians, but in the end they were busied with Aristotle, Averroes, and others, who later gave rise to the Thomases, the Scotuses, and such progeny.[7]

Nor is Luther's caution undeserved, for the Scriptures are the pastor's tools—as it were—which must be used at all times as the situation demands. He is nothing without them, however learned he may otherwise be in the whole encyclopedia of the more humane letters. The Scriptures are like a watchtower: from them we espy all the devious labyrinths of error. They are like a packed storehouse: from them the wise caretaker of souls may draw all things necessary for the work of ministry.

LET THE PASTOR BE SKILLFUL IN TEACHING

The second thing desirable for undertaking the office is for him to be skillful in teaching (*didaktikos*). To be skillful in teaching, let him be equipped with a rich knowledge of divinity. Let him be inclined to share

7. Ibid., 14.

with others what he possesses in his mind; this is the "ready-mindedness" (*prothumia*) that Peter mentions (1 Pet. 5:2). Let him be expertly skilled in accommodating what he knows to each person; this is what "rightly dividing the Word of truth" means (2 Tim. 2:15).

Then he should have "an open door for speaking" (Col. 4:3; cf. 1 Cor. 14:19)—that is, the facility to express freely the thoughts of his mind according to the ability of his hearers, speaking in such a way as to equip others. Many of the most learned exert themselves in teaching others, but since they are hardly capable of communicating their thoughts, you would say they utter nothing but thorns and stones. Then there are others who, no matter how distinctly they can enunciate what they grasp with the mind, nevertheless lack any impulse toward the kind of application that gives "to each his own." They pour themselves completely into general discourse, taking no account of the people they are addressing. However venerable these men may be—and rightly so, considering their gifts—in demanding that the pastor be skillful in teaching (*didaktikos*), the apostle forbids them from undertaking this office. Here the condition of our own church must be deplored. Although there are all kinds of ranks and titles, scholarly degrees, and advanced knowledge, it is not customary to consider whether someone has the kind of gifts that profit the people toward salvation. Consequently many now sit in the pastoral chair who are neither evil nor ignorant, but since they lack any aptitude for feeding the Lord's flock, God has definitely not ordained them to engage in this office.

LET THE PASTOR CONSTRUCT A SOUND THEOLOGY

Third, someone who holds this office must have engraved on his mind "the pattern of sound words" (2 Tim. 1:13). Elsewhere this is called "the form of knowledge" (Rom. 2:20) and "the analogy of faith" (Rom. 12:6). A pattern of sound words or form of knowledge is a brief compendium of what to believe and what to do. The Holy Spirit seems to have collected under these two headings things that are scattered here and there throughout the Scriptures. In the passage mentioned above, these words follow: "in faith and charity" (2 Tim. 1:13). The Scriptures also say: "having faith and a good conscience" (1 Tim. 1:19); "I believe everything that has been written. . . . I train myself to have a conscience without offense" (Acts 24:14–16).

Let this pattern of sound doctrine be arranged systematically. It is very important to classify individual items in their own categories, to distinguish things that are different from things that are the same, to deal with generalities before specifics, and to arrange things in their natural order. Consult the masters of theological method and learn the laws they have established. Study the various systems of theology and seriously evaluate whether they have twisted the straight laws of method. After weighing individual matters with a careful balance, let us follow the system that is most completely in accord with the laws of method.

Let the individual headings or sections that occur in the system be developed with general thesis statements. These theological propositions—wherever they are drawn from—should be defended either from the Scriptures or from divine reason. It will be worth taking the trouble to illustrate with particular care theological propositions in any *loci* that are especially controversial. We should also remove theology from the fractious disputations of men and state it positively; for if it is perceived correctly, something straight is the best indicator of what is straight and what is slanted.

In this theological system, let the errors that are prevalent in our age be noted briefly wherever they pertain, so that we may accurately understand on what division of theology these heresies impinge. When this "form of knowledge" is engraved on the mind, it especially strengthens one's judgment, for when one strand of the whole theology is in view, so too is the logical relationship that the individual parts bear to one another. With this assistance, when we come to the more difficult passages of Scripture, we are guided as it were by a thread, so that we at least render a sense that is consonant with the faith, and do not just keep pounding away at monstrous errors. When we look from the vantage point of the system, we detect whatever errors arise and easily liberate ourselves from them, as long as we adhere to the analogy of faith.

Book II, Chapter 1: On the Public Preaching of the Word

An Explanation of the Pastoral Office

Concerning the exercise of the pastoral office, we must consider how complex it is and also the things that strengthen its performance. The pastor's office is twofold: some things he does singly, some he does in conjunction with others (I do not intend to deal with that here). His duty is single when he is either the mouth of God to the people, or of the people to God. He is the mouth of God to the people both in the dispensation of the Word and in the administration of the sacraments.

Now as to the dispensation of the Word, we should notice in how many ways it should be dispensed and what guidelines serve its dispensation. The Word is to be dispensed either publicly or privately; public dispensation is either primary or secondary; the primary dispensation of the Word is public preaching.

WHAT IS THE PREACHING OF THE WORD?

The preaching of the Word is a divinely ordained means of grace, wherein the things of the kingdom of God are publicly explained and applied to the salvation and edification of the people.

I say it is *a means of grace* because it is a moral instrument that God efficaciously employs, when it is united with faith, to work his grace. Thus it is said to be "the power of God unto salvation for everyone who believes" (Rom. 1:16); it is the "arm of Jehovah" (Isa. 53:1).

It is *divinely ordained* because God has determined not to speak in his own living voice, or the voice of an angel, but that one man should instruct another to salvation. "Whatever they have said, they have said well" (Deut. 5:28)—that is, when they wanted Moses to intercede between God and the people. "Go, teach all nations, teaching them to obey everything I have commanded you," etc. (Matt. 28:19).

What are *the things of the kingdom of God* (see Luke 4:43; 8:1)? The things of the kingdom are law and gospel—the gospel as primary, the law as subservient to it. In the gospel, Christ is offered unto salvation to anyone who believes and repents. The law either leads people by the hand to Christ or directs those who have been drawn to him.

Preaching is *public* first by reason of its location, which ought to be more or less public—a place where people whose hearts God is stirring may gather (e.g., Acts 13:44). Second, preaching is public by reason of the person, for it is delivered by one who has been publicly set apart for this office.

How are these things *explained and applied*? Hidden mysteries have to be explained to be understood, for they transcend the capacity of the natural man. Christ explained how the Scripture at hand was fulfilled in himself (Luke 4:21). When things are explained generally, no one will understand them as addressed to him personally unless the things explained are accommodated for edification according to the various condition of each person. "He who prophesies speaks to men for edification, for exhortation, for consolation" (1 Cor. 14:3).

Finally, preaching is *for the salvation of the people*—that is, so that those who are brought over from death to life may receive the remission of sins and a place among the sanctified (Acts 26:18).

18

Calvin's Theology of Certainty

DAVID B. MCWILLIAMS

FOR MANY YEARS I have committed myself to theologizing within the pastoral context. As I have ministered the gospel to my congregation, the question of assurance of faith has surfaced time and again. Regular reading of the remarkable pastoral theologian John Calvin has provided wonderfully fruitful insights about the questions many of my parishioners have asked: "How can I know that I am a Christian?" "What is faith and how do I know that I believe?" "What does your emphasis on Word and sacrament have to do with my internal struggles with assurance of faith?" "Can we live with certainty in the modern world?"

What follows is a brief and updated summary of my investigations on Calvin and assurance that I pursued many years ago. It is selective, of course, but nonetheless representative of the main issues. I still find Calvin's thinking as helpful in everyday pastoral labor, as well as in my own Christian living, as I did when I began studying his insights on assurance of faith.

Even a cursory reading of Calvin's writings highlights the prominence of three unified themes threading his corpus: *union with Christ, adoption,* and *assurance of faith*. While all of these themes are essential to Calvin's theology, singling out the assurance theme for distinct investigation can be especially fruitful since assurance of faith is a perennial pastoral issue. For Calvin the theme is dominant, though it seldom receives attention from his students in proportion to its prominence in his thought.

The following approach will provide a succinct summary of the pervasive idea of assurance of faith in Calvin's theology, will seek to define the role of the *syllogismus practicus* in Calvin's thought, and finally, will attempt to clarify the relationship of Calvin's doctrine to the Westminster Assembly's confessional standards. We begin by investigating Calvin's definition of faith.

CALVIN'S DEFINITION OF FAITH

Calvin's definition of saving faith virtually equates faith and assurance:

Now we shall possess a right definition of faith if we call it a firm and certain knowledge of God's benevolence toward us, founded upon the truth of the freely given promise in Christ, both revealed to our minds and sealed upon our hearts through the Holy Spirit.[1]

Elsewhere Calvin says similarly, "faith is a firm and solid confidence of the heart, by means of which we rest surely in the mercy of God which is promised to us through the Gospel."[2] In both definitions Calvin inseparably associates faith with assurance. What factors contribute to this equation?

Calvin's definition has been attributed to his resistance to Roman Catholic antagonists on assurance.[3] The dissonance between the Reformed and Rome must be given its due weight. In his "Reply" to Sadolet, Calvin fervently denounces the pastoral bondage and cruelty of Rome's position on assurance.

That confident hope of salvation which is both enjoined by the Word, and founded upon it, had almost vanished. Nay, it was received as a kind of oracle, that it was foolish arrogance, and, as they termed it, presump-

---

1. John Calvin, *Institutes of the Christian Religion*, ed. John T. McNeill, trans. Ford Lewis Battles (Philadelphia: Westminster, 1960), 3.2.7.
2. Calvin, *Instruction in Faith*, 1537 edition, trans. Paul Fuhrmann (Philadelphia: Westminster, 1969), 38.
3. E.g., William Cunningham, *The Reformers and the Theology of the Reformation* (Edinburgh: Banner of Truth, 1967), 111–48.

tion for anyone trusting to thy goodness, and the righteous of thy Son, to entertain a sure and unfaltering hope of salvation.[4]

This pastoral factor unquestionably influenced Calvin's definition of faith.

However, Pastor Calvin was concerned to minister *the Word* to his flock. It was his burning desire to know what the Scriptures say and to teach faithfully the truth to his needy people.[5] His approach was motivated not only by the debate with Rome, but also by his biblically derived doctrines of God and of man. As a sinful human contrasts himself with the majesty of God he sees nothing in himself but what is damnable. God's holiness produces a sense of sin, which in turn repudiates assurance: "Where our conscience sees only indignation and vengeance, how can it fail to tremble and be afraid? or to shun the God whom it dreads? Yet faith ought to seek God, not to shun him."[6] Calvin's motivation in defining faith as he did was polemical. However, his concern was not entirely or even primarily polemical. Calvin was confronting a consuming pastoral issue that challenges believers in every era and will continue to do so until the *parousia*. This becomes evident as we examine the elements comprising Calvin's theology of certainty.

ELEMENTS OF CALVIN'S DOCTRINE OF ASSURANCE

Faith and the Word

Ronald Wallace correctly observed that in Calvin's thought there is reciprocity between faith and the Word.[7] In his definition of faith in the *Institutes*, Calvin speaks of faith "founded upon the truth of the freely given promise in Christ."[8] Similarly, in *Instruction in Faith*, Calvin

---

4. John Calvin, "Reply By Calvin To Cardinal Sadolet's Letter" in *Selected Works of John Calvin—Tracts and Letters,* ed. Henry Beveridge and Jules Bonnet (Grand Rapids: Baker Book House, 1983), 1:57.

5. See B. B. Warfield, "Calvin and the Bible" in *Selected Shorter Writings of Benjamin B. Warfield* (Philadelphia: Presbyterian and Reformed, 1970), 1:399–400. "It was not, however, the homage of his admiration alone that Calvin gave to the Scriptures. He gave them the homage of his faith and obedience. In them he heard the very words of God, as if they were pronounced by his very lips. And to these words he bent his ear, the Spirit in him bearing witness with his Spirit that they are the words of God."

6. Calvin, *Institutes*, 3.2.7.

7. Ronald S. Wallace, *Calvin's Doctrine of the Word and Sacrament* (Tyler, TX: Geneva Divinity School Press, 1982), 130.

8. Calvin, *Institutes*, 3.2.7.

refers to faith as the means by which "we rest surely in the mercy of God which is promised to us through the Gospel." He adds significantly: "For thus the definition of faith must be taken from the substance of the promise. Faith rests so much on this foundation that, if the latter be taken away, faith would collapse at once, or, rather, vanish away."[9] The relationship between faith and the Word is permanent and inseparable: "We must be reminded that there is a permanent relationship between faith and the Word. He [the apostle Paul] could not separate one from the other any more than we could separate the rays from the sun from which they come."[10]

The relationship between faith and the Word is not only permanent and inseparable; it is also exclusive. This foundation of faith in the Word can never be supplanted by any other foundation.

> We make the freely given promise of God the foundation of faith because upon it faith properly rests. Faith is certain that God is true in all things whether he command or forbid, whether he promise or threaten; and it also obediently receives his commandments, observes his prohibitions, heeds his threats. Nevertheless, faith properly begins with the promise, rests in it, and ends in it.[11]

Faith and Justification

Sinful men and women cannot live in assurance before God due to their fallen condition, rebellious and unrighteous hearts. Man's need is such that, in and of himself, he is hopeless:

> For God finds nothing in man's nature but his miserable condition to dispose Him to mercy. If, therefore, when he is first received by God, it is certain that man is naked and bereft of all good, and on the other hand, stuffed and laden with all kinds of evils—on the basis of what endowment, I ask, shall we say he is worthy of a heavenly calling [Heb. 3:1]? Away, then, with this empty dreaming about merits, where God so clearly sets off his free mercy![12]

9. Calvin, *Instruction*, 38.
10. Calvin, *Institutes*, 3.2.6.
11. Calvin, *Institutes*, 3.2.29.
12. Calvin, *Institutes*, 3.17. 4.

Obviously, the works of sinners contribute nothing to their justification:

> We must strongly insist upon these two points: first, that there never existed any work of a godly man which, if examined by God's stern judgment, would not deserve condemnation; secondly, if such a work were found (something not possible for man), it would still lose favor—weakened and stained as it is by the sins with which its author himself is surely burdened.[13]

Again, Calvin underscores our desperation in view of the perfection of the law:

> For since no perfection can come to us so long as we are clothed in this flesh, and the law moreover announces death and judgment to all who do not maintain perfect righteousness in works, it will always have grounds for accusing and condemning us unless, on the contrary, God's mercy counters it, and by continual forgiveness of sins repeatedly acquits us. Therefore, what I said at the beginning always holds good: if we are judged by our own worth, whatever we plan or undertake, with all our efforts and labors we still deserve death and destruction.[14]

Our only hope, in view of our depravity and the curse of the law, is the free justification that comes to sinners by virtue of Christ's accomplishment of redemption:

> But we define justification as follows: the sinner, received into communion with Christ, is reconciled to God by his grace, while, cleansed by Christ's blood, he obtains forgiveness of sins, and clothed with Christ's righteousness as if it were his own, he stands confident before the heavenly judgment seat.[15]

Freedom from the law's condemnation is essential for assurance of faith:

> [In Galatians] Paul . . . strongly insists that believers should not suppose they can obtain righteousness before God by any works of the law, still less

13. Calvin, *Institutes*, 3.14.11.
14. Calvin, *Institutes*, 3.14.10.
15. Calvin, *Institutes*, 3.17.8.

by those paltry rudiments! And at the same time he teaches that through the cross of Christ they are free from the condemnation of the law, which otherwise hangs over all men [Gal. 4:5], so that they may rest with full assurance in Christ alone.[16]

Without this freedom there could be no living but only a grim paralysis:

> See how all our works are under the curse of the law if they are measured by the standard of the law! But how, then, would unhappy souls gird themselves eagerly for a work for which they might expect to receive only a curse? But if, freed from this severe requirement of the law, or rather from the entire rigor of the law, they hear themselves called with fatherly gentleness by God, they will cheerfully and with great eagerness answer, and follow his leading.

To which Calvin adds: "And we need this assurance in no slight degree, for without it we attempt everything in vain."[17]

So indispensable is this free justification for assured living before God that Calvin warns against allowing "ourselves to be drawn even a finger's breadth from this sole foundation."[18] For, "If righteousness is supported by works, in God's sight it must entirely collapse; and it is confined solely to God's mercy, solely to communion with Christ, and therefore solely to faith."[19]

Faith and the Sacraments

The sacraments confirm faith in the Word:

> The sacraments are instituted by God to this end that they might be exercises of our faith both before God and before men. And certainly before God they exercise our faith when they confirm it in the truth of God. For,

16. Calvin, *Institutes*, 3.19.3.

17. Calvin, *Institutes*, 3.19. 5. Regarding works performed by the justified, Calvin says in *Institutes* 3.17.8: "After forgiveness of sins is set forth, the good works that now follow are appraised otherwise than on their own merit. For everything imperfect in them is covered by Christ's perfection, every blemish or spot is cleansed away by his purity in order not to be brought in question at the divine judgment. Therefore, after the guilt of all transgressions that hinders man from bringing forth anything pleasing to God has been blotted out, and after the faults of imperfection, which habitually defiles even good works, is buried, the good works done by believers are accounted righteous, or what is the same thing, are reckoned as righteousness [Rom. 4:22]."

18. Calvin, *Institutes*, 3.15.8.

19. Calvin, *Institutes*, 3.15.1.

the Lord has presented to us the high and heavenly secrets under earthly things, as he knew it to be good for us in the ignorance of our flesh. Not, indeed, that such qualities be inherent in the nature of the things that are offered to us in the sacrament; but because by the Word of the Lord they are marked in this significance. For the promise which is contained in the Word always precedes; the sign is added, which sign confirms and seals that promise and renders it unto us as more certified. . . . [20]

The sacraments both exercise and confirm faith, not because of some innate quality within the sacraments, but because the promise of the Word precedes them. The promise, therefore, belongs to both the Word and the sacraments; both together assure believers of God's goodwill toward them. The inseparable relationship between faith, the Word, and the sacraments is evident in the close parallel between Calvin's definition of faith and his definition of the sacrament. A sacrament "is an outward sign by which the Lord seals on our consciences the promises of his good will toward us in order to sustain the weakness of our faith."[21] The sacraments are in this way akin to the preaching of the gospel sealing to the believer's conscience the promise of God's goodwill, confirming faith in the Word.[22]

> Therefore, Word and sacraments confirm our faith where they set before our eyes the good will of our Heavenly Father toward us, by the knowledge of whom the whole firmness of our faith stands fast and increases in strength. The Spirit confirms it when, by engraving this confirmation in our minds, he makes it effective.[23]

The Word and sacraments, therefore, are ineffectual to produce assurance apart from the accompanying power of the Holy Spirit. This leads to the fourth element in our succinct summary of Calvin's doctrine of assurance.

The Testimony of the Spirit

According to Calvin's definition of faith it is the Spirit who produces saving faith, and this faith finds as its object the Christ who is promised in

20. Calvin, *Instruction*, 67.
21. Calvin, *Institutes*, 4.14.1.
22. Calvin, *Institutes*, 4.14.1, 6.
23. Calvin, *Institutes*, 4.14.10.

the Scriptures. Warfield correctly states Calvin's view when he speaks of the Word as the *objective* factor and of the Spirit as the *subjective* factor. "The whole objective revelation of God lies, thus in the Word." On the other hand, observes Warfield, "the whole subjective capacitating for the reception of this revelation lies in the will of the Spirit."[24]

Moreover, the Spirit accomplishes this "subjective capacitating" as the Spirit of adoption. Calvin strongly emphasizes the idea that "none is a Christian save he who has been taught by the teaching of the Holy Spirit to call God his Father."[25] "The Spirit is the earnest and pledge of our adoption, so that we are surely convinced of God's Fatherly attitude toward us."[26]

Clearly, Calvin does not conceive of the witness of the Spirit in mystical terms.[27] As already noted, Calvin founded faith on the promise of Scripture, which is exercised, confirmed, and increased by the sacraments and made effectual by the Spirit. To the objection that if faith is increased by the sacraments then the Holy Spirit is given in vain, Calvin responds:

> I certainly admit to them that faith is the proper and entire work of the Holy Spirit, illumined by whom we recognize God and the treasures of his kindness, and without whose light our mind is so blinded that it can see nothing; so dull that it can sense nothing of spiritual things. But for one blessing of God which they proclaim, we recognize three. For first, the Lord teaches and instructs us by his Word. Secondly, he confirms it by the sacraments. Finally, he illumines our minds by the light of his Holy Spirit and opens our hearts for the Word and sacraments to enter in, which would otherwise only strike our ears and appear before our eyes, but not at all affect us within.[28]

The Spirit of Christ, then, "never gives us new birth without equally giving testimony and pledge to our adoption, so as to set our hearts free from fear and alarm,"[29] but never apart from the objective Word.

24. B. B. Warfield, "Calvin's Doctrine of the Knowledge of God," in *The Works of Benjamin B. Warfield* (Grand Rapids: Baker, 1981), 5:82–83.

25. Calvin, *Calvin's Commentary on Galatians,* ed. David W. Torrance and Thomas F. Torrance, trans. T. H. L. Parker (Grand Rapids: Eerdmans, 1979), 11:75.

26. Ibid., 120.

27. See T. H. L. Parker, *Calvin's Doctrine of the Knowledge of God* (Grand Rapids: Eerdmans, 1959), 107ff.; Robert Letham, "The Relationship of Saving Faith and Assurance of Salvation," (thesis, Westminster Theological Seminary, 1976), 21.

28. Calvin, *Institutes*, 4.14.8; cf. 4.14.9.

29. Calvin, *Calvin's Commentary on James,* ed. David W. Torrance and Thomas F. Torrance, trans. A. W. Morrison (Grand Rapids: Eerdmans, 1972), 3:274.

Assurance and Election

Perhaps it is Calvin's doctrine of election that can best demonstrate the pervasiveness of his doctrine of assurance and his comprehensive pastoral orientation. In *Instruction in Faith*, Calvin places his discussion of election after his vignette "We Apprehend Christ Through Faith" and before "What True Faith Is."[30] Election is never treated abstractly, that is, simply theoretically, and certainly never in a way calculated to produce pastoral problems! Calvin, rather, insists that election is the ground of the believer's assurance.

Calvin does not mean that the believer may gaze directly into God's eternal decree. Rather, he quotes with favor a passage from Bernard that indicates believers may extrapolate from a present assurance to future blessing and confidently infer that the decree of election is behind it all.[31] Thus, when the doctrine of election is received by faith "it is yet a further and more special token by which we perceive that God intends to be our Father and has adopted us to be his children. . . . For when our Lord intends to assure us of our salvation, he brings us back to this eternal election."[32]

Calvin's view is thoroughly christocentric. An attempt to look directly at the decree in order "to confirm the certainty of our salvation . . . can only worry us with a miserable distress and perturbation."[33] What then is the believer to do? He is to look to Christ in whom he has been chosen!

> Accordingly, those whom God has appointed as his sons are said to have been chosen not in themselves but in his Christ [Eph. 1:4]; for unless he could love them in him, he could not honor them with the inheritance of his Kingdom if they had not previously become partakers of him. But

---

30. Ronald S. Wallace, *Calvin, Geneva and the Reformation* (Grand Rapids: Baker, 1988), 280: "In the first edition of the *Institutes* [predestination] is discussed briefly in connection with belief in the Church. In the following editions it is discussed in connection with providence. In the final edition, however, Calvin separated these two doctrines from each other. He placed his discussion of predestination after he had discussed his doctrine of Christ, and at the climax of his discussion on 'how we receive the grace of Christ.' It may be that through this final arrangement he desired to show the doctrine in a slightly more central position, to show more clearly its practical value for living. It shows moreover that he himself had no desire or inclination to discuss a decree of eternal election before he had discussed fully the person and work of Christ. Thought on predestination must always be subordinate to thought on Christ."

31. Calvin, *Institutes*, 3.13.4.

32. Calvin, *Sermons on Ephesians* (Edinburgh: Banner of Truth, 1973) 23, 25.

33. Calvin, *Instruction*, 37.

if we have been chosen in him, we shall not find assurance of our election in ourselves; and not even in God the Father, if we conceive him as severed from his Son. Christ, then, is the mirror wherein we must, and without self-deception may, contemplate our own election. For since it is into his body the Father has destined those to be engrafted whom he has willed from eternity to be his own, that he may hold as sons all whom he acknowledges to be among his members, we have a sufficiently clear and firm testimony that we have been inscribed in the book of life [cf. Rev. 21:27] if we are in communion with Christ.[34]

In writing against Pighius he affirmed:

But I do not merely send men off to the secret election of God to await with gaping mouth salvation there. I bid them make their way directly to Christ in whom salvation is offered us, which otherwise would have lain in God. For whoever does not walk in the plain path of faith can make nothing of the election of God but a labyrinth of destruction. Therefore, that the remission of sins may be a certainty to us, our consciences rest in confidence of eternal life, and we call upon God as Father without fear, the beginning is not to be made here. We must begin with what is revealed in Christ concerning the love of the Father for us and what Christ Himself daily preaches to us through the Gospel . . . nor is tranquil peace to be found elsewhere than in the Gospel.[35]

A *Syllogismus Practicus*?

Since assurance is found in Christ and not in self, is there no place for self-examination in order to find evidences that confirm a saving relationship with Christ? Is there no *syllogismus practicus* in Calvin's thought?

34. Calvin, *Institutes*, 3.14.5; cf. *Instruction*, 37: "For, as in Christ are elected all those who have been preordained to life before the foundations of the world were laid, so also he is he in whom the pledge of our election is presented to us if we receive him and embrace him through faith. For what do we seek in election except that we be participants in the life eternal? And we have it in Christ, who was the life since the beginning and who is offered as life to us in order that all those who believe in him may not perish but enjoy the life eternal. If, therefore, in possessing Christ through faith we possess in him likewise life, we need no further inquire beyond the eternal counsel of God. For Christ is not only a mirror by which the will of God in presented to us, but he is a pledge by which life is as sealed and confirmed to us."

35. Calvin, *Concerning The Eternal Predestination of God*, trans. J. K. S. Reid (Cambridge: James Clarke and Co., 1982), 113; cf. 127, 130: "Christ therefore is for us the bright mirror of the eternal and hidden election of God, and also the earnest and pledge. . . . If Pighius asks how I know I am elect, I answer that Christ is more than a thousand testimonies to me."

It has often been denied that a *syllogismus practicus* has any place in Calvin's theology.[36] Yet, to say that the works of the believer have nothing to do with assurance does not do justice to Calvin's thought.

In examining the various strands of Calvin's thought on this subject, it is necessary first to understand that to Calvin the promise of God's love and goodwill to sinners is a personal promise to each believer. Calvin frequently uses incredibly strong language on the assurance aspect of faith. Faith does not merely believe that God saves sinners; in faith the believer is assured that God saves *me*. The Scriptures form the basis of "full assurance . . . which puts beyond doubt God's goodness clearly manifested for us."[37] The "chief hinge on which faith turns" is "that we do not regard the promises of mercy that God offers as true only outside ourselves, but not at all in us; rather that we make them ours by inwardly embracing them."[38] Again, "no man is a believer, I say, except him who, leaning upon the assurance of his salvation, confidently triumphs over the devil and death. . . ."[39]

Lest we misunderstand Calvin, it is necessary to see that though he holds that all true faith is certain, personal confidence in God's promise, this does not imply the perfection of faith. Faith grows and matures through Word and sacrament. So Calvin says that faith is mingled with incredulity even while maintaining the certainty of faith.[40] Some have imagined a contradiction in Calvin's thinking on this point.[41] However, it is essential to keep two points in mind. The first is that Calvin's great concern is the unshakeable certainty of the promise on which faith is built.[42] Second, Calvin is careful to clarify and qualify his statements about faith and assurance in light of Christian experience.

Calvin understands that believers can be shaken by the "gravest terrors" and that these temptations do not seem to be compatible with the certainty of faith. "Surely, while we teach that faith ought to be certain and assured, we cannot imagine any certainty that is not tinged with doubt, or

36. E.g., Wilhelm Niesel, *The Theology of Calvin,* trans. Harold Knight (Philadelphia: Westminster, 1956), 170ff.

37. Calvin, *Institutes,* 3.2.15.

38. Calvin, *Institutes,* 3.2.16.

39. Calvin, *Institutes,* 3.2.16.

40. Calvin, *Institutes,* 3.2.4.

41. Cunningham, *The Reformers,* 120–21; cf. R. L. Dabney, "The Theology of The Plymouth Brethren," in *Discussions of Robert Lewis Dabney* (Edinburgh: Banner of Truth, 1982) 2:173.

42. Calvin, *Institutes,* 3.2.7.

any assurance that is not assailed by some anxiety."[43] He cites the example of David before moving on to the Spirit/flesh antithesis in the next division of *Institutes of the Christian Religion*, where Calvin concludes:

> Therefore the godly heart feels in itself a division because it is partly imbued with sweetness from its recognition of the divine goodness, partly grieves in bitterness from an awareness of its calamity; partly rests upon the promise of the gospel, partly trembles at the evidence of its own iniquity; partly rejoices at the expectation of life, partly shudders at death. This variation arises from imperfections of faith, since in the course of the present life it never goes so well with us that we are wholly cured of the disease of unbelief and entirely filled and possessed by faith. Hence arise those conflicts; when unbelief, which reposes in the remains of the flesh, rises up to attack the faith that has been inwardly conceived.[44]

However, the fact that certainty is mixed with doubt does not mean that faith itself is uncertain or essentially confused:

> For even if we are distracted by various thoughts, we are not on that account completely divorced from faith. Nor if we are troubled on all sides by the agitation of unbelief, are we for that reason immersed in its abyss. If we are struck, we are not for that reason cast down from our position. For the end of the conflict is always this: that faith ultimately triumphs over those difficulties which besiege and seem to imperil it.[45]

It is the tension of the Christian who lives between the times that causes the stress to which Calvin alludes (Rom. 7:24, 25). Faith is certain and secure, but not unassailed. The believer cannot fall from the confidence he has in God's mercy.[46] Confidence in God's mercy is never destroyed and the flame of faith never quenched.[47] Indeed, why would the godly cry out for help if they were not convinced the Lord was ready to help?[48] Faith is a

43. Calvin, *Institutes*, 3.2.17.
44. Calvin, *Institutes*, 3.2.18.
45. Calvin, *Institutes*, 3.2.18.
46. Calvin, *Institutes*, 3.2.17: "Yet, once again, we deny that, in whatever way they are afflicted, they fall away and depart from the certain assurance received from God's mercy."
47. Calvin, *Institutes*, 3.2.21.
48. Calvin, *Institutes*, 3.2.21.

light that cannot be extinguished, and which, even at its lowest point, lurks beneath the ashes.[49]

Clearly, Calvin's stress is on the certainty of faith's foundation. Faith is *founded* on the promise of God's Word and not on what the believer discerns or fails to discern within himself. In this way Calvin kept equilibrium as he distinguished faith's *foundation* from faith's *evidence*.

Even though there is a wholesome place for self-examination, Calvin always directed believers away from morbid introspection.

> Surely there is no one who is not sunken in infinite filth! Let even the most perfect man descend into his conscience and call his deeds to account, what then will be the outcome for him? Will he sweetly rest as if all things were well composed between him and God and not, rather, be torn by dire torments, since if he be judged by works, he will feel grounds for condemnation within himself? The conscience, if it looks to God, must either have sure peace with his judgment or be besieged by the terrors of hell. Therefore we profit nothing in discussing righteousness unless we establish a righteousness so steadfast that it can support our souls in the judgment of God. When our souls possess that by which they may present themselves fearless before God's face and receive his judgment undismayed, then only may we know that we have found no counterfeit righteousness.[50]

Calvin's preaching did not keep his congregation fluctuating in despair. He preached that sinners must seek peace "solely in the anguish of Christ our Redeemer."[51] It is not an inward fixation on our works but an outward fixation on God's promises that constitutes the ground of assurance.

> Scripture shows that God's promises are not established unless they are grasped with the full assurance of conscience. Whenever there is doubt or uncertainty, it pronounces them void. Again, it declares that these promises do nothing but vacillate and waver if they rest upon our works.[52]

This does not mean, however, that the works of the believer have no strengthening or confirming role in a believer's sense of assurance. We

---

49. Calvin, *Institutes*, 3.2.21.
50. Calvin, *Institutes*, 3.8.13.
51. Calvin, *Institutes*, 3.8.4; cf. 3.8.3.
52. Calvin, *Institutes*, 3.8.4.

affirm that there certainly is a *syllogismus practicus* in Calvin, but it is a very carefully balanced matter, never confusing the *foundation* of assurance with the *evidences* and never severing the *evidences* from the *foundation*. G. C. Berkouwer is Calvinian when he writes: "He who loses sight of the connection between God's salvation—in His electing mercy—and the sanctification of life, becomes the victim of a serious misinterpretation of the *sola fide*."[53] He is thoroughly congruent with Calvin in his insistence that *sola fide* and the *syllogismus practicus* are not opposites from which to choose but complementary aspects of *sola fide*.

So, Calvin can speak of the believer's works as "aids":

> Although faith is confirmed by all the aids of the graces of God, it does not cease to have its foundation only in the mercy of God. For example, when we enjoy the light, we are sure the sun is shining. If the sun actually shines on the place where we are, we see it more clearly. But even when the visible rays do not reach us, we are satisfied that the sun diffuses the benefit of its brightness to us. So when faith has been founded on Christ, some things can happen to help it; by yet it rests on Christ's grace alone.[54]

Calvin, then, insists that the believer receives "a witness to his faith from his works" and calls them "a subsequent proof." But, he is careful to state, "the certainty of faith dwells only in Christ's grace."[55]

CALVIN'S DOCTRINE AND THE WESTMINSTER CONFESSION

At first blush, Calvin's emphasis and that of the Westminster Confession of Faith seem contradictory. Calvin's writings teach that assurance is in some sense of the essence of saving faith. The Confession, on the other hand, in chapter 18.3, is distanced from this emphasis. "This infallible assurance doth not so belong to the essence of faith, but that a true believer may wait long, and conflict with many difficulties, before he be partaker of it."[56]

53. G. C. Berkouwer, *Divine Election* (Grand Rapids: Eerdmans, 1960), 295; cf. 284–90.

54. Calvin, *Calvin's Commentary on I John*, ed. David W. Torrance and Thomas F. Torrance, trans. T. H. L. Parker (Grand Rapids; Eerdmans, 1978), 5:276.

55. Ibid., 246.

56. See also Westminster Larger Catechism, answer to Question 81: "Assurance of grace and salvation *not being* of the essence of faith, true believers may wait long before they obtain it . . . " (emphasis mine).

Yet, the parallels between Calvin and the Confession should not be overlooked. Both Calvin and the Confession hold that subjective assurance is based on the promise of God's Word, is the work of the Spirit, and is strengthened by means (Confession 18.1–3). Further, the note of adoption is common to both (Confession 18.2), and both confess that no believer is utterly forsaken or left in utter despair even at his weakest (Larger Catechism 81). Both assume that subjective assurance is the *norm* for believers. Calvin could have affirmed along with the Confession that "assurance of God's love, peace of conscience, joy in the Holy Ghost" are "benefits which in this life do accompany or flow from justification, adoption and sanctification" (Shorter Catechism 36). Calvin and the Confession are fundamentally unified.

But, what of Calvin's insistence that assurance is of the essence of saving faith? Is not Calvin at basic variance with the *Confession* here?

It is usually assumed that this is the case. McCleod, for example, thought that the Reformer's successors were faced with a problem in their formulation of assurance and had to find a solution.[57] Can Calvin and the *Confession* be reasonably harmonized?

The Marrow men thought so. The publication of *The Marrow of Modern Divinity* had caused quite a stir at that time. James Haddow of St. Andrews preached against the book, and the Assembly of the Church of Scotland appointed a commission to deal with the controversy surrounding it. The upshot was that in May 1722, Thomas Boston, and those who stood shoulder to shoulder with him were rebuked by the assembly. Boston saw the issue as a defense of the gospel of grace, especially the free offer of the gospel and a biblical concept of saving faith.

Among questions posed by the General Assembly to Boston and those with him was this one:

> Is knowledge, belief and persuasion that Christ died for me, and that he is mine, and that whatever he did and suffered, he did and suffered for me, the direct act of faith, whereby a sinner is united to Christ, interested in him, instated in God's covenant of grace? Or, is that knowledge a persuasion included in the very essence of that justifying act of faith?[58]

---

57. John McCleod, *Scottish Theology In Relation To Church History* (Edinburgh: Banner of Truth, 1974), 27ff.

58. Thomas Boston, "The Occasion of the 'Marrow' Controversy," in *Complete Works of Thomas Boston* (Wheaton, IL: Richard Owen Roberts, 1980), 7:478.

The question is here stated in bold-faced terms. Is assurance that Christ is *my* Savior included in the justifying act of faith?

In answering this question the Marrow men did not demur. They answered unquestionably—*yes*. Moreover, they claimed that this was the overwhelming view of Reformed divines (whose names they cited) and that this was the view necessitated by the confessional documents of the Church of Scotland as well, which speak of sinners "receiving and resting upon Christ alone for salvation, as he is offered to us in the Gospel" (Shorter Catechism 31; cf. Westminster Confession 11.2), where, said the Marrow men:

> . . . it is evident the offer of Christ to us, though mentioned in the last place, is to be believed first, for till the soul be persuaded that Christ crucified is in the Gospel set forth, and exhibited to it as if expressed by name, there can be no believing on him. And when the offer is brought home to a person by the Holy Ghost, there will be a measure of persuasion that Christ is his. . . . [59]

Insisting that the Westminster Assembly had never intended to deviate from this common doctrine, they maintained that the Larger Catechism teaching on justification demands their conclusion. They added:

> . . . the sinner has not always, at his first closing with Christ, not afterwards, such a clear, steady, and full persuasion that Christ is his,—that his sins are forgiven,—and he eventually shall be saved, as that he dare profess the same to others, or even positively assert it within himself; yet, upon the first saving manifestation of Christ to him, such a persuasion and humble confidence is begotten, as is real and relieving, and particular as to himself and his own salvation, and which works a proportionable hope as to the issue; . . . [60]

The Marrow men, also, distinguished the *persuasion* from the *sense* of assurance. "Further, as to the difference between these two kinds of assurance: the assurance of faith has its object and foundation without the man, but that of sense has them within him. . . . The one says, 'I take him for mine;' the other says, 'I feel he is mine.'"[61]

59. Ibid., 479.
60. Ibid., 483.
61. Ibid., 484.

The Marrow men help to point to the broad lines of a solution. While it is not best to speak of "two kinds of assurance," it is clear that the Marrow men were figuratively holding Calvin's *Institutes* in their left hand and the Westminster Confession of Faith in their right.

Is assurance of the essence of saving faith? Calvin answers yes, because his focus is on faith's foundation. The Confession answers no, because its focus is on the subjective persuasion of that assurance. Each is correct when the issue is viewed as one of focus and perspective. Perhaps it is best to say that assurance is of the essence of saving faith in the same way that the tree is contained in the seed. Assurance is of the essence of saving faith *implicitly.* The subjective persuasion of assurance can be cultivated just because of the certainty of its object—*Christ!*

To illustrate: I am a child standing on the edge of a cliff. Dangers surround me. My father, thirty feet below, tells me to jump into his arms for safety. I hesitate. Faith is mingled with doubt. Then, I jump. I believe that my father will catch me. I trust (*fiducia*). Later, I have nightmares. I lose for a time my sense of assurance. In my dreams, I see myself on the edge of the cliff. Will I jump or not? I wake up. Did I jump? Am I safe? Did I trust my father after all? I become oriented to my circumstances and surroundings. I am safe. My sense of assurance and safety returns. The *foundation* of my trust never changed though my *inward sense* of my father's trustworthiness faltered temporarily, but not altogether.

The question of assurance being *in some sense* of the essence of saving faith involves also the question: when I come to Christ do I believe he died for *sinners* generally or for *me* the sinner?

It is frequently claimed that when a sinner comes to Christ he may believe that Christ died for him in particular only if a universal atonement is assumed.[62] This was not the conclusion of the Marrow men or of many other Calvinistic divines who have held to the particular nature of the atonement. Why should adherence to this view demand universal atonement? It is argued that for a sinner initially to come to Christ with the assurance that Christ died for *him* in particular it must be assumed that he died for all men without exception. But, is not faith the supernatural production of the Holy Spirit? And, is not the Holy Spirit the Spirit of adoption? Cannot the Spirit who applies to the elect the work of Christ produce within the

---

62. Cf. McCleod, *Scottish Theology*, 28ff.

sinner saving faith that embraces Christ as *mine* in particular as a fruit of Christ's purchase? When the child jumps, he believes: "My father will catch *me*," not children in general. Faith embraces the promise as its own.

CONCLUSION

We have noted that Calvin's view of assurance is, in part, accounted for by the setting in which he addressed and applied the gospel. Sometimes, indeed, his statements might be considered extreme or imbalanced. Yet, Calvin and the Westminster Confession of Faith are not far apart.

The differences are more apparent than real, and result from differing emphases. Calvin is concerned to distinguish the foundation from the evidence of assurance. The evidence can only confirm an already certain foundation.

We need Calvin's emphasis. We need to be able to say to God's people that because the foundation of faith is certain, the personal persuasion of a saving relationship with Christ should thrive in an atmosphere of certainty. "Believers ought to be sure of their salvation," says Calvin. "They should not remain in suspense."[63] This should be, at least, the norm. Assurance of personal salvation should correspond to the nature of faith's foundation. Of course, Calvin is well aware that a sense of assurance can be shaken. However, "although fear is not completely shaken off, yet, when we flee to God as a quiet harbour, safe and free from all danger of ship-wreck and tempest, fear really is cast out, for it gives place to faith. Therefore, fear is not cast out in such a way that it does not assault our minds; but it is so cast out that it does not disturb us or hamper the peace that we obtain by faith."[64]

The result is incredible boldness in Christian living. The Spirit of adoption seals the testimony of the gospel to us and "raises up our spirits to dare show forth to God their desires."[65]

---

63. Calvin, *Eternal Predestination*, 132.

64. Calvin, *Commentary on 1 John*, 296; cf. this beautiful passage in *Institutes* 3.2.19 which is deserving of lengthy meditation: "It is like a man who, shut up in a prison into which the sun's rays shine obliquely and half obscured through a rather narrow window, is indeed deprived of the full sight of the sun. Yet his eyes dwell on the steadfast brightness, and he receives its benefits. Thus, bound with the fetters of an earthly body, however much we are shadowed on every side with great darkness, we are nevertheless illumined as much as need be for firm assurance when, to show forth his mercy, the light of God sheds even a little of its radiance."

65. Calvin, *Institutes*, 3.20.1.

Hence comes an extraordinary peace and repose to our consciences. For having disclosed to the Lord the necessity that was pressing upon us, we even rest fully in the thought that none of our ills is hid from him who, we are convinced, has both the will and the power to take the best care of us.[66]

When we pray stripped of self-confidence but with confidence in the Lord, we are assured of success in that for which we pray. "We enjoin believers to be convinced with firm assurance of mind that God is favorable and benevolent to them."[67] "We receive this singular fruit of God's promises when we frame our prayers without hesitation or trepidation; but, relying upon the word of him whose majesty would otherwise terrify us, we dare call upon him as Father, while he deigns to suggest this sweetest of names to us."[68]

While due attention should be given to those who may be presumptuous—a concern not absent in Calvin—could it be that this Reformation emphasis on assurance is to varying degrees lacking in preaching and the administration of the sacraments with the result that the Christian ministry is failing in large measure to galvanize God's people for Christian living? If Calvin's words were carefully and critically studied by pastors, the church surely would reap large dividends, not least of which would be more mature faith and greater assurance before God and the world.

Assurance of personal faith is not isolated from the larger question of how one can live with certainty in the world, and perhaps this theme has peculiar application as we face a culture whose worldview is one of relativism, one that affirms radical autonomy and asserts with an inconsistent sense of authority that there can be no ground for certainty. If the church and her members do not live before God in the certainty of faith, can we consistently offer a message to a relativistic culture that turns up its collective nose at the notion of God's authority?

It is in this context that the early Berkouwer spoke of "the self-created problems of modern Protestantism" and called the church to express "the love indignation of the Gospel" that we may speak the message loud and clear.[69] Berkouwer called the church back to the certainty

---

66. Calvin, *Institutes*, 3.20.2.
67. Calvin, *Institutes*, 3.20.12.
68. Calvin, *Institutes*, 3.20.14.
69. G. C. Berkouwer, *Modern Uncertainty and Christian Faith* (Grand Rapids: Eerdmans, 1953), 35.

of the Reformation, the genius of which was "a new reading of the old Word," and to bow before the scepter of Christ.[70] Modern uncertainty is "a falling away of confidence in the possibilities of human reason, . . . the invasion of irrationalism."[71] In other words, modern uncertainty is an expression of doubt about the possibility of truly knowing anything. "This irrationalism wants to build a new house on the ruins of our old culture without conversion to the living God."[72] Berkouwer rightly saw that "the more insecure the world becomes, the more the attack on the assurance of faith will increase. For that assurance seems to others who do not have this faith, to be a kind of pride."[73] However, "*the Church is only attacked when her voice is clear.*"[74] And, Berkouwer understood that "we must stand in the midst of our time, not afraid of any problem, because we still believe that the Word of the Scripture is for science and for all the modern problems of our time a lamp unto our feet and a light unto our path."[75]

It is not difficult to detect in Berkouwer's comments the influence of Herman Bavinck and behind Bavinck, Calvin. Bavinck gave much attention to assurance of faith, especially in his little book *The Certainty of Faith*,[76] and in his *Reformed Dogmatics*.[77] "To the question 'Why do you believe?' Christians reply, 'Because God has spoken' (*Deus dixit*). They cannot indicate another, deeper ground. If you then ask them, 'But why do you believe that God has spoken, say, in Scripture?' they can only answer that God so transformed them internally that they recognize Scripture as the word of God. But having said that, they said it all. The witness of God is the ground, but God's grace, the will, is the cause of faith."[78] And it is when the church rests in this self-authenticating Word from God that she is freed to serve God and man. Assurance of faith is the necessary enabler for ministry and service. Without it, the church and the believers curve inward. Bavinck understood this:

70. Ibid., 40, 46–48.
71. Ibid., 52.
72. Ibid., 53.
73. Ibid., 54.
74. Ibid., 83.
75. Ibid., 57.
76. Herman Bavinck, *The Certainty of Faith* (St. Catherines, Ontario: Paideia, 1980).
77. Herman Bavinck, *Reformed Dogmatics*, 4 vols. (Grand Rapids: Baker, 2003–2008); see especially 1:497–621; 3:536–37; 3:589–95.
78. Bavinck, *Reformed Dogmatics*, 1:582.

As long as we aren't certain and firm in our faith and we still doubt, we will continue to experience anxiety and fear and will not have the boldness and trust of children of God. We will still be far too much concerned with ourselves to be able to devote our attention to works of love toward God and our neighbor. The eye of the soul remains turned inward and does not have a broad, liberated vision of the world. We are still more or less subject to the spirit of fear. We still feel far from God and do not live out of fellowship with Him. Secretly, we still harbor the thoughts that we must please Him with our stature and virtues, and we still act out of legalistic principles; we remain servants, not children.

But if in faith we fasten immediately onto the promises of God and take our stand in His rich grace, then we are His children and receive the Spirit of adoption. This Spirit is appropriate to our sonship; it testifies with our spirit that we are children of God. Then we feel like children; we have the stature and experience of children and as a matter of course do good works, not for wages like servants, but out of thankfulness.[79]

This is Calvin's legacy to us, the liberating proclamation of a well-established faith based on a self-attesting Scripture that enables the church to serve God and man in the context of its God-focused certainty. And, in the church's message to the world, we must insist that, just as with all things of God, certainty cannot be man's attainment but can only be God's gift.

---

79. Bavinck, *The Certainty of Faith*, 92–93.

19

Calvin on Baptism: Baptismal Regeneration or the *Duplex Loquendi Modus*?[1]

JAMES J. CASSIDY

DR. RICHARD GAFFIN'S method of exegeting Holy Scripture was, and remains, inimitable. I observed it firsthand on numerous occasions during my student years at Westminster Theological Seminary. Like all good exegetes, Dr. Gaffin began with the text. But by the time he was finished, one was left with no doubts: the doctrine that he derived from the text was unquestionably heaven-sent—and therefore unquestionably correct. It is surely this careful handling of Scripture—in both the close detail of the immediate context as well as the broader redemptive-historical context—that the *Book of Church Order* of the Orthodox Presbyterian Church has in mind when it speaks of "painstakingly expounding the Word of God." Dr. Gaffin has exemplified such expositional faithfulness to the Reformed faith.

He learned it, at least in part, from John Calvin—a master biblical and systematic theologian himself. For Calvin there was no rift between sound

1. I would like to thank Jeremiah Montgomery for his editorial assistance on this paper.

biblical exegesis, right systematic doctrine, and faithful pastoral ministry. This we see nowhere more clearly than in his teaching on the sacraments, particularly in his treatment of baptism.

We may begin our observations by asking, "What is the relation between baptism and salvation in the thought of John Calvin?" This is a timely question, given that there has been much discussion over this very subject of late. On the one hand, there are those who claim that Calvin taught a form of baptismal regeneration.[2] On the other hand, there are those who insist he taught presumptive regeneration.[3] It should be born in mind, however, that none of these claimants are writing in an agenda-free fashion. It seems that across the board, they are reacting against a perceived trend—in both American Protestantism generally and in American Presbyterianism particularly—toward turning the sacrament of baptism into a "bare sign." It is claimed that baptism is being denigrated into a mere symbol. Consequently, the trend is toward making baptism almost optional in the life and ministry of the church.

As for us, we are sympathetic with such concerns. A marginalization of the sacraments can be sensed in broad evangelicalism, and perhaps even in some quarters of the Reformed church. What, however, is the proper response to a low view of baptism? A high view would seem to be the answer, but how high do we go before running into baptismal regeneration? Does having a high view of this sacrament necessarily entail something close to an *ex opere operato*[4] approach to sacramental efficacy? Certainly if Calvin

---

2. Rich Lusk, "Calvin on Baptism, Penance, and Absolution," n.p. [cited Feb. 3, 2007]. Online: http://www.hornes.org/theologia/content/rich_lusk/calvin_on_baptism_penance_absolution.htm#7b, and http://www.hornes.org/theologia/content/rich_lusk/baptismal_efficacy_the_Reformed_tradition_past_present_future.htm#43b. Also, see his article in *The Federal Vision,* ed. Steve Wilkins and Duane Garner (Monroe, LA: Athanasius, 2004) 89ff. In these discussions it is often correctly pointed out how the term "regeneration" was not used in the sense of the initial effectual call of God by which he makes a sinner to be "converted," but, in a broader sense, to denote the progressive spiritual growth in holiness throughout the life of the believer. However, the way we will be employing it here is in the more narrow sense of the initial working of grace in the heart of the sinner.

3. Lewis B. Schenck, *The Presbyterian Doctrine of Children in the Covenant: An Historical Study of the Significance of Infant Baptism in the Presbyterian Church* (Phillipsburg, NJ: P&R, 2003), 11–13, 16.

4. I am using this term in the way used by Charles Hodge when he says that this view of the sacraments holds that "they have a real inherent and objective value, which renders them effectual in communicating saving benefits to those who receive them," Charles Hodge, *Systematic Theology* (Grand Rapids: Eerdmans, 1982), 3:489. This is the Roman Catholic view at the time of the Counter-Reformation as seen in the Council of Trent, session 6, canon 8 where it says, "If anyone saith, that by the said sacraments of the New Law grace is not conferred *through*

taught baptismal regeneration, this ought to lead us in the direction of answering these questions in the affirmative. Calvin, of course, was not infallible, but given Calvin's high esteem within the Reformed tradition, we ought to give him a serious hearing.

In the spirit of such a serious hearing, the position of this essay is that Calvin did not teach what we commonly call baptismal regeneration. Thus, adhering to a "bare sign" view of baptism is not the only means of breaching faith with the Reformed tradition. Going to the opposite extreme and holding to anything akin to baptismal regeneration is equally unfaithful.

In contrast with both these extremes, Calvin's view might be summed up by the term "baptismal efficacy." In other words, Calvin understood baptism to be a means of grace.[5] According to the Reformers, there are three means of grace in the church: Word, sacrament, and prayer. These three means become effectual in a qualified sense: *they are efficacious only in the lives of the elect when they are received by faith and in the power of the Holy Spirit.*

In other words, for Calvin there is no automatic *ex opere operato* connection between the means of grace and the person receiving them. Grace is not communicated automatically, in a mechanical fashion, to the person receiving its means. This is not what is meant by saying that the sacraments are effectual. Instead, the phrase *means of grace* denotes the earthly and human way through which the Holy Spirit ordinarily communicates grace to the believer. In order to understand this better, we need further to explicate several important qualifications.

THE WORD PREACHED AS MEANS OF GRACE

Before we show how Calvin understood baptismal efficacy, we will illustrate how he applied it to the Word, especially as it is preached.[6] The

---

the act performed (Latin: *ex opere operato*), but that faith alone in the divine promise suffices for the obtaining of grace: let him be anathema," Philip Schaff, *Creeds of Christendom*, 2:121. We will maintain this definition despite pleas from some ecumenical corners to avoid it. See, for instance, S. Joel Garver, "Ex Opere Operato," http://www.joelgarver.com/writ/sacr/exopere.htm [Cited Feb. 3, 2007].

5. The phrase used here (i.e., means of grace) is not one found often in English translations of Calvin's writings. Where he uses it, it is in a much broader way than we are using it here. However, the concept behind the phrase as used here is very much present in his thought.

6. See Roland S. Wallace, *Calvin's Doctrine of the Word and Sacrament* (Grand Rapids: Eerdmans, 1957), 21ff.

first thing to note in this regard is that the three means of grace (i.e., Word, sacrament, and prayer) are effectual only for the elect. Grace is not automatically communicated to any person who is present to receive them. For instance, having a person present at a sermon to hear the Word of God preached does not *necessarily* ensure that he will be blessed by it. In fact, for the reprobate, that sermon (assuming it is faithful preaching) becomes not a means of grace, but rather a means of judgment. Calvin, commenting on Matthew 16:19, says, "There Christ declared that the preaching of the Gospel would not be without effect, but that the *odor* of it would either be *life-giving* or *deadly*."[7] The nature of the effect depends on whether the one who receives the Word receives it in faith or rejects it in unbelief. Again, Calvin puts it clearly:

> Thus, our Savior, while declaring that none can come to him but those whom the Father draws, and that the elect come after they have heard and learned of the Father (John 6:44, 45), does not lay aside the office of teacher, but carefully invites those who must be taught inwardly by the Spirit before they can make any profit. The reprobate, again, are admonished by Paul, that the doctrine is not in vain; because, while it is in them a savor of death unto death, it is still a sweet savor unto God.[8]

Notice that Calvin explains "none can come to him but . . . the elect after they have heard." Here we have the intricate connection between what we today would refer to as election, effectual calling ("whom the Father draws"), and the blessing received from hearing the Word taught ("they can make any profit"). For Calvin, it is the elect alone who are blessed by the preaching of the Word.

Second, being elect is not enough.[9] A person can be elect and sit under the faithful preaching of the Word and not be blessed, if he is

---

7. John Calvin, *Calvin's Commentaries* (Grand Rapids: Baker, 2003) 16:358.

8. John Calvin, *The Comprehensive John Calvin Collection*, CD-ROM (The Ages Digital Library System, 2002).

9. As Gaffin reminds us in his inaugural lecture to the Charles Krahe Chair of Biblical and Systematic Theology at Westminster Seminary, Calvin is adamant that without faith Christ and all his benefits remain outside of us to no effect. "Biblical Theology and the Westminster Standards," *WTJ* 65 (2003): 170. In this context Gaffin is arguing for the essential link between *historia salutis* and *ordo salutis*, and how Christ's work in history is applied to the individual believer. But the relevance to our point here is clear: the relation between election and faith is essential. If election is held up at the expense of the God-wrought faith of the believer, then the

still in a state of rebellion. So the second requirement for the preaching of the Word to be a means of grace is that it is received by faith. In this way an elect person may hear the gospel preached, while in a state of rebellion, and not be blessed. But at a later time, after he has been brought to faith, he will be blessed. According to Calvin, an elect person *will* believe. However, until the Spirit works faith in him, he will not, indeed *cannot*, be blessed by the Word of God. Rather, the Word of God condemns him.

It is important to keep in mind that the Word of God preached is never devoid of effect. If a person does not hear the Word by faith he receives the opposite of blessing: a curse. Wallace summarizes Calvin's position aptly when he says,

> Thus the true preaching of the Word of God, if it does not find a willing response through faith in the hearer, can, instead of bringing blessing and salvation, rouse within men the opposite effect and harden the heart instead of blessing it.[10]

Wallace continues:

> Thus preaching has a twofold effect. It can either soften or harden the heart. It can either save or condemn the hearer. . . . As the Word is efficacious for the salvation of believers, so it is abundantly efficacious for the condemning of the wicked[11]

So, for Calvin, in order for the Word to be an effectual means of grace, the elect must receive the Word by Spirit-wrought faith.

The third thing to note with regard to the preached Word as a means of grace is the power of the Holy Spirit. The Holy Spirit alone can give the faith requisite to make the preaching of the Word a means of grace. From Calvin's perspective, it is "by the inward illumination of his Spirit [that God]

---

danger of hyper-Calvinism lurks at the door. It is this error that we hope to avoid, in staying faithful to Calvin, when we say "election is not enough."

10. Wallace, *Calvin's Doctrine*, 92. Wallace's volume is mostly reliable, though an element of neoorthodoxy can be detected in his treatment of Calvin on the nature of Scripture (see, for instance, 113). A brief, but helpful, critique can be found in J. G. Vos's review in *WTJ* 21 (1959): 103–7.

11. Ibid, 93.

causes the preached Word to dwell in their [i.e., true believers] hearts."[12] Or, elsewhere, he puts it like this:

> This work of the Spirit, then, is joined with the word of God. But a distinction is made, that we may know that the external word is of no avail by itself, unless animated by the power of the Spirit.[13]

The Holy Spirit is needed not only to give faith initially, but throughout the life of the believer. He is needed every time a Christian hears the Word of God preached. The Holy Spirit is needed to illuminate the hearts and minds of his people—to the end that they may hear the Word of God, understand it, and be blessed by it. And yet, the Holy Spirit is sovereign and he may not make the preaching of the Word a blessing to the elect person *at the time of the hearing it*. To give a rough illustration, a person may hear a faithful sermon at age eighteen when he is living in unbelief. That sermon may not become a blessing to him until he is seventy-five, after having come to faith. In other words, the Holy Spirit can choose to make the preached Word a blessing to an elect person *when* and *where* He pleases.

Finally, all this is the case "ordinarily." The means of grace in the preaching of the Word is the way God ordinarily works. Nevertheless, God, being sovereign, may work apart from or besides this means. While he ordinarily blesses his people through Word, sacrament, and prayer, he may choose not to work that way and apply grace directly and immediately to one of his elect. This is the instance often cited by Calvin and others in the case of the death of an infant. The child, if he is elect, would have received full grace upon grace apart from partaking in the ordinary means of grace. But more on this below.

BAPTISM AS MEANS OF GRACE

Having seen how Calvin qualifies the Word of God preached as a means of grace, we are now in a better position to understand his view of baptism. Calvin's teaching on how the preached Word is a means of

---

12. John Calvin, *Institutes of the Christian Religion*, ed. John T. McNeill, trans. Ford Lewis Battles, Library of Christian Classics (London: SCM, 1960), 3.24.8.

13. Calvin, *The Comprehensive John Calvin.*

grace parallels how the sacraments in general are effectual, particularly baptism. Like the preached Word, baptism is a means of grace. And as such it communicates grace. It confers that which it signs and seals: adoption, regeneration, and the washing away of sins.[14] Baptism does not confer grace in an automatic or *ex opere operato* fashion, but only with the following qualifications.

First, baptism is a means of grace, by conferring what it seals and signifies, only for the elect. What Calvin says about the sacraments in general is also true of baptism in particular:

> The Holy Spirit, whom the sacraments do not bring promiscuously to all, but whom the Lord specially confers on his people, brings the gifts of God along with him, makes way for the sacraments, and causes them to bear fruit. [15]

Many reprobate receive the sacrament of baptism. But in such instances it is far from being a means of grace. In fact, it is a means of judgment. This is not to say, however, that it does not provide some external and outward benefit to the reprobate person. It does in some ways. It initiates them into the life of the church. And there they receive many benefits because of the "common operations of the Holy Spirit."[16] To them are given the oracles and ordinances of God, for even the reprobate are "those who have once been enlightened, who have tasted the heavenly gift, and have shared in the Holy Spirit, and have tasted the goodness of the word of God and the powers of the age to come" (Heb. 6:4–5). But, and this is all important, *these are not eternal and internal operations of the Holy Spirit that accompany salvation*. Rather, they are the common works of the Spirit given to all those in the field, whether tares or wheat.

Second, baptism confers what it signs and signifies by faith. Calvin argues:

> Therefore, let it be regarded as a settled principle that the sacraments have the same office as the Word of God: to offer and set forth Christ

---

14. Calvin, *Institutes* 4.16.2.

15. Ibid., 4.14.17.

16. This is language drawn from the Westminster Confession of Faith, 10.4 and the Larger Catechism, 68.

to us, and in him the treasures of heavenly grace. *But they avail and profit nothing unless received in faith.*[17]

Later, Calvin reiterates:

> Let us take as proof of this, Cornelius the centurion, who, having already received forgiveness of sins and the visible graces of the Holy Spirit, was nevertheless baptized. He did not seek an ampler forgiveness of sins through baptism, but a surer exercise of faith—indeed, increase of assurance from a pledge. Perhaps someone will object: why, then, did Ananias tell Paul to wash away his sins through baptism if sins are not washed away by the power of baptism itself? I reply: we are said to receive, obtain, and acquire what, *according as our faith is aware*, is shown forth to us by the Lord, whether when he first testifies to it, or when he confirms more fully and more surely what has been attested. Ananias meant only this: "To be assured, Paul, that your sins are forgiven, be baptized. For the Lord promises forgiveness of sins in baptism; receive it, and be secure." . . . But from this sacrament, as from all others, we obtain only as much as *we receive in faith.*[18]

For Calvin, then, baptism is a sign that ordinarily follows faith. Of course, in an elect infant the case is different: faith follows baptism. For an elect infant who does not have faith at the time of his or her baptism (though Calvin can speak about an infant having a latent faith like that of Jeremiah, David, or John the Baptist),[19] the baptism becomes a means of grace later in life when the child does come to faith. The grace that is signified at baptism is then conferred on him or her. But, and this is crucial for understanding Calvin at this point, *baptism as a means of grace does not end there.* For the elect who are regenerate, baptism continues to be a means of grace as they continue to look back at their baptism and strive to improve it.[20] By faith we look back at our baptism and are encouraged. As Calvin says: "The great truth, for example, of our spiritual regeneration, though but once represented to us in baptism, should remain fixed

---

17. Calvin *Institutes*, 4.14.17, emphasis added.
18. Ibid., 4.15.15, emphasis added.
19. See his argument in *Institutes* 4.16.18–20.
20. For a similar point, consult the Westminster Larger Catechism, 167.

in our minds through our whole life. . . ."[21] Similarly stated, baptism is an ongoing means of grace for the elect. Each time a true believer looks back at his baptism by faith in Christ, the Holy Spirit communicates the grace signified by the sacrament.

Third, baptism confers what it signs and signifies only by the power of the Holy Spirit.[22] Calvin writes:

> We must not suppose that there is some latent virtue inherent in the sacraments by which they, in themselves, confer the gifts of the Holy Spirit upon us in the same way in which wine is drunk out of a cup, since the only office divinely assigned them is to attest and ratify the benevolence of the Lord towards us; and they avail no farther than accompanied by the Holy Spirit to open our minds and hearts, and make us capable of receiving this testimony, in which various distinguished graces are clearly manifested.[23]

Just as was mentioned above with reference to the Word of God preached, likewise with baptism: a means of grace may be efficacious at times other than when it is received. The Holy Spirit is sovereign, and so he may or may not confer the grace signed and sealed in baptism at the time of its administration:

> Whatever God offers in the sacraments, depends on the secret operation of the Holy Spirit. . . . So far, then, is God from resigning the grace of His Spirit to the sacraments, that all their efficacy and utility are lodged in the Spirit alone. . . . Thus the sacraments are effectual only "where and whenever God is so pleased."[24]

Subsequently Calvin makes explicit the connection between baptism and the Word of God as means of grace:

> As the outward voice of man cannot at all penetrate the heart, it is in the free and sovereign determination of God to give the profitable use of the

21. John Calvin, *Commentary on the Book of Psalms* (Grand Rapids: Baker, 2003), 2:435. See also *Institutes*, 4.15.3.
22. Wallace, *Calvin's Doctrine*, 169–71.
23. Calvin, *Institutes*, 4.14.17.
24. Wallace, *Calvin's Doctrine*, 169.

signs to whom he pleases. . . . The external administration of Baptism profits nothing, save only where God pleases it shall.[25]

In other words, God may confer the grace *before* the sacrament is administered, or he may confer it *at the time* of its administration, or he may confer it shortly or long *after* its administration. In answering Westphal's teaching that infants who are baptized are always regenerated, Calvin responds, ". . . that the nature of baptism or the Supper must not be tied down to an instant of time."[26]

Fourth, the grace that is signified in baptism is not necessarily tied to the sign. God is sovereign and may work with or without the sign, even though he ordinarily works through means. Calvin puts it this way:

> The grace of God is not confined to the sign: so that God may not, if He pleases, bestow it without the aid of the sign. Besides, many receive the sign who are not partakers of grace; for the sign is common to all, to the good and to the bad alike; but the Spirit is bestowed on none but the elect, and the sign, as we have said, has no efficacy without the Spirit.[27]

God may certainly confer the grace signed and sealed by baptism apart from or besides the actual administration of the sacrament. While ordinarily this is not how God works, the doctrine of his sovereignty demands that he not be tied down or restricted to the ordinary use of the means of grace:

> [W]e also maintain that it is the ordinary instrument of God in washing and renewing us; in short, in communicating to us salvation. The only exception we make is, that the hand of God must not be tied down to the instrument. He may of himself accomplish salvation. For when an opportunity of Baptism is wanting, the promise of God alone is amply sufficient.[28]

25. Ibid., 170.
26. John Calvin, *Selected Works of John Calvin* (Grand Rapids: Baker, 1983) 2:342.
27. Calvin, *Calvin's Commentaries on the Epistles of Paul to the Galatians and Ephesians*, 320.
28. "Acts of the Council Of Trent, with the Antidote," in *Tracts and Treatises* (Grand Rapids: Eerdmans, 1958) 3:162–63.

The *Signa* and *Res*

Having addressed the qualifications Calvin makes about the efficacy of Word and sacrament, we move on to develop the relationship in his thought between the sign (*signa*) and the thing signified (*res*) with reference to baptism. For Calvin, the relationship between them is so close that, without confusing them, the language of the *res* can be used for the *signa*. In this way, the Reformed and Chalcedonian Christology was helpful as an analogy.[29] As Christ is fully God and fully man, in hypostatic union without separation or confusion, so likewise is the relation between the sign and the thing signified.

In other words, there is a "sacramental union" in baptism. What this means is that, between the sign and the thing signified, the names and effects of the one are attributable to the other. In this way, the Bible can speak about baptism as the washing of regeneration (Titus 3:5) and as that which saves (1 Peter 3:21)—not because the sign *is* the thing itself, but because of the sacramental union. The same is the case with Christ. By reason of the unity of his person, that which is proper to one of Christ's natures is sometimes in Scripture attributed to the person denominated by the other nature.[30] And just as with the two natures of Christ, so with the relation between baptism and regeneration: there is no conversion, confusion, or composition:

> Not that such graces are included and bound in the sacrament so as to be conferred by its efficacy, but only that by this badge the Lord declares to us that He is pleased to bestow all these things upon us. . . . The truth is never to be separated from the signs, though it ought to be distinguished from them. . . . The signs and the things signified are not disjoined but distinct. . . . The sacrament is one thing, the virtue of the sacrament is another. . . . The efficacy and use of the sacraments will be properly understood by him who shall connect the sign and the thing signified, in

29. See Wallace, 167–69. For a helpful treatment of Calvin's Chalcedonian Christology, see Mark A. Garcia, "Imputation and the Christology of Union with Christ: Calvin, Osiander, and the Contemporary Quest for a Reformed Model," *WTJ* 68 (2006): 219–51, and the literature cited there, esp. 226ff. More explicitly on the sacraments in Calvin, see Garcia, "Life in Christ: The Function of Union with Christ in the *Unio-Duplex Gratia* Structure of Calvin's Soteriology with Special Reference to the Relationship of Justification and Sanctification in Sixteenth-Century Context," (PhD diss., University of Edinburgh, 2004), 132–74.

30. This language is borrowed in part from the Westminster Confession of Faith 8.7. It is a fruitful exercise to compare 8.7 with 27.2 to see the analogy between the doctrine of the incarnation and the sacraments as the confession here faithfully follows Calvin.

such a manner as not to make the sign unmeaning and inefficacious, and
who nevertheless shall not, for the sake of adorning the sign, take away
from the Holy Spirit what belongs to him.[31]

Calvin argues that the error of the Roman Catholic Church's doctrine
of baptismal regeneration was the confusion of the sign and the thing
signified. As we will later see, this is why Calvin can write with language
that would lead us to think he is advocating baptismal regeneration—
while at the same time vehemently rejecting the Roman doctrine. In so
doing, he borrows from Scripture a *duplex loquendi modus*: a "twofold
way of speaking" concerning the sacraments.[32] This is part and parcel
of Calvin's hermeneutic with reference to certain passages. The exegesis depends on the audience that Scripture is addressing. If the text is
addressing believers, often the thing signified will be predicated of the
sign. However, if the audience is unbelievers, the text may speak of the
signs as "frigid empty figures."[33] Calvin articulates the *duplex loquendi
modus* this way:

> But the argument, that, because they have been baptized, they have put on
> Christ, appears weak; for how far is baptism from being efficacious to all?
> Is it reasonable that the grace of the Holy Spirit should be so closely linked
> to an external symbol? Does not the uniform doctrine of Scripture, as well
> as experience, appear to confute this statement? I answer, it is customary
> with Paul to treat of the sacraments in two points of view. When he is
> dealing with the hypocrites, in whom the mere symbol awakens pride, he
> then proclaims loudly the emptiness and worthlessness of the outward
> symbol, and denounces, in strong terms, their foolish confidence. In such
> cases he contemplates not the ordinance of God, but the corruption of
> wicked men. When, on the other hand, he addresses believers, who make
> a proper use of the symbols, he then views them in connexion with the
> truth—which they represent. In this case, he makes no boast of any false
> splendour as belonging to the sacraments, but calls out attention to the
> actual fact represented by the outward ceremony. Thus, agreeably to the Di-
> vine appointment, the truth comes to be associated with the symbols.[34]

31. Wallace, *Calvin's Doctrine*, 164–65.
32. Ibid., 173.
33. Calvin, *Institutes*, 4.14.17.
34. Calvin, *Calvin's Commentaries on the Epistles of Paul to the Galatians and Ephesians*, 111.

In sum, Scripture, depending on whom is being addressed in the immediate context, can speak of the sacrament in one of two ways. Either it can speak in language that predicates the *res* for the *signa* if the audience is made up of believers (as in Titus 3:5 and 1 Peter 3:21), or it can speak in a way that emphasizes the distinction between the *res* and *signa* when the spiritual state of the audience is unbelief or questionable. Therefore, since Scripture speaks in two ways about the sacraments (*duplex loquendi modus*), so does Calvin. This understanding of the *duplex loquendi modus* of Scripture will go a long way toward understanding the difficult quotations from Calvin often cited, particularly by those who desire to move his position in the direction of something akin to baptismal regeneration.

ADDRESSING THE TOUGH QUOTATIONS

All of the above notwithstanding, there remains with us a nagging question concerning some of the citations from Calvin's teachings. Despite what we surveyed above, there are some quotations that make us scratch our heads and wonder whether he did not, in fact, believe in baptismal regeneration. A comprehensive survey of all these citations is not possible here. However, we will consider a representative share of them. Then we will propose some sound principles for understanding Calvin's language.

The first and most often quoted citation comes from his *Antidote Against the Decrees of the Council of Trent*:

> We assert that the whole guilt of sin is taken away in baptism, so that the remains of sin still existing are not imputed. That this may be more clear, let my readers call to mind that there is a twofold grace in baptism, for therein both remission of sins and regeneration are offered to us. We teach that full remission is made, but that regeneration is only begun and goes on making progress during the whole of life. Accordingly, sin truly remains in us, and is not instantly in one day extinguished by baptism, but as the guilt is effaced it is null in regard to imputation. Nothing is plainer than this doctrine.[35]

The first point that we need to keep in mind here as we interpret Calvin is the point in history during which he penned these words. Just as with

---

35. Calvin, *Selected Works*, 3:85–86.

any writer, Calvin's thought developed throughout his life. *The Antidote* was written in 1547, twelve years before the final edition of his *Institutes* was published. Whatever he may have believed at this point, we must take our definitive information on his views from his later, more mature writings. They indicate that he held to a close relation between the sign and the thing signified, such that the sign and the thing signified can share common attributes without being identified. In this connection it is essential to remember Calvin's Chalcedonian Christology, discussed above. The *signa* and the *res* are always inseparably joined without being confused.[36] In fact, the two are so closely joined that the characteristics of the one may be predicated of the other in the *duplex loquendi modus*.

The second consideration we must keep in mind is the context. The issue many interpreters of Calvin fail to discern is Calvin's polemical context. In other words, against whom is Calvin writing? Calvin, in the above quotation, is responding to the first decree of the fifth session of the Council of Trent held on June 17, 1546. This decree addressed the topic of original sin. It is made up of five condemnations—or "heads." The first head condemns whomever does not confess that Adam, in his sin, lost his original holiness and righteousness and incurred God's wrath. The second head condemns any who deny that Adam's sin was not just for himself, but for his posterity as well. The third head pronounces an *anathema* on any who say that this original sin may be remedied by human nature or anything

---

36. It is simply good historical theology to be mindful of the intricate interlacing of doctrines in the systematic mind of the sixteenth-century Reformers. Garcia models this approach to understanding Calvin. He writes,

"Sacramental theology is layered theology. It rests, as the sixteenth century perhaps uniquely attests, upon certain christological and soteriological premises. The way one understands the person of Christ, particularly in terms of the *communicatio idiomatum*, is tied to one's view of how this Christ has become our salvation, and, further, how this Christ and this salvation are 'given' in the sacraments. Especially in its formative Reformation expression, the theology of the sacraments rests upon an explicit relationship of interdependence, a fact that points to the sixteenth-century presupposition of the unity of truth. Naturally, then, and as the polemic of this period proves, an attack on one 'layer' is perceived as an attack on them all. From the Reformed literature of the period, one often encounters a line of accusation that typically runs thus: a misunderstanding of Augustine on signification results in the confusion of *signa* and *res*, which leads in turn to a denigration of the real, that is, locally circumscribed humanity of the Mediator. Alternatively: the supposed ubiquity of the humanity of Christ necessarily implies a rejection of Chalcedon, which again obscures the ontological distinction and distance between God and humankind. Yet again: a local, 'corporeal' presence of Christ in the Supper marginalizes the indispensable work of the Spirit for salvation." (132–33).

Garcia reminds us that one may not separate Calvin's Christology from his sacramental theology.

other than the merit of Jesus Christ. The fourth head is to condemn all who say that newborn infants should not be baptized, or that such an infant has no original sin.

With these first four heads Calvin has no problem. He begins his "antidote" here wondering why the council rants about the denial of these doctrines, as if the Reformation were about challenging them. Here, Calvin shows himself shrewd and discerning. He does not condemn Trent in all the council says. In fact, Calvin often will say "amen" to the pronouncements. And concerning these first four heads, he is in full agreement:

> As to these there will be no dispute, and therefore it was obviously mali-
> cious in them to premise that their object was to settle the dissensions
> which have arisen at this time. Of what use was it, pray, to thunder out
> so many anathemas? Just to make the unskillful believe that there really
> was some ground for it; though, in fact, there was not.[37]

However, it is the fifth head of the decree that Calvin challenges. The fifth head anathematizes those who deny that original sin is remitted by the grace of Christ through baptism and assert that the sin nature is not wholly taken away in the regenerate person. What the council means by this is that the regenerate person is one who is completely purified of the sin nature, though there may remain a desire for sin (what the Roman Catholics call "concupiscence"). The council further affirms that this desire, though the apostle sometimes calls it sin, is really not sin! In the regenerate it is not properly called sin, though it is of sin and inclines to sin.

Calvin takes issue over this topic, what we will call here "indwelling sin," and he deals with this in his response, not baptism per se. So Calvin asserts exactly what Trent anathematizes. He asserts that the guilt of sin is taken away in baptism so that the indwelling sin of the believer is not imputed to him. The accent here for Calvin is not on baptism. His dispute with Trent at this point has nothing to do with the sacrament. Rather, his emphasis is on the non-imputation of guilt to the believer despite the fact that the sinner still has indwelling sin—real, natural, and properly called "sin." This point is important because Calvin is echoing the Reformation teaching (expressed so well by Martin Luther) that the believer is *simul iustus et peccator*. In other words, Calvin is speaking imprecisely about the

---

37. Calvin, *Selected Works*, 3:85.

sacrament. One might even say that he is granting Rome's view of baptism for the sake of the argument, so that he might speak precisely on the doctrine of indwelling sin.

Even so, we can understand Calvin's expression on baptism here in light of how he understands the sacraments as a whole. As discussed above, the sign and the thing signified are so closely related, without being confused, that the thing signified can be predicated by the use of the wording for the sign. This is how Calvin interprets the language in 1 Peter 3:21. Therefore, he can concede that "the guilt of sin is taken away in baptism" because it is the sign and seal of the forgiveness of sins. And Scripture often uses the term denoting the sign in connection with the thing signified. In this way Jesus can say "this is my body" with reference to the bread, without confusing the bread with his body. Likewise, Peter can say "baptism . . . now saves you" without confusing the waters of baptism with the internal washing of the Spirit. This goes to the heart of Calvin's sacramental theology. At the very least, we can be confident to conclude that whatever Calvin may mean here, he certainly is not advocating a doctrine of baptismal regeneration or anything that would see grace being communicated through baptism in an *ex opere operato* fashion. While Calvin does not tell us, we can reasonably conclude that he is either granting the language of Trent for the sake of argument, or he is employing the concept of the *duplex loquendi modus*—or both.

Let us move then to the next citation, which is often invoked to show that Calvin believes in baptismal regeneration. It is from the *Institutes* as follows:

> For as in baptism, God, regenerating us, engrafts us into the society of his church and makes us his own by adoption, so we have said, that he discharges the function of a provident householder in continually supplying to us the food to sustain and preserve us in that life into which he has begotten us by his Word.[38]

Again, context is everything. Those who would make Calvin to be a supporter of their position have indeed here taken him out of context. These words find themselves in the chapter on the Lord's Supper, not baptism. Moreover, the section in which these words are found addresses the issue

38. Calvin, *Institutes*, 4.17.1.

we just left above, namely, the relation between the *signa* and *res*. Calvin explains in the sentence before our quotation that bread and wine are signs that represent invisible food. The bread and the wine are the signs. The invisible food of Christ and his blessings are the things signified. Then Calvin proceeds to draw an analogy with baptism in saying what we have already quoted.

At this point it would do us well to pause for a moment and ask: would it make sense for Calvin to identify the sign of baptism with the thing signified by it, when he is using baptism to illustrate what he just said about the Lord's Supper (namely that the sign of bread and wine *represents* spiritual nourishment)? Not only would that be inconsistent with his broader sacramental theology, but it would be inconsistent with his doctrine of the Lord's Supper here immediately considered. Therefore, it makes better sense to interpret Calvin as saying in this quotation that in baptism we have represented God's regeneration of us and his engrafting us into the society of his church. In fact, the phrase in the citation should be taken into serious consideration. Calvin teaches that the new life the Christian has is one begotten "by his Word." In other words, God begets new life in us. He regenerates us through the means of the Word,[39] and then we receive the visible sign of that invisible grace. It is not the baptism that begets us; it is the Word. Baptism visibly points to that regeneration given by the Spirit by means of the Word of God. Or, to put it another way, Calvin here is clearly employing the two ways of speaking, the *duplex loquendi modus*, because he has in view a body of believers. Therefore he can, as Scripture itself does, employ language proper to the *res* for the *signa*.

Finally, we will consider a passage from one of Calvin's sermons on the book of Deuteronomy, a favorite of those who are convinced that Calvin believed in baptismal regeneration:

> So then we must ever come to this point, that the Sacraments are effectual and that they are not trifling signs that vanish away in the air, but that the truth is always matched with them, because God who is faithful shows that he has not ordained anything in vain. And that is the reason why in Baptism we truly receive the forgiveness of sins, we

---

39. There is no dispute here how Calvin is using the term "regeneration," as that once-for-all act of God in the beginning of the believer's new spiritual life. He is using it synonymously with the term "begotten" and sets it over against the "continually supplying" grace that comes through the Lord's Supper.

are washed and cleansed with the blood of our Lord Jesus Christ, we are renewed by the operation of his Holy Spirit. And how so? Does a little water have such power when it is cast upon the head of a child? No. But because it is the will of our Lord Jesus Christ that the water should be a visible sign of his blood and of the Holy Spirit. Therefore baptism has that power and whatsoever is there set forth to the eye is forthwith accomplished in very deed.[40]

It should initially be pointed out how Calvin asks the rhetorical question, "Does a little water have such power . . . ?" and answers in the negative. In other words, "a little water" does not have the power to renew us. Yet he says in the final sentence that "baptism has that power." But we may ask, what power? And the answer is there in the sentence before, namely, to signify the blood of Christ and the Holy Spirit. In this way then Calvin distinguishes between the sign and the thing signified without separating them (the *distinctio sed non separatio* of Chalcedon).[41] The sign is honored, but the sovereignty of God is protected.

He makes the same point in the paragraph before where he is speaking of the laying on of hands found in the New Testament, particularly Paul's comment to Timothy in 2 Timothy 1:6 and the receiving of the gift of tongues in Acts 19:6. He uses these incidents to expound on Deuteronomy 34:9, where Moses imparts wisdom to Joshua by the laying on of hands. Calvin asks whether a man's hands have that power, and answers in the negative. He then proceeds to ask further questions: Did Moses of his own accord choose Joshua? Do ceremonies such as the one in Acts 19 where disciples received the gift of tongues through laying on of hands "have such virtue"? Again and again, Calvin answers in the negative. Concerning the passage in 2 Timothy, Calvin explains that Paul did not claim such power for himself as opposed to the Holy Spirit. But, lest his listeners think that he is trying to make the ceremony of laying on hands a vain thing, Calvin at last qualifies his statements by saying "but he showeth us that the sign which God had appointed unto it, was not vain or uneffectual."

Therefore, here we see again Calvin's biblical balance. He goes through great pains to make clear that the sign does not have power in itself to mechanically bestow the thing signified. Yet the sign is no bare sign, but

---

40. John Calvin, *Sermons on Deuteronomy* (Edinburgh: Banner of Truth, 1987) 1244.
41. See Garcia, *Life in Christ*, 143.

accompanies the thing signified when and where the Holy Spirit chooses.[42] It is in this way, then, that we must read the above quote from Calvin's sermon on Deuteronomy 34. He is zealous to maintain (as we are here) that the sign is not vain. It is not a dead or naked sign, with no reality to give it substance. But at the same time, it has no power in itself. It is an effectual means of grace only when the Holy Spirit accompanies the sign with the thing signified in the elect.[43]

At the same time, however, because Scripture distinguishes between the *signa* and the *res* without separating them, so does Calvin. In this quote, as in the entire discussion in the immediate context of this part of the sermon, Calvin protects against accusations of making biblical signs vain, whether sacraments or other signs such as the laying on of hands.[44] At the same time, he is careful not to confuse the sign with the thing signified—hence the series of terse negative answers to his own questions. Thus he *can* say that in baptism we receive the forgiveness of sins because, by way of the *duplex loquendi modus* applied to believers, he predicates of the sign that which is proper to the thing itself.

CONCLUDING REMARKS

In addressing the issue of what Calvin (or any other theologian in church history) believed concerning a certain topic, we must bear several things in mind. First, we must handle their writing in a way not altogether

42. At this point we should address the criticism given by some concerning how baptism is often administered in our churches. Lusk complains that we spend too much time telling people what the sacraments are not. Yet, Calvin does the same thing here. He knows our hearts are idol factories, and we will turn the sign into an idol and a magical item to mechanically bestow grace if we are not careful. Therefore, it is of pastoral wisdom to be sure that in the administration of the sacrament we do take pains to make clear to the people what is *not* happening in the ceremony. As Calvin does here, we need to make clear that the sacrament is not vain or an empty sign, and that it is not effectual in an automatic and mechanical fashion.

43. So any notion of the sign of baptism being a means of grace and blessing even for the unelect is nonsensical on Calvin's view. The reprobate who receive baptism have the sign of God's judgment, not blessing. It is true, then, that we can say that the sign is always effectual—as a means of grace to the elect, but an effectual means of judgment to the reprobate.

44. To be sure, Calvin here has in mind the accusations of Westphal that Calvin and the Reformers were advancing a doctrine of bare, empty, and vain signs. Calvin continually defended his position against this charge by making clear that he neither confused the sign and the thing signified—which he charged Westphal with doing—nor separated them such that the sign was left meaningless.

different than the way we handle the Bible. In other words, we must interpret a given author's less clear or older comments in light of his clearer and more recent writings. Second, we must read what he says in its *textual* context. Pulling citations out of a person's corpus of writing without regard to the immediate and extended context of what he or she is saying will lead to an unfaithful reading. Third, we must read an author in his *historical* context. A person's opinions change, but what is more frequent, a person's mode of expression changes as well. The way I communicate a thought in writing today is not the way I would have communicated the same thought 10 years ago. What is going on immediately in one's own *sitz im leben* will certainly make a difference in how that person expresses himself.

As we do this with Calvin's writings, we soon see that he cannot possibly be an advocate for what we are calling baptismal regeneration, which involves a mechanical, *ex opere operato*, understanding of the sacrament. When we understand what Calvin *does* mean when he teaches on baptism as well as understand what he *does not mean*, we see that his sacramental theology is not that different from later Reformed orthodoxy as found in the creeds and confessions of the seventeenth century. In this way we can say that those who hold to the view of baptism in the Westminster Standards stand directly in the theological line of John Calvin. Consequently, any view of baptism that adheres to baptismal regeneration is outside the mainstream of Reformed thinking. To say that the Westminster Standards teach baptismal regeneration[45] would be to impute a view to the framers of the standards not held by them (or by Calvin!).

For both Calvin and the Westminster Divines, baptism is a means of grace. As a sign, it communicates and confers the thing signified when—and only when—the Holy Spirit sovereignly works in the hearts of the elect when they come to true saving faith. In this way the sign and the thing signified are kept together without being separated.[46] The doctrine of Rome kept

45. Doug Wilson, *Reformed Is Not Enough* (Moscow, ID: Canon Press, 2002) 103–4. See also Lusk, *Federal Vision*, 96–99, where he uses the Westminster Standards to support collapsing together the sign and the thing signified in baptismal regeneration. It is true that Lusk at times distances himself from the Roman view of baptismal regeneration. However, at other times it is difficult to see how his view differs from Rome's view.

46. See Wallace, *Calvin's Doctrine*, 24ff. Here Wallace argues that Calvin sees the sacraments as a kind of mirror in which Jesus and his grace are communicated to us. The mirror image is apropos for what is being argued here. The person who looks in a mirror receives a real image, real and true information, even if he (or the mirror) does not have the thing being reflected. Likewise with baptism: Christ and his benefits are being communicated to us, even though

the sign and the thing signified together, but did not distinguish them. The Anabaptists separated the sign and the thing signified such that the sacraments become a bare sign and virtually optional in the life of the believer. Calvin, and those following in his theological train, advanced a third way. Theirs is a middle way, one that gave due and biblical honor to the importance and even essential nature of baptism, without going so far as to make it necessary for salvation in a causal fashion.

Finally, while we admit that Calvin *did* use language concerning the sacraments that made it sound like he advocated something like baptismal regeneration, we maintain strenuously that he actually rejected such thinking. Rather, what he does, because of the *duplex loquendi modus* of Scripture, is to employ language that is proper of the *res* when speaking of the *signa*. But even in such instances, he makes clear that the sign is not the thing signified. This doctrine, forged in the fires of debate with Rome, the Lutheran ubiquitarians, and the Anabaptists, produced a sacramentology that avoided both baptismal regeneration *and* "bare sign" anti-sacramentalism. We would do well to follow the great Reformer in his sacramental theology today.

---

baptism is not Christ or his benefits themselves. It is not an empty sign. But it is also not the things themselves.

20

Preaching by Faith, Not by Sight: A Sermon on 2 Corinthians 5:5

JOHN CURRIE

IT HAS BEEN MY PRIVILEGE not only to learn from Dr. Richard Gaffin as his student, but also to serve as the pastor of his church. Friends and colleagues sometimes ask me what it's like to preach when "Gaffin" is in the congregation. I usually relate that when I accepted the call as pastor I asked Dick (as he insisted I call him from then on) how I pastor my professor. He adopted his typical pondering pose (students know what it looks like) and sincerely asserted "Gaffin needs to hear the word preached!" That response gave a young preacher liberty to preach instead of proving his assimilation of class material in every sermon. But it also disclosed a virtue which I've seen lived out again and again. Dr. Gaffin's careful biblical scholarship is wedded to earnest Christian piety. The theology that he has taught to be the truth of God's Word rules the way he relates to his world.

No more profound example could be mentioned than his perseverance in faith, hope, and love in the midst of profound personal suffering. Gaffin has written paradigm-shaping works on eschatology and Christian suffering (*The Usefulness of the Cross*) and, of course, the resurrection (*Resurrection*

555

and Redemption).[1] But, from a pastor's-eye view, I have seen how conviction about the already/not-yet structure of redemption in Christ, exegeted and explicated in those works, results in godliness through the midst of grief.

I highlight this quality in particular because of the sermon which follows. When I was invited to contribute to this volume it was suggested that I present a sermon, written in the colloquial style in which a typical sermon is delivered, which reflects the influence of Gaffin's approach for the pulpit. That influence has, for me, been theology *in biography* as I have seen glorious eschatological realities lived as well as taught. It then seemed that the most appropriate sermon to submit was one in which we consider the apostle Paul's assertion that his conviction about the *yet future* bodily *resurrection* emboldens him for ministry and life while *suffering now*.

CHRISTIAN COURAGE UNDER FIRE: 2 CORINTHIANS 5:5

Winston Churchill said, " '*Courage*' is the first of human qualities. . . . because it guarantees all the rest." Senator John McCain, no stranger to courage under fire, wrote a book titled *Why Courage Matters: The Way to a Braver Life*. In it he writes that "*courage* is not the *absence of fear* but the capacity for action despite our fears."

Through this mini-series from 2 Corinthians it has become clear that the temptation to lose heart, to become *dis*-couraged under fire, is the practical need which prompted the profound theology unfolded in these chapters. It has also become clear that *courage* for Christian life, and Christian ministry, results from knowing and believing all that God has revealed to us in this passage. That was the result in the life of God's servant, Paul, according to 5:6. Knowledge of and faith in the realities detailed through chapters 4–5 equipped this Christian for *courage.*

So I would like to ask you to think about your own need for courage in life and in ministry. Perhaps you fear the pain of strained relationships within your family if you were to live the lordship of Jesus in your home. It may be fear of being marginalized by friends if you were to live for God's glory at school. Maybe you fear the professional or financial consequences at work if you were to conduct yourself according to the culture of Christ's kingdom instead of the kingdom of the world. Not a few of us might fear the

---

1. For full information on these works see Olinger and Muether's bibliography at the end of this volume.

church's future in our culture. It is quite possible that we or our children's generation could experience genuine persecution, if violent religious agendas or immoral legislative agendas prevail.

Whatever *fears* threaten to cripple us or silence us, the teaching and example of Christ's apostle remind us that believing the facts of the faith can give us the capacity to take action despite our fears. The particular fact of faith we will pay attention to in 5:5 is that *God has prepared us for bodily resurrection and guaranteed it to us by the Spirit.* The life-transforming reality to take away from this verse is this: *We should be courageous in Christian life, and ministry, because God has prepared us for bodily resurrection and guaranteed it to us by the Spirit.* Let me unpack this in the following observations.

First, Christian courage under fire is fueled by the fact that God has prepared us for *bodily resurrection.* Paul's focus is still on *the weight of eternal glory* (4:17) which caused him not to *lose heart.* The end of chapter 4 and the beginning of chapter 5 remind us that Paul was genuinely and profoundly suffering. Yet he considered that genuine affliction, which he *could* see, as *passing* and *light* compared with the glory that he could *not* see but which is *eternal* and *weighty.* Through 5:1–4 we were convinced that this unseen, eternal, weighty glory is the putting on of the resurrected body, which is like Christ's resurrected body. That is still his focus in verse 5 when he writes "He who has prepared us for *this very thing* is God." *This very thing* is what he has just described, the resurrection body, the heavenly dwelling he longs for. Focusing by faith on *this very thing* is what fuels courage for a slandered, betrayed, fractured servant of Christ. That much we know so far.

But why was the future bodily resurrection so overcoming for Paul? Why did the vision of putting off this temporary earthly dwelling and putting on the eternal heavenly dwelling embolden him and why ought it to embolden us? Because he knew that the resurrection body is the realization of the very thing we were created for. The vision of future bodily resurrection is so empowering because it is not only the final remedy for sin but the realization of that for which we were created but which sin corrupted.

Turn to 1 Corinthians 15 and follow with me as we look at something quite fascinating. In 1 Corinthians 15, Paul describes *the kind* of body in which believers will be raised. The bottom line is that we will be raised in a body which corresponds to Christ's resurrection body. In 15:45–49 he contrasts the risen Christ with Adam, the first man. As we read that portion you'll see that in the contrast he calls Adam the *first man*, and Christ the *last Adam*.

Here's why that's important. In this passage, the first man, Adam, is described, not as he was *after the fall*, in sin, but in his original created state. In other words, the first Adam is described as he was in Genesis 2, not Genesis 3. Adam is the *natural* man, *from* the earth, *of* the dust, as the living being who bore the image of God. In this passage, the *risen* Christ is contrasted with Adam in that state. Christ is the man of *heaven*, which means in his exalted, glorified resurrected state. So the correspondence is between *created Adam* as the *first* man and *exalted Christ* as the *last* Adam.

Notice how Paul focuses the lens on the *kind* of body in which we will be raised: "Thus it is written, 'The first man Adam became a living being'; the last Adam became a life-giving spirit. But it is not the spiritual that is first but the *natural*, and then the spiritual. The first man was *from the earth*, a man *of dust*; the second man is from heaven. As was the man of dust, so also are those who are of the dust, and as is the man *of heaven*, so also are those who are *of heaven*. Just as we have borne the image of the man of dust, we shall also bear the image of the man of heaven."* (1 Cor. 15:45–49)

Did you catch his point? The *spiritual* body, like Christ's, that we will bear in the resurrection corresponds to the original image we bore in Adam. It's not just a response to our sin-corrupted state. The glory of the resurrection body in the *last* Adam is actually the realization of the image for which the *first* Adam was created.

But it's also more. The resurrection body goes beyond what could even have been imagined in that pre-sin created state. Earlier, in 1 Corinthians 2:9, Paul wrote "no eye has seen, nor ear heard, nor the heart of man imagined, what God has *prepared* for those who love him . . . ." Even they in the Garden of Eden could not have *imagined* the *glory* God has prepared for those raised in Christ.

My point is this: when Paul, who wrote both 1 Corinthians 15 and our text, asserts that God "has prepared us for this very thing," the *very thing* was not *just* a remedy for the corruption of sin. It is that! But it is the *restoration* of and *surpassing* of the original pattern we were created for as humans. What does the apostle say in that famous verse coming up in 2 Corinthians 5:17? If any man is in Christ . . . new *creation*! Faith in the resurrection fueled courage for Paul, at least in part because he knew it realized his purpose for being *created*!

As bearers of God's image, people long for that created purpose. Despite the *illusion of glory* we can build around our life here and now, we still feel the loss of our created purpose deep in our soul. And the loss is *dis*heartening, *dis*couraging, because it is actually *de*-humanizing.

I think there is a great picture of this in George Orwell's description of the world of *1984*. That world is constructed entirely around propaganda, and in one scene Orwell pictures masses of people crammed into an industrial cafeteria as they hear statistics poured out about their prosperity and security. The party line bouncing around the room is that everybody and everything is whizzing rapidly upward. But as the main character sits in the cafeteria and takes up his spoon to dabble with *pale colored gravy* Orwell writes:

> He meditated resentfully on the physical texture of life. Had it always been like this? Had food always tasted like this? He looked round the canteen. A low-ceilinged, crowded room, its walls grimy from the contact of innumerable bodies; battered metal tables and chairs, placed so close together that you sat with elbows touching; bent spoons, dented trays, coarse white mugs; all surfaces greasy, grime in every crack; and a sourish, composite smell of bad gin and bad coffee and metallic stew and dirty clothes. Always in your stomach and in your skin there was a sort of *protest*, a feeling that you had been cheated of something that you had *a right to*.

Here's the connection. The *low-ceilinged, battered, sourish* world cheats us out of the purpose for which we were created. And our soul protests! But the eternal weight of glory for which God has prepared us in Christ restores us beyond anything creation could envision. And if we focus on *this very thing* by faith it will strengthen our heart and fuel our courage as God's image bearers, as Christians, in the low-ceilinged, battered, sourish world of the yet-corrupted creation. That's our first point; Christian courage under fire is fueled by the fact that God has prepared us for *bodily resurrection.*

Second, I'd like you to notice: Christian courage under fire is fueled by the fact that *God* has prepared us for bodily resurrection. There is no firmer ground for courage than the assurance that *God* is for you. Paul is in a position where he is being discredited and disregarded by seemingly strong opponents. So he puts an exclamation mark on the ultimate source of his confidence not to lose heart: *God!* The point really is, "*God* has prepared us for this very thing!"

This is not unlike the great theme in Romans 8:31, "If *God* is for us, who can be against us?" Interestingly, that assurance is a response to the knowledge of certain *glorification*. Those whom God predestined he called, those he called he justified, and those he justified he *glorified* (Romans 8:30). Paul's courage was fueled by the knowledge that, since he was one of those who would be resurrected with Christ, it meant *God* had prepared him for it and therefore *God* was for him. Why should he be disheartened and discouraged by what *man* is saying about him or what *man* is doing to him?

Putting it this way also reveals that our participation in this glorious resurrection is *God's* work. It wasn't Paul's superior intellect, or his powerful ministry that guaranteed him future resurrection. He didn't qualify for resurrection with Christ because he had great religious feeling or even visions, which we hear about later in 2 Corinthians. No, it is *God* who has prepared him and every other Christian for *glory*. The Christian at every stage, including glorification, is the work *of God*.

God's spokesman can't talk very long about the blessings of salvation without going *God*-ward! It's always, in the end, all about *God*. Even as we rejoice and draw courage from the manifold blessings of our salvation, it is ultimately not about us.

There is a sense in which, in the end, it is not even ultimately about our Savior, *God* the Son. In 1 Corinthians 15:28, Paul writes "When all things are subjected to him, then the Son himself will also be subjected to him who put all things in subjection under him, that *God* may be all in all." In God's purposes for history, *God the Son* will even deflect the attention to *God the Father*. This God-centered focus is peppered throughout Paul's argument in 2 Corinthians also, most immediately in 4:15 (cf. 1:20–21; 2:14–15; 3:4–5; 4:1,6). All of salvation through Christ, including *this very thing* of bodily resurrection, is God's work for *God's* glory.

Why is that so? Because, as we have seen already, it is the realization, the *consummation*, of God's work as creator! And that fact fuels Christian courage. If our final glorified state is *God's* work, according to *God's* purpose, for *God's* glory . . . it cannot fail! It cannot be frustrated by the schemes of men or Satan. So we are always of good courage.

Do you notice how the entire Trinity is the source of *this very thing*? *God*, the name Paul is using to refer to *the Father* in distinction from Christ, the Son, has prepared us for bodily resurrection. The entire context shows us it is *through* Jesus *the Son*. And, as we are about to see, it is guaranteed and accomplished by *the Spirit*. The eternal weight of glory that fuels our hope and courage is the work of the Trinity: God the Father, and the Son, and the Holy Spirit.

Third, please notice: Christian courage under fire is fueled by the fact that God has given us *the Holy Spirit* as his guarantee. The apostle's confidence is not simply "whistling in the dark." God has given his *guarantee* of *this very thing* for which he has prepared Christians.

Paul makes this point by drawing on trade language, the language of commerce in his culture. The word "guarantee" refers to a deposit given as security for a future full payment. In this kind of deposit the thing given as down payment is of the same *kind* as the thing to be finally paid. The deposit is a part of the whole.

What this common cultural image communicates is that God has given us a *down payment* which *guarantees* full payment at the appointed time. He has given the first installment of the very thing which is guaranteed to come fully later on. So, this embattled servant's courage and confidence is based on the fact that God, who does not change and cannot lie, and whose purposes cannot be thwarted, has given him a first installment of the full glory yet to come.

Please notice carefully what that guarantee is, or rather *who* it is. The *guarantee* is *the Spirit*! Something similar has already been said in 1:22, " . . . who has also put his seal on us and given us his Spirit in our hearts *as a guarantee*." God the Holy Spirit, in our hearts, is the first installment of the glory that we will receive in full when Jesus returns. God the Holy Spirit, in our hearts, is the guarantee of the bodily resurrection!

Again, Paul uses a similar concept and similar language in another letter, and it will help us to look at it. In Romans 8:23 he discloses how the whole creation groans for the time when Christians' bodies will be redeemed, the resurrection of the body. Romans 8:23 reads, "And not only the creation, but we ourselves, who have the *firstfruits* of the Spirit, groan inwardly as we wait eagerly for adoption as sons, the redemption of our bodies."

In this instance the apostle uses *agricultural* imagery. The "firstfruits" is the initial installment of the whole harvest. It is a small portion taken at the beginning of the harvest which represents the entire harvest to come. And, Paul says, the Spirit is the firstfruits of the whole harvest, which is the redemption of our bodies. A little different imagery, but it communicates the same concept as our passage.

Here's the point. When you believed in Jesus, God gave you the Spirit in your heart. And he gave him to you not just for power for Christian living. He is that, but not *just* that. God gave you the Spirit as *his guarantee* that he will raise you from the dead with a body transformed like Christ's glorified body! The *fact* that the Spirit lives in you means God will raise you bodily in eternal glory. The Spirit, and his work of inner renewal and transformation in you *now*, is the first installment, the *foretaste*, of the final glorious renewal of your entire person when Christ returns. J. B. Lightfoot, a noted New Testament commentator, put it this way, "The actual Spiritual life of the Christian is of the same kind as his future glorified life . . . the present gift of the Spirit is only a small function of the future endowment."

The point, of cosmic proportions, is this: the *Spirit*, who is *now* working out the resurrected life of Christ in our *inner man* by transforming us to Christ's image (cf. 2 Cor. 4:16), is God's *guarantee* to us of the transformation of our *outer man* in eternal glory. Why do I think it matters to press that home? Because we need to realize how central the *Holy Spirit* is to our entire salvation.

Perhaps I can make the point this way. We have just completed Easter, the celebration of the death and resurrection of Christ. For that reason Easter is a celebration which makes sense to us as Christians. Without Christ and his death and his resurrection we have no salvation; there is no Christianity. But there is, in about a month, another celebration on the Christian calendar: Pentecost.

Pentecost celebrates the giving of the Holy Spirit. In our tradition we don't set that time aside for special celebration, and I'm not saying we ought to. There is nothing in Scripture that mandates such things, even a special Easter celebration. But perhaps the church's disparity in its observance of these particular seasons is illustrative of what we think of the Holy Spirit. "*Easter* is indispensable, *Pentecost* a bit of a frill, take it or leave it." In fact, when it comes to the Holy Spirit we may even be a little skeptical. We relegate focusing on him to *other traditions* that are more sensational and emotional.

But, for the apostle, there is no salvation without the Spirit. There is no *Christianity* without the Spirit! Please notice the essential bond between Christ and the Spirit and the Christian in the apostle's theology in Romans 8:9–11:

> You, however, are not in the flesh but *in the Spirit*, if in fact the Spirit of God dwells in you. Anyone who does not have the Spirit of Christ does not belong to him. But if Christ is in you, although the body is dead because of sin, the Spirit is life because of righteousness. If *the Spirit* of him who raised Jesus from the dead dwells in you, he who raised Christ Jesus from the dead will also give life to your mortal bodies through the Spirit who dwells in you.

To be in Christ is to be in the Spirit, to have Christ in you is to have the Spirit in you; without *the Spirit*, we do not belong to Christ.

But, the centrality of the Spirit is also disclosed in the very context of our passage. In 2 Corinthians 3, Paul describes the ministry that he is *courageous* about, the ministry for which the guarantee of bodily resurrection strengthens his heart. And he describes it as essentially a ministry about *the Spirit*. You can see this in 3:3, 6, 8, and especially in 18!

For Paul, the ministry of the new covenant is one where *the Spirit* gives life. *The Spirit* gives glory. *The Spirit* works in us to transform us from glory to glory. In the new covenant the present ministry of Christ and the Spirit are so inseparably tied that he says, "The Lord is the Spirit . . . ." (3:17). He's not confused about distinctions within the Trinity, but it's the Spirit who makes the presence and power of the Lord effective in our lives.

Please understand this: the Holy Spirit is not a frill negotiable to what is otherwise basic to salvation. To focus on him *only* in terms of spectacular phenomena is to make *far too little* of him! *The Spirit* is essential to the very *nature* of our salvation and Christianity itself. So, it is not strange that *he* is the guarantee, *he* is the down payment, of the consummate hope of our salvation. *The Spirit* in our hearts is the first installment in our final resurrection in eternal glory!

Why? Because the final resurrection of our body is also the work of the Spirit.

We've already taken some time in 1 Corinthians 15, and you remember its promise that those who are united to the last Adam follow him in the same kind of resurrection body. Do you remember how it describes the *kind* of resurrection body in which he was raised, and so shall we? A *spiritual* body (vv. 44, 46)! That doesn't mean a "see-through body." It means a body transformed by the Spirit. One of the verses we just read states, "If the Spirit of him who raised Jesus from the dead dwells in you, he who raised Christ Jesus from the dead will also give life to your mortal bodies *through his Spirit* who dwells in you" (Rom. 8:11).

Just as it was the Spirit who transformed the body of Jesus at his resurrection, so it will be the Spirit who will transform our bodies at our resurrection in Christ. That's why *the Spirit* is the guarantee, the first installment, because *he* is the one who pays *in full* at the end! *The Spirit* is the one who brings in the full harvest of our resurrection on that day.

So you see the spiritual logic of God's afflicted spokesman. Having the Spirit in our hearts is the Christian's guarantee from God that we will inherit an eternal weight of glory which surpasses the affliction we experience now. And that guarantee from God gives us confidence and *courage* under fire. The capacity for Christian living and action despite our fears is fueled by believing this fact of the faith: *God has prepared us for bodily resurrection and guaranteed it to us by the Spirit.*

Where is your own need for courage in life and in ministry? Relationships within your family as you live the lordship of Jesus? Consequences among friends or colleagues as you live the culture of Christ's kingdom in the kingdom of the world? *Be courageous* in your Christian life and ministry, because God has prepared us for bodily resurrection and guaranteed it to us by the Spirit!

21

He Offered Up Himself:
A Sermon on Hebrews 7:27–28

WILLIAM F. SNODGRASS

A LONG TIME AGO, there was a king who was also a priest. You may think I am talking about Melchizedek, given that this sermon comes from Hebrews. I am talking about a different king, who was also a priest. I am talking about Adam.

Does that surprise you? Adam was both a king and a priest in the Garden of Eden (Gen. 1:26–28; 2:15). Adam was given a kingly role to rule over the earth, and he was also called to consecrate both himself and the garden-sanctuary as holy to the Lord.

But then something marred his priestly service on behalf of all mankind in the garden. Adam sinned against God by eating from the forbidden fruit, and this original sin resulted in mankind being barred from the holy sanctuary in Eden. Imagine it! The priest-king barred from the sanctuary! What is more, the Lord God clothed him with animal skins—the first sacrifice in redemptive history, one which anticipates the sacrificial system of the Mosaic economy and the substitutionary sacrifice of Jesus Christ.

And God did something else. He placed cherubim at the entrance to the garden, with a flaming sword to guard the entrance to that sanctuary where the Tree of Life was kept (Gen. 3:24). These cherubim took over Adam's priestly role by guarding God's created sanctuary.

Those cherubim would be seen again. They would be represented on the curtain that hung inside a special place, a place where only the high priest could go, and that only once a year. It was called the Holy of Holies. The time when the high priest could enter was the Day of Atonement (cf. Lev. 16). On that day, and that day alone, the representative of the people of God could enter this most holy place (Lev. 16:2ff).

At this point, an important question arises. How does the advent of Jesus Christ affect this situation in the old covenant order? Is the way into the presence of God still guarded from us, those who spoiled the original earthly sanctuary in Adam (cf. Rom. 5:12–19)?

In our previous sermon, we saw the qualifications of our high priest, the Lord Jesus Christ. We saw how his qualifications are *precisely appropriate* to our condition, the condition in which we found ourselves as sinners before a holy God. As Hebrews 7:26 reminds us, "For it was indeed fitting that we should have such a high priest, holy, innocent, unstained, separated from sinners, and exalted above the heavens." Therefore, we not only have a high priest who sympathizes perfectly with us (Heb. 4:14–16), but we have a spotless sacrifice that takes away our sin and enables us to enter the most holy place (Heb. 9:12, 24, 26).

But where exactly is the holy place in which he ministers as our high priest? Adam, like Aaron, was a priest who was stained by sin and ministered in an earthly sanctuary. And Aaron had to offer sacrifices year after year that could never take away sin (cf. Heb. 9:25). What precisely is the role of Jesus Christ in his exalted place above the heavens as our high priest? Hebrews 7:27 provides the beginning of an answer to that question: "He has no need, like those high priests, to offer sacrifices daily."

In other words, Jesus Christ, your heavenly high priest, has offered a sinless sacrifice that needs no repetition, because it is perfect in every way. What invests his sacrifice with this once-for-all perfection and finality? The answer to this question is found in Christ's sinlessness as both high priest and sacrifice.

But wait a minute, you might say. I thought that the high priest offered sacrifices for sins *for himself* too. But now, under the new covenant, I have

a *sinless* priest? How can he help me? If as verse 27 says, "He has no need, like those high priests, to offer sacrifices daily, first for his own sins and then for those of the people," then how can I be sure that my sinless high priest can help me get out from under the weight of my sin?

First, it is important to note something significant about the old covenant sacrifices. They were *repetitive*; they were offered *daily*. When a sacrifice has to be repeated again and again, it is *a sign that it is incomplete and temporary*. The *repetition* of a sacrifice implies that complete atonement has not been made (*pace* Rome). This repetition stands in the sharpest possible contrast with the *once for all* sacrifice of Christ (cf. Heb. 9:25–10:18).

Second, remember that when the old covenant high priest entered that sanctuary to bring sacrifices for sin, he *brought the sacrifices with him*. He was *not* the sacrifice, but he was *the priest offering the sacrifices*. This point is very important. The priest was not the sacrifice in the old covenant order. But what happened when Jesus Christ was sacrificed for our sins (John 1:29)? He offered up *himself* (Heb. 7:27). For the first time in the history of redemption, a high priest *himself* became the sacrifice. Finally, the perfect sacrifice had been offered. Finally, the perfect sacrifice was set before the perfectly holy God to remove His holy wrath.

But notice the order. "He offered up himself" is in the *past* tense. That is why, as verse 27 began to tell us, he has no need, now, to offer sacrifices. Verse 27 looks at the work of Jesus Christ from two standpoints: from the standpoint of the *finished* work of Christ, described for us at the end of the verse, and from the standpoint of the *current* work of Christ, which is how the verse opens.

Yet there is something *still greater* that emerges as we consider this verse from these two points of view. The verse tells us that Jesus did the work of those other high priests. No need for the offering of daily sacrifices, either for his own sins (he had none!) or for those of the people, since he did this once for all when he offered up himself. Jesus Christ *accomplished* the work of the old covenant high priests, and he fulfilled that work in a final and climactic way. In fact, he accomplished it in a way that ensured it never needs repetition, *even by him!* How?

The answer is concrete and tangible. The Lord Jesus Christ became *in himself* the sacrifice for your sins. In other words, he was the sacrifice of sacrifices, the sacrifice toward which all the others pointed, the original sacrifice, next to which all other sacrifices were mere imitations. This is true for one main reason: he was the only *perfectly obedient* priest and sacrifice. You see, all the other sacrifices could only be accepted toward the penalty, passively suffering as the substitute for a sinner. But when the Lord Jesus Christ assumed the role of the sacrifice, he was offering a sacrifice unlike all the others, a sacrifice that fulfilled the law of God on your behalf. Those animal sacrifices offered blood but not obedience; suffering but not righteous suffering. But Jesus offered one sacrifice that encompassed *all* of these elements. When he sacrificed himself, he offered to God a true obedient Son, a life that was surrendered to God for you and sacrificed for you. Jesus gave himself for you.

Can you see how Jesus Christ identified with you in your weakness more closely than any high priest ever identified with his people? This is why the *one* sacrifice of Christ eliminated the need for *the whole Levitical system*. As our passage says, *he did this once for all*. As a result, the Levitical sacrifices are now rendered obsolete.

Verse 28, then, summarizes the argument of the entire chapter. In this verse, the far-reaching difference between the two priesthoods is made clear. There are no fewer than three sets of contrasts, or antitheses, that we must consider here in this final verse of chapter seven.

First, the basis of the Levitical priesthood was "the law," but the basis of the new priesthood is the word of the oath. Second, the old priesthood was comprised of "men" while the new priest is "a Son." Finally, the old priests are characterized as being "in their weakness" as they are appointed, while the Son, by contrast, has been made perfect.

In verse 28, the One who is referred to as "a Son" is set in contrast with "men" (28a). What is more, the Son who is in view here is the Son from eternity past, the Son of God. The point to see here is that the Son who was appointed by the word of the oath was a Son *before* this word of the oath was declared to him.

This makes what has happened even more amazing. Jesus surrendered to the demands of the ceremonial law even though he was in line to be appointed by the greater word of the oath: "'The Lord has sworn and will not change his mind, "You are a priest forever"'" (Heb. 7:21). Jesus, the eternal Son, entered the world of men, to die once for all. And so he has been made perfect forever.

Consider that phrase with me: "a Son who has been made perfect forever" (Heb. 7:28). This language of having been made perfect forever refs to the *exaltation* of Jesus Christ. Jesus Christ now dwells at the Father's right hand (cf. Heb. 1:3). This means that death no longer remains to spoil this perfect sacrifice. The sacrifice, then, has no need of being repeated. The sacrifice has been made once, and the priest who applies the sacrifice *lives to apply it*. In other words, the work in regard to the sacrifice has been done and the work in regard to the priestly duties related to that sacrifice is ongoing and perpetual.

We must always remember that Jesus is *both* the sacrifice *and* the priest. "It is finished," in regard to the sacrifice being made for your sin (John 19:30). We can never pull back from the absolute finality of that statement. Jesus' sacrificial work is *done*, once for all. Yet, at the same time, we can never diminish the wonder of the priestly work of Jesus that continues: "he always lives to make intercession" for believers (Heb. 7:25)!

You see, only the Son could make such a connection. Only the One who could offer up *himself* as a sinless sacrifice could dwell in the heavenly sanctuary and serve there as a priest forever. Only he was qualified, since he was the only one who is "holy, innocent, unstained, separated from sinners, and exalted above the heavens" (v. 26b).

22

Filling Up Christ's Afflictions: A Sermon on Colossians 1:24–29

Eric B. Watkins

Now I rejoice in my sufferings for your sake, and in my flesh I am filling up what is lacking in Christ's afflictions for the sake of his body, that is, the church, of which I became a minister according to the stewardship from God that was given to me for you, to make the word of God fully known, the mystery hidden for ages and generations but now revealed to his saints. To them God chose to make known how great among the Gentiles are the riches of the glory of this mystery, which is Christ in you, the hope of glory. Him we proclaim, warning everyone and teaching everyone with all wisdom, that we may present everyone mature in Christ. For this I toil, struggling with all his energy that he powerfully works within me. (Col. 1:24–29)

Has the apostle Paul gone too far? We read through the words of Colossians 1:24–29, and find Paul hard to understand, and perhaps even harder to believe. He poses two ideas before us that seem hard to swallow: first, that he is in some way fulfilling a lack in Christ's sufferings, and second, that he even finds joy in his own sufferings that accomplish this. We take these in turn.

Can it rightly be said that there is anything lacking in Christ's work on our behalf? These somewhat confusing words come from the very same apostle who says elsewhere that there is only one gospel, and that if he or an angel from heaven should preach otherwise, he should be accursed (Gal. 1:8–9). Is Paul here contradicting the very things that he passionately defends elsewhere? Perhaps of even greater concern, is Paul now suggesting that there is something lacking in Christ's sufferings on the cross that must be somehow completed by him or us? The impact of such a conclusion would be devastating to the Protestant doctrine of the atonement, leading away from Geneva and back to Rome. Indeed, there are those of Roman Catholic persuasion who take this verse to teach exactly that. Should we abandon the doctrine of a perfectly sufficient Savior?

The answer is emphatically, "No!" Paul is not teaching a different gospel than he teaches elsewhere. His teaching here is entirely consistent with what he teaches in other letters and even here in Colossians: there is nothing lacking in Christ's atonement. As he put it earlier in the very same chapter, "you, who once were alienated ... he has now reconciled in his body of flesh by his death, in order to present you holy and blameless and above reproach before him" (1:21–22). Christ's death was definitively effective. It lacks nothing; it needs nothing; it was a once-for-all sacrifice for our sins which has secured our holiness and blamelessness before God. The proof of this is found not only in Christ's resurrection, but in the resurrection work of the Spirit that unites us to Christ and has "delivered us from the domain of darkness and transferred us to the kingdom of his beloved son," as Paul has already mentioned (1:13). What can be added to Christ's work for us? Nothing! We may rest assured that Paul has not caved in. He is still resting in the sufficiency of Christ's work on his behalf, and with him, we may do the same.

Still, we are left wondering what Paul has in mind. He must have something in view, something that was lacking in Christ and now is being completed by Paul. But what is it?

The answer is deep and inspiring. It touches the heart not only of the apostle Paul, but of every minister, indeed every Christian who has tasted anything of the sufferings of Christ and the brokenness of this present evil age. To understand Paul's language here is to understand his theology of suffering and servanthood, which for Paul are inseparable from union with Christ.

Think now about Paul's calling in Acts 9. There the resurrected Lord tells Paul (then Saul) that in persecuting Christ's church, Saul was persecuting Christ himself. So the Lord says to him, "Saul, Saul, why are you persecuting *me*?" (Acts 9:4). The Lord identifies himself as the resurrected Lord who is inseparably united to his church. ". . . I am Jesus, whom you are persecuting" (Acts 9:5). What the Lord was communicating to Saul is unmistakable: he was so intimately bound to those who were suffering for Christ that Saul's persecution of the church was nothing shy of persecuting the Lord of the church. The Lord is bound to his church, and his church bound to him. Saul is instructed as to what he must do, and it is then said of Saul, "he is a chosen instrument of mine to carry my name before the Gentiles and kings and the children of Israel. For I will show him how much he must suffer for the sake of my name" (Acts 9:15–16). What is said of Saul here is in reverse order to the promise of Acts 1:8–9. Whereas the church gathered at that time would be dispersed to "Jerusalem and in all Judea and Samaria, and to the end of the earth," Saul will become Paul, and be sent to the Gentiles *first.* The priority of his ministry will be that he is sent to testify to the gospel of Jesus Christ primarily to the Gentiles. He will be called the "apostle to the Gentiles." This is Christ's call on Paul's life: he is to be a servant of the King of kings and Lord of lords, and in doing so, will take the gospel to those who once were not a people, that they too might become saints and fellow citizens in Christ's kingdom through the preaching of his word.

Paul's call to this, however, has not fully explained his language of "filling up what is lacking in Christ's afflictions." It is at this point that we understand the origin of both Paul's language, and even that of the Savior in Saul's calling. It is here that we listen to the "servant songs" of Isaiah. There are several of these, beginning in Isaiah 42. They sing of the Messiah of the Lord, who is the Lord himself. He will be a "light for the nations" (42:6; 49:6) and will manifest the glory of the Lord. The irony of this servant's work, however, is that it will be accomplished through his own suffering. This servant will be a suffering servant. Isaiah 53 is one of the great Old Testament texts that speak of the Messiah's suffering on behalf of his people. Indeed, it is through his suffering that the wages of their sin shall be paid. Their burdens shall rest upon him; he shall endure their griefs, their sorrows, even their deaths. Though he is righteous in every way and obeys the law in every respect, he shall offer his very life in death so that he will "make many to be accounted righteous" (53:10–11). The King of kings shall become the servant of sinners. This promise of a suffering servant is clearly fulfilled in the person and work of Christ. He came as the one on whom the burden of our sins would fall. He identified himself with us so that we might be identified with him. All that we deserve for our sins fell on him at the cross, so that he might freely give of his righteousness to us. How mysteriously glorious it is that the Lord of the universe should stoop so low as to become our servant and even suffer in our place. Yet he has given so freely, so generously, and even now continues to send his life-giving Spirit to us that we might know and believe the gospel of our Lord Jesus Christ. This is the glorious gospel promised in the days of Isaiah, fulfilled in the coming of Christ, and proclaimed by Paul—the apostle to the Gentiles.

There is still, however, something more that we must understand. The Lord of glory who came as our suffering servant and humble lamb did not fulfill in his earthly life everything promised in Isaiah. To say it differently, aspects of this prophetic promise of Isaiah would not find their fulfillment until Jesus was raised from the dead and sent his Spirit to carry out the work of applying his benefits to a people yet to be brought into Christ's church. We take note of the fact that in Christ's earthly life, he had fairly little interaction with the Gentiles. His commission had more of a focus on the Jews than it did the Gentiles. He went to the lost sheep of Israel and declared that he was the good shepherd who would lay down his life for them, and indeed he did. But what about the Gentiles? In Christ's earthly life, it seems that when the Gentiles begin to come to Christ, he sees this as the end of his work, almost as though he were a relay runner who was prepared to hand off the baton to the next runner. Jesus seemed to indicate as much in John 12:20–26. When a group of Gentiles came to see Jesus, his first response was, "The hour has come . . ." From then on he ceased performing miracles and was headed for the cross. The earthly life of our Lord was coming to an end, but the ministry to Gentiles was just beginning.

The dots begin to connect. The proclamation of the gospel to the end of the earth, even to the Gentiles, would begin in Christ's earthly life but would not find its fulfillment until he had died and been raised. The Spirit would be poured out, and the gospel would be proclaimed by lesser servants, sent by the Lord to the Gentiles of this world. The apostle Paul was clearly such a servant. He was indeed filling up in his flesh what was lacking in

Christ's afflictions—the proclamation of the gospel to the Gentiles. And so he did. The baton of proclamation was handed off. Yet the Lord would work in Paul a rather mysterious thing. Not only would Paul have the privilege of proclaiming the sufferings of Christ with his words, his very life would reflect them. Jesus promised Paul (then Saul) that he would learn what it meant to suffer for Christ's name's sake. Indeed, Paul would. His life would be marked at many times by suffering, rejection, and cross-bearing. He would be beaten, imprisoned, rejected, and eventually condemned for Christ's sake. The sufferings of Christ would be put on display in Paul's life. Paul would learn to understand more that he had died, and that his life was hidden in Christ. This explains Paul's language not only here, but in so many places in his writings where he affirms a union with Christ that is so real and intimate, it seems to cross the line of reason. He describes himself as being "absent in the body, yet I am with you in spirit," as having "not ceased to pray for you," as willing to "endure everything for the sake of the elect," and here as "filling up what is lacking in Christ's afflictions" (Col. 2:5; 1:9; 2 Tim. 2:10; Col. 1:24). What Paul reveals in each of these is simply that he understands his relationship to the church, his prayers, and even his sufferings on behalf of the church as the reality of his union with Christ. The gospel proclaimed by his lips is the gospel evidenced in his life. It is his reference point for all things. It is not only his lens for understanding his trials, but his consolation in the midst of them.

It is for this reason that Paul can say that he endures his own sufferings *joyfully*. Christ Jesus has suffered for Paul's sake. Paul believes this in his heart of hearts. Therefore, whatever Paul might lose in this life is unworthy to be compared with the glory that awaits him (Rom. 8:18). If his loss should lead to the church's gain and Christ's glory, Paul rejoices. Christ, in his goodness, chose to reveal himself to Paul, and to the Gentiles through Paul, as he affirms even here in Colossians 1:27. Paul's privilege is that of being a servant to those whom God is saving for himself. Paul has lost his life only to find it again in Christ, and now Christ must be proclaimed. Gentile men and women must be warned and taught the truth of Jesus Christ. And if the Lord of the church should arm his servants with nothing other than the cross, so be it; it is his right. Never in Paul do we detect a note of cynicism or regret. He fulfills his calling joyfully, because he sees beyond his own cross to the life the Savior has purchased for him. And not even death can separate him from that heavenly land above. There is his treasure; there is his heart.

Is this true only for the apostle Paul? Should it not be for us, his servants as well? It must be, of course. Each of us who belong to Christ is so ultimately because of Christ's definitive work on the cross. But has he not used frail and oft-tried servants to proclaim his word to us? Are we not all Gentiles who have learned of the Servant of the Lord through the work of various servants of the Lord? Are we not also called to take up our crosses and follow after Christ? Christ has not called us to the particular office of apostle, but that does not estrange us from the text. He has not saved any of us through a miraculous encounter like that of the Damascus road, yet we know the Lord who met Paul there. The Savior has said of all of us that, "all who desire to live a godly life in Christ Jesus will be persecuted" (2 Tim. 3:12). The servant is not above his master; if the world has hated Christ, will it not hate those who proclaim his glory among the nations?

It is the privilege of every Christian to live out his or her union with Christ in such a way that when Christ is pleased to lay on us a cross to bear, that we bear it not only faithfully but joyfully. We all have a cross to bear. But the cross we bear will always be so much lighter than that born by our Savior, for his was loaded down by the weight of our sins. It was crushing. The burden we bear, the Savior has promised to make light enough that we might bear it honorably and faithfully. Such a display of perseverance and joy, even in the midst of trials, shall prove to be quite unfamiliar to this world which knows neither our Savior nor the joy of his resurrection. As we bear our own crosses and reflect Christ in us, we have opportunity to wed our words to our deeds, and reflect the glory of the Lord. While this applies to all Christians in a general sense, it applies especially to those who are called to suffer as ordained servants of the word. So here I would speak especially to ministers of the gospel.

Beloved brethren, you are so uniquely called to this. Christ has marked you out as those who fill up in your flesh what is lacking in Christ's afflictions. Your lives will surely bear his reproach at times. You shall know something of those sufferings of which the Lord spoke to Saul on the road to Damascus. But you shall also know the joy of the Lord, even in the midst of your trials. The church is indeed wearisome, and you will endure many things for her sake. At times, the burden of it may seem more than you can bear. Let us look to Christ together at these moments, and find in him not only the source of the command to bear our crosses faithfully, but the joy of knowing that Christ is glorified, even in our weakness, and that his church is indeed being gathered and strengthened. He is saving many for his own name's sake, even as he saved us. He is working powerfully within us, conforming us to Christ's image, so that as men and women look upon us, they see an imperfect reflection of the Savior and his work. As they hear our words, they hear the words of the king who has promised to embolden his servants to proclaim his word with joy and confidence. May this joy and confidence temper your ministry and cause you not to shrink back from adversity nor grow weary in doing good. And as you "toil, struggling with all his energy that he powerfully works within" (Col. 1:29), know that the same Spirit who has worked faith and life in you will work faith and life in others that they too might partake of "the glory of this mystery, which is Christ in you, the hope of glory" (Col. 1:27). Amen.

Appendix: A Comprehensive Bibliography of Publications by Richard B. Gaffin Jr.

DANNY E. OLINGER AND JOHN R. MUETHER

1962

"Calvin and the Sabbath." Th.M. thesis, Westminster Theological Seminary, 1962.

1963

Review of *The Work of Christ*, by R. S. Franks. *WTJ* 25 (May 1963): 231–35.

1964

Review of *The Inspiration of Scripture*, by D. M. Beegle. *WTJ* 26 (May 1964): 230–38.

1965

Review of *The History of the Synoptic Tradition*, by R. Bultmann. *WTJ* 27 (May 1965): 172–77.

Review of *Between Heaven and Earth*, by H. Thielicke. *WTJ* 28 (Nov. 1965): 99–105.

1968

"Paul as Theologian [review article]." *WTJ* 30 (May 1968): 204–32.

1969

"Resurrection and Redemption: A Study in Pauline Eschatology." ThD diss., Westminster Theological Seminary, 1969.

"Contemporary Hermeneutics and the Study of the New Testament." *WTJ* 31 (May 1969): 129–44.

1970

Review of *Grundriss der Theologie des Neuen Testaments*, by H. Conzelmann. *WTJ* 32 (May 1970): 220–28.

1971

"Geerhardus Vos and the Interpretation of Paul." In *Jerusalem and Athens: Critical Discussions on the Philosophy and Apologetics of Cornelius Van Til*, edited by E. R. Geehan, 228–37. Nutley, NJ: Presbyterian & Reformed, 1971.

"The Sabbath: A Creation Ordinance and Sign of the Christian Hope." *Presbyterian Guardian* 40 (Mar. 1971): 40–42.

1974

"The Place and Importance of Introduction to the New Testament." In *Studying the New Testament Today, The New Testament Student*, edited by John Skilton, 1:143–51. Nutley, NJ: Presbyterian & Reformed, 1974.

Review of *Critical Quests of Jesus* and *The Historical Jesus*, by C. C. Anderson. *WTJ* 36 (Spring 1974): 408–10.

Review of *David Friedrich Strauss and His Theology*, by H. Harris. *WTJ* 37 (Fall 1974): 115–19.

1976

"Systematic Theology and Biblical Theology." *WTJ* 38 (Spring 1976): 281–99.

1977

"The Holy Spirit and Charismatic Gifts." In *The Holy Spirit Down to Earth*, 3–25. Grand Rapids: Reformed Ecumenical Synod, 1977.

1978

The Centrality of the Resurrection. Grand Rapids: Baker, 1978.

"The Whole Counsel of God and the Bible." In *The Book of Books: Essays on the Scriptures in Honor of Johannes G. Vos*, edited by John H. White, 19–28. Phillipsburg, NJ: Presbyterian & Reformed, 1978.

1979

Perspectives on Pentecost: Studies in the New Testament Teaching on the Gifts of the Holy Spirit. Phillipsburg, NJ: Presbyterian & Reformed, 1979.

"The Usefulness of the Cross." *WTJ* 41 (Spring 1979): 228–46.

1980

Redemptive History and Biblical Interpretation: The Shorter Writings of Geerhardus Vos (editor). Phillipsburg, NJ: Presbyterian & Reformed, 1980.

"The Holy Spirit." *WTJ* 43 (Fall 1980): 58–78.

Review of *New Testament Theology*, by G. F. Hasel. *WTJ* 42 (Spring 1980): 435–38.

Review of *Vom Verstehen des Neuen Testaments*, by P. Stuhlmacher. *WTJ* 43 (Fall 1980): 164–68.

1982

"Old Amsterdam and Inerrancy?—I" *WTJ* 44 (Fall 1982): 250–89.

1983

"Old Amsterdam and Inerrancy?—II" *WTJ* 45 (Fall 1983): 219–72.

1984

"Running the Race." *NH* 5:6 (June–July 1984): 1.

1986

"Christ, Our High Priest in Heaven" *Kerux* 1:3 (Dec. 1986): 17–27.

"A Sabbath Rest Still Awaits the People of God." In *Pressing Toward the Mark: Essays Commemorating Fifty Years of the Orthodox Presbyterian Church*, edited by Charles G. Dennison and Richard C. Gamble, 33–51. Philadelphia: Committee for the Historian of the Orthodox Presbyterian Church, 1986.

Review of *Election and Predestination*, by P. K. Jewett. *Eternity* 37:11 (Nov. 1986): 71, 74.

1987

Resurrection and Redemption: A Study in Paul's Soteriology. Phillipsburg, NJ: Presbyterian & Reformed, 1987.

"A Response to *The Holy Spirit and His Work* [by J. I. Packer]." In *Applying the Scriptures*, edited by K. Kantzer, 83–89. Grand Rapids: Zondervan, 1987.

1988

Redemptive History and the New Testament Scriptures. Translated by H. De Jongste [reviser], 2nd rev. ed. Phillipsburg, NJ: Presbyterian & Reformed, 1988.

"Adam"; "Baptism of Christ"; "Kingdom of God"; "New Testament Theology"; "Sabbath"; and "Vos, Geerhardus." In *New Dictionary of Theology*, edited by Sinclair Ferguson and David Wright, 3–5, 367–69, 461–66, 606, 713. Downers Grove, IL: InterVarsity Press, 1988.

"The Holy Spirit and Eschatology." In *'N Woord Op Sy Tyd': Teologiese Feesbundel Aangebied aan Prof. Johan Heyns ter Herdenking van Sy Sestigste Verjaarsdag*, edited by C. J. Wethmar and C. J. A. Vos, 43–52. Pretoria, South Africa: NG Kerkboekhandel, 1988.

"Man, Natural" and "New Creation, New Creature." In *Baker Encyclopedia of the Bible*, edited by W. A. Elwell, 1388, 1544–1546. Grand Rapids: Baker, 1988.

"The New Testament as Canon." In *Inerrancy and Hermeneutic*, edited by Harvie M. Conn, 165–88. Grand Rapids: Baker, 1988.

"The New Testament as Canon." In *Koninkryk Gees en Woord*, edited by J. C. Coetzee, 250–64. Pretoria: NG Kerkboekhandel, 1988.

"The New Testament: How Do We Know for Sure?" *Christianity Today* 32:2 (Feb. 5, 1988): 28–32.

1989

"Life in the Spirit: Some Biblical and Theological Perspectives." In *The Holy Spirit: Renewing and Empowering Presence*, edited by G. Vandervelde, 45–55. Winfield, B.C.: Wood Lakes, 1989.

"Total Depravity and Business Ethics." In *Business Principles and Business: The Foundations*, edited by R. C. Chewning, 139–54. Colorado Springs: NavPress, 1989.

" 'So I Said Good-Bye to Them and Went on to Macedonia.' " *NH* 10:6 (June–July 1989): 19.

"The Holy Spirit and Eschatology." *Kerux* 4:3 (Dec. 1989): 14–28.

1990

"Green, Henry (1825–1900)"; "Murray, John (1898–1975)"; "Stonehouse, Ned B. (1902–1962)"; "Vos, Geerhardus (1862–1949)"; and "Young, Edward Joseph (1907–1968)." In *Dictionary of Christianity in America*, edited by D. G. Reid, 499, 785, 1137, 1229. Downers Grove, IL: InterVarsity, 1990.

"Theonomy and Eschatology: Reflections on Postmillennialism." In *Theonomy: A Reformed Critique*, edited by William S. Barker and W. Robert Godfrey, 197–224. Grand Rapids: Zondervan, 1990.

"The Gifts of the Holy Spirit." *The Gospel Witness* 68:22 (Mar. 8, 1990): 8–14.

"The Holy Spirit and Eschatology." *The Gospel Witness* 68:21 (Feb. 22, 1990): 8–14.

"The Holy Spirit and Justification." *The Gospel Witness* 69:4 (May 10, 1990): 8–13.

"The Holy Spirit and Suffering." *The Gospel Witness* 69:5 (May 24, 1990): 8–14.

Review of *The Canon of the New Testament*, by B. M. Metzger. *WTJ* 52 (Spring 1990): 152–55.

1991

"The Sabbath: A Sign of Hope." *NH* 12:2 (Feb. 1991): 5–6.

"How to Interpret the Bible." *NH* 12:5 (May 1991): 2–3.

1992

"Resurrection." In *Encyclopedia of the Reformed Faith*, edited by D. K. McKim, 319–20. Louisville: Westminster/John Knox, 1992.

"Justification in Luke-Acts" In *Right with God: Justification in the Bible and the World*, edited by D. A. Carson. Carlisle, UK: Paternoster; Grand Rapids: Baker, 1992.

"The Gifts of the Holy Spirit." *Reformed Theological Review* 51 (Jan.–April 1992): 1–10.

"Denominations – A Scandal or a Necessity? A Review Article." *NH* 13:6 (June–July 1992): 18–19.

"No Rolling Stones!" *Evangelical Presbyterian* (Oct. 1992): 3–7.

"Response" [to the Majority Report of the "Word and Spirit" Study Committee of the Synod of the Reformed Churches in Australia]. *Theological Forum of the Reformed Ecumenical Council* 20:2–3 (Sept. 1992): 49–56.

"Sharing in Christ's Sufferings: The Church's Calling Before Christ's Return." *Creation Social Science and Humanities Quarterly* 14:3 (Spring 1992): 23–27.

Review of *The Bible's Authority*, by J. C. O'Neill. *Reformed Theological Review* 51:3 (Sept.–Dec. 1992): 113–15.

1993

"Glory, Glorification." In *Dictionary of Paul and His Letters*, edited by G. F. Hawthorne and R. P. Martin, 348–50. Downers Grove, IL.: InterVarsity, 1993.

"Pre-Post-A-Millennialism: What's in a Name?" *Sword and Trowel* (1, 1993): 10–11.

"Eschatology: What's in a Word?" *NH* 14:10 (Dec. 1993): 3–5.

1994

"The Vitality of Reformed Dogmatics." In *The Vitality of Reformed Theology*, edited by J. M. Batteau et al., 16–50. Kampen: Kok, 1994.

"It's That Simple." *NH* 15:11 (Dec. 1994): 21.

"New Paradigm in Theology? [review article]" *WTJ* 56 (Fall 1994): 379–90.

Review of *Justification by Faith*, by Mark A. Seifried. *WTJ* 56 (Spring 1994): 195–97.

1995

"Some Epistemological Reflections on 1 Corinthians 2:6–16." *WTJ* 57 (Spring 1995): 103–24.

"Pentecost: Before and After." *Kerux* 10:2 (Sept. 1995): 3–24.

1996

"A Cessationist View." In *Are Miraculous Gifts for Today? Four Views*, edited by Wayne A. Grudem, 25–64. Grand Rapids: Zondervan, 1996. See also "A Cessationist Response to Robert L. Saucy" (149–55) and "A Cessationist Response to C. Samuel Storms and Douglas A. Oss" (284–97).

"Women Speaking in the Church: A Response." *NH* 17:3 (Mar. 1996): 9–11.

"No Rolling Stones!" *NH* 17:9 (Oct. 1996): 3–4, 8.

1997

"Challenges of the Charismatic Movement to the Reformed Tradition." In *Proceedings of the International Conference of Reformed Churches, South Korea, October 15–23, 1997*, 162–83. Pella, IA: Inheritance, 1997.

"The Gifts of the Holy Spirit." In *Revival and Renewal*, edited by T. Boyle and C. Duffy, 8–22. Tokyo: Hayama Seminar Annual Report, 1997.

1998

Calvin and the Sabbath. Ross-shire, Scotland: Mentor, 1998.

"Challenges of the Charismatic Movement to the Reformed Tradition, Part 1." *Ordained Servant* 7:3 (July 1998): 48–57.

"Challenges of the Charismatic Movement to the Reformed Tradition, Part 2." *Ordained Servant* 7:4 (Oct. 1998): 69–74.

" 'Life-Giving Spirit': Probing the Center of Paul's Pneumatology." *JETS* 41 (Dec. 1998): 573–89.

1999

"Resurrection and Redemption: How Eschatology and the Gospel Relate." *MR* 8:1 (Jan./Feb. 1999): 23–26.

2000

"Glory." In *New Dictionary of Biblical Theology*, edited by T. D. Alexander and B. S. Rosner, 507–11. Downers Grove, IL.: InterVarsity, 2000.

"Herman Bavinck on the Covenant of Works" (translator). In *Creator, Redeemer, Consummator: A Festschrift for Meredith G. Kline*, edited by H. Griffith and J. R. Muether, 169–85. Greenville, SC: Reformed Academic, 2000.

"Redemption and Resurrection: An Exercise in Biblical-Systematic Theology." In *A Confessing Theology for Postmodern Times*, edited by Michael Horton, 229–49. Wheaton, IL: Crossway, 2000.

"Paul the Theologian: A Review Essay." *WTJ* 62 (Spring 2000): 121–41.

2001

"Eclipsing the Canon? The Spirit, the Word and 'Revelations of the Third Kind'" (with R. F. White). In *Whatever Happened to the Reformation?* edited by G. L. W. Johnson and R. F. White, 133–57. Phillipsburg, NJ: P&R, 2001.

"The Great Commission." In *Westminster Theological Seminary*, 15–23. Philadelphia: Westminster Theological Seminary, 2001.

"The Obedience of Faith: Some Reflections on the Rationale for Romans." In *Israel and the Church: Essays in Honour of Allan Macdonald Harman*, edited by D. J. W. Milne, 71–85. Melbourne: Theological Education Committee, Presbyterian Church of Victoria, 2001.

"Where Have All the Spiritual Gifts Gone? A Defense of Cessationism." *MR* 10:5 (Sept./Oct. 2001): 20–24.

2002

"Biblical Theology and the Westminster Standards." In *The Practical Calvinist: An Introduction to the Presbyterian and Reformed Heritage: Essays in Honor of Dr. Clair Davis*, edited by Peter A. Lillback, 425–41. Fearn, Ross-shire: Christian Focus [Mentor]: 2002.

"What about Prophecy and Tongues Today?" *NH* 23:1 (Jan. 2002): 11–12, 22.

"A Reformed Critique of the New Perspective." *MR* 11:2 (Mar./Apr. 2002): 24–28.

"Redemption and Resurrection: An Exercise in Biblical-Systematic Theology." *Themelios* 27:2 (Spring 2002): 16–31.

2003

"Westminster and the Sabbath." In *The Westminster Confession into the 21st Century: Essays in Remembrance of the 350th Anniversary of the Westminster Assembly*, edited by Ligon Duncan, 123–44. Fearn, Ross-shire: Christian Focus [Mentor], 2003.

"A Sign of Hope." *NH* 24:3 (Mar. 2003): 3–4.

"Biblical Theology and the Westminster Standards." *WTJ* 65 (Fall 2003): 165–80.

"Response to John Franke." *WTJ* 65 (Fall 2003): 327–30.

2004

"The Scandal of the Cross: Atonement in the Pauline Corpus." In *The Glory of the Atonement: Biblical, Historical and Practical Perspectives: Essays in Honor of Roger Nicole*, edited by Charles E. Hill and Frank A. James III, 140–62. Downers Grove, IL: InterVarsity, 2004.

"Speech and the Images of God: Biblical Reflections on Language and Its Uses." In *The Pattern of Sound Doctrine, Systematic Theology at the Westminster Seminaries: Essays in Honor of Robert B. Strimple*, edited by David VanDrunen, 181–93. Phillipsburg, NJ: P&R, 2004.

2005

"Promises, Promises." *Australian Presbyterian*, Mar. 2005, 4–8 [an interview concerning the Sabbath by the editor, Peter Hastie].

2006

By Faith, Not by Sight: Paul and the Order of Salvation. Milton Keynes, England: Paternoster, 2006.

"Union with Christ: Some Biblical and Theological Reflections." In *Always Reforming: Explorations in Systematic Theology*, edited by A. T. B. McGowan, 271–88. Downers Grove, IL: IVP Academic, 2006.

Review of *World and Life: As Viewed from the Biblical Theme of Creation, Fall, Redemption*, by Robert Russell Drake. *NH* 27:9 (Oct. 2006): 23.

2007

"Justification and Eschatology." In *Justified in Christ: God's Plan for Us in Justification*, edited by K. Scott Oliphint, 1–21. Fearn, Ross-shire: Mentor, 2007.

"Epistemological Reflections on 1 Corinthians 2:6–16." In *Revelation and Reason: New Essays in Reformed Apologetics*, edited by K. Scott Oliphint and Lane G. Tipton, 13–40. Phillipsburg: P&R, 2007.

"Foreword." In *The God-Breathed Scripture: The Bauman Memorial Lecture for 1966 Delivered at Grace Theological Seminary and College*, by E. J. Young, 7–10. Willow Grove, PA: The Committee for the Historian of the Orthodox Presbyterian Church, 2007.

In These Last Days: Biblical-Theological Teachings on the Sabbath, Eschatology, and the Holy Spirit [in Korean]. Translated by Choe Nack Jae et al. N.p.: Sungyak, 2007.

"The Last Adam, The Life-Giving Spirit." In *The Forgotten Christ: Exploring the Majesty and Mystery of God Incarnate*, edited by S. Clark, 191–23. Nottingham: Apollos/IVP, 2007.

"The Vitality of Reformed Systematic Theology." In *The Faith Once Delivered: Essays in Honor of Dr. Wayne R. Spear*, edited by A. T. Selvaggio, 1–32. Phillipsburg, NJ: P&R, 2007.

"Vos, Geehardus." In *Dictionary of Major Biblical Interpreters*, edited by Donald K. McKim, 1016–19. Downers Grove, IL: IVP Academic, 2007.

"Justified Now and Forever." *NH* 28:2 (Feb. 2007): 8–9.

2008

God's Word in Servant Form: Abraham Kuyper and Herman Bavinck and the Doctrine of Scripture. Jackson, MS: Reformed Academic, 2008.

" 'For Our Sakes Also': Christ in the Old Testament in the New Testament." In *The Hope Fulfilled: Essays in Honor of O. Palmer Robertson*, edited by Robert L. Penny. Phillipsburg, NJ: P&R, 2008.

"Justification and Union with Christ." In *A Theological Guide to Calvin's Institutes: Essays and Analysis*, edited by David W. Hall and Peter A. Lillback. Phillipsburg, NJ: P&R, 2008.

Dennis E. Johnson (PhD, Fuller Theological Seminary) is professor of practical theology and academic dean at Westminster Seminary California.

Bruce K. Waltke (ThD, Dallas Theological Seminary; PhD, Harvard University) is professor emeritus of Old Testament studies at Regent College and professor of Old Testament at Reformed Theological Seminary in Orlando, FL.

Vern Sheridan Poythress (PhD, Harvard University; ThD, University of Stellenbosch) is professor of New Testament interpretation at Westminster Theological Seminary.

D. A. Carson (PhD, University of Cambridge) is research professor of New Testament at Trinity Evangelical Divinity School.

G. K. Beale (PhD, University of Cambridge) is Kenneth T. Wessner chair of biblical studies and professor of New Testament at Wheaton College Graduate School.

Lane G. Tipton (PhD, Westminster Theological Seminary) is associate professor of systematic theology at Westminster Theological Seminary.

C. E. Hill (PhD, University of Cambridge) is professor of New Testament at Reformed Theological Seminary in Orlando, FL.

David B. Garner (PhD, Westminster Theological Seminary) is vice president for alumni relations and educational advancement at Westminster Theological Seminary.

Peter A. Lillback (PhD, Westminster Theological Seminary) is president and professor of historical theology at Westminster Theological Seminary.

William D. Dennison (PhD, Michigan State University) is professor of interdisciplinary studies at Covenant College.

K. Scott Oliphint (PhD, Westminster Theological Seminary) is professor of apologetics and systematic theology at Westminster Theological Seminary.

Jeffrey K. Jue (PhD, University of Aberdeen) is associate professor of church history and department coordinator at Westminster Theological Seminary.

Mark A. Garcia (PhD, University of Edinburgh) is pastor of Immanuel Orthodox Presbyterian Church in West Allegheny, PA.

J. V. Fesko (PhD, University of Aberdeen) is pastor of Geneva Orthodox Presbyterian Church in Woodstock, GA, and adjunct professor of systematic theology at Reformed Theological Seminary in Atlanta.

Jeffrey C. Waddington is a PhD candidate at Westminster Theological Seminary and teacher of the congregation at Calvary Orthodox Presbyterian Church in Ringoes, NJ.

Jonathan B. Rockey (MAR, Westminster Theological Seminary; MA, Villanova University) teaches high school Latin for the North Penn school district in Lansdale, PA.

Philip G. Ryken (DPhil, Oxford University) is senior minister at Tenth Presbyterian Church in Philadelphia and serves on the board of trustees of Westminster Theological Seminary.

David McWilliams (PhD, Highland Theological College) is senior minister of Covenant Presbyterian Church in Lakeland, FL.

James J. Cassidy (MDiv, Westminster Theological Seminary) is pastor of Calvary Orthodox Presbyterian Church in Ringoes, NJ.

John Currie (MAR, Westminster Theological Seminary) is pastor of Cornerstone Presbyterian Church in Ambler, PA, and lecturer in practical theology at Westminster Theological Seminary.

William F. Snodgrass (MDiv, Westminster Theological Seminary) is pastor of Grace Fellowship Orthodox Presbyterian Church in the Germantown section of Philadelphia, PA.

Eric Watkins (MDiv, Westminster Seminary California) is an ordained minister in the Orthodox Presbyterian Church and a church planter in Jacksonville, FL.

Danny E. Olinger (MDiv, Reformed Presbyterian Theological Seminary) is the general secretary for the Committee on Christian Education for the Orthodox Presbyterian Church in Willow Grove, PA.

John R. Muether (MAR, Westminster Theological Seminary; MSLS, Simmons College) is associate professor of theological bibliography and research and library director at Reformed Theological Seminary in Orlando, FL, and serves as historian of the Orthodox Presbyterian Church.